THE LAW OF ENERGY UNDERGROUND

The Law of Energy Underground

Understanding New Developments in Subsurface Production, Transmission, and Storage

Edited by
DONALD N. ZILLMAN,
AILEEN McHARG,
LILA BARRERA-HERNÁNDEZ,
and
ADRIAN BRADBROOK

OXFORD
UNIVERSITY PRESS

OXFORD
UNIVERSITY PRESS

Great Clarendon Street, Oxford, OX2 6DP,
United Kingdom

Oxford University Press is a department of the University of Oxford. It furthers the University's objective of excellence in research, scholarship, and education by publishing worldwide. Oxford is a registered trade mark of Oxford University Press in the UK and in certain other countries

First Edition Published in 2014

Published in the United States of America by Oxford University Press
198 Madison Avenue, New York, NY 10016, United States of America

British Library Cataloguing in Publication Data
Data available

Library of Congress Control Number: 2013952032

ISBN 978–0–19–870318–1

Preface

This book is the seventh collaboration between the Academic Advisory Group (AAG) of the International Bar Association's Section on Energy, Environment, Resources, and Infrastructure Law (SEERIL) and Oxford University Press (OUP). The previous books are *Human Rights in Natural Resource Development: Public Participation in the Sustainable Development of Mining and Energy Resources* (2002); *Energy Security: Managing Risk in a Dynamic Legal and Regulatory Environment* (2004); *Regulating Energy and Natural Resources* (2006); *Beyond the Carbon Economy: Energy Law in Transition* (2008); *Property Law in Energy and Natural Resources* (2010); and *Energy Networks and the Law: Innovative Solutions in Changing Markets* (2012).

The Preface to *Beyond the Carbon Economy* provides a short history of the AAG. The Group has now reached 30 years of age. While much of the original membership has changed, the objective has remained the same: to study analytically developments in energy law from a worldwide perspective. We note with pride that the authors who have contributed chapters to *Energy Underground* are nationals of Algeria, Argentina, Australia, Canada, China, Colombia, Denmark, Germany, Israel, India, Japan, Mexico, Namibia, the Netherlands, New Zealand, Norway, Nigeria, the Republic of South Africa, Russia, Spain, the United Kingdom, and the United States. If anything, that understates the geographic diversity of the authors. Many of them have studied, worked, and taught in nations other than their native countries and in international institutions.

As we noted in *Energy Networks*, '[e]nergy law is regularly changing and rarely dull'. It continues to provide us with a rich supply of topics which are ripe for analysis from a range of disciplinary and jurisdictional perspectives. In choosing the theme for this book, we have been guided by the desire to identify issues on the cutting edge of energy law, which are of interest to legal practitioners and to academics, as well as to students of energy policy more generally. The matters discussed in *Energy Underground*, whilst in some ways returning us to the property law roots of energy law, raise issues which are the active subject of political controversy and legislative and policy development in many parts of the world.

In developing the project, we followed our usual format. This time we met to discuss draft chapters in Raglan, New Zealand in May 2013, and then to present some of those chapters at seminars in Hamilton and Wellington. The authors benefited enormously from these opportunities, and we are extremely grateful to SEERIL, the University of Waikato, and the New Zealand Energy Law Association for the financial support that made the New Zealand experience possible. We are also indebted to Professor Barry Barton and Ms Rene Rewi of the University of Waikato who were marvellous facilitators of our work. As ever, OUP has been extremely efficient and supportive, and the comments from its anonymous reviewers have been helpful in strengthening the project.

Our special thanks go to Mr Simon Beirne of the University of Maine School of Law, Class of 2015, for his enormous help with the final stages of the project. Simon has been research assistant, editor, and coordinator, as well as a crucial point of contact with OUP.

The chapters take account of developments up to 7 October 2013.

Donald N. Zillman, Aileen McHarg,
Lila Barrera-Hernández, and Adrian Bradbrook.

Contents

List of Abbreviations

Chapter 1

CBM	coal bed methane
CCS	carbon capture and storage
CSG	coal seam gas
EIA	Energy Information Administration [United States]
LNG	liquefied natural gas
OECD	Organization for Economic Co-operation and Development
UK	United Kingdom
US	United States

Chapter 3

CBM	coal bed methane
CSG	coal seam gas
UK	United Kingdom
US	United States

Chapter 5

CC	Constitutional Court [South Africa]
CCS	carbon capture and storage
MPRDA	Minerals and Petroleum Resources Development Act
Namcor	National Petroleum Corporation of Namibia (Pty) Ltd
SCA	Supreme Court of Appeal [South Africa]
US	United States

Chapter 6

AfDB	African Development Bank
CCS	carbon capture and storage
CDM	Clean Development Mechanism
CER	Certified Emission Reductions
CESCR	Committee on Economic, Social and Cultural Rights
ECE	Economic Commission for Europe
EIA	Environmental Impact Assessment
Environmental Protocol	1991 Protocol on Environmental Protection to the 1959 Antarctic Treaty
GEF	Global Environment Facility
GHG	greenhouse gas
GoK	Government of Kenya

IAEA	International Atomic Energy Agency
ICCPR	International Covenant on Civil and Political Rights
ICESCR	International Covenant on Economic, Social and Cultural Rights
ICJ	International Court of Justice
IEA	International Energy Agency
ILC	International Law Commission
ISA	International Seabed Authority
ITLOS	International Tribunal for the Law of the Sea
London Protocol	1996 Protocol to the 1972 Convention on the Prevention of Marine Pollution by Dumping of Wastes and Other Matter
LOSC	Law of the Sea Convention
OECD	Organisation for Economic Co-operation and Development
OSPAR	1992 Convention on the Protection of the Marine Environment of the North-East Atlantic
PSNR	Permanent Sovereignty over Natural Resources
Rio + 20	2012 United Nations Conference on Sustainable Development
SREP	Scaling-Up Renewable Energy Programme
UNEP	United Nations Environment Programme
UNFCCC	United Nations Framework Convention on Climate Change
US	United States

Chapter 7

AER	Alberta Energy Regulator
CBM	coal bed methane
MSHF	multistage hydraulic fracturing
URF	Unconventional Resource Framework

Chapter 8

BLM	Bureau of Land Management [United States]
Btu	British thermal units
CBM	coal bed methane
CSSD	Center for Sustainable Shale Development
CWA	Clean Water Act
DEP	Department of Environmental Protection [United States]
DOI	Department of the Interior [United States]
EPA	Environmental Protection Agency [United States]
GEIS	Generic Environmental Impact Statement
GHG	greenhouse gas
HAP	hazardous air pollutants
kWh	kilowatt hour
LEAF	Legal Environmental Assistance Foundation
MPC	Municipalities Planning Code (Pennsylvania)
NEPA	National Environmental Policy Act
NESHAP	National Emission Standards for Hazardous Air Pollutants
NGO	non-governmental organization

NMHC	non-methane hydrocarbon
NPDES	National Pollutant Discharge Elimination System
NY DEC	New York Department of Environmental Conservation
NYCRR	New York Codes, Rules and Regulations
POWT	publicly owned wastewater treatment facility
PUC	Public Utilities Commission [United States]
RICE	reciprocating internal combustion engine
RPS	Renewable Portfolio Standards
RSGEIS	Revised Draft Supplemental Generic Environmental Impact Statement
SDWA	Safe Drinking Water Act
SEAB	Secretary of Energy Advisory Board [United States]
UIC	Underground Injection Control
US	United States
US EIA	US Department of Energy, Energy Information Administration
VOC	volatile organic compounds

Chapter 9

AIC	Autoridad Interjurisdiccional de las Cuencas de los Ríos Limay, Neuquén y Negro (Inter-jurisdictional Authority for the Limay, Neuquén and Negro River Basin)
COHIFE	Consejo Hidrico Federal (Federal Water Council) [Argentina]
COIRCO	Comité Interjurisdiccional del Río Colorado (Colorado River Interjurisdictional Agency)
CTF	Comisión Técnica Fiscalizadora [Argentina]
ICSID	International Centre for Settlement of Investment Disputes
PC	Planning Commission (Comisión de Planificación y Coordinación Estratégica del Plan Nacional de Inversiones Hidrocarburíferas) [Argentina]
US	United States
YPF	Yacimientos Petrolíferos Fiscales [Argentina]

Chapter 10

CLCS	United Nations Commission on the Limits of the Continental Shelf
EEZ	Exclusive Economic Zone
GATT	General Agreement on Tariffs and Trade
JNOC	Japan National Oil Company
JOGMEC	Japan Oil, Gas and Metals National Corporation
METI	Ministry of Economy, Trade and Industry [Japan]
UN	United Nations
WTO	World Trade Organization

Chapter 11

ALNAFT	Agence Nationale de Valorisation des Ressources en Hydrocarbures (Algerian Regulatory Agency for Hydrocarbon Resources Management)

ARH	Agence Nationale de Contrôle et de Régulation des Activités dans le Domaine des Hydrocarbures (Algerian Regulatory and Monitoring Agency for Hydrocarbon Activities)
EFL	Environmental Framework Law (EFL)
EIA	Environmental Impact Assessment
EMP	Environmental Management Plan
ESDL	Law on Environment Protection within the Framework of Sustainable Development
GDP	Gross Domestic Product
JVC	Joint Venture Contract
MEM	Ministry of Energy and Mining [Algeria]
MOE	Ministry of Environment [Algeria]
NCE	National Council for Energy [Algeria]
OPEC	Organization of the Petroleum Exporting Countries
PSC	Production Sharing Contracts
Sonatrach	Société nationale de transport et de commercialisation des hydrocarbures (National Company for Transportation and Trading of Hydrocarbons) [Algeria]
TRR	Technically Recoverable Resources
US EIA	United States Energy Information Administration

Chapter 12

AGA	American Gas Association
ANH	National Hydrocarbons Agency [Colombia]
ANLA	National Environmental Licensing Authority [Colombia]
API	American Petroleum Institute
ASTM	American Society for Testing and Materials
bbl/d	barrels per day
CBM	coal bed methane
COP	Colombian peso
CREG	Commission of Electricity and Gas [Colombia]
E&P	Exploration and production
Gbbl	gigabarrels
Mt	million tonnes
NFPA	National Fire Protection Association [Colombia]
NTC	Norma Técnica Colombiana (Colombian Technical Standards)
RUE	rational and efficient use of energy
TCF	trillion cubic feet
UPME	Mining and Energy Planning Unit [Colombia]
US	United States

Chapter 13

CCS	carbon capture and storage
CfD	contracts for difference
CPS	Carbon Price Support

DECC	Department of Energy and Climate Change [United Kingdom]
ECCSC	House of Commons Energy and Climate Change Committee [United Kingdom]
EEPR	European Energy Programme for Recovery
EIA	Environmental Impact Assessment
EMR	Electricity Market Reform
EPS	Emissions Performance Standard
EU	European Union
EU-ETS	EU Emissions Trading Scheme
FEED	Front-End Engineering and Design
NER	New Entrants' Reserve
NPF	National Planning Framework
SEPA	Scottish Environment Protection Agency
TPA	third-party access
UK	United Kingdom
UKERC	UK Energy Research Centre

Chapter 14

CCS	carbon capture and storage
CCUS	carbon capture, utilization, and storage
CTL	coal to liquids
EOR	Enhanced Oil Recovery
GHG	greenhouse gas
IGCC	Integrated Gasification Combined Cycle
MOF	Ministry of Finance [China]
NDRC	National Development and Reform Commission [China]
NZEC	near-zero emission coal
PC	pulverized coal
R&D	research and development
SME	small and medium-sized enterprises
SOE	state-owned enterprises
UK	United Kingdom
UN	United Nations
US	United States
USC	ultra-supercritical

Chapter 15

CCS	carbon capture and storage
EIA	Environmental Impact Assessment
EU	European Union
IPCC	integrated pollution prevention and control
NIMBY	'not in my back yard'
US	United States

Chapter 16

ACT	Australian Capital Territory
BC	British Columbia
DEA	Danish Energy Agency
HDR	hot dry rocks
NSW	New South Wales
NZ	New Zealand
Qld	Queensland
RES	renewable energy sources
SA	South Australia
SEA	Strategic Environmental Assessment
Tas	Tasmania
TFEU	Treaty on the Functioning of the European Union
US	United States
Vic	Victoria
WA	Western Australia

Chapter 17

ANDRA	National Radioactive Waste Management Agency [France]
BRC	Blue Ribbon Commission [United States]
ERDO	European Repository Development Organisation
EU	European Union
NIMBY	'not in my back yard'
NRC	Nuclear Regulatory Commission [United States]
NUMO	Nuclear Waste Management Organization [Japan]
NWPA	Nuclear Waste Policy Act [United States]
SKB	Swedish Nuclear Fuel and Waste Management Company
UK	United Kingdom
US	United States
WIPP	Waste Isolation Pilot Plant

Chapter 18

UPS	United Power System of the Russian Federation

Chapter 19

CCS	carbon capture and storage
EBN	Energiebeheer Nederland [The Netherlands]
EU	European Union
EU-ETS	European Union Emissions Trading Scheme
IPPC	integrated pollution prevention and control
NL	The Netherlands
PRC	Policy Research Corporation [The Netherlands]

SDE	Stimulering Duurzame Energie [The Netherlands]
TK	Tweede Kamer (House of Representatives) [The Netherlands]
TNO	Nederlandse Organisatie voor Toegepast Natuurwetenschappelijk Onderzoek (Netherlands Organization for Applied Scientific Research)
TPA	third-party access
UGS	underground gas storage

Chapter 20

BBergG	Bundesberggesetz (Federal Mining Act)
BGBl	Bundesgesetzblatt (Federal Gazette)
BGH	Bundesgerichtshof (Federal Supreme Court) [Germany]
BGR	Bundesanstalt für Geowissenschaften und Rohstoffe (Federal Agency for Geo-Sciences and Raw Materials) [Germany]
CCS	carbon capture and storage
EEG	Erneuerbare-Energien-Gesetz (Renewable Energies Act)
EnLAG	Energieleitungsausbaugesetz (Electricity Grid Expansion Act)
ROG	Raumordnungsgesetz (Zoning Act)
SRU	Sachverständigenrat für Umweltfragen (Expert Council for Environmental Matters) [Germany]
UBA	Umweltbundesamt (Federal Environmental Agency) [Germany]
UPR	Umwelt und Planungsrecht (review)
UVP-V	Verordnung über die Umweltverträglichkeitsprüfung bergbaulicher Vorhaben (UVP-V Bergbau) (Ordinance on the Environmental Impact Assessment Regarding Mining Projects)
WHG	Wasserhaushaltsgesetz (Water Resources Act)
ZHR	Zeitschrift für das gesamte Handelsrecht und Wirtschaftsrecht (review)

Chapter 21

ACT	Australian Capital Territory
Cth	Commonwealth
GGS	greenhouse gas storage
LNG	liquified natural gas
NSW	New South Wales
NT	Northern Territory
Qld	Queensland
SA	South Australia
Tas	Tasmania
UK	United Kingdom
Vic	Victoria
WA	Western Australia

Chapter 22

AER	Alberta Energy Regulator
CCS	carbon capture and sequestration

CPR	Canadian Pacific Railway Company
DSA	Designated Storage Area
ERCB	Energy Resources Conservation Board (Alberta)
EUB	Alberta Energy Utilities Board
MMA	Mines and Minerals Act (Alberta)
OGCA	Oil and Gas Conservation Act (Alberta)
UK	United Kingdom

Chapter 23

CCD	EU Directive on the geological storage of carbon dioxide
CCS	carbon capture and storage
CIUDEN	Ministry of Industry's Energy City Foundation [Spain]
ETS	Emissions Trading System
EU	European Union
GSCA	Act on the geological storage of carbon dioxide
HA	Act on hydrocarbons
MA	Act on mines

Chapter 24

ECOSOC	United Nations Economic and Social Council
GDC	Geothermal Development Company [Kenya]
GoAL WaSH	Governance, Advocacy and Leadership for Water, Sanitation and Hygiene [United Nations]
HOWCO	Halliburton Oil Well Cementing Co
MDG	Millennium Development Goals
MWe	Megawatts of electricity
NGO	non-governmental organization
UN	United Nations
UNDP	United Nations Development Programme
UNGA	United Nations General Assembly
UNU-GTP	United Nations University Geothermal Programme
US	United States

Chapter 25

CCS	carbon capture and storage
EU	European Union
UK	United Kingdom
US	United States

List of Contributors

José Alenza is Professor of Administrative Law, Public University of Navarre, Spain. Email: jose.f.alenza@unavarra.es

Nigel Bankes is Chaired Professor of Natural Resources Law, University of Calgary Law School and Adjunct Professor at the University of Tromsø, Norway. Email: ndbankes@ucalgary.ca

Lila K. Barrera-Hernández is Adjunct Assistant Professor of Law, Faculty of Law, University of Calgary, Alberta, Canada. Email: lila.kbh@gmail.com

Barry Barton is Professor and Director of the Centre for Environmental, Resources, and Energy Law, University of Waikato, New Zealand. Email: barton@waikato.ac.nz

Mohammed Abdelwahab Bekhechi was Professor of International Law, University of Oran, Algeria (1974–1994) and Lead Counsel World Bank (1994–2012). He is currently Partner in Sequoia Energy Market Finance LLP in Washington, DC, USA. Email: abekhechi@hotmail.com

Adrian Bradbrook is Emeritus Professor of Law, University of Adelaide, Australia. Email: Adrian.bradbrook@adelaide.edu.au

Michael Crommelin is Zelman Cowen Professor of Law, University of Melbourne, Australia. Email: m.crommelin@unimelb.edu.au

Terence Daintith is Professorial Fellow, Institute for Advanced Legal Studies, University of London, London, UK. Email: Terence.daintith@wanadoo.fr

Jin Feng is a PhD Candidate at the Tsinghua University School of Law, Beijing, China.

José Juan González is Professor of Law, Universidad Autónoma Metropolitana Mexico, Mexico City, Mexico and Director of the Mexican Institute for Environmental Law Research. Email: josejuan@imida.mx

Iñigo del Guayo is Professor of Administrative Law, University of Almería, Spain. Email: iguayo@ual.es

Danielle Hanema is Junior Researcher at the Groningen Centre of Energy Law, University of Groningen, Netherlands. Email: d.m.hanema@rug.nl

Lital Helman is Engelberg Center Fellow, New York University Law School, USA and Assistant Professor, Ono College of Law, Israel. Email: lh1620@nyu.edu

Eric Kimmel is Economist and Senior Advisor, Alberta Energy Regulator, Alberta, Canada. Email: Eric.Kimmel@aer.ca

Gunther Kühne is Emeritus Professor of Mining and Energy Law, Technical University of Clausthal, Germany and Honorary Professor of Law, University of Göttingen, Germany. Email: Gunther.kuehne@tu-clausthal.de

Alastair R. Lucas is Professor of Law, University of Calgary, Alberta, Canada. Email: alucas@ucalgary.ca

Aileen McHarg is Professor of Public Law, University of Strathclyde, UK. Email: aileen. mcharg@strath.ac.uk

Milton Fernando Montoya Pardo is Research Director of Mining and Energy Law Institute, Universidad Externado de Colombia, Bogotá, Colombia. Email: Milton. montoya@uexternado.edu.co

Hanri Mostert is Professor of Private Law, University of Cape Town, South Africa. Email: Hanri.mostert@uc.ac.za

Kazuhiro Nakatani is Professor of International law, University of Tokyo, Japan. Email: nakatani@j.u-tokyo.oc.jp

Yinka Omorogbe is Nabo Graham Douglas Distinguished Professor of Law, Nigerian Institute of Advanced Legal Studies, Abuja, Nigeria. She served as Corporation Secretary and Legal Adviser to the Nigerian National Petroleum Corporation (2009–11). Email: Yinka.omorogbe@gmail.com

LeRoy C. Paddock is Associate Dean for the Environmental Law Studies and Professorial Lecturer in Law, The George Washington University Law School, Washington, DC, USA. Email: lpaddock@law.gwu.edu

Gideon Parchomovsky is Robert G. Fuller Professor of Law at the University of Pennsylvania School of Law, USA and Professor, Bar Ilan, Faculty of Law, Israel. Email: gparchom@law. upenn.edu

Mark Poustie is Professor of Law and Vice Dean (Internationalization), Faculty of Humanities and Social Sciences, University of Strathclyde, UK. Email: mark.poustie@strath.ac.uk

Lavanya Rajamani is Professor, Centre for Policy Research, New Delhi, India. Email: lrajamani@googlemail.com

Catherine Redgwell is Chicele Professor of Public International Law and Fellow, All Souls College, Oxford, UK. Email: Catherine.redgwell@law.ox.ac.uk

Martha Roggenkamp is Professor of Energy Law and Director of the Groningen Centre of Energy Law, Faculty of Law, University of Groningen, Netherlands. Email: m.m.roggenkamp@rug.nl

Anita Rønne is Professor of Law, University of Copenhagen, Denmark and a Member of the Danish Energy Regulatory Authority. Email: anita.ronne@jur.ku.dk

Sergey Seliverstov is Partner, Sokolov, Maslov and Partners and Associate Professor, MGIMO-University, Moscow, Russia. Email: sergey.seliverstov@smplawyers.ru

Endre Stavang is Professor of Law, University of Oslo, Norway. Email: endre.stavang@jus. uio.no

Meyer van den Berg is Research Associate at the University of Cape Town, South Africa and Associate, Koep and Partners, Windhoek, Namibia. Email: Meyer@koep.com.na

Wang Mingyuan is Professor of Law and Director for the Centre for Environmental, Natural Resources, and Energy Law, Tsinghua University School of Law, Beijing, China. Email: wangmy@tsinghua.edu.cn

Theresa Watson, PEng is President of T.L. Watson & Associates, Inc. and a Former Member, Alberta Energy Resources Conservation Board, Canada. Email: TheresaWatson@TLWatson.com

Jessica Anne Wentz is Environmental Program Fellow and Visiting Associate Professor of Law, The George Washington University Law School, Washington, DC, USA. Email: jwentz@law.gwu.edu

Donald N. Zillman is Edward Godfrey Professor of Law, University of Maine School of Law, Portland, Maine, USA. Email: donald.zillman@umpi.edu

1

Introduction

Donald N. Zillman, Aileen McHarg, Lila K. Barrera-Hernández, and Adrian Bradbrook

I. Introduction

The Law of Energy Underground provides a worldwide study of the role of law in directing the new and transformative approaches to using resources beneath the surface of the earth for energy purposes. In this book, we examine the extraction of oil and natural gas from unconventional sources like oil and gas shale, tar sands, and coal bed methane, which often call on technologies like horizontal drilling and hydraulic fracturing ('fracking'). We also examine the use of underground areas not for the extraction of exhaustible resources but for the long-term storage of carbon gases (carbon capture and storage or 'CCS') to mitigate climate change, the use of renewable geothermal energy, the undergrounding of electricity infrastructure, and the long-term disposal of nuclear waste. All of these activities—extractive and non-extractive—provide human and environmental benefits and, at the same time, impose human and environmental costs. Our focus is on the law and public policy that govern development of these activities presently, and that may govern them in the near future. These decisions will shape the world in which we live.

II. The emergence of energy underground

For most of humanity's life on earth, energy needs were simple and were supplied from the earth's surface and from the skies above. The sun made life on the planet possible. Its warmth, light, and enablement of the photosynthetic process required no intellectual or physical effort from humans. Even from the early stages of human existence, however, human intelligence has added to the sun's gifts. The use of fire, fuelled by various forms of plant life, and dried human and animal waste, allowed what we now classify as residential heating, cooking, and lighting. The domestication of animals, such as horses, mules, and camels, enhanced human capacity for moving people and goods. Sailing ships harnessed the wind, enabling long-distance water transport. Power generated from wind and from falling water assisted the development of primitive industries and agriculture. The first uses of subterranean hot water and carbon fuels were also seen.

While a few uses of resources under the surface of the earth for energy purposes date back to antiquity,[1] the energy world of 1750 AD was little changed from that of three millennia earlier.[2] Towards the late eighteenth century, the Industrial Revolution in the west shaped, and was shaped by, an 'energy revolution' that began with the accelerated use of water power. Then came the use of the carbon fuels that are located under the surface of the earth—coal, oil, and natural gas. For a century and a half, these three raw materials provided the majority of the energy used in the transportation, commercial, industrial, and residential sectors of most modern economies.

The emergence of the carbon fuels moved the search for sources of energy from the earth's surface to its subsurface. Underground mining has been the major source of coal production. Uranium, which is used for fabricating the fuel for nuclear electric generating plants, is also mined underground. Oil shale, tar sands, and other so-called 'unconventional' hydrocarbons are mined underground to provide additional energy fuels. Oil and natural gas reserves are almost entirely located and extracted underground.

Beyond the provision of energy raw materials, the earth's subsurface is a useful location for energy infrastructure such as pipelines and electricity transmission and distribution lines, as well as for temporary storage of refined energy products like oil or natural gas. Underground water may be essential for the processing of energy raw materials into usable forms of energy. The underground can also be an attractive place for the storage of energy waste products such as fuel residues, nuclear waste, and undesired carbon gases.

Two aspects of the energy revolution continue to shape energy decision-making today. The first aspect is the need for expensive infrastructure to deliver usable energy products from the underground location of the raw materials to the locations of final human use. From three millennia ago until about 1750, fuel in the form of wood could be gathered locally and with limited expense or use of technology. But in the modern world, in order to supply consumers with fuel in the form of coal, oil, and natural gas, large investments must be made in exploration, extraction, refining, and shipping. Such investments necessitate diverse human expertise and often cost billions of dollars. The second aspect stems from the geographic locations of the underground fuel resources, which are often long distances from the areas where the final products will be used by consumers. Oil and gas discoveries in rural Texas, the Arabian Peninsula, and the North Sea have illustrated this point.

1 B. Black, *Crude Reality: Petroleum in World History* (2012) 21–5.

2 See, M. M. Roggenkamp, L. Barrera-Hernández, D. N. Zillman, and I. Del Guayo (eds), *Energy Networks and the Law: Innovative Solutions in Changing Markets* (2012) 1–2.

III. The challenges of the carbon economy

Many of the contributors to *The Law of Energy Underground* were also contributors to *Beyond the Carbon Economy*.[3] In the latter book, we examined the energy world of 2007 and expressed doubts as to whether the world's energy needs could continue to be supplied by a status quo reliance on the three carbon fuels. We identified five factors that 'drive the need' for legal and public policy 'to look beyond the carbon economy'.[4]

The first factor is the environmental harm resulting from the continued dominance of fossil fuel in the energy picture. The most serious environmental concern is the impact on climate of the burning of the carbon fuels, which releases carbon dioxide (CO_2) and other greenhouse gases into the atmosphere.

The second factor is energy security. We asked whether adequate supplies of the carbon fuels, particularly oil, would continue to be available at reasonable prices in ways that satisfied both producer and consumer nations.

The third factor is the enormous increase in demand for energy. The modern energy lifestyle is ceasing to be the exclusive province of the several dozen economically advanced nations. Most visibly, economic growth in China and India promise a vastly expanded market for automobiles, industrial and agricultural activities, and residential and commercial comforts, including modern climate control and electricity.

The fourth factor is the concern regarding exhausting the supply of the carbon fuels, which are finite and nonrenewable. Can the world rely on a consistently growing supply of both the energy raw materials and the enormously expensive infrastructure needed to move them from the place of extraction to the place of final use?

Finally, the fifth factor is the fact that one-third of the world's population lacks access to modern energy services. Prominent international studies and commissions have concluded that the continued reliance on the present carbon economy cannot serve the needs of these disadvantaged citizens of the world.

Beyond the Carbon Economy was written in 2007—not so long ago! At that time, we would have needed a very accurate crystal ball to predict many of the major impending events that have had a direct impact on energy use and energy law. The list would include: (1) the worldwide economic downturn that invited comparisons with the Great Depression of the 1930s; (2) the increasing evidence of climate change in such events as the rise in sea level, melting of the Arctic ice packs,[5] and major droughts, heat waves, hurricanes, and other so-called natural disasters; (3) the

3 D. N. Zillman, C. Redgwell, Y. O. Omorogbe, and L. K. Barrera-Hernández (eds), *Beyond the Carbon Economy: Energy Law in Transition* (2008) 562.

4 Zillman et al (n 3) at 6–9.

5 See, e.g., Andrew Shepherd et al, 'A Reconciled Estimate of Ice-Sheet Mass Balance' (2012) 338 Science 1183–9. The United States Environmental Protection Agency identifies the primary sources of US greenhouse gas emissions in 2011 as electricity production (33%), transportation (28%), and industry (20%), available at <http://www.epa.gov/climatechange/ghgemissions/sources.html>.

disaster at the Fukushima Daiichi nuclear facility in Japan, which has called into question the future of nuclear electric power; (4) the Arab Spring, with its threats to long-established autocracies in major energy-producing nations in the Middle East; (5) the massive BP oil spill in the Gulf of Mexico; and (6) the rapid advancement of unconventional oil and gas production aided by horizontal drilling and hydraulic fracturing, which offers the prospect of self-sufficiency in oil and natural gas for more nations, as well as changes in longstanding import/export patterns of fossil fuels. This is the world we study in *The Law of Energy Underground*.

IV. Energy in the twenty-first century

Before examining the new reality and potential of energy underground activities, we profile the energy world of the early twenty-first century. This is the world that has the potential to be transformed by the emerging underground activities.

International studies examine energy in terms of energy sources and energy uses. Two of the best documentations of such information are the 'World Energy Outlook 2012' of the International Energy Agency (IEA)[6] and the 'Annual Energy Outlook 2013' of the United States Energy Information Administration (EIA).[7] Both of these organizations compile existing data on sources and uses of energy in order to offer multiple scenarios as to what the next quarter-century of world energy might look like.

The energy sources are the raw materials and processes that can be used to provide energy. The energy uses are the benefits to human beings that come from the development of those raw materials and processes.

A common classification of energy sources includes: the three carbon fuels (coal, oil, and natural gas), the power of falling water (hydropower), the energy from the exploitation of the nuclear process, and a variety of renewable energy sources (solar, wind, biomass, wave, tidal, and geothermal). The sum total of these raw materials and processes provides almost 100% of the energy used in most economically developed nations. About 75–80% of that total typically comes from the three carbon fuels.

The energy uses are divided according to whether the energy is used for purposes of transportation, housing, commerce, or industry. Transportation includes the energy needed to operate automobiles, buses, motorcycles, trucks, aircraft, trains, boats, and ships. Residential (housing) uses serve human habitation needs and include heating and cooling, lighting, cooking, and the energy to operate the ever-growing number of electric devices that are essential or desirable for modern living (e.g., refrigerators, televisions, computers, and smartphones). Commercial uses provide many of the same services as residential uses, but occur in offices, stores,

[6] Available at <http://www.iea.org/publications/freepublications/publication/English.pdf>. See generally, the International Energy Agency, available at <http://www.iea.org/>.

[7] Available at <http://www.eia.gov/forecasts/aeo/pdf/0383(2013).pdf>. See generally, the United States Energy Information Administration, available at <http://www.eia.gov/>.

government buildings, schools, hospitals, stadia, and shopping centres. Industrial uses focus on energy needs for agriculture, mining, and manufacturing, as well as the physical construction of public and private infrastructure. In these industrial uses, the energy raw materials can serve both energy purposes to run the farm or factory and also serve as raw materials for the final manufactured products.[8] Fertilizers, medicines, and plastics are examples of carbon compounds being used as feedstocks.

In most classifications, electricity is typically not treated as a primary energy source or as an energy end use. Electricity is not a raw material extracted from the ground or drawn from the skies. Rather, it is a manufactured product that can be produced from any of the energy raw materials. Likewise, electricity can contribute to any of the four uses—that is, transportation, residential, commercial, and industrial purposes.

Sources and uses of energy vary from nation to nation and region to region. However, as of 2014, a general big-picture classification is as follows:[9]

(1) Coal

Coal was the dominant energy source of the early twentieth century. Located in many geographic areas, it was used for transportation, residential, and commercial purposes, as well as for a wide number of industrial processes. Today, coal is used primarily as fuel to run electricity-generating plants. Coal also serves to enable various industrial processes and to serve as a product component and as a feedstock.

Coal can be transported across national boundaries by truck, train, or ship, although at considerable cost because of its bulk. Another of coal's significant characteristics is its environmental unattractiveness. In addition to the environmental and human hazards of coal mining, the burning of coal to be used as fuel to run electricity-generating and other industrial plants releases far more pollutants than the combustion of either oil or natural gas. The CO_2 release from coal is the most prevalent of all the fossil fuel contributions to climate change.

(2) Oil

Oil (or liquids) is the type of fuel used for more than 90% of transportation activities. Primarily for cost reasons, oil's use for residential and commercial heating, as well as for the manufacture of electricity, has declined over the past half century. Oil remains an important industrial feedstock.

[8] A. Makhijani, *Carbon-Free and Nuclear-Free: A Roadmap for U.S. Energy Policy* (2007) 93. Makhijani identifies the wide range of energy uses in industry, including process heating, steam production, operating machinery, and heating, lighting, air conditioning, as well as fuel for onsite generation of steam and electricity, distillation, and reduction of ores to metal.

[9] EIA, 'International Energy Outlook 2013', Highlights, available at <http://www.eia.gov/forecasts/ieo/more_highlights.cfm>. For a concise summary of the present sources and uses of energy, see Makhijani (n 8) at 28–9.

Oil has been the great energy import/export product for over a century. The United States, the former Soviet Union, Indonesia, West Africa, Venezuela, Mexico, the North Sea, and, most significantly, the Middle East all have large oil reserves. Other developed and underdeveloped nations have not been afforded such reserves. Much of the history of the twentieth century has turned on who has—and who does not have—oil. Oil use is also a large contributor to climate change because of the CO_2 released from tens of millions of automobiles.

(3) Natural gas

Natural gas was the last of the three carbon fuels to achieve market prominence. For much of the first 50 years of the oil era, natural gas, often discovered along with liquid oil, was regarded more as a waste product (and was burned at the well site for safety reasons) than as a valuable energy resource. Following World War II, the development of long-distance pipelines for the transport of natural gas started a boom in the use of natural gas that has continued to the present day. This gas is attractive for residential and commercial heating and cooking, as well as for powering industrial facilities. In recent decades, natural gas has become increasingly attractive as an industrial and agricultural feedstock and, in particular, as a fuel for electricity generation. It is also becoming more attractive in its potential as a transportation fuel.

The development of liquefied natural gas (LNG) has made natural gas an international energy fuel. Major producing regions—North America, the Middle East, and the former Soviet Union—can now move natural gas by either ocean tanker or by pipeline across national boundaries to areas of high demand.

A final plus point for natural gas is its ranking as the least polluting—with the least CO_2 emissions—of the three carbon fuels.

(4) Nuclear energy and renewable energy

Nuclear energy and most renewable energy sources are primarily used to generate electricity. Nuclear power use begins with the mining of uranium ore, located in such widely separated areas as North America, Sub-Saharan Africa, the former Soviet Union, and Australia.[10] The raw uranium is then processed and enriched to be the fissionable fuel that provides an enormous source of heat to operate an electricity-generating plant. Compared with the other three carbon fuels, the actual production of the electricity from a nuclear plant produces minimal CO_2 releases.

The nuclear process can be relied on for steady generation of electric power, unlike renewable energy sources that require water to flow, the sun to shine, and the wind to blow. Nuclear electric power's attractions are weighed against the environmental hazards that can occur throughout the nuclear fuel cycle. Most visibly, the failures of nuclear power plants (e.g., Three Mile Island, Chernobyl, and

[10] Available at <http://www.eia.gov/energyexplained/index.cfm?page=nuclear_where>.

Fukushima Daiichi) create international news, as well as billion-dollar remedial efforts. Less visible is the continuing struggle to decide how to handle the dangerously radioactive and long-lived nuclear waste and spent nuclear fuel.

Hydropower uses the energy of falling water to generate electricity. Hydropower has been an important source of electricity generation for a century or more. In nations rich in water power (e.g., Norway, Canada, and Brazil), hydropower can provide a significant percentage of electricity-generating capacity. While the initial costs of dam and power plant construction are considerable, the cost of the 'fuel' is deemed 'free'. Hydroelectric generation is not itself a contributor to CO_2 release, but hydropower development is not free of human and environmental consequences. The manufacture of hydroelectric equipment and the construction of the dam do cause carbon releases. So do the destruction of forests to make way for the dams and reservoirs. Most importantly, the development of dams and reservoirs also displace local residents (including indigenous people), drown agricultural land, alter recreational uses of the waterways, degrade water quality, and prevent native migratory fish from accessing their spawning and rearing habitat.

Until about a decade ago, other sources of renewable energy were a minute percentage of energy worldwide. Since then, however, the use of wind, solar, biomass, wave, and tidal power has grown considerably. Most of the renewables are contributors to electricity generation. Solar, biomass, and geothermal can also serve heating needs in the residential and commercial spheres. All renewable energy sources offer substantially smaller releases of greenhouse gases than do carbon sources of energy.

V. Restraints on energy projects

All energy sources and uses have positive and negative impacts. In the early years of the growth of the carbon fuels and the development of the law governing underground extraction, only modest attention was paid to the negative impacts. Production often came from lightly populated areas. Typically, the value of the carbon fuels far exceeded the alternative uses of the land—usually agriculture and ranching. The surface owner was as eager as the coal or oil company to share the considerable revenues of a successful mine or well. Political power typically resided with the corporate extractor. The initial legal instruments and legislation to govern subsurface activity reflected those realities.

Today, those realities have changed. We call attention to three factors. First is the rapid expansion of environmental concerns throughout the world. Scientific study has identified a wide range of harmful consequences from the extraction and use of energy resources. Air pollution, water pollution, toxic substances, species harm, and habitat disruption are only some of those consequences. Increased awareness has led to laws regulating the polluting processes. Over the past two decades, the worldwide potential for climate change from the discharge of CO_2 and other greenhouse gases has also become widely known. Few, if any, major energy projects can go forward in today's world without a serious assessment of environmental consequences.

Second, public participation has become an essential part of many resource development projects. In the early years of underground resource development, an extractive venture was the business of the mining, oil, and gas companies, as well as the surface landowner(s) located above the energy resources. In time, agencies of government began to assert regulatory powers over that sort of development. Typically, there was little involvement of ordinary citizens. Today, however, that has changed. A wide variety of statutes and regulations require that information about prospective underground energy developments be provided to the general public. Public hearings are required before the development can go forward. Administrative agencies and courts may have the power to decide citizens' challenges to the development. Beyond formal legal review of development decisions, supporters and opponents of a particular development can take their complaints to a legislative body of the local, state, and national government for relief. Finally, the prevalence of the internet and social media now allow modestly funded activist groups to rally public support without relying on traditional political processes or mainstream media outlets.

Third, international law and international public policy regarding many energy underground issues have grown. In the years since World War II, a wide variety of energy matters became the subject of international treaties, diplomatic agreements, and multinational standards. International agencies help promulgate, implement, and enforce such standards. Non-governmental organizations lead or assist in the process. The majority of the chapters in *The Law of Energy Underground* will reflect the importance of environmental issues, public participation, and international standards.

VI. Predictions for the coming decades

Both the IEA and the EIA recognize that any predictions regarding energy sources and uses over the next 25 to 50 years are subject to a large number of variables. Nonetheless, several predictions stand out. First, world energy consumption will almost certainly increase. The EIA's International Energy Outlook 2013 predicts a 56% increase in world consumption from 2010 figures to those predicted to 2040.[11] The major portion of this increase is expected to come from those nations which are not members of the Organization for Economic Co-operation and Development (OECD), such as China and India, whose growing middle class will demand the transportation and residential comforts available in OECD nations. A vivid statistic looks at both vehicle and computer ownership in China. In 1993, there were 0.9 cars and 1.2 personal computers per 1,000 people in China.[12] By 2012, however, those numbers had risen to 53.4 and 273 per 1,000, respectively. Non-OECD nations will sustain worldwide growth in coal consumption and the use of nuclear power. These non-OECD nations will also provide a major portion of the growth in the use of renewables. In a recent report on wind

[11] See 'International Energy Outlook 2013' (n 9) at 1.
[12] 'China's Growing Middle Class', *Economist*, 27 April 2013, at 9.

energy development in China, for example, the IEA and the Energy Research Institute projected 'wind power capacity reaching 200 GW [gigawatts] by 2020, 400 GW by 2030 and 1 000 [sic] GW by 2050'.[13]

The IEA's World Energy Outlook 2012 began with the bold prediction that '[t]he global energy map is changing, with potentially far-reaching consequences for energy markets and trade'.[14] The Outlook emphasized that the United States is experiencing a resurgence in oil and gas production, with a focus on unconventional sources. The future of nuclear power is in doubt after the Fukushima disaster. Control of climate change is recognized as becoming increasingly necessary, but also as increasingly difficult. The need for energy efficiency has been emphasized as a control on both the increase in energy demand and the increase in carbon releases.[15] Despite these increases in CO_2 emissions, 1.3 billion citizens of the world remain without access to electricity, while 2.6 billion lack access to clean cooking facilities.

The EIA's Annual Energy Outlook 2013 concurs with many of the conclusions of the IEA's 2012 World Energy Outlook. Oil and natural gas production in the United States will increase significantly. Various efficiency measures can reduce both energy demand and carbon releases. Renewables will continue to grow.

VII. New developments underground

As the EIA and IEA Outlooks indicate, traditional underground energy activities will continue to provide the majority of the world's energy for decades to come. While these uses are not without legal issues, many of them have been well defined over the years. Our interest in this book is on new activities in the subsurface that can provide answers to some of the problems raised by the continuation of the traditional carbon economy. These new activities give rise to new legal issues. In some cases, the present state of the law may be an impediment to the advancement of the new underground activities. Depending on the issue, as well as on one's perspective of it, this may be good or it may be bad. Creative use of the law can advance the new activities and help resolve some of the doubts about their value.

In *The Law of Energy Underground*, we look at five new and emerging underground energy activities. We give special emphasis to two developments that have game-changing potential for the energy world of the twenty-first century: (1) the possibility offered by recent initiatives to exploit unconventional oil and gas; and (2) the storage of climate-changing gases underground, rather than releasing them into the atmosphere where they would contribute to climate change. We also consider three other new underground opportunities: (1) the subsurface disposal of spent nuclear fuel and nuclear waste; (2) the undergrounding of portions of the electricity infrastructure; and (3) the new advancements in geothermal technologies to supply both electric and non-electric energy.

13 Available at <http://www.iea.org/publications/freepublications/publication/china_wind.pdf> at 7.

14 See 'World Energy Outlook 2012' (n 6) at 1.

15 B. Barton, 'The Denominator Problem: Energy Demand in a Sustainable Energy Policy' (2013) 9 Policy Quarterly 3, available at <http://igps.victoria.ac.nz/publications/files/8e93a03ba5b.pdf>.

The production of unconventional oil and natural gas—whether shale oil and gas, tight gas, or coal bed methane—appears to have the potential to provide a considerable answer to the fear of running short on affordable carbon fuels over the next half-century or longer. These unconventionals also have the potential to reorder the ranks of energy producer and consumer nations, as significant numbers of nations may have the capability of becoming far more self-sufficient in energy production or even becoming exporters of their own production. The United States, for example, may have the opportunity to move from being an importer of natural gas to an exporter of natural gas.[16] Also, Poland could become a major gas producer for Europe, which would raise questions about Russia's continuing share of that market. The natural gas boom—abundant and inexpensive natural gas that produces only half the carbon emissions of coal—threatens to change the economic position of other fuels. Will coal lose its dominant position as the primary supplier of fuel for electricity generation? Will nuclear power find itself priced out of electricity markets? Will renewable energy sources like wind, solar, and geothermal find their attractiveness undercut?

Major expansion of unconventional oil and gas extraction can make a significant contribution to resolving concerns about supply shortages, demand expansions, and aspects of energy security for both advanced economies and for the energy underserved of the world. By contrast, carbon capture and storage development (CCS) makes sense only in the context of a concerted effort to reduce the release of greenhouse gases. Widespread growth of CCS could help mitigate the consequences of the expected expansion in the use of fossil fuels in the decades to come. CCS could have an industry-saving potential for coal, the dirtiest of the carbon fuels, but CCS development will depend on how seriously governments treat the concerns about greenhouse gas emissions. Despite ever-growing scientific evidence of the threat to the earth from the growing releases of climate-changing gases, the political and legal actions to combat climate change have been inconsistent, at best.

Because multiple studies will consider unconventional oil and gas, as well as CCS, we expand on common features of those topics in the sections that follow, with the aim of avoiding the duplication of materials and thus allowing the individual contributors to concentrate on the distinctive features of their topics. The chapters on nuclear waste disposal, electricity infrastructure undergrounding, and geothermal development will provide background materials within those chapters.

VIII. Unconventional oil and gas development

The newness of initiatives for the extraction of unconventional oil and gas is reflected by the United States National Petroleum Council in its 380-page report

[16] W. Montgomery and S. Tuladhar, 'Macroeconomic Impacts of LNG Exports from the United States' (2013) AGI Energia, available at <http://www.nera.com/nera-files/PUB_Macroeconomic_Impacts_LNG_Exports_0413.pdf>.

from 2007, 'Facing the Hard Truths about Energy'.[17] The report was replete with cautions about the hard truths of the global energy picture in the coming decades. There would be 'no easy, single solution' to the multiple problems the United States would face. The 'concept of energy independence [was] not realistic in the foreseeable future'. While 'unconventional oil and natural gas' were mentioned as one aspect of 'expansion of all economic energy sources', little in the report would have alerted the reader that a 'revolution' in unconventional oil and gas production was in prospect.

Annual production of natural gas in the United States increased from 2006 to 2012, a year in which it set a record high.[18] This increase was 'the result of more efficient, cost-effective drilling techniques, notably in the production of natural gas from shale formations'.

The European Union Joint Research Centre has classified unconventional natural gas resources as those that are 'found in less permeable rock formations, where resource accumulations may be distributed over a much larger area than in conventional gas. Unconventional gas resources typically require well-stimulation measures in order to be made productive, but recovery rates are much lower than in conventional gas—typically of the order of 15–30% of original gas in place.'[19]

The two major technological advancements that combined to open the prospects for large expansions of proven reserves of both gas and oil were horizontal drilling and hydraulic fracturing ('fracking'). The EIA described fracking as 'a technique in which water, chemicals, and sand are pumped into the well to unlock the hydrocarbons trapped in shale formations by opening cracks (fractures) in the rock and allowing natural gas to flow from the shale into the well. When used in conjunction with horizontal drilling, hydraulic fracturing enables gas producers to extract shale gas economically.'[20]

Horizontal drilling and fracking are not new discoveries of the twenty-first century; rather, they were first demonstrated as early as the 1940s. An independent American oilman, George P. Mitchell, boldly experimented with a combination of the two technologies for over two decades in Texas.[21] This experimentation continued when Mitchell sold his company to Devon Energy in 2002.[22] Some

[17] Available at <http://www.npchardtruthsreport.org/download.php>.

[18] Available at <http://www.eia.gov/energyexplained/index.cfm?page=natural_gas_factors_affecting_prices>.

[19] European Union Joint Research Centre, 'Unconventional Gas: Potential Energy Market Impacts in the European Union', available at <http://ec.europa.eu/dgs/jrc/downloads/jrc_report_2012_09_unconventional_gas.pdf> at iv.

[20] Available at <http://www.eia.gov/energy_in_brief/article/about_shale_gas.cfm>. For an industry perspective on fracking, see American Petroleum Institute, available at <http://www.api.org/oil-and-natural-gas-overview/exploration-and-production/hydraulic-fracturing/hydraulic-fracturing-safe-oil-natural-gas-extraction>. API refers to fracking as 'a proven technology used safely for more than 60 years in more than a million wells'. See also, <http://fracfocus.org/> and <http://www.energyfromshale.org/>.

[21] See <http://www.marketplace.org/topics/sustainability/oil-man-who-figured-out-fracking>.

[22] See <http://www.devonenergy.com/Pages/devon_energy_home.aspx> and <http://www.devonenergy.com/AboutDevon/Pages/our_history.aspx>.

federal research dollars also contributed to the development.[23] By 2010, proper combinations of horizontal drilling, fracking, and water use had created a shale gas and oil boom in states as diverse as Texas, North Dakota, and Ohio, as well as in the massive Marcellus shale belt spread across New York, Pennsylvania, and West Virginia. While shale gas was the most attractive target for the new combination of technologies, considerable attention was also given to coal bed methane and tight gas formations. Of potentially equal importance, new technologies also offered the prospect of expanded recovery of oil.

Unconventional oil and gas activity in the United States to date is producing important results.[24] Projections for both oil and gas production have increased markedly. Virtual self-sufficiency in oil for the United States has been predicted to transpire within a decade, as the country has moved to recapture its role as the world's largest oil producer.[25] Natural gas production in the United States may move beyond self-sufficiency to forecasts of the country changing from importer to exporter of natural gas, which is predicted to occur primarily through ocean shipments of LNG.[26] Energy-related emissions of CO_2 in the United States are projected to remain below 2005 levels through 2035 because, in part, of the expanding use of natural gas in the country.[27]

The realities of and the speculation about unconventional gas and oil development have given rise to significant objections to fracking. Typically, fracked wells demand the use of much more water than conventional drilling. Chemicals in the fracking fluid pose a variety of pollution risks. Features distinct to fracking raise concerns about air pollution, including the release of greenhouse gases. The small explosions of a fracking operation raise concerns about earthquakes. Lifecycle emissions issues arise from the pumping of millions of gallons of water under high pressure, trucking millions of pounds of sand from distant locations, and trucking away (or otherwise treating) millions of gallons of waste water.[28] Finally, even though natural gas has trumped coal as an electricity-generation fuel, a glut of inexpensive natural gas has threatened the roles of nuclear and renewable energy.

To date, most of the actual development of unconventional oil and gas has taken place in the United States and Canada, but this is likely to change in the very near future. Geological studies indicate that the prospects for unconventional oil and gas are spread widely over the world.[29] The potential of unconventional gas is indeed global, given the geographic spread of countries involved in domestic exploration

[23] D. Martin, 'George Mitchell, a Pioneer in Hydraulic Fracturing, Dies at 94', *The New York Times*, 26 July 2013, available at <http://www.nytimes.com/2013/07/27/business/george-mitchell-a-pioneer-in-hydraulic-fracturing-dies-at-94.html?pagewanted=all&_r=0>.

[24] See generally, the 'Annual Energy Outlook 2013' (n 7) at 2–6.

[25] See, the 'World Energy Outlook 2012' (n 6) at 1–2.

[26] See, the 'Annual Energy Outlook 2013' (n 7) at 3.

[27] See, the EIA's 'Annual Energy Outlook 2012', available at <http://www.eia.gov/forecasts/aeo/pdf/0383(2012).pdf> at 4.

[28] See EIA, 'What is Shale Gas and Why is it Important?' (n 20).

[29] European Union Joint Research Centre (n 19) at iii.

and production.[30] The most optimistic development scenarios may turn some countries into exporters of liquid and gaseous fossil fuels.

The IEA has reported on the prospects of a 'golden age' of natural gas—driven by shale gas and other developments—in its report 'Are We Entering a Golden Age of Natural Gas?'.[31] In the follow-up report, 'Golden Rules for the Golden Age of Gas', the IEA emphasized the need for legislative and popular support for new extractive techniques.[32] The Golden Rules report acknowledged the wide variety of environmental and land use objections to new development of liquids and gases.[33] Relying upon experiences in the United States and Canada, the IEA's work addresses those issues with an emphasis on best practices and ample public consultation. The IEA estimates that the total Golden Rules activity may add 7% to the cost of exploratory and extractive activity.[34] It remains to be seen whether this 7% solution can satisfy the objections to new development that have already arisen.

IX. Carbon capture and storage

As of 2013, exploitation of unconventional oil and gas has been proven at large scale in parts of the United States and Canada. Development of CCS is less advanced. Again, the IEA, with its 28 members from developed nations, has been a leader in trying to move the technology forward. The IEA describes CCS as a 'family of technologies and techniques that enable the capture of CO_2 from fuel combustion or industrial processes, the transport of CO_2 via ships or pipelines, and its storage underground, in depleted oil and gas fields and deep saline formations'.[35] Such potential gives CCS a 'unique and vital role' in the transition to a 'sustainable low-carbon economy' in power generation and industry.

As with horizontal drilling and hydraulic fracturing, the technology of CCS has been pioneered in various industries for several decades on a small scale. However, only a few industrial operations have reached large scale. None has done so in electricity production.

The IEA views CCS as one part of a low-carbon sustainability agenda that could hold world temperature rise to 2°C by 2050. CCS could contribute one-fifth of the reductions needed in carbon release. That would require 100 CCS projects to be operative by 2020 and over 3,000 such projects to be in place by 2050. And, not all

30 See IEA, 'Are We Entering a Golden Age of Natural Gas?', available at <http://www.worldenergyoutlook.org/media/weowebsite/2011/WEO2011_GoldenAgeofGasReport.pdf> at 57–9.

31 See n 30.

32 Available at <http://www.worldenergyoutlook.org/media/weowebsite/2012/goldenrules/weo2012_goldenrulesreport.pdf>.

33 See also European Union Joint Research Centre (n 19).

34 IEA (n 32) at 10 ('We estimate that applying the Golden Rules could increase the overall financial cost of development [of] a typical shale-gas well by an estimated 7%. However, for a larger development project with multiple wells, additional investment in measures to mitigate environmental impacts may be offset by lowering operating costs.').

35 Available at <http://www.iea.org/topics/CCS/>.

CCS projects yield identical environmental benefits. Small-scale gas-based projects, for instance, provide only modest benefits.

The IEA concludes that CCS 'deployment is dependent on an enabling policy framework' in which 'the quality of the policy matters'.[36] What is needed is both 'national level CCS-specific policy and global climate policy development'. To aid this development, the IEA has taken a lead role in coordinating law and policy at both the national and international levels. Particularly important are the efforts of the IEA to stimulate CCS projects in non-member nations. This is essential, given the estimate that by 2050, as many as 65% of all CCS projects will be located outside OECD and IEA nations, including major energy players like China, Russia, and India.

X. The law of underground energy

The development of new and transformational underground energy technologies will require the confluence of science and technology, adequate financing by the private sector and government, and a receptive legal and public policy structure. Typically, all three of these factors are needed to complete a successful project. Not surprisingly, these three factors influence each other. Without proven technology, financing may be far more difficult to secure. If laws and public policy tend to discourage new initiatives in an effort to address environmental concerns, as well as concerns over existing industry practices, then even the boldest financiers may be stymied.

As was the case in our six previous collaborations with OUP, our primary focus in this book is to examine the legal implications of energy underground. We are, of course, attentive to the real-world consequences of technological, financial, environmental, and public policy matters. However, the law is where our expertise lies and it is quite often that the law will determine, at least in part, the success or the failure of new technologies, financial approaches, or public policies.

The law of energy underground has a fascinating past, present, and future.[37] The location of fossil fuels beneath the surface of the earth raised a number of practical questions that needed legal answers in the late nineteenth and early twentieth centuries. These legal answers came from courts interpreting common law judicial precedents, from legislative action, and from decrees by the executive authority of the nation.

A crucial question was who owned the underground resource and who had the right to exploit it. One answer was government, whether styled the King (hence the origin of 'royalty rights'), the national, state, or provincial government, or 'the people'. This was true even if the land overlying the underground resource was privately owned. The primary alternative to sovereign ownership was to include the underground resource ownership with the ownership of the surface. The farmer or

[36] Available at <http://www.iea.org/topics/ccs/ccsstrategyandpolicy/>.
[37] See Part I of this book.

grazer or private business that owned the surface could extract the resource found beneath the surface. The modern economist reminds us that the difference between government ownership and private ownership of the subsurface resources will have a large impact on the willingness of the private surface owner to support extraction operations.

The issue of ownership of the subsurface resources is made more complicated by the fact that underground liquid and gaseous resources can move around in response to extraction activity. Molecules of oil, natural gas, and water might be found under the boundaries of one landowner but then migrate to a well on an abutting owner's land. In such a situation, who has what rights to resources? A further complication may arise if multiple underground resources are identified under the same parcel of land. What determines priorities of exploitation?

The very same issues of science, technology, and finance that were identified above also compound energy resource extraction, whether the original ownership of the resource lay with a government or with a private surface owner. Successful extraction requires expertise and wealth. Often, it is a speculative financial prospect. The prospect of a 'dry hole' following the investment of millions of local currency in an oil or gas venture is a daunting risk for a landowner or an entity of government. Even if they have the money, they usually lack the expertise to carry out successful extraction. Thus, the familiar pattern of the resource owner entering into a contractual arrangement with the experienced mining or oil and gas company arose. The extensive lease between the parties defined their rights and responsibilities and provided for the division of the financial risk and reward. The lease may or may not clarify the right of surface owners to sue for damage to the surface from underground operations.

Even if ownership issues were resolved between the private parties to the lease, underground activity became increasingly likely to be regulated by government in a variety of ways and for a variety of reasons. Governments often enter the picture as the regulator of the extraction of the energy minerals. This may be done via conditions in the lease, via separate legislation or regulation, or via judicial action.

Conflicting uses of land have been regulated for over a century in most developed nations. An ample body of land use law arose both through judicial decisions and through legislative action to govern where underground activities (with their surface impacts) could take place and under what circumstances. These general permitting laws have been expanded with the growth of specific environmental protection legislation during the past 50 years. Energy activities will need to be assessed for their impacts on such matters as ground and surface water, air quality, species preservation, and toxic substance releases.

These forms of land use and environmental regulation often arise from multiple units of government (localities, state, and national) that desire to regulate and have a legal basis for doing so. Different government entities may take different views towards underground development. For example, a national government or a state government may be eager to encourage the economic development benefits of an underground energy project. The citizens and local government living near the energy project may take a different position towards the land use and environmental consequences. They may be ready to raise both legal and public relations objections to the project.

A further role for government may be to serve as a financial supporter or some other enabler of new energy underground projects and technologies. The government's objectives may include job creation, promotion of national security, advancement of new business activities, development of export markets, and limitation of global warming and other environmental harms. Government's tools to advance the underground project include research and development subsidies, tax benefits to the private enterprises involved, guaranteed government purchases of the energy products, and mandates to produce energy from the favoured technologies.

XI. The internationalization of underground energy law

A half-century ago, government involvement with energy underground activity was limited to the local, state, and national government activities of the types just discussed. Now, national laws have been joined by international laws that address some of the large issues involved in energy underground projects. The rewards and harms of energy projects today often cross national boundaries or implicate matters of global concern. The response to climate change is a highly visible example. So are regulations of international trade, control of air pollution and pollution of the seas, and protection of the sea lanes, as well as other issues such as energy security and the protection of indigenous people impacted by energy development.

Traditionally, some of these issues were addressed through diplomatic channels on a bilateral or multilateral basis. Increasingly, international legislation in the form of treaties identifies real-world problems, sets standards for corrective action, and provides enforcement against violators. These 'hard law' instruments are joined by a growing variety of 'soft law' understandings or agreements that seek the same end results. While these latter instruments may lack means of direct legal enforcement, they may also influence the conduct of such powerful players as international financing authorities and prominent non-governmental organizations with ready access to international media.

In *The Law of Energy Underground*, we explore cross-pollination between national (including local and state) law and international law. National laws help shape international law. Likewise, international law helps shape national laws. The collective views of multiple national states often define the needs for and content of international legal standards. Those international legal standards then bind national actions. Even if the international standards still remain in the posture of 'soft law', those standards can have a considerable impact on the further evolution of national law.

As we examine underground energy developments, we have asked the contributors to consider how existing national and international standards are likely to advance or impede potentially transformational energy activities. We recognize that issues in Germany or Nigeria may not be the same as issues in Canada or China. Nonetheless, efforts to enhance fossil fuel supplies, or to make CCS a major part of the mitigation of greenhouse gas release, or to decide whether solutions to problems of nuclear waste will preserve a nuclear option have worldwide implications and need worldwide legal attention.

XII. The organization of this book

Part I of *The Law of Energy Underground* studies the history and present status of the laws that govern underground energy resources. Barton, Daintith, Gonzalez, and Mostert and Van den Berg explore the application of common law, civil law, and Roman-Dutch law to such issues as ownership of resources and the rule of capture. These different legal systems have developed the basic principles that influence underground energy law in all the contexts that will be discussed in later chapters. The use of new approaches to underground resources will be guided by these fundamental principles of law.

Part II examines the role of international law and practice in the treatment of underground resources. Redgwell and Rajamani provide a wide-ranging look at the relevance of international law to underground energy resource issues. As noted, the contributors examine both existing international law doctrines and doctrines in the formative stages. Those observations also shape the chapters that follow with their emphasis on national laws and new developments.

Part III examines the extraction of exhaustible underground energy resources. Those chapters consider one of the most important developments in new energy underground activity—the growth in extractive practices for facilitating the development of unconventional oil and natural gas resources. Horizontal drilling and hydraulic fracturing have inspired a variety of national responses. Lucas, Watson, and Kimmel, Paddock and Wentz, Barrera-Hernández, Nakatani, Bekhechi, and Montoya study jurisdictions in North and South America, Asia, and Africa, as they cope with the opportunities and drawbacks of a major expansion of oil and gas development using new energy underground processes.

Part IV takes a similar approach to use of the underground for non-extractive processes and renewable processes. While all of these processes raise environmental concerns, they do offer to solve serious environmental problems. McHarg and Poustie, Wang and Jin, and Helman, Parchomovsky, and Stavang provide perspectives on carbon capture. Bradbrook and Rønne provide a transnational look at geothermal energy development—one renewable energy source with an underground location. Zillman examines approaches to siting facilities for the safe underground disposal of nuclear waste products and spent nuclear fuel. Seliverstov introduces us to Russia's efforts to move urban electricity substations to below ground.

Part V studies national and regional approaches to the new extractive and renewable activities discussed in Parts III and IV, focusing on potential conflicts between different underground energy activities and the role of law in managing those conflicts. Roggenkamp and Hanema (for the Netherlands), Kühne (for Germany), Crommelin (for Australia), Bankes (for Canada), del Guayo and Alenza (for Spain),

Crommelin and Omorogbe (for sub-Saharan Africa) track the core principles of law addressed in Part I and the new positive law that expands on and sometimes modifies those core principles.

The conclusion allows the editors to summarize the findings of the prior chapters. More importantly, it allows reflections on the potential impacts of the varied underground developments for the energy world of the decades to come. It stresses the highly important role that the law will play in advancing sensible use of energy.

PART I

PROPERTY RIGHTS IN UNDERGROUND RESOURCES

2

The Common Law of Subsurface Activity: General Principle and Current Problems

Barry Barton

I. Introduction

The common law principles governing property rights to the subsurface and to minerals are fundamental to an understanding of the law governing activities that use geological formations. Some more recent uses of subsurface resources pose novel legal questions; carbon capture and storage is a leading example. Apart from new legislation to make specific provision for such activities, one would expect the legal situation to be relatively stable. In fact, there has been uncertainty on two key points, the general principle that the rights of the owner of land extend vertically downwards, and the rights of mineral owners to use subsurface features for non-mineral purposes. This chapter addresses those points of uncertainty and contention. It argues that, on both matters, principle and authority tend towards a broader role than has been suggested by some writers for the rights of the land owner, and a lesser one for the mineral owner. It is possible to connect this to a distinct long-term trend away from the private ownership of minerals. This chapter pursues these themes, in the context of an overview of the law in common law countries other than the United States, the law of which has taken its own complex path, discussed in chapter 3.

Before we proceed, it may be useful to consider the nature of the inquiry that this chapter undertakes. Why does it emphasize private law and private property, with so little statute law, and so many old cases? The first point to make is that property law affects anything concerning land and its resources, both at the surface and below. All other things being equal, the owner of a parcel of land can sue in trespass or nuisance to repel incursions. He or she may not be able to do so if these underlying rules have been supplanted by legislation authorizing the government or a company to enter on land or use it in a way that would otherwise be trespass. Such legislation is common in many fields of natural resources law. However, the interesting thing is that new uses of the subsurface and new technologies may not be covered by that legislation. For example, a jurisdiction may not have yet passed laws for carbon capture and storage (geosequestration), deep-well disposal of waste, or enhanced geothermal systems. If no new laws have been passed for such activities, then the existing laws will apply. There is no option here; a court must decide the disputes that parties bring to it, according to law, even if the results are unsatisfactory, without waiting for better laws to be passed. This chapter therefore considers the default rules.

Default rules are relevant where new activities are not covered by specific statutory rules, either because an activity is not covered at all, or only around the edges, where some aspects of the activity are provided for but others are not. Default rules are always relevant. As soon as legislation covers one new activity, another one emerges; the next big thing is always just around the corner, and the legislator is often struggling to catch up with it. Default rules are often tort and property law; they are the law that will apply to a land or resources dispute where there is no statute, no contract, and no trust to provide any other legal framework. Property law is also persistent; courts and legislatures are slow to interfere with property rights.[1] Nonetheless, default rules are not necessarily good law, and that is why legislatures often change them. This inquiry does not express any normative preference for default rules; what it seeks is accuracy in understanding them. Nor does it express a preference for common law over statute; what it seeks is to pursue the law whatever its character in the particular matter. In fact, more than in most branches of the law, natural resources law crosses and recrosses the boundary between public and private law. Nor should this inquiry be understood as a historical one. It considers old cases not as antiquities, but as parts of the current law.

II. Rights of ownership of land extend downwards

Little in the law of property and natural resources can be as familiar and as apparently well established as the principle that the rights of the owner of the surface of land extend upwards and downwards. The rights deriving from the ownership or possession of an estate in land are presumed to be capable of exercise on all parts of the land, including upwards and downwards, indefinitely. The Latin phrase that expresses this rule is *cujus est solum ejus est usque ad coelum et ad inferos*; to whom the soil belongs, to that person it belongs all the way to the sky and the depths. There are many exceptions, but this is the general rule. The House of Lords in 1860 declared in *Rowbotham v Wilson*[2] that prima facie the owner of the surface is entitled to the surface itself and everything below it down to the centre of the earth. The main New Zealand text on land law puts it:[3]

[1] 'Next to constitutional rights, property rights are the strongest interests recognised by our law': Hammond J in *White v Chandler* [2001] 1 NZLR 28 at [67].

[2] (1860) 8 HLC 348, 11 ER 463. Also W. Blackstone, 2 *Commentaries on the Laws of England* 18 (1769).

[3] G. W. Hinde, N.R. Campbell, and P. Twist, *Principles of Real Property Law* (2007) 6.002. Footnotes omitted, the main references being to *Corbett v Hill* (1870) LR 9 Eq 671 at 673 and *Wandsworth Board of Works v United Telephone Co Ltd* (1884) 13 QBD 904 at 915 (CA). Generally, see Y. Abramovitch, 'The Maxim "Cuius Est Solum Ejus Usque Ad Coelum" as Applied to Aviation'

The general rule at common law is that the owner of the soil is presumed to be 'the owner of everything up to the sky and down to the centre of the earth' according to the maxim *cujus est solum ejus est usque ad coelum et ad inferos*. Where a parcel of land was granted by the Crown or conveyed from one person to another, the grant or conveyance (unless some contrary indication was shown) passed everything which lay below the surface 'down to the centre of the earth' and everything above it 'up to the sky'.

In the High Court of Australia, Windeyer J in *Wade v NSW Rutile Mining Co*[4] refers to:

> . . . the elementary principle of the common law that a freeholder . . . is entitled to take from his land anything that is his. Except for those minerals which belong to the Crown, the soil and everything naturally contained therein is his.

A consequence of the general rule is that the person in possession of the surface can defend his or her possession of the subsurface. Interference with the landowner's right to possession underground is trespass, just as on the surface. Alderson B once said, 'There is no distinction between trespasses underground and upon the surface.'[5] Thus, in Canadian cases, where construction companies inserted anchor rods under the neighbouring property for temporary support; exemplary damages were awarded against them to deprive them of the profits of its trespass.[6] It was no defence that permission to enter was unreasonably withheld. In New Zealand, *Waugh v Attorney General*[7] dealt with a tunnel that the Navy had used for many years, connecting two of its yards on either side of a ridge. It went under some private properties and streets. There was a period during which the tunnel was unauthorized. The owners of one of the properties sued for damages. That the unauthorized tunnel under their land was a trespass went without argument; the only dispute was the damages. The correct measure was held to be the profit of the Navy gained from using the tunnel rather than using a longer route through the streets. Damages did not need to be measured by the loss suffered by the landowners.

That there are many exceptions to the general rule is often the real legal issue. Several kinds of exception are in the form of mineral rights. Gold and silver are recognized as prerogative minerals vested in the Crown or the state, as decided by the *Case of Mines*.[8] Mineral rights can be severed from the surface by conveyance as a matter of private law, capable of being held as a separate inheritance, in fee, for a term, or as a profit à prendre (i.e., a servitude). In many common law countries, mineral rights have been reserved or excepted to the state upon the grant or patent of land to an individual. Rights to minerals can also be declared by statute to be

(1962) 8 McGill LJ 247; and M. Taggart, *Private Property and Abuse of Rights in Victorian England* (2002) 120. Also 31 *Halsbury's Laws of England* (4th edn) Mines and Minerals, para 19: 'Prima facie "land" or "lands" includes everything on or under the surface.'

[4] (1969) 121 CLR 177 at 185.

[5] *Hunter v Gibbons* (1856) 1 H&N 459 at 465, 156 ER 1281 at 1284.

[6] *Austin v Rescon Construction (1984) Ltd* (1989) 57 DLR (4th) 591 (BC CA) and *Epstein v Cressey Development Corp* (1992) 89 DLR (4th) 32 (BC CA).

[7] [2006] 2 NZLR 812.

[8] (1567) 1 Plowd 310, 75 ER 472.

vested in the state, notwithstanding the terms of any grant, conveyance, or instrument of title. Other exceptions to the general rule of subsurface ownership are not for minerals. As a matter of conveyancing, it is possible to subdivide land into horizontal strata or parcels, whether above the surface or below. The same can be done by statute. Statutory powers can also be used to take particular attributes or characteristics such as pore space or storage capacity and vest them in the state. Alternatively, a statute can grant rights on an agency or company to enter and use the subsurface of land without taking a proprietary right. Finally, it should be noted that underground water, oil, and gas, being fluid and fugitive, are less susceptible to any principle of ownership in situ, and so present something of an exception to the general rule. The exceptions are numerous, but their existence is not in itself a contradiction of the general rule of subsurface ownership.

III. Doubt about the general principle

The validity or breadth of the general principle has been questioned from time to time. Adrian Bradbrook argued that the wide application of the *cuius est solum* doctrine may not be accurate, and suggested that resources at depth constitute a *res nullius* so that ownership will vest in the first person to reduce them into possession.[9] K. Gray and S. F. Gray adopted the argument.[10] Parallel arguments have been made in America.[11] One of the main authorities for the argument needs careful consideration.

Commissioner for Railways v Valuer-General[12] was an Australian case in the Privy Council, and in it Lord Wilberforce gave the maxim *cuius est solum* rough treatment. He called it a tag or brocard, and questioned its standing in Roman law, as well as English law. He said that its use is imprecise and mainly serviceable as dispensing with analysis:

> In none of these cases is there an authoritative pronouncement that 'land' means the whole of the space from the centre of the earth to the heavens: so sweeping, unscientific and unpractical a doctrine is unlikely to appeal to the common law mind.

But it is not necessary to pick a fight with Lord Wilberforce, fortunately, about what appeals to the common law mind, if one finds the *ratio decidendi* carefully. The Privy Council was responding to an argument for a very artificial interpretation of the term 'land' in the Valuation of Land Act 1916, that it meant *only* land that extended upwards and downwards indefinitely, and that if any other parcel lay vertically above or below, then it was not 'land' but a 'stratum' and to be valued

[9] A. J. Bradbrook, 'Ownership of Geothermal Resources' [1987] AMPLA Yearbook 353; A. J. Bradbrook, 'The Relevance of the Cujus Est Solum Doctrine to the Surface Landowner's Claim to Natural Resources Located Above and Beneath the Land' (1988) 11 Adel LR 462 at 473.

[10] K. Gray and S. Gray, *Elements of Land Law* (5th edn, 2009) 18. K. Gray, 'Property in Thin Air' [1991] CLJ 252 criticizes the maxim *cuius est solum*, but in relation to airspace, not minerals.

[11] J. G. Sprankling, 'Owning the Center of the Earth' (2008) 55 UCLA L Rev 979.

[12] [1974] AC 328 at 351 (PC NSW).

under separate rules. What was vital to appreciate[13] was that the application of this interpretation to the subject property (leased premises in a multi-level transport, hotel, retail, and commercial complex in Sydney) included in the valuation only 'strata' areas on each floor above or below which there intruded at some level one or the other of the exceptions from the demise. This left 12 'land islands' where there happened to be no space excepted from the lease at any level. This division was wholly artificial and produced units that were incapable of separate occupation or sale. The company's interpretation of the Act was for a complete dichotomy between 'strata' and land 'in the strict sense', *usque at coelum et ad inferos*—all the way to the heavens and to the depths. It is this strained interpretation of 'land' that the Privy Council was rejecting. Lord Wilberforce was demolishing the proposition that if land was to be valued, it was necessary that it extend all the way up and down. But that was wrong. Horizontal layers or spaces could be valued as land.

Lord Wilberforce may have been impatient with ancient authorities and talk about the centre of the earth, but his decision recognized that subsurface ownership was part of land ownership, and that the *cuius est solum* maxim expressed the principle of the indefinite extension downwards of a freehold. Immediately after his words about what would be unlikely to appeal to the common law mind, he said:

> At most the maxim is used as a statement, imprecise enough, of the extent of the rights, prima facie, of owners of land: Bowen L.J. was concerned with these rights when, in a case dealing with rights of support, he said 'Prima facie the owner of the land has everything under the sky down to the centre of the earth': *Pountney v Clayton* (1883) 11 QBD 820, 838.

Thus, *Commissioner for Railways v Valuer-General* readily accepted that a parcel of land could extend upwards and downwards from the surface, and that it could be defined by boundaries in three dimensions.

IV. Subsurface activity as trespass: *Bocardo v Star Energy*

A case of directional drilling allowed the Supreme Court of the United Kingdom to clarify the vitality of the principle in *Bocardo SA v Star Energy UK Onshore Ltd* in 2010.[14] Bocardo, a land owner, sued Star Energy, an oil company, for trespass for three wells made under its land by directional drilling. All oil and gas in its natural condition was vested in the Crown, by the Petroleum Act 1934 (meaning that Bocardo had no claim to the petroleum), and the oil company and its predecessor, Conoco, held a licence under the Act for petroleum exploration and production.

13 And italicized as such by the judge, at 346. (The Act provided separately for the valuation of strata in order to deal with the conceptual impossibility of determining the unimproved value of premises in an underground complex that existed and could be occupied only because of excavations that were improvements.)

14 [2011] 1 AC 380 (SC(E)), [2010] UKSC 35.

The apex or top point of the oil in this particular field lay below Bocardo's land. Conoco did not drill for the oil vertically, but used directional or deviated drilling from a nearby site to get to the right spot. Two wells were drilled for production and ended at points below Bocardo's land, and the third was for water injection, passing under the land and ending at a point beyond it. The closest that any of the wells came to the surface under Bocardo's land was 800 feet, and their lowest point was 2,900 feet. The company had not sought the land owner's permission. Bocardo's case was simply that the wells, with their casing and tubing, were a trespass; title to the land extended downwards and included everything in it, subject to exceptions such as for minerals.

Lord Hope addressed this basic question of liability in terms that the other four judges agreed with. He referred to the many cases, such as *Rowbotham v Wilson*,[15] where it was said that prima facie the owner of the surface is entitled to the surface itself and everything below it down to the centre of the earth. This principle is often put in terms of the maxim or brocard *cuius est solum eius est usque ad coelum et ad inferos*. The first recognized appearance of the maxim was in Accursius, a glossator of the thirteenth century.

The oil company's defence on liability was to build on *Bernstein v Skyviews & General Ltd*[16] as to airspace, and say that a surface owner should be held to own directly down beneath the boundaries of his or her land as far down as necessary for the use and enjoyment of the surface, buildings, and any minerals not excluded from his ownership. However, the Court found no English authority for such a limitation, and held that it was not helpful to make analogies between the rights of an owner of land with regard to the airspace above it and his or her rights with regard to the strata below the surface. There was some such authority from the United States, but the Court agreed with Sprankling[17] that there is also much authority against it, and that the debate remains alive in American law. The Court cited Smillie[18] that 'there appears to be no case in the Commonwealth where a plaintiff has failed on the basis that the area of subsoil invaded was so deep that the surface occupier's possessory rights did not extend that far'.

Lord Hope concluded that the maxim *cuius est solum* still has value in English law. The reasons for saying it has no place as to airspace are a good deal less compelling as to the subsurface. The approach in *Chance v BP Chemicals Inc*[19] that some kind of physical interference with the surface must be shown, would lead to much uncertainty. It overlooks the point that, at least as to corporeal elements, the question is essentially one of ownership. His interesting dictum was that '[a]s a general rule anything that can be touched or worked must be taken to belong to someone'. The law was 'that the owner of the surface is the owner of the strata beneath it, including the minerals that are to be found there, unless

[15] (1860) 8 HLC 348, 11 ER 463. [16] [1978] QB 479. [17] Sprankling (n 11) at 991.

[18] J. Smillie, ch 9 in S. Todd (ed), *The Law of Torts in New Zealand* (5th edn, 2009) 426.

[19] 670 NE 2d 985 (Ohio 1996). *Coastal Oil and Gas Corp v Garza Energy Trust* 268 SW3d 1 (Tex SC 2008), discussed in chapter 3, also takes a limited view of subsurface trespass.

there has been an alienation of them by a conveyance, at common law or by statute to someone else'.[20]

Lord Hope observed that over time the use of technology has penetrated deeper and deeper into the earth, and there must obviously be some stopping point as one reaches the point where pressure and temperature make the concept of ownership so absurd as to be not worth arguing about. But the fact that the strata in this case, between 800 and 2,900 feet deep, could be worked by wells pointed to the opposite conclusion.

As to possession—necessary for trespass—Lord Hope followed the principle that in the absence of evidence to the contrary, the holder of the paper title is deemed to be in possession, so that the owner was deemed to be in possession of the subsurface. The Crown licence gave no right to trespass. Thus, on liability, underground ownership, and underground trespass, the Court was unanimous. On the measure of damages, which took up much of the judgments, the Court was divided; the majority held that, as it was controlled by a background of the legislation, compulsory acquisition principles applied and prevented the surface owner from claiming value that came only from the oil company's development or 'scheme'.

Bocardo v Star Energy was therefore a strong reaffirmation of the general common law principle that the proprietorship and possession of the surface of land extend downwards. There is no depth limit after which geological formations are owned by the state, or are free of ownership as some kind of *res nullius*. There is no restriction on a claim to the ownership or possession of land below the surface that it must be required for the ordinary use and enjoyment of the surface, or that any invasion of it must have a physical effect on the surface. The principle cannot be avoided by dismissing the *cuius est solum* principle and ownership to the centre of the earth as a whimsy; it is better to say that the ownership of the surface extends downwards indefinitely.[21] Certainly, that ownership is subject to any reservations or exceptions made by statute, grant, or common law, chiefly as to minerals (and it does not generally include water or other fluids). The decision is also a sound basis for an understanding of the relationship between the subsurface rights of the proprietor of the surface and the proprietor of any mineral rights.

V. Property rights in minerals

The corollary of the basic principle of subsurface ownership is that minerals, except for gold and silver, are part of the land itself and belong prima facie to the owner of

20 *Bocardo v Star Energy*, paras 26 and 27.

21 'Indefinitely' seems to cover the matter very well. 'Indefinite' conveys that there is no fixed depth limit, and avoids unnecessary pronouncements on Lord Hope's stopping point where ownership is not worth arguing about. 'Indefinitely' is used in some American legislation and is criticized by Sprankling (n 11) at 1002, but he seems to insist that indefinite means infinite and boundaries free from convergence. Equally there seems to be no logic in his argument that, because no court has dealt with a case more than two miles below the surface, ownership below that level is a blank slate.

the soil. More exactly, it is presumed that the land of which a proprietor of an estate has seisin includes the minerals in the land.[22] The *Case of Mines* is authority.[23] Again, it is desirable to note that there are many exceptions, or ways of rebutting the presumption. The consequence is that the word 'land' is interpreted to include minerals, such as in an agreement for the sale and purchase of land.[24]

It is common for the owner of land to sell land excepting the minerals, or to transfer the minerals separately. The transaction can be the conveyance of an estate in fee simple, or it can be for a leasehold estate, or for a profit à prendre; 'there may be a severance of the mines and minerals from ownership of the surface and . . . the mines and minerals so severed are a separate tenement capable of being held for the same estates as other hereditaments'.[25] Because such a transaction severs the mineral rights from the rest of the land, it is convenient to refer to the conveyance as an instrument of severance.

It is to the instrument of severance that one must look in order to determine what minerals and what rights are held by the mineral owner rather than the owner of the land generally. In the nineteenth century, a great number of cases came to the courts of England and Scotland about what was meant when an instrument of severance caused 'minerals' to come into separate ownership. What substances were included? Many of the cases concerned severances of minerals effected under the Land Clauses Acts and other legislation for railways, canals, and waterworks. They had resulted in different tests for determining the meaning of the term 'minerals'. Some cases had held that minerals included any substance that could be got from the ground for a profit.[26] *Glasgow Corp v Farie*[27] held that, instead, the proper test was what the words meant in the vernacular, but a period of uncertainty followed where the relationship between the two tests was unclear. In 1910, the House of Lords tackled the question, plainly intending to bring the uncertainty to an end and settle the law. In *North British Railway Co v Budhill Coal and Sandstone Co*,[28] the House held that the nature and extent of the mineral rights depend upon the interpretation of the original grant or instrument of severance, reading words as they were meant in the vernacular of the mining world, the commercial world, and landowners, at the time of the grant. The vernacular test supplanted the profit test. *North British Railway v Budhill* is also important for making it clear that reserved or excepted minerals could not be the ordinary rock or soil, otherwise the land owner would have bought, or have left to it, only a few feet of turf and mould.

[22] R. Megarry and H. W. R. Wade, *The Law of Real Property* (5th edn, 1984) 64. The 6th edition (C. Harpum, 2000) 3-052 says '[a]lthough prima facie a tenant in fee simple is entitled to all minerals under his land, this is subject to some exceptions'.

[23] (1567) 1 Plowd 310 at 336, 75 ER 472.

[24] *Hobbs v Esquimalt & Nanaimo Railway Co* (1899) 29 SCR 450 (BC).

[25] *Re Algoma Ore Properties Ltd and Smith* [1953] OR 634 at 640 (CA). (This seems more accurate than the expression of Kellock J in *Berkheiser v Berkheiser* [1957] SCR 387 at 395 (Sask) that two separate estates exist.) Early authorities are *Harris v Ryding* (1839) 5 M&W 60, 151 ER 27 (Exch Ch) and *Humphries v Brogden* (1850) 12 QB 739 (KB).

[26] *Hext v Gill* (1872) 7 LR Ch App 699 (HL Eng).

[27] (1888) 13 App Cas 657 (HL).

[28] [1910] AC 116 (HL Scot).

It is impossible to give an exhaustive definition of the meaning of the much debated words that are to be found in s.70. But I hope your Lordships may assist in their interpretation. In the first place, I think it is clear that by the words 'or other minerals' exceptional substances are designated, not the ordinary rock of the district. In the second place, I think that in deciding whether or not in a particular case exceptional substances are minerals the true test is that laid down by Lord Halsbury in *Lord Provost of Glasgow* v. *Farie*. The Court has to determine 'what these words meant in the vernacular of the mining world, the commercial world, and landowners' at the time when the purchase was effected, and whether the particular substance was so regarded as a mineral.[29]

North British Railway v Budhill made another important point by holding that the burden of proof that a particular substance was, at the date of the document to be construed, or is, at the present day, regarded as a mineral is upon those raising the contention.[30] This onus of proof is a reflection of the rule, or presumption, that the proprietor of the surface is proprietor of everything below. In subsequent cases, the House made it clear that as far as they were concerned, they had settled the law with this 'vernacular test'.[31] Much later, *Lonsdale v Attorney General*[32] reaffirmed the continuing primacy of *North British Railway v Budhill*, and demonstrates something of the complexities of the matter in relation to a claim for petroleum rights. 'Minerals' is not a term that has any ordinary primary meaning.

There is a natural tendency to assume that anything subterranean is in the hands of the owners of mineral rights, but a closer examination shows that this is not the case. Mineral rights are grants of minerals, as understood by the vernacular test; they are not grants of all strata, structures, and phenomena below the surface. Where mineral rights are owned separately, they do not necessarily entail property rights to all things subterranean. The leading case on this point is *Pountney v Clayton*,[33] where a railway company used statutory powers to purchase land (the surface) without the minerals. It was held that this allowed the mineral owner to continue working the minerals. Brett MR observed:

That is a power of election given to railway companies by which they may, if they please, elect to purchase the mines as well as the rest of the land, or only that which is popularly called the surface land, but which really means a right to all the land except the mines.

Bowen LJ said:

Primâ facie the owner of the land has everything under the sky down to the centre of the earth, but there are certain rights of support which follow as incident thereto when nothing is known about the origin of such rights.... What I have said is, I think, consistent with the language of Lord Wensleydale in *Rowbotham v Wilson*... 'prima facie the owner of the

[29] [1910] AC 116 (HL Scot) at 127 per Lord Loreburn LC.

[30] *North British Railway Co v Budhill* at 134.

[31] *Great Western Rwy v Carpalla United China Clay Co* [1910] AC 83 (HL Eng); *Caledonian Rwy Co v Glenboig Union Fireclay Co* [1911] AC 290 (HL Scot); and *Symington v Caledonian Rwy Co* [1912] AC 87 at 90 (HL Scot).

[32] [1982] 3 All ER 579 at 602, 609.

[33] (1883) 11 QBD 820. The quotation from Brett MR is at 833; that from Bowen LJ at 838–40.

surface is entitled to the surface itself and all below it ex jure naturae: and those who claim the property in the minerals below, or any interest in them, must do so by some grant from or conveyance by him, or it may be from the Crown' . . . Now applying what I have said to the grant of the surface of the land, too much stress cannot be laid upon what has been pointed out by the Master of the Rolls, that the surface means not the mere plane surface but all the land except the mines.

This quotation is worthwhile not only because of its confirmation of the general rule, but also because of its affirmation that the ownership of land includes all the land and everything underneath, except the mines or minerals that have been specifically excepted. Even where mineral rights are owned separately, they do not necessarily entail rights to everything in the subsurface.

In *North British Railway v Budhill* itself, Lord Gorell said of the use of the definition of 'minerals' in the railway lands statute in issue that:[34]

The enumeration of certain specified matters tends to shew that its [the Act's] object was to except exceptional matters, and not to include in its scope those matters which are to be found everywhere in the construction of railways, such as clay, sand, gravel, and ordinary stone.

Again, the default position is that the subsurface is in the same proprietorship as the surface, subject only to particular grants of mines and minerals. An understanding of this point makes it possible to deal more readily with questions of the ownership of underground pore space or chambers.

VI. Mine workings and pore space

Some of the newer uses of the subsurface inject fluid into pore space. Pore space comprises the minute voids that exist between the solid grains of minerals that make up rock, filled with fluids such as water, oil, or gas. Carbon capture and storage, gas storage, and deep-well disposal all inject fluids into this pore space. Enhanced oil recovery injects fluids into pore space as part of the extraction of minerals, but other operations are not for the extraction of minerals. In many jurisdictions, the analysis of proprietary rights concerning carbon capture and storage has been couched as a debate between the ownership of pore space by the land owner or the mineral owner.[35] A line of English and Scottish cases (and one Canadian) is often cited in support of the mineral owner, but when read closely the cases do not produce that result, and can be reconciled with general common law principles of subsurface ownership.

The line begins with *Bowser v Maclean*[36] and its facts are typical of the line generally. A surface owner objected to the activities of a mineral owner, who had

[34] [1910] AC 116 (HL Scot) at 134.

[35] O. Anderson, 'Geologic CO_2 Sequestration: Who Owns the Pore Space?' (2009) 9 Wyoming L Rev 97.

[36] (1860) 2 DeG&J 415, 45 ER 682.

coal mine workings which he used not only to extract the coal below the estate of the surface owner, but also to run a tramway to carry coal from his workings under adjoining properties ('foreign coal') and to provide those other mines with drainage and ventilation. The Lord Chancellor held that the miner could not do this, because the land was copyhold, and the copyholder was in possession of the subsoil subject only to the minerals being in the lord of the manor and its lessee. However, the surface owner would have had no complaint in the case of freehold land leased with a reservation of minerals, or freehold land where the surface belongs to one owner and the subsoil, containing the minerals, belongs to another, as separate tenements divided from each other vertically.

Proud v Bates[37] applied *Bowser v Maclean* to an exception in a lease or demise of 'the mines and quarries lying and being within the same [land] . . . with free wayleave and passage to, from and along the same, on foot or on horseback, with all manner of carriages'. The judge construed this to mean that the mine owner could use the mine passages for the transport of foreign coal or for any other purpose. The mines were altogether out of the demise and, never having been demised or parted with, their owners were at liberty to use them as they may think fit. But the judge did not lay down any general rule; he construed the particular demise. *Proud v Bates* was followed in several subsequent cases. *Duke of Hamilton v Graham*[38] applied it in the House of Lords, to an exception of 'all and sundry the said coal and limestone within the bounds of the lands' which was held to give the owner an absolute right to do what he pleased with the mines, and might use them for any purpose beneficial to himself, not merely for the extraction of the coal and limestone in those lands. The mine owner's right was a right of property *in pleno dominio*, and not a right of servitude, like an easement. There was no distinction to be drawn between the law of England and Scotland on the matter. *Ramsay v Blair*,[39] *Ballacorkish Silver, Lead, and Copper Mining Co v Harrison*,[40] *Eardley v Granville*,[41] and *Batten Pooll v Kennedy*[42] all followed the same reasoning. In Canada, it was followed in *Little v Western Transfer and Storage Co*,[43] where a mineral lease recited that the lessor owned 'the coal and surface rights' and granted 'all the said coal'. The Court reasoned that this suggested and indicated a parity of title between the coal rights and the surface rights, so that the grant was one of the property, the stratum or strata, in which the coal was embedded.

Recent literature on carbon capture and storage has picked up on these cases in the form of the 'English Rule'. For example, Campbell, James, and Hutchings say that '[t]he English Rule states that the mineral interest holder is the owner of rights in the mineral formation separate and apart from its rights to remove the

[37] (1865) 34 LJ (Ch) 406. [38] (1871) LR 2 SC&Div 166. [39] (1876) 1 App Cas 701.
[40] LR 5 PC 49. [41] (1876) 3 ChD 826. [42] [1907] 1 Ch 256.
[43] [1922] 3 WWR 356 (Alta SC TD). See N. Bankes, J. Poschwatta, and E. M. Shier, 'The Legal Framework for Carbon Capture and Storage in Alberta' (2008) 45 Alberta L Rev 585 at 604, referring to the 'English' rule and the 'American' rule. Also see B. J. Barton, *Canadian Law of Mining* (1993) 35–6.

minerals'.[44] Plainly, that is not right. The usage started, it seems, in an early natural gas storage case, *Central Kentucky Natural Gas Co v Smallwood*,[45] which cited *Bowser v Maclean* and *Batten Pooll*, accurately, but distinguished them as dealing with solid minerals rather than fugitive ones, where the formation could be exhausted, but the mineral owner still retained the exclusive right to take all the minerals that find their way into the formation, whether by injection or otherwise. Stamm picked up the idea of an English rule that was the opposite of the American rule.[46] Lyndon, in a creditable short student piece, used the terms as well, but studied the British cases and *Little v Western Transfer and Storage*.[47] Stewart analysed the cases in a fine study that stands the test of time.[48] But then follows a group of writings that cite *Central Kentucky*, Stamm, and Lyndon, but not the British cases themselves, and fall into error.[49] Some other writers have sensibly expressed scepticism of the idea of an 'English Rule'.[50]

What, then, can properly be extracted from these old cases about the application of the common law to modern subsurface ownership questions? Certainly they affirmed that a mineral owner could control passageways for purposes unrelated to mining the minerals in the land. *Hamilton v Graham, Ramsay v Blair*, and *Ballacorkish Silver v Harrison* are clear authority and at the highest level; and if there were any rule, perhaps it would be called the Scottish rule. Many of the cases concerned grants of 'mines' and the reasoning in *Proud v Bates* was that mines must be something more than minerals, being where minerals came from. The term 'mines' was understood in a fairly literal manner, unlikely to have lent itself to an

[44] T. A. Campbell, R. A. James, and J. Hutchings, 'Carbon Capture and Storage Project Development: An Overview of Property Rights Acquisition, Permitting, and Operational Liability Issues' (2007) 38 Texas Envtl LJ 169 at 172.

[45] 252 SW 2d 866 (1952); overruled by *Texas American Energy Corp v Citizens Fidelity Bank & Trust Co*, 736 SW 2d 25 (Ky 1987).

[46] A. Stamm, 'Legal Problems in the Underground Storage of Natural Gas' (1957) 36 Texas L Rev 161.

[47] J. L. Lyndon 'Legal Aspects of Underground Storage of Natural Gas' (1961)1 Alberta L Rev 543.

[48] N. J. Stewart, 'The Reservation or Exception of Mines and Minerals' (1962) 40 Canadian Bar Rev 329. The only questions I would ask about his analysis of these cases are whether he overemphasizes the intention of the parties separately from the reading of the documents as objectively understood at the time they were written; and whether his distinction between deep minerals and shallow ones is well grounded.

[49] E. Wilson, 'Managing the Risks of Geologic Carbon Sequestration: A Regulatory and Legal Analysis' (2004) PhD thesis, Carnegie Mellon University, 68; B. Metz, O. Davidson, H. de Coninck, M. Loos, and L. Meyer, *Carbon Dioxide Capture and Storage* (Intergovernmental Panel on Climate Change Special Report, 2005) 256; M. de Figueiredo, *Property Interests and Liability of Geologic Carbon Dioxide Storage* (Special Report to MIT Carbon Sequestration Initiative, 2005) 6; E. Wilson and M. de Figueiredo, 'Geologic Carbon Dioxide Sequestration: An Analysis of Subsurface Property Law' (2006) 36 ELR 10114 at 10121; M. de Figueiredo, 'Liability of Carbon Dioxide Storage' (2007) PhD thesis, Massachusetts Institute of Technology, 287; Campbell, James, and Hutchings (n 44); Interstate Oil and Gas Compact Commission, *Storage of Carbon Dioxide in Geologic Structures: A Legal and Regulatory Guide for States and Provinces* (2007) 19; G. Severinsen, 'Towards an Effective Legal Framework for the Geo-Sequestration of Carbon Dioxide in New Zealand' (2010) 16 Canterbury L Rev 130.

[50] N. Bankes, J. Poschwatta, and E. Shier, 'The Legal Framework for Carbon Capture and Storage in Alberta' (2008) 45 Alta L Rev 585 at 604 and I. Duncan, S. Anderson, and J.-P. Nicot, 'Pore Space Ownership Issues for CO2 Sequestration in the US' (2009) 1 Energy Procedia 4427.

extrapolation to include pore space. The term 'minerals' did not give their owner any right to subsurface chambers and passages except for the working of the minerals granted. 'Minerals' does not comprise the space occupied or formerly occupied by mineral substances. *Eardley v Granville* is entirely clear on that, in a gloss on *Bowser v Maclean*, which was subsequently accepted in *Batten Pooll v Kennedy*.[51] Indeed, there appears to be no case where a grant of 'minerals' has given such rights. Further, every case depended on the construction of the instrument of severance, the grant or demise in question. The courts never erected a rule independent of the facts and the instruments. In some cases they thought the grant to be odd[52] (all the more reason for not finding a general rule), but they construed them as they were. In *Proud v Bates*, for example, it seems entirely clear that mine passageways were meant to be included. Finally, one may observe that virtually all the cases concerned coal, or coal and limestone or ironstone.[53] The context of stratified mineral deposits may have lent itself more readily than others to the conclusion that a grant of a stratum was intended. Extrapolation to oil and gas seems unjustified. In addition, the cases are all about the use of the spaces in a conventional mine; extrapolation to microscopic pore spaces also seems unjustified.

Some related points need to be made. First, the construction of mineral instruments of severance changed with *North British Railway v Budhill* in 1914, and arguably more attention would now be given than in the *Bowser v Maclean* cases to the understanding of the words used in an instrument at the time it was made. A more flexible interpretation might emerge. Second, two cases seem to stand outside the *Bowser v Maclean* line of cases while dealing with the same issues. The first is *Pountney v Clayton*, quoted earlier, dealing with the Railway Clauses Consolidation Act 1845, and emphasizing the primacy of the land owner's rights. The second is *Mitchell v Mosley*, where the defendant's predecessors in title granted a mining lease in 1740, a demise of 'all and every the mines, veins, seams and beds of coal, and cannel' which might be found in the land. Subsequent conveyances had to be interpreted. The following quotation is long but it is valuable for showing what seems to be a modern approach to the operation of the *cuius est solum* principle in relation to the conveyances in question.[54]

> It seems to me quite clear that they are conveyances of everything—conveyances of the land which include (unless you can find something to the contrary) everything down to the centre of the earth. The grant of the land includes the surface and all that is supra—houses, trees, and the like—*cujus est solum ejus est usque ad caelum*—and all that is infra, i.e., mines, earth, clay, &c. It is, however, within the right of the lessees to get the coal and cannel during the term. Subject to that right, so far as it can be and is exercised by the lessees under the lease, it is to my mind quite clear as a matter of construction of the conveyances that not merely the surface rights but the whole substratum to the centre of the earth, even including

[51] *Eardley v Granville* at 834. This is also the position taken in 20 Halsbury, *Laws of England* (1st edn) 504.

[52] *Proud v Bates; Hamilton v Graham.*

[53] *Ballacorkish Silver* concerned a grant of mines and minerals but the company name suggests that it was not a coal case.

[54] [1914] 1 Ch 438 (CA) at 450 per Cozens-Hardy MR.

the vacant spaces from which during the term the coal may have been worked out by the lessees—all that passed by the conveyance to the Mitchells.

The decision meant that rights under the mining lease did not provide consequent rights to control the use of the vacant spaces left. Rights to them, not being held under the mining lease, are held by default by the owner of the land. The 'surface' proprietor is likely to hold rights to subsurface features if those rights do not fall into the mineral rights that have been excepted or reserved. *Mitchell v Mosley* and *Pountney v Clayton* are not easy to reconcile with the old authorities, but they were both referred to in *Bocardo v Star Energy*, and may be more compatible with a modern approach to subsurface ownership.

This analysis may have been lengthy, but it may be enough to explode the fallacy of a general rule of common law in England or anywhere else that a mineral owner has control of a mineral formation for purposes other than extracting minerals. The decisions all concerned coal and, like solid substances, they all depended on the interpretation of the instrument of severance, and the most recent case is from 1922. The key characteristic of the common law is that the ownership of the land owner includes everything downwards indefinitely, subject only to those rights, such as to minerals, that are vested in someone else. The generality of the soil and rock is in the hands of the land owner.

In particular, the cases do not justify any proposition that pore space has a legal status different from any other attribute of subsurface material, or of land ownership generally. If I have two sheds on my land with a gap between them, that space does not have any special legal status. Nor should the spaces between individual grains of rock. 'Pore space' is generally owned and possessed by the land owner, not the mineral owner. What we see is therefore another aspect of a confined role for the mineral owner.

This is the default position, of course. It is often changed, in order to make possible activities that are in the public interest. For example, legislation in several jurisdictions has vested the right to control pore space or storage capacity in the Crown as part of law reform to make geosequestration possible.[55]

VII. The reservation of minerals to the state in common law countries

There is another way that the role of private mineral ownership is confined in many common law countries. Legislation and public land management practices have often prevented mineral rights from falling into private hands, and have secured their return to public ownership or control. The result is that in many common law

[55] Examples from three loyally named jurisdictions are: Queensland, Greenhouse Gas Storage Act 2009, s 27 (greenhouse gas storage reservoirs are property of the state); Victoria, Greenhouse Gas Geological Sequestration Act 2008, s 14 (Crown owns underground geological storage formations below the surface of any land); Alberta Mines and Minerals Act RSA 2000, c M-17, s 15.1 (pore space is vested in the Crown).

countries, public ownership of minerals is much more significant than private mineral ownership. This may not be immediately apparent if one applies the common law principle of minerals as part of the land, in much the same way as the accession theory of the civil law.

In the early days of British colonization and settlement of Canada, Australia, and New Zealand, the basic rule that minerals were part of the land applied to grants of land made by the state to settlers. But in the late 1800s and early 1900s, there spread through such countries a policy of reserving all minerals to the state.[56] In western Canada, for example, grants of land were made subject to a reservation of minerals from 1887. Similar reservations had spread to all states in Australia by 1909.[57] In the United Kingdom, petroleum and coal are vested in public ownership. This policy of reserving or reclaiming mineral rights has led to a pattern that is more akin to the dominial theory than the accession theory. The policy is little studied, but it has been of the first importance to the economic and legal history of those countries.

In fact, the trend away from private mineral ownership continues, both in the common law world and elsewhere.[58] One reason is that it is easier to pursue the principle of permanent sovereignty over natural resources, espoused by many countries,[59] with public ownership than private. A second reason is social equity, if private mineral ownership reflects an unfair allocation of rights to natural resources.[60] A third is efficiency.[61] Private mineral rights are often divided and subdivided, making it difficult to assemble land for exploration. The documents that govern them may be out-of-date in the arrangements they allow. Title is often poorly recorded. Different legislatures have therefore enacted measures to transfer mineral ownership to the state. In some jurisdictions, such as Victoria and Quebec, legislation has simply abolished private mineral rights and vested them in the state. Another route, which Australian legislatures have followed, is to leave private mineral rights in private hands, but to grant the state the power under the mining code to

56 Barton (n 43) at 65; T. Daintith, *Finders Keepers? How the Law of Capture Shaped the World Oil Industry* (2010) 318, 429. The United States was less affected by this policy than other common law countries (see chapter 3), but the conservation movement identified with Roosevelt and Pinchot led to many withdrawals of lands and minerals from sale. The United States administers 635–40 million acres of land, mainly in the west, about 28% of the land in the United States: R. W. Gorte et al, *Federal Land Ownership and Data* (Congressional Research Service, 2012). In some 63 million acres minerals are owned by the federal government, but the surface is privately owned: J. D. Leshy, *The Mining Law: A Study in Perpetual Motion* (1987) 243.

57 J. P. Hamilton, 'Expropriation and Compensation in Relation to Mining' [1985] AMPLA Yearbook 242.

58 J. Otto and J. Cordes, *The Regulation of Mineral Enterprises: A Global Perspective on Economics, Law and Policy* (2002) 2–7.

59 Permanent Sovereignty over Natural Resources, GA res 1803 (XVII), 17 UN GAOR Supp (No 17) at 15, UN Doc A/5217 (1962).

60 The Mineral and Petroleum Resources Development Act 2002 of South Africa is an example; see chapter 5.

61 The classical statement of such objections is the argument by Mirabeau in the National Assembly of France in 1791, against the accession system and in favour of the regalian system. Daintith (n 56) at 312; N. J. Campbell, 'Principles of Mineral Ownership in the Civil Law and Common Law Systems' (1957) 31 Tulane L Rev 303 at 305.

grant rights to those minerals to others.[62] The third policy approach, used in several provinces in Canada, is a mineral land tax levied on privately owned mineral lands in order to induce land owners without any particular intention to explore for minerals to surrender the rights to the Crown.[63]

VIII. Conclusion

This chapter has sought to provide a general introduction to property rights to the subsurface and to minerals in common law countries other than the United States, addressing current legal problems. One of the contentious problems is the principle that the rights of the owner of land extend downwards vertically, with no definite limit. That principle has been shown to continue to be an accurate statement of the law. The mere fact that something is underground does not make it the province of a mineral owner. Nor is it *res nullius*. The generality and simplicity of the principle is not overthrown by the existence of multiple well-known exceptions, such as prerogative minerals, statutory and private reservations of minerals, and different rules for fugacious substances, oil, gas, and water. The second contentious point is the rights of a mineral owner—where mineral ownership exists separately from surface ownership—to workings, pore space, or other features associated with minerals. It has been shown that, generally, the mineral owner has no claim on such features except for the exploration and extraction of the minerals. There is no English rule to the contrary. Neither of these conclusions on contentious matters is normative; they are not arguments for suitable legal arrangements for subsurface resources. They are analyses of the default rules, which often need to be changed. A clear understanding of common law principle and authority makes it easier to ascertain the reforms that are desirable from a policy point of view for gas storage, carbon capture and storage, and emerging subsurface technologies.

What emerges generally is a clearer legal position for the land owner, both as to subsurface activity and as to use of the subsurface for non-mineral purposes. The corollary is a more restricted legal position for private mineral rights than some might argue for.[64] When we look more broadly, we find other restrictions on private mineral rights (whether severed or owned by the surface owner) in favour of the state. There is a significant long-term trend away from private ownership of minerals.

[62] J. Forbes and A. Lang, *Australian Mining and Petroleum Laws* (2nd edn, 1987) 5. See *Wade v New South Wales Rutile Mining Co Pty Ltd* (1960) 121 CLR 177.

[63] Barton (n 43) at 72–4.

[64] Anderson (n 35) at 100 observes that the concept of the dominant mineral estate is often overstated.

3

The Common Law of Underground Energy Resources in the United States

Terence Daintith

I. Introduction

Grimes v Goodman Drilling Co[1] is not a leading case in US mineral law, but it offers a vivid illustration of the way several of its leading principles work. Mr Grimes bought a house in Burkburnett in northern Texas, a town that was then in the throes of an oil boom. Within a short time of his family's arrival, he found an oil company drilling a well in his front yard. No one had told him this was going to happen, still less asked his permission. The noise of the engine driving the drill was so loud that he and his family could only converse by shouting, and the engine's boiler had been placed so close to an outer door giving access to his bedroom that he could not open it. He went to court to get the nuisance removed, but received neither sympathy nor relief. No, said the court, the land on which his house was built was subject to an oil and gas lease, of which he knew, or should have known, and the lessee was entitled to make reasonable use of the surface to get the oil and gas. Burkburnett was a town under intensive development through what was known as 'town lot drilling', with very small leases and several wells to the acre, and if the lessees did not drill in Mr Grimes' yard, they might risk losing the oil and gas under their property to neighbouring lessees, since oil and gas tend to flow through the reservoir strata to any point of low pressure created by drilling. What they did was therefore reasonable, and Mr Grimes and his family must put up with it.

Grimes' misery tells us a lot about US mineral law in general and oil and gas law in particular. In the first place, we should notice that this is a purely private affair between surface owner and mineral lessee. The state is absent because the fundamental principle of US mineral law is that the landowner has rights to all the minerals beneath the surface. This is the accession principle, inherited from England as part of the common law.[2] Once the state makes a grant of land, it is for the grantee to decide how to manage the property, and the options available include separating the mineral interest (termed 'estate' in common law language)

[1] 216 SW 202 (Tex Civ App 1919). [2] See chapter 2.

from the surface enjoyment. Obviously this is what Grimes' vendor, or one of his predecessors, had done. The deed carving out the mineral estate may define the respective rights of the mineral and surface owners, but to the extent that it does not, the law will assume, save in exceptional cases, that mineral owners may make reasonable use of the surface for the purpose of recovering the substances to which the lease entitles them, without any obligation to compensate surface owners. This dominance of the separated mineral estate may seem harsh, but follows logically from the power of disposition granted to surface owners by the accession principle; unless it operated, surface owners would be able to prevent mineral interest holders from exploiting the rights they had received.

We shall see that there may sometimes be room for argument about what it is reasonable for the mineral interest owner to do, but in Grimes' case, this was pre-empted by the application of a third principle, the law of capture. Under this rule,

> [t]he owner of a tract of land acquires title to the oil and gas which he produces from wells drilled thereon, although it may be proved that part of such oil and gas migrated from adjoining lands.[3]

This being the case, no surface owner could maintain, in an oil town like Burkburnett, that it was unreasonable for an oil and gas lessee to drill its lease, whatever its proximity to habitations or other sensitive property, when the consequence of failure to do so might be the total loss of all that lay beneath it.

These three ideas—the accession principle (and its concomitant that legal dealings with minerals in the United States are at root a private law affair); the severability and dominance of the mineral estate; and the law of capture—have together largely shaped the common law of minerals in the United States. The first two principles, and perhaps the third also,[4] are shared with other common law jurisdictions, but in the great majority of those jurisdictions, their significance is today much reduced by the fact that, as chapter 2 makes clear, the state has reserved for itself, or has taken back, the property in all or most mineral resources. By studying the United States, therefore, we can demonstrate how common law principles may, when left to operate with relative autonomy, shape the enjoyment of underground energy resources, including unconventional resources. Such autonomy is of course not absolute. The legislature has intervened at both the state and federal level, and with increasing regularity and intensity, to protect important public interests, such as a healthy environment, and to adjust private interests, in cases where the common law is thought to provide inadequate or inappropriate solutions. This chapter does not pretend, however, to be a comprehensive treatment of substantive US law, and I make no attempt to examine such legislation.[5]

[3] R. E. Hardwicke, 'The Rule of Capture and its Implications as Applied to Oil and Gas' (1935) 13 Texas L Rev 391 at 393. See generally T. C. Daintith, *Finders Keepers? How the Law of Capture Shaped the World Oil Industry* (2010).

[4] For discussion of the rule of capture in relation to Australia and the United Kingdom, see Daintith (n 3) ch 10.

[5] For discussion of the US position on some specific issues, see chapter 8 (hydraulic fracturing) and chapter 16 (geothermal energy).

One caveat to be entered at the outset is that underground energy is very largely a matter of state law. There are 50 state jurisdictions, and while all of them, save Louisiana, are common law jurisdictions, their courts have not necessarily applied the general principles of mineral law in a uniform manner. Some specific variations are highlighted in the discussion that follows, and any generalizations offered about judicial opinion in this chapter do not exclude the possibility of a different view in one or more states.

II. Private mineral ownership: the accession principle

A. The basic principle

The common law that the English colonists brought with them to America included the idea, attributed to Roman law, that land, as a subject of ownership, included both the air above the surface and the minerals beneath it.[6] Blackstone, in his *Commentaries*, put it as follows:

> [W]hatever is in a direct line between the surface of any land, and the centre of the earth, belongs to the owner of the surface; as is every day's experience in the mining countries.[7]

The reference to practice in mining countries could hardly support such an extensive subsurface claim, and indeed in some places, notably the Spanish Empire, the accession principle itself had been displaced by the contrary principle that mines were the property of the sovereign.[8] In Britain, however, the monarch never claimed more than the property in gold and silver,[9] and when successive British monarchs made their grants of land in the New World, they made no reservations of minerals other than gold and silver, in respect of which they would commonly reserve a one-fifth royalty.[10]

The colonial proprietors, their successor governments, and, after federation, the United States government in respect of land beyond the original 13 colonies, adopted a wide range of methods for disposing of land.[11] A common objective was to promote settlement by small-scale grants of land accompanied by the obligation to develop it for agriculture. An alternative policy was to make large-scale sales of land to

[6] *Cujus est solum, ejus est usque ad coelum et ad inferos*: 'Whoever owns the surface also owns up to the heavens above and to the depths beneath.' For a critical history of this notion, see J. G. Sprankling, 'Owning the Center of the Earth' (2008) 55 UCLA L Rev 980 at 982–9, who points out that the *ad inferos* element is a late addition.

[7] 2 *Commentaries on the Laws of England* 18 (1766 edn).

[8] See chapter 4. On the history of state claims to minerals in civil law countries, see generally N. J. Campbell, Jr, 'Principles of Mineral Ownership in the Civil Law and Common Law Systems' (1956) 31 Tulane L Rev 303 at 308–10.

[9] What happened when gold and silver were mixed in situ with other metals such as copper was the subject of the celebrated litigation in the *Case of Mines* (1568) 1 Plowden 310, 75 ER 472.

[10] R. W. Swenson, 'Legal Aspects of Mineral Resources Exploitation' in P. W. Gates, *History of Public Land Law Development* (1968) 701. Exceptionally, a royalty of one-fifteenth on copper was also reserved in Virginia. See also J. Kerr, 'Mines and Minerals' (1894) 50 Albany LJ 253 at 253–4.

[11] See generally Gates (n 10) ch 2.

speculators, often with the help of a little bribery and corruption. Whatever the method of disposal, sales of land were assumed to carry with them the rights to the minerals beneath the land. As Blackstone put it,

> . . . if a man grants all his lands, he grants thereby all his mines of metal and other fossils, his woods, his waters and his houses, as well as his fields and meadows.[12]

This proposition was accepted as part of the law of the American colonies.[13] In the first couple of centuries of settlement, there was relatively little interest in the exploitation of mineral resources, and little expertise in the identification of mineral-rich lands, so it is not surprising that colonial legislatures should have made no attempt to design any special arrangements for granting such lands, beyond reserving precious metals to themselves. When the States came together after the War of Independence in the Continental Congress, their 1785 Land Ordinance—designed for the disposal of lands outside the original colonies—reserved one-third of all gold, silver, lead, and copper mines in any land disposed of. The Ordinance expired, however, on the dissolution of the Continental Congress, and no comparable provision was enacted in the successive land disposal laws of the United States Congress. Instead, these Acts generally withheld 'mineral lands' from disposal by the usual methods,[14] sometimes providing for separate sales at higher prices.

B. The grant and retention of public lands

What colonial and state governments,[15] and Congress in its turn, never contemplated until the twentieth century was the possibility of selling off land for surface settlement while retaining, and then leasing out, any minerals beneath it. In the nineteenth century, people who wanted free access to minerals in public lands were quick to describe leasing as un-American: 'foreign to the spirit of our race and the genius of our institutions',[16] or even as derived from 'the dark ages of the world, or from our Spanish neighbors, a nation that broiled Montezuma for his gold'.[17] This long-standing rejection of the idea of reserving minerals in public grants of land has produced a remarkable contrast between the United States and almost all other countries in the world, where strategic minerals, including energy minerals such as hydrocarbons and coal, are generally in the ownership of, or at least under the control of, the state. This may come about either in implementation of a general principle of law (the so-called 'domanial' or 'regalian' systems of mineral ownership),[18] or because

[12] Blackstone (n 7). [13] Kerr (n 10).

[14] See the listing of such Acts in *United States v Sweet*, 245 US 563 at 568–70 (1918).

[15] There is a major exception in Texas, which had inherited, when part of Mexico, the principles of the Spanish Mining Ordinance of 1783.

[16] Counsel in *Moore v Smaw*, 17 Cal 199 (1861).

[17] Cited by J. E. Wright, *The Galena Lead District: Federal Policy and Practice, 1824–1847* (1966) 80, from an 1841 newspaper published in the Galena lead district.

[18] C. Duval et al, *International Petroleum Exploration and Exploitation Agreements: Legal, Economic and Policy Aspects* (2nd edn, 2009) 17–18.

such ownership and control are mandated by the constitution,[19] or because, in an accession-based jurisdiction, the state has by legislation specifically reserved, or indeed re-taken, mineral rights that would otherwise have been attached to the surface.[20]

In the United States, public ownership and control of minerals is limited to lands retained in federal or state ownership and lands which have been granted by the federal government or by a state with a reservation of mineral rights, a practice which only commenced in the twentieth century with large-scale reservations of coal and petroleum.[21] Access to coal and petroleum in federal lands is now regulated by the Mineral Leasing Act 1920. In addition, offshore minerals are the property of each coastal state out to the limits of territorial waters, and beyond this point, are subject to the sovereign rights, under international law, of the United States as a whole.[22] This very large mineral estate is administered on lines that broadly parallel the management of state-owned or controlled minerals in the rest of the world, and there is no space in this chapter to say more about the legislative arrangements involved, save to point to one vital contrast with minerals under private land.

C. Private land and public land: differing constitutional treatment

Mining companies, as well as oil and gas companies, obtain access to energy minerals[23] in federal lands through grants in the form of leases, and the granting authority, the Secretary of the Interior, is free to determine the scope and nature of the grant, and impose whatever conditions he or she thinks fit. This means that problems likely to arise in mining and drilling—waste, pollution, and other environmental concerns, inefficient management of the resource, sharing of infrastructure, and so on—can be dealt with by the imposition of conditions in the lease or in legislation to which lease rights are made subject. The lessee takes the mineral interest subject to these constraints.

In contrast, securing such public interest goals in relation to the exploitation of privately owned minerals requires legislation which will necessarily restrict whatever property rights in the minerals are recognized by the common law, as declared by the courts. The restrictions on legislative power imposed by the US

[19] As under the Indonesian Constitution of 1945, amended 2002, art 33, invoked by the Indonesian Constitutional Court in a ruling of 13 November 2012, which declared invalid a number of articles of the Oil and Gas Law, Law 22 of 2001.

[20] As in France, under the Law of 12–29 July 1791 relating to mines; in the United Kingdom, under the Petroleum (Production) Act 1934 and the Coal Act 1938, and in Australia, under laws covering most minerals, enacted by the different states in the late nineteenth and early twentieth centuries.

[21] Swenson (n 10) at 725–33.

[22] There are also some state holdings of mineral lands, together with mineral-rich Indian lands under federal administration.

[23] Access to other minerals is still governed by the Mining Law of 1872, incorporating a claim-staking system which results in a transfer to the miner of the whole estate in the land, both minerals and surface, in the event of a productive claim: see J. D. Leshy, *The Mining Law: A Study in Perpetual Motion* (1987). No new grants have been made under the Law since the US Congress enacted a moratorium in 1994.

Constitution, and in particular by the Bill of Rights, may thus significantly constrain public policy regarding underground energy and may indeed pose an insurmountable barrier to certain kinds of measures. State legislation designed to limit the waste of petroleum resources resulting from the rule of capture, which encourages adjoining interest owners to drill competitively in order to be the first to produce oil and gas from new fields while reservoir pressure is still high,[24] was fought every step of the way by less forward-looking producers through constitutional challenges. The process of conservation was thereby considerably slowed, and the solutions adopted by the different states run a very poor second-best to those that could be adopted on federal lands.[25] The decisions of the courts as to what property rights in underground minerals are recognized at common law, what are their incidents, and to whom they belong, thus do not simply serve to settle private disputes between individual claimants; they also serve to set the constitutional limits to legislative policy and regulation in the field.[26]

III. Severance of the mineral estate

A. Surface and mineral estates

It took longer in the United States than in England for the possibility of creating a distinct mineral estate by severance from the surface to receive unambiguous judicial recognition. The leading American case is *Caldwell v Fulton*,[27] an 1858 decision of the Supreme Court of Pennsylvania, considered particularly authoritative across the nation by reason of the extensive experience with mineral law issues in this coal- and iron-rich state. The court made express reference to separate ownership of surface and minerals as an everyday occurrence, and at the same time disposed of an issue that might have cast a shadow over mineral severances:

> Coal and minerals in place are land. It is no longer to be doubted that they are subject to conveyance as such. Nothing is more common in Pennsylvania than that the surface right should be in one man, and the mineral right in another. It is not denied, in such a case, that both are landowners, both holders of a corporeal hereditament. Our English ancestors, indeed, found difficulty in conceiving of a corporeal interest in an unopened mine—separate from the ownership of the surface—because livery of seisin was in their minds inseparable from a conveyance of land, and livery could not be made of an unopened mine. The consequence was, that they were disposed to regard such rights as incorporeal, though they are not rights issuing out of land, but the substance itself. In this state, however, livery

[24] See section IV. [25] Daintith (n 3) ch 9.

[26] For a very recent example, albeit one involving rights in underground water, see *Edwards Aquifer Authority v Day*, 398 S W 3d 814 (Tex 2012), where the Texas Supreme Court refused to dismiss two farmers' constitutional challenge to a regulatory order restricting the amount of water they could take for irrigation from an aquifer underlying their land, on the ground that they enjoyed absolute ownership of the water in place (albeit subject to capture, as with oil and gas).

[27] 31 Pa 475. See also *Adam v Briggs Iron Company*, 61 Mass 361 (1851), making the point that the presumption is that the minerals remain attached to the surface estate in the absence of evidence of severance.

of seisin is supplied by the deed and its registration, and there is nothing incongruous in considering a grant of the *substratum* a grant of land, as much as is a conveyance of the surface itself. It is often by far the most valuable, and sometimes embraces all for which the land is worth owning.[28]

The qualification of the miner's right here as a corporeal, rather than an incorporeal, hereditament was crucial to the decision, since a series of conveyances following the original grant of minerals had purported to divide up the minerals into parcels, and an incorporeal hereditament, consisting of a right to get coal from the land, rather than the coal itself, could not, as the law then stood, be divided up in this way.[29]

B. The dominance of the mineral estate

Once the mineral rights are separated from the surface estate, whether by outright sale or by lease, it is the mineral estate that the law treats as 'dominant', as Mr Grimes of Burkburnett found to his cost. Use by the miner of the surface of the land will, so far as not expressly indicated in the grant, be implied in the grant by the court so far as 'it was necessary to be done for the reasonably proper enjoyment of its property in the minerals'.[30] Access to the land so as to be able to mine it is the most fundamental of these rights, but the court may also find that the miner is entitled to use surface resources such as timber, rocks, soil, and water—including water that might be needed for the purposes of the surface owner such as irrigation[31]—for its mining operations, and to erect buildings, build houses, lay roads and railways, sink shafts, and otherwise modify the landscape.[32]

These rights can bear very heavily upon the enjoyment of the land by the surface owner. Certainly, if the surface owner is the original grantor, he or she can seek protection by limiting permitted uses through the express terms of the grant, and will enjoy whatever royalty, or other compensation for the grant, may be agreed. Many, if not most, surface owners, however, will have acquired their property after the mineral grant or lease has been made, so that they cannot control its terms and will probably also find that their vendor has reserved any royalties accruing from the mineral lease. The same will generally be the case for agricultural lessees. This has led a number of legislatures to pass surface owners' protection acts, normally with the aim of providing compensation for damage and disturbance rather than impairing the dominance of the mineral estate.[33] Courts have also taken hesitant

28 At 481. For parallel English authority, likewise referring to the longstanding practice of severing mineral estates, see *Barnes v Mawson* (1813) 1 M & S 77 at 84; 105 ER 30 at 32.

29 The authority was the old English decision in *Lord Mountjoy's Case* (1582) Godbolt 17, 1 Anderson 307, 78 ER 11. On the corporeal/incorporeal distinction in relation to oil and gas, see nn 44–8 and accompanying text.

30 *Marvin v Brewster Iron Mining Co*, 55 NY 538 (1874) at 565.

31 *Sun Oil v Whitaker*, 483 SW 2d 808 (Texas 1972).

32 See generally D. N. Zillman and J. R. Tyler, 'The Common Law of Access and Surface Use in Mining' (1985) 1 J Energy Law and Policy 267; E. E. Smith, 'The Growing Demand for Oil and Gas and the Potential Impact Upon Rural Land' (2008–2009) 4 Texas J Oil, Gas and Energy Law 1.

33 Such Acts have been passed in North and South Dakota, Montana, West Virginia, New Mexico, Wyoming, Oklahoma, and some other states. A recent Colorado statute goes so far as to enable the

steps in this direction through the development of the so-called 'accommodation doctrine', which was framed in this way by the Texas Supreme Court in 1971:

> [I]f the manner of use selected by the dominant mineral lessee is the only reasonable, usual and customary method that is available for developing and producing the minerals on this particular land then the owner of the servient estate must yield. However, if there are other usual, customary and reasonable methods practised in the industry on similar lands put to similar uses which would not interfere with the existing uses being made by the servient surface owner, it would be unreasonable for the lessee to employ an interfering method or manner of use.[34]

By contrast, courts, following English precedents, have been reluctant to find an inherent right in the miner to remove minerals from beneath the land to the point where subsidence is caused. If the miner wants to be protected against subsidence claims, there will need to be language in the grant expressive of a waiver of this right of the surface owner, such as the grant of a right to remove 'all coals', or of relief from 'any and all claims' arising from the operation of the mine.

The courts may also be sensitive to the question of what mining methods were available, economical, or contemplated by the parties. They have been reluctant to create obstacles to the use of efficient new technology, even though this could not have been in the minds of the parties when the deed under interpretation was made. The longwall method of mining for coal, for example, extensively adopted in the 1980s, employs enormous machines which grind into the coalface leaving behind them a void into which the mine roof collapses, causing an inevitable subsidence of overlying strata and surface land. This provoked much litigation by aggrieved surface owners, but the general reaction of courts was to say that longwall mining was simply a modern method of underground mining, which would be covered by a waiver of subsidence liability even if parties did not have this degree of subsidence in mind. Some courts have been more reluctant to extend the effect of subsidence waivers to cover strip mining, which involves the complete removal of the surface; others—notably in Kentucky, a state heavily dependent on coal mining—have held that standard waivers will extend even to this form of mining.[35]

C. The proliferation of interests[36]

In practice, relations between the holders of surface and mineral estates form only a small part of a dense and massive network of connections between holders of a wide variety of interests. Mineral rights are dealt in as a common-or-garden type of

landowner to insist on exploitation methods that will minimize intrusion (Colorado Revised Statutes 34-60-127 (2012)). Restrictions of this type have been a strong incentive to the adoption of horizontal drilling: see n 63 and accompanying text.

[34] *Getty Oil Co v Jones*, 490 SW 2d 618 (Texas 1971) at 628.

[35] See generally J. J. Lewis, 'Severance Deed Waivers of the Surface Estate's Right to Subjacent Support as a Basis for Longwall Mining Rights' (1990) 6 J Mineral Law and Policy 309; Zillman and Tyler (n 32) at 280–3.

[36] See generally O. L. Anderson and E. E. Smith III, 'The Use of Law to Promote Domestic Exploration and Production' (1999) 50 Inst Oil and Gas Law and Taxation, ch 2.

property in the United States, and come in a bewildering variety of forms. Landowners, as original grantors or successors, may divide and subdivide interests in the surface, and do likewise with interests in the minerals underlying it. Different minerals may be made the subject of separate grants. Distinct deposits of the same material, such as seams of coal or petroleum reservoirs, may be separately granted, so that, for example, one oil and gas lessee's property may lie directly beneath another's and may need to be exploited by drilling through it (but not into it). Simultaneously, surface owners will often separate from their surface conveyances the rights to royalty deriving from a mineral lease, rights which they may retain, dispose of separately, or subdivide, by sale or testament. Similarly, rights to get minerals under leases or grants may be transferred or subdivided, again often subject to the retention of a royalty (known as an 'overriding royalty') by the transferor, which in turn may be transferred and divided. The quantum or nature of an interest such as a reserved royalty may continue to be problematic even today.[37] More important from our point of view is the fact that, over time, through sale and inheritance, interests in a single original property proliferate and ramify, with the consequence that today, enormous numbers of people may be interested in a particular mineral deposit. In the case of oil and gas, royalty holders

> . . . often own interests that begin in the sixth or seventh decimal place. The owner of that small a fractionalized interest will receive less than $10 from production sales of $1 million. . . . In Texas in 1997 . . . the average per-well production was only 7.7 barrels per day. The owners of fractionated royalties in these wells are entitled, at best, to pennies per month, not dollars.[38]

The many problems created by this situation will become evident as we proceed through the chapter.

IV. The rule of capture and the special problem of oil and gas ownership

When the interest in minerals like coal or iron is separated from the surface estate by sale or reservation, the minerals become a separate piece of property, treated as land just as the surface is. There is a problem, however, in applying this simple logic to oil and gas, since from the commercial beginnings of the industry in the United States—and also in the other countries where oil began to be produced in the nineteenth century[39]—operators were aware that the oil and gas that came up through the wells on their leases might not have originated in the subsoil beneath. Oil and gas are fluids, and the earliest conception of their origin was that they

37 See by way of example *Moore v Noble Energy, Inc*, 374 SW 3d 644 (Tex App 2012), an oil and gas case which turned on the difference between a fractional royalty and a fraction of royalty.

38 Anderson and Smith (n 36) at 2–10.

39 Notably in Russia (in what is now Azerbaijan), Romania, and Austrian Galicia: see Daintith (n 3) ch 6.

flowed to the surface from deep underground lakes, perhaps over long distances. Physically, therefore, they were thought to be much more akin to underground streams or percolating water than to substances like coal. Only in the 1880s and 1890s did the true characteristics of oil and gas in their unexploited state come to be understood—that they were held in porous rock strata of limited thickness and area, and migrated within such reservoirs only when these were penetrated by drilling so as to create points of low pressure towards which oil and gas would flow. By this time, however, the idea that taking oil and gas originating from beneath adjoining lands was a natural and indeed inevitable process had become so entrenched in the industry's thinking and practice that the courts saw no alternative to recognizing its legitimacy by enunciating the so-called rule or law of capture. Taking the opposite course, and insisting that it was unlawful to take one's neighbour's oil or gas, might have thrown the industry into chaos.[40]

One might have assumed that if, as a practical matter, the courts were compelled to accept a situation in which one might lose the oil and gas lying beneath one's land if an operator elsewhere drilled into the reservoir first, they would be bound to hold that no one had property in such oil and gas before it was actually brought to the surface, and that ownership would belong, from that moment, to whoever had so produced it. This, after all, was the general rule, inherited from England, applying to underground water.[41] In some states, the courts accepted the logic of the 'no ownership' principle and have stuck to it. The first of these was Indiana; the most important, as a contemporary oil-producing state, is Oklahoma.[42] By holding that an oil company had no property in the oil and gas under its lease until it was actually produced, the Indiana Supreme Court was able to dismiss the company's claim that Indiana legislation forbidding it to flare gas associated with the oil that it wanted to produce (and hence making oil production much more costly) was unconstitutional as a taking of the company's property.[43]

Over time, however, the majority of oil-producing states have adopted the principle that oil and gas can be owned as a mineral like any hard rock mineral, the so-called principle of 'absolute ownership'. Some of them, like Pennsylvania[44] and West Virginia,[45] reached this position after early decisions in the opposite sense; others, like Ohio[46] and Texas,[47] took this view from the start. Decisions in

[40] On these developments see, for more detail, Daintith (n 3) ch 2.

[41] *Acton v Blundell* (1843) 12 M & W 324, 152 ER 1223.

[42] *Rich v Doneghey*, 71 Okla 204, 177 P 86 (1918).

[43] *State v Ohio Oil Co*, 150 Ind 21, 49 NE 809 (1898). The decision as to the constitutionality of the legislation was sustained by the US Supreme Court in the leading case of *Ohio Oil Co v Indiana*, 177 US 190, 20 S Ct 576, 44 L Ed 729, but on the basis of reasoning that did not require the Court to take a view on whether or not oil and gas could be owned in situ.

[44] Compare *Dark v Johnston*, 55 Pa 164 (1867) with *Stoughton's Appeal*, 88 Pa 198 (1878). The courts tended to find that oil was owned as part of the land where this was necessary to protect parties with future interests in the land, such as those who would inherit when the current occupant died.

[45] Compare *Wood County Petroleum Co v West Virginia Transportation Co*, 28 W Va 210, 57 Am Rep 659 (1886), with *Williamson v Jones*, 39 W Va 31, 19 SE 436.

[46] *Kelley v Ohio Oil Co*, 57 Ohio St 317, 49 NE 399, 39 LRA 765 (1897).

[47] *Texas Co v Daugherty*, 107 Tex 226 (1915); *Stephens County v Mid-Kansas Oil & Gas Co*, 113 Tex 160, 254 S W 290 (1923).

this sense were certainly influenced by the fact that some interests—notably those of lessees—might be more easily protected if the basis of dealings in oil and gas interests were the full ownership of the material in place and not just the exclusive right to obtain it, which would be classified as an incorporeal hereditament. This would mean, for example, that a lessee seeking to protect its interest against the lessor or a third party could bring a common law action of ejectment, whereas the incorporeal right that the lessor could grant under the 'no ownership' principle would have to be defended by a less reliable suit in equity. It is noteworthy that in a lively debate about this issue in the law journals in the 1910s and 1920s, the only voice in favour of absolute ownership theory was that of James Veasey, who gave lectures at the University of Michigan but whose day job was as general counsel for the Carter Oil Company, a subsidiary of Standard Oil of New Jersey.[48] Neither Mr Veasey, nor the courts that shared his view, offered any convincing explanation of how the rule of capture could co-exist with full ownership of oil and gas in place: how you could be said to 'own' something that could be lawfully taken away from you at any moment.

It is also clear from a reading of Veasey's articles[49] that a wide range of other factors and doctrines might operate to impair the lessee's security of title and to affect the situation of other oil and gas interest holders, and that there was considerable confusion about the effect of such factors in the reasoning of courts in a number of oil states. While today a strict application of the 'no ownership' and 'absolute ownership' principles might lead to different results in certain quite commonplace situations,[50] in practice the courts cannot be relied upon to follow this logic. The significance, today, of the choice in favour of one theory or the other may perhaps be measured by the fact that in some states courts do not seem very clear about which principle they are applying.[51]

The law of capture encouraged intense competition in drilling when new fields opened up, each lessee drilling as many wells as fast as it could in an attempt to profit from the initially high reservoir pressures and to capture oil from as wide an area as possible. This process wasted both capital and oil through the drilling of far

[48] J. Veasey, 'The Law of Oil and Gas' (1920) 18 Michigan L Rev 445. Contrast J. S. Adams, 'The Right of a Landowner to Oil and Gas in his Land' (1915) 63 University of Pennsylvania L Rev 481; W. L. Summers, 'Legal Interests in Oil and Gas' (1921) 4 Illinois Law Quarterly 12 at 128; J. W. Simonton 'Has a Landowner any Property in Oil and Gas in Place?' (1921) 27 West Virginia Law Quarterly 281; D. E. Greer, 'Ownership of Petroleum Oil and Natural Gas in Place' (1923) 1 Texas L Rev 162.

[49] The article cited at n 48, was the first of a series of four on issues related to leases: the others are at (1920) 18 Michigan L Rev 652 and 749, and 19 Michigan L Rev 161.

[50] Such as the question of what measure of damages for the lessor would be appropriate where the holder of several adjoining leases exploited them so as to drain oil from under the land of that lessor by producing it from his neighbour's lease, where production under the first lease would have been profitable. I am grateful to Professor Owen Anderson for this example.

[51] See *NCNB Texas National Bank v West*, 631 So 2d 212 (Ala 1993) at 223–4, where the court states (1) that Alabama is a no-ownership jurisdiction; (2) that a leading text (H. Williams and C. Meyers, *Oil and Gas Law* (1988), §203.1 at 34) says that 'there is no clear adherence to the non-ownership theory in Alabama'; and (3) that 'gas, is . . . a part of the realty, subject to ownership, severance, and sale'.

more wells than were needed for efficient production, created serious fire risks, and led to massive over-production that brought about a price collapse. It was powerfully reinforced by judicial attempts to protect lessors' royalties by implying into leases obligations for lessees to undertake prompt development and to drill additional wells to 'offset', that is, to limit capture by, wells drilled close to the boundary of neighbouring leases. This made it impossible for a lessee to develop a field rationally by acquiring a block of leases and then choosing where within the block to drill to get the best results.[52]

Economic and physical waste became so serious by the 1920s that most oil operators were prepared to accept an ever-developing programme of conservation measures.[53] The most controversial element of this programme was 'prorationing', controls on the quantity of production, in force in different states from 1915 to about 1970. More interesting today, because it remains at the heart of the system, is the requirement of a minimum distance between wells, and between wells and property boundaries. This type of rule was first imposed in Galicia as a safety measure for the prevention of fires, and eventually adopted in the United States, first on Indian lands under federal supervision, and then in Texas, in response, most likely, to fires in the town of Burkburnett where we began this chapter. The potential of well-spacing as an instrument for avoiding the over-exploitation of oil fields by unnecessary drilling was soon apparent, but a new problem immediately presented itself: that of the very small lease on which, if a given spacing were imposed, it might be impossible to drill any well at all. Since this would amount to the expropriation of the lessee's opportunity to obtain oil or gas from it, and of the lessor's consequent royalties, application of the spacing rule might be unconstitutional as a deprivation of property without due process of law. As a result, it became necessary either to provide for small tract exemptions—which was the course followed in Texas until the 1960s[54]—or to create a system under which mineral interest owners would be encouraged to agree to 'pool' their tracts so as to make up a drilling unit of the necessary size, with provision for allocating the costs and benefits of producing only from some leases while others were left undrilled. This was never an easy process, not least because of the fractionalization of interests to which we referred earlier,[55] so the need for compulsory pooling orders has been accepted in almost all states.

It is important to distinguish pooling, which starts from the division of the surface into lease areas and drilling units, from unitization, under which the aim is to develop the whole reservoir, or a substantial part of it, by placing wells in the best locations regardless of lease boundaries, and distributing costs and production among all mineral interest owners according to formulae reflecting their respective

[52] See M. H. Merrill, *Covenants Implied on Oil and Gas Leases* (2nd edn, 1940). On the current law see the multi-volume treatments in, e.g., Williams and Meyers (n 51); E. Kuntz, *A Treatise on the Law of Oil and Gas* (1962–, looseleaf); W. L. Summers, *The Law of Oil and Gas* (3rd edn, 2008).

[53] See in general Daintith (n 3) ch 9.

[54] Fields discovered before that time still enjoy these exemptions.

[55] Though not every kind of interest enjoys a right to participate in decisions such as those on pooling.

stakes in the field. This, the normal method of exploiting shared fields in states that operate domanial or regalian systems,[56] has never been wholeheartedly accepted in the United States. Fractionalization of interests makes voluntary unitization hard to achieve, and state powers to impose unitization are very limited.[57]

V. How new (and newish) technology challenges the common law

The common law has not been rendered irrelevant by the kind of legislative intervention exemplified by oil conservation regulation, which is superimposed on the structure of common law property rights and indeed assumes the operation of basic principles like the rule of capture.[58] Such principles thus continue to be invoked by the courts to resolve legal problems posed by traditional methods of recovery of energy materials from underground. Despite the legislative attention they have attracted, the new technologies through which unconventional resources—shale oil and gas, coal bed methane, underground storage—are exploited, may likewise demand the application of common law principles and may indeed present the courts with new challenges, which I examine in this section.

A. Shale gas and oil: hydraulic fracturing and horizontal drilling

US courts did not come totally unprepared to adjudicate on the 'new' technologies of horizontal drilling and hydraulic fracturing[59] that now enable us to tap the great quantities of oil and of gas held in underground shale beds and coal seams. These are refinements of practices that have a long history. Early oil producers in Pennsylvania and other northern states frequently tried to remedy reduced flows of oil in a well by 'improving' it: a process which involved dropping a can of nitro-glycerine down the well and relying on the explosion at the bottom to shatter the surrounding reservoir rock so as to make the oil flow more freely. This was held in 1892 to be generally lawful in the face of a complaint that the technique artificially accelerated the process of drainage from the complainant's land to the 'improved' well.[60] Similarly, horizontal drilling, perfected only in the past few decades, is a development of the practice of directional drilling, the deliberate deviation of a well away from the vertical. This was extensively practised in Texas in the 1930s, and the objective, again, was to get more oil than might have been obtained by

[56] Including federal public lands in the United States: Daintith (n 3) at 285–8.

[57] Daintith (n 3) at 288–94. The agreement of up to 85% of interest holders is required before unitization can be imposed on the remainder: see W. F. Carr, 'Compulsory Fieldwide Unitization' (2003) 49 Rocky Mountain Mineral Law Institute, ch 21, Appendix. Texas still has no compulsory unitization statute.

[58] B. M. Kramer and O. L. Anderson, 'The Rule of Capture: An Oil and Gas Perspective' (2005) 35 Environmental Law 899 at 951–4.

[59] For definitions see chapter 1.

[60] *People's Gas Co v Tyner*, 131 Ind 277, 31 NE 59 (1892). But the technique might still amount to a nuisance if practised in an urban area because of the dangers involved: *Tyner v People's Gas Co*, 131 Ind 408, 31 N E 61 (1892).

conventional drilling; but this time the idea was to bottom out one's well under the more productive land of a neighbour. Unlike 'improving' with nitro-glycerine, therefore, it involved an underground invasion of one's neighbour's lease area, and despite anguished protests by its practitioners that it was behaviour hallowed by time, by Texan values, and by popular consent, even Texas courts felt constrained to hold that it constituted an unlawful subterranean trespass.[61]

Contemporary use of hydraulic fracturing is controversial largely because of concerns about its environmental impacts, particularly the fear that the mix of chemicals added to the vast volumes of water injected into the formation under high pressure to crack the rock may penetrate strata carrying potable water.[62] Horizontal drilling, by contrast, offers real environmental advantages in that, by drilling a number of wells from a single production pad and extending the bores horizontally over considerable distances, a far greater proportion of the pay zone may be reached with less surface interference. Increasing restrictions on access to land for the purposes of drilling, especially in the Rocky Mountain states, have provided a substantial stimulus for horizontal drilling in those areas.[63] Both horizontal drilling and hydraulic fracturing may also raise the same kinds of property right issues as did their predecessors.

Unless the lease to be exploited is a large one, making horizontal drilling effective will require the pooling of a number of leases if the end-points at which the wells collect oil and gas from the formation are not to be off-lease—which would mean that such drilling constituted a subsurface trespass. Indeed, since the key applications of horizontal drilling are in shale formations and highly fractured formations that cannot be economically exploited with vertical drilling, each horizontal wellbore will commonly be perforated and fractured at a number of points along its length, so that all leases overlying the bore will need to be pooled.

The consequent problems are well illustrated by cases like *Browning Oil Co Inc v Luecke*,[64] in which the plaintiff lessors claimed all the royalties payable in respect of pooled operations on units comprising their land along with a number of other leases, on the ground that the pooling arrangements were inconsistent with the terms of the leases they had granted. This being the case, they argued that the rule of capture meant that any oil and gas captured via a horizontal wellbore drilled from or perforated within their land was subject to royalty under their leases. The court rejected this view, holding that the rule of capture did not apply in the same way to horizontal as to vertical wells, noting that a major purpose of horizontal wells was efficiently to exploit 'tight' formations like the one in question, in which oil and gas did not migrate in the manner that had produced the rule of capture. The lessors'

[61] *Hastings Oil Co v Texas Co*, 149 Tex 416, 234 S.W.2d 389 (1950); D. F. Prindle, *Petroleum Politics and the Texas Railroad Commission* (1981) 81–91. See also *Bell v Bell View Oil Syndicate*, 76 P 2d 167 (Cal Ct App 1938).

[62] See chapters 7 and 8.

[63] R. P. Thibault et al, 'A Modern Look at the Law of Subsurface Trespass: Does it Need Review, Refinement or Restatement?' [2008] Rocky Mountain Mineral Law Institute 24–01 at 24–5 to 24–9.

[64] 38 SW 3d 65 (Tex Civ App 2000).

royalties should therefore be calculated by reference to the proportion of production that originated from their leases.

A finding in favour of the lessors in *Browning* would have posed a substantial obstacle to shale gas development in Texas,[65] as it might have encouraged lessors to demand a high price where amendment of their leases was necessary to permit a pooled horizontal drilling operation. Development may already be difficult enough; substantial proportions of the Barnett Shale in Texas lie under urban or suburban areas, where the surface has been broken down into small subdivisions. If the subdividing owner has retained the mineral estate and can grant a single lease, this may not pose any special problem; however, if the owners of surface lots retain the mineral estate, then, subject to any applicable compulsory pooling laws, would-be lessees will need to obtain a lease from each lot-owner facilitating horizontal drilling, and surface owners who do not grant leases may be in a position to hold up the whole project.

Horizontal drilling in such situations also raises a basic property right problem which has not yet received an unambiguous solution in the United States. It is clear that if the wellbore is perforated under a particular tract, the mineral interest owner and royalty holder will, in the absence of a compulsory pooling order, need to consent if a trespass is not to be committed. But suppose the wellbore simply traverses a lot or lease area en route to another destination? One or two cases (of directional drilling) have dealt with the situation where the holder of an oil and gas lease cannot get access to the hydrocarbon-bearing strata through the surface above—because, for example, it is a railway right-of-way in which drilling is impossible for safety reasons,[66] or because it is covered by water [67]—and seeks to drill diagonally into and through an adjoining mineral estate to reach its own lease area. The decided cases give inconsistent answers to the question of whether the mineral interest owner can restrain drilling that traverses—without exploiting—the strata in which it has an interest. It is clear that when drilling is vertical, and different horizons within a given area are the subject of different leases, those leasing the lower horizons may legitimately drill through the upper ones (though they must not perforate their well casings so as to extract any oil or gas from those upper strata).[68] Whether the same rule will be applied in relation to non-vertical drilling may depend on such factors as whether the traversing wellbore and its associated surface equipment prejudicially affect the exploration of the mineral interest immediately below.[69] It may also be the case that the terms of the original mineral

65 Texas decisions will be no more than persuasive authority in other oil-producing states, where the regulatory environment may also be different.

66 *Humble Oil and Refining Co v L & G Oil Co*, 259 SW 2d 933 (Tex Civ App 1953).

67 *Chevron Oil Co v Howell*, 407 SW 2d 525 (Tex Civ App 1966).

68 See *Storck v Cities Service Gas Co*, 575 P 2d 1364 (Okla 1977). Here the drilling was through a storage reservoir, but the court appears to have assumed the legitimacy of passage through the relevant strata.

69 See Thibault et al (n 63) at 24–3 to 24–9; J. W. Morrison and W. C. Mann, 'Reservoir Development: Competing Rights of Horizontal and Vertical Developers and other Oddities of Vertical Legal Principles Gone Sideways' (2012) 58 Rocky Mountain Mineral Law Institute 11–01 at 11–23 to 11–25.

lease are such that the surface owner retains the right to admit another adjoining mineral interest owner to drill directionally. The matter thus becomes one of the interpretation of the relevant grants. Certainly the grant of mineral rights, however described, does not convey the entirety of the subsurface.[70]

The rights of the surface owner when the strata beneath his surface are traversed by horizontal drilling might seem to be clearer. Penetration by a wellbore must constitute a trespass to the surface owner's property, certainly if it is not the subject of a mineral lease and probably, on the principle just enunciated, even if it is. The fact that it is hard to identify any damage to the surface owner's interests does not, in terms of established trespass law, excuse the trespass.[71]

Over the past few decades, however, a number of US courts have shown reluctance to prohibit or sanction subsurface trespasses where no specific harm has been shown to ensue. The issue was presented in very clear terms in the recent case of *Coastal Oil and Gas Corp v Garza Energy Trust* in the Texas Supreme Court.[72] Here the alleged trespass was the result not of horizontal drilling, but of hydraulic fracturing. The cracks created by the injection of water, chemicals, and proppants into Coastal's vertical wells to allow oil or gas to escape were alleged by the plaintiffs to have extended beyond the boundaries of Coastal's land, resulting in the extraction of gas from under the Garzas' land: gas, said the Garzas, that rightfully belonged to them. The defendants' response, unsurprisingly, was the same as that of the People's Gas Company to Mr Tyner a century earlier: the rule of capture excused them from any liability for this taking. When the gas flowed from the Garzas' land into Coastal's wellbore, it became Coastal's property. To this the Garzas replied that the fractures constituted a trespass to their land in the same way as would the bottoming by Coastal of a directional well on their land; the rule of capture only operated when drilling was lawful.

While a three-judge dissent accepted the plaintiffs' argument, a concurring opinion rejected it on the ground that the court, with the public interest in view, ought to adjust notions like trespass to the circumstances in which the action complained of occurred, and that causing cracks in the ground and invasions of fluid and ceramic beads two miles down (the depth of the well in question) should simply not be regarded as trespass. The five-judge majority was not prepared to take this radical view of subsurface trespass, asserting instead that while there had been a trespass, the plaintiffs had to show damage to their interests, and this they could not do because the only injury they alleged was the loss of gas occasioned by the fracturing operation, a claim for which was 'precluded by the law of capture.... The gas he claims to have lost simply does not belong to him.'[73] In other words, while for the dissenters the rule of capture could not apply if the fracturing constituted a trespass, the majority,

[70] *Dunn-McCampbell Royalty Interest Inc v National Park Service*, 630 F 3d 431 (5th cir 2011) at 441–2.

[71] This was the view taken in the recent UK Supreme Court decision in *Bocardo v Star Energy UK Onshore Ltd* [2010] UKSC 35, [2010] 3 WLR 654 (SC), in which a landowner was held to have a cause of action for subsurface trespass for unauthorized directional drilling through his land despite the fact that its oil resources were not his property, but that of the state.

[72] 268 S W 3d 1 (Tex 2008).

[73] At 13.

rejecting the directional well analogy, reversed the reasoning and held that the rule rendered any trespass non-actionable in this case.[74] At the same time, the majority endorsed the more general trend to limit the operation of subsurface trespass,[75] asserting that:

> [T]he maxim—*cujus est solum ejus est usque ad coelum et ad inferos*—'has no place in the modern world'.... Lord Coke, who pronounced the maxim, did not consider the possibility of... oil wells. The law of trespass need no more be the same two miles below the surface than two miles above.[76]

On this reasoning, and that of the concurring opinion, traversing someone's subsoil without causing any measurable prejudice would not be actionable.

B. Injection of fluids into the subsoil: gas storage and carbon sequestration

This way of thinking may have considerable relevance to other contemporary underground energy issues. A particular concern of this book is the legal regime states are adopting to facilitate the process of carbon capture and subsequent underground storage.[77] As with hydraulic fracturing and horizontal drilling, the common law issues presented by injection and storage of CO_2 will not be wholly new to the courts. The United States has long and extensive experience of the injection of fluids into the subsoil. Water is injected, and natural gas re-injected, into oil and gas fields to maintain pressure and prolong recovery; CO_2 may be injected either to improve pressure or to reduce the viscosity of oil remaining in place (one of a range of tertiary recovery methods); natural gas is re-injected into exhausted reservoirs and salt formations for temporary storage. In dealing with these activities, the courts have had to address a range of basic questions. Who owns the rights to the underground space into which the fluid is to be injected? In the event of migration from the reservoir, is the injected gas subject to the rule of capture? Is the injector of the fluid liable in damages to anyone suffering loss in consequence of its migration? A brief response to each of these questions may give some sense of how CO_2 storage issues are likely to be addressed in the United States.

The ownership of rights to underground space, in UK law, is discussed in Professor Barton's chapter in this volume,[78] where the reception of that law in the United States is also considered. All that needs to be added here on this topic is that US jurisdictions are divided on the issue, some favouring the claims of the

[74] Hydraulic fracturing might, however, be actionable as trespass in the event, say, that a well on neighbouring land was damaged by the process.

[75] O. L. Anderson, 'Subsurface Trespass after *Coastal v Garza*' (2009) 60 Institute on Oil and Gas Law and Taxation 65.

[76] 268 S W 3d at 11 (footnotes omitted). Compare *Stone and Corwin v Chesapeake Appalachia*, Case 5:12-cv-00102-JPB (District Court, ND WVa, 2013 unreported), refusing to follow *Garza* on the capture issue and reasserting the *usque ad coelum* principle.

[77] See chapters 13 to 15.

[78] See chapter 2.

surface owner, others the mineral owner.[79] Ownership rights are principally of importance in determining who may authorize use of the underground for long-term storage. Where there is some form of production title, the mineral owner or lessee will ordinarily have the right, as an incident of that title, to inject fluids, including CO_2, for other purposes such as enhanced oil recovery. Under state laws, public gas supply utilities may also be able to obtain rights to store gas through eminent domain proceedings (compulsory acquisition) if agreement with the owner of the storage space cannot be reached.[80]

A significant amount of the litigation in US courts relating to underground storage arises from the fact that the injected fluids may not stay within the storage reservoir but may migrate elsewhere. In a number of cases, oil and gas lessees have drilled in the neighbourhood of gas storage reservoirs and recovered gas that had previously been injected there for storage. In such cases, some courts have found it difficult to resist the allure of the rule of capture, and have held, following the much-criticized case of *Hammonds v Central Kentucky Natural Gas Co*,[81] that a storage company has no title to gas that it has injected and that is subsequently produced by drilling on neighbouring property. Under the rule of capture, it is said, such gas, though 'non-native', becomes the property of the person who (re)-produces it.[82] Other courts have held that natural gas once produced becomes personal property and retains this status when injected for storage, so that the rule of capture does not entitle a neighbouring producer to recover it.[83] This, it should be noted, is not necessarily the more just solution, since its effect may be to limit the ability of neighbouring mineral interest holders to recover any native gas with which the stored gas has become commingled through migration from the strata over which the storers have obtained rights.

Stored gas that migrates in a 'personal property' jurisdiction thus presents itself not as a capturable windfall to neighbouring owners but as a nuisance. This is not the only damaging effect that may follow from storage of natural gas in leaky reservoirs: the most spectacular was perhaps the leakage of gas from storage in the Yaggy salt cavern near Hutchinson, Kansas in 2001. The gas travelled several miles before venting through abandoned brine wells in or near the town centre, killing two people and destroying buildings.[84] The risk of damage to neighbouring interests through inadequate containment of injected fluids has been the source

[79] The authorities are comprehensively examined in B. Kramer, 'Horizontal Drilling and Trespass, A Challenge to the Norms of Property and Tort Law' (2012) 58 Rocky Mountain Mineral Law Institute 5–1, and O. Anderson, 'Geologic CO_2 Sequestration: Who Owns the Pore Space?' (2009) 9 Wyoming L Rev 98, Appendix 2. The authors disagree as to whether it would be more efficient for ownership to rest in the surface owner or the mineral owner.

[80] A. Stamm, 'Legal Problems in the Underground Storage of Natural Gas' (1957) 36 Texas L Rev 161.

[81] 75 SW 2d 204 (Ky 1934).

[82] See, e.g., *Bezzi v Hocker*, 370 F 2d 533 (10th Cir 1966); *Anderson v Beech Aircraft Corp*, 237 Kan 336, 699 P 2d 1023 (1985).

[83] *White v NY State Natural Gas Corp*, 190 F Supp 342 (D Pa 1960); *Lone Star Gas Co v Murchison*, 353 SW 2d 870 (Tex Civ App 1962).

[84] M. L. Allison, *Hutchinson, Kansas, A Geologic Detective Story* (October 2001), available at <http://www.agiweb.org/geotimes/oct01/feature_kansas.html>.

of extensive litigation in different state jurisdictions, whose results are clearly of relevance to the development of CO_2 storage. While it has been suggested that leakage from appropriate sites is likely to be 'low',[85] compressed CO_2 is capable of migrating laterally for more than 100 kilometres, and some of it may rise vertically through saline aquifers and some oil fields until it encounters cap rock, clay, or some other barrier.[86] In the absence of such a barrier, it may even reach the surface. Governments in various parts of the world have reacted to these risks by developing elaborate and stringent rules to govern the storage process, including allocation of liability for leakage.[87] In the United States, while the technologies of underground injection are familiar and a wide range of protective legislative measures may be applicable,[88] leakage liability is likely to be addressed by reference to common law rules.

Much of the earlier litigation on subsurface issues connected with the oil industry related to the escape into neighbouring properties of fluids used in a range of oil and gas operations. A classic scenario is furnished by the practice of waterflooding: injecting large quantities of water into a partially depleted reservoir with the aim of restoring pressure and driving more oil towards producing wells. If this goes wrong, other parties' wells successfully tapping the same reservoir may be 'watered out' so that they no longer produce. Courts in different states have generally discussed this sort of issue within the framework of actions for trespass, and have reached contrasting conclusions on such facts: some insisting on a showing of damage, others not.[89]

Legal claims arising out of the malfunction of storage facilities are likely to be treated along the same lines. The clearest situation might be that of a neighbouring gas producer who found that the composition of the gas being produced had changed and that it was being contaminated by CO_2. In such a situation, it might be possible to satisfy the frequently expressed judicial requirement that proof of damage resulting from the trespass be shown.[90] In many other instances, it might be impossible to discharge this burden of proof, not least because knowledge both of leakage itself and of the effects it was producing would be very hard to come by.[91] Alternative bases of liability—like negligence—might be available, but would be subject to even greater difficulties of proof.

[85] J. Moore, 'The Potential Law of On-Shore Geologic Sequestration of CO_2 Captured from Coal-Fired Power Plants' (2007) 28 Energy LJ 443 at 452, citing Massachusetts Institute of Technology, *The Future of Coal: Options for a Carbon Constrained World* (2007) 51.

[86] Moore (n 85) at 454.

[87] See, e.g., the EU's Directive 2009/31/EC of the European Parliament and of the Council of 23 April 2009 on the geological storage of carbon dioxide [2009] OJ L140/114, and the UK Energy Act 2008, ss 17–35.

[88] E.g. federal and state Underground Injection Control (UIC) programmes, the Safe Drinking Water Act, the Resource Conservation and Recovery Act, the Toxic Substances Control Act, and the Comprehensive Environmental Response, Compensation and Liability Act (CERCLA). For discussion of how such legislation bears on CO_2 sequestration, see Moore (n 85).

[89] See authorities cited by Kramer (n 79) and Anderson (n 79).

[90] See for an example of this requirement *Chance v BP Chemicals, Inc*, 670 NE 2d 985 (Ohio 1996).

[91] Moore (n 85) at 477–8.

C. Coal bed methane

Other new sources of underground energy may present a different kind of problem under common law: that of characterization. Coal bed methane (CBM) provides one example.[92] This is natural gas that accumulates in coal seams and is held in the coal. Once it was just a danger and a nuisance, provoking fires and explosions in mines; today, it is seen as a valuable fuel, obtained by drilling wells to remove water from the coal formation and thereby reduce the pressure in the seam and enable the gas to escape. Frequently, but not invariably, this requires the use of horizontal drilling and hydraulic fracturing along the coal seam.

To whom does this gas belong? US courts have on a number of occasions been confronted by a situation where a landowner has at one time sold the coal interests in land, and has later granted oil and gas leases. Landowner and lessee may not at the time have had CBM extraction in mind, but subsequent economic changes and technological advances may make CBM an attractive target.

There seems to be general agreement on the proposition that although CBM is contained within the coal, it is a different substance, and some states have legislated to this effect. This, however, does not resolve the argument in favour of the owner of the gas rights. In the leading Pennsylvania case of *United States Steel Corp v Hoge*,[93] the plaintiff coal-owner successfully argued that since the gas was contained within the coal, a conveyance of 'all the coal' of a particular vein operated to transfer to it the gas within that coal. It noted that it might need to release such gas, if only as a safety measure, and persuaded the court that drilling into the coal seam by third parties such as oil and gas lessees might interfere with full development of the coal, and cause considerable additional costs to the coal operator. In *Carbon County v Union Reserve Coal Co Inc*,[94] by contrast, the Montana Supreme Court rejected this 'container' theory. It had to construe a 1984 deed granting 'all coal and coal rights' under described acreage, along with a 1990 oil and gas lease granting the right to produce from the same area 'oil and all gas including coal seam methane of whatsoever nature or kind . . . '. This court, which was unconvinced of any risk to mining operations from CBM drilling, reached the opposite result from that in *Hoge*: gas (including CBM) being a distinct substance from coal in the eyes of the law,[95] the 1984 deed did not convey any title to CBM, which belonged to the oil and gas lessee. The miner could extract and capture CBM for safety purposes only.

In domanial and regalian jurisdictions, the allocation of CBM between the holders of state-granted rights to oil and gas, on the one hand, and coal, on the other, is likely to be determined either by the terms of the statutory grants or by specific legislative arrangements,[96] and may be treated as raising significant issues of

[92] This is the American term; others, such as the Australians, refer instead to coal seam gas (CSG).

[93] 503 Pa 140, 468 A 2d 1380 (1983).

[94] 271 Mont 459, 898 P 2d 680 (1995).

[95] §82-11-101, Montana Code Annotated. This was later amended (but only prospectively) by §82-1-111, which provides that the expression 'coal' is to be interpreted not to include gas that may be found in any coal formation, unless the clear and express terms of the instrument provide otherwise.

[96] As in Queensland: see Petroleum and Gas (Production and Safety) Act 2004, ch 3.

public policy.[97] In the United States, by contrast, the issue is determined essentially as a matter of interpretation of private conveyances and contracts, influenced, though not wholly determined, by legislative indications[98] and by judicial application—or refusal of application—of presumptions like that represented by the 'container' theory. The choices made by courts in different states—Illinois and Alabama have joined Pennsylvania in adopting the container theory, while Kentucky, Kansas, and Virginia, like Montana, have rejected the use of any such presumption as an aid to interpretation[99]—do not seem to be driven by discernible policy considerations. Technology may in practice be a more important factor: modern longwall mining methods tend to release large quantities of CBM from the coal seam into the adjacent rubble ('gob') left by the process and into the overlying strata, and the application of the rule of capture will mean that such gas can be collected by the oil and gas lessee whatever the approach taken to interpretation.[100]

VI. Conclusion

It does not appear that the unconventional resources under discussion in this book or the new technologies used to obtain them have created any kind of crisis in the process of applying the common law concepts that remain such a central part of US mineral law. Generally speaking, American courts have been very supportive of mineral exploitation. As an early judgment put it:

> The discovery of new sources of wealth, and the springing up of new industries which were never dreamed of half a century ago, sometimes present questions to which it is difficult to apply the law, as it has heretofore existed. It is the crowning merit of the common law, however, that it is not composed of ironclad rules, but may be modified to a reasonable extent to meet new questions as they arise . . . Mining rights are peculiar, and exist from necessity, and the necessity must be recognized, and the rights of the mine and land owners adjusted and protected accordingly.[101]

The remark still rings true. One bright line linking judicial treatments of new technologies, from nineteenth-century 'improvement' of wells to today's waterflooding, hydraulic fracturing, horizontal drilling, and carbon sequestration, is reluctance to impede productive development and a consequent readiness to adjust even long-established concepts like subsurface ownership and trespass. With

[97] P. Johnston, 'Whose Right? The Adequacy of the Law Governing Coal-Seam Gas Development in Queensland' (2001) 20 AMPLA Journal 258 at para 6.1.2, stating that (as of 2001) 'The New South Wales Department of Mineral Resources (DMR) has a stated policy of giving "total priority" to coal mining ahead of the development of a stand-alone CSG industry.' Considerable attention has since been paid in NSW to CSG developments, but no new policy on coal/CSG priorities has yet been announced.

[98] See n 95.

[99] The case-law is summarized in *Central Natural Resources Inc v Davis Operating Company*, 288 Kan 234, 201 P 3d 680 (2009).

[100] *NCNB Texas National Bank v West*, 631 So 2d 212 (Ala 1993).

[101] *Chartiers Block Coal Co v Mellon*, 152 Pa 286, 294–95, 25 A 597, 598 (1893).

legislative intervention in the field of underground property rights complicated by the constraints in federal and state constitutions, courts still enjoy considerable discretion to make such adjustments. This may occasionally be carried to the point of jeopardizing the security of the parties' own contractual arrangements, which perform a much more crucial role in the management of resource development in the United States than they are allowed in state-ownership jurisdictions.[102] Legitimizing the capture of oil and gas was a very early expression of this judicial approach. Today, judicial reluctance, in a range of situations, to treat subsurface trespasses in the same way as surface intrusions, suggests that the courts are increasingly hesitant about giving full effect to the notion of land ownership extending to indefinite depths. The logical conclusion of such a development, of course, would be to ask why courts should recognize surface owners as having any interest at all in minerals two miles beneath their property (the depth of the gas in issue in *Coastal v Garza*), but I know from experience that even to pose such a question is as 'un-American' today as was promoting the leasing of public mineral lands in the nineteenth century.

[102] For examples see n 35 and accompanying text.

4

Civil Law Treatment of the Subsurface in Latin American Countries

José Juan González

I. Introduction

This chapter analyses the treatment of subsurface property rights in civil law countries with special focus on Latin American jurisdictions, and its compatibility with new unconventional uses of the underground. The study is divided into five sections. Section II briefly explains the origins of civil law and its evolution in Latin American legal regimes. Section III surveys the characteristics of the subsurface property regime in the Roman law tradition. This section also studies the process of fragmentation of property rights that took place during the Middle Ages; the idea of property as an absolute and indivisible right postulated by the Napoleonic Code, and the way the Spanish Empire adapted Roman law to its imperial interests. Section IV analyses the difference between surface and subsurface natural resources rights in current Latin American legislation and the exclusion of natural resources from the application of the *cujus est solum* principle. Section V attempts to demonstrate that unconventional uses of the subsurface are ruled by the *cujus est solum* principle. Finally, in section VI the study provides some conclusions.

II. Civil law legal tradition

Civil law has its roots in ancient Roman law,[1] updated and codified in the sixth century AD by Emperor Justinian in the *Corpus Juris Civiles* and adapted in later times by French and German jurists.[2] Civil law is also referred to as Romano-Germanic law. To explain the distinction between both expressions, two main branches can be identified: (a) the Roman branch, modelled on the Napoleonic

[1] The term 'civil law' derives from the Latin *ius civile*, the law applicable to all Roman *cives* or citizens.

[2] See René David and Camille Jauffret-Spinosi, *Los grandes sistemas jurídicos contemporáneos* (trans Jorge Sánchez Cordero, 2010).

Code;[3] and (b) the German or Central European branch, currently represented by German-speaking countries, based on the adoption of the Austrian, the German, or the Swiss Civil Code.[4]

The Napoleonic Code, considered the 'code de propriétaires fait pour les propriétaires',[5] inspired civil codes in almost all Western Europe and the civil codes passed in Latin American countries after their independence from Spain. Thus, the property rights regimes of Latin American countries are very closely based on the French Civil Code of 1804.

The French Code's influence on Latin American law is illustrated by the Civil Codes of Argentina (1869);[6] Bolivia (1830, replaced in 1898);[7] Costa Rica (1841, replaced in 1888);[8] Colombia (1873);[9] Chile (1855);[10] the Dominican Republic (1845/1884);[11] Ecuador (1860);[12] El Salvador (1859);[13] Haiti (1825);[14] Honduras (1906);[15] Mexico (1870/1884 and 1928/1932);[16] Peru (1852 replaced in 1936 and 1984);[17] Uruguay (1868);[18] and Venezuela (1862).[19]

Latin American legal systems inherited from Roman law the idea of property over land as an absolute right. They also adopted the *summa divisio iuris*.[20] The *summa divisio iuris* classified the entire legal system into two branches: public law and private law. According to the classification provided by Ulpiano in the *Digest*, Roman public law (*jus publicum*) regulated the organization of the state, including ecclesiastical organization. Questions of private life, i.e., family, citizens' relations, and business, were regulated by Roman private law (*jus privatum*).[21]

Although the *summa divisio iuris* served as the foundation for jurisprudence and the law in Latin American countries, private law rules on property in the region were complemented and, in some cases, modified by public law. Since the nineteenth century, when Latin American countries became independent, a number of

[3] The Napoleonic Code (French Civil Code of 1804) is recognized as the most successful codification after Justinian's *Corpus Juris*.

[4] Cristian Hertel, 'Legal Systems of the World: An Overview' (2009) 1–2 J International Union of Latin Notaries 130.

[5] A. J. Arnaud, 'Les origines doctrinales du Code civil français' (1974) 26(4) Revue internationale de droit comparé 894 at 897.

[6] Available at <http://www.infoleg.gov.ar/>.

[7] Available at <http://www.iberred.org/legislacion-codigo-civil>.

[8] Available at <http://www.tse.go.cr/>.

[9] Available at <http://www.secretariasenado.gov.co/senado/basedoc/codigo/codigo_civil.html>.

[10] Available at <http://www.diariooficial.cl/>.

[11] Available at <http://www.suprema.gov.do/>.

[12] Available at <http://www.cortenacional.gob.ec/cnj/index.php/component/k2/item/286-biblioteca>.

[13] Available at <http://www.asamblea.gob.sv/>.

[14] Available at <http://juristehaitien.chez.com/pages_textes/droit_haitien/p_code_civil.htm>.

[15] Available <http://www.congresonacional.hn>.

[16] Available at <http://www.diputados.gob.mx/LeyesBiblio/>.

[17] Available at <http://www.abogadoperu.com/>.

[18] Available at <http://www.iberred.org/legislacion-codigo-civil>.

[19] Available at <http://www.asambleanacional.gob.ve/>.

[20] See Alejandro Vergara Blanco, 'La summa diviso iuris publico/privado de las disciplinas juridicas' (2010) 17(1) Revista de Derecho Universidad Católica del Norte 115.

[21] See Miguel Villoro Toranzo, *Derecho Público y Derecho Privado* (1975) 1 at 54.

constitutional provisions, laws, and codes that modify the classic rules of civil codes on the content of property rights have been passed. This trend can be seen in various mining codes, such as the Argentinian code of 1886;[22] the Ecuadorian code of 1886;[23] the Mexican code of 1884 (repealed in 1892 by the Mining Act of the United Mexican States);[24] the Venezuelan code of 1893;[25] and the Peruvian Law of 1895, which established rules applicable to the acquisition of mines.[26] As discussed in section IV of this chapter, during the twentieth century the series of limitations to land property rights imposed by public law gave form to the idea of property having a social function: *social law*. According to the social function, the landowner has not only rights but also duties.

III. Subsurface property in civil law

Unlike common law jurisdictions, countries with civil law systems have comprehensive and regularly updated codes and laws. Given that in the civil law tradition the judge's role is less crucial in shaping the legal order than in common law, in civil law countries the legal status of property is not defined by case-law but by constitutions, codes, and a number of administrative and other laws that modify and complete codified provisions in accordance with political, economic, social, and environmental considerations.

Property law in Latin American countries is the result of a series of influences that adapted the French Code to particular circumstances of the *Orbe Novo,* rich in gold and silver, discovered by the Spanish Crown in the fifteenth century. In that sense, although the provisions governing surface rights do not differ greatly from the French Code of 1804, important modifications were introduced in colonial law regarding the subsurface. After the independence of Latin American countries, colonial law continued to be enforced during the first part of the nineteenth century and guided the orientation of the first national legislations of those countries. Important modifications to property regimes were introduced into Latin American constitutions during the twentieth century. This happened first under the influence of the Weimar Constitution that postulated the social function of property, and then under a United Nations declaration on the environment,[27] according to which environmental protection must be included in the social function of property.

22 Available at <http://www.mineria.gov.ar/codigominero.htm>.

23 Available at <http://www.efemerides.ec/1/marzo/h_petroleo.htm>.

24 Available at <http://biblio.juridicas.unam.mx/libros/1/153/6.pdf>.

25 Available at <http://www.pdv.com/lexico/museo/minerales/legislacion.htm>.

26 Available at <http://www.congreso.gob.pe/ntley/Imagenes/LeyesXIX/1873034.pdf>.

27 Principles 2 at 5 of The Stockholm Declaration on the Human Environment (1972) and principle 15 of the Rio Declaration on Environment and Development (1992) provide the basis for the environmental function of property. See J. Russo and R.O. Russo, 'Induvio pro Natura: Un principio de precaución y prevención a favor de los recursos naturales' (2009) 5(1) Tierra Tropical 23.

A. Roman roots

The legal theory regulating the status of subsurface areas in the majority of countries worldwide was conceived thousands of years ago. Its genesis can be found in Talmudic and Roman law.[28]

Although it has been proposed that the idea of property as an absolute right has its origin in Roman private law, studies demonstrate that ancient Jewish law, the Babylonian Talmud,[29] had already stated that ownership extends 'from the depth of the earth to the height of the sky'.[30]

This idea, according to which the scope of land ownership rights takes the form of a cone down to the centre of the earth, was later adopted by Roman law and expressed in the well-known Latin phrase, *cujus est solum, eius est usque ad coelum et usque ad inferos* ('he who owns the land, has a right from the sky, down into the depths of the earth').[31] Thus, according to the theory of property as an absolute right, subsurface ownership follows ownership of the surface.[32] In consequence, in Roman law, soil and subsoil constituted a single legal unit in which the physical extension of the subsurface was boundless. This idea of property changed during the centuries that followed the end of the Roman Empire.

B. Fragmentation of property during the Middle Ages

During feudalism the idea of vertical, absolute, and indivisible property underwent a substantial change.[33] In feudal law property was not individual, but social. Feudal property was social because individuals were users, but they lacked the rights to use, convey, and exclude as they saw fit. In this regard, it is said that the essence of feudalism is its contention that property in land cannot be 'owned' by anyone; it can merely be 'held' on a temporary basis subject to the overriding good of society.[34] In the feudal system there was only one absolute owner of land: the sovereign. The maxim, 'the King is the sole owner and original proprietor of all

[28] See H. Patrick Glenn, *Legal Traditions of the World* (2010) 99.

[29] The Talmud is a central text of Rabbinic Judaism, considered second to the Torah. It is also traditionally referred to as *Shas* (ש״ס), a Hebrew abbreviation of *shisha sedarim*, the 'six orders' of the Oral Law of Judaism. The Talmud has two components: (a) the Mishnah (Hebrew: המשנה, c 200 AD), the first written compendium of Judaism's Oral Law; and (b) the Gemara (c 500 AD), an elucidation of the Mishnah and related Tannaitic writings that often ventures onto other subjects and expounds broadly on the Hebrew Bible. The terms *Talmud* and *Gemara* are often used interchangeably.

[30] Yehuda Abramovitch, 'The Maxim *cujus est solum ejus usque ad coelum* as Applied in Aviation' (1961–1962) 4(8) McGill LJ 247 at 249.

[31] Haim Sandberg, 'Three Dimensional Partition and Registration of Subsurface Space' (Spring 2003–2004) 37(1) Israel L Rev 119 at 167.

[32] This *maxim,* known also as *Ad coelom,* influenced both common law and civil law traditions, but it has had a different evolution in each one of them.

[33] See John McClaughry, 'Farmers, Freedom and Feudalism: How to Avoid the Coming Serfdom' (1976) 21 South Dakota L Rev 486.

[34] Leo Huberman, *Los bienes terrenales del Hombre* (1973).

lands of the kingdom', summarizes this idea.[35] However, the king normally received the land from other more powerful authorities who, in turn, received it from God. As a result, a king's dominium was neither original nor absolute. Feudal property was a fragmented right. As Booth indicates, '[t]he nobility were tenants-in-chief to the king and they in turn offered tenancies to others. In theory, the chain of ownership could become quite extended. But at every level the principle was the same: the tenant held land in return for services to a superior and was dependent on the superior for his or her continuity.'[36]

During the Middle Ages, whereas the lord had the *domaine éminent* (*direct domain*), the servant possessed the *domaine útile* that allowed him to use and exploit the land.[37] The explanation of the nature of *domaine éminent* is found in its origin. According to one author, there is no territory on the earth's surface that has not been at one time or another taken by force and occupied and attributed to the conquering race. However, winners and masters—precisely because they are winners and masters—are not concerned with cultivating the land, and they only attribute to themselves the legal ownership (*domaine eminent*), leaving to the people the land use in the form of mere occupancy.[38]

Even though in current common law *eminent domain* is associated with the idea of expropriation or takings, the feudal meaning of *domaine éminent* is quite different. As Errera asserts, *dominium*—domain—is associated with the existence of simultaneous, juxtaposed, or superposed rights, that of the owner—*domaine eminent*—and that of those of the different users—*domain útile*.[39] In fact, the common law action of eminent domain also has its origins in the feudal system of property. Bret Boyce asserts in this regard that '[f]eudalism, with its complex network of overlapping rights of kings, manorial lords, ecclesiastical authorities, and municipalities, formed the political and socioeconomic background for the development of expropriation and other kind of property right limitations'.[40]

Up to this point in history, the fragmentation of ownership simply meant the separation of *domaine útile* and *domaine éminent*. Fragmentation between land ownership and subsurface happened centuries later, but the pyramidal feudal property system is at its foundation.

[35] Alipio Valencia Vega, *Fundamentos de derecho político* (1980) 451 and Lina M. Torres Rivera, *Las ciencias sociales en el Mundo contemporáneo* (2004) 16.

[36] Philip Booth, *From Property Rights to Public Control: The Quest for Public Interest in the Control of Urban Development* (2002) 73.

[37] Ben Depoorter and Francesco Parisi, 'Fragmentation of Property Rights. A Functional Interpretation of the Law of Servitudes' (January 2003) 3(1) Global Jurist Frontiers, available at <http://www.mapi.gov.il>.

[38] See Juan de Solorzano Pereyra, *Política Indiana* (1776) 470.

[39] Roger Errera, 'The Right of Property and Freedom of Enterprise in French Constitutional Law' (2009), available at <http://www.rogererrera.fr/libertes_publiques/docs/Droit_de_propriete_St_Petersbourg_09.pdf>.

[40] Bret Boyce, 'Property as a Natural Right and as a Conventional Right in Constitutional Law' (2007) at 216, available at <http://papers.ssrn.com>.

C. The Napoleonic Code

The French Revolution of 1789 marked the beginning of a new era in the property regimes not only of France, but of the rest of Europe as well. The abolition of feudalism implied a transition back from the relativistic and contractual basis of property to the Roman absolute conception of ownership. In this setting, the Roman approach became the model for bourgeois property, conceived as an absolute private right to the enjoyment of one's land.

The French Revolution gradually eliminated complex and hierarchical forms of feudal property, including fragmentation of property rights. After the French Revolution, feudal property tenures were replaced by the concept of absolute property supported by a strong right to property postulated by article 17 of the *Declaration of the Rights of Man and of the Citizen* of 26 August 1789 [the Declaration]. It stated:[41]

> Property being a sacred and inviolable right, no one can be deprived of it unless a legally established public necessity evidently demands it, under the condition of a just and prior indemnity.[42]

This is a unitary concept of property conceived as attached to the person, as part of their *patrimoine* or patrimony.[43]

In the eighteenth and early nineteenth centuries, the reforming aspirations of Enlightenment rulers aligned with jurists' desire to rationalize the law to produce comprehensive, systematic legal codes. This resulted in Austria's 1786 Code of Joseph II[44] and the Complete Civil Code of 1811,[45] Prussia's Complete Territorial Code of 1794,[46] and France's Civil Code (i.e. the Napoleonic Code) of 1804.[47]

[41] Declaration of the Rights of Man and of the Citizen (1789), available at <http://mjmfall2010.wikispaces.com>.

[42] The second part of the provision resulted from the debate that took place in France before and after the abolition of feudalism among Sieyes, Malouet, Ladébat, and Maraton on both (a) the idea of property as a social right; and (b) the abolition of feudal privileges without compensation. See Boyce (n 40).

[43] According to Monreal the Declaration of the Rights of Man and of the Citizen considers property as a natural and imprescriptible right, asserting that its conservation is the aim of all political association. See Eduardo Novoa Monreal, 'Evolución del Derecho de Propiedad ante los actuales textos constitucionales latinoamericanos' (1980) available at <http://biblio.juridicas.unam.mx/libros/1/373/4.pdf>.

[44] Emperor Joseph II ruled from 1780 to 1790.

[45] Joseph II decided that he would enact sections as they were completed rather than wait for a full code to be drafted, so Joseph II's General Civil Law Code, Part I was published on 1 November 1786, to take effect on 1 January 1787, but the full 1811 Austrian General Civil Code was published by Francis II. However, Joseph II's 1786 code was the first part of the full code of 1811, and was also the first set of laws to apply to all Habsburg territories except Hungary, Lombardy, and the Austrian Netherlands. See Miriam J. Levy, 'The Rights of the Individual in Habsburg Civil Law: Joseph II and the Illegitimate' (1991)10 Man and Nature/L'homme et la nature 105, available at <http://id.erudit.org/iderudit/1012627ar>.

[46] The Prussian General Code of 1794 was in effect in about half the territory of Prusia and in a few small territories outside of it.

[47] The French Civil Code was promulgated on 21 March 1804 (i.e. the 30 ventôse, year XII of the Revolution). Bonaparte, the first Consul, was its main instigator. See Catherine Delplanque, 'Origins

Those codes, shaped by the Roman law tradition, are also at the foundations of today's civil law.

When the Napoleonic Code was drafted, article 552 declared that ownership of land included ownership of what is over and under it. That is to say, ownership of land comprised the subsurface. Nevertheless, one should not overemphasize the absolute character of the Napoleonic right to property. The drafters of the Code added exceptions resulting from mining and other laws, and relating to servitudes and other uses which assume that property is subject to regulation for the benefit of society at large. Article 552 of the Napoleonic Code stated:

> Property in the soil imports property above and beneath. The proprietor may put above all kinds of plantations and buildings as he shall judge convenient, saving the exceptions established under the Title *'Of Servitudes and Services related the Land.'* He may put beneath all buildings and excavations as he shall judge convenient, and draw from these excavations all the products as they are capable of furnishing, *saving the restrictions resulting from laws and statutes relating to mines and from laws and regulations of police.*[48]

That French version of the maxim *cujus est solum* adopted by article 552 of the Napoleonic Code made its way into the Codes of Belgium, Austria, Italy, Japan, the Netherlands, Portugal, Spain, Switzerland, Germany, Turkey, and the Province of Quebec, Canada.[49]

Despite its rejection of the feudal system of property, the Napoleonic Code did not fully ascribe to the Roman theory of unrestricted property in the form of a cone down to the centre of the earth, at least for the case of mining. This could be seen as the beginning of the process of fragmentation between surface and subsurface. However, at least for Latin America, the process of fragmentation took its definitive impulse from Spanish colonial law.

D. The influence of Spanish property law

Before the discovery of America by Christopher Columbus in 1492, the *Ordinances of Alcala* of 1348 had already ruled that the King of Castille was the owner of subsurface resources in his kingdom. The riches found in the New World reinforced that principle. During colonial times the subsurface had an extraordinary importance. The natural riches of America—mainly gold and silver—impressed and attracted the first conquerors.

Shortly after the discovery of America in 1492, Pope Alexander VI granted the Catholic monarchs, Ferdinand and Isabella of Spain, ownership—*dominum*—over the lands of the new continent. Indeed, by the bulls *Inter Coetera, Eximie devotionis et Dum si quidem,*[50] the pontiff granted the Spanish sovereigns all lands of the Americas

and Impact of the French Civil Code' [Translated by Edith Horak] (July 2004) Journal of French Association for History of Justice, vol 20, available at <http://www.afhj.fr>.

[48] [Translation by the author; emphasis added.] *The Code of Napoleon or the French Civil Code* (1827) available at <http://files.libertyfund.org>.

[49] Abramovitch (n 30).

[50] All issued in 1493.

already discovered and those to be discovered[51] within certain boundaries.[52] The papal bulls were issued under the condition of catechizing the natives.

Thus, by pontifical acts the Spanish monarchs acquired the *domaine éminent* of American lands and could subsequently convey them to their vassals. Consequently, all distribution of such lands, agreed to by the monarchs, was understood as a conditional concession that could revert to the Crown.[53] Indeed, the Spanish colonization of America took shape under two institutions: the '*encomienda*' and '*mercedes*'. *Mercedes* were lands conveyed by the King to the conqueror as payment. The *encomienda* was established as a right on behalf of the '*encomenderos*' to receive taxes from indigenous inhabitants. In return, the *encomenderos* were obligated to look after the welfare of the indigenous persons in spiritual and earthly matters, ensuring their maintenance and protection, and their Christian indoctrination.[54]

The property regime that applied to the natural resources in the subsoil was more complex. As holders of the *domaine éminent* by pontifical grant, the Spanish monarchs severed those resources from land ownership and imposed on the colonies the *regalian* system of natural resources property.

In the *regalian* system, the King or the state is the owner of all wealth in the subsurface, but that ownership is not absolute. The *regalian* regime assumes that the Crown or the state has the right to grant the privilege to exploit the subsoil, monitor the exploitation's operation, and to receive a *royalty* or tax on the products of such exploitation, but cannot exploit it itself. Thus, in the *regalian* system public ownership of subsurface natural resources does not have a patrimonial connotation but it is an expression of the state's sovereignty.[55]

Accordingly, Gesner and Barrenechea hold that 'the regalist regime is the one in which, while the mines are owned by the State, it is obliged to grant them temporally or definitively to those that fulfil the special conditions set up by the law'.[56] Moreover, in the *regalian* system, as the lords in feudal times, the state does not have full ownership of the natural resources, but it can transmit to private persons the exploitation rights, including the right to any income derived from such exploitation.[57]

As mentioned, in the case of mining resources, the Spanish empire applied the *regalian* system to its American colonies.[58] Articles 1 and 2 of Title V of the Royal

[51] Rodolfo de la Garza, *Temas de derecho mexicano de la energía* (undated).

[52] In order to avoid conflicts with Portugal, the Pope's Bulas granted to Spain the property of discovered lands in a meridian of one hundred leagues to the West of the Azores Islands or Cape Verde.

[53] See Leyes de Indias, available at <http://www.congreso.gob.pe>.

[54] Josefina Piana de Cuestas, 'De encomiendas y mercedes de tierras: afinidades y precedencias en la jurisdicción de Córdoba (1573–1610)' (1992) Tercera Serie: 5 Boletín del Instituto de Historia Argentina y Americana 'Dr. E. Ravignani', available at <http://ravignanidigital.com.ar/_bol_ravig/n05/n05a01.pdf>.

[55] Juan C. Molina, 'El dominio minero en Colombia. La propiedad minera del Estado' (September–October 1945) 4 Revista Trimestral de Cultura Moderna 107.

[56] [Translation by the author.] A. Gesner and P. Barrenechea, *Legislación de Minas* (1928) at 130.

[57] According to Catalano, the regalian system grants the state the *domine eminent*, which is different from the *domine patrimoniale*: E. Catalano, *Curso de Derecho Minero* (1969).

[58] de Avila Martell asserts: 'In the Indies' law on mines regalism was accepted in more general and explicit terms than in Spanish law.' Alamiro de Avila Martell, 'La propiedad minera en el Derecho indiano. Sus bases, constitutción y peculiaridades' (1969) 8 Historia 13 at 17.

Mining Ordinances of New Spain (Mexico)—which were applicable in almost all of Spanish America—illustrate that situation well.[59] They state:

> Article 1. Mines are property of my Royal Crown, as per their nature, their origin and their organization set up by the Law 4, title 13, book 9 of the new compilation.
>
> Article 2. Without taking them out of my Patrimony, I convey their property and possession to my vassals, in a way that they can sell, exchange, lend, donate, or transfer them by inheritance, or by any other way of transmitting the rights they have according to the Law.[60]

There seems to be a contradiction between articles 1 and 2 of the Royal Ordinances, given that the first of these provisions asserted that mines were the property of the Crown, whereas the second conveyed their property to the sovereign's vassals. However, there is no actual contradiction. The assertion that mines were not separated from the Royal Patrimony means that the sovereign expressly reserved for himself the original property—the *domaine eminent*—but conveyed the actual domain—the *domaine utile*—to those who assume the obligation of contributing to the Royal Treasury. Thus, the Royal Ordinances adopted the *regalian* system of natural resources property. This thesis is reinforced by article 3 of the Ordinances according to which concessions over mines could be granted only if two conditions were met: first, those receiving the *domaine útile* had to contribute to the Royal Treasury with the determined portion of metals; and, second, they had to work and enjoy the mines in compliance with that Ordinance.[61] Accordingly, the *regalian* system came to be the force behind fragmentation between surface and subsurface property.

Once Latin American countries became independent from the Spanish Empire, the *eminent domain* passed from the King to the new national states.[62] Thus, the *regalian* system postulated by the Royal Ordinances strongly influenced legislation on subsoil mineral resources passed in Latin America during the last part of the nineteenth century and the first part of the twentieth century.[63] This influence is seen in the Codes on mining and hydrocarbons that were proclaimed during that time.

[59] On 8 December 1785 the Royal Ordinances of New Spain went into force in the Viceroyalty of Peru covering all territories from Panama to Tierra del Fuego (Argentina), excluding Venezuela and part of Brazil, which belonged to Portugal. However, the Ordinances were not immediately applicable to the Viceroyalty of the Plata River established in 1776. In 1857, the Statute of Finance and Credit of the Confederation ordered the entrance into force of the Ordinances in the former Viceroyalty of the Plata River. See Maria Gilli, *Constitución de la Nación Argentina. Comentada y concordada* (2003).

[60] [Translation by the author.] Maria del Refugio González, *Ordenanzas de la minería de la Nueva España, formadas y propuestas por su Real Tribunal* (2013) at 201.

[61] According to Molina, when the Royal Ordinances hold that the Crown conveys the natural resources to its vassals and these can transmit their property to others, the Ordinances recognize the *domanial* system. See Molina (n 55).

[62] For instance, Mexico received all rights that belonged to the Spanish Crown through the Treaty of Peace and Friendship signed by Spain and Mexico in December 1836. See Alejandro Alvarez, 'Latin America and International Law' (2009) 3(2) Am J Int'l L 269.

[63] See Ramón José Bahri Pinto, *La propiedad minera y la propiedad superficial en la legislación Venezolana* (2006), available at <http://servicio.bc.uc.edu.ve>.

For instance, the *regalian* system of property was adopted by nineteenth-century Chilean legislation. In that country, although article 591 of the Civil Code of 1855 (in force in 1857)[64] held that, regardless of the ownership of individuals or corporations of the land's surface, the state owns all mines of gold, silver, copper, mercury, tin, gemstones, and other fossil substances located thereunder. In addition, article 13 of the Mining Code of 1874[65] conveys the property of mines to private persons conditional on their exploitation.

In Venezuela, according to Jesus Mora, the regulations to the Mining Code issued in 1855[66] also introduced the *regalian* system of property in mines. Article 2 of the regulations stated: 'Ownership of all substances mentioned in the previous article corresponds to the State, and nobody can exploit them without a concession issued by the Executive power...' Article 1 of the regulations referred to all inorganic substances susceptible to exploitation, including metals, fuels, or gemstones in the subsoil or on the surface of the land.[67]

According to another author, the *regalian* system in Colombia was introduced by the Law on Exploitation on Behalf of the Nation of Mines and Carbon Deposits of 1868.[68] This Law established in its article 1 that: 'The Republic reserves for itself the property of mines and carbon deposits and such mines and deposits cannot be sold together with the land where they are located.'[69] This provision also established that 'mines can only be exploited on behalf of the Republic through a contract signed by the Executive with the approval of the Congress'.[70] Similarly, in Argentina the National Code of Mining of 1887 adopted the *regalian* system.[71]

In Mexico, in accordance with a ruling of the Mexican Supreme Court of Justice, the Mining Act of the United Mexican States of 1892 vested the nation with the property of subsurface mining resources. The argument of the Supreme Court was based on articles 2 and 3 of the 1884 Code, which held that a concession was necessary for exploiting mines of (a) gold, platinum, silver, mercury, iron, lead, copper, tin, zinc, antimony, nickel, cobalt, manganese, bismuth, and arsenic; and (b) gemstones, rock salt, and brimstone.[72] Thus, the Mining Act of 1892 recognized the *regalian* system in Mexico but just for the case of mining resources;

[64] [Translation by the author.] Código Civil de Chile available at <http://www.diariooficial.cl/>.

[65] Under specified circumstances, ownership of mines could be lost and revert to the state. Código de Minería, available at <http://www.estudiosdelarepublica.cl/plugins/news/images/5_marianne_gonzoz_presentaciooo_de_minero1874_pdf.pdf>.

[66] The Mining Code of 1854 did not refer to property of mines; the regulation addressed that matter.

[67] Jesús Mora Contreras, 'El derecho de propiedad de hidrocarburos en Venezuela: Origen y tradición legal' (2002) 8(2) Revista Venezolana de Economía y Ciencias Sociales 229.

[68] Molina (n 55).

[69] Ley 13 sobre Explotación de Minas y Depósitos de carbón por cuenta de la Nación as cited by Molina (n 55) at 117. [Translation by the author.]

[70] Vicente Olarte Camacho, *Propiedad de las minas de petróleo, carbón e hidrocarburos* (1916) 7.

[71] María Virginia de Moori K, 'Reformas económicas y la inversión en el sector minero argentino' (1999), available at <http://www.eclac.cl/publicaciones/xml/2/4572/lcl1327e.pdf>.

[72] *Compañía de Minas de Fierro 'Las Truchas', SA v Gobierno de los Estados Unidos Mexicanos (1939) Amparo administrativo en revision 8359/37 Register* 329152, available at <http://sjf.scjn.gob.mx/sjfsist/Paginas/ResultadosV2.aspx?Epoca=1e3e1fdfdf8fcfd&Apendice=1fffdfffcfcff&Expresion=329152&-Dominio=Rubro,Localizacion&TATJ=2&Orden=1&Clase=TesisBL&bc=Jurisprudencia.Resultados&TesisPrincipal=TesisPrincipal&Hits=20>.

hydrocarbons continued to be regulated by the *cujus est solum* principle, according to the Mining Code of 1884.

IV. Current Latin American law on subsurface rights

Current Latin American law on subsurface property rights is far from uniform and simple. In that sense, even when all civil codes of Latin America have adopted the Roman maxim *cujus est solum* and in principle recognize that land ownership includes ownership of the subsoil,[73] most of them expressly exclude hydrocarbons and other mineral resources from the extent of land property rights and reserve them to the national domain.

Fragmentation of property rights as inherited from Spain is a constant in Latin American civil law. In fact, this fragmentation of property rights finds its theoretical basis in the differentiation made by feudal law between *domaine éminent* and *domain utile* that gave its foundation to the *regalian* system of property imposed by the Spanish empire in the American colonies and adopted by Latin American independent countries during the nineteenth century.

However, in the twentieth century, Latin America's civil law system built a complex regime of land property rights based on both the *regalian* and the *domanial* systems of property, where private and public law converge. This convergence implies that codes and laws on natural resources modify civil code provisions, but it also means that public law in the national states serves to orient the social function of property. This is discussed further in the following subsections.

A. Coexistence of regalian and domanial systems of property

Since the beginning of the twentieth century, mainly as a result of the domestic political processes in each country, beside the *regalian* system, the *domanial*[74] system also began to exert an important influence on the political constitutions and laws on natural resources and, thus, on the way in which Latin American countries considered subsurface property. Although in both cases ownership of resources is vested in the state, the *regalian* and the *domanial* systems are not synonymous.

The *domanial* regime vests the state with the direct, absolute, exclusive, and inalienable property of subsurface natural resources.[75] It vests it with the right to

[73] See Civil Code of Argentina, article 2518; Civil Code of Bolivia, article 111; Civil Code of Brazil, article 1.229; Civil Code of Costa Rica, article 505; Civil Code of El Salvador, article 569; Civil Code of Guatemala, article 473; Civil Code of Honduras, article 614; Civil Code of Nicaragua, article 618; Civil Code of Paraguay, article 1958; Civil Code of Peru, article 954; Civil Code or Dominican Republic, article 552; Civil Code of Uruguay, article 748; and Civil Code of Venezuela, article 549.

[74] The word domanial comes from 'demanio'. In Spanish law, demanio refers to those assets owned by the state that are designated to provide a public service or to strengthen the national economy and are imprescriptible and non-transferable. See *Enciclopedia Jurídica Básica, Dominio público* (1995) 2610.

[75] Carlos Amado Gutiérrez, 'La propiedad minera' (2010) 3(25) Revista del Instituto de Investigaciones FIGMMG 44.

directly exploit them and, in specific cases defined by the law, the right to grant concessions to private interests.[76] Indeed, various constitutions and laws refer to concessions and contracts as mechanisms to convey natural resources use and exploitation to private parties under temporary basis. Generally, neither concessions nor contracts convey property of natural resources, though in a few cases, such as in Argentina's legislation, the mining concession grants *in rem* rights.[77]

In Mexico the *domanial* model has ruled ownership of hydrocarbons since 1940. In that year, paragraph four of article 27 of the Constitution was amended to forbid granting concessions or contracts for oil exploration and exploitation. However, mining resources received a different treatment. Although they are under the inalienable and imprescriptible ownership of the state, Mexico's constitution allows their exploitation by private parties through concessions granted by Executive Power.

In the case of Bolivia, article 359, paragraph I, of the Constitution (2009) asserts that:

> The hydrocarbons, in whatever state they are found or form in which they are, are the inalienable and unlimited property of the Bolivian people. The State, on behalf of and in representation of the Bolivian people, is owner of the entire hydrocarbon production of the country and is the only one authorized to sell them. The totality of the income received by the sale of hydrocarbons shall be the property of the State.[78]

Article 349 of the Constitution contains the same assertion regarding mineral resources. However, in both cases, the Bolivian Constitution allows the state to enter into agreements with public, private, and mixed national and foreign companies to enable them to conduct certain activities related to natural resources exploitation. In this case, ownership of natural resources also follows the *domanial* system, given that private companies conduct the mentioned activities on behalf of the Bolivian State and the contracts do not transfer rights in property or in possession.

B. The social function of property

During the twentieth century an additional factor influenced the evolution of property rights in Latin American civil law. According to one author: 'since the 1920s, numerous countries in Latin America have promulgated constitutions that adopt a definition of property incorporating the social function'.[79] Leon Duguit asserted that the social function means that property is no longer exclusively a right

[76] Luis González Berti, *Compendio de derecho minero venezolano* (1969).

[77] Alejandro Dulitzky 'La relación entre el estado y la empresas transnacionales y su implicancia en los procesos de desarrollo' (2011) 16 Revista Documentos de investigación social Universidad Nacional de San Martin 30.

[78] Political Constitution of Bolivia [translation by the Embassy of Bolivia, Washington DC], available at <http://www.scribd.com/doc/73770823/Bolivia-2009-Official-Translation>.

[79] See Mirow, 'Origins of the Social Function of Property in Chile' (2011) 80:3 Fordham L Rev 1183 at 1183.

of individuals but that it plays a social function.[80] Although the first constitution in Europe that sanctioned a social function of property was the Weimar Constitution of 1919,[81] it is generally accepted that the Mexican Constitution of 1917 has served as the source for other Latin American constitutions that define property in terms of a social function. The third paragraph of article 27 holds that:

> The Nation shall at all time have the right to impose on private property such restrictions as the public interest may demand, as well as to regulate, for social benefit, the utilization of those natural resources which are susceptible of appropriation, in order to make an equitable distribution of public wealth, to conserve them, to achieve a balanced development of the country and to improve the living conditions of rural and urban population.[82]

The social function of property has been later adopted by other political constitutions of Latin America, including the constitutions of Bolivia (article 56), Brazil (article 5, paragraph XXIII), Colombia (article 58), Ecuador (article 66), El Salvador (article 103), Honduras (article 103), Nicaragua (article 5), Panama (article 46), Paraguay (article 109), and Uruguay (article 32).

Moreover, under the influence of the United Nations Declarations of Stockholm (1972) and of Rio de Janeiro (1992),[83] most Latin American countries have incorporated the right to a healthy environment[84] and, many of them, the principle of sustainability[85] in their constitutions, implicitly or explicitly recognizing that the social function of property includes environmental protection. For instance, article 58 of Colombia's Constitution asserts that property is not a right but a social function that includes environmental protection. The provision reads as follows:

> Property is a social function that implies obligations. As such, an ecological function is inherent to it.[86]

The environmental function of property empowers the national states to impose limitations on private property rights with the aim of protecting the environment.

[80] [Translation by the author.] See Monreal (n 43).

[81] Article 153 of the Weimar's Constitution stated: 'Property implies duties. Its use shall be determined by what is best for the community.' See Gottfriend Dietze, 'In Defense of Constitution' (1995) 122 at 125.

[82] Official translation of the Political Constitution of the Mexican United States, available at <http://www.scjn.gob.mx/leyes/Documents/Political_Mexican_States_2008.pdf>.

[83] See PNUMA-PNUD, *La recepción de los sistemas jurídicos de los países de América latina y el Caribe de los compromisos asumidos en la Conferencia de las Naciones Unidas sobre el Medio Ambiente y el Desarrollo (1992). Propuestas para la cooperación hemisférica* (1996).

[84] See articles 41 of the Argentinian Constitution; 15 and 342 of the Bolivian Constitution; 225 of the Brazilian Constitution; 50 of the Constitution of Costa Rica; 19 of the Chilean Constitution; 79 of the Colombian Constitution; 23 of Ecuador's Constitution; 4 of the Mexican Constitution; 60 of the Constitution of Nicaragua; 114 of Panama's Constitution; 7 of Paraguay's Constitution; 2 of the Peruvian Constitution; and 127 and 128 of the Venezuelan Constitution.

[85] See articles 225 of the Brazilian Constitution; 80 of the Colombian Constitution; 27 of the Cuban Constitution; 25 of the Mexican Constitution; 66–69 of the Peruvian Constitution.

[86] The Constitution of Colombia (1991), available at <http://confinder.richmond.edu/admin/docs/colombia_const2.pdf>. Other political constitutions also refer to the environmental function of property, e.g. the Bolivian Constitution (article 397, paragraph II); the Brazilian Constitution (article 186, paragraph II); the Chilean Constitution (article 19); and the Constitution of Ecuador (articles 26 and 321).

Accordingly, the theory on the social function of property has provided the foundation for surface use regulations in most of the Latin American countries. As a result, it may be possible to build a system of subsurface use regulations on the same principles.

V. The *cujus est solum* maxim and unconventional uses of the subsurface in Latin American legal regimes

Despite the distinction between property over the subsurface and subsurface natural resources, the analysis of the legislation of Latin American countries allows one to assert that while mining and hydrocarbon resources have a comprehensive legal regime, in itself, the subsurface lacks an appropriate legal framework. A survey of Latin American constitutions shows that although most of them consider that property of hydrocarbons and mining resources is vested in the state, with the only exceptions being Colombia, Cuba, and Guatemala, they do not refer to the subsurface per se.

The Colombian Constitution is one of the few in the region that vests the subsurface in the state. Article 332 states: 'The state is the owner of the subsoil and of the natural, nonrenewable resources, without prejudice to the rights acquired and established in accordance with prior laws.'[87]

In the case of Cuba, article 15 of the Constitution holds that the 'Socialist state property, which is the property of the entire people, comprises: a) the lands that do not belong to small farmers or to cooperatives formed by them, the subsoil, mines, mineral, plant and animal resources in the Republic's maritime economic area, forests, waters and means of communications.'[88]

Finally, article 121, paragraph e, of Guatemala's Constitution asserts that 'the subsoil, hydrocarbon and mineral deposits, as well as any other organic or inorganic substances of the subsoil belong to the State.'[89]

Thus, with the only exceptions being Cuba, Colombia, and Guatemala, where both subsurface and subsurface natural resources belong to the state,[90] in most Latin American countries the *cujus est solum* maxim governs subsurface property with the limitations established by constitutions and laws. One of these limitations consists of excluding certain underground natural resources of economic relevance from the scope of the *cujus est solum* principle—such as hydrocarbons, gold, and silver—to vest its dominium in the state as analysed in the previous sections.

[87] See n 86.

[88] [Translation by the author.] Constitution of the Republic of Cuba, 1992 (as amended to 2002), available at <http://www.cubanet.org/ref/dis/const_92_e.htm>.

[89] [Translation by the author.] Constitution of the Republic of Guatemala, 1985 (as amended to 1993) available at <http://www.constitutionnet.org/files/Guatemala%20Constitution.pdf>.

[90] As previously mentioned, in Cuba, Colombia, and Guatemala, subsurface and subsurface natural resources constitute a unity that belongs to the same person; in the cases of Cuba, Colombia, and Guatemala to the state, and in the case of Costa Rica to the landowner, whether private or public.

The implications of such fragmentation of property rights are not limited to the landowners' inability to exploit underground natural resources without the consent of the state. Very frequently, they include limitations to the landowner's land use rights. For instance, article 6 of the Mexican Mining Law asserts:

> The exploration, exploitation and beneficiation of the minerals or substances referred to in this Law are public utilities and *will have preference over any other use or utilization of the land,* subject to the conditions established herein, and only by a Federal Law may taxes be assessed on these activities.[91]

Accordingly, the landowner's rights to use the land are limited by the interest of the concessionaire in exploiting mineral resources in the subsoil.

Due to the land use limitations imposed by the laws, in many countries of the region, the resulting tension between landowners and companies (public or private) interested in exploiting hydrocarbons and mineral resources in the subsoil have ignited social conflicts. Many of these cases involve indigenous peoples that have taken care of the land and its ecosystems for decades and feel that industrial uses of the subsurface threaten the environmental balance. In addition, concessionaries frequently attempt to rent or to buy those peoples' lands for unfair prices.[92]

In addition to this, new uses of the subsurface, such as fracking, carbon capture and storage, etc., could further stress relations between landowners and subsurface natural resources' concessionaries.[93] In contrast to conventional hydrocarbon and mining activities, where the resources have clearly been severed from other land property rights, in these cases the property of the subsurface still follows the *cujus est solum* principle and the land owner may have the power to allow or prevent unconventional uses of the subsurface.

These new unconventional uses of the underground, that in the case of Argentina and Colombia are analysed in chapter 9 and chapter 12, respectively, generally lack a specific normative framework. Such lack of rules could become problematic given the level of concern and criticism that such uses have provoked in the entire region.[94]

However, the role of the landowner in permitting activities, such as carbon capture and storage and other non-conventional uses of the subsurface, depends on the scope of property rights recognized by each national jurisdiction. In other words, it depends on a series of limitations to the extent of the *cujus est soulum* maximum imposed or to be imposed by each national regime.

91 [Emphasis added.] Official translation of the Mexican Mining Law, available at <http://www.economia.gob.mx/files/comunidad_negocios/industria_comercio/ley_minera_mining_law.pdf>.

92 See Anthony Bebbington and Denise Humphreys Bebbington, 'Actores y ambientalismos: continuidades & cambios en los conflictos socioambientales en el Perú' in *Minerìa y territorio en el Perú. Conflictos, resistencias y propuestas en tiempos de globalización* (José de Echave, Raphael Hoetmer and Mario Palacios Panéz, eds, 2009) 434.

93 See, e.g., Paul Johnston and David Santillo, *Carbon Capture and Sequestration: Potential Environmental Impacts* (2007), available at <http://www.greenpeace.to/publications/ccs02-07.pdf>.

94 There are a number of issues associated with these unconventional uses of the subsurface, particularly regarding their environmental impacts, that lack a legal framework.

In this regard, notwithstanding that most Latin American legal regimes consider the subsoil as an extension of the surface land, given the social function of property adopted by Latin American constitutions during the twentieth century, generally, the state has the power to regulate its use. A legal regime governing subsurface uses could reduce the negative environmental impacts of such uses, as well as provide solutions for conflicts between landowners' interests and those of the subsurface resources concessionaries. However, most Latin American countries have yet to exercise those powers. As a result, with the exception of those activities related to the extraction of conventional hydrocarbons and mining resources, the subsurface will continue to be governed by the *cujus est solum* principle.

VI. Conclusion

According to the analysis conducted in this chapter, with a few exceptions, in Latin American civil law there is no fragmentation between land property and subsurface property, and both are still considered by the law as a unity. However, in the majority of Latin American regimes, public law has established a series of limitations to the extent of the *cujus est solum* maxim.

First, in most of Latin America's national regimes, ownership of the subsurface and of natural resources in the subsoil constitute two different subjects of regulation.

Second, in most of the cases, ownership of hydrocarbons and mineral resources is vested in the state. In this respect, whereas a few of the countries adopt the *domanial* system, others follow the *regalian* model inherited from Spanish colonial law. It is also possible to find cases, such as in Mexico, where a country's constitution adopted both models depending on which natural resource is involved.

Third, while national regimes tend to leave ownership of the subsurface to the landowner, the subject is not sufficiently regulated.

Finally, the fragmentation between ownership of the subsurface and ownership of natural resources could generate conflicts between the landowner and those holding a concession or contract to exploit subsurface natural resources, and between environmental preservation and natural resources exploitation.

New unconventional uses of the subsurface are calling the attention of scholars, policy makers, and the general public to the importance of regulating the subsurface in itself, given that competition between traditional and non-traditional uses of the subsurface could stress tensions between conservationists, indigenous peoples, governments, and concessionaries. The law currently in force in the region does not provide an effective legal framework to deal with these issues.

In this regard, the theory on the social function of property adopted by twentieth-century Latin American constitutionalism empowers national states to regulate subsurface uses and exploitation. Thus, it is high time for twenty-first century jurists to build a new theory of property where the subsurface is considered as a matter of legal regulation in itself. Subsurface use regulation has to be the core of a new theory of property whereby the social and environmental functions of property provide the foundations to further limit the scope of the *cujus est solum* maxim.

5

Roman-Dutch Law, Custodianship, and the African Subsurface: The South African and Namibian Experiences

Hanri Mostert and Meyer van den Berg

I. Introduction

Despite significant coal reserves[1] and hitherto largely untapped oil and gas resources,[2] the energy sectors of various Southern African states are persistently unable to meet the needs of their national economies.[3] In attempts to improve the energy independency of the region, attention is increasingly being paid to new technologies for extracting conventional energy sources. This places strain on existing legal frameworks for regulating subsurface use.

As a net importer of petroleum, South Africa is vulnerable to international politics and economics; hence its petroleum extraction sector is strictly regulated.[4] The same applies to Namibia, which is entirely dependent on imports to secure its energy supply.[5] Namibia imports most of its energy from South Africa,[6] where coal and oil comprise 75% and 20%, respectively of the energy sources.[7] In South Africa, the Department of Energy is responsible for administering downstream petroleum (including gas), electricity, renewable fuels, and nuclear minerals.[8] The upstream

[1] South Africa has 5% of the world's recoverable coal reserves. F. T. Cawood, 'Can South Africa Improve on its National Petroleum Strategy?' LLM: Dundee University (2008) 4. Namibia has very little proven coal reserves. Anonymous, 'Geological Survey of Namibia', available at <http://www.mme.gov.na/gsn/fossilfuels.htm>.

[2] Cawood (n 1) at 4.

[3] South Africa must import about 60% of its crude oil needs. See Energy Research Centre (UCT), *Final Report on Energy Security in South Africa* prepared for Global Network on Energy for Sustainable Development (2009) 11, available at <http://www.gnesd.org/upload/gnesd/pdfs/energy%20security/erc%20south%20africa_energy_security.pdf>.

[4] Cawood (n 1) at 3.

[5] R. Shelbourne, *Guide to the Namibian Economy 2010* (2010) 309.

[6] See Minister of Mines and Energy, 'Fossil Fuels', available at <http://www.mme.gov.na/gsn/fossilfuels.htm>.

[7] Nuclear, gas, hydro, and other renewable resources comprise the remaining 5%. See US Energy Information Administration, *South Africa*, available at <http://www.eia.gov/countries/cab.cfm?fips=SF>.

[8] Department of Energy 'What We Do', available at <http://www.energy.gov.za/files/au_frame.html>.

petroleum industry falls under the auspices of the Department of Mineral Resources and is regulated by the 2002 Minerals and Petroleum Resources Development Act (MPRDA). In Namibia, all these sectors are regulated by the Energy Directorate (a division of the Ministry of Mines and Energy), which is responsible for the upstream and downstream petroleum industries (including gas), as well as electricity and renewable energy sectors.[9] The discussion in this chapter focuses largely on the upstream industry, as this is where issues relating to the surface and subsurface are most pertinent.

This chapter examines the regulatory frameworks for exploitation of subsurface energy resources in South Africa and Namibia. It queries the extent to which the principles of the 'mixed' legal family to which South Africa and Namibia belong provide for such regulation. The legal systems of both of these countries are built on a historic mix of common law and civil law principles, due to the bipartite colonial history of Southern Africa. The chapter makes brief reference to this historical context, before focusing on how conventional energy resources are regulated. It then looks more closely at three areas identified as particularly problematic in current legal discourse, namely (i) subsurface trespass and nuisance; (ii) advances in energy production and how these impact on subsurface use; and (iii) the overlap between proprietary and regulatory aspects of current legislation and how this impacts on tenure security in the mineral and petroleum sector.

II. Historical context

Although mineral resource extraction in Southern Africa commenced long before European colonization,[10] the origins of the current system of subsurface regulation can be traced back to the period that commenced roughly around the mid-nineteenth century, with the Namibian guano boom and the diamond and gold rush in South Africa.[11] Regulation of the subsurface in relation to energy resources is founded largely on the concept of ownership and the modes of administering mineral resource extraction introduced into Southern Africa through colonization. The intertwined colonial histories of South Africa and Namibia account for the overlaps in law pertaining to ownership. In both jurisdictions, the local 'common law' is based on the civil law tradition[12] and a key component is the Roman-Dutch law conception of ownership. However, especially as concerns extraction of mineral resources, subsurface laws in these jurisdictions differ in important respects.

[9] Ministry of Mines and Energy, *Mission Statement*, available at <http://www.mme.gov.na/directe.htm>.

[10] See K. Dierks, *Chronology of Namibian History: From Pre-Historical Times to Independent Namibia* (2nd edn, 2002) 5; C. H. Feinstein, *An Economic History of South Africa: Conquest, Discrimination and Development* (2005) 15.

[11] M. Wallace and J. Kinahan, *A History of Namibia* (2011) 66; O. Levinson, *South West Africa* (1976) 12.

[12] G. Visagie, 'Regspleging en Reg aan die Kaap van 1652 tot 1806 met 'n Bespreking van die Historiese Agtergrond' PhD: University of Cape Town (1964) 25; J. C. de Wet, 'Die Resepsie van die Romeins-Hollandse Reg in Suid-Afrika' (1958) 21 Tydskrif vir die Hedendaagse Romeins-Hollandse Reg 84ff.

A. From *cujus est solum* to severance: Dutch/British colonization and the South African subsurface

Due to the manner in which European settlement originally occurred at the Cape of Good Hope,[13] the European *ius commune* as applied in the province of Holland was firmly established there by the end of the eighteenth century.[14] Between 1652 and 1795 there was no noteworthy activity in respect of natural resources such as minerals, oil, and gas. Instead, the territory's economy was linked to the trading post established at the Cape. What little guidance might have been necessary as regards to the law pertaining to the subsurface would have relied on the position in Roman law, which essentially allowed private ownership of mines and minerals to a limited extent and subject to severe restrictions.[15]

On a rudimentary level, the subsurface was subject to and regulated by general private property law principles. Roman-Dutch law accepted the principle *cujus est solum eius est usque ad coelum et ad inferos,*[16] which confirmed the landowner's rights and entitlements to the subsurface.[17] But the largely unitary[18] Roman-Dutch conception of landownership did not allow horizontal layering of property: one person could not have ownership of the surface, while another had ownership of the subsurface.[19]

British occupation and annexation of the Cape of Good Hope from 1795 onwards represented a second wave of colonization. By then Roman-Dutch law was already established, and it was not replaced by the law of the British conqueror.[20] However, the English common law became increasingly influential in matters of state organization and legal practice from 1806 onwards, because of administrative and legal reforms.[21] This affected the understanding and treatment of certain legal concepts and positions, including those concerning the use of the subsurface.

The imperial extension of British authority in Southern Africa[22] was rejected by settler farmers (mostly of Dutch origin),[23] who responded by organizing an exodus

[13] South Africa was governed between 1652 and 1795 by the United East Indian Company, whose employees had strong relations with Dutch Law: J. E. du Plessis, 'The Promises and Pitfalls of Mixed Legal Systems: The South African and Scottish Experiences' (1998) 9 Stellenbosch Law Review 338ff.

[14] See further the discussion by R. Zimmerman, 'Synthesis in South African Private Law: Civil Law, Common Law and *Usus Hodiernus Pandectarum*' (1986) (103) South African LJ 259 272ff.

[15] J. de Boer, *De Winning van Delfstoffen in het Romeinse Recht, de Middeleeuwse Juridische Literatuur en het Franse Recht tot 1810* (1978) 2–10, 53–92, 267.

[16] C. G. van der Merwe, *Sakereg* (2nd edn, 1989) 551; H. P. Viljoen and P. H. Bosman, *A Guide to Mining Rights in South Africa* (1979) 7; B. L. S. Franklin and M. Kaplan, *The Mining and Mineral Laws of South Africa* (1982) 4–5.

[17] J. W. Wessels, *The History of the Roman-Dutch Law* (1908) 486.

[18] A. J. van der Walt, *Property Rights and Hierarchies of Power: A Critical Evaluation of Land-Reform Policy in South Africa* (1999) 64 Koers 259 at 264–8.

[19] H. R. Hahlo and E. Kahn, *The Union of South Africa* (1960) 761–2.

[20] H. J. Erasmus, 'Thoughts on Private Law in a Future South Africa' (1994) 5 Stellenbosch L Rev 105 at 109.

[21] See D. H. van Zyl, *Geskiedenis van die Romeins-Hollandse Reg* (1983) 453ff.

[22] See M. Meredith, *Diamonds, Gold and War: The Making of South Africa* (2007/2008) 2–10.

[23] H. Giliomee, *The Shaping of South African Society* (2nd edn, 1989) 130–44; H. Giliomee and B. Mbenga, *New History of South Africa* (2007) 102–7.

(the 'Great Trek') from the eastern frontier region northwards and eastwards.[24] Of the independent republics established, the Orange Free State and the *Zuid-Afrikaansche Republiek* in the Transvaal were especially resistant to Britain's attempts to re-establish dominance over the area,[25] although the settlers (the 'Boers') eventually capitulated at the end of the Anglo-Boer War in 1902.[26] By then, valuable deposits of diamonds and gold had already been discovered,[27] an initial interest in extracting oil had already been formed,[28] and laws had been put in place in the different territories to regulate the extraction of minerals and oil.[29]

When explorations to uncover the mineral wealth of South Africa began after 1867, the rules governing use of the subsurface all across the territory consisted of no more than a few standard Roman-Dutch principles of property law, supplemented in some parts by British colonial policy.[30] A common theme in an otherwise disparate set of legal mechanisms across the various territories was that statute intervened to regulate the right to mine, generally regarded as a component of the right to the mineral resource.[31] In property law parlance, the 'right to mine' was one of the 'entitlements' comprised by the 'mineral right'. Landowners or mineral right holders were not divested of their interests when the state granted prospecting or mining rights. Instead, the proprietary rights of the landowner and/or mineral right holder provided the basis upon which the regulatory system was established.[32] Apart from the state's permission to conduct mining activities, a miner thus needed to act on the authority of the landowner or mineral right holder.

Where mineral rights were not reserved for the state or the Crown they formed part of the rights of the landowner,[33] emanating from the entitlement to use and enjoy the land, its attachments, and subsurface. As prospecting and mining operations were often unaffordable for individual landowners,[34] the practice soon developed of severing mineral rights from land ownership.[35] The landowner could reserve the mineral rights against the title deed of the land, upon transferring the land to another, or could register a notarial deed of cession in respect of the

[24] T. R. H. Davenport and C. Saunders, *South Africa: A Modern History* (5th edn, 2000) 49–54.

[25] Davenport (n 24) at 206–8.

[26] Giliomee and Mbenga (n 23) at 245–68.

[27] See R. Richardson and J. van Helton, 'The Development of the South African Gold-Mining Industry, 1895–1918' (1984) 37 The Economic History Review 319 at 320.

[28] E. Rosenthal, *South Africa's Oil Search Down the Years* (1970) 11.

[29] More detail in H. Mostert, *Mineral Law: Principles and Policies in Perspective* (2012) 6.

[30] Embodied in the Proclamation on Conversion of Loan Places to Quitrent Tenure, 1813 (6 August 1813) (the 'Cradock Proclamation'), which reformed landholding in the Cape Colony and reserved rights to Crown minerals (e.g. precious stones, gold, and silver) to the state upon the grant of land: Van der Merwe (n 16) at 553 and see Giliomee and Mbenga (n 23) at 486.

[31] Mostert (n 29) at 37–8.

[32] Compare F. T. Cawood and R. C. A. Minnitt, 'A Historical Perspective on the Economics of the Ownership of Mineral Rights Ownership' (1998) J South African Institute of Mining and Metallurgy 369ff.

[33] *Agri South Africa v The Minister of Minerals and Energy/Van Rooyen v The Minister of Minerals and Energy* 2010 (1) SA 104 (GNP) para 7.

[34] Van der Merwe (n 16) at 553.

[35] P. J. Badenhorst, 'Mining and Minerals', Vol 18 in *The Law of South Africa (LAWSA)* (W. A. Joubert and J. A. Faris, eds, 1999) para 40.

mineral rights, transferring these to a new holder, while retaining the ownership of the land.[36] Severance of the mineral rights from the surface rights enabled third parties to become holders of the mineral rights.

From 1881 onwards, the idea that mineral rights can exist independently from the ownership of the land in which they are found became established.[37] It was entrenched in statute from as early as 1883 and 1909.[38] Significantly, this occurred at the same time as the political move towards greater unity between the different Boer Republics and British-run colonies, which culminated in Unification in 1910.[39] By 1911, the practice of severance was confirmed in case-law,[40] probably under the influence of similar principles in English law.[41] It was further entrenched by subsequent legislation.[42]

In the formative years of South African mineral law, i.e, around the beginning of the twentieth century, courts used the ample opportunities that presented themselves[43] to work out the relationship between the landowner and the holders of rights to the subsurface,[44] and the nature of such rights, where they were severed from the ownership of the land. Core notions of South African mineral and petroleum law were hence developed largely by the judiciary. Mineral rights, severed from the land ownership, included[45] the entitlements to enter the land to which they related to search for minerals, and extract and remove these minerals, if found. These mineral rights fitted neither the classification as praedial servitudes (as they were in favour of a person, not a dominant tenement), nor personal servitudes (as they were freely transferable).[46] The judicial solution for this conundrum was to refer to mineral rights as 'quasi-servitudes',[47] a 'label that . . . stuck'[48] even though it was highly contentious.[49] Scholars pointed out the extraordinary dogmatic somersaults[50] required to keep the conceptualization of mineral rights connected to land

[36] Other registration-based methods to achieve severance also existed—see P. J. Badenhorst, H. Mostert, and M. Dendy, 'Minerals and Petroleum' Vol 18 in *LAWSA* (n 35) para 40.

[37] Viljoen and Bosman (n 16) at 10.

[38] Law 1 of 1883, s 14; Registration of Deeds and Titles Act 25 of 1909, ss 30 and 32. See, e.g., *Trojan Exploration Co (Pty) Ltd and Another v Rustenburg Platinum Mines Ltd and Others* 1996 (4) SA 499 (A) ('*Trojan Exploration*') at 509C.

[39] B. L. S. Franklin, 'Mining and Minerals' Vol 18 in *LAWSA* (n 35) para 1.

[40] *Taylor and Claridge v Van Jaarsveld and Nellmapius* 1885–1888 (2) SAR TS 137 at 141; *McDonald v Versfeld* 1885–1888 (2) SAR TS 234 at 236; *Pearce v Olivier and Others and Noyce* 1889–1890 (3) SAR TS 79 at 81.

[41] Viljoen and Bosman (n 16) at 10.

[42] Deeds Registries Act 47 of 1937, s 70(1): repealed by Mining Titles Registration Amendment Act 24 of 2003, s 53 (as amended by the Minerals and Energy Laws Amendment Act 11 of 2005).

[43] E.g. in *Van Vuren v Registrar of Deeds* 1907 TS 289 ('*Van Vuren*'); *Rocher v Registrar of Deeds* 1911 TPD 311; *Le Roux v Loewenthal* 1905 TS 742; *Coronation Collieries v Malan* 1911 TPD 577; *Witbank Colliery Ltd v Malan and Coronation Colliery Co Ltd* 1910 TS 667.

[44] See Mostert (n 29) at 11–13.

[45] *Van Vuren* (n 43) at 294.

[46] '*Trojan Exploration*' (n 38) at 510A.

[47] *Beyers en 'n Ander v Du Preez en Andere* 1989 (1) SA 328 (T) at 336; *Webb v Beaver Investments (Pty) Ltd & Another* 1954 (1) SA 13 (T) at 25A.

[48] '*Trojan Exploration*' (n 38) at 510A.

[49] Van der Merwe (n 16) at 561–2.

[50] The terminology of servitudes was wholly insufficient to conceptualize mineral rights. Mineral rights were freely transferable and inheritable, and did not require exercise *salva rei substantia.* Unlike servitudes, mineral rights did not terminate where the landowner later (re)acquired these rights.

ownership, long after they had been juridically severed. A few lone voices advocated the recognition of mineral *title* as a separate and independent class of right, removed from the servitude context,[51] to no avail. Instead, mineral rights were conceived as limited real rights,[52] which enjoyed precedence in cases of irreconcilable conflict with the interests of the landowner.[53] In situ, the minerals were the property of the landowner; upon being extracted they became the movable property of the landowner.[54]

Since those early years of the twentieth century, South African law pertaining to minerals has been subject to several revisions, the recognizable trend being one of increasing statutory intervention in the rights of the landowner and the mineral right holder.[55] In particular, the right to prospect and mine for natural oil vested in the state from 1942 onwards: the state could prospect for and mine natural oil, and could grant prospecting and mining leases, subject to the payment of compensation to the surface owner and royalties or a share of the profits to the state. A quarter of such royalties or profits fell to the holder of the mineral right, upon which the right to prospect and mine depended.[56] This development rendered the regulatory regime in respect of natural oil even more stringent than that of precious stones and precious metals.[57] The state's right to prospect for and mine natural oil outranked even that of the holder of the mineral rights. Likewise, the regulation of the exploitation of source material associated with nuclear energy (such as uranium and thorium) was very stringent.[58] The state had the exclusive right to search for, prospect, or mine such material. Material acquired was vested in and controlled by the Atomic Energy Board on behalf of the state.[59] These were the 'most comprehensive rights conferred on the state in any South African mining legislation'.[60]

The current dispensation, introduced in 2004 by the MPRDA,[61] represents the zenith of the state's right to intervene in subsurface matters. Mineral and petroleum resources belong to the nation, with the state as custodian being responsible for ensuring that these resources are exploited for the benefit of the nation as a whole.[62] A system of state intervention statutorily envisaged as the exercise of custodial duties may be fraught with difficulty. This is elaborated further at section III.B, once the South African history has been contrasted with that of Namibia.

B. German colonization and state control of the subsurface in Namibia

The common laws of Namibia and South Africa are intertwined, because of these countries' shared political history between 1910 and 1990. However, the countries'

Moreover, a mineral right could e.g. form the object of a usufruct (*Ex Parte Eloff* 1953 (1) SA 617 (T)), thus assuming the role of an 'incorporeal thing'—an impossibility in the eyes of the law. Van der Merwe (n 16) at 24, 25.

[51] Viljoen and Bosman (n 16) at 20.

[52] '*Trojan Exploration*' (n 38) at 510A.

[53] *Nolte v Johannesburg Consolidated Investment Co Ltd Respondent* 1943 AD 295 at 315; *Hudson v Mann and Another* 1950 (4) SA 485 (T) at 488E–F.

[54] *Van Vuren* (n 43) at 295.

[55] Cawood and Minnitt (n 32) at 369.

[56] Natural Oil Act 46 of 1942, s 7.

[57] Hahlo and Kahn (n 19) at 770.

[58] See Atomic Energy Act 35 of 1948.

[59] Atomic Energy Act 35 of 1948, preamble.

[60] Hahlo and Kahn (n 19) at 770.

[61] 28 of 2002.

[62] MPRDA, s 3(1).

differing colonial experiences make for interesting deviations in the ways in which the shared common law applies to mineral and energy resources.

With the British government showing very little interest in the interior along the Southern African West Coast, European penetration occurred gradually and informally, through missionaries, traders, and explorers, and was marked by violent encounters with the indigenous population, which was already internally divided. This sparked frequent appeals to the British Colonial Government at the Cape to extend its protectorate. Unwilling to extend its already troubled domain to what was thought to be worthless, strife-ridden land, however, the British Colonial Government eventually only annexed the guano islands, in 1861, and in 1878, the only good harbour, Walvis Bay.[63]

Meanwhile, however, the indigenous Nama people had already begun granting concessions for the exploitation of minerals, thus opening the area surrounding the bay at Lüderitz to German economic and political interests.[64] Further similar deals[65] motivated the establishment of German colonial rule in 1884,[66] and subsequently the formal declaration of the area as a German protectorate. Only Walvis Bay was incorporated formally into the Cape Colony,[67] Britain having missed the opportunity to annex the entire area.

The German colonial presence in South-West Africa towards the end of the 1880s coincided with the 'Scramble for Africa'[68] and the first discoveries of semi-precious stones and gold deposits and the first promulgations of mining ordinances, which occurred under the guidance of German mining law.[69] The *Deutsche Kolonialgesellschaft für Südwest-Afrika*, under the supervision of the German Empire, held all mining rights.[70] When the Imperial German Government assumed direct military and administrative control of South-West Africa after 1890, it acquired the right to grant concessions.[71] This effectively created a dual system, in terms of which land or mining rights in some areas were granted by indigenous leaders, and in other areas concessions were granted by the German Colonial Government. The 1889 Mining Ordinance vested all mining rights in the Imperial Mining Office, which then could grant prospecting and mining permits—a tenet of Namibian mineral and mining law that persists to this day.[72]

Other ordinances followed. The third ordinance of 1905,[73] modelled on the General Prussian Mining Act of 1865 (*Berggesetz*), established the principle of

[63] Levinson (n 11) at 12–13, 16, 18–23; G. Cockram, *South West African Mandate* (1976) 7–8; Wallace and Kinahan (n 11) at 18–22, 57, 66.

[64] H. Hahlo, 'The Great South-West African Diamond Case: A Discourse' (1959) 76 South African L. J. 151 at 152–3; Wallace and Kinahan (n 11) at 66; Levinson (n 11) at 12, 66–7.

[65] W. Miller *A History of South-West Africa* (1957) 43–5.

[66] P. Katjavivi, *A History of Resistence in Namibia* (1988) 7.

[67] Cockram (n 63) at 9.

[68] Meredith (n 22) at 248–9.

[69] E.g. the Mining Ordinance of 25 March 1888. See further M. D. Bomani et al, *Namibia: Legal Framework and Development Strategy Options for the Mining Industry Namibia Studies Series* (1987) 65.

[70] Hahlo (n 64) at 155.

[71] Bomani et al (n 69) at 64–5.

[72] Dierks (n 10) at 67.

[73] The Imperial Mining Ordinance for German South-West Africa of 8 August 1905. See also Dierks (n 10) at 123.

mining freedom:[74] although title to minerals vested in the Imperial Government outside concession areas, all persons except 'natives and coloureds' could prospect for precious and base metals anywhere in the country.[75] Because of this German influence, rights to exploit mineral and petroleum resources in Namibia have always been treated as separate from land ownership and have been reserved for the state.[76]

Namibia's political history became closely intertwined with that of the Union of South Africa pursuant to the latter's 1915 occupation of South-West Africa at the behest of the British Government.[77] The Union Government also took control of South-West Africa's mineral and mining industry.[78] In 1919 South-West Africa became a mandate of South Africa.[79] Roman-Dutch law was made applicable[80] and the Union Parliament's authority over the grant of rights to minerals confirmed statutorily,[81] while German companies' concession rights were terminated.[82] Control over the mineral and mining industry was placed in the hands of the South African-appointed Administrator. However, the regulatory system of the 1905 Mining Ordinance essentially remained in force until it was replaced by the Mines, Works and Minerals Ordinance of 1954 and a comprehensive Mines Division was established.[83] The 1954 Ordinance included natural oil and gas in the definition of 'mineral'.[84]

Growing international concern about the effect of South Africa's imposition of its Apartheid policy on South-West Africa,[85] and the depletion of South-West Africa's natural resources to the sole benefit of South Africa, caused a decree[86] to be handed down by the Council for Namibia established by the United Nations.[87] It imposed penalties for mining and export of Namibia's minerals without the

[74] Hahlo (n 64) at 155.

[75] Registering an area as a prospecting field ensured exclusive rights, and enabled a later conversion into a mining field. The landowner's permission for the prospecting operations had to be obtained, and compensation was payable to the landowner for loss/reduction of enjoyment of land or its value. Bomani et al (n 69) at 66.

[76] *Namibia Grape Growers and Exporters Association and Others v Ministry of Mines and Energy and Others* 2004 NR 194 (SC) at 209.

[77] Katjavivi (n 66) at 13. Although the former German administrative system was abolished, both the German Civil Code and the German Criminal Code remained in force. See A. du Pisani, *SWA/Namibia: The Politics of Continuity and Change* (1986) 47; G. Naldi, *Constitutional Rights in Namibia* (1995) 1.

[78] Bomani et al (n 69) at 66.

[79] See E. Emmett, 'The Mandate over South-West Africa' (1927) 9 J Comp Legislation and Int'l L 111 at 117.

[80] Proclamation 21 of 1919, s 1(1).

[81] Emmett (n 79) at 118.

[82] Proclamation 59 of 1920, entrenched by the 1921 mandate of the League of Nations and the South West Africa Constitution Act of 1925. Katjavivi (n 66) at 13.

[83] See discussion in Bomani et al (n 69) at 68 of various statutory amendments to the Ordinance.

[84] Section 1 of the Mines, Works and Minerals Ordinance of 1954, *sv* 'mineral'. Reference to natural oil and gas was removed from this definition by the Mines, Works and Minerals Ordinance of 1968, which defined natural oil in an independent section.

[85] See N. Schrijver, 'Sovereignty over Natural Resources: Balancing Rights and Duties in an Interdependent World' LLD: Rijksuniversiteit Groningen (1995) 134–6.

[86] Decree no. 1 for the Protection of the Natural Resources of Namibia of 27 September 1974.

[87] General Assembly Resolution 2248 (S-V) of May 19, 1967.

Council's authority.[88] The colonial laws dealing with mineral and petroleum resources were replaced soon after Namibia gained independence in 1990.[89] The state's right in respect of natural resources is now constitutionally entrenched[90] and all rights in respect of minerals and petroleum are now vested in the state.[91]

III. The different faces of resource regulation in South Africa and Namibia

Modern Namibian law is closely linked with South African law because the South African common law (which was adopted in Namibia and applied from 1919 until 1990) is still binding today. However, the influence of German law on the Namibian system during its formative years means that the laws of the two countries vary in their approaches to the regulation of natural resources. This influence has rendered it beyond contest that minerals and petroleum in situ belong to the state, a position which is much more recent and contentious in South African law. This section deals with the current regulatory frameworks in both countries, considering whether the common law basis remains relevant and, if so, how.

A. The 'nationalized' resources of Namibia

Namibia's Constitution is supreme law. Roman-Dutch common law continues to exist insofar as it is consistent with the Constitution.[92] The Constitution acknowledges Namibia's pre-independence approach to mineral and petroleum resources, in that it reserves all natural resources in, on, or under the land for the state, insofar as these resources are not otherwise lawfully owned.[93] The effect is that natural resources, including subsurface natural resources, are nationalized, although the government hesitates to use this word. The Constitution itself therefore also acknowledges the abrogation of the common law principle of *cujus est solum* in respect of minerals and petroleum.[94]

Mineral and petroleum resources in situ vest in the state, along with all rights in respect of these resources, regardless of where the ownership of the land lies, and the Minister of Mines and Energy may grant licences to search for and extract minerals and petroleum.[95] The wording of the legislation leaves little room to doubt the

[88] Bomani et al (n 69) at 71.

[89] Petroleum (Exploration and Production) Act 1991; Minerals (Prospecting and Mining) Act 1992.

[90] Constitution of the Republic of Namibia of 1990 ('Namibian Constitution'), art 100.

[91] Petroleum (Exploration and Production) Act of 1991, s 2; Minerals (Prospecting and Mining) Act of 1992, s 2.

[92] Namibian Constitution, art 1(6) and art 66.

[93] Namibian Constitution, art 100.

[94] See H. van den Berg, 'Mineral Rights under Development: A Comparative Study of the Evolving Nature of Mineral Rights in South Africa and Namibia' LLM: University of Cape Town (2009) 92.

[95] Petroleum (Exploration and Production) Act of 1991, s 2; Minerals (Prospecting and Mining) Act of 1992, s 2.

state's claim to and authority over the resources. However, the Namibian Government's Minerals Policy of 2002, formulated in an attempt to reform the law, does not refer to the state as owner of mineral resources, but states that the Ministry of Mines and Energy is a custodian of Namibia's mineral resources. This being the first reference to the Ministry's custodial role, the document recognizes the importance of the mining industry in the social and economic development of Namibia,[96] and the need for the state to ensure that mineral resources are exploited for the benefit of the nation as a whole. As custodian, the Ministry facilitates and regulates the exploitation of mineral resources for the benefit of all Namibians.[97] The Minerals Policy also envisages a high level of responsible development of 'national resources', thereby acknowledging the nationalized nature of mineral resources.

These attempts at policy reform are having an impact on the minerals and petroleum industries. One example is that of the changing role of the state petroleum company, the National Petroleum Corporation of Namibia (Pty) Ltd ('Namcor'), which until 1998 was tasked with acquiring data and promoting Namibia's petroleum potential.[98] Today, however, Namcor may take a participatory interest in a petroleum licence if invited by the company applying for or holding the licence, or if the Minister of Mines and Energy requires the petroleum company to offer Namcor a participatory interest. Furthermore, Namcor's mandate now also includes delivering 50% of the country's petroleum product requirements and ensuring an uninterrupted domestic fuel supply.[99]

An even more drastic reform confirming the nationalization of minerals involves the controversial 2011 Cabinet decision to give the state-owned mining company, Epangelo Mining Limited, the exclusive right to strategic minerals (including uranium, gold, copper, coal, diamonds, and rare earth metals).[100] This decision was taken prematurely, as it cannot be accommodated within the existing regulatory framework for mineral resources. As a result, the implementation of this decision is proving problematic.

While Namibian law acknowledges that natural resources belong to the state, the state does not own natural resources in a private law sense.[101] In an *obiter dictum*,[102] the Namibian High Court indicated that Article 100, which contains the reservation in favour of the state, must be read subject to the rest of the Constitution.[103] This enables a nuanced, less literal interpretation of the reservation: as the Constitution vests all power in the people of Namibia, to be exercised through the democratic institutions of the state,[104] natural resources, according to

[96] Van den Berg (n 94) at 74–5.

[97] Ministry of Mines and Energy, *Mission Statement*, available at <http://www.mme.gov.na/directe.htm>.

[98] Ministry of Mines and Energy, *Petroleum Exploration and Production*, available at <http://www.mme.gov.na/energy/upstream.htm>.

[99] More detail available at <http://www.namcor.com.na/index.php?pn=about_us#Scene_1>.

[100] Media Statement by the Minister of Mines and Energy on the Public–Private Partnership in the Mining Sector, 10 May 2011.

[101] *Rostock CC and Another v Van Biljon* 2011 (2) 751 (HC) ('*Rostock*') at para 8. See also Van den Berg (n 94) at para 93.

[102] *Rostock* (n 101) at paras 8–10.

[103] *Rostock* (n 101) at para 9.

[104] Namibian Constitution (n 90), art 1(2).

the court, belong to the people of Namibia and are administered by the state on their behalf. The court further stated, without elaborating, that these resources are either *res publicae* or *res omnium communes*.[105]

These developments demonstrate a shift in the mindset of the Namibian state and judiciary regarding the regulation of natural resources, specifically minerals. Whereas it was uncontested for most of the twentieth century that all aspects of minerals and petroleum vest in the state, the trend increasingly is to qualify this point of departure: mineral and petroleum resources do vest in the state, but the state must ensure that these resources are exploited for the benefit of the nation. Custodianship thinking in the context of Namibian mineral and petroleum law is, however, a very recent development. An opportunity to theorize the notion of custodianship in this context has not yet arisen, and it may be premature to do so here. Nevertheless, South African mineral and petroleum law might provide some preliminary insights.

B. State custodianship of South African resources

Although the MPRDA brought about significant changes to the regulatory regime applicable to mineral and petroleum resources, the common law, property-based matrix remained unquestioned until the recent case of *Agri South Africa v Minister of Minerals and Energy*,[106] which involved a dispute between the Ministry and a lobby organization for commercial farming interests. The argument was that the MPRDA brought about a direct expropriation of certain interests that existed under the previous mineral law regime.[107] The interests in question pertained to mineral rights that were not actively exercised before, and that would expire within one year after the MPRDA entered into force, unless these rights were converted under the MPRDA, which provides only for rights that are actively exercised.[108]

The dispute attacked the core provisions of the MPRDA, among others s 3, which creates the model of state custodianship of mineral and petroleum resources. By basing the regulatory framework on the notion of state custodianship,[109] the MPRDA enables the state 'to achieve broader access to and optimal exploitation of the country's mineral and petroleum resources, without transferring property rights to the state'.[110] The state can award mining or prospecting rights in respect of

[105] *Rostock* (n 101) at para 10. Van den Berg (n 94) at 93 argues that unsevered mineral resources in Namibia must be seen as *res publica*.

[106] *Agri South Africa v The Minister of Minerals and Energy/Van Rooyen v Minister of Minerals and Energy* 2010 (1) SA 104 (GNP) ('*Agri South Africa* interlocutory decision'); *Agri South Africa v Minister of Minerals and Energy and Another* 2012 (1) SA 171 (GNP) ('*Agri South Africa* GNP'); *Minister of Minerals and Energy v Agri South Africa* (458/2011) [2012] ZASCA 93 ('*Agri South Africa* SCA'); *Agri South Africa v Minister for Minerals and Energy* 2013 (4) SA 1 (CC) ('*Agri South Africa* CC').

[107] *Agri South Africa* interlocutory decision (n 106) at paras 2, 3.

[108] MPRDA, s 25(2)(b). More detail in Mostert (n 29) at 87.

[109] See MPRDA, preamble and ss 2–3.

[110] Mostert (n 29) at 133. Cf contra J. D. van der Vyfer 'Nationalisation of Mineral Rights in South Africa' (2012) De Jure 8.

minerals,[111] and exploration or production rights in respect of petroleum,[112] to applicants who meet the criteria laid down by law.[113]

There are few other statutory innovations that have caused as much academic speculation and criticism over the past decade as the notion of state custodianship in South African mineral and petroleum law.[114] A considerable part of the difficulty with conceptualizing state custodianship has to do with the Roman-Dutch property law roots of South African mineral law, which invite attempts to explain state custodianship in private law terms, with results bordering on the absurd. For example, any opinion to the effect that the legislative intent must have been to confer private law type ownership of South Africa's mineral and petroleum resources onto the 'nation' would be spurious or facetious, since 'the nation' lacks legal personality.[115] Instead, considering the many references to the benefit of the nation in the Act as a whole,[116] the legislative intention seems rather to establish a mechanism for regulating mineral and petroleum resources so as to hold the state responsible for administering these resources in a manner that would benefit all the people of South Africa.[117] The legislature's focus is, therefore, less on the question of 'who owns?' and more on the question of 'who is responsible?'.

Even if one accepts, however, that a private law definition is out of the question, the meaning of state custodianship remains problematic. Some scholars consider the state's custodial duties as envisaged by the MPRDA to require that ownership of minerals and petroleum in situ vest in the state. Two arguments are generally raised in favour of this contention, namely, that royalties are no longer payable to the landowner, but rather to the state,[118] and that some of the elements of the contentious public trust doctrine, prevalent in US law, were imported through the MPRDA.[119] Both these arguments may be contested.[120] The fact that the implementation of the new royalties dispensation was delayed,[121] due to the severe economic downturn, may point to how the state views its role as custodian. Besides,

[111] MPRDA, s 17(1). [112] MPRDA, ss 80, 84. [113] MPRDA, ss 16, 79, 83.

[114] E.g. P. J. Badenhorst and H. Mostert, 'Artikel 3(1) en (2) van die Mineral and Petroleum Resources Development Act 28 van 2002: 'n Herbeskouing' (2007) Tydskrif vir die Suid Afrikaanse Reg 469; H. M. van den Berg, 'Ownership of Minerals under the New Legislative Framework for Mineral Resources' (2009) 20 Stellenbosch L Rev 139 at 152; E. van der Schyff, 'Who 'Owns' the Country's Mineral Resources? The Possible Incorporation of the Public Trust Doctrine through the Mineral and Petroleum Resources Development Act' (2008) South African LJ 757 at 767.

[115] See D. Watson, *Ownership of and Custodianship over Unsevered Minerals: The Impact of the MPRDA,* LLB research paper: University of Cape Town (2009); M. Dale et al, *South African Mineral and Petroleum Law* (2005) MPRDA-121 to MPRDA-122; P.J. Badenhorst and H. Mostert, *Mineral and Petroleum Law of South Africa* (1st edn, 2004) 13–3 to 13–5.

[116] See MPRDA, ss 2(c), 3(1), 12(3)(a), 49(1).

[117] Mostert (n 29) at 7, 8.

[118] E. van der Schyff, 'The Constitutionality of the Mineral and Petroleum Resources Development Act 28 of 2002' (2006) LLD, North West University 239–42.

[119] Van der Schyff (n 118) at 236; (n 114) at 758; C. Young, *Public Trust and Res Publicae in South African Law* LLB research paper: University of Cape Town (2009).

[120] Mostert (n 29) at 133–5.

[121] Until 1 March 2010. B. Strydom, 'South Africa—Mining and Petroleum Royalties—The Imposition and Calculation' (2012), available at <http://www.bowman.co.za/FileBrowser/ArticleDocuments/South-Africa-Mining-and-Petroleum-Royalties.pdf>.

given the contentious scope and evasive parameters of the public trust doctrine in the United States itself,[122] appropriate reception thereof into South African law would be problematic.[123] In the interests of coherency and consistency, some argue,[124] the notion of state custodianship must be developed with reference to existing South African law,[125] rather than by importing foreign law.

The Supreme Court of Appeal (SCA), in *Agri South Africa*, acknowledged that there had never before been a need to challenge the common law 'flavour' of South African mineral law, which arose from the 'creative judgments of the courts in characterizing and giving effect to such rights within a framework provided by well-known categories of rights in our law' and which 'disguise[d] the true origins of such [mineral] rights'.[126] The court held that the basis of proprietary rights to minerals had always been the right to prospect and/or mine, and that the matter of expropriation hence did not arise in the present case.[127] In following this line of reasoning, the court deliberately sidestepped the task of giving content to the notion of state custodianship of mineral and petroleum resources. Indeed, it dismissed attempts to unpack the concept of custodianship altogether.[128]

The court is correct in dismissing an analysis within the private law paradigm: if the state were to be the owner of the country's mineral resources, the MPRDA would have authorized it to act as owner; it would have authorized discretionary use and enjoyment and discretionary abilities of disposal. The MPRDA does not authorize such state action. Instead, it attempts to limit discretionary exercise of state power.[129] For this reason, the SCA's rejection of the opportunity to give content to the core notion of state custodianship in current mineral law by positioning it within the ambit of state administration and state liability law is unfortunate.

The Constitutional Court (CC) decision focused largely on the question of whether expropriation requires the state to have acquired the property taken from individuals. The majority judgment treated the right to minerals as a separate form of ownership, unceremoniously breaking with traditional conceptions of the right to minerals as a limited real right.[130] Without engaging in an analysis of the mineral right concept, the court held that the entitlement not to mine, or the ability not to exploit minerals, are essential components of what it calls common law 'mineral ownership',[131] thus setting itself apart from the other branches of the judiciary on this issue. The court of first instance followed the conventional line of thinking, while the SCA favoured an interpretation focusing on the public-law basis of the

[122] Van der Schyff (n 118) at 107.

[123] Van den Berg (n 114) at 147.

[124] Watson (n 115) at 24.

[125] See P. J. Badenhorst, J. M. Pienaar, and H. Mostert, *Silberberg and Schoeman's The Law of Property* (5th edn, 2006) 34; C. G. van der Merwe and A. Pope, 'Property' in *Wille's Principles of South African Law* (F. du Bois, ed, 2007) 417.

[126] *Agri South Africa* SCA (n 106) at para 68.

[127] *Agri South Africa* SCA (n 106) at para 117.

[128] *Agri South Africa* SCA (n 106) at para 86.

[129] See Mostert (n 29) at 90–2.

[130] *Agri South Africa* CC (n 106) at paras 38–39.

[131] *Agri South Africa* SCA (n 106) at paras 44–43.

right to mine. The CC viewed this entitlement *not* to exploit as the main tool in enabling sterilization of mineral resources.

Space precludes full exploration of the reasons that may support the court's intuition on the ownership issue. It suffices to point out that for a constitutionality challenge involving an interference with a proprietary position as strong as ownership to be dismissed, the reason for an interference needs to be particularly persuasive.[132] What was lost must be set off against what was gained.

In developing the reasoning necessary for this response, the court relied on the state custodianship model introduced by the MPRDA. It argued that the state now has the 'power to grant others what could previously have been granted only by holders',[133] but does not provide for the state to be a beneficiary of the new mineral and petroleum dispensation. Instead, the state facilitates broader and equitable access to mineral and petroleum resources. The court then developed its pro-transformation argument to counteract the infringement on the proprietary rights that it found had occurred, but not before it rejected an opportunity to define 'state custodianship'. All the court was willing to admit is that, 'whatever "custodian" means, it does not mean that the state has acquired and thus has become owner of the mineral rights concerned'.[134] This was a surprising move, not least because by the court's own admission,[135] the notion of custodianship plays an important part in its overall justification of a pro-redress approach to the matter. The implication for present purposes is that the matter about the meaning of state custodianship remains largely unsettled.

Two factors contribute to the remaining uncertainties about the current basis of South African mineral law. The first is South African law's rigid reliance on a unitary notion of ownership as found in Roman-Dutch law, and the concomitant judicial unwillingness, over more than a century, to conceptualize rights to minerals as a separate form of *title* (in the sense of a *ius in re propria*) altogether. Mineral law, having been rooted in a property law dictated largely by civil law principles,[136] over time created 'untenable assumptions about [its own] scope and limits'.[137] With the CC's overt break in conventional wisdom on this point, a window of opportunity has arisen for reconceptualization of the relationship between property and state regulation.

The second factor contributing to uncertainty about the current basis of South African mineral law is the (judicial and scholarly) negation of the fact that mineral rights always had a distinct public-law dimension, a consideration which was pointedly ignored in those contexts where the nature of the right was discussed.[138]

[132] *First National Bank of SA Limited t/a Wesbank v Commissioner for the South African Revenue Services and Another; First National Bank of SA Limited t/a Wesbank v Minister of Finance* 2002 (4) SA 768 (CC) at para 110.

[133] *Agri South Africa* CC (n 106) at para 68.

[134] *Agri South Africa* SCA (n 106) at para 71.

[135] *Agri South Africa* SCA (n 106) at para 68.

[136] R. Zimmermann and D. P. Visser, 'Introduction: South African Law as a Mixed Legal System' in *Southern Cross: Civil Law and Common Law in South Africa* (R. Zimmermann and D. P. Visser, eds, 1996) 28.

[137] Mostert (n 29) at 6.

[138] Mostert (n 29) at 159.

The SCA was correct in pointing out that the exercise of mineral rights depended by and large on whether it was permitted by the state.[139] The 'common law' mineral right included the entitlement to search for and extract (mine for) minerals, but to prospect and mine, the mineral right holder needed the permission of the state.[140] This permission took different forms in different generations of mineral law.[141] The point is that even from the earliest days of the Gold Rush, despite territorial and political disparities,[142] the state generally had control over the exercise of rights to precious minerals, even though the rights themselves were very often in private hands. Across four generations of South African mineral law, the right to prospect and mine was regulated by the state in different ways, to serve different policy choices. The common denominator, however, is that state regulation was constitutive of a right holder's ability to prospect or mine at all.[143]

Adopting a public-law based approach to explaining South African mineral law has its own challenges. Ironically, the differences of interpretation on the nature of rights to minerals which have haunted the private law discourse for almost a century are not eradicated when the parameters of the analysis change to the public-law sphere. There seem to be different interpretations from the public-law angle about how exactly the state's regulatory involvement in mineral rights determines the nature of those rights. One view[144] is that extraction of minerals depended on a dual legal layer. One layer concerned *access* to the mining industry, which was controlled by the mineral right holder. These rights were determined under common law. The other layer was about *activation* of those rights, which concerned the state's regulatory regime for minerals. The MPRDA eradicated the boundaries between these layers by giving the state administrative powers and functions to determine both access to the industry and how rights thus obtained could be activated. This view supports a notion of state custodianship that goes beyond affording the state the role, metaphorically, of being merely the referee in a ball game. Instead, the state determines the rules of the game, but also chooses the players.

The SCA's interpretation is somewhat different. Interestingly, despite its rejection of the private law paradigm, the court uses the terminology of private property law to explain its position: under the common law, it argues, the landowner (or presumably also the mineral right holder) could only confer a personal right on another to remove and extract minerals.[145] The court's stance[146] is that the right to remove and extract minerals became a 'real right' through judicial development reinforced by statute. Mineral rights, the court indicated, were founded on the right

[139] *Agri South Africa* SCA (n 106) at para 48.
[140] Van der Vyfer (n 110) at 127; Van den Berg (n 114) at 141–3.
[141] See Mostert (n 29) at 19–38.
[142] See E. van der Schyff, 'South African Mineral Law: A Historical Overview of the State's Regulatory Power Regarding the Exploitation of Minerals' (2012) (64) New Contree 131 at 135–46.
[143] Mostert (n 29) at 157–9.
[144] Mostert (n 29) at 94–5.
[145] *Agri South Africa* SCA (n 106) at paras 33, 61.
[146] *Agri South Africa* SCA (n 106) at paras 39, 49–52, 59, 63, 68, and 83.

to mine.[147] Such private rights as existed were wholly dependent on the authority granted by the state. This essentially inverts the access/activation argument. In terms of the court's view, a mineral right was actually only really fully in existence if it was accompanied by the state authorization to mine.[148] Before that point, no consequences could attach to the right.[149]

The court is correct in its statement that the *value* of mineral rights derived from the allocation of the right to mine.[150] Its finding—that when the legislature decided to abolish the existing system and reallocate the right to mine, the change did not amount to a blanket deprivation of all who previously held or exercised the mineral right[151]—is also persuasive. Yet, the court's conceptualization of the right to prospect/mine may be questioned. The view that a mineral right in its entirety was dependant on the gift of the state does not take cognizance of the fact that in considerable parts of the country the right to minerals was *not* reserved for the state.[152] For considerable parts of the country, and for significant types of minerals, the right to prospect and mine was, in fact, originally an aspect of the common law mineral right, which could be comprised in the land ownership, or could be severed from it. The scope of the right to mine was admittedly determined by the state, and these determinations had varied from time to time, across different legislative periods.[153]

Given how all the decisions in *Agri South Africa* invite criticism for their engagement with mineral law concepts, the directional value of the decisions for issues which may arise in a different context, for example, in regulating underground energy sources, is limited. The custodial role that the state is now expected to play undoubtedly needs more content than the SCA and the CC in the *Agri South Africa* judgments were willing to attribute to it. We advance that the MPRDA is formulated such as to require the state to demonstrate a higher responsibility and duty of care than what is expected of an owner, by acting as custodian,[154] both in relation to managing existing and accommodating new interests. State custodianship imposes constraints on the state, and empowers it to perform the duties that such constraints involve.[155] As a consequence, the state is empowered to control access to the mining industry in a manner that previous generations of mineral law had not envisaged because of their fundamental reliance on the notion of the private law mineral right. Moreover, state custodianship means that the state may regulate the exploitation of mineral resources within confined parameters only. It is expected to fulfil its constitutional duty[156] to reform property

[147] *Agri South Africa* SCA (n 106) at para 28. [148] Minerals Act 50 of 1991, s 5(2).

[149] M. Kaplan and M. Dale, *A Guide to the Minerals Act 1991* (1992) 17. *Agri South Africa* SCA (n 106) at paras 65–76.

[150] *Agri South Africa* SCA (n 106) at para 69.

[151] *Agri South Africa* SCA (n 106) at paras 73, 97.

[152] Badenhorst and Mostert (n 115) at 1–18 to 1–20A.

[153] Mostert (n 29) at 15, 53, 157–9.

[154] Van der Schyff (n 114) at 760; Dale et al (n 115) at MPRDA-124.

[155] Mostert (n 29) at 135.

[156] Constitution of the Republic of South Africa, 1996, s 25.

relations and promote the interests of those who were excluded from benefitting from the system in the past, due to the racialized policies of the Apartheid government.[157]

By introducing state custodianship as the pivot point of the new legislative regime for minerals and petroleum, the South African legislature achieved a far-reaching change of the proprietary relationships underlying mineral law,[158] substituting the earlier relationships with ones aligned to the custodianship model.

IV. Implications of the divergence and convergence of subsurface regulation in South Africa and Namibia

The preceding section shows that, despite a divergence in regulatory regimes affecting the subsurface in South Africa and Namibia, the law of the two systems seems to be converging on the matter of state custodianship of mineral and petroleum resources. Space precludes a thorough analysis of this concept, but in this section we flag some of the possible conceptual and practical implications of the current regulatory trends. It commences with some remarks about the property law and administrative law foundations of subsurface regulation. It then explores the suitability of such regulation to deal with advances in subsurface energy production. Finally, it comments briefly on issues of subsurface trespass and nuisance.

A. Property law and administrative law overlap

Generally speaking, it can be said that the state is heavily involved in the minerals and petroleum sectors because it must ensure that these resources are extracted so as to serve the national interest. How the national interest can best be served depends on political views. These may address environmental, health, and safety concerns. They may (or may not) consider private interests. They may also aim to achieve social transformation.

The latest legislative trends in South Africa and Namibia, in as far as they relate to minerals and petroleum, respond in various ways to the legacy of Apartheid.[159] The South African MPRDA clearly aims at redressing past discrimination and promoting access to the mining industry. In doing so, the legislature made a policy choice in favour of active mining, under the auspices of a state authority to determine who may access the industry. Consequently, the *cujus est solum* principle was modified even beyond the effects achieved through severance. Owners are barred from freely exploiting their subsurface mineral and petroleum resources, through the introduction of a range of administrative measures to regulate access to mineral and petroleum, even where resources are situated on private land.[160]

[157] This argument is made in more detail in Mostert (n 29) at 135.

[158] P.J. Badenhorst, 'Transitional Arrangements in Terms of the Mineral and Petroleum Resources Development Act 28 of 2002: Crossing a Narrow Bridge?' (2002) 23 Obiter 250 at 257–8.

[159] More detail in Mostert (n 29) at 37–8, 51–6.

[160] Mostert (n 29) at 163.

These considerations beg the question about where the rules of the subsurface reside, when they pertain to mineral and petroleum resources. There is an argument to be made for positioning them within administrative law,[161] although it may prove impossible to divorce them completely from the property law context. Even in Namibia, where the positioning of the rules regarding mineral and petroleum resources has been unequivocally within the ambit of administrative law, property law principles have remained influential in matters pertaining to the exploitation of these resources.

B. Advances in energy and subsurface use

Southern Africa's non-renewable mineral and petroleum resources have been actively exploited for over a century. Nevertheless, South Africa and Namibia are but minor players in the petroleum industry, mainly because conventional extraction techniques are insufficient to allow optimal exploitation of the resources available. The decrease in, and unavailability of, conventional sources for oil and gas created a need, however, for alternative and unconventional methods to tap oil and gas sources previously not worth exploiting, such as oil shale and tar sands.

New technologies and technical advances render extraction of some of the petroleum discoveries more commercially attractive, and a better yield from existing conventional wells more likely.[162] One such new method is horizontal drilling, which exposes the wellbore to a far greater surface area than conventional drilling.[163] Another method gaining popularity (and causing great controversy) is hydraulic fracturing, a technological advance in recovery of shale gas that, combined with horizontal drilling, renders a far more cost-effective option.

These new technologies will require rethinking the methods of extraction supported by the existing regulatory regime. The legislative, executive, and judicial approaches in both South Africa and Namibia are still focused strongly on the idea that mineral and petroleum regulation must evolve to ensure that the benefit derived from these resources is spread equally among their populations.[164] However, focus on the social goals underlying regulation appears to have resulted in a disregard for technical issues. Amendments and reforms, regularly implemented,[165] are aimed mostly at streamlining access to the industry, rather than focusing on exploitability of resources. Despite frequent reform initiatives, the legislation is still geared towards conventional methods of exploiting mineral and petroleum resources.

An example may be found in the premature lifting of the moratorium on hydraulic fracturing. South Africa's first encounter with unconventional extraction

[161] See Viljoen and Bosman (n 16) at 7; Van den Berg (n 94) at 111.

[162] H. Wiseman, 'Untested Waters: The Rise of Hydraulic Fracturing in Oil and Gas Production and the Need to Revisit Regulation' (2009–2010) 20 Fordham Env'l L Rev 115ff.

[163] See chapters 7 and 8.

[164] MPRDA, s 3(1). For Namibia, see Minerals Policy, 2002.

[165] See Mineral and Petroleum Resources Development Amendment Act 49 of 2008; Mineral and Petroleum Resources Development Amendment Bill 15 of 2013.

of petroleum arose in 2011, when Royal Dutch Shell ('Shell') applied for rights to explore for shale gas[166] in the Karoo.[167] Although such a venture could bring South Africa closer to self-sufficiency in the context of petroleum resources, the application was controversial, especially with regard to the impact of hydraulic fracturing on the environment and on (already scarce) water resources.[168] An initial moratorium on the granting of hydrofracturing rights was lifted in 2012.

The current legislative frameworks for petroleum exploitation in South Africa and Namibia do not cater to hydraulic fracturing. Both countries draw a clear distinction in their legislation between exploration for and production of petroleum.[169] Both grant different rights in respect of each of these activities: in Namibia, exploration and production *licences* are granted, while in South Africa exploration and production *rights* are granted. In Namibia, there is no indication that the process of hydraulic fracturing will be employed any time soon. In South Africa, *exploration* rights are granted to persons who intend to use hydraulic fracturing to recover petroleum (specifically shale gas).[170] Exploration operations are aimed solely at *locating* a discovery of petroleum,[171] and *not to exploit* it.[172] Exploitation is the purpose of *production* operations. The MPRDA is unclear about what exactly constitutes production of petroleum, but the term may be understood by analogy to the verb 'to mine'[173]—its counterpart in the minerals context—as an operation or activity for the purposes of winning any petroleum.[174] A production right allows production operations, which include activities relating to the exploration, appraisal, development, and production of petroleum.[175]

At least two implications are clear. First, granting a mere exploration right is insufficient to allow hydraulic fracturing. The latter is not aimed at defining a trap and locating a petroleum discovery, but rather at stimulating a reservoir to produce oil or gas, to increase the rate of petroleum production by boosting the flow of oil and gas.[176] Second, hydraulic fracturing is a process for *winning* petroleum, not

166 Exploration licence application WP, intersecting the Western and Northern Cape, PASA Reference No 12/3/219; Exploration license application CP, intersecting the Western and Eastern Cape, PASA Reference No 12/3/220; Exploration licence application EP, intersecting the Northern and Eastern Cape, PASA Reference No 12/3/221.

167 A semi-desert natural region in the South African interior.

168 See, e.g., L. Steyn, 'Fracking Opens Deep Divisions' *Mail & Guardian* (27 May 2011); and the commentaries on Shell's environmental management plan: F. Bekker, *Review of the Draft EMP in Support of an Application for Gas Exploration in the Western Karoo (Central Precinct) by Shell Exploration Company* (2011); L. Havemann et al, 'A Critical Review of the Application for Karoo Gas Exploration Right by Shell Exploration Company B.V.', Haveman Specialist Energy Attorneys Policy Objection (5 April 2011).

169 See the MPRDA, s 1; Petroleum (Exploration and Production) Petroleum (Exploration and Production) Act of 1991, s 1.

170 E.g. Shell was granted exploration rights over the Karoo Basin. Part of their exploration activities may include hydraulic fracturing.

171 See Dale et al (n 115) at MPRDA-44.

172 Dale et al (n 115) at MPRDA-76(1).

173 Dale et al (n 115) at MPRDA-77, with reference to MPRDA, s 69(2)(b)(ii).

174 MPRDA, s 1 *sv* 'mine'.

175 MPRDA, s 1 *sv* 'production operations'.

176 N. J. Hyne, *Nontechnical Guide to Petroleum Geology, Exploration, Drilling, and Production* (2nd edn, 2001) 425; Ground Water Protection Council and ALL Consulting, *Modern Shale Gas Development in the United States: A Primer* (Report prepared for the Department of Energy) (2009), available at <http://www.netl.doe.gov/technologies/oil-gas/publications/epreports/shale_gas_primer_2009.pdf>.

merely for *exploring* for petroleum. Hence, where a company foresees the possibility of using the process of hydraulic fracturing, it should rather be prevailed on to apply for a production right.

Some of the clauses in the recently published Minerals and Petroleum Resources Development Amendment Bill[177] seem to take into account that the exploration and extraction process for gas demand a rethink of some of the MPRDA's provisions.[178] However, the Government is still consulting on this Bill and it is difficult to forecast when these new amendments will be promulgated. Meanwhile, rights to hydrofracturing are being granted in terms of a system that caters to conventional extraction methods. Of particular concern is the fact that environmental clearance for exploration is granted at levels much more relaxed than would be the case for production.[179] There is, accordingly, a real possibility of environmental concerns not being entertained appropriately.

New methods for exploiting subsurface resources for energy purposes aside, the evolving nature of the energy industry also creates new uses for the subsurface. Energy generation results in substantial carbon emissions, especially in South Africa, where 92% of total electricity comes from coal-fired power plants,[180] which emit approximately 400 million tonnes of carbon dioxide (CO_2) annually.[181] Coal also appears to be a driving force for South Africa's energy economy in the foreseeable future.[182] Like many other countries, South Africa therefore faces the challenge of dealing with such emissions to curb the environmental impacts of CO_2. One solution is to capture the CO_2 and to store it in geological formations (pore space) in the subsurface.[183]

In 2009, the South African Government established the South African Centre for Carbon Capture and Storage, a division of the South African National Energy Development Institute.[184] In 2012, the Cabinet approved a carbon capture and storage (CCS) roadmap as one of the Government's plans to reduce carbon dioxide emissions.[185] Nevertheless, CCS is still in its infancy in South Africa and not even a topic of discussion in Namibia. As a result, there are no national laws in either country that deal with CCS. When captured CO_2 is stored in the pore spaces in subsurface geological formations, it raises the question of who owns these pore spaces.

As stated, mineral and petroleum resources in South Africa vest in the nation, with the state as custodian. In Namibia, all natural resources in, on, or under the

177 B15–2013. 178 See in particular clause 25(a) and (b), read with clause 27(a).

179 Compare the provisions for exploration rights under MPRDA, s 80(1)(c) and production rights under MPRDA, s 83(5). Unlike exploration rights, production rights can only be granted if 'the production will not result in unacceptable pollution, ecological degradation or damage to the environment'.

180 D. Khoza, 'Quantifying South Africa's Carbon Storage Potential Using Geophysics' (2012) South African J Science 108ff.

181 Khoza (n 180) at 108; J. Glazewski, A. Gilder, and E. Swanepoel, 'Carbon Capture and Storage (CCS): Towards a Regulatory and Legal Regime in South Africa' (2012) Institute of Marine and Environmental Law (IMEL) and African Climate and Development Initiative (ACDI), University of Cape Town, Cape Town.

182 Glazewski, Gilder, and Swanepoel (n 181).

183 See further chapters 13, 14, and 15. 184 See <http://www.sacccs.org.za/about-us/>.

185 Glazewski, Gilder, and Swanepoel (n 181).

land vest in the state. However, nothing in any South African or Namibian statutes vest the subsurface itself (including pore spaces) in anyone other than the owner of the surface. Absent a statutory regulation of ownership of pore space, the default common law position of *cujus est solum* must apply. The axiomatic consequence is that, unless and until statute provides otherwise, pore space vests in the owner of the surface, even though mineral and petroleum resources in South Africa and Namibia do not.

C. Subsurface trespass and nuisance

Energy exploitation and advances in it may have further implications for subsurface ownership. Because regulation of mineral and petroleum resources has not kept up with the advances in energy, it does not consider the potential repercussions of unconventional methods of petroleum exploitation, especially with regard to subsurface use and ownership. The issues of trespass and nuisance are particularly pertinent.

The holder of a prospecting or mining licence granted under the Namibian Minerals Act may conduct prospecting and mining operations on or under the land in respect of which the licence was granted. Similarly, the holder of an exploration or production licence issued under the Petroleum Act may conduct exploration and production activities exclusively within the designated block(s).[186] A production licence further authorizes its holder to conduct any necessary operation for the production of petroleum.[187] This includes, for example, laying a pipeline from the production point to the point of sale or distribution for the purposes of transport of the produced petroleum. In South Africa, holders of prospecting, mining, exploration, and production rights may explore for and produce minerals and petroleum on or under that land in respect of which the rights were granted.[188] The activities of the holder of a right to petroleum are therefore limited to the area over which the right was granted. As with Namibian petroleum provisions, the holder of a prospecting, mining, exploration, and production right may carry out any other activities incidental to exploration and production operations, if consistent with the MPRDA.[189] The holders of rights to minerals and petroleum in South Africa and Namibia[190] have no rights to enter or use neighbouring land. However, both the MPRDA and the Petroleum Act seem to envisage the exercise of certain activities outside the relevant land—activities that relate to the operations in respect of which the relevant rights are held. Typically, these activities relate to access to the land or transport of extracted resources.

Conventional methods of resource extraction respect the artificial boundaries of mining and production areas. This explains why the technical side of the legislation relating to mineral and petroleum resources continue unaltered with every

[186] Petroleum (Exploration and Production) Act 2 of 1991, ss 29(1), 44(1)(a).
[187] Petroleum (Exploration and Production) Act 2 of 1991, s 44(1)(c).
[188] MPRDA, s 5(3)(b). [189] MPRDA, s 5(3)(e).
[190] Dale et al (n 115) at MPRDA-140(1).

legislative amendment opportunity. New or unconventional methods of resource extraction introduce the possibility that the artificial boundaries of mining or production areas can be traversed below the surface. The likelihood of boundaries being traversed is probably not as imminent with horizontal drilling as it is with hydraulic fracturing. However, because activities take place underground, there is a possibility that horizontal wells may also inadvertently exceed the boundaries of the mineral or petroleum area.[191]

When a fracking job is planned, the design team projects the length of the potential fractures from the well. The estimates of the potential fractures depend on the data available and clues may be obtained from the seismic and other data.[192] These are, however, inaccurate, at best, and nothing can be done to control the fractures.[193] It is therefore possible that the fractures may extend beyond the boundaries of the holder's mineral or petroleum area. With horizontal drilling, the operators control the path of the drill and can therefore ensure that the boundaries of the mining or production area are not exceeded.

It is an incident of ownership that a landowner may deny a person access to the property, within the bounds of law.[194] In accordance with the principle of *cuius est solum*, a landowner may therefore in principle deny a person access over the skies above the land and the subsurface. Furthermore, wrongful interference with property that alters its state is recognized as a delict (tort of trespass) in South Africa and Namibia.[195] The principle of *cuius est solum* has been amended extensively insofar as it relates to airspace in the light of aviation.[196] It has also been abolished with regard to the area below the land in respect of which a mineral or petroleum right or licence has been granted. What is unclear, however, is whether the principle can still be applied with regard to the subsurface of neighbouring land which falls outside the mineral or petroleum area.

A number of potential issues pertaining to trespass on the subsurface of neighbouring land may arise in the context of hydraulic fracturing and horizontal drilling.[197] One question is whether it would be unlawful for the artificial boundaries of the mining or production area to be exceeded. The defence may be that trespass is incidental to these activities, and not wrongful, because these activities were conducted in terms of a validly issued right or licence. Another possible defence is that the fault necessary to constitute a delict is absent.[198]

Legislation currently provides for compensation where damages are suffered by the owner of the land in respect of which the licence was granted, but not for

[191] T. D. Ragsdalet, 'Hydraulic Fracturing: The Stealthy Subsurface Trespass' (1993) 28 Tulsa LJ 311 at 318.

[192] See *Coastal Oil & Gas Corp v Garza Energy Trust* 2006 268 S.W.3d ('*Coastal Oil*') at 5.

[193] *Coastal Oil* (n 192) at 5.

[194] Van der Merwe and Pope (n 125) at 470.

[195] See *Central South African Railways v Geldenhuis Main Reef GM Co Ltd* 1907 1907 TH 270 at 289.

[196] Aviation Act 1962, s 11 (Namibia); Civil Aviation Act 2009, s 8 (South Africa).

[197] Ragsdalet (n 191) at 317.

[198] Delictual liability requires proof of either negligence or intention. See D. Visser, 'Delict' in *Wille's Principles of South African Law* (F. du Bois, ed, 2007) 1122, 1123.

neighbouring owners who may be affected by horizontal drilling and hydraulic fracturing. These owners will have to resort to common law remedies for the appropriate relief.

While the discussion here is not exhaustive, it is obvious that the South African and Namibian legislation dealing with natural resources will have to be amended to accommodate advances in energy and the effect thereof on the subsurface.

V. Conclusion

In both Namibia and South Africa, the colonial approaches to the regulation of minerals, oil, and gas had a noticeable impact on the manner in which common law was applied and adapted in relation to subsurface issues. The rise of constitutional supremacy, likewise, influenced current trends in subsurface regulation as it pertains to minerals, oil, and gas. Interestingly, although the two jurisdictions share the same principles of common law, their positions diverge quite significantly as regards private versus state control of the subsurface. In South Africa, for almost a century, the ability to give access to the subsurface lay in the hands of private parties, landowners and/or mineral right holders. In Namibia, due to the influence of German law during the colonial era, the state controlled access to the subsurface.

These differences in the baseline position influenced post-constitutional law making. The MPRDA in South Africa had to achieve a large-scale overhaul of mineral law. It had to transition from a dual regime in which access to the industry was controlled privately, while activation of resources lay within the power of the state, to a system in which the state controls both the access to the industry as well as the activation of rights to extract resources. This had to be done in a manner that does not reserve private rights to the resources to the state itself, hence the legislature opted for a model of state custodianship. In Namibia, where the position regarding both access to the resources and activation of extraction rights was clearly in favour of full state control, recent judicial, legislative, and executive developments are signifying a trend towards treatment similar to that of state custodianship.

The motivation for preferring the state custodianship model can be found in the social goals of the current South African and Namibian states. True to their constitutional mandates, much emphasis is placed on broader, more equitable access to the two nations' resources, and the empowerment of a broader base of these populations to participate in the creation of wealth offered in the mineral and energy sectors. It is noticeable, however, that the equally important goals of optimal exploitation of mineral and energy resources are not given the same careful consideration in the legislative process. In both countries, the legislation is still geared largely towards conventional extraction methods, which do not cater well for new advances in subsurface energy extraction and production. The immediate task of the legislatures, in giving effect to the states' custodial roles in respect of mineral and energy resources, therefore, will be to consider the implications of unconventional subsurface activities on the constitutional and economic goals of the state.

PART II

THE INTERNATIONAL LAW TREATMENT OF SUBSURFACE RESOURCES

6

Energy Underground: What's International Law Got to Do With It?

Catherine Redgwell and Lavanya Rajamani

I. Introduction

This chapter addresses the international law applicable to 'energy underground'. It considers the extent to which existing treaty and customary law, as well as soft law, are adequate for the regulation of new subsurface energy activities, whether onshore or offshore, and whether new rules and/or institutions have been or should be developed. Of course, energy underground is a wide and diverse category, as the many chapters to this volume attest. From an international law perspective, however, it is possible to identify a number of key questions around which to frame the analysis. These are: (a) where the activity takes place (onshore, offshore, in areas beyond national jurisdiction, or in areas where resources are shared) and the implications for international regulation of the activity, direct or indirect; (b) the potential magnitude of environmental risks, climate change, and social impacts of non-conventional energy underground activities requiring international response; (c) whether specific underground energy activities are expressly prohibited; (d) the role of international law in providing legal frameworks for energy cooperation facilitating energy underground activities; and (e) in providing a stable legal framework for high-risk, high-cost energy underground activities; (f) whether there is an international legal requirement for public participation and consultation in underground energy decision-making with transboundary effects; (g) the role of international law, if any, in determining the ownership of underground energy resources;[1] and (h) whether there is an emerging discrete international policy/institutional framework for new/unconventional underground energy resource development. In addressing each of these questions, examples are drawn from, in particular, unconventional hydrocarbons, carbon capture and storage (CCS), geothermal, and nuclear waste disposal, in order to reflect the important new energy

[1] This is the international legal counterpart to Part I of this volume, on property rights in underground resources. See more generally A. McHarg, B. Barton, A. Bradbrook, and L. Godden, *Property and the Law in Energy and Natural Resources* (2010).

subsurface activities which have emerged and to which the national and regional contributions in this volume are principally addressed.

II. Distinctive international law features of (new) energy underground

A. Where the activity takes place

1. Offshore

The first and most important issue is where the proposed underground energy activity takes place. As CCS illustrates, if it takes place in an internationalized domain, for example transport, injection, and storage of CO_2 offshore, then there will inevitably be international (in addition to national) regulation of that activity.[2] Here we have seen swift amendment of international rules on the disposal of wastes and other matter at sea so as not to foreclose the option of sub-seabed disposal of CO_2 and to address potential adverse effects on the marine environment. Indeed, since it addresses climate change without threatening the dominance of fossil fuels and engaging the politically charged issue of lifestyle change, CCS has quickly come to be considered an essential part of the technology portfolio needed to achieve the necessary global greenhouse gas (GHG) reductions. As a result, states have acted proactively to remove legal barriers to the deployment of CCS.

The principal example of this is in the 1996 Protocol to the 1972 Convention on the Prevention of Marine Pollution by Dumping of Wastes and Other Matter (the 'London Protocol'). The London Protocol prohibits dumping of any material or substance in the sea unless it is listed in its Annex 1. If a substance is so listed, then dumping is permitted subject to the issuance of a permit by the competent authorities in compliance with provisions of Annex 2. As CO_2 streams were not included in Annex 1, the London Protocol prohibited CCS activities offshore. In 2006, however, the States Parties introduced an additional category of substances, 'carbon dioxide streams from carbon dioxide capture processes for sequestration', to Annex 1,[3] thereby removing a legal barrier to the deployment of CCS activities offshore.[4] The Parties also agreed to amendments and subsequent guidelines that,

[2] International rules also apply to the determination of opposite and adjacent maritime boundaries, and to the delimitation of the outer limits of the outer continental shelf, thus determining the limits of state(s). This may be pursuant to general rules of customary or treaty law or by bespoke boundary agreement.

[3] See for a full treatment of these amendments, C. Armeni, 'Legal Developments for Carbon Capture and Storage under International and Regional Marine Legislation' in *Carbon Capture and Storage: Emerging Legal and Regulatory Issues* (I. Havercroft, R. Macrory, and R. B. Stewart, eds, 2011) 145.

[4] States also sought to remove legal obstacles to the deployment of CCS in the North-East Atlantic area through appropriate amendments to the 1992 Convention on the Protection of the Marine Environment of the North-East Atlantic (OSPAR). In 2007, OSPAR was amended to permit CO_2 streams to be dumped into sub-soil geological formations, provided, however, that these are intended to be retained permanently in these formations and will not lead to significant adverse consequences for

in conjunction with other provisions of the Protocol, provide an integrated permitting framework for CCS activities.[5]

In contrast to the relative speed and ease of amendment of these provisions on sub-seabed disposal, export of CO_2 for sub-seabed storage has proven far more controversial. In 2009, a further amendment was introduced to the London Protocol to permit export of CO_2 for sub-seabed storage in another country, but this is yet to enter into force.[6] An additional legal hurdle to CO_2 export, depending on whether CO_2 can be characterized as a 'hazardous waste', is presented by the 1989 Basel Convention.[7] While CO_2 by itself does not fulfil the requirements for categorization as 'hazardous waste' under the Convention, it could apply in the event (yet, and unlikely to, materialize) of the designation by a Party to the Convention of CO_2 as hazardous waste under that Party's national law.[8]

Another, more sluggish, response in relation to CCS was the agreement by the Parties to the Kyoto Protocol in 2011, after first having considered the inclusion of CCS activities in the Clean Development Mechanism (CDM) in 2005, to adopt modalities and procedures for such inclusion in 2011. This decision permits CCS activities to be undertaken collaboratively by developed and developing countries, and for certified emission reductions (CERs) to be generated as a result. The inclusion of CCS projects in the CDM endorses CCS as a legitimate mitigation option and allows for capacity building, financial assistance, and technology transfer to developing countries, where most of the world's new coal plants are likely to be built, and therefore where CCS will most need to be deployed.[9] The inclusion of CCS in the CDM thus has the potential to rapidly expand the use and deployment of CCS technology. However, given the uncertain future of the Kyoto

the marine environment: Amendments to Article 3(2) of Annex II, OSPAR, available at <http://ospar.org/html_documents/ospar/html/ospar_convention_e_updated_text_2007_annex_ii.pdf>.

[5] Parties inserted a new sub-section 4 to the Annex that specifies the conditions under which CO_2 streams can be considered for offshore storage. They also subsequently agreed to two sets of guidelines: 'Risk Assessment and Management Framework for CO_2 Sequestration in Sub-seabed Geological Structures' and 'Specific Guidelines for Assessment of Carbon Dioxide Streams for Disposal into the Sub-Seabed Geological Formations', available at <http://www.imo.org/blast/mainframemenu.asp?topic_id=1615>.

[6] See IEA, *Carbon Capture and Storage and the London Protocol: Options for Enabling Transboundary CO_2 Transfer* (2011) for a detailed analysis of options available under international law to address the current barrier to transboundary CO_2 transfer, pending formal entry into force of the 2009 amendment. See generally 'Transboundary Carbon Capture and Storage Activities', Technical Paper, FCCC/TP/2012/9 (1 November 2012) for an overview of applicable international legal rules.

[7] 1989 Basel Convention on the Control of Transboundary Movements of Hazardous Wastes and their Disposal. Similar, although not identical, issues arise in relation to movements of hazardous wastes within Africa: see 1991 Bamako Convention on the ban of the Import into Africa and the Control of Transboundary Movement of Hazardous Wastes within Africa.

[8] Basel Convention, Art 1(b). The EU CCS Directive (Directive 2009/30/EC) removes CO_2 from the scope of both the Waste Framework Directive (Directive 2006/12/EC, subsequently repealed and replaced by the new Waste Framework Directive 2008/98/EC) and the Regulation on Shipments of Waste (Regulation EC 1013/2006, as amended), suggesting that, in an European context, a national qualification of CO_2 as hazardous waste under Basel might be incompatible with EU law.

[9] IEA and UN Industrial Development Organization, *Technology Roadmap: Carbon Capture and Storage in Industrial Applications* (2011) at 12 envisages that by 2050, 75% of all CCS projects will be in non-OECD countries.

Protocol and the shrinking market for CDM credits,[10] in particular from countries like China and India where the deployment of CCS technology would have the most impact, this inclusion may prove to be of muted significance.

Of greater potential in relation to CCS is the Technology established in 2010 by the United Nations Framework Convention on Climate Change (UNFCCC).[11] Much of the details of this Mechanism are yet to be worked out, but since one of the priority areas identified for the work of the Mechanism is 'deployment and diffusion of environmentally sound technologies and know-how in developing country Parties',[12] it is likely that CCS will form an important part of the work of this Committee Mechanism, especially in countries like China and India. Hence, although there does not exist at present, as chapter 14 argues, an 'effective mechanism' to promote international technology transfer, this may be remedied soon under the UNFCCC framework.

2. *Onshore*

In contrast to underground energy activities such as CCS that may take place in an internationalized domain, underground energy activities within the sovereign territory of the State[13] give rise to fewer international implications. The most obvious one is the customary law duty to prevent, or to mitigate, transboundary impacts arising from activities which may cause significant harm to the environment of other states or to areas beyond national jurisdiction.[14] States may also be party to a wide range of voluntarily assumed treaty obligations limiting and constraining where, and the manner in which, underground energy resources may be exploited. For example, many states are parties to treaties that oblige them to protect and preserve the marine environment,[15] conserve biological diversity,[16] maintain the ecological character of wetlands of international importance,[17] conserve dry lands,[18] conserve sites of natural and/or cultural heritage,[19] and stabilize climate change.[20] Large-scale energy activities in relation to

[10] Art 11(a)(4)–(6) of the 2009 EU Emissions Trading Directive provides a market post-2012 only for CERs from projects in Least Developed Countries. Other non-Annex I countries, such as India, China, and Brazil are required to conclude enabling agreements with the EU in order to be able to trade in the EU ETS market, the largest market for CERs.

[11] Decision 1/CP.16, The Cancun Agreements: Outcome of the Work of the Ad Hoc Working Group on Long-term Cooperative Action under the Convention, FCCC/CP/2010/7/Add.1 (15 March 2011) 18–22.

[12] Decision 1/CP.16 (n 11).

[13] For discussion of 'who owns energy underground', see section II.G.

[14] Additional constraints apply in the case of shared resources, as exemplified by shared water resources (see section II.A.4).

[15] 1982 United Nations Convention on the Law of the Sea (165 State Parties) ('LOSC').

[16] 1992 Convention on Biological Diversity (193 State Parties).

[17] 1971 Ramsar Convention on Wetlands (165 State Parties).

[18] 1994 United Nations Convention to Combat Desertification (195 State Parties).

[19] 1972 Convention Concerning the Protection of the World Cultural and Natural Heritage (103 State Parties) (the 'World Heritage Convention').

[20] 1992 United Nations Framework Convention on Climate Change (195 State Parties) ('UNFCCC') and the 1997 Kyoto Protocol (192 State Parties).

conventional energy have long been recognized as posing a significant threat to the environment, and have been addressed accordingly in environmental treaties. For instance, the World Heritage Convention expressly provides for a 'List of World Heritage in Danger'—sites that are under 'serious and specific danger' from, inter alia, 'large-scale public or private projects'.[21]

Extraction of unconventional energy could pose an even more serious threat to the environment than that of conventional energy. In addition to other impacts, the extraction of shale gas, for instance, is likely to emit CO_2, methane, and, in particular, fugitive methane during drilling.[22] These emissions are regulated under the UNFCCC and Kyoto Protocol. Although the UNFCCC and the Kyoto Protocol do not expressly prohibit the exploitation of shale gas, or dictate sovereign energy choice, they do impose constraints on GHG emissions. Depending on the commitments they have made under the climate regime, states will thus need to account for and likely offset the high GHG footprints of such activities to remain in compliance with their treaty obligations.

3. Areas beyond national jurisdiction

Energy underground activities will also take place in areas beyond national jurisdiction, where international law provides an important conduit for the regulation of such activities. The legal framework for deep seabed mining is found in Part XI of the 1982 Law of the Sea Convention (LOSC), which regulates energy activities in 'the sea-bed and ocean floor and subsoil thereof, beyond the limits of national jurisdiction' (the 'Area'[23]). It proclaims the Area and its resources[24] as the 'common heritage of mankind'[25] and establishes an international framework for their exploration and exploitation, which in practice involves private entities and their sponsoring States, as well as the International Seabed Authority (ISA).[26] While exploiting the resources of the Area was once considered to be technically and economically unfeasible, the ISA has already concluded 11 contracts for exploration[27] and issued regulations governing exploration in the Area for polymetallic

[21] World Heritage Convention, Art 11(4). For further discussions see G. Triggs, 'The Rights of Indigenous Peoples to Participate in Resource Development: An International Legal Perspective' and C. Redgwell, 'The International Law of Public Participation: Protected Areas, Endangered Species, and Biological Diversity' in *Human Rights in Natural Resources Development* (Donald N. Zillman, A. Lucas, and G. Pring, eds, 2002).

[22] British Geological Survey, 'Environmental Impacts of Shale Gas Extraction', available at <http://www.bgs.ac.uk/research/energy/shaleGas/environmentalImpacts.html>.

[23] LOSC, Art 1(1).

[24] LOSC, Art 133(a) defines the resources of the Area as 'all solid, liquid or gaseous mineral resources in situ in the Area at *or beneath the seabed*, including polymetallic nodules' (emphasis added). Amongst other things, the deep seabed is believed to contain significant reserves of 'methyl [methane] hydrate'—frozen natural gas—though there are no imminent plans to exploit: ISA, *Marine Mineral Resources*, available at <http://www.isa.org.jm>. As discussed in chapter 10, Japan is rich in undersea mineral resources and hopes for commercial exploitation of methane hydrate by 2018.

[25] LOSC, Art 136.

[26] LOSC, Arts 156–158. The ISA acts on behalf of 'mankind' (Art 137(2)) and has a general supervisory role with respect to activities in the Area.

[27] With more in the pipeline: see <http://www.isa.org.jm/en/scientific/exploration/contractors>.

nodules, polymetallic sulphides, and cobalt-rich ferromanganese crusts.[28] Article 145 of the LOSC requires the ISA to adopt rules and regulations for the protection of the environment and the adequacy of these regulations for this purpose was considered by the Seabed Disputes Chamber of the International Tribunal for the Law of the Sea (ITLOS) in an Advisory Opinion on the *Responsibilities and Obligations of States Sponsoring Persons and Entities with Respect to Activities in the Area*.[29] Moreover, according to Standard Clause 27.1, the contracts between the ISA and private contractors are governed by international law, including these regulations and the relevant LOSC provisions.[30]

Although it is sometimes incorrectly referred to as another illustration of the application of the common heritage of mankind principle, there is a special international legal regime governing Antarctica—the Antarctic Treaty System[31]—that clearly applies to energy underground.[32] The 1991 Environmental Protocol to the Antarctic Treaty (the Environmental Protocol) is of particular relevance, as it designates Antarctica as a 'nature reserve, devoted to peace and science',[33] prohibits all activities relating to Antarctic mineral resources, except for scientific research,[34] and establishes an enhanced Environmental Impact Assessment (EIA) system for other activities.[35] The Environmental Protocol also strengthens the system of Antarctic Special Protected Areas that restricts access to designated areas to 'protect outstanding environmental, scientific, historic, aesthetic or wilderness values, any combination of those values, or ongoing or planned scientific

[28] Regulations on Prospecting and Exploration for Polymetallic Nodules in the Area, ISBA/6/A/18, 4 October 2000; Regulations on Prospecting and Exploration for Polymetallic Sulphides in the Area, ISBA/16/A/12/Rev.1, 7 May 2010; and Regulations on Prospecting and Exploration for Cobalt-rich Ferromanganese Crusts in the Area, ISBA/18/A/11, 22 October 2012.

[29] Available at <http://www.itlos.org>. For detailed comment see D. French, 'From the Depths: Rich Pickings of Principles of Sustainable Development and General International Law on the Ocean Floor—the Seabed Disputes Chamber's 2011 Advisory Opinion' (2011) 26 Int'l J Marine and Coastal L 525–68.

[30] Standard Clause 27.1 states that the contract 'shall be governed by the terms of the contract, the rules, regulations and procedures of the Authority, Part XI of the [Law of the Sea] Convention, the Agreement and other rules of international law not incompatible with the [Law of the Sea] Convention'. On the possible shared responsibility of states, the ISA, and private entities at international law, see I. Plakokefalos, 'The Practice of Shared Responsibility: The Deep Seabed', SHARES workshop 19 April 2013 (copy on file with the authors).

[31] The term encompasses the 1959 Antarctic Treaty, the 1972 Convention on the Conservation of Antarctic Seals, the 1980 Convention on the Conservation of Antarctic Marine Living Resources, and the 1991 Protocol on Environmental Protection to the Antarctic Treaty (the 'Environmental Protocol').

[32] There is also increasing attention paid to offshore oil and gas activities by the Arctic Council, which itself is evolving as a possible institution for Arctic governance: see further <http://www.arctic-council.org>. These developments are not considered here, since regulation of energy underground remains largely a matter for individual Arctic states, albeit with increasing international cooperation, and may be contrasted with the treaty-based governance regime for the Antarctic: see, generally, D. Rothwell, *The Polar Regions and the Development of International Law* (1996).

[33] Environmental Protocol, Art 1. [34] Environmental Protocol, Art 7.

[35] Environmental Protocol, Art 8. For a detailed discussion of the EIA process, see A. D. Hemmings and L. K. Kriwoken, 'High Level Antarctic EIA under the Madrid Protocol: State Practice and the Effectiveness of the Comprehensive Environmental Evaluation Process' (2010) 10 Int'l Env'l Agreements 187.

research'.[36] Antarctica, therefore, is subject to a high degree of protection. All extractive activities, whether in relation to conventional or unconventional energy, are prohibited in Antarctica.[37]

4. *Shared resources*

The term 'shared natural resources' refers to natural resources that are neither within the exclusive control of one state, nor do they constitute 'common property'. They are natural resources over which geographically contiguous states share rights.[38] There are disagreements between and among states over the identification of shared natural resources and, in particular, over what, if any, rights and responsibilities flow in relation to such resources.

First and foremost, it is unclear what natural resources are to be considered as 'shared'. None of the international instruments that address shared natural resources define and identify particular resources that fall under the term 'shared natural resources'. International watercourses, migratory species, mountain chains, and so on, however, offer some common illustrations of shared natural resources. The International Law Commission's (ILC) Special Rapporteur on Shared Natural Resources had initially proposed addressing transboundary groundwaters, oil, and natural gas under 'shared natural resources', but after considerable resistance from major states, it was decided that oil and natural gas were not suitable topics for the ILC's consideration. The states resisting this discussion argued that oil and gas issues were essentially bilateral in nature, were highly political or technical, and involved diverse regional situations.[39] The resulting draft articles are thus confined to groundwater, and are of relevance for energy underground activities to the extent that underground aquifers may suffer depletion owing to the high volume of water required for hydraulic fracking activities and/or contamination through migration of the chemicals used in fracking or of the released gases (methane, in particular). The draft articles reinforce the customary international law duty to exercise due diligence in preventing significant adverse harm to underground aquifers through activities that have, or are likely to have, such an impact on them.[40]

Second, it is unclear what precise rights and responsibilities flow from the characterization of a particular resource as 'shared'. At the most basic level, states are required to cooperate in the conservation and utilization of shared natural

36 Environmental Protocol, Art 3(1), Annex V.

37 As Antarctica is a vast mineral-rich land mass, comprising 10% of the Earth's surface, states had, prior to the adoption of the Environmental Protocol, negotiated an agreement, the 1988 Convention on the Regulation of Antarctic Mineral Resource Activities, to regulate mining, but this has not entered into force, and is no longer likely to do so.

38 See P. Birnie, A. Boyle, and C. Redgwell, *International Law & the Environment* (3rd edn, 2009) 192–4.

39 S. Murase, 'Shared Natural Resources: Feasibility of Future Work on Oil and Gas', International Law Commission 62nd session Geneva, 3 May to 4 June and 5 July to 6 August 2010 (9 March 2010).

40 2008 Draft Articles on the Law of Transboundary Aquifers, adopted and annexed to GA Res 63/124, Article 6(2); for the obligation with respect to surface water impacts, see the 1997 Convention on the Non-navigational Uses of International Watercourses, Article 7.

resources on the basis of information exchange and prior consultation.[41] The United Nations Environment Programme's 'Draft Principles of Conduct for the Guidance of States in the Conservation and Harmonious Exploitation of Natural Resources Shared by Two or More States', which builds on obligations of transboundary cooperation and equitable utilization in relation to shared natural resources, offers further guidance in this respect.[42] These guidelines, however, while reflective of general practice, do not represent settled law.[43]

In any case, it is unclear what rules, if any, apply to shared reservoirs of oil and gas, of which there are many in, for instance, the North Sea, the Persian Gulf, the Gulf of Guinea, the South China Sea, and the Gulf of Thailand. There are at least two legal approaches to shared oil and gas reservoirs in common law.[44] The first approach is that oil and gas (like water) are distinctive in that they have a fugitive character. As these resources migrate, like wild animals, whoever captures them can claim legal ownership. Characterized as the 'rule of capture', this rule arguably applies to shale gas as well, for although the gas does not migrate, the method of recovery—hydraulic fracturing—has cross-boundary impacts. The process of hydraulic fracturing leads to cracks in geological formations, though the extent of the subterranean impact of these cracks is difficult to gauge. A second approach is that ownership over the surface translates into ownership over all associated subsurface reservoirs. This ownership creates a right to extract these subsurface resources to the full extent, which may cause oil or gas to migrate across property boundaries.

Both these approaches in common law, for those countries that subscribe to it, facilitate legal drainage of oil and gas from a neighbour's property.[45] To the extent that these common law notions can be extended to international law, in the absence of established international legal rules on shared oil and gas reservoirs, it can only lead to (further) disputes over the obligation, if any, to utilize shared oil and gas reservoirs equitably. Although the rule of capture is not explicitly recognized in international law, in the absence of an agreement to the contrary, however, there appears to be nothing to preclude states from maximizing their use of a shared reservoir from their side of the boundary. Given the legal uncertainty regarding straddling oil and gas reservoirs, there is a role for international law—perhaps soft law—in articulating common rules. It is thus to be regretted that in articulating its rules on shared resources, the ILC concentrated on underground aquifers and did not consider oil and gas, nor the potential interplay/conflict between these uses (for example, the potential for shale gas extraction to contaminate groundwater).

[41] See e.g. GA Res 3129 (XXVIII), Co-operation in the field of the environment concerning natural resources shared by two or more States (1973) and GA Res 3281 (XXIX), Charter of Economic Rights and Duties of States (1974).

[42] 17 ILM (1978) 1091.

[43] See Birnie, Boyle, and Redgwell (n 38) at 193, and GA Res 34/186 (1979).

[44] P. M. Gerhert and R. D. Cheren, 'Recognizing the Shared Ownership of Sub-surface Resource Pools' (2013) 63(4) Case Western L Rev 1041. See also chapters 2 and 3 discussing the relevant common law precepts in depth.

[45] See Gerhert and Cheren (n 44).

B. Environmental impacts, climate change, and sustainable energy

1. Environmental impacts

Another basis for distinction between conventional and new, sometimes termed 'unconventional', energy subsurface activities, arises principally from the deployment of new transformative technologies. Here the point of distinction is not (only) where the activity takes place but the potential for adverse (transboundary) effects arising from the technology itself. As unconventional gas extraction illustrates, there are concerns regarding the magnitude of the environmental risks (considered here) and social impacts (see sections II.F and II.G) when compared with conventional extractive activities, which may require international regulatory response. While this section focuses on the regulation of the harmful effects of new underground energy activities, it is well to remember that, as geothermal energy underground illustrates, transformative technologies may facilitate renewable energy developments with positive environmental effects arising from reduced carbon dependence.

The 'no harm' principle is one of a number of key international law principles applicable to energy underground activities whether onshore or offshore. It may be traced to the oft-cited *Trail Smelter Arbitration*,[46] which has been endorsed by, inter alia, the General Assembly,[47] the International Court of Justice (ICJ),[48] the ILC,[49] the Stockholm[50] and Rio[51] Declarations, and various multilateral environmental agreements.[52] The general obligation flowing from the 'no harm' principle to respect the environment of other states and common areas is concretized through the due diligence that States are required to exercise in pursuit of it.[53] The ICJ has found an EIA to be a necessary element of 'due diligence', which is interpreted so as to entail the 'adoption of appropriate rules and measures' as well as 'a certain level of vigilance in their enforcement and the exercise of administrative control applicable to public and private operators, such as the monitoring of activities undertaken by such operators'.[54] More broadly, the degree of diligence required of states depends on the importance of the interest to be protected,[55] and the degree of risk of

[46] *Trail Smelter Arbitration* (1949) 3 Rep Int'l Arb Awards 1903–1982.

[47] 1974 Charter of Economic Rights and Duties of States, GA Res 3281, Art 30.

[48] *Legality of the Threat or Use of Nuclear Weapons, Advisory Opinion*, 1996 (I), ICJ Reports 226 at 241–2, para 29.

[49] See Prevention of Transboundary Harm from Hazardous Activities, in Report of the International Law Commission on its 53rd Session, A/56/10 (2001) (the 'ILC Draft Articles').

[50] 1972 Declaration of the United Nations Conference on the Human Environment (the 'Stockholm Declaration'), Principle 21.

[51] 1992 Rio Declaration on Environment and Development (the 'Rio Declaration'), Principle 2.

[52] See, e.g., UNFCCC, Preamble and Convention on Biological Diversity, Art 3.

[53] See ILC Draft Articles, Art 3 along with commentary (n 49). See also R. Pissillo-Mazzeschi, 'Due Diligence and the International Responsibility of States' (1992) 35 German Y'bk of Int'l L 9 at 38–40.

[54] *Case concerning Pulp Mills on the River Uruguay, (Argentina v Uruguay)* 2010 ICJ Reports 14, para 197 ('*Pulp Mills*').

[55] See *Pulp Mills* (n 54).

transboundary harm.[56] In the context of new energy underground, the more hazardous the extractive activity the higher the standard of care required of states in designing and enforcing policies to prevent or mitigate transboundary harm. It is worth noting, however, that a state's economic level is relevant in determining whether a state has complied with its obligation of due diligence.[57] Developing countries that engage in extractive activities in relation to new energy underground may not, therefore, be held to the same standard as developed countries.[58]

Other principles include the 'precautionary approach or principle',[59] and the principles of 'sustainable development',[60] 'polluter pays',[61] and 'inter- and intra-generational equity'.[62] The literature addressing the normative status, nature, content, and application of these principles is rich.[63] Suffice it to say here that large-scale energy underground activities, given their serious environmental impacts, are likely to attract the application of these principles. Of particular relevance, given the spectre of non-negligible harm and the lack of full scientific certainty in relation to many of the harms associated with new energy underground activities, is the precautionary principle, which requires cost-effective measures to be taken to protect the environment in such circumstances.[64] However, the precautionary principle does not offer clarity either on the concrete measures to be taken or on the scale and/or type of harm that needs to be proven (and how), given the existence of scientific uncertainty, to engage the principle.

2. *Climate change impacts and sustainable energy*

Related to the international transboundary impacts particularly of unconventional energy sources is their climate change impacts, whether from production (for example, the high number of wells needed for unconventional gas extraction) or consumption. Over the past two decades sustainable development has increasingly been confronted with pressure to address climate change, and its implications

[56] *Pulp Mills* (n 54) at 154 noting that '[t]he standard of due diligence against which the conduct of the State of origin should be examined is that which is generally considered to be appropriate and proportional to the degree of risk of transboundary harm in the particular instance'.

[57] *Pulp Mills* (n 54) at 155 noting, however, that 'a State's economic level cannot be used to dispense the State from its obligation under the present articles'.

[58] Drawn from Principle 11 of the Rio Declaration and Principle 23 of the Stockholm Declaration. In practice there may be no distinction: see, e.g., the positions of Uruguay and Argentina in *Pulp Mills* (n 54).

[59] Rio Declaration, Principle 15.

[60] Inter alia, Rio Declaration, Principles 1 and 7; Report of the World Commission on Environment and Development, *Our Common Future* (1987).

[61] Rio Declaration, Principle 16.

[62] Rio Declaration, Principle 3.

[63] See Birnie, Boyle, and Redgwell (n 38) at 115–64 and references contained therein.

[64] In the 2011 *Advisory Opinion on Responsibilities and Obligations of States Sponsoring Persons and Entities with respect to Activities in the Area* (n 30) para 135, the Seabed Disputes Chamber of ITLOS found that the fact that several international treaties and instruments have incorporated the precautionary approach suggest a trend towards making this approach part of customary international law. For further discussion of the legal status of the principle, see 2011 *Advisory Opinion* (n 29).

for energy production and economic growth.[65] As at the domestic level, at international law, debates about unconventional oil and gas in particular are a proxy for consideration of the wider question of sustainable energy.[66]

On the one hand, international law may be seen as facilitating recourse to new and unconventional underground energy resources and the technologies to develop them safely, and fostering a decision-framework (including EIA) within which to assess whether to proceed with development. In the latter context, the ICJ in the *Pulp Mills* case found the requirement to conduct a transboundary EIA to be a distinct and freestanding obligation in international law where significant transboundary harm is threatened.[67] Although the specific content of such an EIA is left to the state's discretion, international law requires that an EIA is conducted and that it bears a relation to the 'nature and magnitude of the proposed development and its likely adverse impact on the environment'.[68] In Europe for members of the Economic Commission for Europe (ECE), the more specific terms of the Espoo Convention in relation to transboundary EIAs will apply to its Parties.[69] Benefits of facilitating recourse to safe development of unconventional energy include enhanced access to energy and promoting energy security, which are two important elements of international energy policy.[70]

On the other hand, development of unconventional resources, particularly hydrocarbons, may be viewed as incompatible with a cornerstone of international energy policy, 'sustainable energy for all',[71] and undermine achievement of the climate change objective of reducing GHG emissions.[72] If moving towards

[65] From relative obscurity in the 1980s, the issue of climate change has today come to be characterized as the 'defining human development challenge for the 21st century', United Nations Development Programme, *Human Development Report, 2007–8, Fighting Climate Change: Human Solidarity in a Divided World* (2007–2008) available at <http://hdr.undp.org/en/reports/global/hdr2007-2008/>. Indeed, the UN Secretary General, has identified climate change—'the defining issue of our time'—as one of his top priorities, see <http://www.un.org/wcm/content/site/climatechange/pages/gateway/secretary-general>.

[66] This can be highly divisive at the national level, as reflected, e.g., in the contrasting conclusions to F. M. Gonnot and P. Martin, *Rapport d'Information*, No 3517, Assemblée Nationale (Paris, 2011).

[67] *Pulp Mills* (n 54); see generally A. Boyle, 'Developments in the International Law of Environmental Impact Assessments and their Relation to the Espoo Convention' (2011) 20(3) RECIEL 227–31.

[68] *Pulp Mills* (n 54) at para 205.

[69] Art 4, and Appendix II, 1991 Convention on Environmental Impact Assessment in a Transboundary Context (the 'Espoo Convention') (45 Parties).

[70] See, e.g., the IEA's four main areas of focus, which are energy security, economic development (including elimination of energy poverty), environmental awareness, and global engagement. See further <http://www.iea.org/aboutus/whatwedo/>.

[71] 'Sustainable Energy for All: A Vision Statement by Ban Ki-moon, United Nations Secretary General', November 2011, available at <http://www.se4all.org>. There are three objectives to be achieved by 2030: universal access to modern energy, doubling the share of renewable energy in the global energy mix, and doubling the rate of improvement of energy efficiency.

[72] For doubts whether expansive shale gas production is compatible with climate change obligations, see J. Broderick et al, *Shale Gas: An Updated Assessment of Environmental and Climate Change Impacts* (2011). On the other hand, other non-hydrocarbon 'unconventionals' such as geothermal clearly contribute to reducing GHG emissions (though, as Bradbrook and Rønne discuss in chapter 16, not without other potentially harmful environmental consequences).

low-carbon energy is one of the main goals of a sustainable energy future,[73] increased reliance on unconventional petroleum in particular might be perceived to undermine this objective and to divert financial and other resources which might otherwise be deployed to develop non-carbon based alternatives (including other non-carbon 'unconventionals' such as geothermal).

Whether perceived as a hero or as villain, there was no direct mention of energy underground or 'unconventionals' in discussion of a sustainable energy future at the 2012 United Nations Conference on Sustainable Development (Rio + 20)[74]—but new energy technologies (and, implicitly, their potential transformative effects) were acknowledged. In the Conference outcome document entitled *The Future We Want* there is the usual latitude afforded to sovereign energy choices, with the text reaffirming the 'support for the implementation of national and subnational policies and strategies, [. . .] using an appropriate energy mix to meet developmental needs, including through increased use of renewable energy sources and other low-emission technologies, the more efficient use of energy, *greater reliance on advanced energy technologies,* including cleaner fossil fuel technologies, and the sustainable use of traditional energy resources'.[75]

There is neither mention of nor debate on energy underground or 'unconventionals' in the ongoing climate change negotiations. However, States recognize the need to arrive at an appropriate energy mix to address cost-effectively both development needs and climate change concerns, and their sovereign energy choices in relation to this mix influence their positions in these negotiations. In the early conceptual work that is currently being undertaken to design the 2015 climate agreement,[76] in recognition of the fact that climate change is a multi-dimensional problem and that the Climate Change Convention can only address a part of the problem, there is a move to strengthen the 'catalytic role' of the Convention. In the past this has meant efforts to encourage 'multilateral bodies, the public and private sectors and civil society, to build on synergies among activities and processes, as a means to support mitigation in a coherent and integrated manner'.[77] Although no specific agenda item yet exists to discuss this, given the concerns raised by possible

[73] See, e.g., the Report of the Secretary-General's Advisory Group on Energy and Climate Change entitled 'Energy for a sustainable future', available at <http://www.unido.org>.

[74] Rio + 20 was convened with the aims of 'secur[ing] renewed political commitment for sustainable development', 'assessing the progress to date and the remaining gaps in the implementation of the outcomes of the major summits on sustainable development', and 'addressing new and emerging challenges'. Resolution 'Implementation of Agenda 21, the Programme for the Further Implementation of Agenda 21 and the outcomes of the World Summit on Sustainable Development', UNGA Res 64/236, 31 March 2010, para 20(a).

[75] United Nations Conference on Sustainable Development, *The Future We Want* (2012) para 127 (emphasis added). The IEA, for example, considers CCS as part of clean fossil fuel technology: IEA, *G-20 Clean Energy, and Energy Efficiency Deployment and Policy Progress* (2011) 8. For further discussion of CCS and sustainable development in the light of Rio + 20, see C. Armeni, 'Carbon Dioxide Storage in the Sub-seabed and Sustainable Development: Please Mind the Gap' (2013) 27 Ocean Yearbook 1.

[76] Decision 1/CP.17, Establishment of an Ad Hoc Working Group on the Durban Platform for Enhanced Action FCCC/CP/2011/9/Add.1 (15 March 2012), launched a process to reach an agreement on climate change by 2015.

[77] Decision 1/CP.13, Bali Action Plan, FCCC/CP/2007/6/Add.1 (14 March 2008), para 1(b)(vii).

wide-scale exploitation of shale gas, the 2015 climate agreement may (in a bid to strengthen the role of the Convention) provide guidance on balancing energy imperatives with climate goals (through, inter alia, the exploitation of unconventional energy).

C. From permission to prohibition

A further issue is the role of international law in directly constraining or facilitating underground energy activities. The extent to which treaty amendments have sought to remove potential obstacles to sub-seabed disposal of CCS—including legal uncertainties—has already been noted in section II.A.1. In other respects, certain energy options are now foreclosed to states in consequence of international law, the most notable example being the disposal of nuclear waste.[78] In addition to the recognition of the Antarctic continent as the first 'nuclear waste free zone',[79] it is widely recognized that the disposal of radioactive waste on or below the seabed is prohibited at international law. This flows either from specific treaty prohibition,[80] or from the more general treaty and customary international law duty to protect the marine environment,[81] with which such disposal is regarded as inconsistent. While this leaves states with the exclusive option of land-based disposal,[82] international law continues to play a role in the regulation of safe disposal of nuclear material, largely through the work of the International Atomic Energy Agency (IAEA). It also plays a role in the transboundary movement of radioactive waste for (land-based) disposal elsewhere, in the transshipment of nuclear fuel for reprocessing,[83] and in the regulation of nuclear liability.[84]

However, it is unclear whether the existing nuclear liability regime would extend to geological or subsurface disposal of high-level nuclear waste and spent fuel. Strict liability is channelled through the operator of a 'nuclear installation' upon proof of nuclear damage.[85] While the definition of 'nuclear installation' under the 1963 Vienna Convention on Civil Liability for Nuclear Damage includes a nuclear

[78] From the fuel cycle during active operations and on decommissioning.

[79] 1959 The Antarctic Treaty, Art 5; 1991 Environment Protocol.

[80] 1959 The Antarctic Treaty, Art 5; 1991 Environment Protocol; see also London Convention, Art IV(1)(a); London Protocol, Art 4(1), OSPAR, Art 3, Annex II.

[81] LOSC, Art 192.

[82] The Moon Treaty rules out disposal there, and as Zillman discusses in chapter 17, disposal in space has never been considered a viable option.

[83] See chapter 17, section IV, for more detailed discussion of international standards, in particular the provisions of the 1997 Joint Convention on the Safety of Spent Fuel Management and on the Safety of Radioactive Waste Management.

[84] Regionally, the 1960 Paris Convention on Nuclear Third Party Liability, the 2004 Protocol to amend the Paris Convention on Nuclear Third Party Liability, the 1963 Brussels Supplementary Convention on Nuclear Third Party Liability, and the 2004 Protocol to amend the Brussels Supplementary Convention on Third Party Liability (collectively the Paris/Brussels regime) (OECD NEA); globally, the 1963 Vienna Convention on Civil Liability for Nuclear Damage and the1997 Protocol to Amend the 1963 Convention (IAEA); linked by 1988 Joint Protocol Relating to the Application of the Vienna Convention and the Paris Convention (the 'Joint Protocol'). Referred to herein as the 'liability regime'.

[85] Vienna Convention, Art II.

reactor, a nuclear factory, or 'any facility where nuclear material is *stored*',[86] there is no explicit reference to disposal. While there is a clear technical distinction between storage, however long-term, and permanent disposal,[87] the legal distinction between them is less clear and could be improved: does 'storage' include 'disposal' for the purposes of the application of the liability regime? Legal certainty could be achieved, for example, were a determination made by the Steering Committee for Nuclear Energy of the Organisation for Economic Co-operation and Development (OECD) that a disposal facility with nuclear fuel or radioactive products or waste is an 'installation' for the purposes of the liability regime.[88]

Whether it should be so extended is another question, given that geological disposal of high-level nuclear waste and spent fuel raises issues different from even the long-term storage of nuclear waste, and may thus require a bespoke legal response. First, long-term surface storage requires active surveillance and maintenance as facilities are likely to degrade over time, and are more vulnerable to human intrusion and natural events than geological disposal, which requires little surveillance or maintenance as it provides 'containment and isolation of radioactive waste from the human environment for the very long periods required'.[89] Second, unlike surface storage, where there is operational experience and a robust knowledge base, geological disposal of high-level nuclear waste and spent fuel, though widely accepted among governments and experts as the preferred option, has yet to be fully operationalized.[90] Given the long time frames involved, we are arguably at the early stage of learning this process—unconscious incompetence—that is to say, we don't know what we don't know. Third, to the extent that there are environmental and other impacts, these may emerge in the near or distant future. In relation to storage, given the necessity of active surveillance and maintenance, there will need to be inter-generational transfer of information, which may or may not occur in a reliable and complete manner. Further, the burdens of surveillance, maintenance, and eventual 'disposal', which is capital cost-intensive, are passed on to future generations. In relation to disposal, there is limited need for the transfer of information, save for the location of the disposal site, and the burden of disposal is dealt with by the current generation. However, first, should there be an incident at some point in the future, it would be difficult to identify an 'operator' to hold liable, creating an inter-generational lack of accountability. And, second, in interring high-level nuclear waste and spent fuel in geological formations, which are likely to remain hazardous for hundreds of thousands of years, the current generations are irreversibly altering a natural system and destroying its integrity. In the absence of

[86] Vienna Convention, Art I(j) (emphasis added).

[87] IAEA, *The Long Term Storage of Radioactive Waste: Safety and Sustainability, A Position Paper of International Experts* (2003) 3, stressing permanence with no intention to remove.

[88] As could be done under the 2004 Protocol to Amend the Paris Convention, Art 1(a)(ii).

[89] See n 87, at 5.

[90] The first geological repositories for high-level nuclear waste and spent fuel are expected to be commissioned by 2025 in the three countries closest to licensing, i.e. Finland, France, and Sweden. See European Commission and EURATOM, *Implementing Geological Disposal of Radioactive Waste Technology Platform, Deployment Plan 2011–2016*, June 2012, 5.

bespoke regulation, international law is ill-suited to address these inter-generational concerns. While the notion of inter-generational equity has some traction in academic writing[91] and in the concern for future generations in the avoidance of irreversible harm through, inter alia, the prohibition of certain activities (e.g., the dumping of radioactive waste at sea and in Antarctica, and the prohibition on mining there), future generations are not currently recognized as possessing justiciable rights in international law.[92]

D. Framework for transboundary energy underground cooperative arrangements

Transboundary movement highlights another facilitative role which international law may play, which is in providing the legal framework for energy cooperation where there is a lack of storage capacity. In the nuclear context, suitable land-based disposal sites may be at a premium or non-existent.[93] Comparable issues arise in other areas, e.g., storage capacity for CCS or for oil, diesel, or gas storage in order to meet the International Energy Agency's stockpiling obligations. Bilateral treaty arrangements (and a domestic legislative amendment removing a prohibition on 'foreign' storage) have been concluded to facilitate Portugal's storage of emergency reserves in Germany, the Netherlands, and Spain, for example.[94]

E. Stable legal framework for high-risk, high-cost energy underground activities

A further facilitative role for international law is in helping to provide a stable legal framework for investment in what are high-cost, high-risk activities. For those instances where legal, economic, environmental, and social conditions are suitable, the private sector has provided investment in unconventional petroleum, facilitated by the extensive framework of investment protection rules which have evolved at international law.[95] Private investors bear the exploration risk. For other unconventional activities, such as geothermal, investment has been facilitated, particularly

[91] Most notably, E. Brown Weiss, *In Fairness to Future Generations* (1989), the cornerstone of whose argument is that each generation must pass the planet on in no worse condition than received. Nuclear waste is one of her case studies.

[92] Birnie, Boyle, and Redgwell (n 38) at 121.

[93] E.g., since 1982 the state utility Taiwan Power Company has stored nuclear waste from its three nuclear power plants at a facility on Orchid Island (Lanyu), a small volcanic island off the coast of the densely populated main island of Taiwan. There is considerable public opposition to the Lanyu facility, and efforts have been exerted by Taipower to locate a suitable offshore (land-based) facility, including reportedly storage in an abandoned coal mine in North Korea. This attracted strong international criticism from, inter alia, South Korea and the United States. In March 2013, 16 years of negotiation pursuant to a 1996 agreement ended with, inter alia, the refusal by the Taiwanese Atomic Energy Council to grant Taipower an export licence. North Korea is now reportedly suing for breach of contract: 'North Korea suing Taipower', *Taipei Times*, 2 March 2013, 1.

[94] IEA, *Oil & Gas Security Emergency Response of IEA Countries—Portugal* (2011) 10.

[95] Extensively canvassed in P. Cameron, *International Energy Investment Law: The Pursuit of Stability* (2010).

in developing states, by international financial institutions. For example, Kenya is one of six pilot countries receiving funding from the 'Scaling-Up Renewable Energy Program [SREP] in Low Income Countries'.[96] In Kenya, it is hoped that concessional financing at the production drilling phase of the proposed Menengai 400 MW geothermal project in the East Rift Valley will pave the way for commercial financing in subsequent stages.[97] This, in turn, may facilitate the necessary insurance underwriting of risk.[98] Financial support by the World Bank Group for geothermal development has grown from US$73 million in 2007 to US$336 million in 2012 and now constitutes nearly 10% of the World Bank's total renewable energy lending.[99] Lending is now on a scale such that a 'Global Geothermal Development Plan' is in preparation.[100] Otherwise, such loans are subject to the general environmental and social safeguard policies[101] for investments which are not specifically tailored to 'unconventional' energy underground, though the policy on environmental assessment is particularly relevant.

F. Public participation and other procedural rights

A recent practitioner-oriented study of shale gas concluded that:

> Technology, innovation and investment can provide solutions or mitigation to most of the environmental issues [of shale gas development] ... while regulation and best practice can

[96] SREP operates under the Strategic Climate Fund, which supports scaled-up transformational action to address climate change. The Strategic Climate Fund is part of Climate Investment Funds, 'which promote international cooperation on climate change and support developing countries as they move toward climate resilient development that minimizes GHG emissions and adapt to climate change'. See <http://www.climateinvestmentfund.org>.

[97] The proposed sequencing of funding sources at the development funding stage is: (1) Detailed Studies—Geothermal Development Company (GDC), Government of Kenya (GoK); (2) Exploration Drilling—GDC and GoK; (3) Appraisal Drilling—GDC and GoK; (4) Feasibility Studies—World Bank; (5) Production Drilling—African Development Bank (AfDB), French Development Agency, and SREP; (6) Steam Field Development—World Bank; (7) Power Plant—International Finance Corporation, private sector, and AfDB; and (8) Transmission/Substation—World Bank.

[98] E.g., the International Finance Corporation has facilitated the development in Turkey of a large database of drilling results available from the geothermal industry. It notes that '[t]he Geothermal Well Productivity Insurance facility for Turkey may be the first example of an international insurance company covering geothermal resource risk outside of continental Europe. The scheme involves local insurance companies providing the immediate coverage and the international insurance company providing reinsurance.' M. Gehringer and V. Loksha, *Geothermal Handbook: Planning and Financing Power Generation*, ESMAP technical report no 2/12 (World Bank, 2012).

[99] Geothermal energy development has also benefitted from Global Environment Facility (GEF) funding.

[100] *Geothermal Handbook* (n 98), and launched in Reykjavik in March 2013: see 'World Bank Calls for Global Initiative to Scale Up Geothermal Energy in Developing Countries', World Bank Press Release 6 March 2013, available at <http://www.worldbank.org/en/news>. This is explicitly tied in with the UN's Sustainable Energy for All initiative, in particular with the goals of universal access to modern energy services and doubling the world's proportion of reliance on renewable energy.

[101] Of which there are currently eight: OP/BP 4.01 on environmental assessment, OP/BP 4.04 on natural habitats, OP/BP 4.09 on pest management, OP/BP 4.10 on indigenous peoples, OP/BP 4.11 on physical cultural resources, OP/BP 4.12 on involuntary resettlement, OP/BP 4.36 on forests, and OP/BP 4.37 on dam safety. Depending on the nature of the project, one or more of these policies will have to be addressed through specific actions and documentation developed as part of the project appraisal process.

ensure that standards are upheld. However, *public opinion* toward shale gas development is ultimately the barometer for judging viability of production.[102]

International law has a role to play here, particularly in facilitating public participation in (national) decision-making on energy underground. The 1998 Aarhus Convention[103] requires Parties to guarantee the rights of access to information, public participation in decision-making, and access to justice in environmental matters.[104] In particular, it requires states to provide for public participation in decisions relating to energy activities.[105] Its provisions are designed to provide the public with early, informed, and effective participation in such decisions. The 1991 Espoo Convention[106] requires states engaged in activities likely to have significant transboundary impacts both to conduct an EIA and to provide the affected public an opportunity to participate in the EIA procedures. Both the Aarhus Convention and the Espoo Convention require states to provide participation opportunities without reference to state borders. The Espoo Convention obliges states not to discriminate between their citizens and those of the affected state,[107] hence according public participation rights to transboundary affected people.[108] The Aarhus Convention obliges states to afford opportunities for public participation 'without discrimination as to citizenship, nationality or domicile'.[109] Both Conventions are also regional instruments,[110] though since 2011, in principle (though not yet in practice) non-ECE members may become parties to Aarhus.[111] There are (non-binding) international instruments that recognize the importance of and provide for, albeit in a more circumscribed way, public participation in decision-making.[112] However, the ICJ in the *Pulp Mills* case did not find a legal obligation to consult with the public.[113] The position, therefore, is weaker outside of the ECE context.

[102] J. Dutton, 'Public Policy and Public Opinion on Shale Gas Development' in *Shale Gas: A Practitioner's Guide to Shale Gas & Other Unconventional Resources* (V. Bakshi, consulting ed, 2012) (emphasis added).

[103] 1998 Convention on Access to Information, Public Participation in Decision Making and Access to Justice in Environmental Matters (the 'Aarhus Convention').

[104] Aarhus Convention, Art 1.

[105] Aarhus Convention, Art 6 (1) read with Annex I.

[106] Espoo Convention, Art 2(3) and 2(6).

[107] Espoo Convention, Art 2(6).

[108] See generally for a discussion of environmental democracy in transboundary contexts, J. Ebbesson, 'A Modest Contribution to Environmental Democracy and Justice in Transboundary Contexts: The Combined Impact of the Espoo and Aarhus Convention' (2011) 20(3) RECIEL 248–56.

[109] Aarhus Convention, Art 3(9).

[110] They have 47 and 45 Parties, respectively.

[111] See Decision IV/5 on accession to the Convention by non-United Nations Economic Commission for Europe member States, ECE/MP.PP/2011/2/Add.1 (2011).

[112] See, e.g., Rio Declaration, Principle 10; 1987 United Nations Environment Programme (UNEP) Goals and Principles of Environmental Impact Assessment, Principles 7 and 8; see generally ILC Draft Articles, Art 13 and commentary therein.

[113] The ICJ noted that Uruguay had consulted with the affected populations of both Uruguay and Argentina, but it did not find that it was under a legal obligation to do so based on the instruments relied on by Argentina, namely, the Espoo Convention, UNEP Goals and Principles, and Art 13 of the 2001 ILC draft Articles on Prevention of Transboundary Harm from Hazardous Activities. See *Pulp Mills* (n 54) at paras 215–219.

In relation to energy underground activities on indigenous peoples' lands, however, the legal case for public participation is stronger. Indigenous peoples have the right to self-determination, and by extension, it is argued, to free, prior, and informed consent in relation to development projects within their lands, and which impact their resources.[114] This point is considered further in the next section.

G. Who owns the energy underground?

1. *Sovereignty over natural resources*

As a matter of both customary[115] and treaty law,[116] international law clearly recognizes the permanent sovereignty of States over their natural resources, including of the territorial sea, and exclusive sovereign rights over the natural resources of the continental shelf and exclusive economic zone.[117] Whether in the exercise of its sovereignty/sovereign rights a state then chooses to vest ownership in the state, or in private actors, is a matter for domestic law. Once private property rights arise, however, there are clearly international rules applicable to the exercise and enjoyment of those property rights,[118] including freedom from interference/deprivation without due process of law.[119]

One of the difficulties in mapping domestically rooted concepts of property rights onto international law is the diversity which exists between municipal concepts, a point well illustrated by Part I of this volume. In the absence of treaty provisions establishing the nature and extent of property rights (and there are many in specialized contexts, such as intellectual property and secured transactions), it is a matter of identifying either customary or general principles of international law. Customary international law requires general and *consistent* state practice as one constituent element for its creation, so this very diversity in national law militates against its evolution. Nor has a general principle of property law emerged at international law.

[114] E. A. Daes, Special Rapporteur on the Rights of Indigenous Peoples, *Prevention of Discrimination and Protection of Indigenous Peoples: Indigenous Peoples' Permanent Sovereignty over Natural Resources: Final Report of the Special Rapporteur*, United Nations, UN Doc E/CN.4/2004/30 (2004) 17.

[115] The ICJ reiterated that the concept of permanent sovereignty over natural resources is part of customary international law in *Case Concerning Armed Activities on the Territory of the Congo (Democratic Republic of the Congo v Uganda)*, judgment of 19 December 2005. See further N. Schrijver, *Sovereignty over Natural Resources: Balancing Rights and Duties* (1997) 377.

[116] See, e.g., 1994 Energy Charter Treaty, Art 18; LOSC, Arts 2, 56, and 77.

[117] For fuller discussion see McHarg et al (n 1).

[118] See, e.g., Art 1 of the First Protocol to the European Convention on Human Rights and Art 21 of the 1969 American Convention on Human Rights.

[119] However, in *Commonwealth v WMC Resources Ltd* the Australian High Court held that the cancellation of an offshore petroleum exploration licence did not amount to the acquisition of property (for which compensation was payable), since the Commonwealth held no radical title to the continental shelf, but 'merely' sovereign rights to explore and exploit the resources of the continental shelf: (1988) 194 CLR 1; for critique, see chapter 21. Whatever the correctness of this decision at domestic law, it raises the question of what property rights, if any, states enjoy, not only in the hydrocarbon resources contained in underground reservoirs but also in the reservoir itself.

The matter thus remains one regulated by competing systems of domestic property rights. Does this mean that states are free at international law to apply their own, potentially conflicting, notions of property rights to straddling resources located on their side of a maritime boundary? The rule of capture discussed earlier, recognized in some jurisdictions but not in others,[120] raises this issue directly, perhaps most acutely in the situation of an undetermined maritime boundary with competing sovereign claims by states to a share of hydrocarbon production and revenue.[121] It has been suggested that where the boundary is determined, and 'in the absence of an agreement to the contrary, a State or international oil company is free to maximize production from its side of the boundary line notwithstanding the policies of neighbouring States which share the same field'.[122] However, practices such as directional drilling may lead to conflict over the resource: in the second Gulf War (1990–1991), Iraq claimed that Kuwait was unlawfully securing Iraqi oil by directional drilling.[123] It is not impossible to imagine future scenarios of conflict over competing uses of a shared reservoir, particularly in the presence of competing national concepts of property and in the absence of clear international rules, hard or soft, on their utilization. There is no international legal obligation to jointly develop straddling fields, though international courts and tribunals have been consistent in encouraging such development.[124]

120 For general discussion of the rule of capture in the United States, see chapter 3. It should be noted that the modern rule of capture is as a preclusion of tortious liability rather than a recognition of proprietary rights in the migrating substance (e.g. water or oil).

121 Licensing of oil and gas activities has not been recognized by the ICJ to constitute a relevant circumstance in maritime boundary delimitation (*Case Concerning the Land and Maritime Boundary Between Cameroon and Nigeria (Cameroon/Nigeria: Equatorial Guinea intervening), ICJ Judgment* (ICJ Reports 2002, 303)) and recourse to such devices in an attempt to cement sovereign claims may risk inflaming a boundary dispute—not to mention placing petroleum companies on the front lines in such disputes (e.g. the threat of the use of force by a Suriname gunboat against a CGX drilling rig undertaking exploratory work for Guyana: see *Guyana v Suriname, Arbitral Award made 17 September 2007*, available at <http://www.pca-cpa.org>).

122 R. Bundy, 'Natural Resources Development (Oil and Gas) and Boundary Disputes' in *The Peaceful Management of Transboundary Resources* (G. H. Blake et al, eds, 1995) 23 at 24.

123 The Iraq–Kuwait Boundary Demarcation Commission's recommendations for the final demarcation of the boundary between Iraq and Kuwait was accepted by UNSC Res 833, 27 May 1993.

124 Specifically in the offshore context, pending final delimitation, Arts 74(3) (EEZ) and 83(3) (CS) LOSC have been interpreted as imposing on parties two obligations: (1) to make 'every effort to enter into provisional arrangements of a practical nature'; and (2) during this period, to 'make every effort... not to jeopardize or hamper the reaching of the final agreement': *Guyana v Suriname* (n 121). 'Every effort' falls short of a substantive obligation, and the jurisprudence appears to support, e.g., the unilateral carrying out of seismic and exploratory drilling activities as consistent with this provision, particularly where there is notice given of such activities and there is sharing of the results: (Aegean Sea Continental Shelf (seismic); Guyana-Suriname (exploratory drilling)). It is, of course, always open to the parties to address the matter: e.g., in Tunisia–Libya the parties voluntarily ceased activities in the overlapping area pending resolution of their maritime boundary dispute before the Court, and Libya and Malta had a 'no drilling' agreement pending the outcome of their ICJ maritime boundary proceedings: Bundy (n 122).

2. *State rights or peoples' rights?*

Historically, the evolution of the principle of permanent sovereignty over natural resources (PSNR) commenced with an acknowledgement of both State and peoples' rights to these resources.[125] While subsequent soft law and treaty iterations of PSNR have omitted reference to 'peoples', and it cannot be considered part of the customary law articulation of this principle, it *does* form part of the collective right of peoples to self-determination.[126] Moreover, in contemporary international law there remains the question of the extent to which indigenous peoples exercise rights in energy resources, including energy underground. A recent illustration of the complex interplay of domestic and international law in this area is the (draft) Nordic Saami Convention.[127] Currently under negotiation with a view to adopting a binding legal text by 2016 (if at all), it builds on a draft text agreed in 2005 by an expert group representing the governments of Norway, Sweden, and Finland, and the Saami parliaments of these states.[128] In the 2005 draft, negotiation of the substantive articles in Chapter IV on the Saami right to land and water, particularly whether such rights included subsurface resources in traditional areas, proved to be highly controversial.[129] In the text, 'protracted traditional use of land or water areas' are recognized as constituting the basis for individual or collective ownership rights, but 'prospecting or extraction of mineral or other sub-surface resources' are not. Rather, the approach taken is one of negotiation, given that such resource activities may constitute interference with or denial of rights. Consequently, the draft protects traditional use of land or water areas, including access thereto, by requiring the public authorities of each state to negotiate with affected Saami, as well as with the Saami parliament, before granting a permit for such prospecting or extraction, and prohibiting such grant if traditional use would be rendered impossible or substantially more difficult.[130] These 2005 provisions on mineral or other subsurface resources draw heavily on existing treaty law, in particular, ILO Convention No 169, Articles 1(2) and 27 of the International Covenant on Civil and Political Rights (ICCPR), as interpreted by the UN Human Rights Committee, and Article 1(2) of the International Covenant on Economic, Social and Cultural Rights (ICESCR), as interpreted by the Committee on Economic, Social and Cultural

[125] Compare UNGA Resolution 545 (VI), 5 February 1952 and UNGA Resolution 1803 (VII) 1962 ('the right of peoples and nations') with UNGA Resolution 3281 (XXIX) 1974 ('every State'). Treaty articulations now use the exclusive 'sovereign right(s) of states' framing, e.g., A LOSC Art 193 and ECT Art 18.

[126] See Triggs (n 21).

[127] Text available at <http://www.regjeringen.no/upload/BLD/Vedlegg_5_d.pdf>. For earlier discussion see Zillman et al (n 21).

[128] For thorough overview, see N. Bankes and R. Koivurova (eds), *The Proposed Nordic Saami Convention: National and International Dimensions of Indigenous Property Rights* (2013).

[129] For a fuller account see M. Ahren, M. Scheinin, and J. B. Henriksen in the special issue of Galdu Cala (Journal of Indigenous Peoples Rights) No 3/2007 on 'The Nordic Sami Convention: International Human Rights, Self-Determination and other Central Provisions'.

[130] Unless with the consent of the Saami parliament and the affected Saami: Art 36 'Utilization of Natural Resources'. There are also provisions on co-management of Saami traditional areas and cooperation between the States and the Saami Parliaments on environmental preservation activities.

Rights (CESCR).[131] Other provisions anticipate the potential evolution of international law.[132]

That new energy underground activities are perceived as threatening to indigenous traditional rights is underscored by another recent development. On 25 January 2013, a Ceremonial Grand Council, comprised of representatives from Native American tribes and Canadian First Nations, concluded an 'International Treaty to Protect the Sacred from Tar Sands Projects' to prevent tar sands projects degrading 'the soil, the waters, the air, sacred sites and our ways of life'. Amongst the adverse effects noted are 'the threat of pipeline and tanker spills' to aquatic ecosystems, 'the negative cumulative health and ecological impacts of tar sands projects on Indigenous Communities',[133] and 'greenhouse gas pollution that could lock the planet into a path of catastrophic climate change' (Article IV). The Treaty calls on the respective non-tribal Governments 'to immediately halt and deny approval for pending tar sands projects' (Article VI) and, with respect to the approval process, the Treaty explicitly invokes the consultation and free informed prior consent provision of Article 32 of the UN Declaration on the Rights of Indigenous Peoples (Article III). However, while Article 36(1) of this (non-binding) UN Declaration recognizes the potential for treaty-making power to be exercised by indigenous peoples under international law, this is undoubtedly de lege ferenda.

H. Policy/institutional framework

Until recently, there has been little specific attention paid to new energy underground in terms of new developments at the international policy or institutional level. As noted earlier, at Rio 20 energy was identified as one of seven critical issues for consideration, with an emphasis on 'Sustainable Energy for All'[134] through universal access to modern energy services, and by doubling the global rate of improvement in energy efficiency and of the share of renewable energy in the

131 Joint Art 1(2) of the ICCPR and ICESCR provides that: 'All peoples may, for their own ends, freely dispose of their natural wealth and resources without prejudice to any obligations arising out of international economic co-operation, based upon the principle of mutual benefits, and international law. In no case may a people be deprived of its own means of subsistence.'

132 E.g., the savings clauses on profit-sharing (Art 37(2)) and restitution/compensation (Art 34(4)), rights to which are not recognized in the 2005 draft. It is assumed that any reference to 'international law' in the 2005 draft is that binding on the (state) parties, i.e. ratified treaties in force and generally applicable customary law. The UN Declaration is not a binding instrument and four key states (Canada, United States, New Zealand, and Australia) initially objected to it, though such objections were subsequently withdrawn (Australia in 2009 and the other three states, individually, in 2010).

133 See International Treaty to Protect the Sacred from Tar Sands Projects, Art IV, available at <http://www.protectthesacred.org/international_treaty>. On effects, see inter alia The Royal Society of Canada Expert Panel Report, *Environmental and Health Impacts of Canada's Oil Sands Industry* (December 2010). The international legal dimensions are largely ignored, however, with reference to international standards largely in terms of EIA and the requirements of international financial institutions (e.g. the EIA was not conducted to World Bank standards).

134 Sustainable Energy for All (n 71).

global energy mix.[135] 2012 was also designated as the 'International Year of Sustainable Energy'[136]—a year in which the World Energy Outlook of the International Energy Agency (IEA) concluded that, even taking into account all new developments and policies, 'the world is still failing to put the global energy system onto a more sustainable path'.[137] In contrast, the IEA has recently turned its attention to energy underground, in particular unconventional gas. In May 2012, a World Energy Outlook special report was issued on unconventional gas, which seeks to establish 'golden rules' to ensure a 'social licence to operate'.[138] This was followed at the end of 2012 with the establishment of a 'High Level Forum for Unconventional Natural Gas Best Practices' for the safe and sustainable development of unconventional natural gas resources.[139] Part of this is a jockeying for position amongst international institutions by the IEA with its 2012 Annual Report, noting that this 'initiative is already helping to further raise interest in the mission of the IEA, with significant unsolicited interest for membership coming from partner countries and industry'.[140]

III. Conclusion

To a large extent new subsurface activities involving new transformative technologies for using energy resources have been addressed within the framework of existing international law and institutions.[141] This is a reflection of at least two factors: (i) a reduced appetite for new law-making and institution-building and the adaptability of existing international law and institutions; and (ii) the underlying absence of 'novelty' in the legal issues posed for international law by the activities addressed in this volume. That said, and as the discussion of unconventional hydrocarbons illustrates, there are heightened concerns regarding the environmental risks and social impacts of upstream unconventional hydrocarbon extraction activities, which are reflected in public opposition and in regulatory responses.

[135] Officially launched by the UN Secretary General at the opening of the UN General Assembly in 2011. The Technical Reports produced by the Secretary-General's High-Level Group on Sustainable Energy for All are available at <http://www.sustainableenergyforall.org>.

[136] UNGA Resolution 65/151, 16 February 2011. In addition to recalling the Millennium Development Goals, the preamble 'reiterates the principles' of the Rio Declaration and Agenda 21, and 'recalls the recommendations and conclusions' of the Johannesburg Plan of Implementation of the World Summit on Sustainable Development, concerning energy for sustainable development.

[137] IEA, *World Energy Outlook 2012* (2012), available at <http://www.oecd-ilibrary.org/energy/world-energy-outlook_20725302>.

[138] IEA, *Golden Rules for a Golden Age of Gas*, World Energy Outlook: Special Report on Unconventional Gas (2012) 19.

[139] IEA, *2012 Annual Report* (2013) 11.

[140] IEA (n 139) at 11. Currently, there are 28 member countries in the IEA, with participation limited to members of the OECD (though not all members of the OECD are IEA members). Outreach to key partner countries outside the IEA is an increasingly important area of IEA activity, with target partner states including China, India, and Brazil.

[141] To a large extent the same is true of domestic law, at least for unconventional gas. The need for new regulatory bodies may have to be considered or, more likely, existing ones may require new resources, functions, and powers. *Golden Rules for a Golden Age of Gas* (n 138) at 49.

There are glimmerings of international policy development through international institutions, and potential to collect and to harmonize best practice, evident in, for example, the IEA's 2012 'Golden Rules' on unconventional gas.[142] Key international regulatory gaps nonetheless remain for some aspects of energy underground, most notably with respect to the current issues regarding (1) transboundary movement of CO_2; (2) the seemingly intractable inter-generational issue of the long-term storage of nuclear waste and liability; and (3) the legal status and use of shared oil and gas reservoirs. While, as noted in section II.A, existing treaty frameworks are already addressing the first issue (for example, the UNFCCC and London Convention/London Protocol), and there exist legal frameworks to address the second, should the political will exist to do so (for example, through the IAEA), it is less easy to see how the regulatory gap on the final point will be addressed within current legal frameworks. One option would be the development of soft law guidance, as was done by the United Nations Environment Programme on shared natural resources, or the aggregation of best practice, as the IEA is currently undertaking in relation to unconventional gas. Until then, whether traditional or unconventional, shared oil and gas resources will continue to be addressed on an ad hoc unilateral or bilateral basis.

142 *Golden Rules for a Golden Age of Gas* (n 138).

PART III

GOVERNING UNCONVENTIONAL OIL AND GAS EXTRACTION

7

Regulating Multistage Hydraulic Fracturing: Challenges in a Mature Oil and Gas Jurisdiction

Alastair R. Lucas, Theresa Watson, and Eric Kimmel

I. Introduction

The adoption and extensive use of multistage hydraulic fracturing through horizontal wells by the upstream oil and gas sector has created a renaissance in the recovery of subsurface hydrocarbon resources within the North American landscape. Oil and gas resources trapped in reservoirs once considered unproductive or in tight geological formations, such as shale, coal, or tight sands, may now be exploited at economically recoverable rates. The resurgence of oil and gas development activities and the associated windfall of economic benefits have been overshadowed by growing public concerns about the real and, in some cases, perceived, risks to human health and safety, and the potential environmental impacts, particularly on water resources. Indeed, this development renaissance has placed regulatory authorities in a challenging position to navigate through the complex challenges of designing a regulatory regime that is responsive to balancing the basic necessity for resource development against managing the inherent development risks to the things that society values.

This chapter is about regulatory adaptation. It assesses the response by an established regulatory regime to a fundamentally new form of activity by the upstream oil and gas sector. By new form of activity, we mean adaptation of known technology to produce a previously unproducible hydrocarbon resource. This takes place in the broader context of regulation by the Alberta Energy Regulator (AER)[1] of the provincial oil and gas and coal industries.

Oil and gas sector regulation by the Regulator is long established. Its experience and expertise are broadly accepted by the industry. The emergence of multistage hydraulic fracturing (MSHF) has required both a technical response and a social

[1] As of June 2013, the Energy Resources Conservation Board established in 1938 was continued in restructured form as the Alberta Energy Regulator: Responsible Energy Development Act, SA 2012, CA 17.3.

justice response by the Regulator. The latter involves protection of the public interest, including broad public goals and aspirations.[2]

The approach that emerges in this context has strong features of what has been characterized as 'decentred' regulation—regulation that is not entirely a matter for the state.[3] The idea is that complexity like that found in the emergence of unconventional resource development and MSHF means that regulation cannot be simply prescriptive and adversarial. It must recognize industry expertise and its interest in effectively managing the sector. Elements of self-regulation must be part of the solution. But this must be in the context of a legal framework. This 'reflexive law'[4] governs industry initiatives and reflects broader social values.

Thus, information and public perspectives need to be part of regulatory solutions. There are important public values that must be addressed. This is another direction in which decentred regulation pushes, namely democratic legitimacy. Today's regulatory agencies must be concerned about fostering legitimacy through public engagement and participation. Regulatory responses to public concerns about hydraulic fracturing must reach out through public involvement in the debate over what fracturing policies and rules should look like and how the regime should work.

The remainder of this chapter begins by looking at the technology of MSHF and its development. Included is the intensity of recent fracturing activity and its strategic importance for energy resource recovery. Then, we identify regulatory roles and assess how these have played out in Alberta's established energy sector. As unconventional energy resource development has soared, hydraulic fracturing has received increasing attention.

This chapter focuses on the credibility gap that has emerged between regulator and public. In this context, we assess the approaches to regulation of hydraulic fracturing developed by AER and the public consultation processes that it has initiated. This reveals a public consultation process that has moved, to a degree, outside the traditional regulatory system and a regulator determined to manage the risks posed by these controversial technologies.

II. Hydraulic fracturing technology

Hydraulic fracturing is not a new technology. It has been used commercially since 1949. Prior to this, wells were often stimulated through down-hole explosions using nitroglycerin.[5] Historically, fracturing was conducted in vertical wellbores

[2] B. Barton, 'The Theoretical Context of Regulation', in *Regulating Energy and Natural Resources* (B. Barton, L. Barrera-Hernandez, A. Lucas, and A. Rønne, eds, 2006) 11 at 18.

[3] J. Black, 'Decentring Regulation, and Self-Regulation in a "Post-Regulatory" World' (2001) 54 Current Legal Problems 102.

[4] G. Teubner, 'Substantive and Reflexive Elements in Modern Law' (1982) 17 Law and Soc Rev 239; Barton (n 2).

[5] C. T. Montgomery and M. B. Smith, 'Hydraulic Fracturing: History of an Enduring Technology' (December 2010) JPT Online 26–41, available at <http://www.spe.org/jpt>.

where a single fracture stimulation was produced, resulting in a bi-wing vertical fracture.[6] Over the years fracturing evolved to use gelled fluids. These viscous fluids could carry proppant, usually sand, that would be left in the fracture to hold the rock open after the stimulation was completed and the fracture fluid was recovered.

With the advent of mud motors in the 1970s, wells could be drilled horizontally for greater distances.[7] This allowed for maximum contact with the reservoir from a single horizontal wellbore. Hydraulic fracturing was adapted to these types of wellbores and applied to multiple intervals along the horizontal section. This new application of an old technology has led to development of reservoirs previously found to be uneconomic due to low porosity and permeability.

Historically, conventional reservoirs in Alberta were allowed to have one well per section for gas reservoirs and one well per quarter section in the case of oil.[8] Tighter reservoirs, or unconventional reservoirs such as shale, tight sands, or coal, need reduced well spacing, or more wells for a given area, to effectively drain the resource. Multistage fracturing in horizontal wells has made the exploitation of these types of resources economic. Without this new application of the technology unconventional reservoirs would require dozens of wells per section from multiple surface locations.

Construction of a horizontal well generally consists of drilling a surface hole, and cementing casing in place deep enough to cover potable groundwater and provide adequate well control. The main hole is drilled vertically to the desired depth and turned 90 degrees. A horizontal section of the wellbore is then drilled through the reservoir, usually at depths greater than 1,000 m and, in Alberta, up to 3,000 m or more in vertical depth. The horizontal section can reach 1,500 m or more.

Casing is then run and cemented in place to protect non-saline water and shallower formations, and provide hydraulic isolation for the production zone. Several intervals along the horizontal section are then opened through the casing to allow hydraulic fractures to be created in each interval. The number of intervals varies depending on the length of the horizontal section and the reservoir parameters, but could be 20 or more.[9]

In hydraulic fracturing, the fractures created are in the order of 1–2 mm in width.[10] Often the fluid is viscosified or 'gelled' using additives such as guar gum. The gelled fluid can then be used to suspend a proppant, usually sand, that will be injected under pressure into the fracture. Additives are used to 'break' the gel after some time so the viscosity is lowered once the fluid is in the formation. This allows the fracture to close on the proppant, which keeps the proppant in place while the fluid is produced out of the well. This fracture becomes a highly permeable pathway for oil and gas to flow from the reservoir to the wellbore where it can be produced.

[6] Montgomery and Smith (n 5). [7] Montgomery and Smith (n 5).

[8] AER, *Energy Development Applications and Schedules*, Directive 056, September 2011. ('Directive 056').

[9] AER, EnerFAQs 14, 'Horizontal Hydraulic Fracturing', available at <http://www.aer.ca>.

[10] See FracFocus, 'Hydraulic Fracturing: The Process', available at <http://www.fracfocus.ca>.

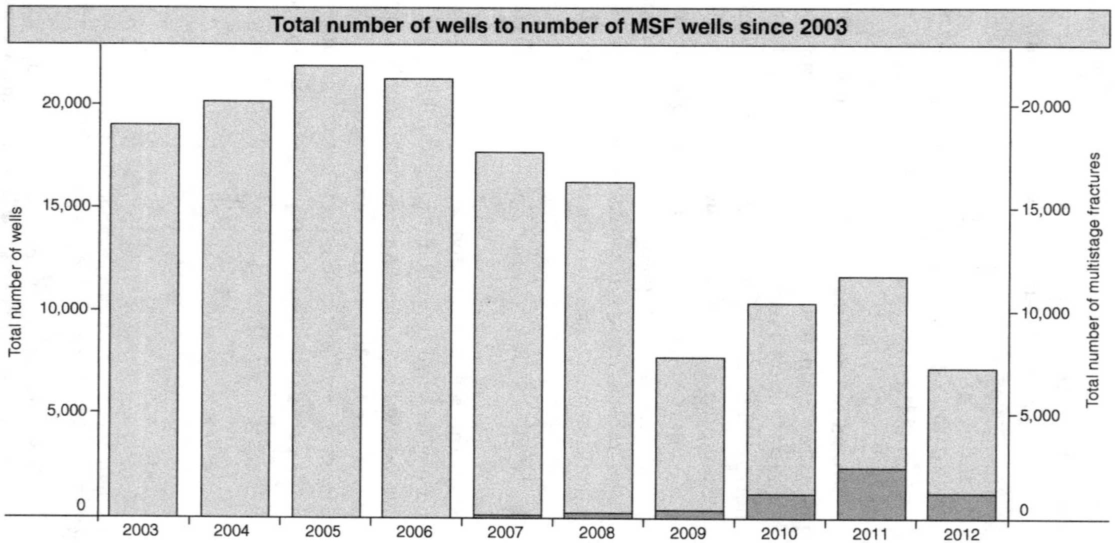

Year	Total wells	MSF
2003	18,978	5
2004	20,116	6
2005	21,756	3
2006	21,180	8
2007	17,632	58
2008	16,226	228
2009	7,747	329
2010	10,350	1,115
2011	11,674	2,414
2012	7,212	1,183

Fig. 7.1 Drilling activity by year with MSHF

Source: AER, available at <http://www.aer.ca>.

A. Snapshot of activity

Figure 7.1 shows the drilling activity in Alberta since 2003. This indicates that MSHF is a relatively new technology application. It was not until 2010 that significant numbers of wells were drilled and completed in this manner. The majority of horizontal wells with MSHF in Alberta are oil wells, either located in previously unproductive areas of known reservoirs, or infill drilling to increase recovery within the developed reservoirs themselves.

B. Strategic importance of enhanced resource recovery

Alberta has been producing oil and gas since 1902. In 1938, the Petroleum and Natural Gas Conservation Board, the precursor to the AER, was established. The Alberta government recognized at that time that unregulated production was leading to resource waste and a significant loss of recoverable resources.[11]

Traditional means of production have been able to produce only up to 20% of oil reserves using primary and secondary recovery methods, such as water flooding. Significant resources are now recoverable in areas with established infrastructure such as pipelines and other facilities. Production through enhanced resource recovery methods in known reservoirs, such as multistage hydraulic fracturing, removes exploration risk, enables further development in areas accustomed to oil and gas activity, utilizes trained workforces, and can access established support services.

In Alberta, the vast majority of the mineral resources are owned by the province (or the people of Alberta). The revenues generated through higher recovery support lifestyle, employment, social services, government, and regulation.

III. Alberta's early experience regulating unconventional resources

Alberta has seen development in its past analogous to the use of MSHF. In the 1990s, coal bed methane production expanded rapidly in the United States. Production in the United States was typically from wet coals that required dewatering before methane could be evolved from the coal. High-density drilling and significant dewatering has detrimental environmental effects in many areas of the United States. This has created public concern related to water handling, disposal, and ground water impacts.[12]

Commercial development of coal bed methane (CBM) began in Alberta in 2002. However, the vast majority of the production in Alberta is from dry coal that does not require dewatering and has limited environmental impacts on ground water.[13] The AER responded to environmental concerns relating to CBM

[11] G. S. Jaremko, *Steward: 75 Years of Alberta Energy Regulation* (2013) 157–60.

[12] J. Squarek and M. Dawson, 'Coalbed Methane Expands in Canada' (2006) 104 Oil & Gas Journal 37–8, at 40–2.

[13] Squarek and Dawson (n 12).

production by developing a suite of regulations specifically designed to address these concerns.

In addition to multiple regulations regarding consultation, wellbore construction, and licensing, Directive 035: *Baseline Water Well Testing Requirements for Coalbed Methane Wells Completed Above the Base of Groundwater Protection*, was released in 2006 to respond to concerns regarding non-saline water production from coal. This directive set strict limits on water production, as well as requiring water well testing for neighbouring wells within 600 m of a CBM well.[14] Directive 27: *Shallow Fracturing Operations—Restricted Operations* was also promulgated in 2006. This directive regulated fracturing operations above the base of groundwater protection, specifically disallowing the use of any toxic substance within these shallow intervals and limiting the size of the fracture stimulation.[15]

Long before the development of these requirements, the AER was protecting non-saline groundwater from oil and gas development. In 1993, Alberta Environment established the *Base of Groundwater Protection in Alberta*, using a total dissolved solids content of 4000 mg/l. To put this in context, the Canadian Drinking Water Standard is less than 500 mg/l.[16] The AER incorporated the protection of groundwater into drilling, completion, and abandonment requirements.

IV. The societal role of the regulator; risk and intervention strategies

For the most part, human behaviours and activities associated with advancing entrepreneurial interests for economic gain introduce risks to social and environmental values and public interest objectives. The market, left to its own devices, may fail to reconcile the incongruence between private and public interest considerations, which results in various forms of societal tension or conflict. There may be more profound ramifications, such as degradation of environmental standards, risks to public safety, erosion of public confidence in governmental institutions, and delay or loss of private and public investment opportunities.

The divergence of private interest pursuits from public interest considerations forms the context of regulatory policy in general, and particularly defines the role of the regulator within a particular economic and political landscape. Regulatory agencies are created by their legislative bodies with a mandate to influence the behaviour of private sector firms to effectively manage risks to public interest considerations that may emerge from economic activities driven by the pursuit of

[14] AER, *Baseline Water Well Testing Requirement for Coalbed Methane Wells Completed Above the Base of Groundwater Protection*, Directive 035, 8 May 2006.

[15] AER, *Shallow Fracturing Operations—Restricted Operations*, Directive 027, 14 August 2009; replaced by *Hydraulic Fracturing—Subsurface Integrity*, Directive 083, 21 May 2013 (the '2013 Fracturing Directive').

[16] Health Canada, *Federal-Provincial-Territorial Committee on Drinking Water of the Federal-Provincial-Territorial Committee on Health and the Environment*, Guidelines for Canadian Drinking Water Quality Summary Table, August 2012.

private interests.[17] In other words, the basis and justification for regulation is the reduction of risk,[18] accomplished through tailored interventions. Regulators' primary role in society is to develop intervention strategies designed to influence commercial operators in managing or reducing risks to social and environmental values. Their administrative duty is to employ regulatory management approaches with the intent to monitor, identify, and evaluate risk, and to design intervention strategies to manage and reduce risk.[19]

The AER has recently made significant efforts to institutionalize changes to its risk and regulatory management protocols to more closely align with the principles advocated by the regulatory reform movement.[20] Proponents of the regulatory reform movement have advanced the idea that governments and their respective administrative bodies need to improve policy and regulatory development practices in particular, and the overall quality of regulatory responses in general.[21] Governments on a global scale have yielded to the promise espoused by the regulatory reform agenda. Canada's 'Smart Regulation',[22] the European Union's 'Better Regulation',[23] and the province of Alberta's 'Enhancing Assurance' and its 'Proposed Unconventional Resource Framework'[24] are examples of a cohesive policy response designed to improve the overall quality of regulations and management of risk.

A risk-based approach to regulatory management provides a framework that enables regulators to rationalize and justify decisions around regulatory interventions, and to ensure that responses are proportionate to the nature of the risk.[25] Risk characterizes an undesirable condition found within the resource development landscape that has the potential to create harm, and depending on the severity of the risk to societal objectives, regulatory intervention may be required. The existence or emergence of a risk that compromises public interest considerations within Alberta's resource development landscape, then, becomes the *prima facie* case or justification for regulatory intervention. This means invoking the coercive powers of the state, bounded by the limitations and authority specified in legislation, to intervene in the market place to induce commercial operators to follow risk reduction strategies.

17 See T. Prosser, *Law and the Regulators* (1997).

18 OECD, *Risk and Regulatory Policy: Improving the Governance of Risk*.

19 See OECD (n 18).

20 See W. Parker, 'The Empirical Roots of the 'Regulatory Reform' Movement: A Critical Appraisal' (2006) 58 Admin L Rev 359.

21 O. Renn with an annex by P. Graham, 'Risk Governance: Towards an Integrative Approach' (2005) White Paper No 1, International Risk Governance Council (IRGC).

22 Privy Council of Canada, *Smart Regulation: A Regulatory Strategy for Canada* (2004), available at <http://publications.gc.ca/site/eng/264209/publication.html>.

23 European Commission, *Mandelkern Report on Better Regulation* (2001), available at <http://ec.europa.eu/governance/better_regulation/documents/mandelkern_report.pdf>.

24 AER Discussion Paper, *Regulating Unconventional Oil and Gas in Alberta*, December 2012, at 12 (the 'Discussion Paper').

25 J. B. Black and R. Baldwin, 'Really Responsive Risk-Based Regulation' (2010) 32 Law and Policy 181.

V. Regulatory interventions for unconventional resource development

Horizontal multistaged hydraulic fracturing presents inherent operational hazards. These have the potential to introduce risk events leading to a range of consequences that may compromise public interest objectives, including environmental standards, public safety, and resource conservation objectives. Alberta's energy regulator recognized that the existing blend of policy instruments and approaches that constitutes the regulatory regime may not be aptly suited to govern the risk profile for an emerging unconventional resource development landscape.[26]

The prevailing government response to emerging and existing industrial risks, and energy development in particular, has been the establishment of prescriptive, uniform, and direct regulatory controls applied to a broad range of activities associated with the recovery of oil and gas resources, complemented with an assessment of compliance with prescribed standards. Regulators, such as the AER, have traditionally used industry's state of compliance to gauge the performance of risk reduction interventions. The regulators' traditional conception of successful risk reduction objectives was to ensure that industry maintained compliance with prescribed standards, engineering and technological specifications, and operating processes. Compliance infers the reduction of risk to social and environmental values.

Historically, the direct control of operators, activities, and business processes has been relatively successful in abating harmful environmental pollutants, controlling public safety hazards, and preventing the waste of valuable marketable commodities.[27] However, this approach has come under considerable scrutiny as *the* optimal solution to managing the risks associated with unconventional development for the following reasons:

(1) Activities-based regulation requires detailed knowledge of industry's business processes, operational risks, corporate behaviours, and capabilities. In many cases, regulators have limited capacity in that regard. Private sector firms operate under differentiated cost regimes, have varying levels of capabilities, and perform development activities that present risk characteristics that are unique to particular resource plays. Uniform, prescriptive regulations do not account for that market and operational variability.

(2) Setting uniform standards does not provide a market incentive for firms to go beyond regulatory compliance and pursue continual improvements to address emerging risks associated with evolving technological innovations. In certain scenarios, this may restrict operators in pursuing cost effective control and mitigation measures.

(3) Regulators have limited resources to monitor compliance effectively in order to influence desired behavioural changes. Assessing simple compliance against

[26] Discussion Paper (n 24) at 1. [27] Discussion Paper (n 24) at 2.

uniform standards applied to a large number of independent firms and licensed operations requires a substantial level of resources and administrative effort. The outcome of assessing simple compliance says little about the effectiveness of risk reduction interventions or the overall state of risk.

(4) Discussion around the role of the regulator with reference to risk management has the potential to lead to a common misconception: regulators directly manage risk. Indeed, regulators do play a role in controlling and reducing risk to broader societal outcomes, and have a visible and substantial role in the governance of risk.[28] However, the risk profile associated with strategic and operational decisions regarding the development of a hydrocarbon-bearing zone is directly managed by the private sector, which implies that the owners and managers of the development and associated infrastructure are in a better position to directly own, manage, and control the risk.

(5) Unconventional resource development introduces unique risk characteristics and challenges which may not fit neatly within a traditional 'command and control', activities-based regulatory regime. Relative to conventional resource development:

a. the scale and intensity of development is large and more intrusive, the technology is more advanced and more complex, and reservoir management is more nuanced;
b. capital investment is large and the market conditions are more volatile;
c. greater water consumption is required;
d. development activities are more visible and are of longer duration;
e. there is a large inventory of offsetting subsurface infrastructure;
f. development often occurs proximal to populated urban and rural centres;
g. there are a large number of heterogeneous industry players with varying capabilities; and
h. there is an emerging class of the global population that is educated, politically astute, and media savvy, which has reservations about the government's and industry's capability to manage and balance the risks to social and environmental values.

Finding the right blend of prescriptive interventions that would induce operators to manage and reduce risks to social and environmental values within a highly diversified, complex, and nuanced unconventional oil and gas landscape is challenging. For that reason, the AER elected to explore alternative intervention strategies, which moved away from uniform standards that control specific activities and to a management-based regulatory approach.[29]

A management-based approach to regulatory interventions directs private sector firms to follow a planning process intended to pursue risk reduction objectives.[30] Management-based regulation does not mandate the application of specific technologies or processes, directly control activities, or assign explicit performance standards in the form of social outcomes. A management-based approach to regulatory intervention requires firms to undertake a planning process that meets and satisfies prescribed criteria to advance the regulator's risk reduction objectives.

[28] See Black and Baldwin (n 25).
[29] Discussion Paper (n 24) at 2.
[30] Discussion Paper (n 24) at 2.

Criteria are the elements that constitute the planning process. These include risk identification, assessment and management, monitoring and reporting requirements, and continual improvement processes. The regulator can either prescribe loosely or tightly defined criteria. For example, the regulator may allow discretion for the firm to identify and assess the salient risk areas, or the regulator may identify the risk areas that merit assessment and mitigation. A management-based approach provides a regulatory platform that mandates firms to identify, assess, and manage the risks associated with their development projects.

The risk profile associated with horizontal multistage hydraulic fracturing consists of operational hazards that occupy the subsurface and surface environment. If not managed appropriately, these operational hazards have the potential to materialize into a risk event that may compromise environmental standards and public safety objectives, erode public confidence in governmental institutions, and delay value added economic activities. The risk areas include:

(1) compromising well integrity or functionality of the well system;
(2) creating unintentional communication between a well undergoing hydraulic fracturing and an offsetting energy well;
(3) for shallow fracturing operations, creating communication between a well undergoing hydraulic fracturing and a non-saline aquifer and/or water well at shallow depths;
(4) improper handling of flow-back materials (storage and disposal of produced fluids);
(5) exceeding source and ambient air quality objectives;
(6) excessive surface footprint associated with oil and gas infrastructure;
(7) excessive traffic volume, noise levels, and general nuisances;
(8) inefficient recovery or waste of oil and gas resources;
(9) erosion of stakeholder confidence in the regulatory system.

The risk profile for hydraulic fracturing has elements in common with conventional development. Generally, the regulatory framework is well equipped to address the risks. However, the AER identified three risk areas that warranted additional analysis, which leads to additional layers of regulatory interventions concerning well integrity, interwellbore communication, and shallow fracturing operations.

Loss of well integrity involves damage to casing, cement, or surface equipment that may compromise the functionality of a well. Maintaining the integrity and functionality of a well contains produced fluids within the internal conduit of the wellbore, thereby isolating produced fluids from the surface and subsurface environment, and creating a barrier between target and non-target formations.[31] Well integrity is a critical operational objective that allows for the safe recovery and

[31] Discussion Paper (n 24) at 29.

production of hydrocarbon resources and acts as the primary line of defence for the protection of groundwater resources from contamination.

Interwellbore communication may involve fluid and/or pressure changes detrimental to an offsetting wellbore that occur during a hydraulic fracture stimulation performed on a well.[32] Communication with an offset well induced by a well undergoing hydraulic fracturing may occur intentionally or unintentionally. This kind of communication may compromise the integrity of an offset well, leading to loss of control and release of fluids at the surface and/or subsurface. It may facilitate the migration of produced fluids between zones, including non-saline aquifers.

Shallow fracturing operations—development activities above the base of groundwater protection (typically zones found between 200–600 m below the surface)[33]—introduce the potential for communication with non-saline or useable water aquifers and/or water wells. This may create a pathway for produced fluids to migrate and interact with water resources. Compromising well integrity, creating interwellbore communication events, and water impacts from shallow fracturing operations all lead to a single risk consequence—adversely impacting the quantity or quality of useable water resources—a vital environmental resource. These are events likely to attract considerable public attention.

The AER selected a management-based regulatory approach as the preferred intervention strategy to influence oil and gas sector firms to manage or reduce the subsurface risks associated with hydraulic fracturing. This aligns with the regulatory approach proposed under the Unconventional Resource Framework (URF) in which the regulator proposes a management regime described as a 'play-focused' approach. A 'play' is 'an area of oil and gas development that is determined mainly by geology, geographic area, the properties of the resource and the technology required to develop that resource'.[34]

The AER's regulatory response specifies the planning elements that operators must consider, and that they be able to demonstrate that the subsurface risks associated with hydraulic fracturing operations are appropriately managed. These requirements direct industry to provide assurances and demonstrate that the risks to social and environmental values (predominately water resources) are safely managed. The regulator abstains from directly controlling the specific activities and technologies applied in the managing of the operational risks, and delegates the duty to firms, which are obliged to show the regulator that hydraulic fracturing operations are being safely managed.[35] The intervention strategy includes the following elements:

(1) Addressing the risks associated with the loss of well integrity—licensees carrying out hydraulic fracturing operations are required to choose the optimal well design system complemented by well integrity testing, and assurances that operational risks unique to the development are assessed and considered

[32] See AER, *Hydraulic Fracturing—Subsurface Integrity*, Directive 083, 21 May 2013, s 3.

[33] *Alberta's Base of Groundwater Protection Information*, AER Bulletin 2007–10: ST55-2007, April 2007.

[34] Discussion Paper (n 24).

[35] AER, Directive 083 (n 32).

in the well design. This response is intended to ensure that well integrity is maintained without prescribing precise construction and testing standards.

(2) Addressing the risks associated with interwellbore communication events—licensees are required to design and execute a risk management plan as part of a licensee's hydraulic fracturing operation programme. The plan is designed to prevent and respond to wellbore intercommunication without prescribing explicit operational standards.

(3) Addressing the risks associated with wellbore intercommunication from a well undergoing hydraulic fracturing operation to a non-saline aquifer—licensees carrying out hydraulic fracturing operations at shallow depths are required to design and execute a risk management plan as part of their fracturing programme without prescribing explicit operational standards.

(4) For shallow fracturing operations, requiring licensees to demonstrate, through an acceptable and established screening process, that their fracturing fluids do not contain any substances that may cause an adverse impact to the quality of water resources—licensees are also required to disclose fracture fluids used in the fracturing process.[36]

A critical component that underscores, and eventually contributes to, the overall success of a preferred intervention strategy, is risk communication.[37] That is usually accomplished by creating a mechanism, such as designing and administering an exhaustive compliance and outcomes assurance programme, which permits the regulator to craft a compelling storyline that shows the progress of risk reduction strategies.[38] In the absence of credible monitoring, evaluation, and reporting mechanisms showing that commercial operators are satisfying (or deviating from) risk reduction objectives, affected stakeholders are likely to question the safety of emerging technologies and challenge the validity of corresponding regulatory responses.

A. Private civil liability for fracturing damage to offset wells

Apart from, but related to, the regulatory perspective, is whether private law liability principles may lead to judicial decisions that influence regulatory approaches.

Should wellbore communication risks be realized, can operators be held liable for damage to offset wells caused by their fracturing activities? Evidence necessary to

[36] Amendments to Directive 059; 'Well Drilling and Completion Data Filing Requirements in Support of Disclosure of Hydraulic Fracturing Fluid Information', AER Bulletin 2012–25, December 2012.

[37] O. Renn, 'The Role of Risk Communication and Public Dialogue for Improving Risk Management', in *Environmental Risk Planning and Management* (S. Gerrard, R. K. Turner, and I. J. Bateman, eds, 2001).

[38] AER, *Compliance Assurance*, Directive 019, September 2010.

establish causation[39] would be a fundamental issue. Public disclosure of the chemical composition of hydraulic fracturing fluid could be a rich source of information.[40]

Another factor relevant to causation is that proof must be of actual injury, not merely proof of drainage. The latter may not be actionable because the rule of capture justifies drainage by the fracturing operation. This would be consistent with the Texas decision *Coastal Oil and Gas Corporation v Garza Energy Trust.*[41] However, in Alberta it is also necessary for the fracturing operator to establish that it owns the oil and gas rights in the target formation.[42] Equity among operators is a statutory objective[43] in Alberta, and the statutory common orders provisions may support a drainage remedy by the regulator.[44] However, the common orders provisions would not bolster a common law claim for damages for drainage.[45]

B. Causes of action

Several causes of action may be relevant. One is negligence.[46] As in other oil and gas cases, the standard of care here would be that of a reasonably prudent operator, exercising due care in the use of fracturing techniques and equipment.[47] The relative newness of fracturing technology may raise the standard that operators must meet. However, the key is the operator's actions. In principle, even customary practices may produce actionable damage if they involve lack of reasonable care.

The tort of private nuisance may also be a basis for action.[48] Strict liability would flow from interference with the property in damaged wells. No element of intention is necessary. Interference with the reservoir is not likely to be sufficient. No liability, apart from negligence, has been found for consequences of water flooding, so long as operations are reasonable and proper.[49] The analogy to fracturing would be strong. Directness of damage would be critical. This underlines the causation issue—proving well communication and the consequence of pressure induced by fracturing operations.

[39] K. Luft, T. O'Leary, and I. Lang, 'Regulatory and Liability Issues in Horizontal Multi-Stage Fracturing' (2012) 50 Alta L Rev 403 at 427.

[40] Luft, O'Leary, and Lang (n 39); AER, 'Amendments to Directive 059, Well Drilling and Completion Data Filing Requirements: Requirements in Support of Disclosure of Hydraulic Fracturing Fluid Information', Bulletin 2012–25, 19 December 2012.

[41] 268 S W 3d 1 (Tex 2008).

[42] AER Decision 2009-068, *CrossAlta Gas Storage and Services Ltd. Application for the Permanent Shut-in and Abandonment of the Crossfield East Basal Quartz A Pool. Crossfield East Field*, 17 November 2009 (the 'CrossAlta Decision').

[43] Oil and Gas Conservation Act, RSA 2000, c O-6, s 4(d).

[44] Oil and Gas Conservation Act, Part 9, Common Carriers, Purchasers and Processes.

[45] N. Bankes (ed), 'Canadian Oil and Gas, Commentaries' (2nd edn, Continuing Services) para 8.8 ['Canadian Oil and Gas'].

[46] Canadian Oil and Gas (n 45), para 8.9; L. Klar, *Tort Law* (5th edn, 2012) 167–8.

[47] Canadian Oil and Gas (n 45), para 8.9; Klar (n 46) 167–8.

[48] Klar (n 46) 759; *Jones v Mobil Canada* [2000] 1 WWR 479 (Alta QB).

[49] Canadian Oil and Gas (n 45) para 8.11.

Another factor is the apparent need in private nuisance actions to establish foreseeability of the harm resulting—a requirement underlined by the House of Lords in *Cambridge Water Company v Eastern Counties Leather*.[50] It is likely, however, that for the purposes of strict liability actions based on the *Rylands v Fletcher* doctrine, oil and gas operations are not a 'non-natural use'[51] of land. But, there may be room for argument on this point because multistage hydraulic fracturing is a relatively new application of fracturing technology, at least used on the scale that has become increasingly common in Alberta.

In a case filed in June 2012, an Alberta landowner alleged that hydraulic fracturing of coal bed methane wells contaminated the landowner's water well.[52] Claims were framed in nuisance, negligence, *Rylands v Fletcher* doctrine, and trespass. Negligence claims against the regulator were included. This case, likely to be heard by the Alberta Court of Queen's Bench in 2013, has become a focus for public opposition to hydraulic fracturing in the province.[53]

C. Statutory cause of action

The regulator has regulatory powers that may be deployed to prevent damage to offset wells by fracturing operations. A key power is to use 'any means . . . necessary or expedient in the public interest to prevent the flow escape' [of oil, gas, or water from a well].[54] In *The Queen (Can) v Saskatchewan Wheat Pool*,[55] the Supreme Court of Canada made it clear that there is no tort based on breach of statute. However, breach of statutory provisions such as s 44 of the Oil and Gas Conservation Act may be relevant to establishing and defining the appropriate duty of care in a negligence action.

The result is that private civil actions are unlikely to be a significant factor in Alberta regulatory responses to hydraulic fracturing. Proof is the major problem. But overall, the paucity of litigation concerning drilling operations leaves major uncertainties.

Regulatory requirements outlined below are significant and have another implication for potential private rights of action. Operators who propose to use fracturing technology must obtain well licences from the regulator. The Regulator has conditioned a well licensee to limit fracturing pressure and required reporting of both pre- and post-fracturing pressure. It refused to enjoin fracturing operations in the absence of evidence that drainage was reasonably likely.[56] Application for a well licence must be preceded by a participant involvement programme—a series of public consultation activities outlined in the AER's Directive 56.[57] This includes

50 [1994] All ER 53 (HL). 51 Canadian Oil and Gas (n 45) para 8.11.

52 *Ernst v Encana Corporation and Energy Resources Conservation Board*, Alberta Court of Queen's Bench, Judicial Centre of Drumheller, 25 June 2012, #0702-00120.

53 See A. Nikiforuk, 'How Alberta Will Fight Fracking Folk Hero Jessica Ernst', The Tyee, 16 January 2013 at 7, available at <http://thetyee.ca>.

54 Oil and Gas Conservation Act, s 41(1). 55 [1983] SCR 205.

56 'CrossAlta Decision' (n 42). 57 Directive 056 (n 8).

notification to persons identified in the directive.[58] Personal notification is required for surface owners and occupants within 0.3 km of a proposed well. Final notification must go only to Crown disposition holders, a category which would include leaseholders for wells in the vicinity; however, no distance is specified for the latter notification.

D. Regulatory implications

Potentially, private legal actions provide a forum for hydraulic fracturing dispute resolution apart from the developing regulatory regime. There are no decided Canadian cases. A judicial decision in the *Ernst* case may provide some guidance, but that case deals with coal bed methane, and not shale formation fracturing.

E. Regulatory requirements

Failure to comply with any requirement of the regulator's Directive 027, *Shallow Fracturing Operations—Restricted Operations*,[59] replaced by Directive 083: *Hydraulic Fracturing—Subsurface Integrity* in 2013,[60] may result in enforcement action by the regulator. Specific requirements for fracturing operations are imposed, including vertical distances from water wells and assessments to support shallow fracturing. The Directive imposes specific technical and operational requirements. Damage to offset wells will result in compliance assurance action. What this action may include is spelled out in Directive 019.[61]

For fracturing, a play-focused approach to regulation like that proposed by the regulator in its Discussion Paper, *Regulating Unconventional Oil and Gas in Alberta*[62] and addressed in the 'At-risk Offset Well Control Plans' and 'Subject Well/At-risk Offset Well Licencee Engagement' requirements[63] in the AER's Hydraulic Fracturing Directive, does not fundamentally change the regulatory compliance tools available. It does, however, include play-specific requirements, as well as assessments and design to support 'life cycle' wellbore integrity requirements designed to minimize risk. Some compliance elements such as conformity to plans or increased audits would be tailored to plays. The result would be a risk assessment, and a plan for each well that addresses well control, monitoring, and response.

But compliance actions that may include a range of instruments, would still be based on the regulator's statutory powers to prevent or control escape of hydrocarbons[64] and to shut down or close wells where the regulator has determined that a regulated party has failed to comply with the Act, the regulations, or a regulator order.[65] This would include requirements of fracturing directives and any regulator orders made under authority found in the directives.

58 Directive 056 (n 8). 59 '2013 Fracturing Directive' (n 15).
60 '2013 Fracturing Directive' (n 15). 61 AER, *Compliance Assurance*, Directive 019 (n 38).
62 Discussion Paper (n 24). 63 '2013 Fracturing Directive' (n 15) ss 3.3.3–3.3.4.
64 Oil and Gas Conservation Act, s 41. 65 Oil and Gas Conservation Act, s 44.

Part of the play-focused approach to regulation of fracturing involved addressing a notification difficulty. Notice requirements for well licence applications have been based on surface proximity to a proposed well.[66] But a key issue for potential fracturing damage is wellbore intercommunication—a subsurface matter. The result was that notification requirements did not necessarily alert landowners or other well owners to potential damage to existing wells, and resulting health or environmental harm. Well owner notice has been addressed by the offset well licence engagement and regulator notification of fracturing operations requirements in the 2013 Fracturing Directive.[67]

VI. Public engagement and change

A. Factors fostering public participation

Public participation and consultation has become fundamental for energy regulators. In the past half-decade, the significance, and certainly the intensity and immediacy of public engagement, have increased. The latter two appear to be the result of more intense media scrutiny and consequent broader public knowledge, as well as increasing experience and relative sophistication of public organizations. Perhaps most important is the development of social media that have contributed to improved citizen communication and often made local issues national and international in their reach. In many ways, the action has moved outside established regulatory processes and entered a kind of informal public realm. The regulatory model is being challenged by a kind of dispersed governance model. Hydraulic fracturing issues in new energy jurisdictions, such as New York, Pennsylvania, and Quebec, are beaming straight to the living rooms and handheld devices of Alberta citizens.[68]

The explosion of public interest in hydraulic fracturing is a result of all of these factors. In particular, conventional media focus, along with social media communication, has meant that Quebec, US, and even European fracturing issues and disputes are all part of the information mix available to local citizens. Issues are shared and generalized, sometimes without sufficient acknowledgement of very different energy, environmental, and socio-political contexts.

Writing in 2000, before the social media revolution, Barry Barton reminded us that public participation is much more than a process—more than merely a variety of citizen voluntary activity. He said that:

> It is a subject where comparison is difficult, because the extent, to which there should be public participation, and how it should occur, go straight to the heart of a nation's political

[66] The application form requires distance to the nearest surface development and Directive 56 (n 8), Schedule 2.

[67] See '2013 Fracturing Directive' (n 15), s 3.3.4, 8.

[68] E.g. M. Lowey, 'US Researcher Exposes "Four Myths" of Fracking, Calls for a Moratorium' Enviroline, 20 January 2013, available at <http://envirolinenews.ca/201301201>; Andrew Nikifovuk, 'The Fracking Continues', Vueweekly.com, 7 March 2012, available at <http://vueweekly.com>.

values, its concept of the state and the state's relationship with its citizens, and its concept of how public business is properly carried out. These underlying values are more relevant to public participation than to more technical matters that we encounter in energy and natural resources law, such as royalty regimes or mechanisms for emissions trading...[69]

Energy activities, such as hydraulic fracturing, have particular resonance with the public. First, they often involve public lands and draw in the broader development and sustainable use issues concerning public land management. Second, individual landowners are often affected to different degrees, with concerns ranging from health and local environment to compensation. With their constitutionalized aboriginal and treaty rights and resulting consultation and engagement rights, aboriginal people are a special group with distinct legal support for effective participation.

There is evidence that consultation efforts outside the traditional regulatory system are particularly compelling for regulation of hydraulic fracturing. Two reasons are Alberta's significant population growth and pace of energy development. Fracturing technology use is not limited to hinterland regions. It is common in historic fields located in settled areas. More generally, some citizens have questioned intensive energy development, but often with little thought about broader community benefits.

A second reason is the increasing public awareness of potential for serious health and environmental damage. This is fuelled by the intense debates concerning oil sands development and worry about the risks of high carbon energy futures. Perceived risks of both oil sands and fracturing are seen as symptoms of energy growth thought to be unsustainable. The importance of public perception cannot be underestimated.

A third reason is more nebulous and difficult to articulate. This is increased public demand for and understanding of human and political rights and the corresponding duties of public officials. These include political and regulatory officials. There is considerable ambivalence. Increased citizen expectations that regulators will protect public health and quality of life interact with reservations and suspicions about regulators' motives and commitment.

B. The credibility gap: public concerns and the regulatory response scepticism

The result is that public concerns are gaining traction in a media domain that is fuelled by scepticism concerning both the energy industry and the regulator. In response, the AER has reached out through a Multi-Stakeholder Advisory Committee that recommended an assessment of effects of hydraulic fracturing. This led to a revised Fracturing Directive, and the further revised 2013 Fracturing Directive.

[69] B. Barton, 'Underlying Concepts and Theoretical Issues in Public Participation in Resources Development' in *Human Rights in Natural Resource Development* (D. Zillman, A. Lucas, and G. Pring, eds, 2002) 77.

The 2013 Directive does address public concerns about safety and environmental harm. Well licence applicants are required to implement measures to prevent loss of well integrity, to assess risks, plan and mitigate risks of interwellbore communication, and to notify operators of potentially affected wells. Set back distances from water wells and from aquifers have been increased. A related issue—disclosure of fracturing fluid composition—was addressed by 2012 requirements.[70] But there are no requirements for notification of surface landowners, even if offset wells that may potentially be impacted by fracturing operations are located on their lands.

The new 2013 Fracturing Directive is part of a broader proposed change for regulation of unconventional resource development. This points to a shift from licensing and regulating specific wells to 'play-focused' regulation, in which operators in a play area will be required to produce risk assessments and plans. It contemplates engagement involving local communities and stakeholders throughout the life cycle of the project. The Discussion Paper states that operators in a play must develop 'comprehensive stakeholder engagement plans' concerning how the public, landowners, and municipalities will be involved at different play stages.[71] Disclosure, open dialogue, and methods of evaluating public engagement activities are noted for consideration and action. But there are no proposals for specific legal requirements.

Broader public concerns about participation by potentially affected landowners and communities in Alberta energy regulatory decisions are also relevant to regulation of hydraulic fracturing. These concerns have centred on the replacement in 2012 of statutory rights of 'directly and adversely affected' persons to trigger well licence application hearings[72] with powers in the Regulator to grant hearings in its discretion.[73] The debate about whether these changes are likely to result in fewer hearings and less overall public involvement in energy regulatory processes has been heated. This has contributed to public distrust and scepticism about energy regulation generally and accordingly has coloured responses to the Regulator's approach and the actions it has taken to manage multistage hydraulic fracturing in the province.[74]

[70] See n 36. [71] Discussion Paper (n 24) at 27–8.

[72] Energy Resources Conservation Act, s 26(2), replaced by the Responsible Energy Development Act, SA 2012, c R-17.3 (note that the entire Energy Resources Conservation Act was repealed and replaced).

[73] Responsible Energy Development Act, ss 33 and 34. The latter section provides that the Regulator may decide on applications with or without a hearing but must conduct a hearing... (b) when required by the rules; or (c) under circumstances prescribed by the regulations. There are no relevant regulations and the Rules (Alberta Energy Regulator) of Practice, Alta Reg 99/2013, s 7, state that the Regulator may make a decision on an application without a hearing if: the person filing a statement of concern has not demonstrated that the person may be directly and adversely affected by the application; the Regulator considers the statement of concern to be frivolous, vexatious, or without merit, or the Regulator determines that the objection raised in the statement of concern has been addressed.

[74] See Shaun Fluker, 'Bill 2 and its Implication for Landowner Participation in Energy Project Decision Making' ABlawg, 13 November 2012, available at <http://ablawg.ca>; Nickie Vlavianos, 'An

VII. Conclusion

The convergence of prominent socioeconomic forces running in parallel with the emergence of unconventional resource development is challenging Alberta's conventional upstream oil and gas regulatory regime. The immediate challenge confronting policy makers is to figure out the appropriate regulatory model to accommodate the changing patterns of resource development, which rely heavily on the extensive application of innovative technologies, such as multistage hydraulic fracturing through horizontal wells, in a political environment that is being rapidly transformed by changing societal preferences and expectations, including:

- a heightened level of awareness of how citizens value their living environment and perceive risk associated with unconventional resource development, which is gaining greater prominence in policy discourse;
- greater public demands for an expanded level of assurance and accountability from governmental agencies within a political environment rampant with cynicism and suspicion towards the perpetuation of a high carbon energy future; and
- an appeal from broader segments of the population for a meaningful voice that shapes the future patterns of unconventional resource development beyond the traditional and narrowly defined participation involvement frameworks.

These changes apply persistent pressure on regulators to deliver on a mandate that imposes an obligation to balance competing and, in some cases, irreconcilable, public interest considerations (e.g., enable resource development while protecting valued societal and environmental objectives).

The AER's URF proposes an expanded role for public involvement that affords an opportunity to shape the future patterns of resource development with a particular emphasis on regional planning and cumulative effects (i.e., play-based approach), risk management, performance reporting, and continual improvement processes. The URF embodies a public engagement process that deviates substantially from the current consultation and notification requirements prescribed in current regulations. The latter approach underscores an engagement process that is designed, in part, to assure potentially directly affected parties are identified and confirm non-objection to a single development project. The process was designed to ensure closure and certainty with a licensing process for activities that, for the most part, are well established with predictable outcomes (e.g. single, vertical wells in traditional reservoirs).

The former engagement process emphasizes a collaborative approach to plan for and manage the unique risk characteristics of a particular unconventional resource

Overview of Bill 2: Responsible Energy Development Act—What are the Changes and What are the Issues?' ABlawg, 15 November 2012, available at <http://ablawg.ca>.

play. This refined process acknowledges that the scale of development is larger (e.g., multiple wells, multiple pads, and supporting infrastructure) and the recovery process and associated risk may vary (e.g., hydraulic fracturing, water use, traffic, variable public perceptions, etc).

The public engagement model proposed under URF informally concedes that Barton's view on public participation is gaining traction within Alberta's regulatory landscape. That is, public engagement is more than merely satisfying compliance with regulatory requirements—it goes 'straight to the heart of a nation's political values, its concept of the state and the state's relationship with its citizens, and its concept of how public business is properly carried out'.[75]

The AER's URF, along with a refined engagement approach, remains largely at a conceptual stage, with ongoing efforts to implement it into operational reality. In the interim, the AER has taken concrete regulatory measures to address the immediate subsurface risk that aligns with the spirit of URF. Operators carrying out hydraulic fracturing operations must demonstrate that the well system maintains integrity and is not functionally compromised, manages the risks associated with interwellbore communication, and takes measures to protect non-saline aquifers and water wells. The AER's regulatory response remains consistent with a risk-based approach to regulatory governance and incorporates elements of a management-based approach to risk prevention, mitigation, and planning.

[75] Barton (n 69).

8

Emerging Regulatory Frameworks for Hydraulic Fracturing and Shale Gas Development in the United States

LeRoy C. Paddock and Jessica Anne Wentz

I. Introduction[1]

Hydraulic fracturing in the United States is a complex issue that is becoming increasingly controversial as the natural gas industry continues to grow rapidly. Because natural gas is displacing coal for power generation, some environmental organizations support expanded drilling while others strongly oppose hydraulic fracturing due to concerns about water use, wastewater disposal, aquifer contamination, the use of hazardous chemicals, and landscape and habitat disruption, among others. An interesting new development is the emergence of a new collaborative initiative, the Center for Sustainable Shale Development, which in March 2013 announced consensus performance standards for shale development in Pennsylvania and committed to continuous improvement to these standards.[2]

From an economic perspective, hydraulic fracturing has transformed the United States from a net importer of natural gas to a country that may become a significant natural gas exporter. President Barack Obama highlighted this debate in his State of the Union Address on 12 February 2013:

> . . . the natural gas boom has led to cleaner power and greater energy independence. We need to encourage that. And that's why my administration will keep cutting red tape and speeding up new oil and gas permits. That's got to be part of an all-of-the-above plan. But I also want to work with this Congress to encourage the research and technology that helps natural gas burn even cleaner and protects our air and our water.[3]

[1] The authors would like to thank Brian Levey (The George Washington Law School, JD, expected May 2015) for his contribution to this chapter, and in particular his research on the federal regulatory framework for hydraulic fracturing.

[2] Center for Sustainable Shale Development, available at <http://www.sustainableshale.org>.

[3] Barack Obama, President of the United States, State of the Union Address, 12 February 2013, available at <http://www.whitehouse.gov/state-of-the-union-2013>.

This chapter focuses on two subjects: the evolving Federal regulatory landscape for hydraulic fracturing, and a comparative analysis of how two states—Pennsylvania, one of the leading states for hydraulic fracturing gas production, and New York, where a long-standing moratorium on hydraulic fracturing remains in place—have regulated, or propose to regulate, fracturing operations. The United States differs from many other legal systems in that natural gas resources are privately owned unless they are located under publicly owned land. Under state law, the individual or organization who owns the surface property typically owns the mineral resources underneath, and may sell or lease those mineral rights to third parties.[4] Thus, natural gas extraction tends to be a private activity which involves a mix of private contract law and public regulation of exploration and extraction practices. State law is especially important, since onshore oil and gas exploration and production have historically been regulated at the state level. In presenting the state regulatory regimes, this chapter also highlights areas where the Center for Sustainable Shale Development's (CSSD) new performance standards compare to the state approach.

II. Shale gas development in the United States

Hydraulic fracturing is not new to the United States. As early as 1949, Standolind Oil and Gas Company granted Halliburton a commercial licence to develop a method of production known as the 'Hydrafrac Process'.[5] However, recent improvements in horizontal drilling and hydraulic fracturing have unlocked vast reserves of unconventional natural gas resources in the United States. This has led to the rapid expansion of shale gas production. From 2008 to 2011, the United States natural gas production from shale increased from 2.3 trillion cubic feet to 7.8 trillion cubic feet, and the US Energy Information Administration (US EIA) anticipates total US natural gas production to increase from 23.0 trillion cubic feet in 2011 to 33.1 trillion cubic feet in 2040, a 44% increase. Almost all of this increase in domestic natural gas production is due to projected growth in shale gas production, from 7.8 trillion cubic feet in 2011 to 16.7 trillion cubic feet in 2040.[6]

Figure 8.1 shows the location of major shale gas and oil plays in the United States.[7] Figure 8.2 shows the increasing percentage of gas production coming from shale formations where hydraulic fracturing is required to stimulate production.[8]

4 For a discussion of how states define property interests in oil and gas, see 1A *Summers Oil & Gas* §§ 7:3, 7:4 (3rd edn, 2012). Common pool resources like natural gas are also subject to the rule of capture, under which 'there is no liability for drainage of oil and gas from under the lands of another so long as there has been no trespass'. Black's Law Dictionary 1448 (9th edn, 2009).

5 *Wiseman v Halliburton Oil Well Cementing Co*, 301 F.2d 654, 655 (10th Cir 1962).

6 US EIA, 'Annual Energy Outlook 2013' (2013), at 148, available at <http://www.eia.gov/forecasts/aeo/pdf/0383(2013).pdf>.

7 US EIA, 'Lower 48 States Shale Plays', available at <http://www.eia.gov/oil_gas/rpd/shale_gas.pdf>.

8 US EIA, 'Annual Energy Outlook 2013 Early Release' (2013) at 2, available at <http://www.eia.gov/forecasts/aeo/er/pdf/0383er(2013).pdf>.

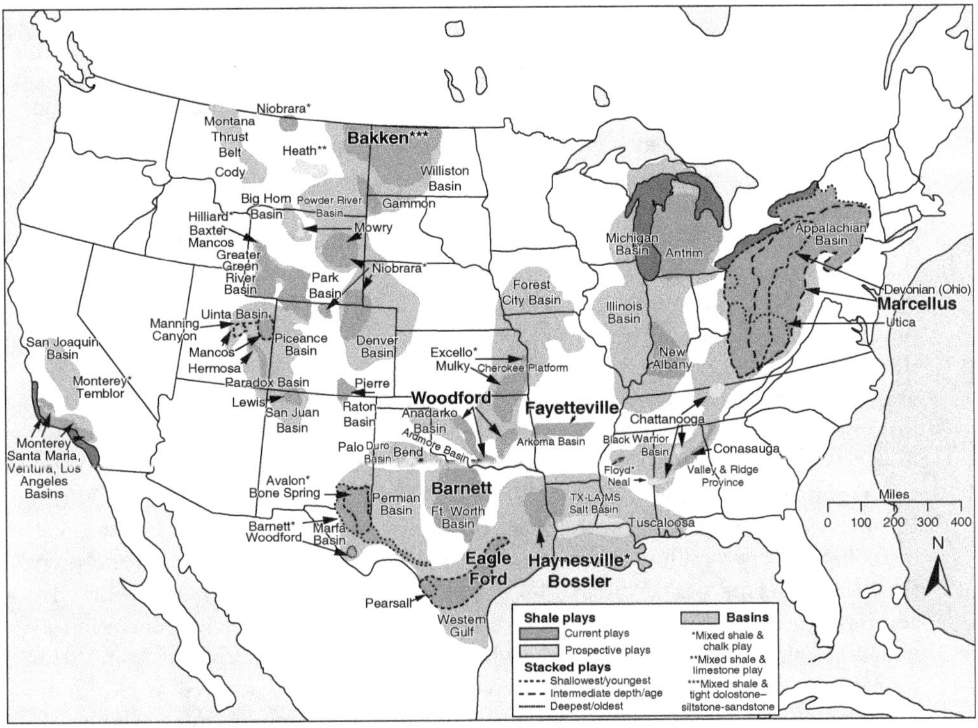

Fig. 8.1 Lower 48 states shale plays

Source: US EIA, 'Review of Emerging Resources: U.S. Shale Gas and Shale Oil Plays', July 2011, available at: <http://www.eia.gov/analysis/studies/usshalegas/pdf/usshaleplays.pdf>.

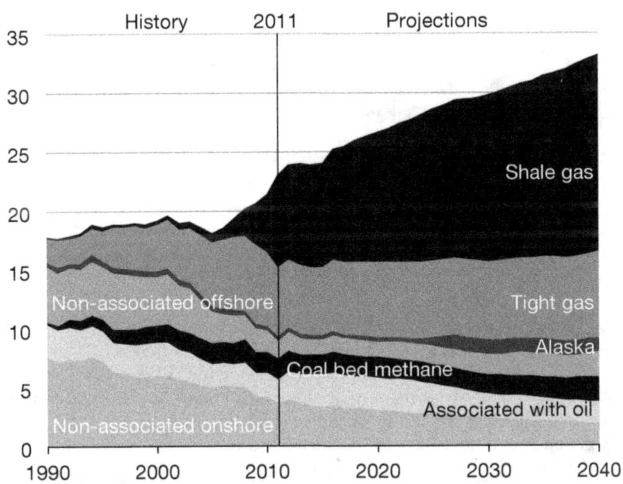

Fig. 8.2 US dry natural gas production by source, 1990–2040 (trillion cubic feet)

Source: US EIA, 'Annual Energy Outlook 2013 Early Release' (2013) at 2, available at <http://www.eia.gov/forecasts/aeo/er/pdf/0383er(2013).pdf>.

Increased natural gas production from shale reserves has reduced natural gas prices, spurring a predicted increase in use of natural gas in industrial and electric power sectors over the next 15 years.[9] Natural gas prices have already declined from approximately US$8 per million Btu in 2008 to US$2.7 per million Btu in 2012.[10] The US EIA predicts that natural gas prices will remain below US$4 per million Btu (2011 dollars) through 2018, and then will increase steadily as lower-cost resources are depleted, reaching approximately US$5.40 per million Btu in 2030 and US$7.83 per million Btu in 2040.[11] Based on these prices, the US EIA predicts that industrial consumption will increase from 6.8 trillion cubic feet per year in 2011 to 7.8 trillion cubic feet per year in 2025, and that overall industrial production will grow more rapidly.[12] In addition, the US EIA predicts that relatively cheap and abundant natural gas will also reach other markets, for example, 'as fuel for heavy-duty freight transportation (trucking), and as a feedstock for producing diesel and other fuels'.[13]

In the electricity sector, the US EIA predicts that the natural gas share of electric generation will rise from 24% in 2010 to 27% in 2020 and 30% in 2040.[14] Relatively cheap natural gas will impact electricity prices, which are expected to fall from 9.9 cents per kWh in 2011 to as low as 9.2 cents per kWh in 2015, and then rise to 10.1 cents per kWh in 2035, and 10.8 cents per kWh in 2040.[15] In addition, the US EIA predicts that coal consumption for electricity generation—which has already declined sharply—will continue to decrease from 41% in 2011 to 35% in 2040, due to competitively priced natural gas, as well as the State Renewable Portfolio Standards (RPS) and federal environmental rules, which will increase construction and operation costs for coal-fired power plants.[16]

The transition from coal to natural gas for electricity generation will likely reduce energy related CO_2 emissions in the United States, since natural gas produces about half as much CO_2 per MWh as coal.[17] According to US EIA projections, energy-

9 'Annual Energy Outlook 2013 Early Release' (n 8) at 5.

10 US EIA, 'Natural Gas Prices', available at <http://www.eia.gov/dnav/ng/ng_pri_sum_dcu_nus_a.htm>.

11 'Annual Energy Outlook 2013 Early Release' (n 8) at 5.

12 'Annual Energy Outlook 2013 Early Release' (n 8) at 8.

13 'Annual Energy Outlook 2013 Early Release' (n 8) at 1.

14 'Annual Energy Outlook 2013 Early Release' (n 8) at 1.

15 These prices are approximately 3–5% lower than the predicted prices in the 2012 outlook, which did not anticipate as much growth in shale gas development. See 'Annual Energy Outlook 2013 Early Release' (n 8) at 6.

16 See 'Annual Energy Outlook 2013 Early Release' (n 8) at 11–12.

17 Natural gas produces, on average, 1135 lbs/MWh of CO_2: whereas coal produces approximately 2,249 lbs/MWh of CO_2: US Environmental Protection Agency (EPA), 'Air Emissions: Natural Gas', available at <http://www.epa.gov/cleanenergy/energy-and-you/affect/air-emissions.html>. However, there is some concern that the relatively cheap and abundant supply of natural gas will displace renewable energy generation in the short-term, since wind and solar technologies may become less cost-competitive. Whether natural gas competes with renewables or complements their deployment (e.g., as a source of base-load power that can balance intermittency associated with wind and solar energy production) will probably depend on state policies to promote renewable energy, such as Renewable Portfolio Standards (RPS), as well as the continuation of federal tax and research subsidies for these technologies. For additional information, see 'Summary Maps, Database of State Incentives for Renewables and Efficiency (DSIRE)', available at <http://www.dsireusa.org/summarymaps/index.cfm?ee=1&RE=1>.

related emissions in the transportation, commercial, and residential sectors will be lower than previously predicted, due in part to the abundance of low-cost natural gas.[18] Replacing coal with natural gas will also reduce emissions of traditional air pollutants, since natural gas plants produce less than one-third as much nitrogen oxides and one percent as much sulphur oxides as coal-fired generation plants.[19] This is an especially important consideration for urban areas with chronic air pollution problems. The benefits of switching to natural gas have already been documented in a variety of contexts. For example, a coal-to-gas conversion of two older electric generation plans in Minneapolis and St Paul, Minnesota, as well as the upgrades to a third nearby coal plant, produced dramatic reductions in several air pollutants, including a 93% reduction in sulphur dioxide and a 91% reduction in nitrogen oxides.[20]

The new supply of relatively cheap and abundant natural gas will also have far-reaching implications for national security in the United States. Historically, the United States has been heavily dependent on foreign oil imports from the Middle East and other regions. In the past decade, however, the nation's dependence on foreign imports has already fallen rapidly. This trend is expected to continue due to increases in both shale gas and tight oil production. Specifically, the US EIA predicts that the United States will become a net exporter of natural gas by 2020, and net exports of natural gas will rise to 3.6 trillion cubic feet in 2040.[21] During this time, oil production from tight oil plays is also expected to increase to an estimated 2.8 million barrels per day in 2020, leading to a reduction in net imports.[22] However, the US EIA does not anticipate that the United States' total oil supply will exceed demand in the coming decades, even with the growth in tight oil production. To the extent that low-cost, natural gas-fired power plants facilitate the increased use of electric vehicles or fleets are repowered to use natural gas rather than petroleum, increased natural gas production also displaces imported oil.

In addition to the economic and environmental prospects discussed here, shale gas development will also create new challenges for state and federal regulators. Most states have comprehensive regulations which govern conventional drilling, but are only beginning to address the specific concerns associated with horizontal drilling and hydraulic fracturing. These include:

- *Water use and conservation*: Hydraulic fracturing requires large quantities of water to be injected into the shale rock formation—between 2 and 8 million

[18] 'Annual Energy Outlook 2013 Revised' (n 8) at 12.

[19] US EPA, 'Natural Gas: Environmental Impacts', available at <http://www.epa.gov/cleanenergy/energy-and-you/affect/natural-gas.html>.

[20] Specifically, the conversions and the upgrade resulted in the following reductions in air pollution emissions: sulphur dioxide 93%; nitrogen oxides 91%; mercury 81%; particulates 55%; carbon dioxide 21%.

The project at the same time increased generating capacity 300 megawatts, while it cost consumers an average of only US$3.50 per month. See Minnesota Metro Emissions Reduction Project, 'Xcel Energy', available at <http://www.xcelenergy.com/Environment/Doing_Our_Part/Clean_Air_Projects/MN_MERP>.

[21] 'Annual Energy Outlook 2013' (n 6) at 3.

[22] 'Annual Energy Outlook 2013' (n 6) at 81.

gallons of water per well.[23] Thus, there are significant concerns about water withdrawals associated with shale gas development, and the extent to which they may deplete local water supplies or adversely impact local watersheds.

- *Wastewater management*: Hydraulic fracturing also creates large quantities of wastewater, which contains the chemicals used in hydraulic fracturing fluid as well as trace amounts of naturally occurring substances in the shale rock formations, including heavy metals, volatile organic compounds, and radioactive materials. Many municipal wastewater treatment facilities are not equipped to process such wastewater, and thus managing this waste is another significant issue for regulators.
- *Chemicals use and disclosure*: A variety of chemicals is added to hydraulic fracturing fluid in order to improve flow, including some chemicals that are known to be dangerous to human health.[24] This raises concerns about the possibility of an accident or spill occurring during the transportation of these chemicals to the well site, the injection of fluids into the well, or the storage, treatment, and disposal phase. Two key issues for regulators are whether and under what circumstances to require disclosure of these chemicals, and whether to restrict the use of certain chemicals in hydraulic fracturing.
- *Water contamination*: One of the primary concerns about hydraulic fracturing is that the fluids used and generated during the process (including flowback fluid and wastewater) may migrate from the well and contaminate local surface and ground water resources. In addition to the chemicals used in the hydraulic fracturing fluid, there are harmful substances located in the fracked rock formations (e.g., methane and heavy metals), which may also migrate to water resources. Regulators have attempted to reduce the risk of water contamination by imposing stringent construction requirements for well casings and well pads, and also by requiring setback distances between fracked wells and surface and ground water resources.
- *Site disturbances and habitat impacts*: As with other drilling activities, shale gas development causes surface disturbances at the well site, which can lead to habitat loss and fragmentation, soil impairment, erosion, and sedimentation.[25]

[23] This figure is based on estimates from three different sources: US EPA, Draft Plan to Study the Potential Impacts of Hydraulic Fracturing on Drinking Water Resources, 7 February 2011 at 19 (2–4 million gallons of water per well); North Carolina Division of Energy, Mineral and Land Resources, 'North Carolina Oil and Gas Study', 30 April 2012 at 3 (3–5 million gallons of water per well); New York Department of Environmental Conservation, 'New York Revised Draft SGEIS on the Oil, Gas and Solution Mining Regulatory Program: Executive Summary', 7 September 2011 at 8 (2.4–7.8 million gallons of water per well).

[24] 'Chemical Use in Hydraulic Fracturing: What Chemicals are Used', FracFocus, available at <http://fracfocus.org/chemical-use/what-chemicals-are-used>.

[25] For a description of spatial disturbance and habitat impacts from horizontal hydraulically fractured wells, see The Nature Conservancy, 'An Assessment of the Potential Impacts of High Volume Hydraulic Fracturing on Forest Resources', 19 December 2011, available at: <http://www.nature.org/ourinitiatives/regions/northamerica/unitedstates/newyork/ny-hydrofracking-impacts-20111220pdfnull.pdf>.

- *Fugitive emissions*: Fugitive emissions of methane, volatile organic compounds (VOCs), and other hazardous air pollutants (HAPs) are released from the wellhead during the flowback period following injection. These fugitive emissions are only slightly greater than those generated during conventional drilling, but are nonetheless an important issue for regulators given the rapid expansion of shale gas development.[26] In addition, concerns have been raised about fugitive emissions that are generated during the processing, transport, and storage of natural gas.
- *Air pollution*: Air pollution from equipment operation at drilling sites, especially from diesel engines, has been identified as an issue of concern. A recent study identified over 50 non-methane hydrocarbons (NMHCs) near unconventional wells in Colorado, many of which can be traced back to the industrial equipment used during the gas production process.[27] Some concerns have also been raised about air emissions caused by increased truck traffic.[28]
- *Public engagement*: In addition to the environmental impacts described above, shale gas development also has a number of local impacts such as increased vehicular traffic, noise pollution, and decreased land value. Thus, many local communities feel that they should have some authority over the nature and extent of shale gas development activities in their county or municipality. One key issue for regulators is how to design a uniform regulatory regime for shale gas development while also accommodating the regulatory interests of local governments.

The manner in which state regulators have responded to these concerns varies widely depending on the political and economic context within the state. Some states, like Pennsylvania, have taken a relatively aggressive approach to developing the state's shale gas reserves, with thousands of wells already in place, and have already modified their oil and gas statutes to specifically accommodate and regulate shale gas development. Others, like New York, have taken a more cautious approach, imposing a moratorium on hydraulic fracturing pending further study about the environmental impacts of hydraulic fracturing. During this time, New York has developed an extensive set of draft regulations for hydraulic fracturing. As discussed in the following section, there are certain federal laws which also regulate certain aspects of hydraulic fracturing, and the federal role is gradually evolving in this context.

[26] F. O'Sullivan and S. Paltsev, 'Shale Gas Production: Potential vs. Actual Greenhouse Gas Emissions' (2012) 7 Envt'l Research Letters 044030.

[27] T. Colborn et al, 'An Exploratory Study of Air Quality near Natural Gas Operations' (2012) Human and Ecological Risk Assessment: An International Journal, DOI: 10.1080/10807039.2012.749447.

[28] E.g., the RSGEIS estimates that there will be approximately 3,950 heavy-duty and 2,840 light-duty one-way truck trips per horizontal well with heavy-duty hydraulic fracturing: New York Department of Environmental Conservation, 'New York Revised Draft SGEIS on the Oil, Gas and Solution Mining Regulatory Program: Executive Summary', 7 September 2011 at 6–303.

III. Federal regulation of hydraulic fracturing

The rapid expansion of shale gas development has led to an ongoing debate within the United States about how to balance environmental concerns with commercial and economic development. One key issue is whether the federal government should play a larger role in the regulation of hydraulic fracturing and horizontal drilling. As noted earlier, the states are primarily responsible for regulating oil and gas exploration and production. However, the federal government has broad authority to regulate environmental matters of national scope, and also retains authority over all resources located beneath federal lands. This section discusses the limited extent to which the federal government has exercised its regulatory authority, as well as recent and ongoing studies looking at the role the federal government should play in this area.

A. Underground Injection Control (UIC)

The Safe Drinking Water Act (SDWA) of 1974 provided the US Environmental Protection Agency (EPA) with a limited statutory framework to protect both surface and drinking water. The Act only applied to certain aspects of oil and gas exploration and production, and the hydraulic fracturing process was not a central focus of the legislation. The SDWA authorizes the EPA to set national standards for drinking water to protect against 'natural-occurring and man-made contaminants'[29] and, in doing so, it also provides the structure for the Underground Injection Control programme or 'UIC'. This programme is responsible for regulating the construction, operation, permitting, and closure of injection wells that place fluids underground for storage or disposal.[30] While EPA sets the minimum requirements under the SDWA, states are generally responsible for administering and enforcing the UIC programme once the state programme has been approved by EPA.

The EPA developed a classification system (Classes I, II, III, IV, V, and VI) for various types of injection wells, which require graduated permitting procedures, depending on the toxicity of the materials and the depth of the injection. Classes I and II encompass wells which normally inject waste or fluids into geological formations well below underground sources of drinking water.[31] Such wells are drilled rather than dug or bored, and use casing and cementing to prevent injected

[29] EPA Office of Water, 'Understanding the Safe Drinking Water Act', EPA 816-F-04-030, June 2004, available at <http://water.epa.gov/lawsregs/guidance/sdwa/upload/2009_08_28_sdwa_fs_30ann_sdwa_web.pdf>.

[30] Underground Injection Control Program, available at <http://water.epa.gov/type/groundwater/uic/index.cfm>.

[31] EPA Office of Drinking Water, 'Statement of Basis and Purpose: Underground Injection Control Regulations', May 1980, at 4, available at <http://www.epa.gov/ogwdw/uic/pdfs/rept_uic_statemt_basis_purpose_uic_1980.pdf>.

fluids from escaping into sources of drinking water.[32] More specifically, Class II permits regulate the injection of fluids used in the 'enhanced recovery of oil or natural gas', and those 'which are brought to the surface in connection with natural gas storage operations, or conventional oil or natural gas production'.[33] The statute was unclear as to whether injecting fluids for the purpose of hydraulic fracturing would need a Class II permit.

In 1997, this issue was raised in court by the Legal Environmental Assistance Foundation (LEAF). LEAF sued, contending Alabama's state UIC programme was deficient because it did not regulate hydraulic fracturing activities. The EPA responded by arguing that hydraulic fracturing does not fall within the regulatory definition of 'underground injection', which only includes those wells whose 'principal function' is the underground emplacement of fluids.[34] In its brief to the Eleventh Circuit, the EPA noted '. . . if this Court were to conclude that all production well drilling activities using fracture fluids and drilling muds should fall within the scope of the UIC regulations, both EPA and authorized states would have to greatly expand the nature of their regulatory programmes. Such expansion might come—given increasingly scarce resources—at the expense of more traditionally regulated and dangerous activities.'[35] The Eleventh Circuit held that hydraulic fracturing activities used as a production enhancement technique by oil and gas industry were subject to regulation by the EPA.[36]

Following this ruling, the EPA attempted to circumvent the Eleventh Circuit's decision by approving a revised version of Alabama's UIC programme under a different portion of the SDWA.[37] In 2001, LEAF once again challenged this interpretation of the law, and although the court accepted the EPA's interpretation of the alternative demonstration programme, it still held that hydraulic fracturing must be classified under one of the regulated categories.[38] These decisions forced industry and the EPA to re-evaluate the possibility of the Federal regulation of hydraulic fracturing.

The EPA responded by conducting a scientific study to determine whether the injection of hydraulic fracturing fluids into coal bed methane (CBM) wells (the same type of well under discussion in the LEAF case) posed any potential danger to contamination of drinking water.[39] The final EPA study concluded that the injection of 'hydraulic fracturing fluids into [CBM] wells poses little or no threat to [drinking water]',[40] but it did express some concern about using diesel fuel as a hydraulic fracturing fluid.

[32] See n 31. [33] 40 CFR § 144.6(b)(1)–(2).

[34] *Legal Envtl Assistance Found Inc v US EPA*, 118 F.3d 1467, 1469 (11th Cir 1997).

[35] Brief for Respondent at 28, *Legal Envtl Assistance Found Inc v US EPA*, 118 F.3d 1467 (11th Cir 1997) (No 95-6501).

[36] See n 35.

[37] *Legal Envtl Assistance Found Inc v US EPA*, 276 F.3d 1253, 1256 (11th Cir 2001).

[38] R. W. Watson, 'Hydraulic Fracturing and Water Supply Protection—Federal Regulatory Developments' (2012) Rocky Mountain Mineral Law Foundation Paper No 6 at 5.

[39] B. M. Kramer, 'Federal Legislative and Administrative Regulation of Hydraulic Fracturing Operations' (2012) 44 Tex Tech L Rev 837 at 853.

[40] 'Evaluation of Impacts to Underground Sources of Drinking Water by Hydraulic Fracturing of Coalbed Methane Reservoirs', Chapter 7: Conclusions and Recommendations, EPA 816-R-04-003,

The natural gas and oil industry began to engage in a lobbying effort to 'minimize federal involvement in the regulation of hydraulic fracturing'.[41] One of the leading environmental concerns was the use of diesel fuel and its associated chemicals in the hydraulic fracturing process.[42] In 2003, BJ Services Company, Halliburton Energy Services, Inc, and Schlumberger Technology Corporation signed a Memorandum of Agreement with the EPA in which the companies agreed to eliminate the use of diesel fuel in exchange for recognition of their achievements and the EPA's cooperation informing the public and Congress of the actions taken by industry under the agreement.[43]

In light of the LEAF decisions and the EPA study of hydraulic fracturing, states and industry urged Congress to exempt hydraulic fracturing from the SDWA and amend the Act's definition of 'underground injection'.[44] The original Act, provided under §1421(d) or 42 U.S.C. 300h(d), defined 'underground injection' as follows:

(1) The term 'underground injection' means the subsurface emplacement of fluids by well injection. Such term does not include the underground injection of natural gas for purposes of storage.[45]

The Energy Policy Act of 2005, introduced by Representative Joe Barton (R-TX) excluded hydraulic fracturing from the legal definition of 'underground injection'. The original House bill, passed on 21 April 2005, excluded all fluids, including diesel fuel:

(1) UNDERGROUND INJECTION.—The term 'underground injection'—
(A) means the subsurface emplacement of fluids by well injection; and

June 2004, at 5, available at <http://www.epa.gov/ogwdw/uic/pdfs/cbmstudy_attach_uic_ch07_conclusions.pdf>.

41 Kramer (n 39) at 853.

42 Specifically, '[d]iesel fuels may be used in hydraulic fracturing operations as a primary base (or carrier) fluid, or added to hydraulic fracturing fluids as a component of a chemical additive to adjust fluid properties (e.g., viscosity and lubricity) or act as a solvent to aid in the delivery of gelling agents. Some chemicals of concern often occur in diesel fuels as impurities or additives. Benzene, toluene, ethylbenzene, and xylene compounds (BTEX) are highly mobile in ground water and are regulated under national primary drinking water regulations because of the risks they pose to human health.' EPA Office of Water, FACT SHEET: Underground Injection Control (UIC) Program Permitting Guidance for Oil and Gas Hydraulic Fracturing Activities Using Diesel Fuels, EPA 816-K-12-001, May 2012, available at <http://water.epa.gov/type/groundwater/uic/class2/hydraulicfracturing/upload/hfdieselfuelsfs.pdf>.

43 Memorandum of Agreement, EPA—BJ Servs Comp, Halliburton Energy Servs, and Schlumberger Tech Corp, 'Elimination of Diesel Fuel in Hydraulic Fracturing Fluids Injected into Underground Sources of Drinking Water During Hydraulic Fracturing of Coalbed Methane Wells', 12 December 2003 at 4.

44 Specifically, the lobbyists noted that: '[s]tates are concerned about the implications of the [Eleventh Circuit] court's decision. States recognize the large threat of the decision to state UIC regulatory programs. Currently, the two state organizations with the greatest involvement in oil and gas regulation—the Interstate Oil and Gas Compact Commission (IOGCC) and the Ground Water Protection Council (GWPC)—support the need for legislation to resolve the issue and return the SDWA to its original intent.' The Energy Policy Act of 2005: Hearings Before the Subcomm On Energy & Air Quality of the H Comm on Energy & Commerce, 109th Cong 380, 2005 (statement of Lee Fuller, VP of Gov't Relations for the Independent Petroleum Association of America).

45 42 USCA § 300h(d).

(B) excludes—
(i) the underground injection of natural gas for purposes of storage; and
(ii) the underground injection of fluids or propping agents pursuant to hydraulic fracturing operations related to oil or gas production activities.

The final bill that was signed into law on 8 August 2005 included the exemption for hydraulic fracturing fluids used in oil and gas production, but did include an exception for diesel fuels:

(1) Underground injection—The term 'underground injection'—
(B) excludes—
. . .
(ii) the underground injection of fluids or propping agents *(other than diesel fuels)* pursuant to hydraulic fracturing operations related to oil, gas, or geothermal production activities.[46]

By excluding the fluids and propping agents pursuant to hydraulic fracturing operations, the EPA and, thus the Federal government, no longer had the regulatory authority to require companies to disclose the chemical composition of their hydraulic fracturing fluids, or provide information regarding the fluids' potential effects on human health or the environment.

B. Clean Water Act

The EPA has authority under the Clean Water Act (CWA) to protect surface water from the disposal of flowback liquids. After the hydraulic fracturing process is complete, anywhere from 30–70% of the fluid is recovered; this is referred to as 'flowback'.[47] The flowback will generally contain the original additives used in the initial mixture, 'as well as substances that dissolve into the water from the rock formation that is fractured. These substances can include salts, naturally occurring radioactive materials, and dissolved solids.'[48] Discharge of flowback water would be considered a 'point source' discharge of a pollutant under the CWA, thereby requiring treatment at a permitted wastewater disposal facility or underground injection at a site that holds the necessary UIC permit. Any direct discharge of untreated or treated flowback water that contains a 'pollutant' would, under the CWA, require the operator to obtain a National Pollutant Discharge Elimination System (NPDES) permit either from the EPA or an approved state agency.[49]

[46] 42 USCA § 300h(d) (West) (emphasis added). See also, Kramer (n 39) at 855.
[47] A. J. Daniel, L. Bruce, and D. Alleman, 'An Overview of Modern Shale Gas Development in the United States', ALL Consulting (2008) 21.
[48] K. B. Hall, 'Hydraulic Fracturing: What Are the Legal Issues?' (2012) 59 La BJ 250 at 251.
[49] 33 USCA § 1342 (National pollutant discharge elimination system).

C. Clean Air Act

On 18 April 2012, the EPA released the first federal air rules for natural gas wells that are hydraulically fractured.[50] The final standards are designed to significantly reduce emissions of air pollutants. The new rules cover 'onshore well[s] drilled principally for production of natural gas'.[51] After considerable input from stakeholders, the final rules mandate the use of technologies, as well as 'processes already in use at approximately half of the natural gas wells in the United States', to achieve air quality goals.[52] The new technologies will reduce 95% of the harmful emissions that contribute to smog and lead to health impacts, including emissions of VOCs, benzene and hexane. In addition, the new technologies are expected to reduce fugitive methane emissions from natural gas operations, thus addressing some of the concerns about greenhouse gas (GHG) emissions from hydraulic fracturing operations.

Emissions from diesel engines have also been a concern at hydraulic fracturing sites, both from onsite generators and from the large number of trucks that deliver water and other supplies to the drilling site. On 14 January 2013, the EPA finalized amendments for the National Emission Standards for Hazardous Air Pollutants (NESHAP) and the reciprocating internal combustion engine (RICE) standard. The EPA estimates there are over 1 million of these engines used to generate electricity and power industrial equipment, typically in sparsely populated areas, including those used for the production of oil and gas.[53] The updated RICE standard enforces annual hourly limits on non-emergency use and replaces emissions limits with management practices or equipment standards, depending on the quantity of horsepower.[54] These standards are expected to have a significant impact on emissions from new and retrofitted stationary diesel engines, but likely will not have a major impact on the thousands of diesel engines that are already in use and that will remain in use for several years. As for trucks, newer diesel engines must meet stringent Federal emissions standards for both criteria pollutants and GHG emissions, but most of the truck fleet in the United States still uses older, higher emission engines.[55]

[50] EPA, Press Release, 'EPA Issues Updated, Achievable Air Pollution Standards for Oil and Natural Gas', 18 April 2012, available at <http://yosemite.epa.gov/opa/admpress.nsf/d0cf6618525a9efb85257359003fb69d/c742df7944b37c50852579e400594f8f/>.

[51] Oil and Natural Gas Sector: New Source Performance Standards and National Emission Standards for Hazardous Air Pollutants Reviews; Final Rule, 77 Fed Reg 49490 (16 August 2012) (to be codified at 40 CFR pts 60 & 63), available at <http://www.gpo.gov/fdsys/pkg/FR-2012-08-16/pdf/2012-16806.pdf>.

[52] EPA, Press Release, (n 50).

[53] Fact Sheet: Final Amendments to the Emissions Standards for Reciprocating Internal Combustion Engines, EPA Office of Air & Radiation, Policy & Guidance, 15 January 2013, at 1, available at <http://www.epa.gov/ttnatw01/rice/20130114overviewfs.pdf>.

[54] Fact Sheet (n 53).

[55] For a complete description of regulations for both heavy-duty and light-duty trucks, see EPA, 'Transportation and Air Quality: Heavy Trucks, Buses and Engines', available at <http://www.epa.gov/oms/hd-hwy.htm>.

D. Current federal studies on the potential impacts of hydraulic fracturing

In response to growing public concern, in 2010, Congress requested that the EPA conduct a comprehensive scientific study to examine the relationship between hydraulic fracturing and drinking water resources. In November 2011, the EPA released its research plan for the *Study of the Potential Impacts of Hydraulic Fracturing on Drinking Water*. The study, which is currently underway, is composed of 18 large research projects including analyses of existing data, scenario evaluations, laboratory studies, toxicity assessments, and five case studies (Las Animas and Huerfano Counties, Colorado; Dunn County, North Dakota; Bradford County, Pennsylvania; Washington County, Pennsylvania; and Wise County, Texas).[56]

Although the final report is not expected to be released until 2014, in December 2012, the EPA released a Progress Report highlighting the five stages of the hydraulic fracturing process included in their research: (1) water acquisition; (2) chemical mixing; (3) well injection; (4) flowback and produced water; and (5) wastewater treatment and waste disposal.[57] The Progress Report does not contain any specific findings about the environmental impacts of hydraulic fracturing, but does describe the universe of data that is available to assess these issues, as well as the research projects that are currently underway.

E. Secretary of Energy Advisory Board recommendations

The Secretary of Energy Advisory Board (SEAB) provides advice and recommendations to the Secretary of Energy on a wide range of issues. At the direction of President Obama, Secretary Chu brought together members of SEAB to form a Subcommittee of Shale Gas Production to make recommendations to improve the safety and environmental performance of hydraulic fracturing in shale formations. The subcommittee included a diverse group of industry experts, environmental advocates, academics, and former state regulators. After holding multiple public meetings, the Subcommittee produced its final report on 18 November 2011.[58] The principal near-term recommendations of the Board included:

- improving public information about shale gas;

[56] EPA, 'Study on the Potential Impacts of Hydraulic Fracturing on Drinking Water Resources: Progress Report', December 2012, at 10, available at <http://www.epa.gov/hfstudy/pdfs/hf-report20121214.pdf>.

[57] EPA. Progress Report, (n 56) at 8.

[58] Secretary of Energy Advisory Board, Shale Gas Production Subcommittee, 'Second 90 Day Report', 18 November 2001, available at <http://www.shalegas.energy.gov/resources/111811_final_report.pdf>.

- reducing air pollutants, ozone precursors, and methane as quickly as practicable;
- enlisting a subset of producers from industry to design and field a system to collect emissions data;
- encouraging industry to use current technology to reduce air emissions;
- launching additional field studies on possible methane migration from natural gas wells to reservoirs;
- disclosing of fracturing fluid composition;
- elimination of diesel fuel use as a hydraulic fracturing fluid.

F. Hydraulic fracturing on public lands

The Bureau of Land Management (BLM) is an agency within the Department of the Interior (DOI), which manages nearly 250 million surface acres of Federal lands. The agency also is responsible for 700 million acres of subsurface minerals that are found beneath both Federal and Non-Federal land.[59] Domestic production from over 63,000 Federal onshore oil and gas wells accounts for 11% of the nation's natural gas supply and 5% of its oil.[60] The BLM leases and provides permits for natural gas and oil exploration within and on this land, therefore all Federal land oil and gas extraction activities, including hydraulic fracturing, are subject to BLM permitting requirements.

In May 2012, the BLM released a proposed rule governing hydraulic fracturing which contained three elements. First, it would require companies to disclose the chemicals used in hydraulic fracturing operations on Federal lands. Second, it would increase wellbore integrity requirements and construction standards. And third, it would require operators to implement appropriate plans for managing flowback waters.[61]

After receiving criticism from industry and other stakeholders,[62] the BLM announced on 18 January 2013 that it was going to revise the proposed rule and issue a new draft within the first quarter of 2013.[63] On 16 May 2013, the BLM released the revised version of the proposed rules. According to the BLM press release, the new proposal maintains the three main components of the initial proposal, but also responds to industry concerns by 'improv[ing] integration with existing state and tribal standards, and increas[ing] flexibility for oil and gas

[59] 'Mineral and Surface Acreage Managed by the BLM', available at: <http://www.blm.gov/wo/st/en/info/About_BLM/subsurface.html>.

[60] BLM, 'Oil and Gas', available at <http://www.blm.gov/wo/st/en/prog/energy/oil_and_gas.html>.

[61] Department of the Interior, BLM, 'Proposed Rule: Oil and Gas; Well Stimulation, Including Hydraulic Fracturing, on Federal and Indian Lands', 11 May 2012, at 4, available at <http://www.doi.gov/news/pressreleases/loader.cfm?csModule=security/getfile&pageid=293916>.

[62] E.g., industry argued that the cost of compliance would be too large and that state regulations were sufficient.

[63] A. Kovski and T. Baltz, 'BLM to Pull Back Proposed Hydraulic Fracturing Rule, Will Issue Revised Version in First Quarter', *Bloomberg BNA*, 22 January 2013, available at <http://www.bna.com/blm-pull-back-n17179871950/>.

developers'.[64] For example, the revised proposal includes a variance process that allows federal regulators to defer to states and tribes that already have standards in place to regulate hydraulic fracturing, so long as those standards meet or exceed the federal standards.[65] The proposal also revises the types of cement evaluation tools that operators may use to protect water resources from contamination.[66] Finally, the proposal modifies the requirements for claiming a trade secret exception to chemical disclosure.[67]

IV. State regulation of hydraulic fracturing

A. Regulation of hydraulic fracturing in Pennsylvania

Approximately two-thirds of Pennsylvania is located above the Marcellus Shale, the nation's largest untapped natural gas reserve. The state also has access to the Utica and Upper Devonian shale formations. In 2010, the US EIA estimated that Pennsylvania had 10,708 billion cubic feet of proved shale gas reserves.[68] Thus, improvements in horizontal drilling and hydraulic fracturing have allowed Pennsylvania to dramatically expand its natural gas production.[69]

Pennsylvania's first shale gas was produced in 2005 and, since then, over 6,000 unconventional wells have been drilled.[70] The proliferation of the shale gas industry has provided significant economic stimulus for the state,[71] but has also given rise

[64] Department of the Interior, BLM, Press Release, 'Interior Releases Updated Draft Rule for Hydraulic Fracturing on Public and Indian Lands for Public Comment', 16 May 2013, available at <http://www.blm.gov/wo/st/en/info/newsroom/2013/may/nr_05_16_2013.html>.

[65] Department of the Interior, BLM, 'Supplemental Notice of Proposed Rulemaking and Request for Comment, Oil and Gas; Hydraulic Fracturing on Federal Lands', 43 CFR Part 3160, 11 May 2012 6–7.

[66] Supplemental Notice (n 65) at 7–8.

[67] Under the original proposed rule, well operators were required to submit all information about chemicals to the BLM, to segregate trade secrets, and to justify the assertion of trade secret protection. Under the revised proposed rule, operators would not be required to disclose trade secret information to the BLM or on FracFocus. Instead, operators would submit an affidavit stating that the withheld information is entitled to withholding from the public under Federal statute or regulation. The BLM would retain authority to require operators to submit the claimed trade secret information. See Supplemental Notice (n 65) at 32.

[68] Proved resources include those resources which can be estimated with reasonable certainty to be commercially recoverable from known reservoirs and under current economic conditions, operating methods and government regulations. This figure has dramatically risen from 3,790 billion cubic feet in 2009 and 88 billion cubic feet in 2008. See US EIA, Shale Gas, available at <http://www.eia.gov/dnav/ng/ng_enr_shalegas_dcu_spa_a.htm>.

[69] E.g., Pennsylvania's natural gas production more than quadrupled between 2009 and 2011. US EIA, 'Horizontal Drilling Boosts Pennsylvania's Natural Gas Production', 23 May 2012, available at <http://www.eia.gov/todayinenergy/detail.cfm?id=6390>.

[70] Pennsylvania Department of Environmental Protection (DEP), 'Oil and Gas Reports', available at <http://www.portal.state.pa.us/portal/server.pt/community/oil_and_gas_reports/20297>.

[71] A recent study by Pennsylvania State University estimated that, in 2009, the state's Marcellus shale gas industry provided a direct economic stimulus of approximately 3.8 billion dollars, and created more than 21,000 jobs. T. J. Considine, R. Watson, and S. Blumsack, 'The Economic Impacts of the Pennsylvania Marcellus Shale Natural Gas Play: An Update' (2010) The Pennsylvania State University College of Earth and Mineral Sciences, Department of Energy and Mineral Engineering.

to concerns about impacts to the environment and local communities. In particular, many citizens initially felt that the state's general rules for oil and gas development did not provide sufficient protection against the special dangers associated with hydraulic fracturing and horizontal drilling.

Between 2005 and 2012, Pennsylvania regulators took a number of incremental steps to address these concerns. These included the imposition of new water management requirements for operators planning to drill in the Marcellus shale formation,[72] revised treatment standards for wastewater discharges from natural gas exploration and production operations,[73] and more stringent design requirements for unconventional wells.[74] Between 2008 and 2010, the Pennsylvania Department of Environmental Protection (DEP) also 'doubled the number of oil and gas inspection staff and implemented new water quality standards and other changes concerning Marcellus Shale operations'.[75]

The most significant regulatory development came in 2012, when Governor Corbett signed House Bill 1950 ('Act 13') into law. Act 13 amends Title 58 (Oil and Gas) of the Pennsylvania Consolidated Statutes, to provide a comprehensive regulatory framework for hydraulic fracturing and shale gas development. The Act reflects a compromise between Pennsylvania's economic and environmental interests. It enables shale gas development by creating a uniform set of rules for unconventional well owners and operators, and by pre-empting local regulatory authority. At the same time, it strengthens the environmental standards for unconventional wells, and authorizes local governments to impose an 'impact fee' on wells that are located within their jurisdiction. Some of the key provisions of Act 13 are discussed later.

Another promising development in Pennsylvania has been the emergence of the CSSD, an independent non-profit organization based in Pittsburgh, Pennsylvania.

[72] In 2008, the Bureau of Oil and Gas Management imposed a new obligation on operators planning to drill in the Marcellus shale formation, requiring them to submit special water management plans, which identified where water would be withdrawn and the volumes of withdrawal. 'State Review of Oil & Natural Gas Environmental Regulations (STRONGER), Pennsylvania Hydraulic Fracturing State Review, 2010', available at: <http://www.strongerinc.org/sites/all/themes/stronger02/downloads/PA%20HF%20Review%20Print%20Version.pdf>.

[73] In 2010, the Environmental Quality Board modified the regulations which permitted discharge of treated wastewater into the state's surface waters, requiring that discharges from natural gas exploration and production operations be treated at a centralized wastewater treatment facility, and establishing specific standards for concentrations of chlorides, barium, and strontium in the treated wastewater. L. K. McKay, R. H. Johnson, and L. A. Salita, 'Science and the Reasonable Development of Marcellus Shale Natural Gas Resources in Pennsylvania and New York' (2011) 32 Energy LJ 125 at 133 (citing 40 Pa.B. 4835, 21 August 2010).

[74] In 2011, the House and Senate Environmental Resources and Energy Committees approved further amendments to the state's administrative regulations governing oil and gas, which 'strengthened well-design requirements to prevent gas migration incidents', and imposed 'additional obligations on operators for well control, immediate response to gas migration complaints, and routine inspection of existing wells'. 41 Pa.B. 805, 5 February 2011, available at <http://www.pabulletin.com/secure/data/vol41/41-6/239.html>.

[75] McKay et al (n 73) at 132–3, citing D. Gilliland, 'Pennsylvania Department of Environmental Protection Chief Defends Regulation of Marcellus Shale Drilling', *Patriot-News*, 11 September 2010, available at <http://www.pennlive.com/midstate/index.ssf/2010/09/Pennsylvania_department_of_env_1.html>.

The CSSD's mission is to support continuous improvement and innovation in shale gas development practices by developing performance standards, as well as third-party certification processes. The CSSD develops these standards through extensive collaboration with regulators, industry representatives, and environmental non-governmental organizations (NGOs).[76] As of June 2013, the CSSD had developed 15 performance standards for shale gas development, including surface and groundwater performance standards, as well as air and climate performance standards.[77]

B. Regulation of hydraulic fracturing in New York

1. Shale gas resources in New York

New York shares the Marcellus shale formation with Pennsylvania, Ohio, and West Virginia.[78] The State government estimates that it may receive 1,700 to 2,500 permit applications during peak years, with drilling expected to persist for about 30 years.[79] The RSGEIS estimated that the 'total direct and indirect impacts on employee earnings are projected to range from US$621.9 million to US$2.5 billion per year during peak production'.[80] Significant portions of the Marcellus formation lie below the watersheds that supply New York City and the city of Syracuse.

2. The moratorium

New York, in stark contrast to Pennsylvania, has taken a go-slow approach to exploiting the same Marcellus shale resources that exist in Pennsylvania. After it became clear around 2005 that hydraulic fracturing would be an available means of recovering large quantities of natural gas, the idea of using hydraulic fracturing in New York began to surface in 2007.[81] In 2008, New York Governor David Patterson ordered the Department of Environmental Conservation (NY DEC) to update the state's 1992 'Generic Environmental Impact Statement' on oil and gas drilling to take the new hydraulic fracturing method into account.[82]

New York law established what is often referred to as a 'little NEPA'[83] process that requires environmental impact review whenever a direct state action (e.g.,

[76] 'Center for Sustainable Shale Development', available at <http://www.sustainableshale.org/>.

[77] 'Center for Sustainable Shale Development: Performance Standards', available at <http://www.sustainableshale.org/performance-standards/>.

[78] The deeper Utica shale formation is also found in the state, but most of the focus is on drilling in the Marcellus formation.

[79] Preliminary Revised Draft Supplemental Generic Environmental Impact Statement on the Oil, Gas and Solution Mining Program: Well Permit Issuance for Horizontal Drilling and High-Volume Hydraulic Fracturing to Develop Marcellus Shale and Other Low-permeability Gas Reservoirs, New York Department of Environmental Conservation, 1 July 2011, at 4 (RSGEIS).

[80] RSGEIS at 17.

[81] See P. Kiernan, 'An Analysis of Hydrofracturing Gubernatorial Decision Making' (2012) 5 Alb Gov't L Rev 769 at 771.

[82] Kiernan (n 81) at 770.

[83] Sixteen states, as well as the District of Columbia, Puerto Rico, and Guam, have 'little NEPAs', which contain similar environmental review requirements as those that are contained in the National Environmental Policy Act (NEPA). Whereas the federal NEPA only imposes procedural requirements

building a highway) or indirect state action (e.g., issuing a permit) has the potential for significant adverse environmental impact.[84] In New York, environmental review procedures vary. Some projects are excluded from review because they are not expected to result in significant adverse impacts,[85] so-called 'Type II' projects. Other projects are subject to screening environmental reviews to determine if they may result in a significant environmental impact. If the agency determines the project will not result in a significant impact or if that impact can be mitigated, the agency may issue a 'negative declaration'.[86] Projects that follow the screening process may still have significant environmental impacts that require the completion of a full Environmental Impact Statement before a state action (authorizing a project or issuing a permit) can proceed.[87] To avoid duplicative Environmental Impact Statements on recurring actions that have the potential for the same or similar impacts, New York law provides for the preparation of Generic Environmental Impact Statements (GEISs). While GEISs are not site-specific, they provide information about whether a specific project can proceed without any additional environmental review or whether additional steps need to be taken, including the preparation of a site-specific environmental review.[88]

The 'supplemental' GEIS for oil and gas was completed in 2009 with more than 130,000 comments submitted to the NY DEC. As one commentator noted, hydraulic fracturing had become a 'white-hot commercial, environmental and political controversy in New York'.[89] As a result of the controversy, the New York legislature passed a bill in November 2010, placing a moratorium on hydraulic fracturing until 15 May 2011. The Governor vetoed the bill but issued an Executive Order[90] at the same time as the veto on 13 December 2010, which required additional environmental review.[91] The 'revised' SGEIS was released for public comment in July 2011, followed by public hearings and an extended public comment period that ended on 11 January 2012.[92] The environmental review concluded that groundwater contamination from hydraulic fracturing operations is 'highly unlikely' if wells are properly constructed,[93] although this conclusion has been challenged.[94]

The RSGEIS also concluded that a 'no action' alternative that would suggest the state should not approve the use of hydraulic fracturing 'is not preferable because

regarding environmental review, some of the state equivalents impose substantive requirements on agencies and developers to mitigate their environmental impacts and/or choose more environmentally friendly alternatives to projects and actions when such alternatives are available and feasible. Some examples of states with substantive 'little NEPAs' include Minnesota, New York, and California.

84 NY Envtl Conserv Law § 8-0109 (McKinney 2005 & Supp, 2013).

85 6 NYCRR § 617.5 (2013). 86 6 NYCRR § 617.2(y) and (h).

87 6 NYCRR § 617.3. 88 6 NYCRR § 617.10.

89 Kiernan (n 81) at 771.

90 See Governor David Patterson, Executive Order 41, available at <http://www.governor.ny.gov/archive/paterson/executiveorders/EO41.html>.

91 Executive Order 41 (n 90) at 780. 92 Executive Order 41 (n 90) at 781.

93 RSGEIS at 11.

94 See Comments of Anthony Ingraffea on the New York High Volume Hydraulic Fracturing Proposed Regulations, 8 January 2013, available at <http://www.psehealthyenergy.org/data/NYS_DEC_Proposed_REGS_comments_Ingraffea_Jan_2013.pdf>.

significant adverse impacts from high-volume hydraulic fracturing can be fully or partially mitigated'.[95] Rather, the environmental review advocates a phased permitting approach under which important water resources would be shielded from drilling.[96]

Despite the long process, New York Governor Cuomo extended the moratorium in late September 2012 for an indefinite period to further study the public health impacts of hydraulic fracturing.[97] In March 2013, the New York Assembly passed a bill extending the hydraulic fracturing moratorium until May 2015. As of the time this chapter was written, the New York Senate had yet to act on the proposed legislation.

While environmental review was proceeding, the NY DEC drafted a comprehensive set of regulations for hydraulic fracturing operations.[98] These rules were also the subject of an extensive public comment period that ended in January 2013. Again, thousands of comments were received. As of the time this chapter was written, it is unclear when and under what conditions New York will allow hydraulic fracturing operations.

V. Analysis of differing approaches to critical regulatory issues

A. Waste use and conservation

1. Pennsylvania

Act 13 prohibits the withdrawal or use of water for drilling or hydraulic fracture stimulation of any natural gas well completed in an unconventional gas formation, except in accordance with a water management plan approved by the department.[99] The DEP must review and approve water management plans 'based on a determination that the proposed withdrawal, when operated in accordance with the withdrawal operating conditions set forth in the plan, including conditions relating to quantity, withdrawal rate, and timing and any pass-by flow conditions, will: (i) not adversely affect the quantity or quality of water available to other users of the same water sources; (ii) protect and maintain the designated and existing uses of water sources; (iii) not cause adverse impact to water quality in the watershed considered as a whole; and (iv) include a reuse plan for fluids that will be used to hydraulically fracture wells'.[100] These criteria shall be 'presumed to be achieved if the proposed water withdrawal has been approved by and is operated in accordance with conditions established by the Susquehanna River Basin Commission, the

[95] RSGEIS (n 79) at 27. [96] RSGEIS (n 79) at 27.

[97] D. Hakim, 'Shift by Cuomo on Gas Drilling Prompts Both Anger and Praise', *New York Times*, 30 September 2012, available at <http://www.nytimes.com/2012/10/01/nyregion/with-new-delays-a-growing-sense-that-gov-andrew-cuomo-will-not-approve-gas-drilling.html?pagewanted=all>.

[98] NY DEC, 'High Volume Hydraulic Fracturing Proposed Regulations', available at <http://www.dec.ny.gov/regulations/77353.html>.

[99] 58 Pa.C.S. § 3211(m)(1). [100] 58 Pa.C.S. § 3211(m)(2).

Delaware River Basin Commission, or the Great Lakes Commission, as applicable'.[101]

2. New York

New York's proposed regulations would require applications for drilling permits to indicate the source of fresh water for the drilling operation and indicate the status of water withdrawal permits for that water. As discussed later, New York's proposed regulations also require operators to test local water quality before a well is spud to establish a baseline.

B. Wastewater management

1. Pennsylvania

The Water Management Plans, discussed earlier, require operators to detail their plans for reuse and recycling of wastewater. Operators must also keep records of the transportation and disposal of wastewater from any unconventional well, but this information only needs to be submitted to the DEP upon request.[102]

In terms of substantive requirements, Act 13 requires well operators to control and dispose of brines produced from drilling, alteration, or operation of an oil or gas well in a manner consistent with the Clean Streams Law and implementing regulations.[103] In addition, Act 13 imposes some new restrictions on the placement of pits or other storage of hazardous waste or waste materials, as well as new protection standards for hazardous chemicals or materials and new containment standards for prevention of offsite spills.[104]

2. New York

Wastewater at hydraulic fracturing sites can include storm water, drilling fluids and cuttings from the bore, and flowback water and brine that is returned to the surface upon completion of a well (an estimated 216,000 to 2.7 million gallons per well).[105] The proposed regulations require preparation of a Storm Water Pollution Prevention Plan.[106] Flowback and brine may be stored in onsite pits that meet specific construction standards.[107] Drilling fluids and cuttings must be stored in a 'closed-loop' tank system rather than in pits.[108]

[101] 58 Pa.C.S. § 3211(m)(3). [102] 58 Pa.C.S. § 3218.3.

[103] 58 Pa.C.S. § 3217(a). The Clean Streams Law sets standards for discharge of industrial wastes and requires that permits be obtained for any waste that will flow into the water. See, e.g., 35 Pa.C.S. § 691.5.

[104] 58 Pa.C.S. § 3215, §3218.2. [105] RSGEIS (n 79) at 8.

[106] NY DEC, 'Proposed Rule' ('Draft New York Rules') § 750-3.6 (e), available at <http://www.dec.ny.gov/regulations/77353.html>.

[107] Draft New York Rules § 750-33.7(l) and 560.6(c)(27).

[108] Draft New York Rules § 750-3.7(n).

Flowback water may not be discharged to the ground.[109] Wastewater from a hydraulic fracturing operation may only be accepted by a permitted publicly owned wastewater treatment facility (POTW) and, even then, only after a 'headworks' analysis has been completed that demonstrates the hydraulic fracturing wastewater will not result in a violation of the POTW's discharge permit.[110] A treatability analysis is required before a private wastewater treatment facility is authorized to accept the hydraulic fracturing wastewater.[111] On-site wastewater treatment would be permitted under the draft rule.[112] However, the draft rules prohibit discharges to waters of the state. The proposed rules require owners and operators to state in their drilling plans that they will maximize the reuse and/or recycling of used drilling mud, flowback water, and production brine to 'the maximum extent feasible'.[113]

New York's proposed rules require the use of a 'Drilling and Production Waste Tracking Form' for any used drilling mud, flowback water, production brine, and drill cuttings removed from the well site. If the waste is disposed of rather than recycled or reused, the operator must make the form available to the public on an accessible website.[114]

3. CSSD

The performance standard provides that operators will 'maintain zero discharge of wastewater (including drilling, flowback, and produced water) to Pennsylvania and other state waters until additional standards for treating waste water are developed'.[115] The standard also requires operators to have a plan to recycle flowback and produced water 'to the maximum extent possible'. The standards call for recycling a minimum of 90% of flowback and produced water within two years.[116]

C. Chemicals use and disclosure

1. Pennsylvania

Although it does not impose any substantive restrictions on the use of particular hydraulic fracturing chemicals, Act 13 does impose stringent requirements on both operators and other entities regarding the disclosure of hydraulic fracturing chemicals. First, service providers who perform 'any part of hydraulic fracturing treatment' and vendors who provide hydraulic fracturing additives directly to the operator must give the operator specific information about those additives within 60 days of the commencement of the hydraulic fracturing.[117] Then, within 60 days

[109] Draft New York Rules § 750-3.12.

[110] Draft New York Rules § 750-3.12(c)(2).

[111] Draft New York Rules § 750-3.12(d).

[112] Draft New York Rules § 750-3.12(e)(1).

[113] Draft New York Rules § 554.1(1).

[114] Draft New York Rules § 560.3(f).

[115] CSSD Performance Standard 1, available at <http://037186e.netsolhost.com/site/wp-content/uploads/2013/03/CSSD-Performance-Standards-3-13R.pdf>.

[116] CSSD Performance Standard 2, available at <http://037186e.netsolhost.com/site/wp-content/uploads/2013/03/CSSD-Performance-Standards-3-13R.pdf>.

[117] 58 Pa.C.S. §3222.1(b)(1).

after the conclusion of hydraulic fracturing, the operator of the well must complete a chemical disclosure registry form and post the form on the chemical disclosure registry in accordance with regulations to be promulgated under the Act, 'in a format that does not link chemicals to their respective hydraulic fracturing additive'.[118]

Act 13 further specifies that, '[i]f the vendor, service provider or operator claims that the specific identity of a chemical, or the concentration of a chemical, or both, are a trade secret or confidential proprietary information, the operator of the well must indicate that to be the case on the chemical disclosure registry form, and the vendor, service provider, or operator shall submit a signed written statement [to that effect]'.[119] Although the operator need not disclose a chemical that is a trade secret, 'the operator shall include in the chemical registry disclosure form the chemical family or similar description associated with the chemical'.[120]

Operators must include in their reports: (1) a 'descriptive list of the chemical additives in the stimulation fluids'; (2) the 'trade name, vendor and a brief description of the intended use or function of each chemical additive in the stimulation fluid'; (3) a list of 'chemicals intentionally added to the simulation fluid'; and (4) 'the maximum concentration, in percent by mass, of each chemical intentionally added to the stimulation fluid'.[121] The reports must also describe the 'total volume of the base fluid', a 'list of water sources used under the approved water management plan and the volume of water used', the 'pump rates and pressure used in the well', and 'the total volume of recycled water used'.[122] Finally, the well record must identify whether methane was encountered in other than a target formation, and the country of origin and manufacture of tubular steel products used in the construction of the well.[123]

Disclosure of chemicals is not required if: (1) the manufacturer, vendor, or service provider did not disclose the chemicals; (2) the chemicals were not intentionally added to the stimulation fluid; or (3) the chemicals occur incidentally or are otherwise unintentionally present in trace amounts (e.g., as the incidental result of a chemical reaction or constituents of naturally occurring materials that become part of a stimulation fluid).[124]

Act 13 also provides an exception to the disclosure rule, in the event that 'a health professional determines that a medical emergency exists and the specific identity and amount of any chemicals claimed to be a trade secret or confidential proprietary information are necessary for emergency treatment'.[125] Under such circumstances, the vendor, service provider, or operator must 'immediately disclose the information to the health professional upon a verbal acknowledgement by the health professional that the information may not be used for purposes other than

[118] 58 Pa.C.S. § 3222.1(b)(2).
[119] 58 Pa.C.S. § 3222.1(b)(3).
[120] 58 Pa.C.S. § 3222.1(b)(3).
[121] 58 Pa.C.S. § 3222(b.1)(1)(i)–(iv).
[122] 58 Pa.C.S. § 3222(b.1)(1)(v)–(viii).
[123] 58 Pa.C.S. § 3222(b.1)(2).
[124] 58 Pa.C.S. § 3222.1(c)(1)–(3).
[125] 58 Pa.C.S. § 3222.1(b)(11).

the health needs asserted and that the health professional shall maintain the information as confidential'.[126]

2. *New York*

New York has focused much of its environmental review and permit rules on the disclosure of hydraulic fracturing chemicals, management of chemical-laden wastewater, and encouraging 'greener' alternatives to traditional chemicals. The state found that 332 chemicals have been identified for use in hydraulic fracturing in the state.[127] Proposed rules would require detailed disclosure of the chemicals to the NY DEC.[128] The proposed rule would also provide that the NY DEC will disclose to the public the information it receives on hydraulic fracturing chemicals, unless the person supplying the information requests the information be protected as a trade secret.[129]

The proposed rules require an 'alternatives analysis' as part of the permit process that examines chemical additives that 'exhibit reduced aquatic toxicity and pose at least as low a potential risk to water resources and the environment as all known alternatives . . . '.[130] An owner or operator *must* use the alternatives that are effective in the drilling operation.[131]

The rules also require owners or operators to prepare a fluid disposal plan and to test nearby residential wells located within 1,000 feet of a well pad for a variety of contaminants to establish background conditions and periodically after the well has been completed. Any significant deviations from baseline conditions must be reported to the NY DEC within five days.[132]

3. *CSSD*

The performance standard commits operators to disclose chemical constituents used in well stimulation fluids and identify:

- the well;
- the operator and dates of stimulation;
- the type and amount of proppant;
- all chemical additives; and
- the actual or maximum concentration of each chemical.[133]

The disclosure must be provided to the relevant state agency and posted on <http://www.fracfocus.org>. The standard does provide protection for trade secrets.[134] The performance standard prohibits the use of diesel fuel as an additive.[135]

126 58 Pa.C.S. § 3222.1(b)(11).
127 RSGEIS (n 79) at 22.
128 Draft New York Rules § 760.3(d)(1).
129 Draft New York Rules § 760.3(d)(2).
130 Draft New York Rules § 750-3.69(k)(2).
131 Draft New York Rules § 750-3.69(k)(2).
132 Draft New York Rules § 560.5(d).
133 CSSD Performance Standard 7, available at <http://037186e.netsolhost.com/site/wp-content/uploads/2013/03/CSSD-Performance-Standards-3-13R.pdf>.
134 CSSD Performance Standard 7 (n 133).
135 CSSD Performance Standard 7 (n 133).

D. Water contamination

1. Pennsylvania

Act 13 contains a number of provisions which are intended to protect Pennsylvania's surface and ground water resources from adverse impacts associated with hydraulic fracturing. These include permitting guidelines, which require the DEP to consider impacts on public resources before issuing well permits; rules relating to the location and construction, and abandonment of unconventional wells; liability and bonding requirements for well owners and operators; and the imposition of an impact fee which is used, in part, to fund emergency planning and response programmes in the event of an accident or spill.

(a) Issuance of permits

Act 13 requires the DEP, when determining whether to issue a well permit, to consider the impact of the proposed well on public resources, including, but not limited to: (1) publicly owned parks, forests, game lands, and wildlife areas; (2) national or state scenic rivers; (3) national natural landmarks; (4) habitats of rare and endangered flora and fauna and other critical communities; (5) historical and archaeological sites listed on the Federal or State list of historic places; and (6) sources used for public water supplies.[136] The Act does not specify how the DEP's analysis of these impacts should influence its final decision, but rather instructs the Environmental Quality Board to develop regulations for the DEP 'for conditioning a well permit based on its impact to the public resources' identified here, and 'for ensuring optimal development of oil and gas resources'.[137]

(b) Well siting

As a general rule, unconventional gas wells may not be drilled within 500 feet from an existing building or water well, unless the applicant receives written consent of the owner of the building or water well.[138] In addition, unconventional wells may not be drilled within 1,000 feet of any existing water well, surface water intake, reservoir, or other water supply extraction point that is used by a water purveyor, without the written consent of the water purveyor.[139]

If such consent is not obtained, and 'the distance restriction would deprive the owner of the oil and gas rights of the right to produce or share in the oil or gas

[136] 58 Pa.C.S. § 3215(c)(1)–(6). [137] 58 Pa.C.S. § 3215(e)(1).

[138] Setback distances are measured horizontally from the vertical well bore. For comparison, the general setback requirement is 200 feet for conventional wells. 58 Pa.C.S. § 3215(a).

[139] 58 Pa.C.S. § 3215(a).

underlying the surface tract', the Act requires the DEP to grant a variance from the distance requirement 'upon submission of a plan identifying the additional measures, facilities or practices as prescribed by the department to be employed during well site construction, drilling and operation'.[140] The variance must contain 'additional terms and conditions required by the department to ensure safety and protection of affected persons and property, including insurance, bonding, indemnification and technical requirements'.[141]

The Act also imposes additional siting restrictions on unconventional wells drilled near streams, springs, and other bodies of water,[142] wetlands,[143] and floodplains.[144] As with the consent-based restrictions, some of these requirements may be waived.[145]

(c) Well construction and abandonment

The Act requires all unconventional well sites to be designed and constructed to prevent spills,[146] and specifies a number of general requirements for containment practices.[147] In addition, permit applicants must submit a plan to the department which details the precise containment practices that will be utilized to prevent migration of fluids, spills, blowouts, explosions, and fires.[148] Containment systems are required wherever any of the following are stored: drilling mud, hydraulic oil,

[140] 58 Pa.C.S. § 3215(a). [141] 58 Pa.C.S. § 3215(a).

[142] Specifically, the following setback distances are required: '300 feet from the vertical well bore or 100 feet from the edge of the well site, whichever is greater, measured horizontally from any solid blue lined stream, spring or body of water, as identified on the most current 7 1/2 minute topographic quadrangle map of the United States Geological Survey'. 58 Pa.C.S. § 3215(b)(1). Moreover, '[t]he edge of the disturbed area associated with any unconventional well site must maintain a 100-foot setback from the edge of any solid blue lined stream, spring or body of water'. 58 Pa.C.S. § 3215(b)(2). The DEP is also authorized to establish 'additional protective measures for storage of hazardous chemicals and materials intended to be used, or that have been used, on an unconventional well drilling site within 750 feet of a solid blue lined stream, spring or body of water identified in the most current 7 ½ minute topographic quadrangle map of the U.S. Geological Survey'. 58 Pa.C.S. § 3215 (d.1).

[143] 'No unconventional well may be drilled within 300 feet of any wetlands greater than one acre in size, and the edge of the disturbed area of any well site must maintain a 100-foot setback from the boundary of the wetlands.' 58 Pa.C.S. § 3215(b)(3).

[144] 'No well site may be prepared or well drilled within any floodplain if the well site will have a pit or impoundment containing drilling cuttings, flowback water, produced water or hazardous materials, chemicals or wastes within the floodplain; or a tank containing hazardous materials, chemicals, condensate, wastes, flowback or produced water within the floodway.' 58 Pa.C.S. § 3215(f).

[145] Specifically, the DEP is required to waive the setback requirements from surface waters and wetlands upon a submission of a plan that identifies the 'additional measures, facilitates or practices to be employed during well site construction, drilling and operations'. Such waiver must impose any 'conditions necessary to protect the waters of this Commonwealth'. 58 Pa.C.S. § 3215(b)(4).

[146] 58 Pa.C.S. §§3211.7, 3218.2, 3218.4, 3219.

[147] Specifically, containment practices must meet the following requirements: (1) be instituted on the well site during both drilling and hydraulic fracturing operations; (2) be sufficiently impervious and able to contain spilled material or waste until it can be removed or treated; (3) be compatible with the waste material or waste stored or used within the containment; (4) comply with additional practices as promulgated in regulation by the Environmental Quality Board. 58 Pa.C.S. § 3218.2(a)(1)–(4). In addition, §3218.2(d) contains specific requirements for containment capacity.

[148] 58 Pa.C.S. § 3218.2(b).

diesel fuel, drilling mud additives, hydraulic fracturing additives, or hydraulic fracturing flowback.[149]

Upon abandoning a well, owners and operators are required to plug the well in a manner prescribed by DEP regulations, so as to stop the vertical flow of fluids or gas within the well bore.[150] There is an exception to this rule for wells that have been granted inactive status or that have been approved by the DEP as orphan wells.[151]

(d) Liability for water contamination and bonding requirements

Act 13 requires 'a well operator who affects a public or private water supply by pollution or diminution [to] restore or replace the affected supply with an alternate source of water adequate in quantity or quality for the purposes served by the supply'.[152] A landowner or water purveyor suffering pollution or diminution of water supply as a result of drilling, alteration, or operation of an oil or gas well may so notify the DEP and request that an investigation be conducted.[153] The Act identifies specific circumstances under which the DEP should presume that the well operator is responsible for pollution, as well as defences that can be used to rebut that presumption.[154] If the DEP finds that the contamination was caused by the well operator, it must issue a compliance order requiring that water supplies be replaced.

To ensure that remediation funds will be available in the event of an accident or spill, the Act also requires owners and operators to 'file with the department a bond covering the well and well site'.[155] The required size of the bond depends on the number of wells owned or operated by the permit applicant, as well as the total well bore length.[156] Owners and operators continue to be liable under the bond until the well has been properly plugged for a period of at least one year.[157]

The Act reserves the right of landowners and water purveyors claiming pollution or diminution of a water supply to seek other remedies at law or in equity.[158] Municipalities and counties may also bring actions in equity for an injunction to restraint a violation of this chapter or rules and regulations promulgated under the chapter to restrain a public nuisance or detriment to health.[159]

New York's proposed regulations do not contain a similar liability provision.

(e) Impact fees

Act 13 authorizes county and municipal governments to impose impact fees on unconventional gas wells that have been spud in the county.[160] These fees provide

149 58 Pa.C.S. § 3218.2(c)(1)–(6).

150 58 Pa.C.S. § 3220(a).

151 58 Pa.C.S. § 3220(a).

152 58 Pa.C.S. § 3218(a).

153 58 Pa.C.S. § 3218(b).

154 58 Pa.C.S. § 3218(c), §3218(d).

155 58 Pa.C.S. § 3225.

156 58 Pa.C.S. § 3225(a)(1).

157 58 Pa.C.S. § 3225(a)(3).

158 58 Pa.C.S. § 3218(f).

159 58 Pa.C.S. § 3254(b).

160 58 Pa.C.S. § 2302(a). A county may impose such a fee by passing an ordinance, and must also notify the Public Utilities Commission (PUC) and give public notice of its intent to adopt the ordinance. §2302(a.1). If the county fails to enact such an ordinance, then municipalities in the county 'may compel the imposition of an unconventional gas well fee on each unconventional gas well spud in the county by adopting resolutions'. §2302(a.4)(1). If such resolutions are enacted by municipalities representing at least 50% of the population of the county, the fee shall take effect.

Table 8.1 Calculation of impact fees on unconventional gas wells

Average annual price of natural gas (in US$)	Year 1	Year 2	Year 3	Year 4–10	Year 11–15
≤ 2.25	40,000	30,000	25,000	10,000	5,000
2.25–2.99	45,000	35,000	30,000	15,000	5,000
3.00–4.99	50,000	40,000	30,000	20,000	10,000
5.00–5.99	55,000	45,000	40,000	20,000	10,000
≥ 6.00	60,000	55,000	50,000	20,000	10,000

funding for a number of state and local programmes intended to mitigate the impacts of shale gas development. Impact fees are to be imposed 'on every producer and shall apply to unconventional gas wells... regardless of when spudding occurred'.[161] The Act provides specific instructions on how to calculate the unconventional gas well fee, which depend on the calendar year following the year in which the unconventional gas well is spud, as well as the annual average price of natural gas.[162] The initial calculation is shown in Table 8.1.[163]

All impact fees are collected and deposited into the Unconventional Gas Well Fund, and then allocated between the County Conservation Districts, the DEP, and the Public Utilities Commission (to cover the costs of administering the Act), and a variety of other state agencies, in accordance with guidelines set forth in §2314. US$750,000 of the fees collected and deposited for the fund is to be allocated to the Pennsylvania Emergency Management Agency for emergency response planning, training, and coordination related to natural gas production from unconventional wells.[164]

New York has not yet proposed an impact fee.

2. *New York*

(a) Well siting

The principal difference in New York on well siting is the existence of proposed 'no drill' areas. The New York environmental review process concluded that hydraulic fracturing 'is not compatible with the preservation' of watersheds that are used as a source for unfiltered drinking water.[165] Most municipal water supplies in the

§2302(a.4)(2). Counties and municipalities that fail to adopt fee ordinances or resolutions are prohibited from receiving funds under §2314(d), which specifies how impact fees are to be distributed to local and state entities. §2302(a.4)(5).

161 58 Pa.C.S. § 2302(b). 162 58 Pa.C.S. § 2302(b).

163 58 Pa.C.S. § 2302(c). The Act directs the Pennsylvania PUC to annually adjust these fee amounts to reflect any upward changes in the Consumer Price Index for all Urban Consumers for Pennsylvania, New Jersey, Delaware, and Maryland.

164 58 Pa.C.S. § 2314(c.1)(4).

165 RSGEIS (n 79) at 20. In addition to unfiltered drinking water supplies, New York will restrict hydraulic fracturing operations that are within 500 feet of any of the 18 primary aquifers in the state, although horizontal drilling under the aquifer likely will be authorized. RSGEIS at 20.

United States must be treated at filtration plants to ensure the water meets drinking water standards. New York City has long been able to use unfiltered water because the City has carefully protected its reservoir system from contaminants.[166] The New York City drinking water reservoir system that extends 125 miles north and west of the City provides 1.2 billion gallons of water a day[167] to 9 million[168] residents. If the City needed to install filtration, the cost is estimated to be over US $8 billion.[169] In light of the value of the New York City and other unfiltered water systems in the state, it is not surprising that the state has taken a precautionary approach by proposing to ban hydraulic fracturing operations in these watersheds. In addition, Forest Preserve land in the Adirondack and the Catskills Mountains are off limits for hydraulic fracturing. These areas are protected from all development by the New York State Constitution.[170]

New York's draft hydraulic fracturing regulation, like its Pennsylvania counterpart, also establishes setbacks from certain types of water resources such as unfiltered drinking water supply watersheds (4,000 feet), a primary aquifer (500 feet), a public drinking water supply well (2,000 feet), and private water wells (500 feet), among others.[171] In some cases, these setbacks are more stringent than those found in the Pennsylvania regulations.

E. Site disturbances and habitat fragmentation

1. Pennsylvania

Some of the provisions of Act 13 discussed here also provide for the protection of the state's other natural resources, including species and habitats. These provisions include the permitting guidelines for the DEP, required setback distances and locational restrictions, and the impact fees. Specifically, the permitting guidelines specify that the DEP must also consider the impact of the proposed wells on publicly owned parks, forests, game lands, and wildlife areas; national natural landmarks; habitats of rare and endangered flora and fauna and other critical communities; and historical and archaeological sites listed on the Federal or state list of historic places. The setback distances also protect habitat insofar as they impose additional siting restrictions on unconventional wells drilled near streams, springs and other bodies of water, wetlands, and floodplains.

[166] See Renee Cho, 'Maintaining the Superiority of NYC's Drinking Water', *Water Matters: News from the Columbia Water Center*, 29 July 2011, available at <http://blogs.ei.columbia.edu/2011/07/29/maintaining-the-superiority-of-nyc's-drinking-water/>.

[167] NYC Department of Environmental Protection, 'Drinking Water', available at <http://www.nyc.gov/html/dep/html/drinking_water/index.shtml>. See also, New York City's Water Supply System Map, available at <http://www.nyc.gov/html/dep/html/drinking_water/wsmaps_wide.shtml>.

[168] New York State Department of Health, 'Drinking Water Program: Facts and Figures', available at <http://www.health.ny.gov/environmental/water/drinking/facts_figures.htm>.

[169] Cho (n 166). [170] RSGEIS (n 79) at 2. [171] Draft New York Rules § 750-3.3(a).

Finally, a significant portion of the impact fees collected under Act 13 are allocated to County Conservation districts for municipal infrastructural projects, as well as environmental projects.[172] If funds remain after the initial allocation, a certain percentage of those funds is also allocated to the Environmental Stewardship Fund, which provides grants for projects relating to land conservation and species protection.[173] Act 13 further requires that money in the Oil and Gas Lease Fund (which is funded by royalties from the leasing of oil and gas on state lands) is to be allocated to the Environmental Stewardship Fund as follows: US$20,000,000 in 2013, and US$35,000,000 in each year thereafter.[174]

Act 13 also imposes specific requirements for well site restoration. As a general rule, '[e]ach oil or gas well owner or operator shall restore the land surface within the area disturbed in siting, drilling, completing, and producing the well'.[175] The owner or operator must prepare an erosion and sedimentation control plan in accordance with the Clean Streams Law, which sets forth the control measures that will be implemented during and after all 'earthmoving or soil disturbing activities', including siting, drilling, completing, producing, and plugging the well.[176] The Act also establishes the manner and timeframe in which certain restoration activities must occur.[177] For example, the owner or operator must 'remove or fill all pits used to contain produced fluids or industrial wastes and remove all drilling supplies and equipment not needed for production' within nine months of the completion of drilling activities.[178]

2. New York

New York's 'no drill' areas, including protected areas in the Adirondack and Catskills Mountains, afford some protection for species and habitats. New York's draft regulations also include site preparation requirements dealing with site soil removal,[179] best management practices for dealing with invasive species,[180] and site reclamation.[181]

[172] US$250,000 of the fees are allocated to Country Conservation districts in 2011, US$500,000 in 2012, and US$750,000 each year thereafter. 58 Pa C S § 2314(c).

[173] Specifically, 10% of the remaining 40% of funds (after allocation) are to be set aside for the Environmental Stewardship Fund. 58 Pa.C.S. § 2315(a.1)(2).

[174] 58 Pa.C.S. § 2505(b)(1).

[175] 58 Pa.C.S. § 3216(a).

[176] 58 Pa.C.S. § 3216(b).

[177] 58 Pa.C.S. § 3216(c)–(d).

[178] 58 Pa.C.S. § 3216(c). There is a limited exception to this requirement: 'Drilling supplies and equipment not needed for production may be stored on the well site if express written consent of the surface landowner is obtained.'

[179] Draft New York Rules § 560.6 (a).

[180] Draft New York Rules § 560.3(a)(16).

[181] Draft New York Rules § 560.3(a)(17).

F. Methane releases

1. Pennsylvania

Act 13 does not impose any substantive requirements on well operators or owners to mitigate methane releases. However, it does require owners and operators to submit a source report to the department, which identifies and quantifies actual air contaminant emissions from any air contamination source.[182]

2. New York

The RSGEIS proposes that owners and operators prepare a GHG emission impacts plan to reduce emissions. The plan would be expected to include:

- a list of best management practices for GHG emissions at a well site;
- use of US EPA's 'Natural Gas Star';[183]
- use emissions that provide for recovery of methane instead of flaring whenever a gas line is available;
- a commitment that the operator will provide the NY DEC with a copy of the GHG report required by US EPA.[184]

The New York proposed rule provides that no gas from any well shall be permitted to escape into the air, except in a few very specific circumstances.[185]

New York anticipates that air pollution permits will be required for typical well pad configurations limiting nitrogen oxide and fine particulate emissions.[186]

3. CSSD

Beginning in January 2014, the performance standards require an operator to direct all pipeline-quality gas produced during well construction to a pipeline for sales. Any other captured gas must be flared.[187] Flaring devices must achieve a 98%

[182] Draft New York Rules § 3227(a). Such reports must be submitted to the department by 1 March for emissions during the preceding calendar year unless a different reporting schedule is required by the Clean Air Act. Draft New York Rules § 3227(d).

[183] See US EPA, 'Natural Gas Star Program', available at <http://www.epa.gov/gasstar/index.html>.

[184] RSGEIS (n 79) at 24. Information on US EPA's greenhouse Gas Reporting Rule can be found at US Environmental Protection Agency, 'Greenhouse Gas Reporting Program', available at <http://www.epa.gov/ghgreporting/>.

[185] Draft New York Rules § 556.1(b). One commentator has suggested that the methane emissions rule proposed by the NY DEC is insufficiently protective and has suggested more specific requirements. Ingraffea (n 94) at 7.

[186] RSGEIS (n 79) at 15–16.

[187] CSSD Performance Standard 9, available at <http://037186e.netsolhost.com/site/wp-content/uploads/2013/03/CSSD-Performance-Standards-3-13R.pdf>.

destruction rate.[188] Flaring is limited to 14 days for development wells and 30 days for exploratory or extension wells.[189]

G. Air pollution

1. Pennsylvania

Act 13 requires owners and operators to submit to the DEP a 'source report identifying and quantifying actual air contaminant emission from any air contamination source', including nitrogen oxides and VOCs.[190] The specific content and schedule for such reports is to be determined by DEP regulations. Act 13 does not contain any substantive restrictions or mitigation requirements for air emissions, but it does reserve the right of any person to bring a judicial action to abate a public or private nuisance caused by air or water pollution.[191]

2. CSSD

The performance standards focus a great deal on air pollution issues associated with drilling operations. They require that an increasing percentage of stationary diesel engines meet advanced US EPA standards so that 95% of the engines meet the standards within four years. All such engines must use low sulphur diesel fuel.[192] The standards support the conversion of diesel pumping engines to dual-fuel, electricity, or natural gas.[193]

The performance standards also place limits on emissions from compressor engines,[194] require that storage tanks install controls that reduce volatile organic emission by at least 95%,[195] and mandate that within one year 80% of the transport trucks meet advanced EPA engine emission standards and within three years 95% of the trucks meet the EPA standard.[196]

H. Public engagement and the role of local governments

1. Pennsylvania

Act 13 contains a number of provisions which are intended to ensure that affected landowners and local governments will have notice of proposed well sites and that

188 CSSD Performance Standard 10, available at <http://037186e.netsolhost.com/site/wp-content/uploads/2013/03/CSSD-Performance-Standards-3-13R.pdf>.

189 CSSD Performance Standard 10 (n 188).

190 58 Pa.C.S. § 3227(a),(c).

191 58 Pa.C.S. § 3257.

192 CSSD Performance Standard 11, available at <http://037186e.netsolhost.com/site/wp-content/uploads/2013/03/CSSD-Performance-Standards-3-13R.pdf>.

193 CSSD Performance Standard 11 (n 192).

194 CSSD Performance Standard 12, available at <http://037186e.netsolhost.com/site/wp-content/uploads/2013/03/CSSD-Performance-Standards-3-13R.pdf>.

195 CSSD Performance Standard 13, available at <http://037186e.netsolhost.com/site/wp-content/uploads/2013/03/CSSD-Performance-Standards-3-13R.pdf>.

196 CSSD Performance Standard 15, available at <http://037186e.netsolhost.com/site/wp-content/uploads/2013/03/CSSD-Performance-Standards-3-13R.pdf>.

the public will have access to information about unconventional wells in the state. That said, the Act also pre-empts local authority to regulate shale gas development—a decision which has outraged many municipalities in the state.

(a) Participation in the permitting process

The Act requires unconventional well permit applicants to provide notice of their application and to forward a copy of the proposed plat to a number of different parties, including, *inter alia*, the surface landowner, the municipality in which the unconventional well is located, each municipality within 3,000 feet of the proposed wellbore, and all surface landowners or water purveyors whose water supplies are within 3,000 feet of the proposed wellbore. A plat is a map which shows the plot of land and actual or planned features, such as streets and building lots.[197]

The Act also specifies the circumstances in which third parties may file objections to permits. For example, if a well is to be located on a tract whose surface is owned by someone other than the operator, the surface landowner may file objections to the issuance of a permit if the well location violates the Act's requirements, or if the information in the application is untrue in any material respect.[198] The surface landowner must file these objections within 15 days of the receipt of the plat under s 3211(b).[199]

During the permitting process, the local municipality may also submit written comments 'describing local conditions or circumstances which the municipality has determined should be considered by the department in rendering its determination on the unconventional well permit'.[200] Such comments must be submitted to the department within 15 days of the receipt by the municipality of the plat under s 3211(b). Storage operators that are located within 3,000 feet of the proposed unconventional vertical wellbore may also submit written comments of the same nature as those that municipalities may submit, and within the same timeframe.[201] Although the DEP is required to review these comments, 'no municipality or storage operator shall have a right of appeal or other form of review from the department's decision'.[202]

(b) Record-keeping requirements

By 1 April of each calendar year, unconventional gas producers must submit payment of their impact fees and must also provide a report with information on: (1) the number of spud unconventional gas wells of a producer in each municipality within each county that has imposed a fee under this chapter; and (2) the date that each of those wells was spud or ceased the production of natural gas.[203] In addition, each unconventional well operator must file with the department a 'semi-annual report specifying the amount of production on the most well-specific basis available', as well as the status of each well, except that in subsequent years, only changes

[197] 58 Pa.C.S. § 3211(b)(2).
[198] 58 Pa.C.S. § 3212.
[199] 58 Pa.C.S. § 3212.
[200] 58 Pa.C.S. § 3212.1(a).
[201] 58 Pa.C.S. § 3212.1(b).
[202] 58 Pa.C.S. § 3215(d).
[203] 58 Pa.C.S. § 2303(b)(1),(2).

in status must be reported.[204] The information contained in these reports is publicly available on the DEP's website.[205]

(c) Local pre-emption

The most controversial aspect of Act 13 is the fact that it expressly supersedes 'all local ordinances purporting to regulate oil and gas operations' that are regulated under Chapter 32 of Title 58 (relating to oil and gas development), with the exception of ordinances adopted pursuant to the Municipalities Planning Code (MPC) and the Flood Plain Management Act.[206] In addition, the Act prohibits ordinances adopted pursuant to the MPC and the Flood Plain Management Act from imposing 'conditions, requirements or limitations on the same features of oil and gas operations regulated by Chapter 32 or that accomplish the same purposes as set forth in Chapter 32'.

In addition to those restrictions, the Act requires that 'all local ordinances regulating oil and gas operations shall allow for the reasonable development of oil and gas resources'.[207] As defined in the Act, this means that local governments:

- must authorize oil and gas operations, other than activities at impoundment areas, compressor stations, and processing plants, as a permitted use in *all zoning districts*;
- must authorize impoundment areas used for oil and gas operations as a permitted use in all zoning districts, 'provided that the edge of any impoundment areas shall not be located closer than 300 feet from an existing building';
- must authorize natural gas compressor stations as a permitted use in agricultural and industrial zoning districts, if the natural gas compressor meets specified standards;
- may not increase setback distances set forth in the Act;
- may not impose limits or conditions on subterranean operations or hours of operation of compressor stations and processing plants or hours of operation for the drilling of oil and gas wells or the assembly and disassembly of drilling rigs;
- may not impose restrictions or conditions on the construction of oil and gas operations that are more stringent than those imposed on construction activities for other industrial uses within the geographic boundaries of the local government;
- may not impose restrictions or conditions on the heights of structures, screening and fencing, lighting, or noise relating to permanent oil and gas operations

204 58 Pa.C.S. § 3222(a.1). § 3222(b) and (b.1) also contain additional details on reporting requirements, including record-keeping requirements, instructions on how to convey information to the department, and the substantive requirements for reports.

205 See Pennsylvania Department of Environmental Protection (DEP) Oil and Gas Reports, available at <http://www.portal.state.pa.us/portal/server.pt/community/oil_and_gas_reports/20297>.

206 58 Pa.C.S. § 3302.

207 58 Pa.C.S. § 3304(a).

that are more stringent than those imposed on other industrial uses or other land development within the particular zoning district;

- must have a review period for permitting uses that does not exceed 30 days for complete submissions or that does not exceed 120 days for conditional uses.[208]

Notwithstanding these requirements, local ordinances 'may prohibit, or permit only as a conditional use, wells or well sites . . . within a residential district if the well site cannot be placed so that the wellhead is at least 500 feet from any existing building'.[209]

2. New York

The proposed New York rules provide for public and local government engagement in several ways. In addition to the requirements for disclosing hydraulic fracturing chemicals noted in section C, the rules also require the NY DEC to notify local governments about drilling permit requests located within the local government's territory.[210] The NY DEC is also required to notify Indian Nations of any well permit application located within one mile of their reservation.[211] Public notice of well permit applications are required to be posted on a public website allowing comments on local and site-specific issues that were not covered in the GEIS.[212]

New York law does not pre-empt local bans of hydraulic fracturing. More than 100 municipalities in New York have imposed either hydraulic fracturing moratoria or bans. Companies interested in developing hydraulic fracturing operations in New York have challenged these local bans and moratoria. The first of these challenges has just reached the New York Supreme Court Appellate Division.

VI. Conclusion

The approaches of New York and Pennsylvania illustrate some of the major developments in state regulation of shale gas development. Pennsylvania's liability provisions and New York's restricted areas provide examples of regulatory tools that can be used to mitigate the risk associated with hydraulic fracturing and horizontal drilling.

Significant questions still remain about the best practices for regulating hydraulic fracturing and horizontal drilling. For example, New York and Pennsylvania have taken a dramatically different approach with respect to the pre-emption of local bans and restrictions on hydraulic fracturing. To the extent that state regulations differ on important issues such as local control over hydraulic fracturing, setback requirements, and air pollution requirements, these differences will provide an

[208] 58 Pa.C.S. § 3304(b)(1)–(11).
[209] 58 Pa.C.S. § 3304(b)(5.1).
[210] Draft New York Rules § 560.3(e)(3).
[211] Draft New York Rules § 560.3(e)(4).
[212] Draft New York Rules § 560.3(e)(5).

opportunity for experimentation and thus may prove useful for other states that are adopting a wait-and-see approach.

The emergence of the CSSD consensus standards is also a promising development in what had become a growing divide between hydraulic fracturing proponents and hydraulic fracturing opponents. The dialogue demonstrates both the importance of natural gas in displacing coal-fired electricity generation and the importance of maintaining a positive corporate sustainability profile.

Finally, as indicated by both the research being undertaken at US EPA and the incorporation of EPA regulations in the CSSD Performance Standards, federal law is likely to play an increasing role in the management of hydraulic fracturing operations.

9

Sleeping with the Enemy: The Legal Landscape of Unconventional Gas Development in Argentina

Lila K. Barrera-Hernández

I. Introduction

Argentina's oil and gas sector has been struggling for a decade to survive a lack of investment, as well as unpredictable government action such as the imposition of price caps and swift nationalization. The news about the country's formidable unconventional reserves—Argentina's technically recoverable shale gas reserves are the third largest in the world after the United States and China[1]—has stirred a lot of interest in the private sector, which is looking again at investing in Argentina. On the other hand, local opposition to development of extractives is growing at unprecedented levels. The question addressed in this chapter is whether the country's legal landscape is ready to facilitate the sector's revitalization while also tackling the challenges inherent in unconventional resource development and the use of controversial new technologies.

As discussed in the following sections, creating a clear and investment-friendly legal and regulatory environment implies tackling complex jurisdictional questions touching upon every single aspect of natural resource development, including investment conditions, water management, and environmental protection. The legal and regulatory framework in place must be able to instil confidence amongst the investment community, as well as amongst an increasingly vocal public worried about environmental and social impacts.

II. Energy is politics

Energy self-sufficiency to support economic development and adequate standards of living is a desirable policy goal; so is widespread access to energy. The two do not

[1] US Energy Information Administration, 'Country Analysis Briefs, Argentina', 24 July 2012, available at <http://www.eia.gov/countries/cab.cfm?fips=AR>.

necessarily go hand in hand. That is patently obvious when looking at the landscape of the energy sector in Argentina today, and is particularly true in relation to natural gas, which supplies over 50% of the country's primary energy needs. While local production of natural gas has dwindled steadily, forcing the government to resort to imports at a huge cost, demand has grown unbridled due to the government's insistence on securing access to cheap energy for its constituents through price caps.

Clearly, in Argentina today, access trumps self-sufficiency. Artificially low prices downstream, combined with export restrictions and increasingly high export duties, have resulted in over 4% yearly decreases in gas production since 2006. In addition, until the recent discovery of huge unconventional reserves, Argentina's gas horizon only extended up to 2023, as proven conventional gas reserves have more than halved since 2000, including a 7% decline in 2011 alone.[2] In contrast to the bleak supply scenario, benefiting from cheap energy inputs, the country's industry experienced steady growth,[3] plunging Argentina into the first of several gas crises in 2004. To avoid frequent blackouts and rationing, the energy deficit has been met with imported substitutes that are heavily subsidized by the government.[4] But sustained levels of growth demand a long-term solution to securing energy supplies. The recent discovery of massive reserves of unconventional gas has the potential to fundamentally alter the current scenario of energy supply and demand in Argentina.[5] For the government, the discovery came at a time when the growing prices of imported substitutes may justify an injection of capital into the upstream at home.[6] However, developing unconventional resources is significantly more costly than conventional production,[7] already stagnant due to lack of investment. Developing unconventional gas also faces other obstacles that relate to its environmental impact and a significant increase in water demand compared to conventional production.

[2] The Neuquén basin surpassed the national average at 58%. See Information Handling Services, 'Proven Hydrocarbon Reserves Continue to Decline in Argentina', 17 August 2012, available at <http://www.ihs.com/products/global-insight/industry-economic-report.aspx?id=1065970674>.

[3] The World Bank, 'Argentina Overview', undated, available at <http://www.worldbank.org/en/country/argentina/overview>.

[4] A. Martinez, 'Los recursos no convencionales y la política petrolera' November 2012, Revista del Instituto Argentino de Energía 'General Mosconi'—Proyecto Energético, Año 28, Numero 96, 5, available at <http://sitio.iae.org.ar/minisites/proyectoe/revistas/Proyecto_Energetico96_IAEMOSCONI.pdf>; J. Webber, 'YPF: So What's the Game Plan?', 5 June 2012, available at <http://blogs.ft.com/beyond-brics/2012/06/05/ypf-so-whats-the-game-plan/#axzz2KeTicnUy>.

[5] C. Cain McGowen, AAPG Explorer, 'Argentina Vaca Muerta Draws GTW Spotlight', January 2013, available at <http://www.aapg.org/explorer/2013/01jan/regsec0113.cfm>.

[6] J. Hidalgo Pallares, 'Suben el precio para el gas en boca de pozo', 29 November 2012, available at <http://www.lanacion.com.ar/1531518-suben-el-precio-para-el-gas-en-boca-de-pozo>.

[7] At US$8–15 million per well, with each pilot consisting of a cluster of 15–20 wells. See Rionegro.com, 'El desafio de movilizar Vaca Muerta', 29 October 2012, available at <http://www.rionegro.com.ar/diario/el-desafio-de-movilizar-vaca-muerta-995051-9532-nota.aspx>.

III. The money trail: nationalization of Yacimientos Petrolíferos Fiscales

In 2012, faced with recurrent energy crises and the catastrophic impact of the country's economic policy (in place since 2001) on the energy sector, Argentina's politicians sought to pin the blame entirely on the private sector and the neoliberal economic model. There was no better target than Yacimientos Petrolíferos Fiscales (YPF), the former national oil and gas company privatized at the peak of the neoliberal wave that swept the country in the 1990s, and owned by the Spanish company Repsol. At the time (2012), YPF-Repsol was the largest oil producer in the country and accounted for 20% of total gas production, a close second after Total.[8] Its nationalization would give the government control over a significant share of the sector.

To achieve YPF's nationalization, the Fernández Kirchner administration promoted Law 26,741 on Hydrocarbon Sovereignty. The law, proclaimed in May 2012, declares hydrocarbon self-sufficiency, as well as all stages of hydrocarbon development (from exploration to commercialization) of public interest and national priority (Article 1). With self-sufficiency as its objective, it goes on to declare of public interest and subject to expropriation in accordance with Article 17 of the Constitution and under the terms of Law 21,499 on legal expropriation, 51% of YPF's patrimony in the hands of Repsol (Articles 7 and 12).[9] At the same time that Law 26,741 was presented to the legislature, the Executive issued a special 'urgent' decree appointing a high-level team of government officials to intervene directly in the company and conduct an investigation into its practices, effectively taking over the company about a month prior to the passage of the nationalization law (26,741).[10] According to the government, the measure was necessary to uncover the evidence that would justify the nationalization. Interestingly, the intervention's report, known as the Mosconi Report, issued in June 2012, does not record any findings of illegal behaviour on the part of the company.[11] Rather, it tells the story of how the company, faced with decreasing profitability due to the government's policies of price controls and increasing export duties, decided to direct its exploration and production investments to other markets where the ability

[8] US Energy Information Administration, Argentina, Country Analysis Brief, 24 July 2012, available at <http://www.eia.gov/countries/cab.cfm?fips=AR>.

[9] Ley 26,741, Declárase de Interés Público Nacional el logro del autoabastecimiento de hidrocarburos. Créase el Consejo Federal de Hidrocarburos. Declárase de Utilidad Pública y sujeto a expropiación el 51% del patrimonio de YPF S.A. y Repsol YPF Gas S.A., Boletín Oficial, 4 May 2012; also available at <http://infoleg.gov.ar/infolegInternet/anexos/195000-199999/196894/norma.htm>.

[10] Two separate decrees cover both oil and gas subsidiaries: Decreto Nacional 530/2012, Decreto de Necesidad y Urgencia que Dispone la Intervención Transitoria de Yacimientos Petrolíferos Fiscales, Buenos Aires, Boletín Oficial, 16 April 2012; and, Decreto Nacional 557/2012 Decreto de Necesidad y Urgencia que Amplia los Alcances del Decreto 530/12 sobre Intervención Transitoria de Yacimientos Petrolíferos Fiscales a Repsol YPF Gas S.A, Boletín Oficial, 19 April 2012.

[11] It does include references to environmental harm, but they are not tied to sanctions or other punitive or remedial action on the side of the authorities.

to trade freely at international prices signified a better return on its investments. Nevertheless, the Report's conclusion echoes the Executive's words in the message that accompanied the presentation of the nationalization bill to the legislature, asserting that: 'the group's [Repsol-YPF] international expansion was based, fundamentally, on the predatory policies implemented in Argentina by Repsol'.[12] As a result, the nationalization was considered to be fully justified and YPF continued to be under the direct control of the government. Having not yet received fair compensation as required by the Constitution as a prerequisite for a lawful expropriation,[13] Repsol is suing the federal government for unlawful confiscation[14] and has launched a complaint with the World Bank's International Centre for Settlement of Investment Disputes (ICSID).[15]

Meanwhile, as a result of YPF's nationalization, the government has gained control over a significant portion (12,000 out of 30,000 km^2) of what is believed to be the country's richest shale gas area, known as Vaca Muerta, in the Neuquén basin. Given that natural resources are vested in the provinces, the nationalization gives the Federal government control over resources that it would not otherwise have. The potential value of the Vaca Muerta concession is a perfect instrument to leverage the government's position when it comes to attracting fresh investments from industry.[16] In fact, acting as *de facto* policy-maker, YPF's new government-appointed management immediately set out to design a strategy to attract investment to the hydrocarbon sector, particularly in the Vaca Muerta area. The 2013–2017 strategy, announced at the end of August 2012, requires investment of US$37,200 million over the five-year period, with US$6,500 million going to gas development. It also contemplates granting a 50% share of net production to potential partners in shale development.[17]

To further incentivize investors, the government continues to signal its willingness to allow gas prices to inch closer to international market prices. Thus, while 2008 saw the launching of the Gas Plus incentives programme which allowed price

[12] Informe Mosconi, available at <http://www.mecon.gov.ar/informe-mosconi/>, at 31 [translation by the author].

[13] J. Lapeña, 'Una brevísima reflexión a seis meses de la estatización de YPF' November 2012, Revista del Instituto Argentino de Energía 'General Mosconi'—Proyecto Energético, Año 28, Número 96 at 4. This case is in progress as at the time of writing, but it has been reported (on 26 November 2013) that Argentina has reached an agreement in principle with Spain regarding compensation for Repsol's expropriation.

[14] Note that only Repsol's shares were targeted for expropriation. M. Cantón, iEco, 'Repsol inicia su primer juicio por YPF en el país', 8 June 2012, available at <http://www.ieco.clarin.com/economia/Repsol-inicia-primer-juicio-YPF_0_715128533.html>.

[15] Repsol, SA and Repsol Butano, SA v Argentine Republic (ICSID Case No ARB/12/38) available at <http://icsid.worldbank.org/ICSID/FrontServlet>. The case is pending the constitution of an arbitral panel. See also Reuters, 'World Bank Tribunal Accepts Repsol Complaint over YPF Takeover', December 21, 2012, available at <http://uk.reuters.com/article/2012/12/21/argentina-repsol-idUKL1E8NL1PR20121221>.

[16] See section VII of this chapter, on the YPF-Chevron deal.

[17] YPF, Plan Estratégico, available at <http://www.enerclub.com.ar/upload/archivos/YPF_PLAN_ESTRATEGICO_127.pdf>; <http://www.mercadoelectriconet.com.ar/web/index.php?option=com_content&view=article&id=400:ypf-estrategia-de-gestion-2013-2017&catid=1:latest-news>; <http://www.ypf.argentina.ar/dia-por-dia/C88-ypf-plan-estrategico-2012-2017.php>.

increases for the case of new or unconventional production,[18] recent reports reveal that the government signed a private agreement with YPF to buy gas for US$7.50 per million Btu, about half the price of Bolivian imports, but three times the average well-head price of conventional gas. According to the announcement made by Fernández Kirchner, Argentina's President, at the Industrial Union's (UIA) meeting in November 2012, the same offer may be extended to other suppliers for any new production resulting from new injections of capital.[19]

IV. A spanner in the works: Decree 1,277 and Law 20,680 on domestic supply of goods and services

Notwithstanding the appeal of Argentina's unconventional gas potential and the promise of better returns due to increasing price flexibility, the legal framework governing upstream activities has undergone a radical transformation; the changes introduced might have investors thinking twice about doing business in Argentina. Indeed, Decree 1,277 of July 2012[20] effectively dismantled the deregulated framework governing upstream operations to make way for implementation of a *National Plan on Hydrocarbon Investment* (the Investment Plan). It does so, amongst other things, by repealing important provisions of the 1990s liberalization regulations: Decree 1,212/89, Decree 1,055/89, and Decree 1,589/89. The repealed sections provided for: (i) the free disposition of hydrocarbons; (ii) the freedom to set prices, allocate volumes, and transfer values and/or incentives of the different stages of the activity; (iii) the freedom to export and import hydrocarbons, without prior approval and free of duties; and (iv) the freedom to dispose of foreign currency which enabled the producers not to repatriate up to 70% of foreign currency proceeds of hydrocarbon exports.

Decree 1,277 solidly places hydrocarbons in the 'strategic goods' category, understood as a category in which management decisions prioritize political concerns over market signals.[21] Surprisingly, the single most important goal of Argentina's energy policy, as asserted in the Decree, is to attract new players to the hydrocarbon market. Indeed, it declares the increase in, and maximization of, investments in oil and gas to be the strategic axes of the forthcoming Investment Plan.

[18] Its mirror programme for oil has been suspended. See further <http://cyt-ar.com.ar/cyt-ar/index.php/Gas_Plus>; Resolución 24/2008, 6 March 2008, available at <http://www.infoleg.gov.ar/infolegInternet/anexos/135000-139999/138628/texact.htm>; <http://www.ieco.clarin.com/economia/Preven-importaciones-record-gas-licuado_0_821917819.html>.

[19] Pallares (n 6); iEco, 'Aumentan el precio del gas para estimular la exploración', 29 November 2012, available at <http://www.ieco.clarin.com/economia/Aumentan-precio-gas-estimular-exploracion_0_819518093.html>.

[20] Decreto 1277/2012, Apruébase la reglamentación de la Ley 26.741, available at <http://www.boletinoficial.gov.ar/Inicio/index.castle?s=1&fea=27/07/2012>.

[21] J. Rigane, 'Análisis del Decreto 1277/12 de Soberanía Hidrocarburífera' August 19, 2012, available at <http://adnrionegro.com.ar/2012/08/analisis-del-decreto-127712-de-soberania-hidrocarburifera-●-jose-rigane/>.

Under the Decree, the Investment Plan is to be designed and implemented by a new federal agency, the Comisión de Planificación y Coordinación Estratégica del Plan Nacional de Inversiones Hidrocarburíferas, housed within the Ministry of Economy and Finances (hereafter the 'Planning Commission' or 'PC'). The Planning Commission is given broad powers to oversee the sector, including the power to review, evaluate, and enforce companies' *mandatory annual investment plans* to ensure that they align with the targets set in the Investment Plan. Moreover, the PC has power to periodically publish reference prices for the sale of hydrocarbons on the basis of what it determines to be reasonable production costs and returns.

Decree 1,277 has come under fire from numerous critics, who point out that:

- its underlying ideology is at odds with a market economy and the sector's private nature, which is made subject to undue government intervention;[22]
- it is unconstitutional because, amongst other reasons, it encroaches on provincial jurisdiction and is contrary to Law 26,197 regulating the 'provincialization' of hydrocarbon resources;[23] and
- the Planning Commission is redundant, as its mandate could be carried out by the existing Energy Secretariat, also within the same Ministry, but presided over by an official with a background and expertise in the energy sector, and therefore better positioned for the job.

While the jury may still be out on whether the Argentine government is making a full shift towards a planned economy model for the energy sector, the federal assault on provincial jurisdiction seems blatant. Article 124 of the amended 1994 Constitution, in force today, vests natural resources, including hydrocarbons, in the provinces, while general law- and policy-making powers remain in federal hands.[24] The federal government's law-making powers are derived from the national legislature's power under the Constitution to issue laws of general application and, specifically, the Mining Code, which includes hydrocarbons within its scope (Article 75, ss12 and 126).[25]

Notwithstanding the unambiguous constitutional mandate contained in article 124 of 1994, its implementation took over a decade to complete and the provinces had no effective control of the resources until the passage of Law 26,197 in 2007.

[22] J. Lapeña, 'El Decreto PE N° 1277, Reglamentación de la Ley 26741' (undated) Revista del Instituto Argentino de Energía 'General Mosconi' available at <http://web.iae.org.ar>.

[23] 'Gil Lavedra denunció que el Decreto 1277 viola la Ley Corta de Hidrocarburos', 1 August 2012, available at <http://www.elextremosur.com/archives/4251>.

[24] *Constitución de 1994*, available at <http://pdba.georgetown.edu/Constitutions/Argentina/argen94_e.html#title2>; Cassagne Abogados, 'La Propiedad de los Yacimientos de Hidrocarburos. Su Relación con las Potestades Nacionales y Provinciales', available at <http://www.cassagne.com.ar/publicaciones/Cassagne/La%20propiedad%20de%20los%20yacimientos%20de%20hidrocarburos-uv.pdf>; Corte Suprema de Justicia de la Nación, Fallos 301:341.

[25] J. A. Zapata, 'Framework Paper. Oil and Gas in Argentina' paper delivered at World Bank, 3 and 4 March 2010, available at <http://siteresources.worldbank.org/EXTOGMC/Resources/336929-1266445624608/Argentina_Final.pdf>.

Known as the Short Law, Law 26,197 effected the transfer to the provinces of all hydrocarbon resources formerly under federal control together with any pre-existing legal relations arising therefrom.[26] However, despite the transfer, the coexistence of provincial ownership with federal law- and policy-making power, and a deeply ingrained centralist tradition, has been the source of much uncertainty regarding the extent of each jurisdiction's powers, including the power to collect royalties, taxes, and other payments.[27]

The lack of clear-cut jurisdictional criteria provides fertile grounds for continued federal advances on provincial turf, and current Supreme Court reasoning seems to encourage those tendencies. Indeed, according to the Court's latest position, the combination of federal jurisdiction to decide on hydrocarbon policy and issue laws of general application, and the public interest nature of the sector, justifies far-reaching federal jurisdiction.[28] Therefore, it is not surprising to find that, emboldened by the Supreme Court's dicta, Decree 1,277 transfers virtually all decision-making vis à vis the developers and their duties to the federal PC. Under the new regime, the federal authorities decide on who invests, how, and when, while the provinces are limited to collecting their share of the proceeds and acting as the federal authorities' enforcement agents. As in the past, this could lead to protracted wrangling between the provinces owning the resources and their federal managers, while industry is caught in between.[29]

Adding to the murkiness of this scenario is the fact that the all-powerful PC is headed by the Vice-Minister of Economy, A. Kicillof,[30] who is also a member of YPF's newly appointed Board of Directors. As a result, the Vice-Minister and, through him, YPF, have access to all the information that hydrocarbon companies must disclose to the PC in order to comply with the requirements of Decree 1,277 and the Investment Plan. That information includes all the technical, quantitative, and financial information that may be necessary to assess the sector's progress, as well as to evaluate a company's annual investment plan and its ability to meet the requirements of the national blueprint issued by the PC. The clear conflict of interests is contrary to the ethical rules applicable to the public administration under Law 25,188[31] and has already been denounced by Shell, which lodged a formal administrative complaint with the federal authorities.[32]

26 L. Barrera-Hernández, 'Are We There Yet? The Long Road to South America's Energy Future' in *Beyond the Carbon Economy* (Zillman et al, eds, 2008) 133.

27 See, e.g., Corte Suprema, Caso 328:1580, Tecpetrol s/inhibitoria (2005) (on provincial right to collect royalties); PAE Inhibitoria (en Neuquén contra PAE) Dictamen del 2005; and Neuquén contra Chevron (2008) (on compensation to surface owners when the owner is the province).

28 J. Lahitou, 'Definiendo la frontera hidrocarburífera entre Provincias & Nación' (2010) available at <http://todosobrelacorte.com>.

29 See n 27.

30 Resolución 1/2012, Comisión de Planificación y Coordinación Estratégica del Plan Nacional de Inversiones Hidrocarburíferas, Boletín Oficial, 3 September 2012, available at <http://www.diputados.gov.ar/leyes/buscarNormasXNumLey.jsp?id_norma=59140>.

31 Ley de Etica de la Función Pública, available at <http://www.infoleg.gov.ar/infolegInternet/anexos/60000-64999/60847/texact.htm>.

32 Energía del Sur, 'Eran previsibles los conflictos por el rol de 'doble agente' de Kicillof', 17 October 2012, available at <http://energiadelsur.blogspot.com/2012/10/eran-previsibles-los-conflictos-por-el.html>;

From an investor's point of view, and even though provincial authorities have been quick to announce that they do not consider that Decree 1,277 unconstitutionally trumps their powers,[33] the Decree is certainly not a propitious piece of regulation.[34]

Added to a federal government intent on micromanaging the sector, and the uncertainty resulting from potential clashes with provincial authorities, is the reinstatement of a 1974 law dedicated to ensuring adequate levels of domestic supply of goods and services: Law 20,680.

Law 20,680 on Domestic Supply (Ley de Abastecimiento)[35] applies to all goods and services that may serve to satisfy the population's general and common needs, either directly or indirectly. The original purpose of the law issued in 1974 was to secure supplies of essential household goods and services (such as transportation) through direct government intervention in their production and sale in times of critical shortage. The law authorized the Executive, amongst other things, to: fix or cap prices; regulate sales, intermediation, distribution, and production; force production, industrialization, commercialization, or distribution of goods and provision of services; ban or restrict exports; intervene temporarily and directly, *inter alia*, in mining activities (including hydrocarbons) and industrial establishments; and demand access to all accounting and administrative documentation, as well as undertake audits. The law contemplates applying stiff penalties, including up to four years, imprisonment to anyone who unduly raises prices; hoards raw materials or products; destroys goods or products; or obstructs the provision of services; denies or restricts the sale of goods or provision of services without reasonable justification; or unduly reduces or does not increase normal production after receiving an order to that effect; diverts supplies from one area to another; refuses to sell those goods that are subject to fixed or controlled pricing and offers replacement goods of a different quality and price; and generally fails to abide by the orders issued under Law 20,680. It also declares of public interest and subject to immediate expropriation all property that may be necessary to prevent supply shortages, hoarding, and any speculative dealings concerning essential goods and

'Alfonso Prat Gay denuncia a Kicillof', 8 September 2012, available at <http://www.losandes.com.ar/notas/2012/9/8/alfonso-prat-denuncia-kicillof-665846.asp>.

[33] The declarations were issued in exchange for the quick implementation of the provinces' participation in YPF through signature of the Federal Agreement on Hydrocarbons. Energía del Sur, 'Acuerdo federal para la implementación de la Ley 26,741', 16 August 2012, available at <http://energiadelsur.blogspot.com/2012/08/documentoacuerdo-federal-para-la.html>; Petrolnews.com, 'La Ofephi firmó el Pacto Federal Hidrocarburífero' (undated), available at <http://petrolnews.net/noticia.php?ID=wcakmqhd&r=18931>; 'Gobierno neuquino afirma que decreto 1277 'no avasalla derechos de las provincias'' August 8, 2012, available at <http://noticias.terra.com.ar/gobierno-neuquino-afirma-que-decreto-1277-no-avasalla-derechos-de-las-provincias,92869a947c709310VgnVCM3000009acceb0aRCRD.html>.

[34] J. Webber, 'Argentina's Unconventional Conundrum' (undated) available at <http://www.newsbase.com/newsbasearchive/cotw.jsp?pub=latamoil&issue=426>; I. Mount, 'Argentina's New Oil Rules "Worse than Nationalization"', 30 July 2012, available at <http://blogs.ft.com/beyond-brics/2012/07/30/argentinas-new-oil-rules-worse-than-nationalisation/#axzz2KeTicnUy>.

[35] Ley 20,680, Boletín Oficial, 24 June 1974, available at <http://www.infoleg.gov.ar/infolegInternet/anexos/55000-59999/58603/texact.htm>.

services. To make matters worse, it covers all government action under the law with a blanket of secrecy, as it requires maximum confidentiality from all government officers charged with its implementation.

To trigger its application, the federal legislature must declare a supply emergency. Although the law had not been invoked since 1991, a 1999 presidential decree declaring a state of emergency reinstated its applicability and it continues to be used to date. The legality of its continued application beyond the 1999 emergency situation has been called into question,[36] but that has not deterred the current administration, which uses it as the central premise to justify its frequent intervention in hydrocarbon operations, particularly downstream. As a result, the Supreme Court has seen an extraordinary number of cases involving Law 20,680 in recent years.[37] However, both the lower courts and the Supreme Court have meticulously avoided any decision regarding the legality of its application, and resolved the cases on other grounds.[38] In addition, even if the application of Law 20,680 were to be struck down by the courts on the basis of the inapplicability of the 1999 decree, the government may be able to garner enough votes in the legislature to re-launch it, and even target the energy sector specifically, by declaring a state of emergency in the supply of energy. The ease with which a new state of emergency could be declared is illustrated by the fact that the administration has been able to secure passage of several extensions to the general Economic Emergency Law 25,561 of 2002, which is still in force today.[39]

V. Federalism, environment, water, and the public

The legal framework governing environmental protection in Argentina is also a common concern of federal and provincial authorities. Under the 1994 Constitution, the federal government has power to enact norms setting minimum

[36] L. D. Barry, 'Verdaderos alcances de la Ley de Abastecimiento', available at <http://www.colabogados.org.ar/larevista/>.

[37] E. G. Arnáez, Diario Judicial, 'Ley de Abastecimiento: la Corte ya tiene más de 60 causas para definir su vigencia' (3 February 2011), available at <http://www.diariojudicial.com/contenidos/2011/02/03/noticia_0002.html>; iProfesional.com, 'Metrogas: intervención, dudas legales y caída bursátil' (7 July 2007), available at <http://www.iprofesional.com/index.php?p=nota&idx=49305>.

[38] See, e.g., Corte de Apelación, Caso 23,207/2010, Shell Compañía Argentina de Petróleo S.A. c/ EN -S.C.I.- RESOL. 295/10 s/Medida Cautelar (Autónoma), Buenos Aires (5 October 2010), available at <http://www.ambito.com/diario/aw_documentos/archivospdf/2005/id_doc_5574.pdf>; and, S. 392. XLV, Shell Compañía Argentina de Petróleo S.A. s/inf. ley 20.680, Buenos Aires (27 September 2011), available at <http://ar.vlex.com/vid/-322737599> referring to the opinion of Argentina's Attorney General, available at <http://www.mpf.gov.ar/dictamenes/2010/casal/abril/s_c_a_de_p_s_190_l_xlv.pdf>.

[39] Law 26, 729 extends it through the end of 2013, Boletín Oficial, 28 December 2011. Currently, under the Economic Emergency law the government can, *inter alia*, fix prices and renegotiate contracts. See also CEPASE, 'La Ley de Abastecimiento y los precios de los combustibles', August 2010, available at <http://www.cepase.com.ar/noticias/index.php?q=node/185>; and, S. Gastaldi et al, 'Las injustificaciones de los Superpoderes y de la ley de Emergencia Económica', September 2008, available at <http://www.fundacionege.org/de_interes/Superpoderes_y_Ley_de_Emergencia_Economica.pdf>.

environmental protection standards, while the provinces have authority to enact complementary rules, and have general enforcement power (Article 41). This has been interpreted to mean that the provinces may issue regulations that are more stringent than, but do not contradict, the general federal norms.[40] Accordingly, the federal Congress proclaimed several framework laws dealing with differing aspects of environmental protection, including a law on principles of general application (Law 25,675); on environmental water management (Law 25,688);[41] on waste (Law 24,015 and Decree 831: hazardous; and, 25,612: non-hazardous);[42] and on glacier protection (26,639).[43] Law 24,585 of 1995[44] added a section to the federal Mining Code dealing with environmental protection in mining activities. As mentioned earlier, the federal Mining Code is the framework law applicable to the mining sector, including the hydrocarbon sector, across the country. As an extension of those rules, the federal government has also issued environmental regulations directed specifically to oil and gas activities. On the other hand, the provinces have come up with their own batteries of rules and regulations, some of which may overlap and conflict with federal regulation. Though federal norms will generally preempt provincial ones, in practice it is not so easy to determine what is or is not a minimum standard and therefore a legitimate exercise of federal or provincial power. That was evident in a highly publicized Supreme Court case challenging Chubut province's statutes requiring environmental assessment of mining activities (Law 4032) and banning open pit mining and cyanide mining in the province (Law 5001). There, the Supreme Court confirmed the constitutionality of the Chubut statutes arguing that provinces are allowed to go beyond the precepts set in federal law because to 'complement' federal norms in the sense of Article 41 of the Constitution per force implies 'adding' further requirements.[45] On the other hand, the Supreme Court has recently decided in favour of the applicability of stringent federal standards in a suite of cases challenging the constitutionality of selected sections of the federal Glacier Protection Law which ban mining in glacial and periglacial areas across the country. According to the plaintiffs, Barrick Exploraciones Argentina SA and Exploraciones Mineras

[40] Jose A. Martinez De Hoz (Jr),'Seaweed Turbulence in the South? Provincial and Municipal Involvements in Oil and Gas Development the Argentine Experience' 17–19 March 1999, 1999 Rocky Mountain Mineral Law Foundation, Special Institute; I.M. de la Riva, 'Dominio y jurisdicción sobre hidrocarburos en nuestro sistema federal: un auténtico rompecabezas para armar', 19 September 2008, El Derecho, 5.

[41] Ley 25.688, Régimen de Gestión Ambiental De Aguas, Boletín Oficial, 3 January 2003, available at <http://www.elaw.org/node/2679>.

[42] Ley 24,015, Residuos Peligrosos, Boletín Oficial, 17 January 1992; Ley 25,612, Gestión integral de residuos industriales y de actividades de servicios, 25 July 2002, available at <http://www.infoleg.gov.ar/infolegInternet/anexos/75000-79999/76349/norma.htm>.

[43] Ley 26.639, Régimen de Presupuestos Mínimos para la Preservación de los Glaciares y del Ambiente Periglacial, 28 October 2010, available at <http://www.infoleg.gov.ar/infolegInternet/anexos/170000-174999/174117/norma.htm>. The law aims at protecting glaciers for their environmental value and as potential water sources. Glaciers are declared to be public goods.

[44] Código de Minería, available at <http://infoleg.mecon.gov.ar/infolegInternet/anexos/30000-34999/30096/norma.htm>.

[45] Villivar, Susana Noemi c/Pcia. de Chubut y otros, available at <http://ebookbrowse.com/gdoc.php?id=89475663&url=6e713380c129c62f136c01d330694ccf>.

Argentinas SA, those sections violate the companies' acquired rights to undertake mining activities in the Pascua Lama concession area in the province of San Juan.[46] The province joined the suit as a co-plaintiff, adhering to the companies' arguments and adding that the Glacier Protection Law was contrary to articles 41 and 121 of the Constitution and ultra vires the federal government. So far, the Supreme Court has only ruled on the admissibility of the precautionary measures sought by the plaintiffs and granted by the lower court. The precautionary measures suspended the operative sections of the law until a decision on its constitutionality is made. In the Supreme Court's decision, the Glacier Protection Law's immediate applicability was upheld based on the argument, *inter alia*, that the plaintiffs failed to provide evidence of potential damage to the mining companies as a result of its application. Most importantly, the Supreme Court admonished the lower court judge for disregarding the impact of his decision to suspend the application of a law on the constitutional division of powers. To avoid overstepping the judiciary's boundaries, according to the Supreme Court, the case needed to be narrowly construed. While, per se, constitutionality is not discussed, in striking down the precautionary measures granted by the lower court, the Supreme Court's reasoning seems to stem from the presumption that, in case of conflict, the need to protect certain public goods of national significance prevails over private interests and provincial power to manage natural resources.[47]

Although the cases discussed do not draw a clear line between what may or may not be considered a minimum standard, they do favour environmental protection over economic development. On the other hand, the Court emphasizes restraint and respect for the constitutional division of powers. As a result, the cases seem to suggest that any provincial law banning fracking may withstand a constitutional challenge. Conversely, fracking could be banned by the federal legislature under the Constitution any time that the protection of certain common public goods, such as glaciers, may be a stake.

This is of significance, given the remarkable level of local activism and opposition to mining and fracking activities. The phenomenon first made the national stage when a grassroots movement succeeded in blocking gold mining in Esquel, in the province of Chubut.[48] Led by the grassroots organization 'Asamblea de Vecinos Autoconvocados de Esquel por el No a la Mina', activists challenge

46 The law was also challenged in its entirety on procedural grounds. Barrick Exploraciones Argentinas S.A. y otro vs Estado Nacional s/Acción Declarativa de Inconstitucionalidad, available at <http://www.ecolex.org/server2.php/libcat/docs/COU/Full/Sp/COU-157343.pdf>.

47 Barrick Exploraciones Argentina S.A. y otro c/Estado Nacional s/Acción declarativa de inconstitucionalidad; Minera Argentina Gold S.A. y otros c/Estado Nacional s/Acción declarativa de inconstitucionalidad; and, A.O.M.A. y otras c/Estado Nacional p/Acción declarativa de inconstitucionalidad, available at <http://www.cij.gov.ar/nota-9417-La-Corte-Suprema-revoco-las-medidas-cautelares-que-frenaban-la-aplicacion-de-la-Ley-de-Glaciares.html>. See also <http://www.pagina12.com.ar/diario/elpais/1-197895-2012-07-04.html>.

48 See n 45. The year 2013 marks 10 years since the citizens of Esquel rejected mining in their municipality in a plebiscite which eventually led to passage of the provincial law banning open cyanide and pit mining challenged in the Villivar case. See also, D. Aranda, 'Esquel sigue haciendo historia' March 25, 2013, available at <http://www.ecoportal.net/Eco-Noticias/Esquel_sigue_haciendo_historia>.

'extractivism'[49] as a model for economic development. Their opposition is based on the argument that mining and hydrocarbon activities, particularly those that involve fracking, have no long-term economic benefits for the local economies, while local communities suffer as a result of changes in land use and impacts on the environment and water resources. Extractivism, they argue, sacrifices the way of life of many for the benefit of a few.[50] Prominent in the argument against extractive activities is their impact on indigenous groups, their territories, and their lifestyle. However, opposition to extractives is not limited to indigenous groups; activism also encompasses farmers and city dwellers that see the advance of extractivism in Argentina as a threat to their lifestyles and, most importantly, that of their descendants.

Emboldened by their success, and fuelled by multiple incidents of environmental harm and blatant cases of environmental injustice,[51] activists have grown louder and stronger, staging regular protests across the country and gaining notoriety both at home and internationally.[52] In some cases, activists have been involved in direct confrontations with government supporters and unionized workers, who often take the side of mining and hydrocarbon interests as potential new sources of revenue and employment.[53] Their differences have proved to be particularly explosive, resulting in highly publicized reports of violent clashes between supporters of both sides.[54]

[49] For an explanation of the term, see: <http://elearning.uni-bielefeld.de/wikifarm/fields/ges_cias/field.php/Main/Unterkapitel53>. See also C. R. Marrero, 'The New Latin American 'Progresismo' and the Extractivism of the 21st Century' (17 February 2011), available at <http://www.cipamericas.org/archives/4025>.

[50] See website of Asamblea de Vecinos Autoconvocados de Esquel, <http://www.noalamina.org>; see also website of Observatorio Petrolero del Sur, <http://www.opsur.org.ar/blog/quienes-somos/>.

[51] See, e.g., Cámara de Apelaciones en lo Civil y Comercial [Capel. CC Nqn.] 2/3/1997, 'Menores Comunidad Paynemil/acción amparo (Menores) (Arg.), available at <http://www.escr-net.org>.

[52] Argentina Indymedia, 'Movilización por la amenaza del fracking y la megaminería', 6 February 2013, available at <http://argentina.indymedia.org/news/2013/02/830729.php>; Asamblea de Vecinos Autoconvocados de Esquel por el No A La Mina, 'Presentaron amparo contra el fracking en Comodoro', 13 February 2013, available at <http://www.noalamina.org/mineria-argentina/mineria-chubut/presentaron-amparo-contra-el-frecking-en-comodoro>.

[53] M. Gavalda and H. Scandizzo, *Patagonia petrolera, el desierto permanente* (Huemul Producciones, 2008). The authors report incidents of violence and intimidation protagonized by mercenaries hired by developers. See also 'Abrazo chubutense a la legislatura para que no haya megamineria', 18 October 2012, available at <http://www.ecoportal.net/Eco-Noticias/Abrazo_chubutense_a_la_legislatura_para_que_no_haya_megamineria>.

[54] The most recent example of a violent clash took place between the police force of Neuquén and activists protesting the deal struck between provincial authorities and Chevron to implement the YPF-Chevron agreement. Emol.economia, 'En medio de intensas protestas, legislatura de Neuquén aprobó acuerdo YPF-Chevron', 29 August 2013, available at <http://www.emol.com/noticias/economia/2013/08/29/616958/provincia-petrolera-argentina-aprueba-inversion-de-chevron-en-medio-de-disturbios.html>; Argentina Indymedia, 'La UOCRA golpeó a los antimineros y la oposición no quiere sesionar', 28 November 2012, available at <http://argentina.indymedia.org/news/2012/11/826327.php>; Argentina Indymedia, 'Represion a vecinos que luchan contra la megamineria', 11 May 2013, available at <http://argentina.indymedia.org/news/2012/07/817935.php>; Asamblea Permanente del Comahue por el Agua, 'Urgente!! Patotas de APACHE en Allen!!!', 31 October 2012, available at <http://apca.noblogs.org/post/author/mallkukunturi/>.

Another visible sign of their action can be found in a bill currently under review by the federal Congress which prohibits fracking in oil and gas development.[55] Also, in one particular instance, local authorities passed a resolution outlawing the activity in their municipality of Cinco Saltos, province of Rio Negro. Cinco Saltos is located in the rich Neuquén unconventional gas basin, and although the resolution was vetoed by the mayor, it provides a clear illustration of the challenges that a developer of unconventional reserves might face when seeking its social licence to operate.[56]

In addition to its potential to cause significant environmental damage, hydraulic fracking technology demands large amounts of water. It is estimated that producing gas from the Vaca Muerta formation would require 144,000 million litres for 7,500 wells.[57] However, the resource is far from abundant in the area and water management is another area where the constitutional division of powers combined with provincial ownership of resources may pose a challenge. As mentioned earlier, all natural resources, and therefore water resources, are vested in the provinces. On the other hand, most water bodies are not confined by geopolitical lines and are often shared between two or more jurisdictions, whether local or international. Nevertheless, there is very little federal law of general application to water bodies aside from that which applies to the regulation of navigation and coastal waters beyond provincial jurisdiction. The only federal water law, in force since 2003, is Law 25,688, which charges federal authorities with defining minimum protection, conservation, and use standards. Not surprisingly, as a result of a long tradition of local water management, Law 25,688 has met much opposition from the provinces and remains, for the most part, unregulated.[58]

Federal authorities, i.e. the Under Secretariat of Water Resources[59] and the Office of Environmental Management of Water Resources,[60] play a very limited role in water management, even at the level of policy-making, a role that since 2003 is reserved to the Federal Water Council (Consejo Hidrico Federal—COHIFE), an agency integrated by representatives of the provinces and the federal government

55 'Iniciativa en el Congreso busca prohibir el fracking en Argentina', 8 October 2012, available at <http://www.aimdigital.com.ar/aim/2012/10/08/iniciativa-en-el-congreso-busca-prohibir-el-fracking-en-argentina/>.

56 M. Matze, 'Rio Negro Town Bans "Fracking"', 10 January 2013, available at <http://www.argentinaindependent.com/currentaffairs/rio-negro-town-bans-'fracki>; Asamblea de Vecinos Autoconvocados de Esquel por el No A La Mina, 'Intendenta vetó la ordenanza que prohibía el fracking en Cinco Saltos', 19 February 2013, available at <http://www.noalamina.org/mineria-argentina/mineria-rio-negro/intendenta-veto-la-ordenanza-que-prohibia-el-fracking-en-cinco-saltos>.

57 On the basis of a conservative estimate of 19 million litres/well. Aol, 'Argentina impulse mineria e hidrocarburos, pero le falta agua', 10 January 2011, available at <http://noticias.aollatino.com/2011/10/01/argentina-impulsa-mineria-e-hidrocarburos-pero-le-falta-agua/>.

58 Marisa Arienza et al, Green Cross, 'Agua. Panorama general en la Argentina', available at <http://www.gcint.org>; V. Pochat, CEPAL, 'Entidades de gestión de agua a nivel de cuencas: experiencia de Argentina', October 2005, available at <http://www.eclac.org/publicaciones/xml/5/22905/lcl2375s.pdf>.

59 For additional information, see the website of Argentina's Undersecretary of Water Resources at <http://www.hidricosargentina.gov.ar>.

60 For additional information, see the website of Argentina's Environmental Office for Water Resources at <http://www.argentina.gob.ar/directorio/130-secretar%C3%ADa-de-ambiente-y-desarrollo-sustentable.php>.

and charged with general policy-making and harmonization of water management principles. Although COHIFE has come up with a set of general principles to guide water management across the country, its impact does not appear to be significant.[61] On the other hand, while provinces have their own laws and institutions governing local water resources, inter-jurisdictional management is, for the most part, in the hands of basin agencies made up by representatives of the corresponding governments. The basin management agencies respond to provincial authorities and their mandates generally cover water allocation and protection.

A good example of a well-established basin management agency that is relevant to the Vaca Muerta play is the Colorado River Interjurisdictional Agency (Comité Interjurisdiccional del Río Colorado (COIRCO)). The Colorado River and its tributaries are a vital source of water to a 48,000-km^2 semi-arid basin which partially overlaps Argentina's main oil and gas basin—i.e. the Neuquén basin—and hosts a thriving agricultural economy. As early as 1956, the five provinces in the Colorado River basin, Mendoza, Neuquén, Río Negro, La Pampa, and Buenos Aires, together with the federal government, joined forces to ensure adequate management of the basin's water resources. Their activities resulted in the creation of COIRCO.[62] COIRCO's main objective is to manage and protect water resources for direct human consumption and farming. With the intensification of hydrocarbon activities in the area, and after a series of pollution incidents in the late nineties, COIRCO joined forces with the federal Energy Secretariat and formed a compliance monitoring body, the Comisión Técnica Fiscalizadora (CTF). Through the 1997 agreement establishing the CTF, the provinces delegate to CTF environmental compliance monitoring of hydrocarbon activities. CTF is charged with monitoring upstream and transportation activities vis-a-vis their impact on the basin's water resources, as well as with monitoring and assessing the quality of the water environment in the basin. CTF works closely with the companies to address environmental protection issues, but it has no power to impose administrative or other penalties.[63] Unfortunately, that weakness may help to explain the steady escalation of pollution incidents as reported by CTF itself.[64]

Another example of a basin management agency, located in close proximity to the Colorado River basin, is the Inter-jurisdictional Authority for the Limay, Neuquén, and Negro River Basin (Autoridad Interjurisdiccional de las Cuencas de los Ríos Limay, Neuquén y Negro (AIC)). The Río Negro basin, including the River's tributaries Neuquén and Limay, is a highly developed basin of about 120,000 km^2. Its waters flow from the Andes to the Atlantic Ocean across three provinces: Neuquén, Río Negro, and Buenos Aires. It is a highly impacted area, as it provides irrigation to Argentina's most important fruit growing area and covers most of the Neuquén hydrocarbon basin, including the Vaca Muerta area. It is also

[61] See the website of COHIFE at <http://www.cohife.org.ar>.

[62] See COIRCO at <http://www.coirco.gov.ar>.

[63] Confirmed by Pochat (n 58).

[64] CTF identifies the intensification of activities as a contributing factor, which could point to a need for additional resources.

home to several major hydroelectricity developments: Alicurá, Piedra del Águila, Pichi Picún Leufú, El Chocón and Arroyito, on the Limay River, and Cerros Colorados, on the Neuquén River. The area is also famous for its scenic value and an important international tourism destination. The privatization of the hydroelectricity developments in the 1990s spurred the three provinces, together with the federal government, into reinforcing their alliance under AIC in order to oversee the hydroelectricity concessions, previously in the hands of a federally owned operator.[65] As a result, AIC was given broad powers to manage both the use and conservation of the basin's water resources, including the design, implementation, control, and enforcement of a programme to use and allocate water resources (formalized by means of interprovincial agreements); issuance of recommendations on environmental protection regulations; and, construction and maintenance of pollution detection and control facilities. While the power to issue and enforce environmental norms remains vested in the provinces, AIC has extraordinary oversight powers and may impose monetary sanctions to a province whenever it fails to take measures to stop or control water pollution. AIC also acts as the regulatory agency in charge of controlling and enforcing the hydroelectricity concessionaires' contractual commitments regarding water management, security, and environmental protection.

Both COIRCO and AIC are examples of basin management agencies with a recognized track record of sound management. Their existence, and that of similar agencies in other basins, bodes well for potential new users with large demands for water resources (that may have impacts beyond the immediate point of extraction or discharge), such as unconventional hydrocarbon developers, as they provide well-established fora for joint decision-making on water use and management. Their recommendations will serve to unify criteria and coordinate decisions on allowable uses (quality and quantity) across the jurisdictions involved and will provide a heightened level of confidence to developers who can reasonably rely on the application of uniform standards and requirements as a result. The potential role to be played by basin management agencies is brought to light by Neuquén's newly enacted regulations on water use in unconventional hydrocarbon operations, Decree 1483.[66]

With limited exceptions, the new regulations issued by Neuquén ban the use of underground water in fracking operations and mandate use of fresh water, but only under permit issued by provincial authorities. Presumably, as the activities in the rich hydrocarbon basin of which the province is a part accelerate, their impact in terms of water allocation and use will have to be discussed and decided upon amongst the provinces sharing the resources. COIRCO and AIC can help jump start the process in their respective basins. However, as noted earlier, the powers of the basin management agencies are limited and the implementation and enforcement of their recommendations rests, for the most part, with provincial authorities which may or may not display similar levels of diligence.

65 See AIC at <http://www.aic.gob.ar/aic/default.aspx#v>.

66 Available at <http://w2.neuquen.gov.ar/index.php?option=com_content&view=article&id=3311:decreto-para-preservar-el-recurso-hidrico&catid=2:noticias&Itemid=39>.

VI. More disquieting news

Despite the recent flurry of news announcing new investment agreements-in-principle with several international companies such as Bridas and others,[67] YPF's balance looks bleak,[68] and its ability to raise funds through issuing bonds is severely curtailed by Argentina's heavily eroded credibility and the ongoing 'battle of the vulture funds', whereby the country is facing a multi-billion dollar lawsuit instituted in a US jurisdiction by a small percentage of powerful creditors that refuse to join the majority in renegotiating the terms of Argentina's debt.[69] Moreover, YPF's former owner, Repsol, is suing (and has vowed to sue all) those companies that are entering into agreements with YPF on the grounds that the agreements have been entered into with illegitimate representatives of YPF and that, as a result, they constitute illegitimate attempts at appropriating a third party's assets.[70] On the other hand, in keeping with recent action regarding YPF, the government demonstrates an increasing tendency to take over private companies, particularly if the companies are involved in the provision of public services. Such was the case of Transportadora de Gas del Norte and of Metrogas, respectively gas transport and distribution companies, as well as Autopistas del Sol, a highway concessionaire.[71]

VII. Conclusions

The legal framework that applies to unconventional gas development in Argentina is murky, to say the least. Developers interested in investing in Argentina seem to be caught in a 'Catch-22' type scenario: Moving in to secure their share of the country's huge unconventional potential too soon may put them at the mercy of a powerful and unpredictable federal administration and an obscure legal landscape, while providing no guarantee of reasonable returns. On the other hand, if they move in too late, they may miss out altogether.

[67] See, e.g., El Mundo.es, 'Argentina sustituye a Repsol por Chevron en Vaca Muerta', 14 September 2012, available at <http://www.elmundo.es/america/2012/09/14/argentina/1347647446.html>; K. Graziana, 'UPDATE 3-Argentine YPF, Bridas in shale investment deal', 28 December 2012, available at <http://www.reuters.com/article/2012/12/28/ypf-bridas-idUSL1E8NS4D420121228>.

[68] Energía del Sur, 'El extraño caso de YPF, la petrolera que ya debe dos veces lo que vale' November 19, 2012, available at <http://energiadelsur.blogspot.com/2012/11/el-extrano-caso-de-ypf-la-petrolera-que.html>.

[69] J. Ghosh and M. Vernengo, 'Why Argentina is Now Paying for its Dangerously Successful Economic Story', 3 December 2012, available at <http://www.guardian.co.uk/commentisfree/2012/dec/03/argentina-paying-economic-vulture-fund>; and Reuters, 'Argentina's Bond Holders Seek Fresh Halt on Court Ordered Payments' (26 November 2012), available at <http://www.reuters.com/article/2012/11/26/us-argentina-debt-idUSBRE8AP0LD20121126>.

[70] lapoliticaonline, 'Por Vaca Muerta, Repsol le inició juicio a los Bulgheroni', 5 January 2013, available at <http://www.lapoliticaonline.com/noticias/val/87804-7/por-vaca-muerta-repsol-le-inicio-juicio-a-los-bulgheroni-.html>.

[71] R. Beller and M. Campbell, 'Argentina' in *The Restructuring Review* (C. Mallon, ed, 5th edn, 2012) 1.

Recently, Chevron decided to bet on Argentina, though not without significant concessions on the government's part. In July 2013, Chevron signed a deal with YPF to invest US$1.24 billion to develop the Vaca Muerta play.[72] The agreement's signature immediately followed issuance of Decree 929/2013, instituting a special investment promotion regime benefiting those companies investing a minimum of one billion dollars over the first five years of their investment plans.[73] According to the Decree, after five years, qualifying companies will be able to export up to 20% of their production, free of applicable export duties. Additionally, those companies will not be required to repatriate exports' earnings. For the case that domestic supply needs preclude exports, the companies will have the right to sell the exportable production domestically at export prices, and are exempted from currency controls.

The YPF-Chevron deal also follows a decision by Argentina's Supreme Court to reverse a lower court's order freezing Chevron's assets as required by indigenous plaintiffs in a case brought against the company in Ecuador, where it was ordered to pay US$19 billion in damages.[74]

YPF's agreement with Chevron drew criticism from several fronts. Indigenous peoples living in the Vaca Muerta area have denounced the deal on the basis of lack of consultation. They also oppose it on the basis of Chevron's poor environmental and social impact record, as well as the company's refusal to comply with the penalties imposed by the Ecuadorian courts and by the Interamerican System.[75] Adolfo Pérez Esquivel, the 1980 Nobel Peace Prize holder, has added his voice to that of indigenous peoples and local communities. He argues that, in addition to trumping indigenous rights and favouring a company with a proven track record of disregard for the environment and local communities, the deal reverses Argentina's move towards energy sovereignty, as it removes any potential disputes from the jurisdiction of the Argentine courts.[76]

Chevron's bold move cannot detract from the fact that the legal framework is rife with uncertainty. In addition, five years is a very long time, given the pendular nature of Argentine politics and the fact that Fernández Kirchner's mandate expires in December of 2015. After all, as Pérez Esquivel reminded the public in a recent interview concerning the YPF-Chevron deal, Argentina is the country that faces the highest number of suits in Washington's ISCSD.[77]

[72] *Financial Post*, 'Chevron, Argentina's YPF Sign US$1.24B Shale Deal', 13 July 2013, available at <http://business.financialpost.com/2013/07/17/chevron-argentinas-ypf-sign-us1-24b-shale-deal/?__lsa=dbd9-fc93>.

[73] Decreto 929/2013, Créase el Régimen de Promoción de Inversión para la Explotación de Hidrocarburos, available at <http://www.boletinoficial.gov.ar/Inicio/Index.castle>.

[74] La Nación, 'La Corte Suprema revocó el embargo sobre Chevron', 5 June 2013, available at <http://www.lanacion.com.ar/1588736-la-corte-suprema-revoco-el-embargo-sobre-chevron>.

[75] Servindi, 'Argentina: Mapuches rechazan presencia de contaminadora Chevron en sus territorios', 11 July 2013, available at <http://servindi.org/actualidad/90333>.

[76] Servindi, 'Argentina se comporta como una semicolonia con acuerdo YPF-Chevron que lesiona soberanía', 25 July 2013, available at <http://servindi.org/actualidad/90995>.

[77] Servindi (n 76).

10

Japan's Undersea Mineral Resources and Its New Mining Act

Kazuhiro Nakatani

I. Introduction

Japan's Mining Act of 1950 gave no consideration to the undersea mineral resources that would become a great asset to the country. Accordingly, the 61-year-old Act was amended in July 2011 in order to recognize these resources, as well as to address other important changes to Japanese energy and minerals policy.

The author of this chapter acted as the Chair of the Working Group of the Amendment of the Mining Act for the Advisory Committee for Natural Resources and Energy of the Japanese Government. This chapter surveys Japan's undersea mineral resources. It then reviews the main contents of the Old and New Mining Acts, followed by some observations about Japanese legislation. Lastly, it examines the future of Japan's energy and mineral policies and the importance of Japan's undersea mineral resources.

II. Japan's rich undersea mineral resources

Because the land area of Japan produces almost no mineral resources, most of the mineral resources the country consumes—oil, gas, and heavy and rare metals—are imported. According to recent scientific research, however, Japan appears to be very rich in undersea mineral resources, such as methane hydrate, cobalt-rich manganese crusts, and hydrothermal deposits. Including its territorial sea and its Exclusive Economic Zone (EEZ), Japan has the sixth largest sea area in the world, approximately 4,470,000 km^2.

Methane hydrate is a crystalline solid, like ice, which stores gas molecules, usually methane. A cage of water molecules surrounds each flammable gas molecule. Methane hydrates can be found under the permafrost of polar regions and in the sediments of deep-sea regions where the temperature is low and the pressure is great. A cleaner fuel than coal or oil, methane gas is used as municipal gas and as fuel for vehicles and fuel cells.

Deposits of methane hydrate have been reported in marine sediments in the Nankai Trough off the Pacific coast of central Japan, where the water depth is more than 500 metres. Japan Oil, Gas and Metals National Corporation (JOGMEC) and its predecessor, Japan National Oil Company (JNOC), have researched methane hydrates since 1995.[1] The methane reserves in the Naikai Trough are estimated to be 77 trillion m^3,[2] while the methane reserves worldwide are estimated to be between 1,000 trillion and 50,000 trillion m^3.

At a depth of 800–2,400 m, cobalt-rich manganese crust covers the slope or the top of seamounts like asphalt. They contain deposits of nickel, copper, cobalt, and, of course, manganese. Cobalt-rich manganese crust is composed of ferromanganese oxides. The crust covers the bedrock on the slope or the top of seamounts with a thickness ranging from several millimetres to tens of centimetres. The average cobalt content of this crust is three times as great as manganese nodules, and may sometimes contain ore-grade platinum.[3]

Hydrothermal deposits consist of heavy metal derived from hot water, which has vented from the seafloor at a depth of 1,500–3,000 m, and contain deposits of copper, lead, zinc, gold, and silver. Hydrothermal deposits are distributed along the spreading centre axis of the seabed in areas such as the East Pacific Rise, the Central Atlantic Ridge, and the North Fiji Basin in the South Pacific. They are also found in back-arc basins. JOGMEC has researched and surveyed manganese nodules, cobalt-rich manganese crusts, and hydrothermal deposits for more than 30 years.[4]

In June 2012, Professor Yasuhiro Kato (of the University of Tokyo) found a large deposit of rare earth minerals, including dysprosium (Dy), in an area near Minimitorishima Island, a Japanese island located some 2,000 km southeast of Tokyo. It is estimated that the deposits would supply Japan's high-tech industries for more than 200 years.[5]

The United Nations Commission on the Limits of the Continental Shelf (CLCS) adopted a recommendation in April 2012 that allowed Japan to extend its claimed continental shelf area. As a result, approximately 310,000 km^2 of seabed was added to Japan's continental shelf beyond 200 sea miles.[6] In March 2013, highly concentrated deposits of rare earth elements were confirmed in the mud from the seafloor near Minamitorishima Island. The figure is about 10 times higher

[1] JOGMEC, 'Promoting the Development of Methane Hydrate', available at <http://www.jogmec.go.jp/english/oil/technology_015.html>.

[2] Wonn Soh, 'Exploring the Unknown Possibilities of Methane Hydrates', available at <http://www.jamstec.go.jp/jamstec-e/30th/part6/page5.html>.

[3] JOGMEC, 'Deep-Sea Mineral Resources', available at <http://www.jogmec.go.jp/english/metal/technology_018.html>.

[4] JOGMEC (n 3).

[5] Available at <http://dawn.com/2012/06/29/japan-finds-major-rare-earth-deposits-researcher/print> and <http://ajw.asahi.com/article/economy/business/AJ201206290121>.

[6] On the submission by Japan in November 2008 and the recommendation of the Commission on the Limits of the Continental Shelf (CLCS), see <http://www.un.org/Depts/los/clcs_new/submissions_files/submission_jpn.htm>.

than that of the inland deposits in China,[7] which are rich in rare metals and rare earths.

In December 2011, the Ministry of Economy, Trade and Industry (METI) published its Priority Measures to Ensure Stable Supply of Natural Resources and Fuel. Developing natural resources in the marine areas of Japan is one of the main objectives of METI. The following three actions are cited as priority measures:

(1) *Promoting geophysical explorations and exploratory drilling for oil and natural gas in marine areas of Japan.* The government will: (a) systematically promote the three-dimensional geophysical exploration of between 5,000 and 6,000 km^2 annually until 2018; (b) select promising marine areas; and (c) conduct exploratory drilling expeditiously.

(2) *Promoting research and development of methane hydrate.* Unlike conventional natural gas, methane hydrate cannot be made to flow using current production technologies. Accordingly, exploiting methane hydrate will require the development of new production technologies. The government will steadily promote research and development that includes conducting marine production tests in 2012, with the goal of establishing technologies for commercial production of methane hydrate around 2018.

(3) *Promoting exploration of seafloor hydrothermal deposits.* For seafloor hydrothermal deposits, the government will promote detailed evaluations and further exploration of promising deposits, the acquisition of necessary technologies, and the establishment of methods for measuring environmental impact. It will then promote projects for the commercialization of deposits by around 2018, based on the Plan for the Development of Marine Energy and Mineral Resources. In addition, the government will promote exploration of cobalt-rich crusts, which is a form of deposit that is rich with cobalt and requires exploration in accordance with the Plan. The government will conduct evaluations of potential rare earth deposits in Japan's EEZ and, based on deposit characteristics, it will also promote research and development of exploration, lifting, and smelting.

In March 2013, JOGMEC announced that it had successfully extracted methane hydrate from the seafloor about 80 km off the coast of Aichi Prefecture. The Corporation had been preparing for the first offshore production test off the coasts of Atsumi and Shima peninsulas when it started a flow test applying the depressurization method and confirmed production of methane gas, estimated from methane hydrate layers.[8] This was an important step toward the commercialization of methane hydrate in Japan by 2018. It is estimated that Japan has methane hydrate deposits, 10% of which are found in the seafloor, sufficient to cover domestic consumption of natural gas for 100 years.

[7] Available at <http://www.yomiuri.co.jp/dy/national/T130321004680.htm>.

[8] JOGMEC, 'Gas Production from Methane Hydrate Layers Confirmed', available at <http://www.jogmec.go.jp/english/news/release/release0110.html?recommend=1>.

III. Japan's Mining Act of 1950

Japan enacted the Old Mining Act in 1950.[9] While exploitation of limestone along the coast was authorized, this first Mining Act did not consider seriously the development of undersea mineral resources.

As promulgated in Article 1, the purpose of the Act is 'to provide for the basic system of mining to contribute to the improvement of public welfare by developing mineral resources in a reasonable manner'. Article 2 gives the state power 'to grant the right to mine and acquire minerals that are yet to be mined'. Article 3 provides that the applicable minerals are ores of gold, silver, copper, lead, bismuth, tin, antimony, mercury, zinc, iron, iron sulfide, chrome iron, manganese, tungsten, molybdenum, arsenic, nickel, cobalt, uranium, thorium, and phosphate. Also covered are graphite, coal, lignite, oil, asphalt, combustible natural gas, sulfur, gypsum, barites, alunite, fluorine, asbestos, limestone, dolomite, silica, feldspar, agalmatolite, talc, fireclay, and placer. Article 5 explains that the mining right encompasses the right both to mine and to acquire title to registered minerals, as well as to other minerals that occur in the same type of ore deposit in the area of certain registered land. Article 11 provides that mining rights include prospecting rights and digging rights. Article 12 provides that mining rights shall be deemed as real rights.[10]

The Old Mining Act is based on laissez-faire and 'first-come, first-served' policies. As to the right of priority, Article 27 provides: 'When the areas of land where mining applications are filed overlap, the person whose date of sending his/her application is earlier shall have the right of priority concerning the creation of mining right for the overlapped area of land.' This provision could prevent the most technically and financially capable company from acquiring the mining right. The New Act changed this provision completely, as will be explained later.

Article 17 restricts foreign investment in Japan's mineral resources. It provides: 'Mining rights shall be held only by the people of Japan or juridical persons of Japan.' While it seemingly prevented foreign companies from acquiring mining rights, it was possible for them to establish a subsidiary in Japan that acquired the mining right. Therefore, it has been a very limited restriction.

Article 18 provided that the duration of a prospecting right would be two years from the date of registration (paragraph 1). That period may be extended twice or, in the case of oil, three times (paragraph 2).

IV. Japan's New Mining Act of 2011

The main points of the New Mining Act of 2011[11] are as follows.

[9] Act No 289 of 1950. A provisional translation of the Old Act is available at <http://www.japaneselawtranslation.go.jp/law/detail/?ky=recovery&re=02&page=27>.

[10] These provisions have not been changed in the New Mining Act.

[11] Act No 84 of 2011 (promulgated on 22 July 2011 and came into force on 21 January 2012). The provisional translation of the New Act is available at <http://www.isa.org.jm/files/documents/EN/NatLeg/JapMiningAct.pdf>.

First, Article 6-2 defines 'specified minerals' as 'minerals which are oils, combustible natural gases, and other minerals important for the national economy and which are specified by Cabinet Order as minerals particularly requiring reasonable development'. According to the Cabinet Order (dated 20 December 2011), 'other minerals important for the national economy' are defined by classifying them into the following three categories: (1) submarine hydrothermal polymetallic ores (gold, copper, lead, bismuth, tin, antimony, mercury, zinc, iron, iron sulfide, manganese, tungsten, molybdenum, nickel, and cobalt); (2) submarine sedimentary deposits (copper, lead, zinc, iron, manganese, tungsten, molybdenum, nickel, and cobalt); and (3) asphalt. It is apparent that the specified minerals are mainly undersea minerals.

Second, as to the specified minerals, the New Act introduces substantial requirements for granting mining rights, which were absent in the Old Act. The first-come, first-served (first-to-file) policy for the granting of the mining right under the Old Act is abolished and the designation system is introduced. The primary designation requirements are sufficient financial basis, technical capability, and the social credibility of the applicant.

Article 29 paragraph 1 provides:

The Minister of Economy, Trade and Industry may not permit any application filed pursuant to the provision of Article 21, paragraph (1), unless he/she finds that such application satisfies the following requirements:

(i) The mining applicant of the relevant application has a sufficient financial basis and technical capability to properly carry out reasonable development of minerals;

(ii) The mining applicant of the relevant application has sufficient social credibility;

[(iii)–(vii) omitted]

(viii) The mining . . . is found to have economic value, is not harmful to health, and does not destroy facilities for public use or any facility equivalent to the above, disrupt the protection of cultural properties, parks or hot spring resources, or impair the interests of agriculture, forestry and other industries, and have an extremely adverse effect on public welfare; and

(ix) In addition to what is listed in the preceding items, the mining . . . is not extremely inappropriate in light of domestic and foreign social and economic circumstances, nor is it likely to hinder the promotion of public interest.

The more precise elements of provision (ix) are considered to be one or both of the following: (1) the mining is not likely to hinder the securing of the stable supply of mineral resources; or (2) it is not likely to hinder the appropriate implementation of Japan's mineral resources policy.[12]

Under the Old Act, there were frequent applications for mining rights by brokers that lacked these requirements and which were sought only for the resale to third

[12] 'On the Future of Japan's Mining Law' (in Japanese, 2011), report of the working group of the amendment of the Mining Act at the Advisory Committee for Natural Resources and Energy, available at <http://www.meti.go.jp/committee/sougouenergy/kougyou/bunkakai_goudou/002_03_00.pdf>27–28.

parties. The New Act is expected to close this loophole and promote development by appropriate applicants.

Sufficient financial and technical capability are also new requirements of the holder of the mining lease right. Article 77 paragraph 3 provides that the Minister of Economy, Trade and Industry may not authorize any application for mining lease rights unless the person who intends to become a holder has a sufficient financial basis and technical capability to properly implement the economical development.

Third, while the Old Act had no rules concerning exploration, the New Act establishes permission for an exploration system. Exploration requires investigations into the geological structure, etc. that are necessary for developing mineral resources and which employ the seismic method or a method specified by the Ordinance of the METI. It is limited to investigations that are undertaken in a fixed area and that do not accompany mining activities (Article 100–2). The Ordinance addresses seismic methods (measuring the reflected waves by artificially creating seismic waves), electronic methods (measuring the change in the electronic magnetic field by creating electronic magnetic waves near the ocean floor), and concentrating sampling exploration methods (intensively collecting bottom materials).[13] Article 100–2 provides that those who intend to carry out an exploration of minerals must file applications with and obtain permission from the Minister of Economy, Trade and Industry.[14] Furthermore, according to the Ordinance for Enforcement (Article 44–8), one of the requirements for granting permission for exploration is that the regime to implement the proper exploration is established. The New Act also introduced a provision, absent from the 1950 Act, on the release of data obtained from the exploration by private actors. Namely, Article 100–11 provides that when the Minister of Economy, Trade and Industry finds it necessary to understand the scope of the mineral resources or to secure the proper implementation of the exploration, the Minister may order the person who has obtained the permission to report that information.

Fourth, the New Act changes the duration of a prospecting right. Article 18 of the Old Act provided that the duration would be two years and might be extended twice (in the case of oil, three times). Article 18 of the New Act provides that the duration will be two years (in the case oil or natural gas, four years) and the period may be extended twice (each period is two years). Since the modern prospector needs to make more complicated and time-consuming preparations, such as for the introduction of offshore drilling rigs, the substantial extension of the duration of prospecting rights assists reasonable development.

Lastly, the New Act expanded the size of a mining area. Under the Old Act, the size of a mining area could not exceed 350 hectares, with no exceptions. The New

[13] Hiroaki Takahashi, 'The Mining Act of Japan Amended for the First Time in 61 years', available at <http://www.martindale.com/natural-resources-law/article_Davis-LLP_1536688.htm>.

[14] In this chapter, exploration of minerals is defined as investigations into the geological structure, etc that are necessary for developing mineral resources (limited to investigations that do not accompany the mining of minerals) and which employ the seismic method or a method specified by the Ordinance as that which uses a fixed area on a continuous basis.

Act provides that when needed for reasonable development of minerals, the 350-hectares rule is not applicable (Article 14(3)). As the undersea mineral resources often exist over a wide area in a block, the abolition of the upper limit of mining area allows for reasonable development of undersea mineral resources.

V. Some observations on the New Act

The following points about the New Mining Act should be highlighted.

First, from the point of comparative law, by enacting the New Mining Act, Japan has at last caught up to the so-called global standard. The Working Group on the Amendment of the Mining Act studied the mining laws and regulations of four major mining nations (United States, United Kingdom, Australia, and Norway) and found that they had already adopted the points mentioned in the previous section.

Second, the New Mining Act is completely in accordance with international law. It is in accordance with OECD Code of Liberalization of Capital Movements, as Japan has lodged reservations relating to investment by non-residents in mining in accordance with Article 2 of the Code. The New Mining Act does not prevent a Japanese subsidiary of a foreign company from acquiring the mining right. Although the prohibition is possible under international law and the Working Group of the Amendment of the Mining Act considered the prohibition, it finally declined to adopt it. The general policy of the Government of Japan to welcome more investment was predominant.

The New Act also is in accordance with World Trade Organization (WTO) rules. The study group considered the possibility of requiring producers of the undersea mineral resources to supply them for domestic use in Japan predominantly. It declined to do so. It was felt that such a measure might become inconsistent with the WTO rules and particularly Article 11 of GATT (General Agreement on Tariffs and Trade) (general elimination of quantitative restrictions) and might not be justified by its Article 20 (general exceptions).

Third, the *lacunae* in legislation governing the exploration of marine mineral resources were filled by the New Mining Act. Article 56 paragraph 1 of the UN Convention on the Law of the Sea provides that in the EEZ, the coastal state has sovereign rights for the purpose of exploring, exploiting, conserving, and managing the natural resources of the waters superjacent to the seabed, and of the seabed and its subsoil. Article 77 of the Convention provides that the coastal state exercises over the continental shelf sovereign rights for the purpose of exploring it and exploiting its natural resources. Under the Old Mining Act, this sovereign right under the EEZ and continental shelf was not enforceable due to the lack of domestic law. The New Mining Act enables Japan to exercise this sovereign right.

Marine scientific research is discussed in Part XIII of the Convention. The New Mining Act does not mention marine scientific research and it does not prejudice the existing rules in the Convention. The exploration of the Japanese EEZ or continental shelf by foreign ships for marine mineral resources could be carried out under the pretence of undertaking marine scientific research. However, this is exploration and requires the permission of the government of Japan. If the exploration is made without permission, then the Minister of Economy, Trade and Industry may order the discontinuance of the work, remove the device or item used for the exploration, or restore the original state (Article 100–6). This is completely legal under the Convention. Article 246 paragraph 2 provides that marine scientific research in the EEZ and on the continental shelf must be conducted with the consent of the coastal state. Paragraph 5 provides that coastal states may at their discretion withhold their consent to the conduct of a marine scientific research project of another state or competent international organization in the EEZ or on the continental shelf of the coastal state if that project is of direct significance for the exploration and exploitation of natural resources, whether living or non-living.

Fourth, although the preservation and protection of the ecosystem in the hydrothermal polymetallic ore zone offshore is important as the ecosystem is different from that of the land, the New Mining Act does not deal with this problem. This is mainly for bureaucratic reasons. It is not the Ministry of Economy, Trade and Industry but the Ministry of Environment that has the mandate on the environmental matter. On the marine pollution resulting from the development and exploration of undersea mineral resources, the Act Relating to the Marine Pollution and Maritime Disaster (Act No 136 of 1970) is applicable, but the preservation and protection of the ecosystem is not within the range of the Mining Act. A few members of the Working Group of the Amendment of the Mining Act were not happy with the result, and it is hoped that new regulations on the preservation and protection of the ecosystem in the hydrothermal polymetallic ore zone will be adopted in the near future.

Fifth, from my experience as the Chair of the Working Group of the Amendment of the Mining Act, the following points are of note. (1) The amendment of the Mining Act was done exceptionally swiftly, in only eight months. The consensus among the stakeholders and the strong motivation of the industries to explore and develop marine mineral resources made the revision of the out-of-date Mining Act possible. (2) There was no substantial change to the rules on some conventional minerals like limestone. Most of limestone is produced on land and most of the holders of the mining rights in limestone are small companies. It is a small and fragile industry. The Working Group took into consideration the situation of the limestone industry and maintained the *status quo*. (3) From my perspective as an international lawyer, I strongly believe that the adoption of the New Mining Act will be beneficial. As mentioned earlier, under the regime of the 1950 Mining Act, the sovereign rights under the EEZ and continental shelf provided by Articles 56 and 77 were not enforceable due to the lack of domestic law. The national wealth was not well preserved.

Lastly, the New Mining Act is based on the clear premise that Japan's mineral resources are the wealth of its nationals. The lack of this consciousness was the major flaw of the 1950 Mining Act. The New Mining Act embodied this consciousness and it is revolutionary in this. It is anticipated that the New Mining Act will protect the wealth of Japan's nationals and serve as a solid legal basis for the development of Japan's undersea mineral resources.

VI. Japan's future energy and mineral policies and the importance of undersea mineral resources

The Great East Japan Earthquake and the accident at TEPCO's Fukushima Daiichi Nuclear Power Station in March 2011 revealed the vulnerability of Japan's energy system. Although Japan had been striving for an optimum energy mix,[15] dependence on nuclear energy has had to be reconsidered after Fukushima. As of August 2013, the Japanese Government has not determined its new energy policy, mainly because public opinion is divided over nuclear policy. Although a formal decision has not yet been made, Prime Minister Abe seems to desire to step back from any major abandonment of nuclear electric generation. As the results of July 2013 Upper House elections indicate, the Prime Minister has legislative support to do this.

Despite its unclear nuclear policy in general, Japan is eager to conclude bilateral nuclear energy agreements, even after Fukushima, with some non-OECD countries, such as Kazakhstan (entered into force in May 2011), Vietnam (entered into force in January 2012), Jordan (entered into force in February 2012), Russia (entered into force in May 2013), United Arab Emirates (signature in May 2013), Turkey (fundamentally agreed to in May 2013), and Saudi Arabia (started negotiation in April 2013). Japan intends to export nuclear reactors and supply related services to these countries through these agreements.

After Fukushima, the operation of most nuclear power plants in Japan was suspended. This necessitated dependence on old and obsolete thermal power plants because these plants were the only available alternative. Otherwise, huge blackouts followed by panic would have been unavoidable. Greater dependence on thermal power plants resulted in an increase in import of oil and natural gas. In 2011, the increase in the import of oil and natural gas to Japan amounted to approximately US$54 billion, in comparison with 2010. This increase in the cost of fossil fuel energy was almost half of the trade deficit of approximately US$115 billion, an amount Japan had not experienced since 1971.

This situation prompted the Japanese Government to adopt its Strategy to Ensure Natural Resources in June 2012. The two main pillars of the Strategy are to strengthen ties with countries rich in mineral resources and to help Japanese companies invest in the upstream energy sector.

In May 2013, the Japanese Government decided to repeal its quantified economy-wide greenhouse gas emissions targets for 2020. In January 2010, Japan had

[15] See Kazuhiro Nakatani, 'In Search of the Optimum Energy Mix: Japanese Laws Promoting Non-Fossil-Fuel Energy', in Don Zillman et al (eds), *Beyond the Carbon Economy: Energy Law in Transition* (2008) 481–96.

committed to a 25% reduction of greenhouse gases by 2020.[16] This commitment followed former Prime Minister Hatoyama's sudden announcement of the reduction at the UN General Assembly in September 2009. When it was announced, Japanese business interests criticized the reduction as too ambitious, too unrealistic, and harmful to the economy. Fukushima proved that Hatoyama's idea was nothing but 'pie in the sky'. In 2011, the emission of greenhouse gases in Japan increased 3.9%, compared with 3.6% in 2010, when compared with the base year 1990. The repeal of the Hatoyama proposal is not a breach of international law. The commitment was non-binding and was premised on the establishment of a fair and effective international framework in which all major economies would participate and agree on ambitious targets. These conditions have not been satisfied. Furthermore, *rebus sic stantibus* can be applied to the particular situation after Fukushima, although this has not been formally invoked by the Japanese government.

The year 2011 will go down in Japanese history as a memorable one for energy and minerals policy. As mentioned, the ultimate consequences of the Fukushima disaster remain uncertain as of the summer of 2013. Far more positive consequences are likely to result from the enactment of the Mining Act of 2011. The Act has modernized and internationalized Japanese energy and minerals law to blend nicely with the geographic expansion of Japan's control of offshore resources and the solid evidence of the presence of minerals and energy resources beneath those offshore areas. Japan is moving ahead vigorously with both government-sponsored research and privately funded exploration to identify the resources and their economic potential.

The most immediate results are likely to result in the realm of metals, and strategic metals in particular. The latter are of particular value to Japanese high-tech industries. To date, Japan has been importing most of these essential metals. It seems realistic to expect that within a decade, Japan will have measurably lower dependence on imports of these metals. The domestic minerals production is likely to further encourage development of the domestic industries that rely on these strategic metals. Those domestic industries can serve both internal and export markets.

As to the subsurface energy resources, development may come more slowly and less predictably. The Mining Act of 2011 provides the legal framework to encourage major exploration of Japanese oil and natural gas offshore. Some of the oil and gas resources may be extractable by conventional methods. Unconventional forms of oil and natural gas may be produced using such technologies as horizontal drilling and hydraulic fracturing. The distinctive undersea methane hydrate resources offshore offer the challenges of the large cost, as well as the technical difficulties and the uncertainty of success of the extraction. A prediction of oil and gas self-sufficiency for Japan in the near future is too optimistic. However, good results from research, exploration, and production could place Japan in a very different position from today's near-total dependence on imports of oil and gas.

[16] Note verbale to the Secretariat of the UN Framework Convention on Climate Change on 26 January 2010 (JB 15/2010).

11

Evolution of Algeria's Legal and Regulatory Framework for Unconventional (Shale) Hydrocarbon Development with Emphasis on Environmental Aspects

Mohammed Abdelwahab Bekhechi

I. Introduction

Algeria is the world's twelfth largest hydrocarbon producer.[1] In addition to its proven conventional hydrocarbon reserves, Algeria is believed to possess[2] more than 707 trillion cubic feet of Technically Recoverable Resources (TRR) of shale gas,[3] making it the third largest country in terms of deposits after China (1115 TRR) and Argentina (802 TRR).[4] For shale oil, Algeria is believed to possess 5,700 million barrels of TRR,[5] making it the thirteenth largest in terms of deposits.[6] For the purpose of this chapter, the term 'unconventional hydrocarbons' refers to both shale gas and shale oil.

Algeria relies heavily on its hydrocarbon sector. In 2011, the oil and gas sector generated about 97% of overall export resources and 70% of budget receipts. During the same year, the sector represented about 37% of GDP.[7] Production has fallen in recent years, however, resulting in reduced hydrocarbon exports and a lower contribution to GDP.[8] This downward trend is the consequence of (i) repeated delays in implementing new hydrocarbon-related infrastructure projects and other necessary investments; (ii) the absence of an advanced technological base;

[1] Available at <http://www.forbes.com/pictures/mef45glfe/12-sonatrach-2-7-million-barrels-per-day-3/>.

[2] United States Energy Information Administration (US EIA), *Technically Recoverable Shale Oil and Shale Gas Resources: An Assessment of 137 Shale Formations in 41 Countries Outside the United States* (2013), available at <http://www.eia.gov>.

[3] US EIA (n 2) at 6. For comparison, proven conventional natural gas reserves are estimated at 159 billion cubic feet.

[4] US EIA (n 2) at 6. [5] US EIA (n 2) at 8.

[6] On Algeria's oil and gas sector, see <http://www.eia.gov/countries/cab.cfm?fips=AG>.

[7] African Economic Outlook, Report (2013), available at <http://www.africaneconomicoutlook.org/en/countries/north-africa/algeria/> at 3.

[8] African Economic Outlook (n 7) at 3.

(iii) uncertainties of global markets; and (iv) the limited interest from investors in undertaking new oil and gas projects under the terms offered in the last three licensing rounds.[9] In addition, population growth, improved living standards, subsidized energy prices in the domestic market, the development of energy-intensive industries, and implementation of a major seawater desalination programme to meet the growing demand for water have all combined to create a very rapid increase in domestic consumption of natural gas and oil,[10] thereby reducing Algeria's petroleum and natural gas export capacity.

Against this background, the government has taken steps to promote a more favourable business environment for the oil and gas sector and to open the field to development of unconventional hydrocarbon sources. Accordingly, the Algerian parliament recently approved amendments (the '2013 Amendment') to the current hydrocarbon law[11] (the '2005 Law') and introduced fiscal and other incentives to entice foreign companies to take on new ventures, particularly exploration in offshore areas and in onshore areas containing unconventional hydrocarbons. This seems to be a promising option, as illustrated by the example of other countries, including the United States, which are demonstrating that unconventional hydrocarbons can be developed under strict environmental and technical conditions to become significant sources of energy in the near future.

Algeria remains an important player in the international hydrocarbon market and any changes to its legal and regulatory framework provide useful information to global oil and gas investors and operators, and are watched closely by other hydrocarbon-producer countries, including other members of the Organization of Petroleum Exporting Countries (OPEC).

The aim of this chapter is to examine the new legal and regulatory framework in Algeria in its application to unconventional hydrocarbon development, and to consider how effectively and successfully it addresses the challenges that this poses. This chapter (i) provides a general overview of the legal and regulatory framework applicable to the hydrocarbon industry in Algeria; (ii) explains the specific rules applicable to unconventional hydrocarbon development; and (iii) discusses the domestic legal challenges facing unconventional hydrocarbon development in Algeria, focusing on environmental issues.

[9] C. Coats, 'Algeria Pledges Energy Diversification but New Law Narrows Focus' Forbes, 11 October 2012, available at <http://www.forbes.com/sites/christophercoats/2012/10/11/algeria-pledges-energy-diversification-but-new-law-narrow-focus/>.

[10] 'Natural gas and oil account for almost all of Algeria's total energy consumption. The country's only other sources are very small and insignificant amounts of hydro power, coal, solar power and traditional biomass'—US EIA (n 2) at 1.

[11] Law 13-01 dated 20 February 2013 modifying and completing Law 05-07 of April 2005 related to hydrocarbons, in Algerian (the '2013 Amendment') in Government Official Gazette (Journal Officiel de la République Algérienne Démocratique et Populaire (JORADP)) No 11 of 24 February 2013, 4–20. Law 05-07, which remains in effect after its amendment by the 2013 Amendment, can be found in JORADP No 11 of 19 July 2005, 3–28 (the '2005 Law'). All Algeria's laws and regulations applicable to the hydrocarbons sector can be found at <http://www.mem-algeria.org/francais/index.php?page=hydrocarbures-2>.

II. Algeria's legal and regulatory framework for the hydrocarbon sector: an overview

In 1999, long before unconventional hydrocarbon exploitation was contemplated, Algeria embarked on a complex process of reform of the legal and regulatory framework for the hydrocarbon sector. Initially, that process was part of a wide-ranging programme of economic reforms promised by the current Head of State, Abdelaziz Bouteflika, during his first presidential election campaign. One of the main tenets of his programme was to reform the hydrocarbon sector and open it to foreign investments. At that time, Algeria's petroleum and gas sector was governed by a 1986 Law,[12] under which the state-owned national hydrocarbon company, Sonatrach,[13] was mandated to act both as a commercial entity handling government participation in petroleum contracts and as the regulatory agency for the entire hydrocarbon sector, including the upstream and downstream components. Given the economic importance of oil and gas in Algeria, Sonatrach is the dominant force in the national economy and has been characterized as a 'State within the State'.[14]

Sonatrach enjoyed this regulatory mandate despite the fact that Algeria already had a Ministry of Energy and Mining (MEM) and National Council for Energy (NCE). The latter was established in 1995, and is chaired by the Head of the State with a membership including major ministers and the Governor of the Central Bank, with a broad mandate including the power to monitor all of Sonatrach activities.[15] To date, however, the NCE has never met, influenced, or reviewed any national hydrocarbon policies, because such policies have remained under the purview of Sonatrach, the MEM, and the Presidency.

The 1986 Law granted Sonatrach a mandatory majority participation in all petroleum-related contracts through Production Sharing Contracts (PSC) covering the entire upstream oil business. In addition to PSCs, the 1986 Law also permitted Joint-Venture Contracts (JVCs) and/or Service Contracts to be used to structure

[12] Law 86-14 of 19 August 1986 related to the prospection, exploration, exploitation, and transportation by pipeline of hydrocarbons, in JORADP No 35, 1986, 1019.

[13] Sonatrach was established by Decree 63-491 of 31 December 1963, approving the statutes of the Société nationale de transport et de commercialisation des hydrocarbures (National Society for Transportation and Trading of Hydrocarbons) (Sonatrach), as further amended by Decree 66-296 of 22 September 1966 and by Decree 98-48 of 11 February 1998 related to the Statutes of Sonatrach, in JORADP No 07 of 15 February 1998 and finally by Decree 2000-271 of 23 September 2000 in JORADP No 57 dated 24 September 2000. See M. Benchikh, *Les Instruments Juridiques de la Politique Algérienne des Hydrocarbures* (1973), and by the same author, 'La nouvelle loi pétrolière algérienne: direction publique et économie de marché' (2013) Année du Maghreb, 103, available at <http://anneemaghreb.revues.org/103>.

[14] Indeed, a well-respected economist has declared that 'Sonatrach is Algeria and Algeria is Sonatrach': A. Mebtoul, 'Polémique entre le ministère de l'énérgie et le PDG de Sonatrach', MarinDZ, 28 December 2012, available at <http://www.lematindz.net/news/10657-polemique-entre-le-ministre-de-lenergie-et-le-pdg-de-sonatrach.html>.

[15] Decree 95-102 of 8 April 1995, establishing a National Council for Energy, JORADP 1995, No 21, Arts 5 and 6.

cooperation between Sonatrach and foreign entities willing to invest in Algeria's rich oil and natural gas resources.[16] Foreign entities had to work in partnership with Sonatrach, which has majority ownership in every PSC. In 1991, the Government amended the 1986 Law in response to a severe financial crisis with mounting international debt and rapidly falling hard currency revenues. The 1991 Law[17] aimed to (i) make the tax regime more attractive; and (ii) allow foreign petroleum companies to enter into partnerships with Sonatrach to improve the outcomes of existing petroleum deposits under exploitation.

Although lauded by many analysts and petroleum specialists,[18] this legal and regulatory framework governing hydrocarbons was judged to be dysfunctional in 1999 by experts supporting the Government of Algeria's and President Bouteflika's call for reform.[19] According to these experts, the regime had created disincentives for foreign companies to invest in Algeria's oil and gas sector and Sonatrach's dual role had led to excessive institutional and regulatory complexity. Some of these experts pleaded for a 'third change' which, they said, was necessary to enable Algeria to adapt 'to the evolution of the global gas and oil scene'[20] and to encourage foreign investments.[21]

In 2001, a draft law related to hydrocarbons was presented by the Minister of Energy and Mines as a critical piece of legislation demonstrating the Government's commitment to engage in a transition towards a competitive market economy and align its energy policy with international best practice. Usually, draft legislation is not officially published. However, this particular draft was leaked to the public.[22] Strong opposition was expressed by the main Algerian labour organization and the oldest and dominant political party, FLN, along with other social and political forces. Consequently, the 2001 Draft Law had to be reviewed and amended before being re-submitted to the Parliament in 2005.

The 2005 Law resulted in substantial changes, including (i) an improved tax system attractive to foreign investors; (ii) the liberalization of access to hydrocarbons resources; and (iii) a substantial change to the status of Sonatrach to enable it to use its financial and technical potential in the global hydrocarbon market and operate as an international commercial entity without being constrained by its

[16] A. Kefaifi, 'la Loi sur les hydrocarbures, les pratiques pétrolières et le lourd héritage de Chakib Khelil', La Nation, 1–7 May 2012, available at <http://www.lanation.info/2011-2012-La-loi-sur-les-hydrocarbures-les-pratiques-petrolieres-et-le-lourd-heritage-de-C-K_a615.html>.

[17] Law No 91-21 dated 4 December 1991, modifying and completing Law 86-14 of 19 August 1986 related to the prospection, exploration, exploitation, and transportation by pipeline of hydrocarbons, in JORADP No 63 dated 7 December 1991, 1958.

[18] See Kefaifi (n 16); N. Zouiouèche, 'La politique de Khelil a augmenté la vulnérabilité de Sonatrach', El Watan, 29 May 2013, available at <http://www.elwatan.com/actualite/la-politique-de-khelil-a-augmente-la-vulnerabilite-de-sonatrach-29-05-2013-215522_109.php>.

[19] A. Mebtoul, M. Oubouzar, D. Rouag, and M. Mekkideche, 'Algerian Preliminary Draft of Hydrocarbon Law: Between the Imperative of National Development and the Challenges of Globalization' (2003) Revue Internationale Périodique de l'Association Algérienne de l'Economie de Marché (RIPAADEM) 104.

[20] Mebtoul et al (n 19) at 104.

[21] See <http://www.thefreelibrary.com/ALGERIA+-+Abdelaziz+Bouteflika.-a0159510747>.

[22] Mebtoul et al (n 19).

status as a State Owned Enterprise. Under the 2005 Law, Sonatrach no longer acts as a regulatory agency, its dual role having been judged to have undermined its dynamism as a commercial entity. Instead, the 2005 Law established two 'independent' regulatory agencies with separate mandates,[23] which have inherited the regulatory and governmental roles previously performed by Sonatrach.

The first regulatory agency (Association Algérienne pour le Développement de l'Economie de Marché (Algerian Association for the Development of Market Economy) (ALNAFT)),[24] is mandated to: (i) enhance Algeria's hydrocarbon resource potential and promote investment in the hydrocarbon sector, focusing on upstream investments; (ii) manage access to Algeria's hydrocarbon resources; (iii) establish and manage upstream data banks; (iv) issue prospecting permits; (v) review and approve development plans for hydrocarbon fields and grant exploration and exploitation acreages; (vi) select potential hydrocarbon fields to be put up for auction,[25] evaluate bids for exploration and production contracts, and enter into exploration and exploitation contracts; (vii) monitor and supervise the execution of exploitation and/or exploration contracts in accordance with the 2005 Law;[26] and (viii) assess and collect taxes.

The second regulatory agency, the Agence Nationale de Valorisation des Ressources en Hydrocarbures (Algerian Regulatory Agency for Hydrocarbon Resources Management) (ARH), enjoys the mandate to regulate and monitor all technical aspects of hydrocarbon-related activities at all stages—exploration, research, production, and transportation. The ARH is mandated to issue regulations on hydrocarbon transportation tariffs and third-party access to pipelines and storage facilities, construction specifications, health, safety, and environmental matters in general.[27] It also enforces technical specificities, norms, and standards defined in all applicable laws, regulations, and permits. The 2005 Law specifies that, beyond applicable laws and regulations, the ARH has the power to define, adopt, and enforce norms and standards based on 'best international practice'.[28]

Because the 2005 Law was well received by the markets, foreign oil operators have steadily increased their participation in exploration and production. For some observers, this was mainly due to the fact that the 2005 Law (i) cancelled the mandatory majority participation of Sonatrach in PSCs and JVCs; and (ii) reduced the role of Sonatrach—and hence its influence—in the operation of joint ventures formed with foreign companies.[29] However, under the 2005 Law, Sonatrach may exercise an option to participate in oil and gas ventures with a 20 to 30% stake when ALNAFT, the regulatory authority, approves the development plan for any discovery made under a PSC. This was a substantial change from the 1986 Law.

[23] 2005 Law, Art 12.

[24] ALNAFT seems to derive from the contraction of Al Djazair and Naft (respectively Algeria and petroleum in Arabic).

[25] 2005 Law, Arts 12 and 14.

[26] 2005 Law, Art 14.6. This provision appears to create an overlap in the respective roles of ALNAFT and ARH, which it would be desirable to clarify.

[27] 2005 Law, Art 13. [28] 2005 Law, Art 13.5.

[29] See: <http://www.carnegieendowment.org/publications/index.cfm?fa=view&id=50726>.

Nevertheless, only a few months after the enactment of the 2005 Law,[30] the government decided to shift away from a liberal policy of access to Algeria's hydrocarbon resources. A 2006 Amendment to the 2005 Law (i) granted Sonatrach the right to exercise an option to acquire a majority participation (51%) in all hydrocarbon ventures, including hydrocarbon transportation systems; (ii) established a specific windfall tax on what the Algerian government called 'super-profit' generated by foreign oil operators and producers whenever the price of oil exceeds US$30 per barrel; (iii) clarified and completed the rules related to the respective administrative structures and operation of ALNAFT and the ARH; and (iv) offered an incentive-based scheme to companies willing to invest and develop marginal oil and gas deposits.[31]

The Algerian Government gave three reasons for these changes. First, it considered that the country was attractive to large oil companies because of the high quality and accessibility of its oil and gas. Second, it wished to preserve resources for future generations. And third, it claimed foreign oil and gas companies had not raised any fundamental opposition to the 51% rule.

However, the effects of the 2006 Amendment were the opposite of what the Government expected. First, the 51% rule was considered a hindrance by many international petroleum companies, some of which have expressed their reluctance to invest in Algeria because they would not be able to assess the financial, managerial, and technical capabilities of Sonatrach to participate in the operations to be undertaken under contract with them. Second, the incentives offered by the 2006 Amendment were not considered sufficiently attractive by major oil and gas companies. On the contrary, the change was perceived to indicate an uncertain investment climate and hence companies lowered their investments or cancelled plans to invest in marginal deposits. Finally, the windfall tax created a quasi-retroactive effect that was challenged by numerous companies before arbitration courts.[32]

In sum, the 2006 Amendment has dampened international companies' interest in any future bidding rounds in Algeria. As a consequence, hydrocarbon production steadily declined over the period between 2007 and 2012, with no major discoveries made to replace existing oil and gas deposits,[33] which are believed to have reached their peak in 2009. 'Concerns over depletion of natural gas reserves have begun to be felt in Algeria [and] policy makers [are] scrambling to address

[30] Ordinance 06-10 of July 28, 2006 amending some provisions of the 2005 Law.

[31] C. Vock, 'Algeria: Recent Developments Since the Adoption of the New Hydrocarbons Law in July 2005' (2006) 1 Texas Journal of Oil, Gas and Energy Law 175.

[32] See request for arbitration by: (1) the US-energy company Anadarko (<http://www.ft.com/cms/s/0/c74801f6-4b39-11e0-b2c2-00144feab49a.html#axzz2YBAb2NyV>); and (2) the global energy and logistics company Maersk (<http://www.maerskoil.com/documents/Maersk_Annual_Report_2009_extract.pdf>).

[33] M. Mekideche, 'Sonatrach en 2011: résilience mais obstacles persistants à surmonter', Liberté, 13 July 2011, who states that in 2010, 29 oil discoveries were announced in Algeria, two of which were made in partnership with large international oil companies, available at <http://www.liberte-algerie.com>.

them.'[34] In its March 2011 licensing round, only two out of the 10 oil and gas permits on offer were awarded, one of which went to Sonatrach. The announcement of the plan to start developing unconventional hydrocarbons is perceived as a major response to the steady decline of Algeria's reserves of conventional gas and oil and rapid increase in domestic demand mentioned earlier.

In December 2011, the Algerian energy minister announced the Government's intention to make further changes to the 2005 Hydrocarbon Law to boost foreign companies' interest in exploration and exploitation investments, including in unconventional hydrocarbons. The announcement was the first official acknowledgement that substantial changes are needed to (i) correct the policies introduced by the 2006 Amendment; and (ii) offer new and additional incentives to revive international hydrocarbon companies' interest in research, exploration, and production investment in both conventional and unconventional hydrocarbons.

III. Unconventional hydrocarbon exploration and production in Algeria

As early as 2009, Algeria planned to develop technology-intensive shale hydrocarbon production to address growing demand, with a role for foreign oil companies in helping to achieve that goal.[35] According to the 2013 US EIA Report, Algeria has seven basins believed to contain 11 shale formations,[36] some containing both shale gas and shale oil. Sonatrach and its partners have undertaken a comprehensive effort to complete characterization studies of major shale hydrocarbon deposits. These studies are intended to help (i) define the size and quality of its shale gas (and oil) resources; and (ii) establish a database of older cores, logs, and other data, complemented by information from new shale well logs in the main shale basins of Algeria. A first pilot well within this shale resource assessment programme seems to be well advanced for the Berkine (Ghadames) Basin, followed by test wells in the Illizi, Timimoun, Ahnet, and Mouydir Basins.[37] There are regular news reports that prospecting/exploration permits have been granted by ALNAFT. ENI and Sonatrach also issued a press release announcing a licence granted to them jointly by ALNAFT in 2011 to start shale gas exploration and production.[38] Interestingly, the press release noted that ENI and Sonatrach have 'extensive experience in exploration and production of unconventional oil [and] will jointly implement

[34] A. Aissaoui, 'Algeria's Natural Gas Policy. Beware of the Egypt Syndrome' (2013) 8 Apicorp Economic Commentary, available at <http://www.apic.com/Research/Commentaries/2013/Commentary_V8_N7_2013.pdf>.

[35] See <http://www.law-now.com/law-now/2012/shaleupdate14aug12.htm>.

[36] US EIA (n 2) Table A.1 and Annex XV-2.

[37] See A. Rahmani, M. Kaced, and M. Arab, 'The Potential of Shale Gas Plays in Algeria' and A. Kaddour, 'Shale Gas Development in Algeria: Possible Synergy with Conventional,' papers presented to the Sonatrach Amont-International Gas Union Shale Gas Workshop, Oran, Algeria, 2012.

[38] See <http://www.eni.com/en_IT/media/press-releases/2011/04/2011-04-28-Eni_Sonatrach_accordo_gas_Algeria.shtml>. The terms of the licence itself have not yet been disclosed.

activities to assess the technical and commercial feasibility of exploration and operational initiatives in shale gas [to] enable both companies to make important discoveries which will enhance the gas potential of the country'.[39] The terms of the agreement between ENI and Sonatrach and the licence granted to them were not disclosed. They were also concluded and granted before Algeria's authorities announced that they were developing 'an appropriate regulatory regime (both environmental and fiscal) to encourage investment to access the country's enormous shale hydrocarbon reserves'. At the same time, however, the authorities committed not to authorize any '... exploitation ... until the required technology and necessary means are acquired to avoid any negative impact on the environment'.[40] The first step taken to fulfil that promise and establish the required regulatory regime is the 2013 Amendment to the 2005 Law, which was prepared by the Government and adopted by the Parliament.

Learning the lessons from the fiasco of the 2006 windfall tax and regulatory reforms, the Algerian Government has defined two major objectives for the 2013 Amendment: (i) improving the investment climate in anticipation of an expanded hydrocarbon licensing round due in the near future;[41] and (ii) providing an appropriate legal basis for the expansion of shale hydrocarbon exploration and production. Under the 2013 Amendment, the Government has put forward a 'package deal' in the form of an incentive-based plan to attract investors in unconventional hydrocarbons, which include tax breaks and the sharing of costs and risks between foreign investors and Sonatrach.

The provisions which form the substance of the 2013 Amendment include 59 articles modifying provisions of the 2005 Law, as well as 10 new articles. Ten of the new or modified provisions deal specifically with unconventional hydrocarbons including: (i) the definition of shale formations (Article 5(10) and (21)); (ii) the reservoir and duration of exploration permits (Articles 35 and 38); (iii) the pilot phase of production for shale hydrocarbons (Article 46(3)); (iv) the content of the development plan of shale hydrocarbon deposits (Article 47(7)); (v) the use of water for the purpose of non-conventional hydrocarbons production (Article 53(2)); (vi) a tax incentive (Article 84); and (vii) the authorization of shale hydrocarbons-related activities for conventional hydrocarbon title holders (Article 110bis). In total, as expected by observers and oil companies, the new provisions cover permitting processes, tax, and environmental issues which are of interest to investors seeking business in shale formations or who make shale discoveries in the course of conventional hydrocarbon exploration.

Under the 2013 Amendment, the regulatory burden on foreign companies is eased and their dealings with ALNAFT, the ARH, and Sonatrach are facilitated. The 2013 Amendment has not modified the position of Sonatrach, which is

[39] See n 38.

[40] A. Kefaifi, 'La décision prématurée sur les gaz non-conventionnels: avant l'heure ce n'est pas l'heure, (le gaz de schiste) et, après l'heure ce n'est plus l'heure', 26 September 2012, available at <http://www.lanation.info/La-decision-prematuree-sur-les-gaz-non-conventionnels_a1424.html>.

[41] Expected before the end of 2013.

expected to remain the dominant player in the overall hydrocarbon sector, including shale hydrocarbons.[42] However, Sonatrach now shares all risks connected to exploration for unconventional hydrocarbons, which constitutes a substantial difference from the situation with conventional hydrocarbons, where Sonatrach takes no exploration risk.

Owing to the strong reservations expressed by academics, experts, and domestic and international NGOs about the environmental impacts of shale hydrocarbon development both in general and in the specific Algerian context,[43] section IV discusses the environmental conditions associated with the development of hydrocarbons in general and unconventional hydrocarbons in particular.

IV. Algeria's environmental law and hydrocarbon sector development

The 1986 Law included broad provisions on conservation of hydrocarbon reserves[44] and obligations on hydrocarbon licence holders to comply with applicable laws and regulations.[45] These provisions appear to assume that, as a general rule, environmental laws and regulations apply to all hydrocarbon activities. However, over its five-decades-long history, the hydrocarbon industry has been seen primarily as a generator of fiscal revenues, which means that the government is less inclined to address environmental and/or natural risk issues connected to hydrocarbons exploration and/or production, and focuses instead on fiscal and other tax-related issues.[46] In fact, although the 1983 Environmental Framework Law (the '1983 EFL')[47] is mentioned in the preamble to the 1986 Law, there are no provisions dealing with environmental compliance in the main body of the law itself. Indeed, Article 5 states that '*future* laws and regulations shall govern the activities related to prospection, research, exploitation, and transport of liquid hydrocarbons' (emphasis added). This general approach was maintained under the 1991 Law and, accordingly, the applicability of relevant environmental laws and regulations to hydrocarbon operations remained uncertain unless they were spelled out in specific implementing regulations and/or contracts between the competent Algerian agency

[42] It seems that in practice, oil companies (Sonatrach and its partner companies) which have already explored given shale gas deposits under a prospecting/exploration for a conventional hydrocarbon permit or contract, and fulfilled other prescribed obligations, will enjoy a priority right to sign a contract with respect to shale hydrocarbon production. No tender for granting production rights for the same deposit may be held by ALNAFT.

[43] E.g., Algerian and international environmental groups demonstrated against fracking for unconventional gas and oil during a visit of the Algerian Minister of Energy to London to present the 2013 Law to British and other international oil companies, see <http://platformlondon.org/2013/04/17/gaz-de-schiste-cest-fasciste-fracking-algeria/>.

[44] Law 86-14 related to the activities of prospection, research, exploitation, and transport by pipelines of hydrocarbons, in JORADP, No 35 of 27 August 1986, 1019–26, Art 14.

[45] Law 86-14, Arts 15 and 30.

[46] Title VI Tax Regime' constitutes almost two-thirds of the whole text.

[47] Law 83-03 of 5 February 1983 related to environmental protection, in JORADP No 6, 1983, 250.

and hydrocarbon licensees.[48] This approach was substantially modified through the 2003 Law on Environment Protection within the Framework of Sustainable Development (ESDL)[49] and the 2005 Law, to better consider environmental aspects connected to hydrocarbons exploration and production, including unconventional hydrocarbons.

A. Algeria's general environmental protection regime

Algeria has a fairly comprehensive legal and regulatory framework for environmental management and protection. The country was among the very first Third World countries to enact a comprehensive environmental legislation (the '1983 EFL'), which was supplemented by numerous implementing regulations. The 1983 EFL was replaced by the 2003 ESDL. Except if otherwise stated in the 2003 ESDL, the implementing regulations adopted in connection with the 1983 EFL remain in effect and include those related to: (i) pollution control procedures, norms, and standards;[50] (ii) control of emission of air pollutants;[51] (iii) norms and standards related to emission of liquid industrial effluents;[52] (iv) classified facilities;[53] and (v) environmental impact assessment (EIA).[54] Other regulations were adopted in connection with the 2003 ESDL including: (i) new EIA regulations[55] and specific EIA rules for hydrocarbon projects;[56] (ii) the use of chemical products that deplete the ozone layer;[57] (iii) rules and procedures applicable to safety in the handling of hazardous chemicals and pressured gas containers;[58] and (v) conservation of oil and

[48] M. A. Bekhechi, 'International Investment and Environmental Protection: Notes on the Environmental Conditions of Investments in the Oil and Mining Sectors' in International Investment and Protection of the Environment: the Role of Dispute Resolution Mechanisms (International Bureau of the Permanent Court of Arbitration, ed, 2001) 73.

[49] Law No 2003-10 of 19 July 2003 related to environmental protection in the framework of sustainable development, available at <http://www.joradp.dz/FTP/jo-francais/2003/F2003043.pdf>.

[50] Decree 06-12 of 7 January 2006 related to air quality and atmospheric pollution control, in JORADP No 1 of 8 January 2006.

[51] Decree 06-138 of 15 April 2006 governing emission in the atmosphere of gaseous particles, fumes, vapours whether liquids or solids including conditions of their control, in JORADP No 24 of 16 April 2006.

[52] Decree 06-1412 of 19 April 2006 related to the standards applicable to the emission of liquid industrial effluents, in JORADP No 26 of 23 April 2006.

[53] Decree 06-198 of 5 May 2006 defining regulations applicable to classified facilities in view of protecting the environment, in JORADP No 37 of 4 June 2006.

[54] Decree 90-78 of 27 February 1990 on Environmental Impact assessment, in JORADP No 10 dated 7 March 1990, 318 (the '1990 EIA Decree'), which remained in effect until the issuance of Decree 07-145 of 19 May 2007 related to the scope, the content, and modalities of approval of environmental impact notices and studies, in JORADP No 58 of 22 May 2007, 105 (the '2007 EIA Decree').

[55] Decree 07-145 (n 54).

[56] Decree 08-312 of 5 October 2008 on conditions of approval of EIA for activities related to hydrocarbon sector, in JORADP No 34 dated 22 May 2008.

[57] Decree 13-110 of 17 March 2013 related to the use of substances that deplete the ozone layer, in JORADP No 17 of 27 March 2013, 5.

[58] Decree 10-19 of 12 January 2010 amending and modifying Decree 03-451 of 1 December 2003 defining safety rules applicable to activities pertaining to hazardous chemicals and pressured gas containers, in JORADP No 4 of 17 January 2010, 5.

gas deposits, including their associated aquifers.[59] In addition, numerous other laws of greater or lesser importance in terms of safeguarding environmental protection during hydrocarbons operations apply, notably laws related to water conservation, waste, and atmospheric pollution.[60]

B. Application of environmental law in the hydrocarbon sector

As mentioned earlier, the government was not inclined to subject the hydrocarbon industry, especially the upstream part of it, to the general environmental law regime. Instead, it acted under the general principle of *lex specialis generalibus derogant* and considered, in practice, that the hydrocarbon industry was generally subjected only to those environmental principles included in the hydrocarbon sector legislation and regulations *stricto sensu*. The 1986 and 2005 Laws, including their various amendments, remained vague enough to allow the petroleum sector to develop without being subjected to any stringent obligations. Sonatrach and its foreign partners were not obliged to demonstrate the environmental quality of their projects and activities but only to 'comply with rules and methods to preserve the hydrocarbon deposits, ensure their conservation and reach the maximum economic profitability, notably through use of available recuperation methods'.[61] The 'maximum economic profitability' was considered to be key in this provision.

A 1988 Decree to implement the 1986 Law, defining the conditions for granting, renouncing and withdrawing hydrocarbon prospection, research, and exploitation titles, failed to refer to any environmental condition(s).[62] Other implementing decrees for both the 1986 Law and 2005 Law confirm the opinion that the government has chosen to remain vague in terms of environmental management and protection in connection with hydrocarbon operations.

An example can be found in Decree 07-184 related to the procedures for the conclusion of contracts for hydrocarbon research and exploitation and contracts for

59 Decree 05-158 dated 27 April 2005 related to the rules of conservation of hydrocarbons deposits and associated aquifers, in JORADP No 49 dated 13 July 2005, 20, which replaced Decree 94-43 of 30 January 1994.

60 These laws and regulations are listed in the 'Whereas' sections of the 2013 Law and they include: (i) ordinance no 76-04 of 20 February 1976 related to rules applicable to safety and fire risks; (ii) law no 83-17 of 16 July 1983, related to the water code; (iii) law no 84-12 of 23 June 1984, related to forests; (iv) law no 85-05 of 16 February 1985 related to the protection and promotion of public health; (v) law no 87-17 of 1 August 1987 related to phytosanitary protection; (vi) law no 90-25 of 18 November 1990, on land policy; (vii) law no 98-04 of 15 June 1998 related to the protection of cultural heritage; (x) law no 99-09 of 28 July 1999 related to energy control; (viii) law no 2001-19 of 12 December 2001 related to waste management; (xii) law no 2001-20 of 12 December 2001 related to land use planning and sustainable development.

61 1986 Law, Art 14. Later in 1994, the government issued Decree 94-43 on the conservation of hydrocarbon deposits and protection of the associated aquifers: JORADP No 8 dated 13 February 1994. This decree provided indications on 'technical' criteria to be used in addressing the protection of the deposits and their associated aquifers and was later amended and completed by Decree 05-158 (n 59).

62 Decree no 88-34 of 16 February 1988 relatif aux conditions d'octroi de renonciation et de retrait des titres miniers pour la prospection, la recherche et l'exploitation des hydrocarbures, in JORADP No 007 of 17 February 1988, 207.

exploitation of hydrocarbons following a bidding process.[63] Article 19 of this Decree states that hydrocarbon fields to be offered for bidding shall be selected on the basis of: (i) the availability of technical data; (ii) the opening of underdeveloped areas; (iii) the need for specific technologies; and (iv) the global energy environment. The first criterion (technical data) is further detailed in Annex B to the Decree, which includes environmental aspects and requires proponents to describe in their proposals: (i) 'particular environmental challenges' that they have faced in their hydrocarbon exploration projects[64] during the previous seven years, and the same for the hydrocarbon development and/or exploitation;[65] and (ii) their health, safety, and environmental management capacity.[66] As such, these provisions do not impose any obligation on proponents in connection with environmental management and protection. They merely seek information on the proponent's experience and capacity to deal with environmental issues.

Similarly, the Decree on conservation of hydrocarbon deposits and associated aquifers[67] states in Article 6 that 'notwithstanding application of the provisions of Article 2 herein above, where the role of operator is not fulfilled by the national company (Sonatrach), the latter is obliged to communicate the legal and regulatory texts in effect with which its partners must comply'.[68] Article 2 goes further, stating that the operator must demonstrate its capacity to take into account technical progress in exploration and evaluation of hydrocarbon resources and to undertake any geological, geophysical, and geochemical studies related to hydrocarbon sites. There is no mention of environmental management capacity. No further reference is made to environmental norms, rules, and/or standards that would be complied with and/or implemented by the operator. Article 9 of the same decree states that the operator must demonstrate its 'technical and financial capacities' to be allowed to undertake prospection and research activities. Also, although Article 9 mandates the Minister to enact additional specific regulations, no additional or implementing rules were adopted, leaving the scope of this article open to interpretation. Decree 94-43, even as amended and completed by Decree 05-158,[69] remains weak as it only obliges operators to restore the area after the end of the activities and does not provide for independent monitoring and/or enforcement, disclosure, or reporting of any kind.

In addition, the 1990 Decree on EIA adopted under the 1983 EFL did not subject hydrocarbon-related activities to any mandatory environmental assessment,[70] although its Article 2 stated that 'all facilities or works which, by their size or importance of their impact, may directly or indirectly affect the environment, including public health, agriculture, natural areas, wildlife, flora, or conservation of monuments are subject to a prior environmental impact study'. This principle, widely considered as a general principle of environmental law, was not

[63] Decree 07-184, full text in JORADP No 40, dated 17 June 2007, 15–19.
[64] Decree 07-184, Annex B 'Aspects techniques', Para A.i. [65] Decree 07-184, Para A.ii.
[66] Decree 07-184, Para A.iii. [67] Decree 94-43 (n 61).
[68] Decree 94-43, Art 2. [69] Decree 05-158 (n 59).
[70] Decree no 90-78 of 27 February 1990 relatif aux études d'impact sur l'environnement, JORADP No 10 of 7 March 1990, 318.

consistently applied to the hydrocarbon industry in Algeria. Article 3 of the same Decree stated that activities, facilities, and works listed in the Annex to the Decree are not subject to EIA and will be governed by 'specific laws and regulations'. Mining was listed and it was assumed that hydrocarbons are included within the mining sector.

These examples clearly show that environmental protection was not considered a fundamental issue in any of the policies and laws that were developed and promulgated by the government to govern hydrocarbon industries. The fact that these regulations do not explicitly include specific mandatory and stringent obligations, clear processes and institutional arrangements for implementation, monitoring compliance, and enforcement can certainly be perceived as a way of lowering the regulatory burden on Sonatrach and its partners. By adopting these provisions, the government has effectively shielded hydrocarbon operations from any third-party scrutiny, environmental control, and liability that may arise from such operations.

This overall framework was substantially amended by the 2005 Law, which has helped make some progress in this regard. Article 2 of the 2005 Law states that no hydrocarbon permits, licences, and/or contracts can be issued without a prior review by several Government agencies, including the Ministry of Environment (MOE).[71] Article 16 requires that hydrocarbon activities must be conducted in a precautionary manner to prevent risks. Article 18 imposes an obligation on hydrocarbon project proponents to prepare and submit an EIA to the ARH, as well as an Environmental Management Plan (EMP), which must 'describe prevention measures [...] for the management of risks associated with their activities'. In addition, the same law imposes a duty on hydrocarbon exploration and production proponents—who are already operating—to comply with existing environmental and industrial safety laws and regulations, and it grants them a seven-year period in which to achieve this objective.[72]

These provisions constitute a very positive step towards better environmental management and protection in Algeria's hydrocarbon sector. However, they were not followed by regulations to clarify implementation and enforcement modalities. A 2007 Decree on the issuance of hydrocarbon research and production titles[73] merely states that applications for hydrocarbon titles must be accompanied by a description and maps of the site and a justification for the geographical limits of the site. Applications are subject to review of various agencies and authorities, including the MOE and the competent local governor (the 'Wali').[74] Ministers and Wali have

[71] Hydrocarbon exploration or exploitation permits are issued by ALNAFT, which is obligated to seek the opinion ('avis' in French) of the ministers in charge of 'national defence, interior, finances, mines, water resources, environment, agriculture, culture, industry, tourism as well as walis (local governors) of the areas in which is located the hydrocarbon field sought by the requested permit'.

[72] 2005 Law, Art 109.

[73] Executive Decree No 07-185 of 9 June 2007 on conditions of issuance of mining titles for hydrocarbons exploration and/or production, in JORADP No 40 of 17 June 2007.

[74] Executive Decree No 07-185 of 9 June 2007 (n 73), 21–3.

a two-month timeframe to provide the regulatory agency with their feedback and comments, although their opinions are not binding.

Similarly, another 2007 Decree,[75] on the procedures and modalities of issuance of exploration permits, states that the proponent can undertake activities such as 'geological, geophysical and geochemical methods, including stratigraphic drilling'. If and when the requested permit is connected to a sensitive area (e.g., close to a national park or to an underground water table), then the Decree states that these activities can be conducted without providing any prior environmental documentation, whether in the form of a simple analysis of issues to be addressed, or of a proposal of environmental mitigation measures associated with the methods to be used, or of any other environmental protection instrument.

By not imposing clear and specific obligations on environmental protection, the regulations issued through this 2007 Decree can be seen as lowering the environmental standards which the 2005 Law aimed to promote. The regulations merely require that the site must be restored at the end of the activities.[76]

The government and the petroleum companies appear to be sticking to the principle that only those environmental rules explicitly and specifically included in hydrocarbon-related laws, regulations, and contracts apply to their activities. Nevertheless, it can be argued to the contrary that nothing in this can be construed as exempting hydrocarbon companies from compliance with applicable laws and regulations including those related to environmental protection, industrial, health, and safety norms and standards when dealing with unconventional hydrocarbon exploration and production.

C. Shale hydrocarbons and environmental law in Algeria

The question of particular importance to this analysis is to understand whether the described environmental legal and regulatory framework for environmental management is adequate to cover shale hydrocarbon-related activities in Algeria. This issue is highly relevant when considering the gaps in and weaknesses of the legal and regulatory framework for environmental protection discussed above.

A number of particular questions arise. For example, are permits for shale hydrocarbons exploration and production subject to environmental assessment? Are the risks of fracking taken into account? If so, how are they dealt with? Are issues of water use and pollution in connection with fracking adequately covered by existing legislation? Are these permits subject to full disclosure in draft form in order to allow for public review and comment? Are environmental permits disclosed to allow compliance monitoring of shale hydrocarbon-related operations with appropriate and required environmental conditions? These questions need to

[75] Executive Decree No 07-294 of 26 September 2007 on procedures and conditions of granting authorization for the prospection of hydrocarbons, in JORADP No 62 of 3 October 2007, 17.

[76] Executive Decree No 07-294, Art 6 states the request must include a commitment to restore the site within three months of the end of the works period. Minutes will be established between ALNAFT and the permit holder to document the restoration of the site.

be addressed because of the potentially harmful impacts associated with shale hydrocarbons operations. Answering them will help identify the required environmental safeguards to fill potential gaps in the current environmental legal and regulatory framework.

In fact, the potential environmental concerns associated with unconventional hydrocarbon exploration and production (particularly fracking), are well known and controversial.[77] For a water-stressed country like Algeria, the most problematic issues relate to water use and pollution. Using large amounts of existing underground aquifers may impact negatively on natural aquatic habitats, especially those likely to be tapped in the northern part of the Sahara desert.[78] These aquifers may potentially be polluted by accidental release, spill, or leak of harmful chemicals, or by faulty well construction. Fracking will result in large amounts of wastewater contaminated by harmful chemicals, which will require additional treatment before release into the environment or reuse. In addition, these wastewaters are generally disposed of by injection into deep wells which can cause earthquakes large enough to be felt and cause damage.[79] Finally, it is proven that methane release in the atmosphere can occur as a consequence of water injection during fracking operations.

It is worth noting that even before shale hydrocarbons became the subject of new policies in Algeria, Decree 94-43[80] had opened the door to regulation of fracking. Article 80 mandates that hydrodynamic tests and studies of the characteristics of the reservoir be undertaken before any fracturing operation (pressure of the deposit, filling, vertical and lateral heterogeneity of permeability) and it authorizes fracking under certain conditions, such as low-permeability reservoirs, deposits with important pressure (including if such pressure improves at significant distance from the well), and when the same efficiency is observed if the layers were sealed during drilling. However, if fracking has limited effect on the productivity of the deposit, then its repetition must be questioned on technical and economic grounds (Article 85).

[77] See n 43 and also n 79.

[78] Environmental law subjects water resources uses to stringent standards and refers to the relevant water legislation for implementing these standards. In fact, under the 2003 EFL, the protection and conservation of water resources must take into account conflicting interests (Art 48) including water supply, water uses, and their impacts on public health and the environment (Art 48.1), the balance of aquatic ecosystems (Art 48.2), the recreational aspects, and water flow and conservation (Art 48.3 and 4). All water resources are assessed on a regular basis to document their quantity and quality, including their pollution loads in order to address any quality issue. Specific regulations shall be issued to govern the quality of surface or underground water. Art 50 states that discharge facilities must comply with specific guidelines and rules set by regulations of the Ministry in charge of water, in particular rules to: (i) prohibit spills, discharges, releases, direct or indirect deposits of materials or substances which may affect the quality of surface, groundwater and/or coastal waters; and (ii) monitor the physical, chemical, biological and bacteriological water discharge and the conditions under which sampling and sample analyses are carried out.

[79] E.g., in the United States, the injection wells typically discharge the wastewater into non-potable salt-water aquifers. For discussion of fracking, see <http://www.eia.gov/energy_in_brief/article/about_shale_gas.cfm>; J. D. Furlow and C. V. Snow, 'In the Wake of the Shale Revolution: A Primer on Hydraulic Fracturing Fluid Chemical Disclosure' (2013) Texas Journal of Oil, Gas and Energy Law 249; and <http://www.earthworksaction.org/issues/details/hydraulic_fracturing_101#.UhHs48u9KSM>.

[80] Decree 05-158 (n 59).

The same decree also stipulates that before any fracking can take place, the wells must be carefully cleaned (Article 83). The Decree mandated the MEM to authorize any fracking request that contains a detailed programme of the envisioned operation (Article 87).

Although not stated clearly, the 2013 Amendment confirms the high risks posed by fracking, and owing to such risks, it provides that studies related to 'hazards' posed by the activities governed by the Law must define and justify the 'prevention and protection measures to be implemented' to address such hazards (Article 18(6)). These studies are subject to review and approval of the ARH, in compliance with regulations to be further enacted (Article 18(9)), and must be updated every five years (Article 18(8)). The appropriate instrument for applying these prescriptions is an EIA. The 2013 Amendment has also added a new Article 23 bis to the 2005 Law, which transfers responsibility for authorization of fracking activities from the MEM to the Council of Ministers. This provision, which amends Decree 94-43[81] discussed earlier, may also be interpreted as limiting the mandate of the ARH.

In addition to addressing the fracking aspect of unconventional hydrocarbon exploration and production, the 2013 Amendment addresses other aspects of environmental protection connected to shale hydrocarbon-related activities. It: (i) defines 'unconventional hydrocarbons', which are those hydrocarbons contained in shale formations[82] or 'reservoirs';[83] (ii) reiterates the general principle that the operator (whether 'party to a contract or concessionaire') must comply with all laws and regulations;[84] and (iii) mandates the ARH to issue all technical regulations applicable to hydrocarbons activities governed by this Law,[85] including regulations related to 'health, industrial safety, environment and major risks preventions, notably protection of aquifers and underground waters in connection with the implementation of hydrocarbon-related activities',[86] 'use of chemicals',[87] and 'carbon dioxide'.[88] It is expected that additional regulations will help clarify and complete the existing legal and regulatory framework to address thoroughly environmental protection issues. In fact, by virtue of the 2013 Amendment, the ARH is mandated to implement, adopt, and enforce standards and norms consistent with best international practices. In addition, ALNAFT must ensure that all issued contracts and permits are in compliance with applicable laws and regulations in effect, including those related to 'environmental protection' (Article 17(2)).

By empowering the ARH to enact any regulations needed in connection with shale gas exploration and exploitation, as well as hydrocarbons in general, the Government seems to intend to enact new regulations on unconventional hydrocarbons as and when needed. The Government shows openness to the principle that, if the prospecting/exploration or production of unconventional hydrocarbons impacts on the environment in a manner not regulated under the currently binding law, any such loophole will be addressed through amendments to the environmental laws currently

[81] See n 68. [82] Article 5(10). [83] Article 5(21). [84] Article 7(3).
[85] 'This Law' refers to the 2005 Law, including the 2013 Amendment; cf. Art 13(1)(1) and 13(2).
[86] Article 13(1)(3). [87] Article 13(1)(4). [88] Article 13(1)(5).

in effect by regulations to be enacted by the ARH and/or contractual provisions to be negotiated by ALNAFT with any foreign oil companies and Sonatrach.[89] This is different from the Government's previous attitude, which did not show any intention to adopt any law specifically concerning the environmental issues associated with unconventional hydrocarbon activities. The adoption of the principle to submit hydrocarbon-related operations to a prior EIA is an interesting demonstration of the new approach being developed by the Government.

D. Environmental impact assessment and hydrocarbon activities

Decree 07-145 implementing the 2003 ESDL (the '2007 EIA Decree') subjects hydrocarbon development-related projects to a prior EIA.[90] This Decree was followed by the adoption of the sector-specific 2008 Decree defining a process for the review and decision related to EIAs for hydrocarbon projects.[91] Under the 2013 Law, the ARH is the regulatory agency in charge of environmental aspects of hydrocarbon-related activities. It is empowered to identify and register consulting firms that will be authorized to conduct EIAs in the hydrocarbon sector in accordance with the 2008 decree.[92]

The EIA applies to both exploration and production activities. The EIA content for exploration activities is described in Article 7 for exploration and Article 8 for production project. In both cases,[93] the EIA report must: (i) provide a thorough review and analysis of water use and pollution, as well as describe impacts on the soil, the biosphere, and the atmosphere;[94] and (ii) include an EMP[95] defining measures for the prevention and management of environmental risks associated with hydrocarbon-related activities 'in compliance with applicable environmental laws and regulations'.[96]

The EIA processes, including public consultation and disclosure, cannot be considered good practice. In fact, the public is invited to comment in the affected area during a one-month period without a mandatory disclosure of the EIA and EMP.[97] The 2007 EIA Decree states that the competent Wali will make the EIA study available 'upon request from interested stakeholders',[98] but these 'interested stakeholders' are not defined.

[89] 2013 Amendment, Art 13. [90] Annex 1, items 21 and 23 of Decree 07-145.

[91] Decree 08-312. [92] Decree 08-312, Art 4. [93] Decree 08-312, Art 2.1.

[94] Decree 08-312, Art 6.1–6.4.

[95] The EMP must include mitigation measures, contingency plans to address oil pollution, sites, and soil contamination and monitoring and evaluation plan (Art 6.5) and finally a decommissioning and restoration plan after the end of the operations.

[96] Decree 08-312, Art 2.2.

[97] It is the Wali of the project area in which the project is to be implemented who will authorize a public inquiry process governed by the 2007 EIA Decree, Arts 9-15 and Decree 08-312, Art 15.

[98] The public participation process described in the Algerian legislation is far from constituting good practice. To be effective, the right to participation must include an entitlement to access the proposed project or activity files and reports. In addition, there must be sufficient time for participation, and the results of the consultation must be accurately documented in the final decision.

The EIA is to be submitted for review by the ARH and if and when found acceptable, the ARH must circulate it, along with its own report, to ministerial departments and Walis for their feedback and opinion (Article 14). The outcome of the public consultation and the opinions of the various ministerial departments will then be forwarded to the ARH within 45 days (Article 16).[99]

If substantial reservations are expressed by the various authorities and stakeholders during the consultation process, the proponent is required to amend the EIA and resubmit it to the ARH (Article 17). The amended EIA must again be circulated for review and feedback from the same stakeholders. If no reservations are expressed, the ARH must notify the proponent and issue an environmental authorization upon receiving the final non objection ('visa') from the MOE (Article 19.2). Finally, it is the ARH which is mandated to monitor implementation of the EIA and to enforce the laws and regulations in case of noncompliance (Article 20).

However, it is not clear whether, in practice, the EIA system operates as intended, as no public information is available on EIAs for the hydrocarbon sector. Some EIAs do appear to have been prepared by international oil companies,[100] but under what conditions and processes they were implemented, and what mitigation measures, including monitoring and supervision, were adopted, remain unknown.

This confirms the general approach taken by Algeria's Government that, even where EIAs are developed, they are not subject to public disclosure and consultation and the terms of environmental permits remain unclear. This is not consistent with best international and industry practice, as a transparent, effective, and enforceable EIA process is known to be the best way to reduce, mitigate, and/or offset negative and harmful impacts of all hydrocarbon-related operations and activities, including those connected to unconventional exploration and production. However, transparency and effectiveness seem not to be major qualities of the EIA process in Algeria for hydrocarbon activities, and more generally.

E. Implementation and enforcement of environmental law in relation to shale hydrocarbons development

Algeria's current environmental legislation, although formally well developed, is not enforced consistently. Information and data about environmental management of the hydrocarbon sector are lacking, and a lack of enforcement capacity, coupled with a certain 'laissez-aller, laissez-faire', is well documented. It is not clear whether the government commissioned any studies on the potential environmental impacts of shale hydrocarbon development in the Sahara Desert or elsewhere before the 2013 Amendment was adopted.

[99] This process does not provide for the relevant documentation to be disclosed as early as possible to allow interested parties and citizens to access it in an easily accessible manner, eg, via a website.

[100] E.g., the consulting firm ERM claims that it has prepared EIAs for the Spanish oil company REPSOL and the Japanese IHI Corp Ltd, respectively—see <http://www.erm.com/en/Analysis-and-Insight/Case-Studies/Case-Study-Repsol-Exploration-Algeria-SA/> and <http://www.erm.com/en/Analysis-and-Insight/Case-Studies/Case-Study-IHI-Corporation/>.

Since no full EIA report has been released, and no EMP for any oil development has been disclosed and monitored, questions and concerns about environmental protection in the hydrocarbon sector are legitimate and cannot be circumvented by general statements on the willingness of Algeria's authorities to enforce environmental legislation. Algeria's overall framework for environmental protection has numerous provisions that must be taken into account when dealing with shale hydrocarbon development and exploitation,[101] the application of which are yet to be clarified and monitored effectively in the absence of any full publicly released EIA report or specific report on water use and pollution in the course of shale hydrocarbon-related operations or any other hydrocarbon exploration or production operation. How, for example, water permits are issued, monitored, and enforced by the competent authority (Ministry of Hydraulic in charge of water resources management) is yet to be monitored in practice, including for those permits to be issued for the injection of hydraulic fracturing fluid[102] into the shale.

V. Concluding remarks

Algeria has proceeded with decisions to authorize fracking for shale hydrocarbon development and to include, in the 2013 Amendment, general provisions to address the harmful impacts of fracking. This legislation constitutes a positive first step. However, appropriate implementing regulations and effective enforcement are also required. Future developments should include the introduction of those principles that govern: (i) public consultation and participation in decision-making processes related to hydrocarbon development, including shale; and (ii) transparency of the negotiation processes for and outcomes of investments in the hydrocarbon sector and disclosure of all relevant documentation, including EIAs and EMPs. These principles will certainly help strengthen implementation of and compliance with policies, laws, and contracts related to the hydrocarbon sector—a sector which constitutes the backbone of the Algerian economy.

Algeria would be well advised to follow the practice of other countries (such as Poland, Bulgaria, the United Kingdom, and South Africa), which commissioned comprehensive studies, including public consultation, before deciding whether to authorize shale hydrocarbon development in specific areas of their territory.[103]

[101] In particular, see n 58, n 60, and n 78.

[102] Fracking uses fluids that contain a mixture of sand and chemical substances. In Algeria, the obligations associated with the use of chemical substances derive from the legislation on classified establishments and other regulations that are under the purview of different authorities. Any person who uses a chemical substance, either on its own or in a mixture, in the course of industrial or professional activities must comply with legislation and regulations that govern the matter. The general principle is that any person must identify and apply adequate measures to control the risks associated with such chemicals, and report to the competent authorities all information connected to the use of said chemicals.

[103] See CMS Cameron McKenna, 'Shale Gas: Legal Developments in Some Key Jurisdictions', Law-Now 23 April 2012, available at: <http://www.law-now.com/law-now/2012/shalegasapril2012.htm>.

Algeria should also draw upon other countries' experiences to develop a programme to strengthen compliance with current legislation, international environmental conventions, and newly developed good industry practices which the ARH has the mandate to identify. The authorities must accept the principle that no compromise be made on the requirement for each energy project to be subjected to a detailed EIA, which thoroughly addresses potential impacts and assesses alternatives. A legal effort must be part of this endeavour, which will include setting clear and stringent standards and developing adequate institutional and technical capacity to monitor shale hydrocarbon development by training staff in the various agencies involved, including strengthening enforcement bodies.[104]

[104] These must include: petroleum regulatory bodies ARH and ALNAFT, ministries in charge of energy and environment, the judiciary, state-owned and foreign companies involved in shale hydrocarbons development, and other civil society institutions.

12

Regulation of Unconventional Reservoirs in Colombia

Milton Fernando Montoya Pardo

I. Introduction

Potential exploration and exploitation of unconventional reservoirs has emerged as an important alternative in Colombia to strengthen the growth of the oil industry. The current energy policy has supported this possibility and, recently, there have been major regulatory reforms that introduce clear rules to promote the birth and growth of this industry. However, environmental concerns have not been cleared. Consequently, environmental licensing of these projects represents one of the main challenges faced by authorities.

This chapter presents the legal and institutional regime for exploration and development of unconventional reservoirs in Colombia, the country's current potential, the advances in public procurement, the authorities' concerns, and the main challenges that the industry is facing.

II. Importance of the hydrocarbon industry

In Colombia, the hydrocarbon industry has experienced significant growth over the past eight years, especially the oil industry. Several reasons explain this intense development, which has allowed local governments to obtain greater financial resources, as well as increased exports and the possibility for Colombia to become one of the top three oil-producing countries in South America, after Venezuela and Brazil.

The reasons for the oil industry's expansion in Colombia can be summarized as follows:

1. a drastic institutional and regulatory change in the hydrocarbons sector;[1]
2. a significant improvement in the country's physical security;

[1] See section III.

3. the development and growth of the oil industry as a permanent energy policy objective of the last two governments;[2]
4. the rise in international commodities' prices.

These four factors have meant that, as discussed in this chapter, there has been continued growth in oil production indicators. In fact, the oil industry is currently one of the country's main economic activities.[3] By December 2012, Colombia had proven reserves equivalent to 2,377 million barrels[4] (the fourth largest in South America), and in the same year reached an average production of 944,000 barrels per day (bbl/d).[5] In January 2013, the country finally reached a historical record production of 1,015,000 bbl/d.[6]

It has been estimated that in 2013 the oil production would range from 1,030,000 bbl/d and 1,060,000 bbl/d.[7] The target is to consolidate Colombia as one of the 20 countries in the world that produce more than one million barrels per day.[8]

Regarding natural gas, average production in 2012 was 1,155 million cubic feet per day.[9] Gas production has maintained constant growth levels over the past five years, but its intensity is not that of the oil sector, mainly because production is linked to demand.[10]

Taking into account the importance of the hydrocarbon industry in the current energy policy, the priorities for oil and gas, according to the National Development Plan,[11] are to:

- strengthen incentives to attract investment to the hydrocarbon sector through the following actions: (i) maintain the economic, security, and contractual rules in force; (ii) expand the level of knowledge of the subsoil; (iii) evaluate industrial safety regulations; and (iv) *identify and exploit the potential in unconventional reservoirs*;[12]
- implement projects to expand transport capacity and ensure third-party access to transport infrastructure and petroleum products;

[2] Under Alvaro Uribe Velez and Juan Manuel Santos: Uribe (2002–2006, 2006–2010), Santos (2010–2014).

[3] Asociación Nacional de Empresarios de Colombia, 'Colombia: Balance 2012 y Perspectivas' (2013) 23, available at <http://www.andi.com.co>. In 2012, the Colombian energy industry (mining, oil, gas and electricity) represented around 15% (US$55,000,000,000) of the Gross Domestic Product (GDP), in which the oil industry participates with a 9% share.

[4] Agencia Nacional de Hidrocarburos, 'Indicadores de Gestión y Estadística de la Industria a Mayo de 2013', available at <http://www.anh.gov.co>.

[5] Agencia Nacional de Hidrocarburos (n 4).

[6] Agencia Nacional de Hidrocarburos (n 4).

[7] Agencia Nacional de Hidrocarburos (n 4).

[8] Agencia Nacional de Hidrocarburos (n 4). For instance, in March 2013, the daily oil production reached 1,012,000 bbl/d (in March 2012: 947,000 bbl/d).

[9] Agencia Nacional de Hidrocarburos (n 4).

[10] Asociación Colombiana del Petróleo, 'Informe Estadístico Petrolero' (2011) 28, available at <http://www.acp.com.co>.

[11] Departamento Nacional de Planeación, 'Plan Nacional de Desarrollo "Prosperidad Para Todos" Resumen Ejecutivo, 2010–2014' (2010) 18, available at <http://www.dnp.gov.co>. This plan was developed by Law 1450/2011.

[12] Emphasis added.

- design and implement a policy to consolidate the natural gas sector, including issues such as storage, expanding exploration, the destination or end use of the gas, the institutional framework, and reliability of supply.

These strategies have resulted in the foreign direct investment in mining, gas, and oil reaching a record amount of US$12,500,000,000 in 2012.[13] Alone, the oil industry reached a record of more than US$6,500,000,000.[14] Regarding the economic gains resulting from mining and hydrocarbons activities, Colombia received $10,540,000,000 Colombian pesos (COP) (approx US$57,000,000) in royalties in 2012, of which COP$8,500,000,000 came from the hydrocarbons industry.[15]

The favourable outlook described here is also the result of a transformation that occurred in 2003 in the institutional structure of the hydrocarbon sector, including its regulation, in Colombia. Those changes targeted greater investment in exploration. Today, the rationale behind promoting increased exploratory activities (for both conventional and unconventional hydrocarbons) is to find reserves that are large enough to allow the country to guarantee its self-sufficiency in the medium-to-long term. According to the predictions, the proven reserves (2,377 million barrels) indicate self-sufficiency for nearly seven years.[16]

It is important to note that, to date, a new oil field the size of the three main fields in the country (Caño Limon (1983), Cusiana (1989), and Cupiagua (1993)) has not been found. These wells are still in production but they are no longer the largest production areas. Wells like 'Campo Rubiales', 'Castilla y Castilla Norte', 'La Cira', and 'Quifa' lead the current oil production.

III. Institutional and legal framework

A. Institutional framework

The institutional framework for the planning, promotion, development, and administration of unconventional reservoirs is based on the same institutional structure that governs conventional hydrocarbons. Direction is provided mainly through five government authorities, which are:

1. Ministry of Mines and Energy

The Ministry of Mines and Energy is the authority responsible for formulating and implementing public policy on mines and energy, including the oil and gas

13 Portafolio, 'Inversión Extranjera Llega a US$15.481 Millones en Colombia' (2012), available at <http://www.portafolio.co>.

14 Presidencia de la República, 'Inversión Extranjera Directa en el Sector Petrolero Será de Más de 6.500 Millones de Dólares en el 2012' (2012), available at <http://www.presidencia.gov.co>.

15 El Nuevo Siglo Minero Energético, 'Record en Meta de Regalías del Sector Minero Energético', Bogota, April 2012, 12.

16 Portafolio, 'Las Reservas Colombianas de Petróleo Suben 5,22%' (2013), available at <http://www.portafolio.co>.

sector.[17] The Ministry must formulate, direct, and coordinate the national policy on exploration, production, transportation, refining, processing, and distribution of hydrocarbons.[18]

Based on these general functions, Article 1 of Resolution 181495 of 2009[19] established that the Ministry of Mines and Energy must regulate the activities relating to the exploration and exploitation of unconventional reservoirs. The Resolution included one of the first definitions of 'unconventional reservoirs', defined as those where the accumulation is predominantly regional, extensive, and often independent of structural or stratigraphic traps. Mentioned in the definition is that the development of unconventional reservoirs requires advanced technology and that the duration of the production phase may take decades. Referred to as unconventional reservoirs are tight gas, coal bed methane (CBM), shale gas, and gas hydrates, among others.[20]

2. *Mining and Energy Planning Unit (UPME)*

UPME is a technical authority in charge of planning the development and use of all of Colombia's mining and energy resources, including oil and gas. It is also responsible for the organization and management of the energy and mining information system.[21] UPME was created in 1992 and, as mentioned, is the government authority responsible for keeping all statistics regarding energy and hydrocarbons' production, exports, imports, demand, supply, etc.[22]

The functions of this authority are defined in Law 143 of 1994. Among those is the determination of the country's energy requirements and the definition of a plan to meet those requirements, taking into account the existing energy resources, both conventional and unconventional, and according to economic, social, technological, and environmental criteria.[23]

3. *National Hydrocarbons Agency (ANH)*

The National Hydrocarbons Agency (ANH, after its name in Spanish) was created in 2003 as a response to the critical situation that Colombia went through due to declining oil reserves, which put the country on the verge of becoming an oil

[17] According to art 332 of the 1991 Constitution, the state is the owner of the subsoil and non-renewable resources.

[18] The functions of the Ministry of Mines and Energy are defined in multiple regulations as established in Law 489/1998 and Decree 0381/2012. Article 6 of this Decree states the obligation of the Ministry to participate in the formulation and implementation of strategies for the rational and efficient use of energy (RUE) and the promotion of non-conventional energy sources.

[19] Resolution 181495/2009, Ministry of Mines and Energy, art 1.

[20] Resolution 181495/2009, Ministry of Mines and Energy, art 6.

[21] UPME was created by Decree 2119/1992.

[22] M. Montoya and G. Mancero, 'Colombia' in *Oil Regulation in 33 Jurisdictions Worldwide* (2013) 47 at 48.

[23] Law 143/1994, art 16.

importer.[24] Decree 1760 of 2003 eliminated the power of the state-owned company, Ecopetrol,[25] to regulate and administer hydrocarbons. That function was given exclusively to the ANH. Since then, Ecopetrol is exclusively dedicated to exploring, producing, transporting, refining, and trading oil.

Among the various functions that were granted to the ANH are the power to manage and assign areas for exploration and exploitation; to assess the country's potential in hydrocarbons; to design, negotiate, conclude, and manage new exploration and production; to administer the state's share, in cash or in kind, of the hydrocarbons' volumes from new contracts; and to collect royalties and financial compensation for the state from the exploitation of hydrocarbons.[26]

The rights to explore and produce are granted through a public auction process managed by the ANH. The corresponding terms of reference include the areas to be granted, the participation requirements, and the awarding criteria. Once an area is awarded, the ANH signs the corresponding exploration and production (E&P) contract with the contractor.[27]

The E&P contract replaced the traditional association agreements for which there was a joint venture scheme between the private company and Ecopetrol. Under traditional association agreements, the risks of exploration activities were borne exclusively by the private partner. Once a commercial discovery was made (and deemed as such by the private partner and Ecopetrol), Ecopetrol reimbursed (in oil) its private partner half of the cost of the exploration wells that entered production and Ecopetrol received 50% of the production after royalties, set at 20%. That regime was in force between 1974 and December 2003.[28]

More recently, December 2012 saw the end of 'Round Colombia 2012', which resulted in 49 new blocks assigned to 27 companies, and commitments in oil exploration for USD $2,631,000,000 for the next six years. In the round launched on 21 February 2012, the ANH offered 31 blocks of unconventional hydrocarbons (not including CBM and bituminous sands) and there were five blocks awarded.[29] For these five new unconventional E&P contracts, the ANH will also be the authority in charge of the contracts' management.

Currently, one of the main activities of the ANH is the preparation of terms of reference for the round to be held in the last semester of 2013 or the first semester 2014 for CBM.

4. *Ministry of Environment and Sustainable Development*

Following a recent structural reform, the Ministry of Environment and Sustainable Development[30] defines the national environmental policy and manages the

24 Agencia Nacional de Hidrocarburos (ANH), 'Historia', available at <http://www.anh.gov.co>. The ANH was created by Decree 1760/2003.

25 Ecopetrol SA is a public oil company. The national government holds a participation of 89%.

26 Decree 1760/2003, art 5. See also Decree 714/2012.

27 Montoya and Mancero (n 22).

28 *Latin America Oil & Gas Handbook, Colombia* (2012) 60.

29 *Latin America Oil & Gas Handbook, Colombia* (n 28).

30 Decree 3570, 27 September 2011.

environment and renewable natural resources. It is in charge of guiding and regulating environmental planning, and defines the policies and regulations on recovery, conservation, protection, management, supervision, and sustainable use of renewable natural resources to ensure their sustainable development.

5. *National Environmental Licensing Authority (ANLA)*

The National Environmental Licensing Authority (ANLA, after its name in Spanish) is responsible for projects, works, or activities subject to licensing or permitting to ensure compliance with environmental regulations.[31]

Its main functions are to grant or deny environmental licences and permits, to track licences, permits, and environmental procedures, to encourage citizen participation in the licensing processes, and to run the preventive and punitive investigation procedure related to the compliance and enforcement of environmental obligations.[32]

As a result, this authority is responsible for processing and issuing environmental licences for exploration and exploitation of unconventional reservoirs. Indeed, one of the main concerns in relation to developing projects in unconventional reservoirs is that of strengthening the ANLA's technical knowledge in order to issue environmental licences without unjustified delays or excessive conditions. Environmental concerns are discussed in section VI.

B. Legal framework

The legal framework for development of unconventional hydrocarbons in Colombia has recently changed and combines different stimuli in terms of royalties, operating criteria in coal deposits, and provisions of the E&P model contract that specifically apply to unconventional reservoirs as discussed here.

1. *Decree 2100/2011*

This Decree aims to promote the supply of gas in the country and it allows gas producers in unconventional reservoirs (shale gas and CBM) to freely market the gas under the contracts defined in the regulation, or they can use the special marketing mechanisms defined by the regulator of the gas and electricity sector, i.e., the Regulatory Commission of Electricity and Gas (CREG). Also, this regulation allows gas producers in unconventional reservoirs (or producers who are also gas marketers in unconventional reservoirs) to produce thermal electricity directly and simultaneously if their primary source is the gas they produce.[33]

This Decree specifically allows other authorities such as the ANH, the Ministry of Mines and Energy, and the CREG, to define other stimuli in order to promote the exploitation and marketing of gas from unconventional reservoirs. It also orders

[31] This authority was created by means of Decree 3573/2011.
[32] Decree 3573/2011, art 3. [33] Decree 2100/2011, arts 12 and 15.

the Ministry of Mines and Energy to issue technical standards for the exploration and exploitation of unconventional gas reservoirs and the rules for coexistence with mining activities. In addition, it directs the ANH to develop special contract rules for exploration and exploitation of unconventional reservoirs and the definition of a model contract for those hydrocarbons.[34]

2. *Resolution 180742/2012*

Based on Decree 2100 of 2011, the Ministry of Mines and Energy issued special technical regulations for the exploration and exploitation of hydrocarbons in unconventional reservoirs,[35] taking into account the industry's best practices. As a result, the local regulation and national and international standards should be applied in any operations, especially those recommended by the American Gas Association (AGA), American Petroleum Institute (API), American Society for Testing and Materials (ASTM), National Fire Protection Association (NFPA), Colombian Technical Standards (NTC) (Norma Técnica Colombiana), and others.[36] In addition, the exploration and exploitation of unconventional reservoirs must meet the national regulations for the protection of natural resources, the environment, ethnic and cultural minorities, health, and industrial safety.[37]

The Resolution includes a definition of 'unconventional reservoir' that is clearer than the one set out in Resolution 181495 of 2009. According to this definition, unconventional reservoirs are rocky formations with low porosity and permeability, which is why they require stimulation to improve mobility conditions and hydrocarbon recovery. It also adds that the typical unconventional reservoirs include tight sands and carbonates, methane gas associated with coal seams, gas and oil shale, and tar sands.[38]

Finally, the regulations define the procedure to be followed in the event that the area of unconventional hydrocarbon exploration overlaps partially or totally with an area where there is a mining title or an area of conventional hydrocarbons. In that case, the contractor interested in the exploration and exploitation of unconventional reservoirs should reach an agreement with the title's owner. If there is no agreement on the conditions for the coexistence of operations, the Ministry of Mines and Energy will choose an expert from two résumés proposed by the parties who disagree. The expert will be hired by the contract holders and mining title owners, and remuneration will be paid equally by the two parties.[39]

[34] Decree 2100/2011, art 16.

[35] The procedures that are not governed by this regulation with regard to the exploration and exploitation of unconventional reservoirs are governed by the general technical regime established by Resolution 181495/2009.

[36] Resolution 180742/2012, arts 1 and 3.

[37] Resolution 180742/2012, art 4.

[38] Resolution 180742/2012, art 5. In the contract model of Round 2012, unconventional reservoirs are defined as a rock formation with low primary permeability requiring stimulation to improve the mobility and recovery of hydrocarbons. ANH E&P Contract, Definitions.

[39] Resolution 180742/2012, arts 18 and 19.

Within six months, the expert must provide the Ministry of Mines and Energy with a technical report with the best option to optimize the natural resources to exploit. Subsequently, the Ministry of Mines and Energy, along with mining and hydrocarbons authorities, must define, by administrative act, the work to be performed by each of the parties.

3. Law 1530/2012

By this regulation governing the national system of royalties, a discount of 40% on the payment of royalties has been granted for the case of hydrocarbons produced from unconventional reservoirs.[40] Currently, royalties vary from 8 to 25%, depending on the size of each oilfield: for production less than or equal to 5,000 bbl/d, royalties are 8%; for production between 125,000 bbl/d and 400,000 bbl/d, royalties are 20%; and for production greater than 600,000 bbl/d, royalties are 25%.[41]

4. ANH E&P Contract

The main rights and obligations of the companies involved in the exploration and exploitation of unconventional hydrocarbons are regulated by the E&P Contracting Model of 2012,[42] drafted by the ANH.[43]

This model contract, which applies to both conventional and unconventional reservoirs, has special clauses that apply to exploration activities in unconventional reservoirs. For example, if a block has been granted for exploration in conventional reservoirs, the contractor may request the ANH's permission, based on the studies and technical tests carried out, to modify the initial contract and develop the site as an unconventional reservoir.[44]

With regard to contract terms, the duration permitted for exploration and for production will vary depending on whether or not the reservoir is conventional. If the contract is for a conventional reservoir, its duration is 6 years for exploration and 24 years for production. Conversely, if the contract is for a non-conventional field, the duration for exploration is 9 years, and for production, 30 years.[45] Moreover, in the subsequent exploratory programme, the contractor is obligated to drill, in each

[40] Article 14, Law 1530, 17 May 2012 and also Article 14, Decree 4923, 26 December 2011.

[41] Act 756, 23 July 2002.

[42] Also, companies holding E&P contracts must comply with the Agreement 04 of 2012 by the ANH establishing the criteria for the administration and allocation of areas, as it defines the contracting statute and sets directives for the administration and supervision of contracts.

[43] Before the 2012 E&P Contract, there were some other E&P contracts in which the exploration and production of unconventional reservoirs were, literally, forbidden; in some others there was no mention about the possibility to explore and produce unconventional hydrocarbons and in other models it was possible, but there was no mention about the duration of the phases of exploration and production. The 2012 E&P Contract clarified this situation, defining rules and procedures for future projects of unconventional hydrocarbons. However, there is still a regulatory challenge to clarify what happens with the past E&P contracts where there was no mention about the possibility to explore and produce unconventional hydrocarbons. Are the companies allowed to do this? Under what terms and conditions?

[44] ANH E&P Contract, art 1, s 5.

[45] ANH E&P Contract, arts 4.1. and 4.2.

phase, one A-3 type exploratory well for conventional reservoirs and two exploratory wells for unconventional reservoirs.[46]

There is also a difference in treatment regarding: when a discovery should be disclosed to the ANH;[47] the extension of the evaluation programme;[48] the declaration of commerciality;[49] payment to the ANH for production sharing, in cases of an extension of the production period (5%);[50] the cost of the non-contractual liability insurance (US$30 million);[51] the rights of the ANH, in case market prices exceed contracted prices;[52] and the participation of the ANH in the production after royalties.[53]

IV. Unconventional hydrocarbon potential in Colombia

A. Coal bed methane

One of the earliest documents highlighting Colombia's potential vis-à-vis unconventional reservoirs is Document 3517 of the National Economic and Social Policy Department, which in 2008 presented a series of recommendations to allocate rights of exploration and exploitation in CBM. This document was the initial response to a situation that was common in Colombia's mining and energy activities, i.e., a need for regulatory clarity in those cases in which the owner of a coal mining site also had the possibility of exploiting methane gas in the mine site, or when a licence to exploit methane gas was obtained for an area that already held a mining licence for coal.

Regarding CBM potential in Colombia, Document 3517 asserted that reserves were 4.7 trillion cubic feet (TCF). Probable reserves in the regions with the greatest potential were estimated at 17 TCF. However, recent studies indicate that CBM potential ranges between 11 and 35 TCF,[54] though recoverable reserves are estimated to be 7.5 TCF.[55] Among the regions with the greatest potential are the provinces of Cesar, La Guajira, Boyacá, and Cundinamarca.[56]

It should be mentioned that Colombia is the country with the largest coal reserves in Latin America. It has potential resources of 16,436 million tons (Mt),

[46] ANH E&P Contract, art 9. [47] ANH E&P Contract, art 14.

[48] ANH E&P Contract, art 14.4. [49] ANH E&P Contract, art 15.

[50] ANH E&P Contract, art 42. [51] ANH E&P Contract, art 50.10.

[52] ANH E&P Contract, Annex D, Economic Rights. The price defined in the Annex D for liquid hydrocarbons associated to unconventional reservoirs was $81 USD/Bl.

[53] ANH E&P Contract, Annex D, Economic Rights.

[54] R. Guzman, 'Potential Resources of Unconventional Hydrocarbons in Colombia' (2011), ANH Unconventional Hydrocarbons Workshop, Arthur D Little presentation (ADL), slide 4, available at <http://www.bnamericas.com>.

[55] D. Jiménez, 'Gas Shale en Colombia: El inicio de una Nueva Época' (2012), Agencia Nacional de Hidrocarburos, Slide 38, available at <http://www.ciien.org>.

[56] Source Jiménez (n 55). The Universidad Nacional de Colombia has also developed a study on the potential of hydrocarbons in Colombia. Regarding the potential of CBM, there are three production scenarios ranging between 725 billion cubic feet and 77,511 billion cubic feet: C. Vargas, 'Potencial de Hidrocarburos en Colombia', Presentación XIV Congreso Colombiano de Petróleo y Gas, Universidad Nacional (2011), slide 29, available at <http://www.anh.gov.co>.

of which 6,508 Mt are measured, 4,571 Mt are indicated, 4,237 Mt are inferred, and 1,209 Mt are hypothesized resources.

The coal industry in Colombia has grown significantly over the past decade and is one of the main economic activities nationwide. For example, between 2005 and 2011, coal production showed an increase of 43.78%, from 59 Mt to 85.8 Mt per year. Also, Colombia is the fourth largest exporter of thermal coal in the world, with a share of 10.01%, or 73.21 Mt of coal per year (2011), and is the tenth largest producer with a production of 74.35 Mt during 2010.[57]

The potential for CBM exploitation in Colombia will be the focus of a new bidding process led by the ANH. It is expected that the terms of reference will be published in the second semester of 2013 or in the first semester of 2014. According to estimates, production of gas associated with coal will start in 2015, although in moderation.[58]

B. Shale gas and shale oil

The current potential for shale gas production has been estimated at approximately 32 TCF in the Mid Magdalena Basin, which is one of the most important recoverable reserves, followed by the Eastern Cordillera Basin and the Cesar Rancheria Basin. Recoverable shale oil resources are estimated at 14 gigabarrels (Gbbl), potentially in the region of Magdalena and the Pacific Coast.[59]

C. Tight gas, tar sands, and gas hydrates

Tight gas does not seem to be abundant in Colombia, although the Mid Magdalena region has been identified as a possible source with a potential of 1.2 TCF.[60]

Regarding tar sands, the regions of Florence, San Vicente, Rio Guejar, Rio Nare, and Sogamoso have been identified as holding recoverable tar sands oil reserves estimated at 20 to 40 Gbbl.[61]

Finally, the potential of Colombia in gas hydrates is estimated at 434 TCF in the Caribbean and pacific coast basins.[62]

V. Ongoing projects

Unconventional reservoir contracts and projects have focused mainly on resources such as shale gas and shale oil. However, as mentioned, it is expected that in 2014 significant progress will be made in CBM regulation.

[57] Unidad de Planeación Minero-Energética (UPME), 'Cadena del Carbón' (2012) 8 at 9, available at <http://www.simco.gov.co>. With the current rate of coal exploitation in Colombia, reserves ensure more than 92 years of production, and, in 2010, this activity accounted for 47% of the country's mining and for 1.57% of gross domestic product with more than 7,05 billion pesos.

[58] Unidad de Planeación Minero-Energética (UPME), 'Escenarios de Oferta y Demanda de Hidrocarburos en Colombia' (2012) 18, available at <http://www.upme.gov.co>.

[59] UPME (n 58), slide 8.

[60] Source Guzman (n 54), slide 7.

[61] Guzman (n 54), slide 9.

[62] Guzman (n 54), slide 10, available at <http://www.bnamericas.com>.

According to information provided by the Ministry of Mines, the existing unconventional hydrocarbons projects, awarded before Round Colombia 2012, and their situation as of July 2013 are as follows.

A. Rio Rancheria Association Agreement

This CBM contract involves the companies Ecopetrol and Drummond. Its start date was November 2000, and it covers an area of 31,497 hectares in the province of La Guajira.[63] The contract is in its exploration phase (three exploratory wells) and has an estimated potential of three to five TFC of gas. However, it has been suspended several times due to its overlap with coal mining.[64]

B. La Loma E&P Contract

The holder of this CBM contract is Drummond. The start date was November 2009 and it covers an area of 158,816 hectares in Cesar province.[65] The contract is in its exploration phase and has an estimated potential of three TFC of gas.[66]

C. Chiquinquira E&P Contract

The holder of the contract is Nexen, the start date was November 2009, and it covers an area of 119,189 hectares in the provinces of Cundinamarca and Boyacá. The resource to explore is shale gas. This contract is under exploration (drilling of one well).[67]

D. Sueva E&P Contract

The holder of the contract is Nexen and the start date was November 2009. It covers an area of 96,106 hectares in the municipalities of Bogotá, Cáqueza, Chipaque, Fómeque, Gachetá, Gama, Guasca, Guatavita, Junin, La Calera, and Machetá Blanket Tibiritaand Ubaque, as well as the province of Cundinamarca. The resource being investigated is shale gas. This contract is in the exploration phase.[68]

E. Barbosa E&P Contract

The holder of the contract is Nexen. This contract is in the exploration phase. The site is located in the eastern mountains basin.[69]

63 In the municipalities of Fonseca and Barrancas.

64 J. C. Vera, 'Perspectivas de los Hidrocarburos No Convencionales en Colombia', XIII Congreso Nacional y IV Internacional de Servicios Públicos, Ministerio de Minas y Energía Presentation (2011) slide 10, available at <http://www.andesco.org.co>.

65 In the municipalities of Chiriguaná, Becerril, and Jagua de Ibirico.

66 Vera (n 64), slide 11.

67 Vera (n 64), slide 12.

68 Vera (n 64), slide 13.

69 In the municipalities of Arcabuco, Briceño, Buenavista, Caldas, Coper, Chiquinquira, Chitaraque, Gachantivá, Maripì, Moniquira, Pauna, Raquira, Saboya, San Jose de Pare, San Jose de Serna, Santa Sofia, Santana, Sutamarchan, Tinjaca, Togüi, Tununga, Simijaca, Susa, Albania, Barbosa, Bolivar, Chipatá, Florian, Guavata, Guepsa, Jesus Maria, Puente Nacional, Sucre, and Vélez. Nexen, Annual

F. Garagoa E&P Contract

The holder of the contract is Nexen. This contract is in the exploration phase. The influence area is located in the eastern mountains basin.[70]

During Round Colombia 2012, five E&P contracts were signed for the exploration of unconventional reservoirs, not including for CBM and tar sands. The E&P Contract requires the contractor to report immediately to the ANH[71] any discoveries of CBM or tar sands.

The following sets out the information regarding these contracts at July 2013:

1. CAT 3 Contract

The holder of the contract is the company Ecopetrol, the start date was 12 December 2012, and it covers an area of 153,875 hectares in Norte de Santander.[72] This contract is in phase zero. During this phase, which lasts for one year, the contractor agrees with the ANH to identify ethnic communities present in the area of interest and, if there are any, consultation with these communities must take place before exploitation.[73]

2. COR-62 Contract

The contract holders are Ecopetrol and ExxonMobil. The start date was 27 November 2012 and it covers an area of 81,863 hectares in the provinces of Antioquia and Norte de Santander.[74] The contract is in phase zero.

3. VMM-5 Contract

The holder of the contract is Ecopetrol, the start date was 12 December 2012, and it covers an area of 146,485 hectares in the province of Tolima.[75] It is currently in phase zero.

Information Form, 15 February 2012, available at <http://www.nexencnoocltd.com/en/AboutUs/Investors/AnnualReports.aspx>.

[70] In the municipalities of Almedia, Aquitania, Bermeo, Campohermoso, Cinavita, Garagoa, Gaquete, Guayatá, La Capilla, Miraflores, Macanal, Miraflorez, Paez, Pachavita, San Eduardo, Somondoco, Sutatenza, Tenza, Zetaquirá, Gachetá, Gama, Junin, Machetá, Manta, Tiribita, and Ubalá.

[71] ANH E&P Contract, art 1, s 2.

[72] In the municipalities of Bochalema, Chinacota, Cucuta, Durania, El Zulia, Gramalote, Herran, Los Patios, Pamplonita, Ragonvalia, Salazar, San Cayetano, Santiago, Sardinata, and Villa del Rosario.

[73] ANH E&P Contract, art 4.0.

[74] In the municipalities of Puerto Berrio and Yondo in Antioquia and Barrancabermeja, Cimitarra, and Puerto Parra in Santander.

[75] In the municipalities of Cunday, Villarica, Purificación, Melgar, Icononzo, Carmen de Apicala, Dolores, and Prado.

4. VMM-16 Contract

The holder of the contract is Ecopetrol, the start date was 12 December 2012, and it covers an area of 116,565 hectares in the provinces of Antioquia, Boyaca, Cundinamarca, Caldas, and Tolima.[76] This contract is also in phase zero.

5. VMM 29 Contract

The contract holders are Ecopetrol and ExxonMobil, the start date was 12 December 2012, and it covers an area of 177,813 hectares in the provinces of Cundinamarca and Tolima.[77] The contract is in phase zero.

VI. Environmental concerns

It should be noted that obtaining an environmental licence in Colombia is mandatory in cases where an individual or legal entity (public or private) wants to develop any activity likely to bring about serious deterioration to renewable natural resources or to the environment, or introduce significant or noticeable modifications to the landscape.[78] Consequently, the vast majority of mining and energy sector activities require environmental licences.

Currently, the ANLA and the Ministry of Environment and Sustainable Development are undertaking internal studies in order to clarify and gain in-depth knowledge of the technical details of the exploration and exploitation of unconventional reservoirs. This has led to delays in environmental licensing. The delays are due to the fact that, for these authorities, it is first necessary to be clear about the nature and risks posed by the activities before making decisions.

ANLA's current position on environmental licensing for unconventional hydrocarbon projects may also be explained by the warning issued in September 2012 by the General Comptroller of the Republic to the Minister of Environment, the Minister of Mines and Energy, the Director of the ANLA, and the Director of the ANH on their need to take into account the precautionary principle in environmental licensing for unconventional hydrocarbons projects. Also, this principle should be taken into account regarding the drafting of the environmental technical regulation for these projects.[79]

[76] In the municipalities of Sonson in the province of Antioquia; Puerto Boyaca in Boyaca, Norcasia, Victoria and La Dorada in the province of Caldas; Puerto Salgar in Cundinarmarca and Mariquita, Lerida, Honda, Armero, and Falan in the province of Tolima.

[77] In the municipalities of Anapoima, Anolaima, Apulo, Arbelaez, Beltran, Cachipay, Fusagasuga, Guataqui, Jerusalen, La Mesa, Nilo, Quipile, Puli, Rioseco, Tibacuy, Tocaima, and Voita in Cundinamarca and in the municipalities of Melgar, Alvarado, Ambalema, Armero, Coello, Lerida, Icononzo, Piedras, and Venadillo in the province of Tolima.

[78] Constitutional Court Ruling C-035 of 1999. The environmental licence application process is mainly regulated by Law 99/1993, Law 790/2002, Decree 2016/2003, and Decree 2820/2010.

[79] This warning was issued on 9 September 2012, File 2012EE0060874.

For the Comptroller, the precautionary principle[80] should be applied to these activities because of the risk that hydraulic fracturing poses to the environment, particularly due to the potential contamination of groundwater and other water sources, risks for urban areas, public health, and geological risk. In this sense, the Comptroller warned the authorities of potential environmental hazards related to the exploration and exploitation of unconventional reservoirs and advised them to adopt necessary and sufficient regulations to enable the exploitation of non-renewable natural resources in a sustainable manner. The warning spurred additional social debate in Colombia about the environmental consequences of unconventional hydrocarbon projects, with participation of the guilds, communities, and journalists. Since the media's coverage lacked enough technical information, the focus of the debate was on the risks and dangers associated with the exploration and exploitation of unconventional reservoirs. The debate highlighted the need to study the topic using reputable scientific sources to avoid speculation.

Notwithstanding this, the ANLA has issued environmental permits for unconventional hydrocarbon projects, such as the licence granted in August 2011 to Nexen Petroleum in the Chiquinquira Block, which was aimed at finding shale resources (mainly shale gas).[81] Also, in March 2011, the ANLA issued Nexen another environmental licence,[82] this time for Sueva Block's unconventional hydrocarbons project.

As mentioned, one of the main difficulties facing the unconventional hydrocarbons industry is the delay in the issuance of environmental licences. However, it is expected that in the second semester of 2013 or first semester of 2014, there will be a new environmental regulation focused exclusively on the terms and conditions for environmental licensing of unconventional reservoirs.[83]

VII. Conclusion

The hydrocarbon sector in Colombia is one of the main drivers of the national economy. A stable institutional and regulatory structure has been put in place

[80] In the Colombian legal system the precautionary principle is defined in Law 99 of 1993, Art 1, in the following terms: 'The formulation of environmental policies take into account the outcome of the scientific research process. However, environmental authorities and individuals will apply the precautionary principle under which, if there are threats of serious and irreversible damage, the lack of full scientific certainty should not be used as a reason for postponing cost-effective measures to prevent degradation of the environment.' (Translation by the author.) This principle has been widely developed in the national jurisprudence, such as Constitutional Court ruling C-293 of 2002, which established that the environmental authority can apply this principle by motivated administrative act, in case it sees a risk of serious and irreversible injury, or there is a hint of scientific certainty, even if it is not absolute and the decision is conceived in order to prevent environmental degradation (Constitutional Court Judgment C-293, 23 April 2002).

[81] Environmental Licence awarded by Resolution 1734, 26 August 2011.

[82] Environmental Licence awarded by Resolution 0363, 3 March 2011.

[83] In order to solve the delays in the environmental licensing and clarify the procedures, some think it is necessary to issue new, specific environmental regulation for unconventional reservoirs. However, others consider it is not necessary, at least regarding the first phases of exploration, because there is not a big difference between this and conventional exploration and because current legislation intensively regulates this initial exploratory activity.

which encourages domestic and foreign investment in hydrocarbon exploration. In addition, improvements in physical security conditions, sustained economic growth in recent years, legal stability, and flexibility in the conditions of E&P contracts have favoured the growth of the hydrocarbon sector.

Current Colombian energy policy supports research, exploration, and exploitation of unconventional reservoirs. This decision was highlighted during Round Colombia 2012, in which 31 blocks were offered for unconventional reservoirs and five contracts were signed.

Since 2008, progress has been made in defining the regulatory framework for the exploration and exploitation of unconventional reservoirs by adjusting the terms of the E&P contract, the enactment of special technical regulations for exploration and exploitation, provision of royalty-related incentives, issuance of rights and rules for CBM fields, and enhancement of institutional coordination.

The development and growth of unconventional hydrocarbon projects in Colombia will depend, to a large extent, on the environmental authorities' efficiency in the analysis, processing, and issuance of environmental licences, which requires adequate technical knowledge of the peculiarities of this industry.

Finally, one of the main challenges facing the authorities and the industry is to engage and educate communities on the technical characteristics of exploration and exploitation of unconventional reservoirs. Today there is widespread ignorance about the subject, which can generate considerable resistance and fear about unconventional reservoirs and their exploitation techniques.

PART IV

ADDRESSING ENVIRONMENTAL AND SUSTAINABILITY ISSUES UNDERGROUND

13

Risk, Regulation, and Carbon Capture and Storage: The United Kingdom Experience

Aileen McHarg and Mark Poustie

I. Introduction

The dominant narrative surrounding carbon capture and storage (CCS) is one of risk and uncertainty.[1] As an early stage and still developing technology, with capital-intensive and unusually long-lived assets, which is not yet proven at commercial scale anywhere in the world, CCS presents clear *technological* and *financial* risks. Since its commercial viability is almost wholly dependent upon government policy,[2] it also carries a very high degree of *regulatory* risk. At the same time, while it is potentially very attractive as a climate change mitigation option in both power generation and certain industrial applications, it poses significant *public policy* risks if it proves to be more expensive or less effective than anticipated.

For some of the underground energy technologies discussed in this book, the law has had to play catch-up with industry practice. In relation to CCS, by contrast, it seems unlikely that commercial deployment will proceed *unless* a suitable legal and regulatory framework is already in place which enables the associated risks and uncertainties to be minimized or managed. According to a recent UK Energy Research Centre (UKERC) report:

> The resolution of all uncertainties is not required for CCS to be financeable . . . Similarly, the derailing of plans to realize the potential of CCS may not require everything to go wrong—but this could be caused by a 'critical mass' of uncertainties persisting for too long.[3]

In a number of jurisdictions, work to put in place appropriate regulatory frameworks is already well advanced, considerably ahead of commercial need. However,

[1] Risk and uncertainty are technically distinct, since risk is quantifiable but uncertainty is not (see J. Black, 'The Role of Risk in Regulatory Processes', in *The Oxford Handbook of Regulation* (R. Baldwin, M. Cave, and M. Lodge, eds, 2010) 302 at 210). However, they are related in the sense that both involve lack of assurance about future events.

[2] Captured CO_2 has some commercial applications, such as for enhanced hydrocarbon recovery, but these are too limited to drive major investment in CCS.

[3] J. Watson (ed), *Carbon Capture and Storage: Realizing the Potential* (2012) 2 (the 'UKERC Report').

whereas much of this work has focused on what might be termed *regulation of* CCS—that is, the process of installing and operating CO_2 capture equipment and transport and storage infrastructure—it is becoming increasingly clear that *regulation for* CCS is also required—that is, the provision of incentives to encourage investment in CCS. While the two are obviously connected—unsuitable or unclear permitting and operational rules being likely to act as a disincentive to investment—more is required to actively encourage investors to incur the costs of CCS and to reassure them that they are likely to see a return on their investment. Nevertheless, in conditions of high uncertainty, there is also a risk that premature regulatory commitment may itself be a source of policy failure. In particular, this may fail to strike an appropriate balance between public and private risk. The task facing regulators and policy makers is therefore a complex one.

In this chapter, we focus on CCS regulation in the United Kingdom. According to the Global CCS Institute, '[t]he UK has been one of the strongest global advocates for the role that CCS will play in its energy portfolio'.[4] It was the first jurisdiction to put in place, via the Energy Act 2008, a regulatory regime for offshore CO_2 storage (since amended and extended by the EU CCS Directive)[5] and it is also a world leader in the provision of commercialization support, most notably at the post-demonstration stage.[6]

The actual implementation of CCS in the United Kingdom, however, has yet to move beyond the pilot stage.[7] The first commercialization competition, which was launched in November 2007 with the intention that demonstration plants would be operational by 2014, collapsed in October 2011. The government ended negotiations with the sole remaining bidder (Scottish Power's Longannet plant), claiming that the project was too expensive and that it could not agree to acceptable terms on the allocation of risk. A damning National Audit Office report concluded that:

> Procuring a demonstration plant was a challenging, high-risk undertaking. The [government] wanted industry to take up a commercial contract, for a large and potentially costly developmental project, with considerable uncertainty over its design and costs. The competition took place against an evolving background of economic, policy and regulatory uncertainty. . . . The [government] did not engage sufficiently early with the commercial risks involved and their consequences on cost.[8]

Although the commercialization programme was relaunched in April 2012,[9] and significant reform of the wholesale electricity market is being undertaken to

[4] <http://www.globalccsinstitute.com/location/united-kingdom>.

[5] Directive 2009/31/EC, [2009] OJ L140/114, 23 April 2009.

[6] Department of Energy and Climate Change (DECC), *CCS Roadmap: Supporting Deployment of Carbon Capture and Storage in the UK* (2012) 26; Global CCS Institute, *The Global Status of CCS 2012* (2012) 2, available at: <http://www.globalccsinstitute.com/publications/global-status-ccs-2012/online/48166>.

[7] A 5-MW post-combustion coal project was launched at SSE's Ferrybridge plant in November 2011.

[8] National Audit Office, *Carbon Capture and Storage: Lessons from the Competition for the First UK Demonstration*, HC 1829, 2010–12, 8.

[9] DECC (n 6).

promote low carbon generation,[10] there has nevertheless been further delay, as well as an apparent scaling back of ambition for the size of the CCS demonstration programme.[11] There is also considerable ongoing uncertainty about the future shape of the generation market and the direction of energy policy.

Our aim in this chapter is to evaluate how successfully the current UK regulatory framework manages the risks and uncertainties associated with CCS. In so doing, we hope to draw some more general lessons about the key risks that need to be addressed to secure commercialization of CCS and avoid policy failure, and about the role of law in handling those risks. Before analysing the UK regulatory framework, we begin by discussing the role of CCS in UK energy policy, and then explore in more depth the nature of the risks posed by CCS.

II. CCS and UK energy policy

The strongest policy driver behind the United Kingdom's attempts to promote CCS is emissions reduction. The United Kingdom has a legally binding target to reduce greenhouse gas emissions by 80% by 2050.[12] As the major current source of CO_2 emissions, and the key to future decarbonization of other sectors, such as heat and transport, electricity generation is an important focus for early emissions reduction efforts. Indeed, the Energy Act 2013 empowers ministers to set a so-called 'decarbonization' target for electricity generation for 2030, although this will not be exercised (if at all) before 2016. CCS is therefore being promoted as part of a low carbon generation mix, along with renewables and nuclear power. The current aim is to establish one or two full-scale CCS demonstration projects by 2016–2020, with a view to commercial deployment in the power sector, and the establishment of transport and storage infrastructure, during the 2020s, before being extended to other industrial sectors in the 2030s and beyond.[13] The government envisages that there could be up to 13 GW of CCS-equipped generation capacity by 2030, and 40 GW by 2050.[14]

It is important to emphasize, however, that there is no commitment to particular technology-based targets. Whether CCS is deployed on a commercial basis at all

[10] DECC, *Planning Our Electric Future: A White Paper for Secure, Affordable and Low-Carbon Electricity* Cm 8099 (2011); Energy Act 2013.

[11] The commercialization programme will support up to two projects, whereas the government's Coalition agreement promised public support for four—HM Government, *The Coalition: Our Programme for Government* (2010) 16, available at <http://www.gov.uk/government/uploads/system/uploads/attachment_data/file/78977/coalition_programme_for_government.pdf>.

[12] Climate Change Act 2008, s 1; Climate Change (Scotland) Act 2009, s 1.

[13] DECC (n 6).

[14] DECC, *Gas Generation Strategy*, Cm 8407 (2012) 24. The CCS Association predicts 20–30 GW of CCS capacity by 2030. Projected total installed capacity for 2030 is 123–156 GW—National Grid, *UK Future Energy Scenarios* (2011), available at: <http://www.nationalgrid.com/NR/rdonlyres/86C815F5-0EAD-46B5-A580-A0A516562B3E/50819/10312_1_NG_Futureenergyscenarios_WEB1.pdf>.

and, if so, in what quantities, will depend entirely on its ability to compete with other forms of low carbon generation in terms of price and public acceptability:

> The Government's aim is . . . to run a low carbon technology race between CCS, renewables and nuclear power. Diversity will bring competition between technologies that will drive innovation and cost reduction, and will hedge against the risk of one technology failing to reduce costs or become publicly acceptable. The low carbon power that can deliver at least cost will gain the largest market share.[15]

Nevertheless, there are reasons why the government may be particularly keen to see CCS succeed. These include potential commercial benefits for British industry as an international leader in the development and supply of CCS technology, from using captured CO_2 for enhanced hydrocarbon recovery in the UK continental shelf, and from exploiting the UK's abundant offshore storage capacity[16] to store carbon captured overseas. Deployment of CCS is also likely to be vital as a global emissions reduction strategy, particularly in emerging economies such as India and China, which are heavily dependent on fossil fuels. The United Kingdom is therefore committed to promoting international development of CCS through knowledge-sharing and bilateral and multi-lateral engagement.[17]

By far the most important of these additional reasons, though, is the benefits that CCS offers in terms of diversity and security of supply. Fossil-fuelled generation has the major advantages of flexibility and certainty over (continuous) nuclear power and (intermittent) renewables, thus enabling system balance to be maintained more easily. Without CCS, emissions limits would permit only a very small role for fossil fuels by 2050, as back-up capacity.[18] Deployment of CCS would also allow the United Kingdom to exploit its unconventional gas resources, thereby enhancing security of supply.[19]

However, the future role of gas generation adds a deeper level of uncertainty to UK energy policy. While CCS is essential to continued use of gas in the long term, in the short term the government does not want to deter investment in new gas capacity by imposing additional costs and regulatory burdens. The December 2012 *Gas Generation Strategy*[20] was therefore highly ambivalent about the future share of unabated gas in the generation mix. This is also an important reason why the government (particularly the Treasury) has so far resisted attempts to force it to set a decarbonization target for 2030, despite a strong recommendation from the

[15] HM Government, *The Carbon Plan: Delivering Our Low Carbon Future* (2011) 72.

[16] Estimated at up to 70 billion tonnes of CO_2 (equivalent to 100 years' worth of current emissions from the energy sector), in both depleted oil and gas reservoirs and saline aquifers—DECC (n 6) at 15.

[17] See DECC (n 6) at 13–14.

[18] HM Government (n 15) at 71.

[19] A moratorium on hydraulic fracturing was lifted in December 2012 (*Written Ministerial Statement by Edward Davey MP: Exploration for Shale Gas*, HC Vol 555, col 44WS, 13 December 2012), and generous tax breaks for shale gas production were proposed in July 2013 (HM Treasury, *Harnessing the Potential of the UK's Natural Resources: A Fiscal Regime for Shale Gas* (2013), available at <http://www.gov.uk/government/consultations/harnessing-the-potential-of-the-uks-natural-resources-a-fiscal-regime-for-shale-gas/harnessing-the-potential-of-the-uks-natural-resources-a-fiscal-regime-for-shale-gas>). There is, however, significant public opposition to onshore shale gas exploration.

[20] DECC (n 14).

Committee on Climate Change—the statutory body created to advise on achievement of climate change targets—that it should do so.[21] The other main complicating factor in energy policy is concern about affordability for consumers. In fact, the Treasury has already insisted on an informal limit on the level of subsidy for low carbon generation through the so-called Levy Control Framework,[22] again sending mixed signals about the government's commitment to decarbonization.

III. Risk, regulation, and CCS

In developing an appropriate regulatory framework for CCS, it is important to understand (a) both the nature and the range of risks and uncertainties that it poses; and (b) the role(s)—and the limits—of legal regulation in responding to those risks and uncertainties.

A. Risk and CCS

The risks associated with CCS can be divided into private or investment risks and public or policy risks.

1. Investment risks

Investment risks refer to the possibility that investors may fail to secure adequate returns on their investment, either because there turns out to be no (or insufficient) demand for the product ('stranded assets') or because the costs are greater than expected. If not adequately addressed, investment risks may raise the cost of capital (to the detriment of consumers) or deter investment altogether.

(a) Economic risk

To some extent the risks faced by investors in CCS are similar to those found elsewhere in the energy sector, arising from the fact that capture equipment, and transport and storage infrastructure all involve high, upfront capital costs,[23] long lead-times (particularly for storage) and have long asset lives. However, economic risks are particularly acute in relation to CCS. As regards capture equipment, risk is increased, first, by the fact that it is not yet clear which of several competing capture

[21] Letter from the Committee on Climate Change to Edward Davey MP, 13 September 2012, available at: <http://www.theccc.org.uk/publication/letter-the-need-for-a-carbon-intensity-target-in-the-power-sector/>; letter from Lord Deben to Edward Davey MP, 25 February 2013, available at: <http://www.theccc.org.uk/wp-content/uploads/2013/02/Ed-Davey-February13.pdf>.

[22] This is contained in the Public Service Agreement between the Treasury and DECC. A cap of £7.6 billion (in 2012 prices) has been set for 2020—DECC, *Government Agreement on Energy Policy Sends Clear, Durable Signal to Investors*, 23 November 2012, available at <http://www.gov.uk/government/news/government-agreement-on-energy-policy-sends-clear-durable-signal-to-investors>.

[23] Transport costs may in some cases be reduced by reusing existing pipelines.

technologies will turn out to be the cheapest, most reliable, or most effective, and second, by the substantial energy penalty imposed by CCS,[24] which also raises generators' operating costs. For transport and storage, the main problem is rising economies of scale, which gives them (particularly transport) natural monopoly characteristics. The existence of a suitably located and sized transport and storage network is therefore a public good, which would facilitate, and reduce the costs of, deployment of CCS.[25] However, uncertainty about the scale, location, and timing of that deployment is likely to lead to under-investment in infrastructure to avoid the risk of stranded assets. This network effect may also expose capture operators to the risk of market power.[26]

(b) Liability risk

A second set of investment risks which are perceived to be particularly serious for CCS projects—especially storage—are liability risks. These have emerged as one of the major obstacles to investment in CCS, although Clarke argues that CO_2 storage is neither particularly novel nor particularly dangerous and should therefore 'fit relatively easily into the existing industrial landscape and the various liability rules that go with it'.[27]

The liability risks associated with CCS are threefold: first, environmental, health, and safety risks associated with construction and operation of all parts of the CCS chain; second, localized risks to human health and ecosystems from leakage or migration from transport or storage facilities; and third, risks to the global climate from large-scale leakages.[28] There is general agreement that the risks of leakage or migration from storage are small if facilities are properly sited and managed, and that in any case they diminish over time as CO_2 stabilizes in the geological formation.

However, what seems to exacerbate the perceived importance of these risks is,[29] first, the fact that the impact of the leakage risk, if it materializes, is likely to be

[24] i.e., it takes more primary fuel to generate the same amount of electricity compared with unabated plants.

[25] In fact, almost half the potential reduction in the cost of CCS by 2028 is expected to come from the increasing scale and utilization of CO_2 infrastructure—CCS Cost Reduction Task Force, *The Potential for Reducing the Costs of CCS in the UK: Final Report* (2013) 53, available at <http://www.gov.uk/government/uploads/system/uploads/attachment_data/file/201021/CCS_Cost_Reduction_Taskforce_-_Final_Report_-_May_2013.pdf>.

[26] See generally N. Bankes and R. Nilson, 'Economic Regulation and the Design of a Carbon Infrastructure for Alberta' in *Energy Networks and the Law: Innovative Solutions in Changing Markets* (M. M. Roggenkamp, L. Barrera-Hernandez, D. N. Zillman, and I. del Guayo, eds, 2012) 231; International Energy Agency, *A Policy Strategy for CCS* (2012) 28–30, available at <http://www.iea.org/publications/freepublications/publication/name,20564,en.html>.

[27] C. Clarke, 'Long-Term Liability for CCS: Some Thoughts about Specific Risks, Multiple Regimes and the EU Directive' in *Carbon Capture and Storage: Emerging Legal and Regulatory Issues* (I. Havercroft, R. Macrory, and R. Stewart, eds, 2011) 179 at 179.

[28] J. Meadowcroft and O. Langhelle, 'The Politics and Policy of Carbon Capture and Storage' in *Caching the Carbon: the Policy and Politics of Carbon Capture and Storage* (J. Meadowcroft and O. Langhelle, eds, 2009) 1 at 4.

[29] Clarke (n 27) at 180–1 notes a range of potentially relevant factors, including the controversial nature of CCS.

serious; second, the fact that the storage risk has to be managed over a very long timescale; and third, the anomalous fact that the financial cost of the climate risk may increase rather than decrease over time. If storage operators are required to purchase emissions permits to offset any leakages, in the context of an expected rising carbon price, the cost of any leakage may significantly outweigh the financial benefit gained by avoiding the carbon price at the time of capture.[30]

(c) **Political and regulatory risk**

The final set of investment risks—political and regulatory risks—are also familiar ones in the energy sector, but again they are particularly serious in relation to CCS. With the limited exception of capture projects linked with enhanced hydrocarbon recovery, investment in CCS represents purely a cost to generators rather than a business opportunity. Accordingly, unless there is a regulatory incentive or imperative do so, there is no commercial reason to install capture equipment, or use CO_2 infrastructure. If, therefore, the governing regulatory framework is unclear, or excessively burdensome, or there is perceived to be a risk of it changing in unpredictable ways, this will again raise the cost of capital, or discourage investment completely.

CCS projects are also vulnerable to political opposition from groups worried, for instance, about the effect on energy prices or the environmental impact of CO_2 infrastructure, or who are sceptical about its effectiveness and concerned that it will lead to 'carbon lock-in' by enabling fossil fuels to remain in the generation mix.[31] This kind of opposition could raise the cost and uncertainty of seeking regulatory approval for particular projects, and heighten the risk of regulatory change.

2. *Public policy risks*

Political opposition to CCS reflects the fact that its promotion as part of a low carbon energy mix in conditions of technological and commercial uncertainty creates risks not only for private investors but also for the achievement of important public policy goals.

(a) **Environmental risk**

The risk of leakage from CO_2 transport or storage facilities is problematic not just for their operators, but also for government. Not only may government—whether *de facto* or *de jure*—have to bear some or all of the remediation costs, but a leak which causes serious injury or environmental damage, or which endangers carbon targets, may catastrophically undermine public support for CCS. As already noted, there is also a serious risk to carbon targets if new fossil fuel generation is built in anticipation of CCS becoming commercially viable, but this fails to materialize. This is a particularly significant risk in the UK context, where an impending

[30] Clarke (n 27) at 189.

[31] For criticisms of CCS, see Meadowcroft and Langhelle (n 28) at 13–14.

security of supply crisis makes it imperative to invest in new generation capacity,[32] and gas-fired plants are the quickest and cheapest to build in the short term.

(b) Economic risk

Promotion of CCS also exposes the public to economic risks. As well as the potential liability risk from storage leaks, the most obvious is the risk to consumers or taxpayers that the cost of subsidizing CCS turns out to be higher than expected. This is again a particularly serious risk in an age of budget austerity and concern about energy affordability.[33] It also carries the consequential risk of diverting public funding from other low carbon energy sources. On the other hand, if CCS is not (widely) deployed, and (unabated) fossil fuels are thereby excluded from the generation mix, there is also an economic risk in terms of increased system balancing costs, and greater likelihood of supply failure.

B. Risk and regulation

1. Risk as a justification for regulation

In recent years, the idea of risk as the object of, and justification for, regulation has become increasingly popular amongst both academic commentators and policy makers.[34] Certainly, in the energy sector, we can see a shift over the past decade or so from an overwhelming emphasis on economic regulation—promotion of competition and regulation of natural monopoly—towards a greater concern with the societal risks associated with the energy industries, particularly in relation to climate change, security of supply, and affordability.

However, the mere existence of risk does not justify regulatory intervention. As the UKERC report puts it:

> When discussing technologies like CCS that are characterized by pervasive uncertainties, it is tempting to feel that all risks must be dealt with by government before progress can be made. But that assumption is mistaken, and forgets that the private sector routinely deals with multiple risks.[35]

Thus, according to the UK's Better Regulation Commission, individuals should be responsible for managing risks 'where they have the knowledge to make an

---

[32] See A. Buchanan, 'Will GB's Lights Stay On and Will the Gas Keep Flowing? A Look at the Next Decade', 19 February 2013, available at: <http://www.ofgem.gov.uk/Media/keyspeeches/Documents1/LECTURE%20-%2019TH%20FEBRUARY%202013.pdf>.

[33] In addition to carbon targets, the UK and Scottish Governments have legally binding obligations to eradicate fuel poverty: Warm Homes and Energy Conservation Act 2000; Housing (Scotland) Act 2001, s 88.

[34] See generally E. Fisher, 'The Rise of the Risk Commonwealth and the Challenge for Administrative Law' [2003] PL 455; Black (n 1); R. Baldwin, M. Cave, and M. Lodge, *Understanding Regulation: Theory, Practice and Strategy* (2nd edn, 2012), ch 6. Risk as a justification for regulation needs to be distinguished from risk-based regulation, for an example of which see chapter 7, and see generally, Baldwin, Cave, and Lodge, ch. 13.

[35] See Watson (ed) (n 3) at 43. Private risk management devices include insurance and limited liability incorporation.

informed assessment of the risk, consider the risk to be acceptable, and regard the cost of mitigating the risk to be affordable or insurable'.[36] Government should only intervene if it really is in the best position to manage risk,[37] and its role 'is not to remove all uncertainties, but to identify those risks that would not be tackled in the absence of intervention'.[38] Nevertheless, there is clearly a large subjective element both to the identification, and the perceived importance, of specific risks.[39] In particular, the risk regulation literature indicates that new risks are treated more seriously than pre-existing risks. Accordingly, a novel process such as CCS is likely to generate demand for greater reassurance, and hence require more extensive regulatory intervention than more familiar energy activities before it can be successfully deployed.

2. *The functions of regulation in responding to risk*

In responding to the risks posed by CCS, there are at least three functions for regulation.

(a) **Risk reduction**

First, and most obviously, regulation may seek to reduce risks by providing as much certainty as possible. This may be achieved in various ways, for instance, by providing clarity as to relevant legal and regulatory rules and processes, by defining and limiting costs and liabilities, by providing co-ordination mechanisms (for example, between capture operators and infrastructure providers), or by providing information to assist with private decision-making.

(b) **Risk management**

Where it is impossible, or inappropriate, to provide certainty, an alternative function for regulation is to provide a stable and predictable framework within which risks can be managed. This may refer to decision-making processes, for instance, the establishment of permitting procedures which allow the risks associated with particular projects to be assessed and addressed case by case. But it could also refer to the substantive policy framework. For example, the International Energy Agency (IEA) has recommended setting CCS policy within a stable framework in which the broad architecture and rules of policy evolution are clear, with predetermined 'breakpoints' or 'policy gateways' establishing when and if policy will move to a new stage, and what policies will be adopted within each stage (such as when public subsidy will cease, or CCS will become mandatory).[40]

(c) **Risk allocation**

A third important role for regulation is in allocating risks, whether between economic actors, or between government and the private sector. In so doing,

36 Better Regulation Commission, *Risk, Responsibility, Regulation: Whose Risk is it Anyway?* (2006) 29.
37 Better Regulation Commission (n 36) at 38.
38 Watson (ed.) (n 3) at 43.
39 See Black (n 1) at 311–23.
40 IEA (n 26) at 12.

regulators must take into account not only who is in the best position to bear the risk, financially or otherwise, should it materialize, but also who is in the best position to mitigate the risk, and thereby to prevent it occurring: '[b]eing too ready to pick up the pieces can . . . lead to moral hazard, and thus inadvertently exacerbate risk'.[41] Considerations of equity, including inter-generational equity, are also likely to be important in ensuring that risk allocations are politically acceptable.

3. Difficulties in designing an appropriate regulatory regime

While the regulatory framework is likely to be a crucial factor in determining the success or failure of CCS, there are also particular difficulties in designing an appropriate regulatory regime. The first arises from the pervasive uncertainties associated with CCS. Although some of these uncertainties can be resolved by legal fiat (for example, questions regarding ownership of pore space, or allocation of liability for leakages), regulation cannot eliminate the fundamental economic and technological uncertainties at stake. At best, it can facilitate learning about these uncertainties by providing a cushion against the risks of experimentation. The second problem is the multiple and inter-related nature of the risks involved, and the existence of conflicting policy imperatives. In this context, there is a danger that regulatory intervention simply *displaces* risk rather than reduces it.[42] For example, the provision of public guarantees against the costs of investing in CCS may simply substitute political risk for economic and liability risk.

Consequently, CCS regulation carries a high institutional risk—that is, a high chance that regulation will fail to meet its objectives.[43] This may arise from regulatory error; in particular, there is a high risk of regulators making premature commitments (for instance, to a particular capture technology, scale of investment, or liability regime) which therefore lack credibility. Equally, though, institutional risk may arise from regulatory inaction; from failure to provide investors with sufficient certainty to enable them to invest, or failure to provide the public with sufficient reassurance that their interests will be protected. The key—more easily stated than achieved—is therefore to strike the right balance between regulatory commitment and regulatory flexibility.[44]

IV. The United Kingdom regulatory framework: regulating for CCS

The question for the remainder of this chapter is how successfully the current United Kingdom regulatory framework has negotiated the various risks and uncertainties associated with CCS. In this section, we examine the incentive structures established to encourage investment in CCS, distinguishing between incentives for

[41] Black (n 1) at 329. [42] See Watson (ed) (n 3) at 2.
[43] Black (n 1) at 305, 327. [44] See IEA (n 26) at 12.

power generators to reduce their emissions via CCS, and support for investment in CO_2 infrastructure. In section V, we discuss regulation of the installation and operation of CCS, distinguishing between capture installations, transport, and storage facilities. In both sections, we consider the interplay of EU and domestic requirements.

A. Incentivizing low carbon fossil generation

There are four elements to the incentive framework for CCS generation, some of which are still evolving, comprising a mixture of carrots and sticks.

1. Carbon pricing

The most basic element of any low carbon regulatory framework is a mechanism to establish a price for carbon emissions. UK power generators are therefore required to participate in the EU Emissions Trading Scheme (EU-ETS),[45] which supports investment in CCS in two ways. First, it gives generators a direct incentive to reduce their carbon emissions, so as to avoid having to purchase emissions permits, or enabling them to sell surplus ones. Second, the carbon price raises the wholesale price of electricity, thus enabling low carbon generators to compete more equally with unabated fossil generators.

Some economists argue that, once a carbon pricing mechanism has been established, it should then be left to the market to decide how best to achieve emissions reduction.[46] In practice, though, there is widespread agreement that the EU-ETS alone will be insufficient to bring about the degree of technological transformation that is needed to meet long-term carbon targets, and is particularly unlikely to promote investment in high-cost and risky technologies like CCS. The reasons are twofold.

First, due to an over-supply of emissions permits, the EU-ETS price (around €5/tCO_2e at the time of writing) is currently too low and too volatile to drive significant investment in low carbon generation. Although it has been successful in encouraging a switch from coal to gas generation,[47] according to the European Commission, a carbon price of €40 or more would be required to drive CCS deployment without any other incentives.[48] In response to this problem, the UK government has introduced, as part of its Electricity Market Reform (EMR) process,[49] a Carbon Price Support (CPS) mechanism, which came into effect on 1 April 2013.[50] Via the Climate Change Levy, this creates a minimum carbon price

[45] Directive 2003/87/EC, [2003] OJ L275/32, 25 October (as amended).

[46] See, e.g., J. B. Wiener, 'Global Environmental Regulation: Instrument Choice in Legal Context' (1999) 108 Yale LJ 677; D Driesen, 'Economic Instruments for Sustainable Development' in *Environmental Law for Sustainability* (G. Richardson and S. Wood, eds, 2006).

[47] House of Commons Energy and Climate Change Committee (ECCSC), *Electricity Market Reform*, 4th Report 2010/12, HC 742, para 13.

[48] European Commission, *The Future of CCS in Europe*, COM (2013) 180 final, 20.

[49] See n 10. [50] Finance Act 2011, s 78, sch 20.

for fossil fuel generators, starting at £16/tCO_2e in 2013, rising to £30 in 2020 and £70 in 2030.[51] Plants which install CCS are exempt from the CPS in proportion to the amount of CO_2 captured and stored.

Although this should help create a more realistic carbon price, it is nevertheless potentially problematic. For one thing, by making fossil generation more expensive, it could result in the premature closure of, or deter further investment in, fossil generation before CCS becomes commercially viable.[52] More generally, it introduces an additional element of political risk into the electricity market,[53] while the adoption of a unilateral price floor within the context of an EU-wide carbon market also creates the risk of simply displacing emissions to other countries.[54] In the absence of more fundamental reform of the EU-ETS, however, unilateral measures are arguably unavoidable.[55]

The second reason why the EU-ETS by itself is unlikely to incentivize investment in CCS is because, even if the carbon price were higher, it would still only address one of the market failures inhibiting the growth of low carbon generation (carbon externality).[56] Market mechanisms of this sort tend to favour cheaper technologies which are close to commercial viability (such as onshore wind), and risk locking out early-stage technologies which may have greater long-term abatement potential, but which are currently more expensive and not guaranteed to reduce emissions in the short term. In order for such technologies to secure deployment, and thereby gain the experience and economies of scale necessary to reduce their costs to a commercially competitive level, additional support is required (infant industry support).

2. *Capital support*

The second essential element of the CCS support framework is therefore capital support for research, development, and demonstration. This is justified on two grounds.

First, it is well established that, since knowledge is a public good, private companies will tend to under-invest in research and development. Accordingly, the government's 2012 *CCS Roadmap*[57] announced a £125 million, four-year co-ordinated research and development and innovation programme. In addition, knowledge acquisition and transfer is an explicit aim of the commercialization programme, which seeks not only to promote technological and economic learning, but also regulatory testing.[58] Indeed, despite the failure of the first demonstration

[51] HM Treasury, *Carbon Price Floor Consultation: the Government Response* (2011), available at: <https://www.gov.uk/government/uploads/system/uploads/attachment_data/file/190279/carbon_price_floor_consultation_govt_response.pdf>.

[52] The introduction of the CPS contributed to the failure of the first commercialization competition, as Scottish Power regarded it as a risk to the continued operation of Longannet: National Audit Office (n 8) 32.

[53] ECCSC (n 47) para 156.

[54] ECCSC (n 47) para 145.

[55] ECCSC (n 47) para 148.

[56] See N. Stern, *The Economics of Climate Change* (2006), esp chs 15 and 16.

[57] DECC (n 6).

[58] DECC (n 6) at 7, 36, 38.

competition, the government made publicly available the results of the Front-End Engineering and Design (FEED) studies for the Kingsnorth and Longannet projects, describing the amount of information made available as going 'beyond anything previously undertaken globally, in the context of CCS knowledge transfer'.[59]

The second reason why capital support is required is because their high capital costs and uncertain returns mean that there is no (or very limited) commercial funding available for the first demonstration projects.[60] The government has therefore also made available £1 billion to fund up to two demonstration projects through the commercialization programme. The second competition is open to a wider range of technologies than the first,[61] and in March 2013 two preferred bidders (out of eight) were announced: Peterhead, in Aberdeenshire, an existing gas-fired power station, and the White Rose project in Yorkshire, a new supercritical coal-fired plant. FEED studies are now underway, and final investment decisions will be taken in 2015.[62]

However, while the amount of public money committed to the commercialization programme is clearly very large, it is questionable whether it is sufficient to ensure that CCS demonstration does go ahead. For instance, the capital costs of the collapsed Longannet project were estimated at £1.3–£1.5 billion.[63] It has also been argued that at least four demonstration projects are required to provide the critical mass for testing alternative technologies,[64] and to enable the regulatory, legal, and commercial framework to develop sufficiently to allow post-demonstration phase projects to be commercially funded.[65]

Additional capital funding is available at EU level under two programmes: the European Energy Programme for Recovery (EEPR) and the New Entrants' Reserve 300 (NER 300) programme. Six projects, including the UK's Don Valley project, received funding under the EEPR, but none has yet received a final investment decision. Up to eight CCS projects were expected to receive (partial) funding under NER 300; however, none was successful in the first bidding round. There are two main problems with these programmes. First, since the NER 300 is funded by the sale of 300 million EU-ETS permits in the New Entrants Reserve, the money available for the programme has plummeted due to the collapse of the carbon price.[66] Second, there is poor alignment between domestic and European funding programmes.[67] For instance, the Don Valley capture project received funding

59 IEA, *Carbon Capture and Storage: Legal and Regulatory Review* (3rd edn, 2012) 61.

60 ECCSC (n 47) at paras 12, 22, 23, 26; Cost Reduction Taskforce (n 25) at 28.

61 It was limited to 300 MW post-combustion coal projects.

62 DECC Press Release, 20 March 2013, available at <http://www.gov.uk/government/news/preferred-bidders-announced-in-uk-s-1bn-ccs-competition>.

63 National Audit Office (n 8) at para 3.1.

64 Committee on Climate Change, *Meeting Carbon Budgets—2012 Progress Report* (2012) 27.

65 Carbon Connect, *Future Electricity Series Part I: Power from Fossil Fuels* (2013) 11, 36.

66 European Commission (n 48) at 16.

67 European Commission (n 48) at 17.

under the EEPR and was top-ranked in the first NER 300 bidding round, yet failed to reach the shortlist for the UK commercialization competition.[68]

3. *Revenue support*

The third element of the United Kingdom's incentive framework for CCS is long-term revenue support. This is particularly important for post-demonstration phase projects, but will also be available for projects in receipt of capital funding. Again, there are two justifications for revenue support. The first is that the cost of carbon is only one part of the cost differential between abated and unabated fossil generation. As noted earlier, there is a significant energy penalty associated with CCS projects, and their capital costs are necessarily higher than those of unabated generators.[69] Second, because low carbon generators have higher capital costs, they are more exposed to electricity price movements than unabated generators. Accordingly, a stable revenue stream is important to enable them to attract funding.[70]

Through its EMR programme, the UK government is attempting to put in place a sustainable market framework for low carbon generation. The key reform is the introduction of feed-in tariffs with contracts for difference (CfDs).[71] These will be long-term contracts (10 years for CCS) guaranteeing a price (the 'strike price') for low carbon generation.[72] Strike prices will initially be set administratively, through individual negotiation for CCS projects, later moving to technology-specific tenders or auctions, and eventually to technology-blind competitions, before being phased out in the late 2020s. CCS projects could also benefit from the introduction of a capacity market,[73] which is intended to reward the availability of flexible capacity[74] at times of system stress. At least initially, however, CCS generators which receive CfDs will not be eligible to enter the capacity market, although provision may be made for them to receive capacity payments for switching off their capture equipment when system margins are tight.

The EMR programme represents 'the first comprehensive attempt globally to set a policy to drive CCS deployment beyond the first demonstration facilities'.[75]

[68] European Commission (n 48) at 27; Committee on Climate Change, *Meeting Carbon Budgets—2013 Progress Report* (2013) 96.

[69] ECCSC (n 47) at para 154.

[70] ECCSC (n 47) at para 221.

[71] Energy Act 2013, Pt 2, ch 2; DECC, *Electricity Market Reform: Annex A: Feed-in Tariffs with Contracts for Difference: Operational Framework* (2012), available at <http://www.gov.uk/government/uploads/system/uploads/attachment_data/file/65635/7077-electricity-market-reform-annex-a.pdf>.

[72] If the wholesale market falls below the strike price, generators will receive the difference; if it is higher, they will have to pay the difference.

[73] Energy Act 2013, Pt 2, ch 3. DECC, *Electricity Market Reform: Annex C: Capacity Market Design and Implementation Update* (2012), available at <http://www.gov.uk/government/uploads/system/uploads/attachment_data/file/65637/7104-emr-annex-c-capacity-market-design-and-implementat.pdf>; DECC, *Electricity Market Reform: Capacity Market—Detailed Design Proposals* (2013), available at: <http://www.gov.uk/government/uploads/system/uploads/attachment_data/file/209280/15398_TSO_Cm_8637_DECC_Electricity_Market_Reform_web_optimised.pdf>.

[74] Initially generation capacity, but ultimately including storage and demand-side measures.

[75] Global CCS Institute (n 6) at 2.

Nevertheless, it has been extensively criticized.[76] This is partly directed at the delay in implementing the reforms, and continued uncertainty over their details, which have had a significant chilling effect on investment.[77] As regards CCS specifically, there is also some concern about the design of CfDs, and about the appropriateness of moving towards a standardized approach to the award of contracts. In particular, the economic characteristics of CCS projects are different from renewables and nuclear generators, and fixed price contracts might actually expose them to greater economic risk, by reducing their ability to pass fuel price risk onto consumers.[78] In addition, in order to protect consumers, there will be a statutory limit on the cost of CfDs. As with support for demonstration projects, there are therefore concerns about funding shortfalls,[79] and the prospect of rationing of CfDs adds what the House of Commons Energy and Climate Change Committee has called an 'unacceptable level' of political risk.[80]

4. *Other supports*

Finally, there are some non-financial incentives to support investment in CCS, both via the introduction of an Emissions Performance Standard (EPS) for new generators as part of the EMR programme and via the land-use planning system.[81] The EPS has initially been set at 450kg CO_2/MWh as from 2013, which excludes new unabated coal generation from the market,[82] while continuing to permit unabated gas. In fact, this simply reinforces the existing position under planning policy: in England and Wales, no new coal-fired power stations will be authorized without CCS;[83] in Scotland, new coal-fired generators must currently demonstrate CCS on at least 300 MW of their capacity, moving to their full capacity from 2020, with a requirement for full retrofit of existing coal stations by 2025–30.[84] In both jurisdictions, all other new fossil generators over 300 MW must demonstrate 'carbon capture readiness'.[85]

[76] See generally, ECCSC (n 47) and ECCSC, *Draft Energy Bill: Pre-Legislative Scrutiny*, 1st Report 2012–13, HC 275-I.

[77] Committee on Climate Change, *Next Steps on Electricity Market Reform—Securing the Benefits of Low Carbon Investment* (2013) 8, available at: <http://www.theccc.org.uk/wp-content/uploads/2013/05/1720_EMR_report_web.pdf>.

[78] ECCSC (n 47) at para 119; Watson (ed.) (n 3) at 11; IEA (n 26), at 23; Cost Reduction Task Force (n 25) at 30. It has been suggested that a fixed premium above market price might be more appropriate.

[79] Carbon Connect (n 65) at 99.

[80] See ECCS (n 76) at para 74.

[81] Energy Act 2013, pt 2, ch 8.

[82] CCS demonstration plants will be exempt from the EPS.

[83] See DECC, *National Policy Statements for Energy Infrastructure* (2011), available at: <http://webarchive.nationalarchives.gov.uk/+/http://www.decc.gov.uk/en/content/cms/meeting_energy/consents_planning/nps_en_infra/nps_en_infra.aspx>.

[84] Scottish Government, *Electricity Generation Policy Statement* (2012), available at: <http://www.scotland.gov.uk/Resource/0038/00389294.pdf>.

[85] Directive 2001/80/EC, [2001] OJ L309/1, 27 November Art. 9A, inserted by Directive 2009/31/EC (n 5). See DECC, *Carbon Capture Readiness: A Guidance Note for Section 36 Electricity Act 1989 Consent Applications* (2009), available at: <http://whitehall-admin.production.alphagov.co.uk/government/uploads/system/uploads/attachment_data/file/43609/Carbon_capture_readiness_-_guidance.pdf>.

In its current form, therefore, the EPS will do little to promote CCS,[86] and could even be counterproductive. Although there are signals that it might be tightened in the future,[87] controversially, the level at which new plants are consented will be 'grandfathered' until 2045.[88] This has been justified as a measure to remove regulatory risk from the new generation,[89] but by doing so it creates a serious risk of carbon lock-in, and indeed risks triggering a new 'dash for gas' as developers seek to pre-empt any future tightening of the EPS. Moreover, since the commitment is incompatible with the achievement of long-term carbon targets, it may not in fact alleviate the perceived risk of regulatory change.[90]

However, planning policy can provide more positive support for CCS development by establishing a presumption in its favour in the development consent process. The planning system in England and Wales has been criticized for not clearly doing so,[91] but in Scotland, the statutory National Planning Framework (NPF)[92] designates so-called 'national developments', the need for which cannot subsequently be questioned.[93] Thus, NPF2 designated a coal-fired power station with CCS for Hunterston,[94] while the draft NPF3 designates gas CCS projects at Peterhead and Grangemouth, including pipeline developments, along with new or refurbished clean fossil fuel plants at Longannet and Cockenzie by 2030.[95] Such designation is not, however, uncontroversial, as there are limited consultation rights,[96] and it reduces effective participation later at the consent stage. In fact, the Hunterston designation was subject to legal challenge for inadequate consultation and, although the challenge was unsuccessful,[97] the application for development consent for the power station was subsequently withdrawn, partly due to extensive public opposition.[98]

B. Incentivizing CO_2 infrastructure

Currently, regulatory support for CCS is entirely focused on generators, with no separate incentives for investment in transport and storage infrastructure. Early

86 The Energy and Climate Change Committee described it as 'pointless': ECCSC (n 47) at 4. See also European Commission (n 48) at 21.

87 Watson (ed.) (n 3) at 10.

88 I.e., there will be no tightening of the EPS for those generators: Energy Act 2013, s 57(2).

89 DECC 'Davey Sets Out Measures to Provide Certainty to Gas Investors', Press Notice 12/025, 17 March 2012, available at <http://www.gov.uk/government/news/davey-sets-out-measures-to-provide-certainty-to-gas-investors>.

90 ECCSC (n 76) at 5.

91 Cost Reduction Task Force (n 25) at 2.

92 Planning (Scotland) Act 2006, s 1.

93 Although whether NPF designations are binding in relation to electricity consents has been doubted: *William Grant & Sons v Scottish Ministers* [2012] CSOH 98, para 17; *McGinty v Scottish Ministers* [2013] CSIH 78, paras 45 and 58.

94 Scottish Government, *National Planning Framework for Scotland 2* (2009), available at <http://www.scotland.gov.uk/Resource/Doc/278232/0083591.pdf>.

95 Scottish Government, *Ambition, Opportunity, Place—Scotland's Third National Planning Framework, Main Issues Report and Draft Framework* (2013) paras 1.12, 2.7, 2.37-2.44, available at <http://www.scotland.gov.uk/Resource/0042/00421073.pdf>.

96 See, e.g., M. Poustie, 'Planning Reforms in Scotland' [2007] JPL 489 at 492–4.

97 *McGinty v Scottish Ministers* (n 93).

98 The project was also unsuccessful in securing funding.

projects are expected to involve single, point-to-point, full-chain configurations, with capital funding and revenue payments to generators therefore covering both the costs of capture and associated transport and storage costs. Thereafter, the government's strategy for CO_2 infrastructure is that it will be funded through private investment, and will develop piecemeal in response to demand, reusing existing pipelines where possible. Eventually, however, it wants those piecemeal developments to become integrated into a network, and expects that regional clusters of CCS projects will develop with shared infrastructure, which other emitters will be able to tap into in the future.[99]

Although it will consider supporting the construction of over-sized infrastructure in anticipation of future demand as part of the commercialization programme,[100] the government has stated that (for now at least) it has no intention of planning the development of a transport and storage network.[101] Instead, integration is to be secured via the Third Party Access (TPA) regime,[102] and the co-ordinating and facilitative functions performed by the Crown Estate as owner of the seabed.[103]

Given the current uncertainty surrounding the future prospects for CCS, this approach is clearly motivated by the desire to avoid stranded assets. Nevertheless, it is potentially problematic. First, it has been suggested that support via CfDs may not be suitable for both capture plant and infrastructure, since they have different cost and risk profiles, and hence that separate funding mechanisms for the transport and storage sectors might be needed.[104] Second, the lack of any strategic vision for the development of CO_2 infrastructure undermines the credibility of capture readiness assessments, and hence their utility as a means of enabling future retrofit of CCS.[105]

Finally, a decentralized approach may fail to realize economies of scale in infrastructure development. It has been argued that a strategic approach could help to identify 'least regret' sizing of pipeline infrastructure,[106] and that a central or regional infrastructure monopoly would have lower funding costs.[107] However, although the government has recognized the potential benefits of a more centralized approach, and remains open to the possibility of different arrangements in the future,[108] it claims that a central agency is unlikely to be more effective in making decisions about the scale, location, and timing of infrastructure investments than

99 DECC (n 6) at 20, 23; *CCS Roadmap: Building Networks: Transport and Storage Infrastructure* (2012) para 3.4, available at <https://www.gov.uk/government/uploads/system/uploads/attachment_data/file/48322/4905-ccs-roadmap--transport-and-storage-infrastructure.pdf>.

100 DECC (n 99) at para 2.6.

101 DECC (n 99) at para 1.3.

102 See section V.B.2.

103 e.g., it has developed, along with the British Geological Survey, an online database of mapped C02 storage capacity: <http://www.co2stored.co.uk>.

104 Cost Reduction Taskforce (n 25) at 30–1.

105 Committee on Climate Change (n 64) at 105; Carbon Connect (n 65) at 10, 12, 24.

106 Committee on Climate Change (n 64).

107 Cost Reduction Taskforce (n 25) at 29.

108 DECC, *Developing Carbon Capture and Storage Infrastructure: Consultation on Implementing the TPA Provisions of the CCS Directive and Call for Evidence on the Long-Term Development of CCS Infrastructure* (2010) ch 3; DECC (n 99) at para 3.4.

individual market actors, given the current state of uncertainty. Bankes and Nilson agree that a suitably designed TPA regime should be able to secure sufficient co-ordination.[109] Nevertheless, there is arguably still a role for government to promote certainty by articulating a clear vision for long-term infrastructure development.[110]

V. The United Kingdom regulatory framework: regulation of CCS[111]

The United Kingdom has adopted a proactive approach to the development of a regulatory framework to govern the establishment and operation of CCS projects. In 2007, the UK government established the CCS Regulatory Taskforce to identify gaps in existing regulations, and a subsequent review exercise by the Scottish government in 2010 resulted in the publication of a *Carbon Capture and Storage Regulatory Test Toolkit*,[112] which has been endorsed as a model of best practice.[113]

The 2007 review identified the most significant regulatory gaps as relating to carbon storage. Accordingly, as noted earlier, the Energy Act 2008, Part 3 provided for the licensing of offshore carbon storage facilities. This was then amended to ensure compliance with the 2009 CCS Directive,[114] before detailed regulations were made under the Energy Act to implement the Directive.[115] The CCS Directive is also primarily focused on the regulation of storage, although it requires the adoption of a TPA regime for both transport and storage. That apart, regulation of capture and transport has largely been achieved through application or extension of existing regulatory regimes. In relation to all three aspects of the CCS chain, regulation is principally through conventional command and control mechanisms.

A. Capture installations

Capture installations required the least regulatory innovation, since they can easily be accommodated within existing land-use planning and environmental control regimes, and do not raise any particular challenges regarding the acquisition of ownership rights. As with most industrial activities, two permits are required for the capture of CO_2. For new generating installations, consent would be required under the Planning Act 2008 (for England and Wales) or the Electricity Act

109 Bankes and Nilson (n 26) at 237–8, 250–1.

110 Committee on Climate Change (n 64) at 105; Cost Reduction Taskforce (n 25) at 2; M. Lewis and N. Westaway, 'Public Participation in UK CCS Planning and Consent Procedures', in Havercroft, Macrory, and Stewart (eds), (n 27) 277 at 286.

111 International law aspects of the regulation of CCS are considered in chapter 6.

112 <http://www.scotland.gov.uk/Resource/Doc/917/0113634.pdf>.

113 IEA, *Carbon Capture and Storage: Legal and Regulatory Review* (2nd edn, 2011) 57.

114 See n 5.

115 Storage of Carbon Dioxide (Amendment of the Energy Act 2008 etc) Regulations, SI 2011/2453; Energy Act 2008 (Storage of Carbon Dioxide) (Scotland) Regulations, SSI 2011/224.

1989 (for Scotland). In addition, an environmental permit would be required, which regulates the processes and techniques used in the installation to reduce and minimize pollution, and would therefore encompass capture operations.[116] The environmental permit regimes make detailed provision for permit applications, public participation, and enforcement.[117] For existing generators, a variation to the existing environmental permit would be required which could be triggered either by the operator, the relevant regulator (the Environment Agency, for England and Wales, or the Scottish Environment Protection Agency) or by a direction from the relevant Minister. As part of the land-use planning processes, the capture operation is subject to formal Environmental Impact Assessment (EIA) processes enabling more extensive public participation than otherwise would be the case.[118] However, as discussed earlier,[119] national planning policy may undercut full and effective public participation by establishing *a priori* the need for CCS.

B. CO_2 pipelines

1. *Pipeline authorization*

The approach adopted to the authorization of CO_2 pipelines has simply been to extend existing legislation to them: the Pipe-Lines Act 1962, which governs the construction of onshore cross-country pipelines;[120] and the Petroleum Act 1998, which governs offshore pipelines. For new onshore pipelines, the 1962 Act provides that pipelines cannot be constructed without ministerial consent, and also provides for the acquisition of compulsory rights over land. Where the intention is to reuse an existing pipeline, the owner may apply to the Secretary of State for a compulsory rights order enabling the conversion to go ahead. For offshore pipelines, a lease must be obtained from the Crown Estate, as well as consent from ministers under the 1998 Act, and again provision has been made for the conversion of existing pipelines.[121] The construction or conversion of pipelines for CO_2 transport and associated booster stations is also subject to EIA requirements during the authorization process.[122]

[116] Environmental Permitting (England and Wales) Regulations 2010, SI 2010/675, sch 1 (amended by SI 2011/2043); Pollution Prevention and Control (Scotland) Regulations 2012, SSI 2012/360, regs 11,12, 20, sch 1, para 6.10.

[117] SI 2010/675, reg 13(3), sch 5, pts 1 and 4; SSI 2012/360, reg 13, sch 4, pts 1, 6, and 10.

[118] Town and Country Planning (Environmental Impact Assessment) Regulations 2011, SI 2011/1824, sch 1, para 23; Town and Country Planning (Environmental Impact Assessment) (Scotland) Regulations 2011, SSI 2011/139, sch 1, para 22. Elements of environmental assessment also form part of the environmental permit application process: SI 2010/675 (n 116), sch 7, para 4; SSI 2012/360 (n 116), sch 1, para 1(1)(e)–(n).

[119] See section IV.A.4.

[120] As amended by the Energy Act 2011, s 108. Nationally significant cross-country pipelines in England and Wales, including those originating in Scotland, are subject to the provisions of the Planning Act 2008, ss 14(1)(g) and 21.

[121] Energy Act 2008, s 30B, inserted by the Energy Act 2011, s 107. The effect is to relieve previous operators of decommissioning liabilities.

[122] SI 2011/1824 (n 118), sch 1, para 16; SSI 2011/139 (n 118), sch 1, para 16. See also the Infrastructure Planning (Environmental Impact Assessment) Regulations 2009, SI 2009/2263 as

2. *Third-party access*

Although existing pipeline legislation already imposed third-party access (TPA) requirements, the UK government enacted new regulations to provide a common set of TPA rules for both CO_2 transport and storage, and also to comply with the transparency requirements of the CCS Directive.[123] TPA requirements apply at two stages: at the point at which consent for new infrastructure is being sought, and to the operation of existing infrastructure. In common with the existing approach, this is a system of negotiated rather than regulated TPA; that is, it is for those seeking access to infrastructure to negotiate agreement with the owner, with powers for the UK/Scottish government to intervene only if agreement cannot be reached. At the consent stage, the relevant consenting authority may require that the capacity of the pipeline or storage facility is greater than proposed by the applicant, that the design be modified, or the route of a pipeline changed to accommodate demand from third parties. Such variation conditions may only be imposed where it will not prejudice the safety, environmental integrity, or efficient operation of the infrastructure, and any additional costs may be recoverable from the party seeking access. Similar provisions apply in relation to existing infrastructure, but an access notice must not prejudice the rights of existing users, nor can it require an increase in the total authorized capacity of a storage site.

Because this is negotiated rather than regulated TPA, infrastructure owners are not obliged to publish tariffs, but they do have a duty to publish information annually relating to available capacity and to the technical and operating requirements for access. However, a further recommendation to improve the co-ordination of infrastructure development, through the imposition of so-called 'open season' requirements on developers,[124] has not been adopted. This would have required developers to make their plans known to other potential users before finalizing design and applying for consent. It is not clear why this proposal was rejected, but the general aim appears to have been to minimize the regulatory burden on infrastructure providers, and indeed, there is a duty to review the TPA regulations every five years, which is clearly deregulatory in intent.[125]

C. Carbon storage

1. *Storage authorization*

Although onshore storage remains a possibility, the focus of the UK storage strategy is on offshore storage, which is abundantly available, raises no complex property

amended by SI 2011/2741. EIA requirements apply to pipelines above 800 mm in diameter and at least 40 km in length.

[123] Storage of Carbon Dioxide (Access to Infrastructure Regulations) 2011, SI 2011/2305.

[124] DECC (n 108) at para 3.18; Bankes and Nilson (n 26) at 237–8, 250–1.

[125] SI 2011/2305 (n 123), reg 2. The review must assess, *inter alia*, whether the objectives of the regulatory system remain appropriate and, if so, whether they could be achieved in a less burdensome manner.

rights issues,[126] and is less likely to attract public opposition. Thus, the Energy Act 2008 vested ownership of storage rights in the UK continental shelf in the Crown Estate,[127] from whom a storage lease is therefore required,[128] and established a system of storage licensing. In order to comply with the CCS Directive, the licensing system was later extended to include storage onshore and within internal waters,[129] and a further requirement to seek a storage permit was added.[130] Again, provision has been made for the conversion of existing facilities,[131] and the planning regime has been amended in line with the CCS Directive to provide for EIA of storage sites.[132]

A licence must first be obtained (from the UK government) for an area to enable exploration of it and the possible selection of a storage site. If such a site is selected, it must then be the subject of a permit application (to UK or Scottish Ministers, as appropriate). Only a licence holder may apply for a storage permit, and only when any exploration required by the licence has been completed and the other conditions of the licence fulfilled.[133]

The key aims of the permitting process are to ensure that both the proposed site and the proposed operator are suitable, and that appropriate plans are in place for site monitoring and for corrective measures should leakage occur. The permitting authority may approve the proposed monitoring and corrective measures plans with such modifications as it considers necessary.[134] Before deciding to grant a permit, however, it must seek and take into account the opinion of the European Commission.[135] If a permit is granted, it must contain extensive prescribed contents including operational requirements such as the total amount of CO_2 authorized to be stored, the monitoring plan, provisions for reporting leakages, a provisional post-closure plan, and provisions relating to financial security.[136]

Although, as is normal with environmental command and control regimes in the United Kingdom, there is provision for a public register, the contents of the register

126 For discussion, see chapter 2.

127 Energy Act 2008, s 1.

128 The Crown Estate's policy is not to impose any additional regulatory burdens on developers through the leasing process. A storage lease must not interfere with the rights of existing petroleum licence holders in the area. See DECC, *CCS Roadmap: Storage Strategy* (2012) 8, available at <https://www.gov.uk/government/uploads/system/uploads/attachment_data/file/48320/4904-ccs-roadmap--storage-strategy.pdf>; see also <http://www.thecrownestate.co.uk/energy-infrastructure/carbon-capture-and-storage/what-we-do/>.

129 Energy Act 2008, s 17(3A) and (4).

130 Storage of Carbon Dioxide (Licensing etc) Regulations 2010, SI 2010/2221; Storage of Carbon Dioxide (Licensing etc) (Scotland) Regulations 2011, SSI 2011/24. The CCS Directive requires both an 'exploration permit' and a 'storage permit'.

131 Energy Act 2008, s 30A, inserted by Energy Act 2011, s 107. Again, this relieves previous operators of decommissioning liabilities.

132 SI 2011/1824 (n 118), sch 1, para 22; SSI 2011/139 (n 118), sch 1, para 21.

133 SI 2010/2221 (n 130), reg 6(1), (2); SSI 2011/24 (n 130), regs 6(1),(2). A licence expires at the end of its term if no application for a storage permit is made by that date or an application for a storage permit is refused: SI 2010/2221 (n 130), reg 4; SSI 2011/24 (n 130), reg 4. Detailed provision is made for the contents of a licence: SI 2010/2221 (n 130), reg 5, sch 1; SSI 2011/24 (n 130), reg 5, sch 1.

134 SI 2010/2221 (n 130), reg 7(5), (6); SSI 2011/24 (n 130), reg 7(5),(6).

135 SI 2010/2221 (n 130), reg 7(7); SSI 2011/24 (n 130), reg 7(7).

136 SI 2010/2221 (n 130), reg 8, sch 2; SSI 2011/24 (n 130), reg 8, sch 2.

are somewhat narrower than in other regimes, notably in that applications for licences, and permits are not advertised and placed upon the register to facilitate public participation. Instead, only the particulars of the licences and permits, together with reports sent to the authority, directions given by the authority, and post-closure arrangements are to be included on the register.[137] Aside from any applicable EIA processes, there are thus much more limited opportunities to participate in licensing and permitting decisions than in other environmental regimes. The fact that in practice such licences and permits are likely to be confined to marine areas is not necessarily an adequate justification for this, as a variety of interests are potentially affected by such developments including fisheries, energy undertakings, grid operators, conservation groups, and shipping undertakings. Given the importance of stakeholder engagement in maintaining trust and confidence in environmental decision-making, this could potentially prove to be problematic.[138]

2. *Storage operation and closure*

Should leakages or other significant irregularities arise during the operation of a storage facility, the relevant authority has powers to require the operator to take corrective measures. If it fails to do so, the authority must take those corrective measures itself and may recover its costs from the operator.[139] There are also powers to modify or revoke the permit, where the authority becomes aware of any (risk of) leakages or significant irregularities, breaches of any terms or conditions of the permit, or any scientific finding or technological development which has a bearing on the conduct of operations at the storage site.[140]

Where a permit is revoked the authority must either close the storage site or consider an application for a new licence (and, if that is granted, for a new storage permit) in respect of the site.[141] Until the site is closed or a new storage permit granted, responsibility for discharging the obligations in relation to the acceptance and injection of CO_2, monitoring, corrective measures, the surrender of allowances under the EU-ETS legislation, and liability for prevention and remediation under legislation implementing the Environmental Liability Directive transfers to the authority.[142]

Assuming the permit is not revoked and the site proceeds to the end of its life, the provisional post-closure plan approved at the time the permit was granted must be revisited and approved when the operator wishes to close the site.[143] The

[137] Energy Act 2008, s 29(1), SI 2010/2221 (n 130), reg 9(1)–(4). The Secretary of State has discretion to include other prescribed categories of information: SI 2010/2221 (n 130), reg 9(5)(b). Surprisingly, the Scottish regulations contain no comparable provisions.

[138] Watson (ed) (n 3) at 21 and 37; and see generally M. Lee et al 'Public Participation and Climate Change Infrastructure' (2013) 25 JEL 33.

[139] SI 2010/2221 (n 130), reg 10; SSI 2011/24 (n 130), reg 9.

[140] SI 2010/2221 (n 130), reg 11, (5); SSI 2011/24 (n 130), reg 10(5).

[141] SI 2010/2221 (n 130), reg 12(1), (2); SSI 2011/24 (n 130), reg 11(1),(2).

[142] SI 2010/2221 (n 130), reg 12(4); SSI 2011/24 (n 130), reg 11(4). See further section V.C.3.

[143] SI 2010/2221 (n 130), reg 13, sch 1, para 3; SSI 2011/24 (n 130), reg 12, sch 1, para 2.

operator's obligations relating to monitoring, corrective measures, the surrender of EU-ETS allowances, and potential liability under the Environmental Liability Directive remain with them for a minimum of 20 years following closure,[144] although there is some flexibility to bring that date forward if the authority is satisfied that all the available evidence indicates that the stored CO_2 will be completely and permanently contained.[145] Responsibility for the site thereafter transfers to the authority, although the operator may retain some residual responsibility if there has been fault.[146]

3. *Liability for leakage*[147]

A suitable liability regime in this context must strike a balance between ensuring that CCS can proceed by not imposing unduly onerous burdens on operators and providing certainty as to when and for how long liability will arise, on the one hand, and ensuring adequate risk management and environmental protection, on the other hand, in order to ensure public confidence in CCS.[148] One key issue is thus the forms of liability that may arise. The other is the transfer of liability between operator and government. Given the length of time that CO_2 will be stored, it is not realistic to expect operators to take on completely open-ended liabilities. In addition, given that commercial entities may not survive indefinitely, it makes sense to transfer liability to the state. However, if transfer takes place too readily it may not ensure adequate public protection and may not be politically acceptable.

Liability may take several forms. First, there is regulatory liability under the CCS legislation itself, discussed in section V.C.2. This is comparable to other environmental regimes, although post-closure monitoring and corrective obligations extend over a longer timescale than normal. Second, there is liability for environmental damage, including climate damage, which is provided for in the CCS Directive by amendments to the Environmental Liability Directive[149] and EU-ETS Directive.[150] The former covers environmental damage[151] and damage to protected species and habitats or the imminent threat of such damage caused by the operation of storage facilities both onshore and offshore. The relevant regulators,

144 SI 2010/2221 (n 130), reg 14, sch 1, para 4; SSI 2011/24 (n 130), reg 13, sch 1, para 3.

145 Directive 2009/31/EC, art 18(1).

146 Directive 2009/31/EC, art 18, 18(7).

147 For fuller discussion see, e.g., Clarke (n 27); A. Haan-Kamminga, 'Long-Term Liability for Geological Carbon Storage in the European Union' (2011) 29 JERL 309.

148 Clarke (n 27) at 181.

149 Directive 2004/35/EC, [2004] OJ L143/54, 30 April, Annex III, para 14. This has been implemented by the Environmental Damage (Prevention and Remediation) Amendment Regulations 2010, SI 2010/587 and the Environmental Liability (Scotland) Amendment Regulations 2011, SSI 2011/116.

150 Directive 2003/87/EC (n 45).

151 Environmental damage is defined as: damage to protected species or habitats which is such that it significantly adversely affects reaching or maintaining the favourable conservation status of such species or habitats; water damage which is such that it significantly adversely affects the ecological, chemical, and/or quantitative status of water and/or its ecological potential; and land damage which is land contamination which creates a significant risk of human health being adversely affected: Directive 2004/35/EC (n 149), art 1.

the Environment Agency (England and Wales) and SEPA (Scotland), can require operators to prevent or remedy such damage and, should they fail to do so, take direct action themselves to do so and recover their costs from the operator.[152] Remediation may be primary, complementary, or compensatory and could potentially thus involve significant costs.

As regards climate damage, the EU-ETS Directive applies to CO_2 capture installations, pipelines, and storage facilities,[153] but only when CO_2 is actually emitted.[154] Thus operators must surrender the appropriate number of EU-ETS allowances only when there is leakage. This should provide a powerful incentive to ensure that there is no leakage, but as noted, it is actually a considerable risk for developers in the context of an expected rise in the carbon price.[155] However, the CCS Directive attempts to manage that risk and provide operators with some degree of certainty by requiring that they put in place financial security to cover such liabilities.[156] In addition, as noted earlier, liability under both the Environmental Liability Directive and the EU-ETS will ultimately pass to the government, albeit not irrevocably.

There is, however, a third category of liability which is not dealt with under the CCS Directive, and where member states therefore have discretion as to how to treat CCS operators. This includes liability for other forms of damage, such as to persons and property at common law (in nuisance, negligence, or trespass). It may also include liability under other domestic environmental law regimes, such as the environmental permitting regime in England and Wales (and its Scottish equivalents)[157] and the contaminated land regime,[158] and under health and safety legislation.[159] Here, unfortunately, there is considerable uncertainty both for operators and for those who may suffer damage from CO_2 leakage. The common law has not responded well to liabilities arising out of technological developments in an environmental context, and judges have tended to indicate that in complex areas (which are likely to include CCS), Parliament ought to produce a legislative solution.[160] There is also no provision for transfer of these categories of liability to government.

Exclusive statutory regimes for personal injury and property damage do exist for certain hazardous activities, such as nuclear installations[161] and marine oil transportation.[162] It may be that the risks of CO_2 leakage are not regarded as

[152] Environmental Damage (Prevention and Remediation) Regulations 2009, SI 2009/153 (as amended, see n 149), pts 2–4; Environmental Liability (Scotland) Regulations 2009, SSI 2009/266 (as amended, see n 149), regs 8–18.

[153] Directive 2003/87/EC (n 45), Annex I.

[154] Directive 2003/87/EC (n 45), art 4.

[155] See section III.A.1.b.

[156] Directive 2009/31/EC (n 5), art 19.

[157] See e.g. SI 2010/675 (n 116), regs 58–59 or, in Scotland, e.g., Water Environment (Controlled Activities) (Scotland) Regulations 2011, SSI 2011/209, regs 32–33; and SSI 2012/360 (n 116), reg 57.

[158] Environmental Protection Act 1990, Pt IIA.

[159] See, e.g., Health and Safety at Work etc Act 1974, ss 33, 36 and 37; Pipelines Safety Regulations 1996, SI 1996/825.

[160] See, e.g., *Cambridge Water Co v Eastern Counties Leather plc* [1994] 2 AC 264 per Lord Goff at 305.

[161] Nuclear Installations Act 1965.

[162] Merchant Shipping Act 1995; Merchant Shipping (Pollution) Act 2006.

comparable, and hence do not justify a specific statutory regime. But while there may be limited risks of injury and property damage if storage is confined to offshore areas, accidents in the oil and gas industry clearly indicate that such damage and injury can arise, and there may also be risks arising out of pipeline accidents onshore, even if storage is exclusively undertaken offshore. Hence clarification of the extent and scope of liability through a statutory regime would be a means of further enhancing investor confidence.

VI. Evaluation and conclusions

We have argued in this chapter that a regulatory regime for CCS needs to strike a careful balance between providing sufficient certainty to enable investors to commit to CCS with reasonable confidence, and sufficient flexibility to ensure that public policy objectives are not compromised. Comparatively, the United Kingdom has a very well-developed CCS regulatory framework, with few remaining gaps, which encompasses both the permitting and operation of capture, transport and storage installations and, crucially, the provision of regulatory incentives to invest in CCS. Clearly, however, this regulatory effort has not yet been sufficient to move CCS from a theoretical to a practical climate change mitigation option. Where, then, in terms of the key risks and uncertainties identified here, do the continuing problems with the UK regulatory framework lie?

As far as investment risks are concerned, a degree of economic risk will remain until the details of the EMR programme are finalized. More fundamentally, there is room for concern about the adequacy of the support being provided, particularly for infrastructure investments. Liability risk is also frequently cited as a major barrier to investment. The liability regime adopted under the CCS Directive provides some degree of certainty for CCS operators, and the United Kingdom has adopted a fairly generous approach to the transfer of liability to government.[163] However, operators currently face an indefinite liability risk at common law for property damage and personal injury, and under other statutory regimes. While the prospect of such liability actually materializing may be small, investor confidence would be enhanced by putting in place a comprehensive statutory liability regime.

However, perhaps the most serious remaining investment risks are political and regulatory risks. One issue here is the complexity of the proposed CCS support mechanisms. While multiple regulatory instruments are justified to meet multiple market failures, each additional instrument adds another element of political risk. Complexity also increases the risk of regulatory failure if interactions among regulatory instruments produce unintended consequences.[164]

A second issue is the government's refusal to make CCS mandatory. Its reluctance to 'pick winners' is motivated by an understandable concern to minimize costs to consumers and not to jeopardize climate change targets by backing a low

163 In France and Germany, liability transfers after 30 years: IEA (n 113) at 11.
164 ECCSC (n 47) at paras 228–231.

carbon generation option which may turn out to be more expensive or less effective than others. Some commentators also argue that any mandating of CCS would be premature at this stage.[165] However, in order to avoid 'picking losers' by default, current policy must attempt to maintain an uneasy balance between technology-neutral and technology-specific support, which both increases regulatory complexity and is a significant source of ongoing uncertainty. Thus, for instance, the IEA argues that a technology-specific approach, particularly in the form of a quantity-based target, would be better suited to the economics of CCS, and would provide greater certainty for those investing in transport and storage facilities.[166] Underpinning the reluctance to commit to CCS is also a deeper perceived ambivalence in the government's commitment to decarbonization of electricity generation. This will probably not be resolved unless or until it adopts a legally binding decarbonization target, although developments at EU level could force its hand.[167]

Turning to the public policy risks, the government's ambivalence about decarbonization, as manifested in the decision to grandfather the EPS until 2045, also poses a clear environmental risk, by creating a danger of carbon lock-in from new, unabated gas-fired generation. There do, however, appear to be relatively robust processes in place to manage the environmental risks from carbon leakage, with the commercialization programme also providing an opportunity for regulatory testing. Nevertheless, a potential issue here is the relatively limited opportunities for public participation in planning and permitting decisions. This could impact on the legitimacy of, and public confidence in, the regulatory regime, thereby increasing political risks.

The final issue is economic risk to consumers and taxpayers, the desire to minimize which has obviously been a key factor shaping the design of the CCS support framework. Ultimately, however, the need for consumers and/or taxpayers to shoulder the burden of investment in low carbon generation is inescapable. Arguably, a simpler and more committed regulatory framework would prove both cheaper and more effective in the long run. Moreover, without CCS generation, and the transport and storage networks to facilitate industrial CCS, meeting long-term carbon targets is likely to be a lot more expensive, if not impossible, both domestically and globally.

[165] Watson (ed) (n 3) at 45. [166] See IEA (n 26) at 24.

[167] The Commission is required to consider whether CCS should be made mandatory when it reviews the operation of the CCS Directives in 2015: Directive 2009/31/EC (n 5), art 38(3).

14

Carbon Capture and Storage Development in China

Wang Mingyuan and Jin Feng

I. Introduction

China is the world's largest developing country. Under any scenario, China's need for energy will increase over the next decades. Those energy uses will also increase the environmental consequences of energy use. Those environmental harms include first-generation releases of such pollutants as SO_X, NO_X, and particulates, which are mostly local burdens, as well as second-generation issues, such as climate change caused by the release of greenhouse gases (GHG). Addressing both energy supply and environmental harms are high priorities for China.

Energy underground activities will play a major role in China's response to both energy needs and environmental harms. China offers rich potential for shale gas development. China also has the potential to be a world leader in the development of carbon capture and storage (CCS). Because 70% of China's energy consumption is supplied from coal, which is the dirtiest source of the GHG, CCS has the potential to be a major response to the environmental impacts of the country's energy use.

In theory, either shale gas or CCS could be the primary solution to China's energy and environmental needs. In reality, China, like most other nations, will need to call on a wide variety of energy solutions. These include nuclear power, as well as renewables such as hydropower, solar, and wind energy. Each energy source brings distinctive environmental problems.

This chapter centres on CCS in China. We address the role of CCS, the current state of CCS development and the difficulties such development presents, and the national plans to advance CCS and the progress of those plans.

II. The significance of CCS development in China

With its vigorous industrialization and urbanization, China's economy will keep growing for the foreseeable future. During that time, its citizens' income and quality of life will continue to improve. It is inevitable that energy consumption and carbon emissions will continue to increase. As one of the major current and future GHG emitters, China has great potential for utilizing CCS. CCS is one of the most effective solutions to the effects of GHG in the coming decades. CCS could also provide national energy security at low cost for a long time.

A. Safeguarding China's energy security

China is a country with lots of coal but little oil and gas. Coal accounts for over two-thirds of China's primary energy production and consumption. Although the ratio of renewable energies and cleaner energies has increased, experts predict that by 2050, coal will still account for over 50% of China's energy.[1] BP's energy statistics indicate that China has about 114.5 billion tons of coal reserves, which account for around 13.5% of the total coal reserves in the world, but China has only 2.1 billion tons of conventional oil reserves and 66.54 billion m^3 of conventional natural gas reserves, which account for 1.3% and 1.1% of the world's reserves, respectively. For a long time into the future, coal will play an important role in the overall energy picture in China.[2] Moreover, due to rapid economic growth and a sharp increase in energy consumption, GHG emissions will also increase significantly.[3]

Concerning the conversion of energy resource forms (particularly coal to liquids (CTL)), CCS is also very important. The data from the China General Administration of Customs shows that China imported around 271 million tons of crude oil in 2012, with 6.8% growth over 2011.[4] Due to rapid economic growth, China's energy demands maintain a high rate of growth. The import of crude oil continues to break records. Sinopec, the largest refinery in China, relies on 80% crude oil imports. Analysts estimate that China's imports of crude oil will amount to 285 million tons in 2013 and more than 60% of its oil supply will be from imported crude oil. The total demand for crude oil in China by 2020 might potentially be over 700 million tons, of which two-thirds will need to be imported.[5]

In this context, CTL technology has attracted more and more attention. Experts predict that by 2020, CTL technology could produce 35 million tons of oil annually, which would replace imported oil. Although there are still many impediments to CTL development, such as crude oil prices, water resources, coal prices, and technology risks, CTL is of major strategic significance to the energy security of China. However, since the process of CTL emits large volumes of GHG, it will be

[1] China Economic Information Network: Report on the Coal Industry of China (Year 2011), available at <http://wenku.baidu.com/view/fa69b38f680203d8ce2f2491.html>.

[2] British Petroleum Statistical Review of World Energy 2012, available at <http://www.bp.com/productlanding.do?categoryId=9041910&contentId=7075397>.

[3] Cheng Changnhui, 'Preliminary Analysis on Status Quo and Prospects of CCS in China' (2010) 2 Journal of Faculty of Jianghan University of Petroleum 70.

[4] Data from General Administration of Customs of the People's Republic of China, available at <http://www.customs.gov.cn/tabid/7841/mid/24699/ctl/infodetail/infoid/353577/default.aspx>.

[5] Zhu Fagen, 'Status Quo, Prospects and Obstacles of CCS Development in China' (2011) 1 Journal of Energy, Technology and Economy 56.

necessary to attempt to reduce those volumes. Sensible development of CTL and CCS is a very important technological challenge.[6]

While domestic production of technology to be used in power generation plants is increasing in China, some technologies, such as gasification furnaces and high temperature and pressure-resistant materials, still depend on imports. The importance of CCS technology for energy development and climate protection should encourage international trade in CCS technologies. Advanced power generation technologies such as CTL and Integrated Gasification Combined Cycle (IGCC) are of strategic significance to China. China could become a major manufacturing centre for such technologies and become a major exporter of the technologies based on its advantages of manufacturing costs, talented labour force, and access to capital. CCS development should produce engineering expertise that will be relevant to such fields as chemicals, power generation, and geology. The study, development, and demonstration of CCS will guide the rapid development of these fields, thus mobilizing innovation in a large number of relevant areas.[7]

B. The potential for business development

The development of CCS will benefit a variety of business enterprises, such as the developers and manufacturers of CCS technology, the implementers of CCS projects, and the beneficiaries of the commercialization of CCS technology. These CCS businesses will be motivated to get involved in the development of CCS technologies. Power generation and petroleum enterprises, as well as the equipment manufacturers for power and petroleum enterprises, have a particular interest in CCS.

The electric power sector is currently the major field for CCS application. The CO_2 from the combustion of fossil fuels is the main source of GHG. The emissions from the electric power sector are the largest contributor. In 2007, the emissions from the power sector were around 2.8 billion tons. The annual emission of CO_2 from a single medium-sized coal-fired power plant (400MW–600MW) is several million tons. The power sector is characterized by high energy consumption and centralized CO_2 emissions. By contrast with vehicle and household emissions of CO2, centralized stationary emissions in large volumes can be contained in a centralized way. Therefore, the power sector should become an important field for CCS application in China.[8]

Coal mining, processing, and utilization are also important fields for CCS application. In the entire lifecycle of coal, it is not only coal-fired power plants that will release CO_2. The stages of extraction, processing, and transportation will also generate CO_2 and coal bed methane. Coal bed methane's main content is

6 Wang Yongying, Zhou Jianming, et al, 'Preliminary Analysis on CO_2 Capture and Storage Technology' (2011) 3 Journal of Technology of Coal 57.

7 Han Dongsheng, Ren Jiping, et al, 'Summary of Carbon Capture and Storage Technologies' (2012) 2 Sichuan Chemical Industry 96.

8 International Climate Organization, 'CCS in China—Status Quo, Challenges and Opportunities', July 2010, available at <http://www.docin.com/p-281504316.html>.

CH_4 gas, which has a greenhouse effect 24 times that of CO_2.[9] Normally, the CO_2 generated from these processes exists in the form of by-products of high concentration, which need less energy to capture than that needed to capture CO_2 from coal-fired power plants. Therefore, it will be beneficial to China if cleaner processing can be realized over the entire lifecycle, from coal mining to the utilization of the coal.

The conversion of coal to liquid fuel also offers considerable potential for CCS use. Given that China has extensive coal reserves but limited conventional oil and natural gas reserves, CTL allows both the use of plentiful fossil fuel reserves and less carbon pollution from the final CTL product. Presently, China has close to 1,000 CTL plants. The United States and Japan, both big coal consumers, have three plants and one plant, respectively.

A further important product of CCS development will be businesses supplying and servicing the CCS infrastructure. Once CCS is commercialized, there will be a huge demand for relevant equipment and technical services. In the research and pilot project stages, equipment manufacturers and technical service providers need to judge the direction of technology development, market trends, demands of equipment and technical services, and the need for further R&D. Active cooperation between power equipment manufacturers and large energy enterprises will be beneficial to the improvement of their products. Once CCS is in large-scale operation, the suppliers who provide CCS equipment could rapidly become wealthy. Power equipment manufacturers in China, such as Dongfang Electric Corporation, Harbin Boiler Works Industrial Company, and Shanghai Electric, have paid active attention to CCS equipment and technical service markets.[10] In addition to these enterprises, with the improvement of the overall processing capacity in China, some small and medium-sized enterprises (SMEs) might also become equipment and technical suppliers when the market is expanded.

C. Other factors

With the current technologies, the capture cost of CO_2 is US$13–51 per ton, with variations depending on the technologies selected. For example, the cost of post-combustion capture by a conventional coal dust power plant is US$29–50 per ton. The capture cost of the CO_2 separation system with pure oxygen combustion is US $21–50 per ton. The emission reduction cost of the IGCC system with prior combustion capture is about US$13–37 per ton. Looking long term, costs will decline with the technological progress while the trading price of GHGs will gradually increase, thus making CCS more and more economical.[11]

Although China started quite late in the development of CCS, it has made progress in both technology R&D and pilot projects. CCS could promote the

[9] International Climate Organization (n 8).
[10] International Climate Organization (n 8).
[11] Dennis Besta and Brendan Becka, 'Status of CCS Development in China' (2011) 4 Energy Procedia 6141–7.

development and integration of industries. CCS technologies are a combination of multiple interdisciplinary technologies, involving coal exploitation and utilization, power generation, transportation, geological exploration, and so on. Although there have long been barriers to interdisciplinary cooperation, CCS requires close and highly effective inter-departmental cooperation. Therefore, development of CCS will not only promote the development of CCS technologies per se, but will also provide platforms for inter-departmental cooperation.

CCS could become an important way for China to mitigate GHG emissions. China will soon be the largest market for CCS. If China is not competitive in the development of CCS technologies and their application, it will face the dilemma of relying on imported technologies. On the other hand, if China starts to develop strategic technology reserves, it will not only hold its domestic market, but could also develop overseas markets for its CCS technologies.

III. Present CCS development in China

As mentioned, compared to other countries, China started quite late in developing CCS. However, in recent years, the government, business enterprises, and research institutes have paid great attention to CCS, with active progress made in policy development, technology R&D, pilot projects, and international cooperation on CCS.

A. Policy development

Government policies have explicitly expressed support for the development of CCS. On 9 February 2006, the State Council issued the Phase One Outline of Medium and Long-Term Program of Science and Technology Development (2006–2020), which incorporates the 'development of cleaner fossil energies of high-efficiency and near zero emission of CO_2' into the area of advanced energy technologies.[12] On 4 June 2007, the National Development and Reform Commission (NDRC) issued China's National Climate Change Program, which proposed to 'devote efforts to the development of CO_2 capture, utilization and storage technologies'.[13] On 14 June 2007, line ministries, such as the Ministry of Science and Technology (MOST), NDRC, and others, jointly issued China's Specific Scientific and Technical Action of Addressing Climate Change, which addresses 'CO_2 capture, utilization and storage' among the key tasks.[14] On 29 October 2008,

[12] The State Council, *Outline of Medium and Long-Term Program of Science and Technology Development (2006–2020)*, 9 February 2006, available at <http://www.gov.cn/jrzg/2006-02/09/content_183787.htm>.

[13] NDRC, *China's National Climate Change Program*, 4 June 2007, available at <http://www.ccchina.gov.cn/WebSite/CCChina/UpFile/File189.pdf>.

[14] The MOST and NDRC, and others, *China's Specific Scientific and Technical Action of Addressing Climate Change*, 14 June 2007, available at <http://www.zhb.gov.cn/gkml/hbb/gwy/200910/t20091030_180716.htm>.

the Information Office of the State Council published 'China's Policies and Actions for Addressing Climate Change'. It points out that 'China has determined to conduct major researches on GHG mitigation technologies including CO_2 capture, utilization and storage technologies'.[15] In July 2011, MOST and related ministries jointly issued the National 12th Five-Year Plan of Science and Technology Development. In February 2012, MOST issued the National 12th Five-Year Specific Program of Science and Technology Development of CO_2 Capture, Utilization and Storage.

The Outline of the Medium and Long-Term Program of Science and Technology Development (2006–2020) views the 'emission control and disposal technologies for GHG such as CO_2 and methane in key sectors' as one of the priority fields for the environment, and sets forth the direction of 'developing clean fossil energy utilization technology of high efficiency and near zero emission'.[16] The ten parts of the Outline Program include: (1) guidance and policies; (2) development goals; (3) key areas and prioritized topics; (4) key specific programmes; (5) cutting-edge technologies; (6) basic research; (7) reform of science and technology institutions; (8) establishment of national innovation systems; (9) input of science and technology; and (10) capacity-building. The technology of CCS is regarded as one of the cutting-edge technologies by the Outline Program.[17]

China's National Climate Change Program points out that 'efforts should be devoted to the development of conversion technologies such as coal liquefaction and gasification and coal chemical industry, co-production technologies based on coal gasification, and CCS technologies'.[18] The National Program identified the specific targets, basic principles, key areas, and relevant policy measures for addressing climate change by 2010. This was the first national program on climate change published by a developing country. The National Program regards CCS as one of the key issues in GHG mitigation.[19]

China's Specific Scientific and Technical Action of Addressing Climate Change proposed to 'develop technologies of GHG emission control and climate change mitigation such as CCS technologies'.[20] Fourteen line ministries, including MOST, NDRC, and the Ministry of Foreign Affairs, jointly issued China's Specific Scientific and Technical Action of Addressing Climate Change, with the aim of integrating and co-ordinating scientific research and technology development in the field of climate change in order to improve the national science and technology capacity for addressing climate change. The Specific Program regards CCS as one of the key areas of GHG emissions control.[21]

[15] The Information Office of the State Council, *China's Policies and Actions for Addressing Climate Change*, 29 October 2008, available at <http://www.gov.cn/jrzg/2011-11/22/content_2000047.htm>.

[16] State Council (n 12). [17] State Council (n 12).

[18] The National Development and Reform Commission (NDRC), *China's National Climate Change Program*, 4 June 2007, available at <http://www.ccchina.gov.cn/WebSite/CCChina/UpFile/File189.pdf>.

[19] State Council (n 12). [20] MOST and NDRC, and others (n 14).

[21] MOST and NDRC, and others (n 14).

The National 12th Five-Year Program of Science and Technology Development points out that 'technologies such as carbon sinks of forestry and grassland, GHG reduction by soil utilization and agriculture as well as CCS should be developed' and 'the ultra-supercritical (USC) cleaner coal power generation technologies of higher parameters should be actively developed, CCS of CO_2 from coal-fired power plants, as well as pollutant prevention should be developed, and pilot projects of coal fuel improvements should be carried out'.[22] MOST joined with NDRC, Ministry of Finance (MOF), Ministry of Education, China Academy of Sciences, China Academy of Engineering, National Natural Science Foundation, China Association for Science and Technology, and State Administration for Science, Technology and Industry for National Defence issued the National 12th Five-Year Plan of Science and Technology Development to implement the medium- and long-term outline program of science and technology, education and talents, and make full use of the supportive role of scientific progress and innovation in transforming economic growth patterns. The Program seeks to enhance the technical research and development of CCS, including viewing CCS technology as one of the key technologies to help cultivate and develop the new strategic industries of energy conservation and environmental protection, which could also serve as technical measures to support sustainable development and effectively address climate change.[23]

B. Technology research and development

Ever since the 10th Five-Year Plan, the national basic research program, the national high-tech development program, and the national science and technology supportive programmes have all made a point of addressing relevant matters. These subjects include: (1) basic research; (2) technology R&D; (3) pilot projects for the mitigation potential of CCS technology; (4) bio-conversion and utilization of CO_2; (5) CO_2 enhanced oil recovery; and (5) geological storage relating to different CO_2 emission sources, different capture technologies, and different modes of CO_2 conversion and utilization. The key national specific research program, 'Development of Large-Scale Oil and Gas Fields and Coal Bed Methane', made arrangements concerning technology R&D and pilot projects for CO_2 enhanced oil recovery and coal bed methane. Preliminary figures show that during the 11th Five-Year Plan period, relevant national specific science and technology programmes made arrangements for about 20 projects of basic research and technology R&D on CCS, with a total expense of over one billion Yuan, 200 million of which comes from public finance. In the 11th Five-Year Plan period, the investment in the demonstration of the entire process increased significantly. In 2011, the relevant national science and technology programmes and specific programmes

[22] The Ministry of Science and Technology (MOST), *The National 12th Five-Year Program of Science and Technology Development*, July 2011, available at <http://www.most.gov.cn/mostinfo/xinxifenlei/gjkjgh/201107/t20110713_88230.htm>.

[23] MOST (n 22).

arranged about 10 projects, with a total budget over two billion Yuan, with 400 million of this coming from public finance.[24]

The key national specific programmes mainly conduct research on the key technologies such as CO_2 capture, transport, enhanced oil recovery, conditions and potential for storage, and standards and safety of storage. Chinese enterprises and research institutes have strength in the field of CCS. This expertise includes:

- *Capture.* Research has been conducted on key technologies, such as absorption of low energy consumption and technical routes of capture, with the development of the commercialization of amine absorbents, and the establishment of industrial pilot projects of coal-fired power plants of 10,000 t/y and 100,000 t/y CO_2 capture. The national assessment of the geological storage potential for CCS has been started. Preliminary results show that the main type of space for geological storage of CO_2 that has huge potential is in deep salty water layers. Pilot projects of storage in salty water layers at an industrial scale have been started.
- *Transport.* The application of low-pressure CO_2 transport engineering projects has been carried out in oil and gas at high pressures and low temperatures.
- *Utilization.* Research has been conducted on theories and key technologies focusing on different utilization paths. Examples are CO_2 enhanced oil recovery and coal bed methane recovery, as well as bio-conversion and chemical synthesis of CO_2. Industrial experiments on CO_2 enhanced oil recovery have been carried out, and pilot plants using microalgae biodiesel small-scale production of degradable plastic made from CO_2 have been set up.

With efforts in recent years, China has established a solid foundation of R&D on key technical components of CCS. However, if compared with advanced international levels, China still lags behind, especially in research concerning theories of CO_2 enhanced oil recovery and geological storage, core technologies for monitoring and warning of CO_2 storage, and experiences with large-scale engineering projects for CO_2 transport and storage.[25]

C. Pilot projects

Due to the large volume of centralized stationary emission sources, the power sector has become the main area of CCS demonstration projects in China. In July 2008, the demonstration of CCS in the Beijing Thermal Power Plant under the China Huaneng corporation was formally put into operation. There, CCS technology was applied for the first time in the Chinese power sector. The designed annual capacity of CO_2 is 3,000 tons.

[24] *Report on CCUS Technology Progress in China*, compiled by MOST, September 2011, available at <http://wenku.baidu.com/view/a06af534f111f18583d05ad2.html?from_page=view&from_mod=download>.

[25] *Report on CCUS Technology Progress in China*, compiled by MOST (n 24).

China Huaneng is the largest power enterprise in China and its coal-fired power generation units account for 88.85% of its total installed capacity for power generation. The CCS activities in China Huaneng mainly focus on the commercialized utilization of CCS capture and non-storage. After one year of successful operation of its capture equipment of 3,000 tons per year, China Huaneng kicked off its second pilot project of CO_2 capture—Phase II of No. 2 Power Plant, located in Shidongkou, Shanghai, with an annual capacity of CO_2 capture reaching 120,000 tons. These two projects both use post-combustion capture technologies. The captured CO_2 is mainly used for industrial purposes, such as CO_2 used for carbonated beverages (the price is 800 Yuan/ton) and the use of CO_2 as a raw material in chemical enterprises. In addition, under China Huaneng, the Green Coal Company plans to introduce the pre-combustion capture technology in phase two of the project and combine it with IGCC to test the technical feasibility of IGCC, plus CCS.

Shenhua Group is the largest coal production enterprise and coal supplier in the world. Shenhua has conducted a demonstration of CCS in the CTL demonstration engineering project Erdos of Inner Mongolia, which applies pre-combustion technology. Since CO_2 per se is the by-product from the CTL process, it does not consume any energy or result in other costs to capture CO_2. Therefore, it has significant advantages concerning capture costs.

PetroChina is the largest petroleum enterprise in China and has carried out some experiments on improving oil recovery with CO_2. For example, Daquing Oil Field started to promote CO_2 enhanced oil recovery in 40 crude oil wells in an area of 25,000 km^2. By May 2009, the enhanced oil recovery technology had increased crude production by 4,000 tons. The Mid-China Oil Field started to produce CO_2 with exhaust emission from a refinery in 2002. In 2006, the key scientific research project of Sino-Pec—the pilot of CO_2 enhanced oil recovery in low permeability reservoirs—started in the Mid-China Oil Field. Experiments show that the injection of close to 10,000 tons of liquid CO_2 into the underground reservoir could increase crude oil production by 2,700 tons.[26]

Currently, it is mainly large-sized state-owned enterprises (SOEs) that are involved in the CCS demonstration projects. China Huaneng is the outstanding representative in the power sector, China Shenhua in the coal sector, and PetroChina in the oil sector.

D. International cooperation

International cooperation projects on CCS are being carried out vigorously. The main Sino-foreign co-operations on CCS include the Sino-UK Near Zero Emission Coal (NZEC) Project, the Sino-EU COACH Project, the Sino-EU STRACO Project, and the Sino-EU GeoCapacity and Sino-Australian CAGS Projects. These projects are related to multiple aspects of CCS, such as development policies,

[26] International Climate Organization (n 8).

capture technologies, and storage assessment, and provide support in fields such as funds and technologies.[27]

IV. Difficulties and issues

A. The immaturity of the technology

The technologies of pre-combustion capture, post-combustion capture, and oxygen-enriched combustion have advantages and disadvantages with respect to application range, energy consumption, and cost. Because all of the technologies are not mature, it is hard to determine which kind of technology will eventually be used in large-scale operations with CCS in the future.

There is more than one way to develop the technology at each link of CCS. Given current technologies, it is difficult to choose the CCS program that is most suitable to China's development. In choosing technology for each link of CCS, important factors include not only cost, energy consumption, site transportation, and geological conditions, but also the general orientation of the whole energy supply chain. Major efforts should be concentrated to develop the technologies most suitable to China's actual situation in energy supply. Capture technology, for example, whether it adopts pre-combustion or post-combustion capture technology, has a close relation to developing the supercritical power plant or IGCC power plant in China's future coal power industry. Whether storage is done in abandoned oil and gas fields, in salt water layers, with Enhanced Oil Recovery (EOR), or in the sea will affect the location of new plants in the future. Since all forms of CCS technology have their shortcomings, China should carry out parallel research, development, and demonstration, gradually finding the technology combination most suitable to China's development, and then concentrate all possible resources to overcome that technology's challenges.[28]

B. Security issues

Large-scale application of any technology will have some impact on the environment. The environmental risks that may be brought about by large-scale application of CCS technology include global environmental impact and local environmental impact. The global impact mainly refers to the fact that the transported and stored CO_2 may leak into the air and reduce the potential for CCS to mitigate climate change. The local risks mainly include the adverse impact of CCS technology on the local environment and human health in such ways as groundwater pollution. These impacts can be seen in all of the major

[27] *Report on CCUS Technology Progress in China*, compiled by MOST (n 24); International Climate Organization (n 8).

[28] International Climate Organization (n 8).

links—capture, transport, and storage. Some of the impacts are particularly prominent in certain links.[29]

The environmental impact at the capture stage arises from extra energy consumption. Present CO_2 capture technology would give rise to higher energy consumption. High energy consumption not only consumes more fossil fuels, it also emits more pollutants including NO_X, SO_2, power coal ash, and other solid wastes. If a chemical absorption method is adopted in capture technology, large amounts of chemicals will also be consumed, such as the ammonia and limestone used by Pulverized Coal (PC) power plants in controlling emissions of NO_x and SO_2.[30]

The environmental impact at the transportation link is from infrastructure construction and potential CO_2 leakage. No matter whether it is tanker transport, pipeline transport, or shipping, all transportation infrastructure construction in CCS projects will have an impact on the environment. Further, no matter what kind of transportation is adopted, container damage may cause CO_2 leakage. Once CO_2 leakage occurs, the increase of CO_2 in the local environment may cause ocean acidification (shipping), soil damage (pipeline), or even human CO_2 poisoning (road transport).[31]

The biggest environmental risk of CCS exists in the process of geological storage. The risks are again from potential CO_2 leakage. A large amount of CO_2 leakage will hinder the control of climate change. A high concentration of leaked CO_2 can also endanger human health. If the CO_2 in storage contains H_2S, SO_2, NO_2, and other pollutants, their harm to health and the environment will be even more serious than that caused by the leakage of pure CO_2.

The storage of CO_2 may also trigger earthquakes. Injecting CO_2 into rock layer pores may increase formation pressure. If the injection pressure exceeds formation pressure, formation fracture and fault movement may occur and produce two kinds of risks. First, the high-pressure fracture zone and related micro earthquakes will increase the permeability of the fracture zone and provide a channel for CO_2 leakage. Second, the high-pressure fault movement may trigger a harmful, larger earthquake. An earthquake occurring at the bottom of the sea may trigger a tsunami. These earthquake possibilities have been an important reason for doubts about CCS technology.

Further environmental concerns with CCS development involve environmental justice and intergenerational equity issues. The risks of CCS technology make it likely that CCS projects will be located in geographic areas populated by less-advantaged citizens. The storage of the undesirable waste CO_2 will also deprive future generations of the use of exhaustible energy resources and pass on the risks of CO_2 leakage to them. These concerns are worsened by public ignorance of climate

[29] See, for example, *Air Pollution Impacts From Carbon Capture and Storage (CCS)* (European Environment Agency Technical Report, 2011) available at <http://www.eea.europa.eu/publications/carbon-capture-and-storage> 23–4.

[30] IEA, 'Bottlenecks of Global Development of CCS Projects', China Energy News, 5 October 2011, available at <http://news.xinhuanet.com/energy/2011-10/05/c_122121524.htm>.

[31] IEA (n 30).

change and CCS. At present, CCS discussion is limited to experts and technicians. Public participation in these important decisions is lacking.[32]

In summary, environmental, health, and security risks exist at all stages of CCS technology.[33]

C. Cost considerations

The Intergovernmental Panel on Climate Change's Special Report on CCS shows that CCS application would cause coal-fired power generation efficiency to decline by 20–30%. For a power plant with 40% efficiency, CCS application would reduce its efficiency to 25–30%. In China, if a power plant runs with post-combustion capture technology, the cost of power generation would increase by 20–30%. Therefore, to produce the same amount of power, the coal consumption of a power plant with CCS would be 25% higher than for the plant without CCS. China's coal consumption in 2008 was 2.72 billion tons, including 1.18 billion tons used in power generation. Based on these calculations, if all power plants were equipped with CCS, total annual coal consumption would increase by 290 million tons. Increased coal consumption will increase manpower, capital, and transportation costs, which would be a serious extra burden to an already costly coal industry. If the external costs of coal, such as environmental and security costs, is added, the burden is even greater.

The high costs of CCS technology appear in the capture, transport, and storage stages. Each stage consumes large amounts of expensive energy. Because the incentive policy for CCS is not sound and the business prospects for CCS are not clear, most funds for China's CCS projects have come from national science and technology programmes, SOE's contributions, and international cooperation projects. These funds have been modest and have not met the demand for rapid development of CCS technology. For-profit business enterprises have been reluctant to invest in CCS technology. The lack of attractive returns on investment and policy incentives needs to be addressed to encourage for-profit business enterprises to conduct CCS research and demonstration projects.[34]

D. Policy and legal shortcomings

In addition to technological and economic challenges, China's adoption of CCS also struggles with public policy and legal issues. As will be discussed later, the adoption of appropriate legal structures may be crucial for the future of CCS.

Although the appeal of CCS is very high around the world, international climate change negotiations have fallen short of adopting binding legal documents. This deters individual nations from adopting commitments to emissions reductions. Without those firm national targets, a business enterprise has limited motivation to reduce emissions, let alone to give priority to installing high-cost CCS technology.

[32] IEA (n 30). [33] IEA (n 30).

[34] He Gang, 'Obstacles and Prospects of Carbon Capture and Storage', October 2009, available at <http://www.chinadialogue.net/article/show/single/ch/3296>.

As already discussed, there are threats to the environment and human health at all stages of CCS. Governments must write laws and regulations to reduce those risks. The laws and regulations should define the responsibilities of parties, set up CCS project examinations and monitoring programmes, and determine emergency measures and treatment methods were a disaster to occur. The present lack of such laws in China results in risks in finance and reputation to businesses considering CCS projects.

A further problem is the lack of effective mechanisms to promote international technology transfer in CCS. The transfer of intellectual property rights in environmentally friendly technology has been a hot topic at UN climate change negotiations. Little hard law has been made, however. Countries with emerging economies, like China and India, will be the countries leading in the use of CCS technology. They will be helped by the ability to employ international advances in CCS technology beyond their own R&D. So far, however, there is no effective mechanism to promote international technology transfer. This is a big obstacle to CCS development.[35]

Finally, CCS development is harmed by a lack of cross-enterprise co-ordination and cooperation. The CCS industrial chain includes almost all parts of energy production and consumption. It also involves chemical production. Under current market structures, problems of benefit allocation exist between coal, oil, electric power, and chemical industries. If sensible co-ordination does not take place, these enterprises may be less willing to participate in CCS activities. Negative attitudes at any part of the CCS chain will hinder overall CCS development.

V. The National Five-Year Specific Plan

In February 2013, the Ministry of Science and Technology issued its most recent plan for CCS development. This is the National 12th Five-Year Specific Plan for Carbon Capture Utilization and Storage Technology Development (hereinafter, the Plan). The Plan was drafted mainly for the purpose of implementing the Outline of the National Program for Medium and Long Term Scientific and Technological Development (2006–2020) and the National 12th Five-Year Plan for Scientific and Technological Development.

The Plan includes six sections: (1) situation and demand; (2) status quo and trend; (3) principle and target; (4) key tasks; (5) priority directions of development; and (6) safeguard measures. We briefly summarize each section.

A. Situation and demand

The Plan states that CCS is an important technological option in response to global climate change. Developing CCS technology would be a strong asset for China in developing a low-carbon green economy and mitigating climate change.

[35] Cheng Changnhui, 'Preliminary Analysis on Status Quo and Prospects of CCS in China' (2010) 2 Journal of Faculty of Jianghan University of Petroleum 70.

B. Status quo and trends

The Plan concludes there are still some problems retarding CCS development. Among them are high-cost, high-energy consumption, and the long-term security and reliability of the technology in its present state. The technology needs to be improved through continuous development and integrated demonstration. The R&D base has already been built in to a certain degree for each link of China's CCS technology. However, the development is unbalanced between the links. There is a long way to go to realize scale and whole-process demonstration and application.

C. Principle and target

The Plan sets out the following principles:

(1) Following the development of CCS technology worldwide and advancing international exchanges and cooperation.
(2) Making breakthroughs in key technologies of CO_2 capture, transportation, utilization, and storage.
(3) Strict observance to the security standards for CCS demonstration projects.
(4) Enhancing human talents in CCS technology and improving CCS technology innovation.

The overall targets of the Plan include: breakthroughs in several key basic CCS theories and technologies; securing a remarkable drop in cost and energy consumption; building up the capacity of designing and integrating a one-million-ton CCS system; establishing CCS R&D capability; and completing a process-integrated demonstration system for CCS with a capacity at the level of 300,000 to 500,000 tons/year.

D. Key tasks

The Plan gives priority to five tasks: (1) solving some problems of basic scientific theory; (2) making breakthroughs in some key technologies; (3) conducting whole-process systematic integration and demonstration of CCS technology; (4) promoting the study of policies, laws, and regulations for the development of CCS technology; and (5) enhancing the capacity for CCS technological innovation.

E. Priority development

The Plan gives priority to five key technological sectors: (1) large-scale and low energy consumption CO_2 separation and capture technology; (2) safe and highly effective CO_2 delivery engineering technology; (3) large-scale and low-cost CO_2 utilization technology; (4) safe and reliable CO_2 storage technology and large-scale CCS technology integration and demonstration; and (5) whole-process demonstration projects to be constructed by studying the suitability and compatibility between elements of CCS technology to test economy, reliability, and safety.

F. Safeguard measures

The Plan puts forward five safeguard measures:

(1) Improving overall co-ordination of science and technology—this includes establishing a co-ordination group of carbon capture, utilization, and storage (CCUS) experts, with members from state departments of science and technology, macro-economic management, energy, land and resources, environmental protection, and others. The co-ordination group seeks to strengthen overall arrangements for CCS technology innovation, promote co-ordination of technology innovation with industrial policies and management measures, and coordinate and mobilize the resources of all sectors and localities to implement the Plan.

(2) Increasing investment in science and technology, giving more support to CCS technology R&D and demonstration, and encouraging localities and related industrial sectors to increase investment.

(3) Intensifying international scientific and technological cooperation, grasping the trend of world CCS technology development, enhancing international scientific and technological cooperation in CCS, and incorporating CCS technology into multilateral and bilateral international cooperation in science and technology.

(4) Establishing a strategic alliance of industrial technology innovation and creating a stable organization and operation mechanism.

(5) Making greater efforts to build up innovation teams and talent forces and driving and improving operations with relation to CCS technology.

VI. Essential steps for the next stage of CCS in China

Although the Plan sets an overall policy framework for China's CCS technology and its relation to industrial development, it is hard to predict the direction of policy implementation. The Plan is a frame-type design without strict legal force. It is also issued solely by the Ministry of Science and Technology, which has a complicated administrative structure that makes it hard to coordinate with other branches of government.

In the sections that follow, we analyse the Plan and other existing policies governing CCS. We offer the following suggestions for the next essential steps in making CCS a key element of Chinese energy, environmental, and industrial policy.

A. Promote R&D and demonstration

The co-ordination and cooperation among the government, business enterprises, scientific research institutions, and other main participants should be strengthened.

The goal is to promote joint development of key technologies for CO_2 capture, transport, and storage. It is also desirable to propel the use of captured CO_2 in petroleum and other fields, and to guarantee economic benefits obtained from demonstration projects.

In studying CCS, the R&D and demonstration programmes should examine such matters as the energy consumption of different capture technologies, different storage methods, and the development potential of different technologies and their rates of return on investment. This will identify the technologies that are worthy of being popularized on a large scale as soon as possible and the ones that can ultimately be commercialized.

- *Capture technology*: the goal is to combine CCS technological advances with China's national needs. Capture technologies (pre-combustion, post-combustion, oxygen-enriched combustion, coal chemical conversions) should be compared and prioritized. Key factors for assessment should include low energy consumption and low costs.
- *Transport technology*: there is no technical difficulty in transport technology itself. However, environmental harm and energy consumption should be highly emphasized. CO_2 source–sink matching should also be researched.
- *Storage technology*: the goals of R&D and demonstration are to gain more experience in the selection of storage locations, to establish the standards of site selection, to develop site investigation technologies, to improve the accuracy of analog computation of long-term storage, to conduct research on the methods for evaluating site stability, to formulate the requirements for long-term monitoring of storage sites, and to develop emergency measures and remedies to prevent and correct CO_2 leakage. Although China's CCS technology has developed rapidly, it would still benefit from extensive and effective international collaboration. For example, more demonstration projects may be launched in China, or Chinese engineers may become deeply involved in the demonstration projects in other countries. The acceleration of the transfer of intellectual property will help China to enhance its R&D capabilities and to accumulate experience in engineering. In terms of funding, the private sector in China is still not investing in key CCS technology. Thus, it is still necessary for the government or large SOEs to invest in R&D and to formulate policies to promote access to capital from the private sector.[36]

B. Launch a geological survey

Research on carbon storage should be strengthened. China has relatively complex geological conditions. Thus, geological research regarding onshore and offshore basin structures that may be used for carbon storage, such as coal-bearing basins, gas-bearing basins, oil-bearing basins, and deep salt formations, should be

[36] Wu Yimin, 'Discussion on Carbon Capture and Storage and Its International Legal Issues' (2012) Journal of Shanghai University (social science edition) 12.

enhanced. A comprehensive survey and evaluation should be carried out on aspects of stratum structure, storage potential, leakage risks, monitoring needs, etc. The evaluation of China's CO_2 storage potential should be carried out so as to prepare primary sources for the eventual introduction of clear and quantified standards for site selection for storage.

C. Establish and perfect investment and financing mechanisms

The domestic funds that can be invested in CCS are currently limited. Thus, international financial investment and support become very important. The transfer of funds is mainly achieved through the international carbon market at present. The Clean Development Mechanism (CDM), one of the three mechanisms of the Kyoto Protocol, plays an important role in encouraging the participation of developing countries in the global emission-reduction actions. From 2009, the Executive Board began to discuss whether CCS should be incorporated into CDM projects, but not without major debate. The opponents argue that the possible emission reduction due to CCS would weaken the validity of certified emission reduction (CER) markets under the CDM mechanism. Even if the CCS is incorporated into CDM, the price of CO_2 in the current market is much lower than the cost of CCS (50–100 euros/ton) and the funds needed by the CCS must be raised through other means. In addition, the fluctuating CER price also makes it more difficult to attract stable investors to CCS.[37]

Although the emissions reduction mechanism may incorporate the electric power industry into the goal of carbon reduction as a whole, it is still under research and exploration. Therefore, the international agreements on climate change must seek new financial mechanisms to meet the needs of full-scale development of CCS.

D. Strengthen international cooperation

The international development of CCS continues. The United Kingdom requires newly built coal-fired power plants to install CCS. Otherwise, power plants without CCS will not be allowed to feed their electricity generated into a power network. The United States will spend one billion dollars to restart the 'Future Gen' project and it will focus on the construction of the IGCC, in addition to a CCS demonstration plant in Illinois. The European Union's Economic Stimulus Plan will invest €1.05 billion in the development of seven power plants, and a CCS alliance consisting of 12 demonstration power plants will be established in 2015.[38] In July 2009, China and the United States also proposed the establishment of the US–China Clean Energy Research Centre. Along with further deepening of Sino–US, Sino–Canada, Sino–UK, Sino–EU, Sino–Japan, Sino–Australian, and other bilateral or multilateral cooperation agreements on climate change in the CCS field, China will establish connections with global CCS counterparts, in order to

[37] International Climate Organization (n 8). [38] He (n 34).

track progresses, understand the dynamics, and exchange experience and know-how to lay the foundation for their efforts for mastering CCS technology and participating in the global response to the challenges of climate change. Taking the joint projects launched by China and other countries as a platform, China's exchanges and cooperation with foreign institutions can be strengthened and foreign technology and capital can be introduced to improve the technical level of China's CCS. At the same time, efforts should be made for the establishment of a mechanism for transferring relevant intellectual properties in the climate negotiations, so as to accelerate the promotion of CCS technology.[39]

E. Create a legal structure

The need to formulate a series of laws and regulations to avoid risks before popularizing CCS technology has been recognized. Laws, regulations, and incentive policies should be prepared regarding CCS project application and approval, environmental impact assessment, site closure conditions, accident emergency treatment, and other special procedures. Tax refunds and subsidies on CCS equipment, the raising of electric power prices, carbon taxes, CCS commercial insurance, CCS trust funds, and other incentive measures should be designed, so as to provide an operational and relatively complete legal and policy system to encourage large-scale implementation of CCS.

At present, there are almost no domestic laws and regulations in China directly related to CCS. Although laws and regulations in petroleum, mining, and other industries provide guidance, specific CCS laws and regulations will help CCS participants to clearly determine their responsibilities, standardize CCS projects, reduce the risks of storage, and reduce public concerns. A complete regulation of the management of CCS projects must fully understand China's current project management system and the limits of the power of national and local authorities. The new laws and regulations should include the development of relevant environmental monitoring and impact assessment standards, the supervision and inspection of CCS projects, the site closure conditions for CCS projects, the operator's responsibility after site closure, the emergency plan for accidents at CCS projects, the management of personnel, responsibility, and authority, remedial measures, implementation, and other key issues concerning accidents and emergency treatment.[40]

F. Improve public participation

Research on public attitudes towards CCS should be increased. Mass education regarding CCS should be carried out. Public concerns about CCS should be

[39] He (n 34).

[40] Richard K. Morse, Varun Rai, and Gang He, 'The Real Drivers of Carbon Capture and Storage in China and Implication for Climate Policy' (working paper), Freeman Spogli Institute for International Study, August 2009, available at <http://wenku.baidu.com/view/0e1dc4db6f1aff00bed51e0a.html>.

addressed, with the goal of increasing public approval ratings for CCS, in order to prepare for the large-scale commercial promotion of CCS technology. Because the public still knows little about the CCS technology and CCS involves various kinds of risks, the acceptance level of CCS in society is currently relatively low. Resistance from the public has become a main obstacle to the development of CCS in some countries. It is necessary to plan ahead while formulating policies, including providing publicity on many aspects of CCS through the media and other channels. The public needs to understand the role of CCS in mitigating climate change. Open, equal, and convenient public participation is essential. Effective public participation should seek public opinion, set deadlines for soliciting that public opinion, give feedback on that opinion, determine strategies to deal with potential environmental risks of CCS, and comment on public participation in environmental impact assessment reports.

15

Dynamic Regulation and Technological Competition: A New Legal Approach to Carbon Capture and Storage

Lital Helman, Gideon Parchomovsky, and Endre Stavang

I. Introduction

Climate change presents a serious challenge for humanity. It is the cause of severe droughts, rising food prices, new endangered species, and numerous other hazards. Carbon capture and storage (CCS) has emerged as a key solution to the climate change crisis, at least in the short term. CCS is the process by which carbon dioxide (CO_2) is captured from the emissions of large industrial facilities such as coal, oil, and gas,[1] purified, and compressed into a liquid state.[2] The CO_2 is then transported, typically through pipelines,[3] and injected into deep, underground rock formations for permanent storage, instead of being emitted to the atmosphere.

The level and scope of CCS activities, as well as the ensuing environmental and other effects of CCS projects are largely dependent on the applicable legal rules. In this chapter, we propose legal policies that encourage the adoption of environmentally sensitive CCS techniques. Specifically, we advance the idea of technological updating through a dynamic and self-adjusting standard for CCS technologies. In addition, we propose to reward carbon emission abatement resulting from CCS based on actual net environmental effect and not on the gross emission reduction, and to design liability for CCS-related harm to optimize precautions, including

[1] There are three approaches to carbon capture from fossil fuels: pre-combustion, post-combustion, and oxy-combustion. See Norman Shilling, 'Carbon Capture and Storage—An Equipment Manufacturer's Perspective' in *Carbon Capture and Storage: Emerging Legal and Regulatory Issues* (Havercroft, Macrory, and Stewart, eds, 2011) 29.

[2] More accurately, the CO_2 is transferred to a supercritical phase (between liquid and gas), to prevent pipe corrosion.

[3] Pipelines are the cheapest option for large volumes, greater distance and longer time frame. However, lorry is used for transportation for smaller volumes, e.g., to provide CO_2 to the soft drink industry in Europe, and ships might be the cheapest transportation method for long-distance small-volume and short-term projects. See Martha M. Roggenkamp and Avelien Haan Kamminga, 'CO_2 Transportation in the European Union: Can the Regulation of CO_2 Pipelines Benefit From the Experiences of the Energy Sector?' in Havercroft, Macrory, and Stewart (eds) (n1) 108, FN 4.

choices of storage sites. We are mindful of non-environmental considerations affecting the CCS question, such as financial, economic, public policy, and employment concerns. Our guidelines take those concerns into account, but first and foremost, they are designed to ensure that environmental values are properly addressed.

En route to devising legal policies that cover these aspects, we revisit some of the most often discussed legal and regulatory questions of CCS, such as long-term liability, and trans-boundary CCS. Although in this chapter we cannot provide answers to all the different legal and regulatory questions pertaining to CCS, our framework's dynamic nature can provide guidance as to how to address them.

In section II we explain the theoretical foundation of our CCS legal framework, and discuss its benefits. In section III, we propose specific policy recommendations pertaining to: the inclusion of CCS in energy policy; the capture process; and the long-term storage of CO_2. A short conclusion follows.

II. Theoretical foundations

High levels of emissions of CO_2, the primary greenhouse gas emitted through human activities, are believed to have a devastating influence on the environment. The objective of CCS is to address this problem. Yet, the adoption and implementation of optimal CCS policies has proven to be a real challenge.

The appeal of CCS is understandable. On the one hand, curbing worldwide emissions of greenhouse gases can mitigate the adverse effects of climate change. On the other hand, economic development, population growth, and improving living standards constantly increase the demand for energy. CCS appears to provide the best way of balancing the competing interests: it allows for continued use of energy, while reducing the emission of CO_2 to the atmosphere.

Notwithstanding its potential for emission avoidance, CCS also carries serious environmental hazards. These hazards range from direct ones (e.g., the energy expended in the capture process) to indirect ones (e.g., prolonging the use of fossil fuels), and from short-term (e.g., the footprint created by transporting CO_2 to storage) to long-term (e.g., the risk of leakage and migration of CO_2 from the storage site).

As a result of the complex mixture of promises and risks, the current debate over CCS is extremely polarized. Proponents hold hopes that the CCS market will be able to provide 'clean coal' while maintaining energy security. Opponents have no faith in 'clean coal' and are concerned that CCS would prolong the use of fossil fuels and delay the development of renewable energy sources.

We reject both categorical approaches. Because the potential effect of CCS on the environment is mixed, CCS projects can prove to be environmentally beneficial, neutral, or harmful, depending on how they are carried out and on the legal and regulatory framework that governs them. Our aim in this chapter is to propose legal policies that would create incentives to private and state actors to avoid CCS projects that are overall harmful to the environment, and to pursue CCS projects in a way that is good for the environment.

There are two reasons for concern that without such policies, CCS practices may be detrimental to the environment. The first is the public good nature of climate mitigation policies. Indeed, the earth's atmosphere is a public good: it can be used simultaneously, and states who do not participate in climate mitigation efforts cannot be effectively excluded from the benefits it produces. This public good nature renders governments and market players under-incentivized to adopt optimal CCS policies.

The public good nature of climate mitigation means that states bear the full economic cost of climate mitigation measures they adopt,[4] but do not receive the full environmental benefit (or environmental costs) of those measures. As a result, countries have an incentive to free ride on the efforts of others to reduce emissions. For example, if a state operates a nuclear energy facility, it bears the full costs of creating and running the facility, yet the benefit of emission reduction (as well as the environmental risks associated with the facility) would be distributed all over the world, skewing the state's incentive to fulfil the project's environmental goals.

This incentive structure is reflected in the approaches that states adopt towards CCS, which often reflect non-environmental self-interests much more than they reflect worldwide environmental goals. This phenomenon manifests itself in more than one way. Some governments adopt a NIMBY ('not in my back yard') approach, and do not pursue CCS projects at all, despite the environmental effect CCS can produce.[5] At the other end of the spectrum, some governments are set to carry out CCS projects for reasons other than the avoidance of emissions. For example, states may wish to continue the use of coal as a primary energy source,[6] or protect the energy economic sectors in their territory.[7] States may also wish to gain a competitive advantage from being a first mover on CCS technologies, if they assume other states will follow suit later on, and that they will then be in a position

[4] While we use the term 'country' or 'state' throughout this chapter, it can apply equally to smaller or bigger jurisdictional entities, such as provinces or federal territories, depending on the allocation of responsibilities that exists in each jurisdiction.

[5] The basis for India's reluctance to CCS best exemplifies this approach: 'The widespread deployment of CCS technology will have global carbon benefits, but it does not offer co-benefits in terms of local environmental quality, economic development, energy access, energy security and poverty reduction.' See Lavanya Rajamani, 'India and Climate Change: Contextualizing India's Approach to CCS Technology' in Havercroft, Macrory, and Stewart (eds) (n1) at 211–12.

[6] See, e.g., chapter 14 (explaining that the interests of China in CCS stem, inter alia, from the large coal reserves it has compared to other, cleaner, energy sources).

[7] In Canada, for example, the political support for CCS in some provinces stems to a large extent from the fiscal benefit these provinces expect from the use of CCS not less from its environmental effects. In Alberta, for example, the Carbon Capture and Storage Funding Act, SA 2009 c C-25, designed to encourage and expedite CCS projects, reflects the prominence of fossil fuel production to the local economy and the position of the gas and oil industries, as well as the mining and coal-fired electricity generation—as a prominent employer in the province. See Henry J. Krupa, 'The Legal Framework for Carbon Capture and Storage in Canada' in Havercroft, Macrory, and Stewart (eds) (n1) 39, at 46.

to export their expertise and know-how to those other states.[8] The existence of non-environmental interests in CCS is not a problem in itself (and can even be an advantage in certain circumstances). Yet, because governments worldwide do not internalize the full environmental effects of their CCS policies, CCS projects may end up sacrificing environmental ends in order to promote other, non-environmental objectives.

This analysis is all the more true with regards to private industry players, in particular fossil fuel-based energy companies that emit large quantities of CO_2. In the absence of substantial carbon prices, private industry players have little incentive to participate in CCS at all. Clearly, ownership of the CCS technologies they themselves develop may provide some incentive for industry players to conduct CCS research. The public pressure in some countries to reduce emissions may further enhance this incentive. Yet, generous monetary incentives by governments are essential for the adoption of CCS projects in virtually all countries.[9] Privately run companies also expect that governments will co-shoulder the legal risks of CCS.[10] Even effective command-and-control regulation and carbon tax or cap and trade programmes will have only a limited effect on the private production of CCS technologies, unless the credit (or other benefits) received under these programmes both fully incorporates the environmental benefits of CCS, and offsets the costs and the risks of employing CCS. Because of the considerable uncertainty concerning the scope of risks associated with CCS at this stage, and the low (or non-existent) cost of carbon relative to it, even the most effective regulatory systems cannot provide sufficient incentive for private parties to engage in CCS, let alone to tie their CCS practices to the actual effect these practices would have on the environment.

The second reason CCS practices may be detrimental to the environment without adequate policies in place is that the CCS regulation is likely to be undermined by information-problems[11] and interest group pressures.[12] Indeed, CCS projects are technical by nature; they are scientifically complex and financially expensive. In addition, CCS projects often involve a number of private and public participants, usually prominent energy corporations which are important economic actors and large employers with long-standing ties to politicians. As self-interest maximizers, such companies are likely to use their political clout to influence CCS

[8] This approach characterizes, to a large extent, the approach taken by the United Kingdom, Norway, and the United States.

[9] See, e.g., Shilling (n 1) at 35. [10] See Shilling (n 1).

[11] CCS as a solution for emission reduction has not been carried out commercially, although the elements that compose CCS have been done in other contexts. See nn 16–17 and accompanying text. Today, a number of experimental CCS projects are taking place around the world, although none is yet on a commercial scale. Thus, injection of CO_2 underground is being carried out onshore in the United States and offshore by Norway; commercial-scale capture projects are under construction in Canada and in the United States, and China is rapidly developing pilot CCS projects, and is set to invest US$1 billion in a CCS project in Texas.

[12] See James Buchanan and Gordon Tullock, *The Calculus of Consent* (1962); Bruce Ackerman, 'Beyond Carolene Products' (1985) 98 Harv L Rev 713, at 723–6 (observing the advantage concentrated interests have over diffuse ones); see also Roger G. Noll, 'Economic Perspectives on the Politics of Regulation' in *Handbook of Industrial Organization* (Richard Schmalensee and Robert D. Willig, eds, 1989) 1265.

regulation. What is more, CSS regulation is susceptible to the problem of planning horizons. While the cost of CCS regulation must be incurred at present, the benefits will only in the future, a number of years down the road.[13] Together, these factors may cause non-environmental considerations to overshadow the environmental ones, and lead to the adoption of CCS policies that have a negative effect on the environment. Mechanisms that encourage states or private industry players to conduct CCS projects in a way that reflects the real, overall environmental effect of the project are essential.

III. Framework applications

There are three important decision-points in the development of CCS policy that require legal intervention in order to ensure environmentally friendly policies and practices. First, there is the planning stage at which the government must decide whether to include CCS in its climate mitigation portfolio. The second stage consists of managing CO_2 capture and transportation. The third and final stage consists of selecting a storage site and managing the long-term liability issues that may arise over time. In the following sections, we discuss ways to enhance the environmental performance of these different CCS phases.

A. Stage A: inclusion of CCS in the state's energy policy

The first stage is the decision by a state to include CCS in its climate mitigation portfolio.[14] Our aim is for governments to select CCS projects that will generate the highest environmental return for the lowest cost.

To this end, we propose that prior to including CCS in its climate mitigation portfolio, the state government should set up a specialized panel that will set standards for CCS technologies. Technological developments are a critical part of CCS. While CCS does not require entirely new innovation,[15] it stretches existing expertise on CO_2 capture, separation, compression, transportation, and long-term storage, and on the links between these processes.[16] All of these technologies must be developed further in order to improve the environmental performance of CCS.

[13] In states where issues regarding capture and the other challenges we discuss are especially severe, legislation or regulation of our proposal in the state level may be unlikely. In those states, it might be better to include our proposals in higher-level jurisdictions, such as the European Union or international treaties.

[14] While we use the term 'state' throughout this discussion, it can apply equally to smaller or bigger jurisdictional entities, such as provinces or federal territories, depending on the responsibilities assigned to the different governments in the state's law or constitution.

[15] The oil industry has many years of experience injecting CO_2 into declining oil or natural gas wells to improve their yields (EOR—Enhanced Oil Recovery); and gas has been transported throughout the United States via pipes and in Europe via lorry to be utilized by the soft drink and other industries, cf the Shell refinery in Rotterdam. See also Shilling (n 1).

[16] Carbon Capture and Storage—Model Regulatory Framework, 2010, available at <http://www.iea.org/publications/freepublications/publication/model_framework.pdf>. In some projects, reports showed that the capture chemical reaction during the capture process was not exactly as expected, and that more time, more investment, and more projects are needed in order for the desired goals to be reached.

This panel would be tasked with weighing all reasonable alternatives for each of the processes needed for CCS, and identifying a list of the existing technologies that generate the greatest environmental benefit at the lowest cost.[17] There may be different lists of technologies for different types of projects, sectors, or industries.

Determining the effectiveness of a technology from an environmental point of view must be comprehensive.[18] The panel would need to identify all the relevant effects a project may have on the environment, and quantify them. Each benefit and harm should be allocated a weight, and factored by the probability that it would manifest in reality. The environmental impact can then be denoted as a fraction, with the expected environmental returns (the benefits multiplied by the probability they would occur) as the numerator and the expected environmental harms (the harms multiplied by their probability) as the denominator.

Thus, the panel would need to weigh the direct environmental benefit of a suggested project, i.e., the emission reduction it produces,[19] against its direct and indirect environmental costs. Direct costs include the energy consumed for the capture, pressing, liquefying,[20] and transportation to storage of the CO_2. Indirect harms include the energy consumed for the building of CO_2 pipelines,[21] and the risks of overpressure of CO_2, leakage or migration, and soil and groundwater disruption. Finally, the panel would need to assess the likelihood that CCS would prolong the use of traditional energy sources,[22] and the probability that approving the project being considered would encourage new CCS projects around the world.[23] This is not an easy task. Not only are some of the effects of CCS contingent upon future events that may or may not occur, but CCS is also a relatively new process, whose environmental effects are yet to be seen. Assessing the effects of separate technologies on the process is even more difficult.

[17] Of course, cost should be part of the equation as well. Some environmental decisions can come at too high a cost—financially. There is some point on the cost continuum that is not worth it anymore, and this should be taken into account.

[18] The CCS Directive in Europe identifies and groups the risks from CCS into three groups: (i) global risks, i.e., the risk of leakage; (ii) local risks, i.e., the risk of migration and its effects; (iii) upstream risk, i.e., the risks associated with the continued use of CCS.

[19] This benefit is different between different projects. For example, if CCS is installed on gas power plants, the environmental utility is lower than if it is installed on coal power plants, where it can capture much more CO_2.

[20] More accurately, the CO_2 will be transformed to a supercritical phase (see n 2).

[21] It is estimated that a large number of new pipelines will need to be constructed during each CCS project. See Roggenkamp and Kamminga (n 3) at 108. Building of pipelines would have non-environmental costs as well, such as the costs associated with clearing property rights and the actual building of the pipelines. Building of the pipeline may, in some situations, have an environmental benefit as well, if these pipelines can later be used for other environmentally beneficial activities.

[22] The NER 300 process in Europe (pursuant to Article 10a(8) of the Revised Emissions Trading Directive), for example, created 300 million allowances to support commercial CCS and innovative RES demonstration projects. Seven CCS projects competed with RES on allowances and funding (none was selected). See also C. Littlecott, 'New Year, New Resolve for Carbon Capture and Storage?' *GreenPeace UK*, 3 January 2013, available at <http://www.greenpeace.org.uk/newsdesk/energy/analysis/new-year-new-resolve-carbon-capture-and-storage>.

[23] Clearly, there is a limitation to how far we can expand the concept of indirect effects. For example, environmental effects may result from the need of different nations to negotiate with each other in the CCS context. The remoteness of these factors renders them unable to be measured in any way.

Importantly, in order to ensure that all relevant considerations are included in the process, and to minimize public choice problems, the decision-making process must allow for participation by members of the public,[24] environmental organizations, and even representatives of other states.[25]

Clearly, there could be more than one technology considered suitable at any given time, if more than one technology arrives at the same ratio between the benefit and the cost to the environment. Thus, the panel does not have to denote a single technology, but rather decide on a list which includes a range of technologies, each of which would satisfy the standard.

When a concrete CCS project is examined later on, the project operators would be required to adopt the technologies that were chosen by the panel, or alternatively, to show that the technology they wish to implement is at least as environmentally beneficial as those technologies selected by the panel of experts.[26] Only projects that satisfy this standard for all the technologies that they are using would be granted permit or funding of any kind. In the case of utilities, only projects that satisfy the standards for all their technologies would be allowed to increase the utility bill on their clients in order to cover the cost of the project. If a project offered for review a *better* technology than those chosen by the panel for a process, the new technology would *replace* the old one as the requisite technological standard, and all new projects would need to perform at least as well from that moment on. The panel may also reconvene periodically to revisit the list and update it as new and improved technologies emerge, as well as when new projects are put forward.

This process would encourage project proponents to justify their projects on environmental grounds. Projects that cannot show a positive environmental prospect will need to improve their capture rate or curb their risks better in order to be

[24] Much has been written about the need to involve the public in regulatory processes. (See, for example, Peta Ashworth and Craig Cormick, 'Enabling the Social Shaping on CCS Technology' in Havercroft, Macrory, and Stewart (eds) (n1) at 251–75.) States have in fact done so quite frequently, but usually in the context of involving local communities before issuing a permit to storage sites, and not at the outset, as hereby suggested. The EU CCS directive also allows participation by anybody who holds expertise in the area, and Directive 2011/92/EU of 13 December 2011 on the assessment of the effects of certain public and private projects on the environment encourages public involvement.

[25] Indeed, broad, inclusive engagement may have disadvantages as well. It can delay and increase the costs of projects that are environmentally desired—by objections of bodies that are across the board against CCS, private interest parties, or competitors. However, such objections, if they indeed occur, would pose a problem even without including the opposing parties in the early stages of the CCS regulation, especially in litigious jurisdictions like the United States. See Les Lo Baugh, 'Legal and Regulatory Challenges of Geological Carbon Capture and Sequestration: US Hurdles to Reducing CO_2 Emission' in Havercroft, Macrory, and Stewart (eds) (n1) 67–80 (discussing possible grounds for litigation under US law for CCS). In fact, there is a good reason to assume that including the objecting parties in the early stages may actually reduce—though definitely not eliminate—the probability of judicial challenge later on.

[26] Enabling project proponents to suggest their own technologies is necessary for at least two reasons. First, many of the CCS technologies are proprietary by other industry players, and may not be widely available. Second, CCS projects tend to be site-specific, industry-specific, and even plant-specific, and technologies that work well in one area may be inapplicable to a different type of plant, industry, or geographical region.

reconsidered. This would encourage industry players and third parties to invest in measures that would enhance CCS environmental benefits and reduce environmental harms. This, in turn, would spur competition among technology providers to come up with CCS technologies that are increasingly better for the environment.

The technological standard we propose is dynamic and self-adjusting. As better CCS technologies are developed, they would replace older and less efficient ones. Over time, this process would lead to the emergence of cleaner and cheaper technologies to be employed at a lower cost by industry players. The adoption of our proposal would spur competition over the development of improved CCS technologies, providing both regulated companies and outsiders with an incentive to come up with environmental solutions which are superior and more cost-effective than those we currently have.

We are mindful of the high initial cost of compliance with our standard. Existing plants could not be forced to retrofit to the new technologies right away, as this would be unrealistic considering the costs involved. For this reason, we propose that existing plants be given a grace period to adjust their technologies to the new environmental standard. It should be born in mind that under our proposed framework, we expect CCS technology to improve and become more cost-effective over time.[27] If our expectation materializes, existing plants will find it in their own self-interest to adopt the new technologies in order to remain competitive.

We believe that our system is potentially superior to the regulatory schemes that exist today, which have specific rules that govern CCS and the permitted or expected outcomes from CCS projects.[28] In Canada, for example, the storage permits that governments issue include a set of predetermined rules and quotas that control the CO_2 that would be stored in the site. Similarly, the European Union has created a set of requirements in the EU CCS Directive,[29] including, for example, the permitted level of leakage from a storage site annually. These rules are now being transposed and implemented by the EU Member States.

In comparison, adoption of our dynamic standard would yield three key advantages. First, it would create an incentive for state and private actors to constantly try to improve the environmental performance of their CCS projects. This is a dynamic standard that would evolve with technology: as new technologies emerge to perform better CCS, i.e., CCS that has a lower overall environmental impact, the policy would promote the use of the better technology over higher-risk existing technologies. As CCS improves, parties that operate these functions would adopt them.

The second advantage of our proposed standard is that it eliminates the need for costly political updates. Our technological standard would constantly update itself via the periodic review of our panel of experts and various industry initiatives. Under a dynamic standard, industry players would have an incentive to implement

[27] In section III.B we propose incentives for retrofitting.

[28] For a report of the current CCS regulatory status in various states, see International Energy Agency, *Carbon Capture and Storage—Legal and Regulatory Review* (2nd edn, 2011). See also International Energy Agency, *Carbon Capture and Storage—Model Regulatory Framework* (2010).

[29] Directive 2009/31/EC on the geological storage of CO_2 [2009] OJ L140/114.

new knowledge without a top-down regulatory mandate, and would have the incentive dynamically to incorporate this new knowledge to guide their use of specific CCS solutions.

The third advantage of our proposal lies in its potential to improve competition in the technology sector. This advantage is rooted in the dynamic nature of the standard. Indeed, the downside of predetermined standards is that they can easily become a ceiling, instead of a floor, and stifle the incentive for researchers or technology companies to come up with new technologies that would reduce the environmental effects of CCS. Under our dynamic standard, third-party technology companies, scientists, and other private actors would have an incentive to constantly come up with technologies that offer better environmental performance. Regulators would have the ability to incorporate these improved technologies, and plants would have an incentive to retrofit to include them.[30] This dynamic would spur innovation for both maximizing the benefits of CCS and minimizing its risks.

Our mechanism may not fit the early 'demo' stage of projects, where a large number of CCS projects are required for the cost of the process to drop and for efficiency to increase and to become apparent. It may also be impossible to quantify the risks of the project at this early stage. There may therefore be a need and a justification under our model to flex the examination for the demo phase of the CCS lifecycle. However, if governments decide to follow this route and apply a more lenient standard for the demo phase, so that the project can operate even though the government does not know at the time of issuing the permit that its environmental effect is positive, governments should include an obligation to retrofit to better technologies later on if appropriate, by either enhancing the environmental benefits of the process or minimizing its environmental harm.

B. Stage B: capture and transportation

The second critical stage of CCS projects involves the capture and transportation of CO_2. This stage is challenging not only technologically but also financially and legally. The capture and transformation of CO_2 to liquid form is the most expensive part of the entire CCS process, and needs to be covered by either government funding or by a substantial increase of the utility bills to consumers.[31] In the European Union, CO_2 capture is controlled by the IPPC Directive[32] and the EIA Directive,[33] while transportation is generally left to Member States to regulate, similarly to the model of natural gas transportation.[34] At this stage, our goal is to

[30] See section III.B.

[31] Estimated at US$60 to US$95 per metric ton of CO_2 captured; these costs could add 81% or more to consumer power bills in the United States.

[32] Directive 2008/1/EC of 15 January 2008 concerning integrated pollution prevention and control.

[33] Directive 85/337/EEC of 27 June 1985 on the assessment of the effects of certain public and private projects on the environment.

[34] Martina Doppelhammer, 'The CCS Directive, Its Implementation and the Co-financing of CCS and RES Demonstration Projects under the Emissions Trading System (NER 300 Process)' in Havercroft, Macrory, and Stewart (eds) (n1) 94, FN 6.

create an incentive for the plant owner that operates a CCS project to be environmentally conscious, namely, to capture as much CO_2 as possible, while using as little energy as possible in the process.

Clearly, part of this goal has already been addressed via the previous stage, namely, the selection of CCS projects. Indeed, according to the process delineated there, states would only grant a permit for CCS projects whose environmental effect is positive. Yet, since the selection process includes other factors as well, that process is not sufficient in order to assure that the plant applies the most cost-effective measure available for the capture and transportation mechanisms, and that existing projects improve the environmental performance of their capture process over time.

To achieve these goals, our proposal is to tie credits and benefits that plants receive for applying CCS to the net environmental outcome they create. The most straightforward application of this principle is in jurisdictions that apply carbon tax or cap and trade programmes. Indeed, some of jurisdictions already implement some of these ideas.

The first stage is to grant the plant emission reduction credits for the emission avoidance it creates. This policy would correlate the credit with the amount of emissions the plant was curbing, and would enhance the incentive of plants to apply CCS, especially if carbon price is high. Yet, the plant should not receive this credit in full. In order to preserve the incentives of plants to consume less energy in the capture process, we suggest that the plant would need to surrender credit allowance corresponding to the energy consumed by the capture and compression of the CO_2. This mechanism would create an incentive for the plant to seek ways to maximize emission reduction and minimize the energy consumed in the capture process.

Our credit programme would also create an incentive for the plant to retrofit, namely, to switch to more environmentally efficient technologies that may emerge during the lifetime of the project. Such technologies may increase the amount of carbon captured, or decrease the energy consumed in the process. Indeed, if credits are granted according to the emission avoidance minus the energy utilized in the process, plants have an incentive to switch to a more environmentally efficient technology, as this would give them more credits. As a result, the impetus for either the plant or third-party technology companies to continue the development of energy-efficient capture mechanisms would be maintained, even after the project is underway.[35]

[35] A similar credit system may also apply to states' incentives, although the international obligations on states are now virtually non-existent, since the Kyoto protocol has expired and the Copenhagen Accords has not come into effect. Had states assumed emission target obligations, however, a similar programme could apply, with some interesting twists. Scholars and practitioners debate whether to allocate credit to the state that undertakes the carbon capture or on the state that stores the CO_2. Our position is that in order to create an incentive for a state to undertake the more expensive (either to the state itself or to its citizens via utility bills or commodity prices) carbon capture projects, the state that captures CO_2 in its territories should also enjoy the emission reduction credits, regardless of where the storage site is located. The reason for that is twofold: first, we aim to incentivize the state to use CCS on the most polluting plants, and so we want to correlate the credit with the amount of emission the state

We further require that credit for CCS would be conditioned upon verification that the captured CO_2 has actually remained underground. Thus, CCS credit should be offset by the CO_2 that leaks to the atmosphere. The reason for this is that although the storage site is likely to be outside of the plant's control, plants should have an incentive to assess the suitability of the storage site to which the CO_2 it captures is transported. In the absence of such rules, there may be an incentive to rush through a project while ignoring the quality of the storage site, in order to collect the CCS credits that the capture and transportation of the CO_2 would generate.

In cases where no carbon price programmes are in effect, devising an appropriate incentive structure is more challenging. Clearly, lack of carbon accountability is a broader problem, which creates various inefficiencies in climate change management beyond the CCS context. Our solution in such cases is to use monetary incentives to achieve the same goal that carbon credits otherwise achieve. Thus, some of the funds that states would allocate to a CCS project would be contingent on the ratio between the emission avoided and the energy that was consumed in the process.

C. Stage C: suitability of the storage site

The final stage we have identified is the long-term storage of CO_2. The question of long-term liability of CCS is considered one of the most difficult issues of CCS law. Indeed, without a safe solution for storage that assures that CO_2 will be completely contained for the indefinite future, CCS emission reduction may be severely undermined by CO_2 leakage and migration.[36] Leakage is an event where contained CO_2 is released back into the atmosphere, while migration is the relocation of CO_2 below the ground surface, which could cause severe environmental (and other) harms.[37]

Under the right design, liability for environmental damages from CCS projects can be the primary tool for incentivizing industry players to minimize those environmental and other risks. Currently, liability rules vary between different jurisdictions. In two Australian jurisdictions, for example, the storage site operator remains subject to long-term liability indefinitely.[38] Other jurisdictions, including the European Union, place liability on the site operator, yet they allow states to assume liability after a period of time, provided that some conditions have been

is curbing. Second, granting credits only for states that hold the storage sites in their territories may incentivize states to offer storage sites in their territories, even if they are not the best sites possible.

[36] But see Shilling (n 1), arguing that permanent, indefinite storage is an unrealistic expectation. Several states set a standard of no more than 1% leakage per 1,000 years.

[37] More accurately, leakage is not an environmental harm, but rather offsets the benefit of the emission reduction that CCS aimed to achieve. Migration, on the other hand, could ruin aquifers by causing them to become saline or acidic, or by contaminating them with metals released by such acidity.

[38] See Meredith Gibbs, The Regulation of Geological Storage of Greenhouse Gases in Australia, in Havercroft, Macrory, and Stewart (eds) (n1) 167.

met.[39] Other mechanisms that were raised include imposing liability on the original CO_2 producer, or implementing industry liability-pooling plans, similar to the American Price-Anderson Nuclear Industries Indemnity Act.[40]

We propose a different route. Our starting point is that liability should be placed upon the least-cost avoider, namely, the entity that can avoid the accident—in this case leakage or migration—at the lowest cost.[41] Imposing liability on the least-cost avoiders would create an incentive for that party to take efficient measures to avoid leakage or migration of CO_2 from the CCS storing sites.

In case of leakage or migration of CO_2 from a storage site, the least-cost avoider is usually the site operator. The operator has full access to the site and has the tools and the expertise to monitor it in order to assess whether the injected CO_2 is behaving as expected, and whether any migration or leakage is occurring. But damage can occur not only because of poor management of the storage site ex post, but also because the government did not select a suitable storage site ex ante. Both the state and the site operator have roles in selecting the storage sites. The operator should have the incentive to offer for consideration only storing sites that to the best of the operator's knowledge can be safe for the indefinite storage of CO_2. The state, on the other hand, needs to issue a permit to storage sites only after state officials are persuaded that the site is safe and suitable for permanent storage of CO_2.[42] In this case, placing the entire liability on the plant's shoulder may be inefficient. It will push site operators to a risk-averse disposition and to over-investing in precautions. Insurance mechanisms may also not be available for such a broad liability. What is more, governments should also be encouraged to conduct a rigorous site selection process.

We therefore suggest that in case of leakage, migration, or other harms that occur from the storage of CO_2, the operator will assume full liability, unless it can show that the monitoring of the site was done flawlessly, in which case, it will be assumed that the selection of the storage site was inappropriate, and the state would share the liability with the site operator. Our proposal maintains the incentive for states and operators to better perform their part, and thus to maintain the reliability of storage sites.

Importantly, under our proposal as set forth in section III.B of this chapter, the original emitter also pays a price if the storage site incurs leakage or migration, in the form of surrendering emission reduction credits, as discussed earlier. This way, the original emitter will also have an incentive to verify the suitability of the storage site for the CO_2 the emitter sends there, although it carries no liability.

39 CCS Directive, §18(1)(b). The reason for this is that there is no insurance and that some party needs to be responsible when anything goes wrong, even if the company ceases to exist.

40 Under this scheme, the operator would have individual insurance, and each operator will also contribute to the industry statutory cap. Beyond industry contributions, the federal government will take responsibility for damages.

41 See Guido Calabresi, *The Costs of Accidents: A Legal and Economic Analysis* (1970) 139.

42 For geological criteria for site suitability, see The Bellona Foundation, 'Fact Sheet: CO_2 Storage', at 1.

1. Trans-boundary CCS

Trans-boundary CCS is the process of storing carbon that was produced in one country in the territory of another country. We encourage trans-boundary CCS, in order to spur competition between states and to increase the availability of suitable storing sites beyond national borders.[43] In our view, states should ratify the relevant treaties and take the necessary legal measures in order to enable trans-boundary CCS. The EU CCS Directive also provides for cross-border CCS, in which an emitter from one EU country should have the opportunity to inject and store CO_2 in the territory of another Member State.[44]

The challenge, however, is to determine which country needs to be responsible for leakage in the case of cross-boundary CCS. We suggest that in most cases, placing liability for leakage on the storing state would be more efficient, not only because the storing state is the least-cost avoider (the storage site is under its territorial control), but for environmental efficiency as well. First, the storing state would have the incentive to examine the risk of leakage from a storing site that competes for a permit for CCS storage in another country. This way, out-of-state storage sites would request permits only if they project low possibility of leakage in relation to their competitors. Second, a clear rule for liability would increase legal certainty, especially in this context, where one storage site may store CO_2 that originates in more than one state—an activity the law should wish to encourage if indeed the storage site is suitable.

IV. Conclusion

To face the challenges climate change poses to humankind, it is necessary to adopt a portfolio approach—that is, to adopt multiple tools to address the problem, rather than a single one. CCS can be an important part of the portfolio. Until new sources of alternative energy become widely available, CCS can play a critical role in curbing emissions while providing the ever-increasing energy needs worldwide. Since 2008, governments worldwide have committed a staggering amount of US $22.5 billion to supporting CCS,[45] but towards the close of 2010, many projects were cancelled or postponed and the fate of several others remains doubtful.[46]

[43] For the current state of the law on trans-Boundary CCS, see Hans Christian Bugge, 'Trans-Boundary Chains for Carbon Capture and Storage: Allocation under the Climate Regime between the States Parties of Emissions due to Leakage' in Havercroft, Macrory, and Stewart (eds) (n1) 123–34.

[44] The CCS Directive however, explicitly forbids trans-boundary CCS outside of the territorial scope of the Directive because it cannot be guaranteed that the requirements of that Directive or other EU legislations will be met.

[45] In 2010, Leaders of the Group of Eight, which includes the United States, Russia, and Japan, embraced in 2008 a goal to launch 20 large-scale CCS demonstration projects by 2010 with 'broad deployment' of the technology by 2020. President Barack Obama unveiled a goal to bring 5 to 10 commercial-size CCS demonstration plants on line in the United States by 2016.

[46] For example, American Electric Power (AEP) put on hold the planned CCS project in Mountaineer, a coal-fired plant in West Virginia in 2011, citing a weak economy and the 'uncertain status of U.S. Climate policy'. See 301 Corporate Counsel's Monitor 22 (September 2011).The Australian

In the light of an overriding concern for maximizing the environmental benefits of CCS, and for minimizing its environmental harms, we have identified in this chapter three key points in the CCS process—the inclusion of CCS in the state's energy policy; the capture process; and long-term storage of CO_2—at which legal intervention is most needed. In these key points, we have proposed specific policies that we believe would generate better environmental results through creating policies that can incentivize industry participants to adopt more environmentally friendly policies.

We are of course aware that the success of any regulatory framework depends on a host of real-world factors. Actual results stem from hard bargaining and balancing exercises involving many competing and often conflicting concerns, including those that may originate in other principles. We think, however, that our dynamic principle could spur new thinking about some of the most difficult CCS legal issues.

ZeroGen CCS project was cancelled by the government in Queensland, after investing AU$150 million in it. Additional cancellations include Bismarck, North Dakota-based Basin Electric Power Cooperative, and Omaha-based Tenaska Inc's plans to build a power plant in Taylorville, Illinois, in the United States.

16

New Advances in Geothermal Energy Law: A Comparative Analysis

Adrian Bradbrook and Anita Rønne

I. Introduction and overview

A. The nature and history of geothermal energy

Humankind's knowledge and exploitation of geothermal resources has a very long history. The first recorded use of geothermal energy dates back to the first century BC, during which the Romans exploited hot springs for a variety of purposes.[1] The first use of geothermal energy for the generation of electricity also occurred in Italy, where in 1904 a geothermal steam-driven engine at Lardarello lit five electric lamps; by the late 1930s the same geothermal field was producing almost 100,000 kW of electric power.[2]

Despite its long history, geothermal energy may realistically be regarded as one of the major energy resources of the future. It has the potential to be one of the major energy technologies to combat climate change. The worldwide potential of the resource is virtually limitless. The amount of geothermal heat in the outer 10 km of the earth's crust has been calculated to be 10^{26} calories, which is more than 2,000 times the heat output of the total coal reserves in the world. The potential of the resource has been examined closely in the United States, where a recent report by the Massachusetts Institute of Technology concluded that it would be economically feasible to generate one hundred gigawatts (GW) of electricity or more by 2050.[3] This makes the proven oil reserves of the United States (25.2 billion barrels) look modest by comparison.[4] On a worldwide basis, scientists have calculated that if

[1] B. Bjorge, 'The Development of Geothermal Resources and the 1970 Geothermal Steam Act—Law in Search of Definition' (1974) 46 U Colorado L Rev 1 at 3. See also <http://www.conserve-energy-future.com/GeothermalEnergyHistory.php>.

[2] <http://geoheat.oit.edu/bulletin/bull25-3/art2.pdf>.

[3] MIT, *The Future of Geothermal Energy* (2007); available at <http://en.wikipedia.org/wiki/world_energy_resources#Geothermal>. See also T. R. Naumann, 'Form over Function: The Law of Hot Water' (1983) 4 J Energy L and Policy 205 at 209; and IEA *Technology Roadmap Geothermal Heat and Power* (2011) at 9–11; available at <http://www.iea.org/publications/freepublications/publication/Geothermal_Roadmap.pdf>

[4] <http://www.eia.gov/naturalgas/crudeoilreserves> (as at 31 December 2010).

means could be found to reduce the temperature of the earth's core by 0.6°C, sufficient energy would be generated to power all existing power plants for 20 million years.[5]

Where are geothermal resources located? First and obviously, they are found in areas of volcanic activity and geological instability. Such areas usually occur on or close to the border of the tectonic plates into which the earth's crust is divided. New Zealand and Iceland are perhaps the most spectacular illustrations of these areas, and considerable reserves of geothermal energy exist in both countries. Geothermal resources also exist in commercial quantities in many other parts of the world which are geologically stable. Illustrations of this are the United Kingdom and Australia. In the United Kingdom, the Carnmellis region in Cornwall can produce heated water with a recoverable temperature at the surface of 63°C. In Australia, geothermal resources exist in southern Victoria, the southern half of South Australia, central Queensland, the eastern highlands of New South Wales, coastal parts of Western Australia, and the Great Artesian Basin.

The reason for the availability of geothermal resources in geologically stable areas is that volcanic or magmatic reserves and vapour-dominated systems, which are associated with instability in the earth's crust, are only two of the five identified types of the resource.[6] The other three types are geopressured systems, hot groundwater, and hot dry rocks (HDR). Geopressured systems are frequently found in subsiding basins containing young sedimentary rock, while hot groundwater is found in a variety of different underground terrains. The HDR resource is exploited by the injection of cold water into the earth through drilled holes. This water becomes superheated on contact with underground heated rock and is discharged at the surface in the form of steam.

The potential of geothermal energy for satisfying the world's energy requirements is enormous. In the United States, for example, recoverable reserves of heat energy in the earth in the 90°C to 150°C range has been estimated at the equivalent of 900 billion barrels of oil, which is twenty times the proven oil reserves in that country.

B. The role of the law

Simply put, the role of the law is to promote the public policy of reducing reliance on fossil fuels (and thereby preserving remaining fossil fuels for future generations) and minimizing harmful environmental effects caused by the generation and use of energy, while at the same time ensuring that there is little or no adverse economic effect. This is an application of the principle of sustainable development; that is, the exploitation and development of resources while ensuring that adverse environmental effects are negated or minimized.

[5] G. Vranesh and J. D. Musick, 'Geothermal Resources: Water and Other Conflicts Encountered by the Developer' (1977) 13 Land and Water L Rev 109 at 115, n 24.

[6] For a discussion of the various types of geothermal resources, see S. Sato and T. D. Crocker, 'Property Rights to Geothermal Resources' (1977) 6 Ecology L Q 250 at 255.

It is submitted that the primary role of the law in achieving this goal is to ensure that a favourable investment climate exists for the resource. Investment and prospecting for geothermal resources is a high-cost, high-risk enterprise. It is unrealistic to expect that significant investment will occur in this area unless investors are confident that there is an established system of legal rights and responsibilities in effect. This can only be achieved if the law settles the ownership issue and establishes a detailed regime for the exploitation and development of the resource. Geothermal exploration and development in many ways resembles that of petroleum exploration and development. Petroleum exploration and development did not proceed without the prior creation of a legal management regime. The same is required for the geothermal industry.

Any new legislative regime must also address environmental issues.[7] As geothermal energy is usually regarded as a renewable energy resource, there appears to be a general assumption that adverse environmental effects are minimal, but unfortunately this is not the case. A number of environmental problems associated with the development and exploitation of geothermal resources can be identified.

II. New legal responses in common law countries to developing geothermal energy

Geothermal legislation could be enacted either through amendments to existing mining and petroleum legislation or through the enactment of new legislation. Examples of both approaches exist in common law jurisdictions. It is submitted that the better approach is to enact new geothermal legislation. The adaptation of existing legislation to geothermal energy would involve either grossly misclassifying one or more of the different types of the resource (for example, to declare hot groundwater to be a 'mineral' or the HDR resource to be 'groundwater'), so as to ensure that all types of geothermal resources fall within the same legislation, or to classify the various types of resources differently (for example, to treat the HDR resource as a mineral and hot groundwater as groundwater). Neither of these approaches would appear to be desirable.

A. The common law approach in the absence of legislation

As geothermal energy was not exploited in modern times until the twentieth century, it is axiomatic that in common law countries no common law rules were developed historically to govern the resource and no legislation existed prior to that time.

[7] For a general discussion of environmental issues associated with geothermal energy, see K. Zaidi, 'Environmental Mitigation Aspects of Water Resources in Geothermal Development' (2010) 23 Georgetown Int Env L Rev 97; A. J. Bradbrook, 'Environmental Controls over Geothermal Energy Exploitation' (1988) 4 EPLJ 5.

It is submitted that an effective and comprehensive legal regime for managing and exploiting geothermal resources should contain three major elements: a resolution of the ownership of the resource; rules controlling its exploration and exploitation; and environmental protection controls. In the absence of legislation, there are no common law rules in relation to exploration and exploitation. As for environmental protection, the only safeguards would be the common law of nuisance, which is generally considered by environmental lawyers as an ineffective remedy.

The ownership issue would be determined by common law rules concerning the respective rights of the surface landowner and the state as to underground resources. In jurisdictions without legislation regulating minerals, gas, or groundwater, the issue would be resolved under the doctrine of *cujus est solum, ejus est usque ad coelum et ad inferos* (discussed in detail in chapter 2).[8] Under this doctrine, the landowner owns all the subsoil, including minerals, down to the centre of the earth. The only common law exception relates to precious metals (that is, gold and silver). As this exception clearly has no application to geothermal energy, at common law geothermal resources would belong to the surface landowner, but only if the resource is classed as a 'mineral'. As mentioned later, conflicting views and decisions exist on this point. If the resource is considered as a 'gas' or 'groundwater', common law is silent.

Fortunately, in the light of this underlying uncertainty, legislation regulating minerals, gas, and groundwater does exist in all major common law jurisdictions. The issue there is to determine which legislation applies to geothermal resources. Geothermal water or steam could be considered by legislation to be a 'mineral', 'gas', or 'groundwater', so as to attract the operation of the legislation regulating minerals, oil and gas, or groundwater (respectively). In the United States, the sole country where this issue has been litigated, precedents exist for all these alternative approaches. Some states declare the resource to be 'water',[9] some declare it to be a 'mineral',[10] while the United States Court of Appeals for the Ninth Circuit, held in *Reich v Commissioner of Internal Revenue*[11] that the resource is a 'gas' for the purpose of securing entitlement to the depletion allowance in the US Internal Revenue Code.[12] The answer at common law may well depend on which of the five types of geothermal energy is being considered. Thus, for example, there is enough in common between the HDR resource and minerals generally to justify the conclusion that the minerals legislation includes the HDR resource. Similarly, the obvious similarities between hot groundwater and groundwater reserves used

[8] See A. J. Bradbrook et al, *Australian Real Property Law* (4th edn, 2011) at [16.130]ff.

[9] Wyoming: Wyo Stat, s 41-121(b); Nevada: Nev Rev Stat s 534A.040.

[10] Hawaii Rev Stat, s 182-1(1); Texas Rev Civ Ann Stat art 1435a, s 4(2). This approach was adopted by the USA Court of Appeals in *Rosette Inc v United States* (2002) 277 F.3d 1222: see S. R. McNutt, 'Rosette Inc v United States: Is The United States Full of Hot Air When it Comes to Reservation of Geothermal Resources as a "Mineral?"' (2003) 8 Great Plains Nat Res J 44.

[11] (1972) 454 F.2d 1157.

[12] See P. McDevitt and D. Wells, 'Energy Market Impacts of the Legal Definition of Geothermal Energy in the Western United States' (1982) 22 Nat Res J 391 at 392ff.

for irrigation purposes may lead to a conclusion that this groundwater is within the existing groundwater statutory regime. However, on closer analysis the similarities among geothermal resources and minerals, gas, and groundwater break down. Geothermal resources are fundamentally different from groundwater as it is the heat energy, rather than the liquid content, which constitutes the resource. Fundamental differences also exist between geothermal resources, on the one hand, and minerals, oil, and gas, on the other hand, as the latter must be burned or processed in order to produce heat energy, while the former is heat energy and hence requires no such processing. An additional factor is that minerals, oil, and gas can be utilized directly, while the geothermal resource can only be exploited indirectly by means of steam or water which conveys the heat energy to the land surface.[13]

We now consider the types of geothermal legislation that have been enacted in modern times in common law jurisdictions. In reality there are considerable differences between all jurisdictions that have legislated in this area. For the purposes of space we will focus on Australia, and compare Australian law with its counterparts in Canada and New Zealand. New Zealand is a unitary jurisdiction and legislation has been enacted at the national level. In Australia and Canada, legislation has been enacted at the state level.

B. Laws in Australia

Legislation affecting geothermal energy has been enacted in recent years in all six states and two territories, except for the Australian Capital Territory, where the resource does not exist. The form and scope of the legislation differs significantly among the jurisdictions.

A minimal approach to the issue has been adopted in New South Wales and Tasmania. In the former jurisdiction, the definition of 'mineral' in the Mining (General) Regulation 1997 (NSW), schedule 1, was amended by the addition of the following:

> A reference in Schedule 1 or 2 to a geothermal substance is a reference to any substance occurring naturally or artificially underground that is heated by the natural processes of the earth to a temperature in excess of 100 degrees Celsius (other than any other substance referred to in those Schedules, and other than petroleum, coal, oil, shale and uranium).

The effect of the inclusion of geothermal energy as a 'mineral' is to confer ownership of the resource in the Crown and to destroy any argument that the resource belongs to the surface owner by virtue of the *cujus est solum* doctrine. Evidently, however, the legislation applies only to steam (over 100°C) and does not cover hot groundwater reserves, from approximately 40°C upwards. This is a very serious omission as the bulk of the geothermal resource in Australia consists of hot groundwater. The ownership of this water is unresolved by law at present.

[13] J. W. Aidlin, 'Representing the Geothermal Resources Client' (1974) 19 Rocky Mt M L Inst 27 at 30–1.

In Tasmania, the same approach is taken, but the legislation is more embracing. Section 3 of the Mineral Resources Development Act 1995 (Tas) defines 'geothermal substance' as meaning:

> . . . a substance occurring naturally or introduced underground which is heated by the natural processes of the earth to a temperature in excess of 40° Celsius.

This clearly includes all commercially exploitable hot groundwater reserves, as well as the other forms of geothermal energy. Thus all geothermal reserves belong to the Crown.

In both New South Wales and Tasmania, the mining legislation to which geothermal resources are subject establishes a comprehensive legal management for exploration and production.[14] This legislation establishes prospecting licences and exploration and retention licences for potential developers. Mining leases are created for projects in the development stage. Rent and royalty provisions are established, and a system of compensation for damage caused to surface landowners is in place. While using the mining legislation as a vehicle for state control of geothermal development may be questionable in the light of the physical differences between steam and hard rock minerals, the Acts create legal certainty for investors and geothermal developers. In Tasmania, which has no separate petroleum legislation, it is perhaps understandable that the mining legislation has been used in this context.

The major weakness with the geothermal legal regimes in New South Wales and Tasmania is that, with one exception, the mining legislation does not address environmental issues. The exception relates to abandoned facilities, for which the legislation mandates that the onus of rehabilitating the land to its former condition be on the leaseholder.[15] The other environmental issues are not addressed. While the generally applicable state environmental legislation would apply, this does not directly address the issues affecting geothermal development and, in many cases, it would be difficult to frame an action against developers under this legislation.

Western Australia and South Australia have adopted the approach of applying geothermal legislative controls to the existing state legislation regulating onshore petroleum exploration and production. The relevant legislation is the Petroleum and Geothermal Energy Resources Act 1967 (WA) and the Petroleum and Geothermal Energy Act 2000 (SA).

The definition of the resource in Western Australia and South Australia is far more straightforward and comprehensive than in New South Wales and Tasmania. Section 9 of the Western Australian Act states: '*geothermal energy* means thermal energy that results from natural geological processes and is contained in geothermal energy resources'. The legislative definition in South Australia is to similar effect.[16]

[14] Mining Act 1992 (NSW), Parts 3–6; Mineral Resources Development Act 1995 (Tas), Parts 2–4.

[15] Mining Act 1992 (NSW), s 239; Mineral Resources Development Act 1995 (Tas), ss 180–182.

[16] Petroleum and Geothermal Energy Act 2000 (SA), s 4.

The issue of ownership is settled by a section declaring the resource to belong to the Crown.[17]

The effect of the Western Australian and South Australian legislation is that geothermal resources are subject to the special controls regulating the exploration and production of petroleum. These are separate from the mining legislation controls, which are located in different enactments. The controls are comprehensive and are certainly sufficient to satisfy any investor's desire for legal certainty prior to embarking on a high-risk enterprise. The inclusion of geothermal resources within the petroleum rather than the general mining legislation would seem more appropriate in light of the fact that the resource is in liquid form and is subject to similar issues of migration. The method of drilling for and otherwise developing geothermal sites also closely approximates that traditionally adopted in the onshore petroleum industry.

The Western Australian and South Australian Acts differ markedly in their approach to environmental issues. The former contains no special provisions dealing with the environmental concerns of the industry, discussed earlier. Part 12 of the South Australian Act, however, contains comprehensive environmental controls which, while not specifically referring to the environmental issues discussed earlier, nevertheless seek to address them in a different manner. Section 97 requires developers to prepare an environmental impact report in all cases of low-impact development, while sections 102 and 103 state that for medium- and high-impact developments, a formal environmental impact assessment is required under the terms of section 8 of the Development Act 1993 (SA). All developers must prepare a statement of environmental objectives under section 99, and by section 105 it is a mandatory condition of every geothermal licence that the licensee must comply with its terms (subject to a penalty of AU$120,000). In the event of environmental harm of any nature, section 108 empowers the relevant Minister to direct the licensee to take specified action to prevent or minimize damage. This latter provision could be used to address the major environmental concerns relevant to the geothermal industry.

Legislation specific to the geothermal industry has been enacted in the remaining jurisdictions—Queensland, Victoria, and the Northern Territory. The most comprehensive enactment is the Geothermal Energy Act of the Northern Territory. This Act not only deals with the ownership issue and establishes a management regime for the resource, but it also contains detailed environmental protection provisions that are unique in Australia. The Act creates a general obligation to take care of the environment (section 84) and establishes legally binding environmental obligations on the geothermal operator (section 85). A variety of environmental offences is created in sections 90–95. These include serious environmental harm or material environmental harm caused by either recklessness or negligence by the operator, as well as a statutory offence of environmental nuisance. 'Serious environmental harm', 'material environmental harm', and 'environmental nuisance' are

[17] Petroleum and Geothermal Energy Resources Act 1967 (WA), s 9; Petroleum and Geothermal Energy Act 2000 (SA), s 5.

defined in section 83 in such a way as to include liability for all the environmental issues associated with geothermal exploration and production discussed earlier.

The Queensland and Victorian Acts also resolve the ownership issue and establish a legal management regime for the resource, but fail to deal with environmental issues, except (in Queensland) in the case of environmental damage caused by decommissioning.[18] The Victorian Act expands on the legal management regime in respect of the resource by adding provisions on unit development, which do not exist elsewhere in Australia.

C. Laws in Canada and New Zealand

The only Canadian province where geothermal resources have been discovered is British Columbia, and for this reason, this province is the only jurisdiction with geothermal legislation. The relevant enactment is the Geothermal Resources Act, which was first enacted in 1973 and predates all the Australian state legislation.[19] It has been amended several times since its inception.

The resource ownership issue is expressly covered by the definition of 'geothermal resource' in section 1(1):

> ... the natural heat of the earth and all substances that derive and added value from it, including steam, water and water vapour heated by the natural heat of the earth and all substances dissolved in the steam, water or water vapour obtained from a well, but does not include (a) water that has a temperature less than 80°C at the point where it reaches the surface...

This definition is more comprehensive than many of the Australian enactments as it would include all types of geothermal energy, including HDR. However, it is limited in scope by the reference to a minimum water temperature of 80°C. The original 1973 legislation imposed a minimum requirement of 120°C, which excluded all hot groundwater. While the later amendment to 80°C is an improvement in the coverage of the legislation, the Act has not changed to keep pace with technological and engineering developments, which now allow geothermal hot water to be commercially exploited at much lower temperatures.

The British Columbia legislation includes a comprehensive legal management regime for the exploration and development of the resource, modelled largely on the province's petroleum legislation. There is a separate section (section 17) establishing a royalty payment wherever geothermal energy production (other than testing occurs), and there are provisions (in sections 18–19) allowing the relevant Minister to make a unitization order for the unitized operation of part or all of a field.

Comprehensive environmental controls affecting the exploitation of geothermal energy are contained in the legislation. Interestingly, these controls extend to the

[18] Geothermal Energy Act 2010 (Qld), ss 200–202.

[19] For a detailed discussion of the British Columbia legislation, see S. Martin, 'The Geothermal Resources Act: A Case Study in Resource Management' (1985) 19 UBC L Rev 1.

requirement for the operator to practice energy conservation. This requirement is included in section 4(1), which prohibits the production of geothermal energy unless the operator does so in accordance with a plan submitted to and approved by the Minister. The plan must specifically include a consideration of energy conservation. This requirement goes beyond any of the Australian enactments.

Unlike the Australian legislation, the environmental issues associated with geothermal energy exploitation are dealt with in the regulations made under the Act rather than in the Act itself. There are two relevant sections in the Act. Section 23 authorizes the Minister to make regulations of general application or an order related to a specific location or well, governing a range of matters of environmental concern. These are primarily concerned with preventing blowouts and water pollution. Section 24 authorizes the Lieutenant Governor in Council to make further regulations concerning the whole geothermal operating process. The specified powers accorded to the Minister and the Lieutenant Governor in Council are itemized in the respective sections. It is unclear why there are two separate regulation-making powers. The only environmental issue that is not directly covered by the Act is the issue of abandonment of wells. Presumably, however, the Minister may insist that the plan required to be submitted prior to production approval contain adequate provision in relation to the later abandonment.

New Zealand has taken a unique approach to regulating geothermal energy development. Although being one of the earliest common law jurisdictions to legislate on this matter, in the Geothermal Energy Act 1953,[20] this legislation was repealed in its entirety in 1991 and not replaced by any specific geothermal legislation. Instead, geothermal development was placed under the operation of the Resources Management Act 1991, a comprehensive enactment designed to deregulate and abolish national planning controls and regulate all resource development activities. The government of the time desired to amalgamate and coordinate development in all sectors and it was apparently concerned that there was insufficient reason to exclude geothermal energy from this overall reform.[21]

By section 354 of the 1991 Act, Crown rights over geothermal energy under the 1953 Act have been expressly preserved. The 1953 Act gave the Crown 'the sole right to tap, take, use and apply geothermal energy' (section 3(1)).[22] Thus, while avoiding the use of the word 'ownership', as a practical matter, geothermal energy development is under Crown control. Significantly, however, the Resource Management Act treats geothermal resources as a water resource. The effect of this is that the control and management of geothermal resources are vested in regional councils by virtue of the Water and Soil Conservation Act 1967, which

[20] The earlier Geothermal Steam Act 1952 was repealed and replaced by the 1953 legislation on the basis that the earlier Act was not sufficiently comprehensive. The 1952 Act only vested ownership of geothermal steam 'for the purposes of generating electricity' in the Crown.

[21] See R. Boast, 'Geothermal Resources in New Zealand: A Legal History' (1995) 6 Canterbury L Rev 1.

[22] Section 354(2) defines 'geothermal water' as 'water heated within the earth by natural phenomena to a temperature of 30 degrees Celsius or more; and includes all steam, water, and water vapour, and every mixture of all or any of them that has been heated by natural phenomena'.

nationalized all water rights and vested control in regional water bodies. The New Zealand Court of Appeal affirmed in *Keam v Minister of Works and Development*[23] that geothermal development applicants required two separate approvals: a licence under the Geothermal Energy Act 1953 and a water right under the 1967 Act from the regional water board.

The 1991 Act also contains the environmental controls and developmental processes of geothermal resources. Again, both are effectively regulated by regional councils. The main environmental controls are contained in section 30, which grants to regional councils 'the control of the taking and use of geothermal energy' and 'the control of discharges of contaminants into or onto land, air, or water and discharges of water into air'.[24] As for development controls, the distinguishing feature of the New Zealand legislation is that the regional councils are obliged to take account of the Treaty of Waitangi, as well as Maori rights and concerns. For example, sections 61(2) and 66(2) require regional councils to have regard to Maori planning documents. In addition, councils are obliged to consider the desirability of preparing a regional plan where there is evidence of Maori cultural heritage being affected by proposed development, including geothermal development.

The vesting and control of geothermal management and development by regional councils thus markedly distinguishes New Zealand law from that enacted in Australia and Canada.

III. New European responses to developing geothermal energy

A. European Union

1. Introduction

Traditionally, the laws of the world have been grouped into different legal families and the most common in the Western world has been the division between common law and civil law systems. Classifications may serve a good purpose when you compare different legal regimes, but they are also subject to criticism. Under all circumstances it is important to emphasize that the boundaries between the legal families have never been sharp and that categorizations are not static and have less influence today than in the past.[25] The world is changing all the time and so is the law. In Europe, a comprehensive europeanization has taken place under the auspices of the supra-national grouping of the European Union that comprises both traditional common law legal systems (e.g., the United Kingdom) and civil law systems (e.g., France).[26]

[23] [1982] 1 NZLR 319. [24] See also ss 14 and 15.

[25] H. P. Glenn in *The Oxford Handbook of Comparative Law* (M. Reimann and R. Zimmermann, eds, 2006) and K. Zweigert and H. Kôtz, *An Introduction to Comparative Law* (3rd edn, 1998).

[26] P. Craig and G. de Búrca, *The Evolution of the EU Law* (2nd edn, 2011) and S. Weatherill, *Cases & Material on EU Law* (9th edn, 2010).

2. *Policy developments*

In Europe, developments are driven by both national and EU policies. 'Greening' energy is at the very forefront of the political agenda and a long list of policy action plans and legal initiatives have been taken at both the regional and national levels. Increasingly, focus is put on the energy systems needed to support development that is more climate-friendly and resource-efficient, while also ensuring competitiveness, energy at fair prices, and a safe and reliable energy supply at all times.

The EU and the case studies of Denmark and Iceland together with reference to other European jurisdictions like Germany and the Netherlands, described in other chapters of this book, provide examples of a region and countries that want to change energy patterns in a more sustainable way and to promote developments in renewable technologies. Geothermal energy is looked upon as one of the renewable alternatives to be further promoted.

In the European Union just 1% of renewable power generation derives from geothermal energy, and geothermal heat in the European Union accounts for no more than 3% of total renewable heat. However, geothermal energy features in the Smart Cities Initiative,[27] with the objective to develop enhanced geothermal systems and to go deeper than 3 km. The volcanic areas (Sicily, Portugal, Greece, Canary Islands) show potential. Moreover, Iceland is involved in bringing geothermal energy to the European Union, together with seven other Member States assessing their potential for geothermal energy production, particularly in Central and Eastern Europe.[28]

As part of its action on climate change, the European Union has agreed that renewable energy will comprise 20% of the European Union's total energy consumption by 2020. In January 2008, the Commission presented a major legislative package on climate and energy. It included proposals for new (later adopted) directives on the promotion of renewables and emissions trading, and new guidelines for state aid. The legislative initiatives also covered harmonization of the allocation of national targets for increased use of renewable energy sources (RES) that later became Directive 2009/28/EC. The Directive is intended to remove unnecessary barriers to the growth of renewable energy—for example, by simplifying the administrative procedures for new renewable energy development.

Another important initiative is the publication of a new energy strategy in 2010, followed by a comprehensive range of other initiatives.[29] This strategy sets out the European Commission's energy strategy to 2020. In addition, 'A Roadmap for

27 <http://setis.ec.europa.eu> under: Set-Plan Implementation>Technology Roadmaps> European Initiative on Smart Cities.

28 <http://www.energylivenews.com/2012/05/31/icelands-volcanoes-could-power-uk-homes>. The EU has provided support for research in new technologies and implementation of pilot projects for a number of years, cf <http://ec.europa.eu/research/energy/eu/research/geothermal/index_en.htm>; <http://ec.europa.eu/research/energy/nn/nn_rt/nn_rt_geo/article_1134_en.htm>; Renewable Energy Technologies, EU Commission (2007) 90–7, available at <ftp://ftp.cordis.europa.eu/pub/fp7/energy/docs/synopses_res_en.pdf>.

29 *Energy 2020—A strategy for competitive, sustainable and secure energy*, COM(2010)639; *Energy Roadmap 2050*, COM(2011)88. *Renewable Energy: a major player in the European energy market*, COM (2012)271.

moving to a competitive low-carbon economy in 2050', the EU Commission's Communication of March 2011, defines pathways to reach the European Union's objective of cutting greenhouse gas emissions by 80–90% of 1990 levels by 2050.

On 6 June 2012, the European Commission presented a Communication on its renewable energy policy outlining options beyond 2020.[30] It confirms the need for the growth of renewables in the decades after 2020. The Communication also calls for a more coordinated European approach in the establishment and reform of support schemes and an increased use of renewable energy trading among Member States. The Council's conclusions stress, *inter alia,* the importance of providing stimulus and certainty to investors. This is partly reflected in the RES Directive, but it also make clear that a long planning process and ensuring economic and environmental stability is essential, together with affordable consumer prices.

The most recent Green Paper that discusses future climate change and energy policy targets for 2030[31] was published on 27 March 2013.[32] It sums up and assesses the effect and aspirations of existing policy documents and legislation in meeting the European Union's climate and energy targets for 2020 against the background of a different economic climate from just a few years ago when the original energy policies were drafted. Although not expressly referring to geothermal energy, the Green Paper does refer to renewable energy in the context of the energy mix. It is highlighted that the 20% RES target is implemented through policy instruments at the EU level within the framework of an internal competitive market, as well as at the Member States' level where different national approaches, support schemes, and energy and CO_2 taxation exist. The Green Paper raises a set of highly relevant questions, including how coherence between different policy instruments can be attained, and how the different capacities of Member States to take action can be taken into account. It is beyond doubt that the Commission has increased its focus on the promotion of renewables and achieving improved RES operation by establishing RES clusters using different technologies, including geothermal, to support other volatile sources like wind and solar. At the same time, however, focus is increasingly put on the existing differences between Member States in terms of financial supporting schemes. It seems quite clear that the issue of harmonization is gaining more and more attention.

3. *Ownership and access to the resources*

The Treaty on the Functioning of the European Union (TFEU)[33] (EU Treaty as amended by the Lisbon Treaty, 1 December 2009), confirms the increasing

[30] COM(2012)271.

[31] GREEN PAPER, *A 2030 framework for climate and energy policies* COM(2013) 169, available at <http://www.eur-lex.europa.eu/LexUriServ/LexUriServ.do?uri=CELEX:52013DC0169:EN:NOT>.

[32] The consultation period ran out on 2 July 2013 and the concluding report is soon to follow: <http://www.ec.europa.eu/energy/consultations/20130702_green_paper_2030_en.htm> <http://www.ec.europa.eu/clima/policies/2030/documentation_en.htm; <http://www.europa.eu/rapid/press-release_IP-13-272_en.htm>; <http://www.europa.eu/rapid/press-release_MEMO-13-275_en.htm>.

[33] Treaty on the Functioning of the European Union [2008] OJ C115/47.

priority of the energy sector by including a special title devoted to energy (XXI). Member States are required to coordinate among themselves the policies pursued at the national level. TFEU Article 194 includes the objectives of the EU energy policy: 'In the context of the establishment and functioning of the internal market and with regard for the need to preserve and improve the environment, Union policy on energy shall aim, in a spirit of solidarity between Member States, to' develop new and renewable forms of energy, among other aims. It adds that 'Such measures shall not affect a Member State's right to determine the conditions for exploiting its energy resources, its choice between different energy sources and the general structure of its energy supply.' The Member States' sovereignty over primary energy sources is also confirmed by Directive 94/22/EC on the conditions for granting and using authorizations for the prospecting, exploration, and production of hydrocarbons.[34]

However, Community rules emphasize the need for sustainable development and for promoting measures at the international level to deal with regional and global environmental problems and, in particular, combating climate change.[35] TFEU also includes authority to adopt measures significantly affecting a Member State's choice between different energy sources and the general structure of its energy supply if the Council is acting unanimously in accordance with a special legislative procedure and after consultation.[36]

4. *Legal management regime*

(a) The Renewables Directive

As indicated earlier, Directive 2009/28 is the main directive driving the development of renewables.[37] Energy from renewable sources is defined in Art 2(a), and 'means energy from renewable non-fossil sources, namely wind, solar, aerothermal, geothermal, hydrothermal . . . '. More specifically, geothermal energy 'means energy stored in the form of heat beneath the surface of solid earth' (Art 2(c)). The definition of geothermal resources is thus very comprehensive.

The scope of the Directive is to establish a common framework for the promotion of energy from renewable sources (Art 1). Mandatory national targets are set for the overall share of energy from RES in gross final consumption of energy. In this connection, Member States are required to establish a national renewable energy action plan,[38] and should encourage local and regional authorities to set targets in excess of national targets, and involve local and regional authorities in drawing up plans and in raising awareness of the benefits of energy from RES.[39]

Member States are required to remove administrative barriers and to ensure that any national rules concerning the authorization, certification, and licensing procedures are proportionate and necessary (Art 13.1). Moreover, these procedures

[34] See Preamble to Directive 94/22/EC of 30 May 1994.

[35] Arts 11 and 191.

[36] Art 192(2)(c).

[37] Directive 2009/28/EC of 23 April 2009 on the promotion of the use of energy from renewable sources and amending and subsequently repealing Directives 2001/77/EC and 2003/30/EC.

[38] Recital 19 and Art 4.

[39] Recital 23.

should be coordinated and streamlined with transparent timetables, and any information on these issues should be properly published. It is also emphasized that rules must be 'objective, transparent, proportionate, do not discriminate between applicants and take fully into account the particularities of individual renewable energy technologies' (Art 13.1(d)). This is a sensible approach, as the different RES have varying environmental impacts.

(b) Hydrocarbon licensing and the procurement directives

There are other directives that deal with licensing and contracting in the energy sector and therefore may be relevant to the legislation applicable to development of geothermal resources.

It follows from the title of Directive 94/22/EC on the conditions for granting and using authorizations for the prospection, exploration, and production of hydrocarbons that it is only applicable to oil and gas resources and not to geothermal energy.

Directive 2004/17 (as amended) regulates the contracting by entities operating in the water, energy, transport, and postal services sectors and complements the hydrocarbon licensing directive in the energy sector. It applies to public procurement contracts for supplies, services, or works which are not expressly excluded by the Directive. The purpose of the Directive is to ensure open competition in the contracting process and a fair balance in applying the rules for granting contracts in the mentioned sectors due to the variety of ways in which national authorities can influence the behaviour of the entities in these special sectors, and the closed nature of the markets in which they operate.

The activities that the Directive applies to are set out in Articles 3 to 7. Specifically regarding heat and gas, the Directive applies to: 'The provision or operation of fixed networks intended to provide a service to the public in connection with the production, transport or distribution of gas or heat; or the supply of gas or heat to such networks' (Art 3(1)). Annex 1 includes a list of entities providing transport and distribution of heat and gas, and it is only directed to the so-called 'down stream activities' and not to the exploitation of the natural resources as such. Pursuant to Art 7(a): 'This Directive shall apply to activities relating to the exploitation of a geographical area for the purpose of exploring for or extracting oil, gas, coal or other solid fuels.' Geothermal energy is not mentioned in this connection. Under all circumstances, contracts awarded are no longer subject to the Directive if effective competition exists. The scope of the Directive also excludes works and service concessions in the sectors of activity concerned and service contracts awarded on the basis of an exclusive right in the field of the exploration or extraction of oil, gas, coal, and other solid fuels (Arts 18 and 25).

Even when the activities connected to extraction of geothermal energy are not covered by the legislation mentioned, contracting authorities from Member States would still have to comply with the internal market rules of the TFEU when granting a licence.[40]

[40] *Commission Interpretative Communication on the law applicable to contract awards not or not fully subject to the provisions of the Public Procurement Directives*, 23 June 2006, 2, available at <http://www.

5. *Environmental protection*

Plans, programmes, and projects likely to have significant effects on the environment are subject to an environmental assessment prior to their approval or authorization. Environmental Impact Assessments (EIA) for individual projects can be undertaken on the basis of the codified Directive 2011/92/EU (EIA Directive)[41] and for public plans or programmes ('Strategic Environmental Assessment' (SEA)) on the basis of Directive 2001/42/EC (SEA Directive). Consultation with the public is a key feature of environmental assessment procedures.

The EIA Directive has been in force since 1985 and applies to a wide range of public and private projects, which are defined in Annexes I and II. Whereas all projects listed in Annex I are considered as having significant effects on the environment and require an EIA, national authorities have to decide whether an EIA is needed for projects listed in Annex II. This decision is made via a screening procedure, which determines the effects of projects on the basis of thresholds/criteria or a case-by-case examination (Art 4(2)).

With respect to exploration and production of geothermal energy, Annex II includes the extraction industry, and under 2(d): 'deep drillings, in particular: . . . geothermal drilling'. Moreover, the specific section related to the energy industry (section 3) includes industrial installations for the production of electricity, steam, and hot water (projects not included in Annex I) and 'industrial installations for carrying . . . hot water'. An EIA is thus not mandatory for the exploitation of geothermal energy but is left to the decision of the individual Member States.

B. Legislation in Denmark, Germany, the Netherlands, and Iceland

1. *Introduction and new policy framework*

The following discussion is designed to focus on different jurisdictions and the relevant legislation to the governance of exploitation of geothermal energy. Denmark will provide the starting point for the analysis, but Germany and the Netherlands, discussed in other chapters of this book, will be referred to when relevant. Iceland is not a Member State of the EU, although it is associated via the Economic Association Agreement, but it is also discussed here due to the vast geothermal resources found in its jurisdiction.

Compared to, for example, Germany,[42] Denmark[43] has had a favourable approach to the development of geothermal resources and has been focusing on

ec.europa.eu/internal_market/publicprocurement/docs/keydocs/communication_en.pdf>. An action for annulment of the Communication was dismissed as inadmissible, 20 May 2010, available at <http://www.eur-lex.europa.eu/LexUriServ/LexUriServ.do?uri=CELEX:62006TJ0258:EN:HTML>.

41 The EIA Directive 85/337/EEC of 1985 has been amended three times: in 1997, in 2003, and in 2009.

42 See chapter 20.

43 Danish Energy Agency <http://www.ens.dk>, *Oil and Gas Production in Denmark 2011* (May 2012) 15–16; <http://www.ec.europa.eu/research/index.cfm> under: Themes>Energy>Energy

the opportunities this might provide for energy security and carbon dioxide reduction. Activities were initiated in the early 1980s, much earlier than in several other Member States, by the state-owned company DONG Energy. The public has not really raised its voice in protest despite the use of the fracking technique (which has also been used for oil and gas offshore). There has been much more controversy in relation to the potential exploitation of shale gas.

A geothermal plant emits no direct emissions to the environment—no CO_2, NOx, SOx, particulates, heavy metals, etc. Overall emissions can be greatly reduced by replacing district heating based on coal and natural gas with geothermal heating. However, pumps driven by electricity are required in order for the water to circulate in the system, and this does lead to some greenhouse gas emissions.

Reports and investigations confirm that substantial quantities of geothermal energy are present throughout much of the Danish subsoil, even though no volcanic activities are present in this region. In Denmark, the temperature in the subsoil layers typically increases by 25 to 30°C for every 1,000 metres of depth. Below a depth of around 800 m, the formation water is hot enough for the purpose of district heating. With depth, however, the sandstone layers become less porous and permeable, so although the water contained in the layers becomes hotter with depth, there is a maximum depth at which it ceases to be cost-effective to extract geothermal heat. Danish experience has shown that this limit is normally around a depth of 2,500 m.[44]

It is anticipated that in the future, geothermal energy could play a role as a heat source in many existing district heating grids in Denmark. Reports of the Danish Energy Agency (DEA) state that there is potential to establish geothermal energy production in 32 existing district heating grids, with a heat supply of more than 400 TJ/year. More detailed analyses are, however, necessary in order to determine whether it would be attractive to establish geothermal energy production at a given location.[45]

2. *Ownership and access to the resources*

As early as 1932 it was established in Denmark's first Subsoil Act that natural resources in the Danish subsoil belong to the State of Denmark. At this time, the Act only included the land and territorial sea, but in 1963, sovereignty was claimed over the Danish continental shelf area as well. The Subsoil Act of 1932 did not include all the natural resources of the subsoil, but limited its scope to the resources

Research>Research>Other renewable energies>Geothermal; Danish District Heating Association <http://www.dff.dk>; Dansk Fjernvarmes Geotermiselskab <http://www.geotermi.dk>; A. Mahler and J. Magtengaard, *Country Update Report for Denmark, Geothermal reserves and sustainability in the Greater Copenhagen Area,* Proceedings World Geothermal Congress 2010, available at <http://www.geotermi.dk/getfile.php?objectid=43778> and <http://www.geotermi.dk/getfile.php?objectid=49601>.

44 <http://www.ens.dk>.

45 The Danish Energy Agency has published two reports, *Geothermal Energy—heat from the interior of the Earth, status and possibilities in Denmark* (Oct 2009) and *Geothermal Energy—heat from the interior of the Earth, international experience, financial issues and the challenges of geothermal heat production in Denmark* (May 2010).

that had not been produced commercially before 23 February 1932 (to avoid disputes on expropriation), on which date the law came into force. The ownership of geothermal resources is thus clearly determined.

The Subsoil Act was entirely revised by the adoption of a new Act in 1981,[46] which constituted an important part of Denmark's energy goals expediting self-sufficiency in energy by increasing the exploration for and production of oil and natural gas from the Danish subsoil. Starting in 1983, it also provided a simple licensing system for the development of geothermal energy. A substantial, detailed amendment with new chapters was implemented in 2011 to allow new uses of the underground for carbon capture and storage and to focus the regulation on exploitation of geothermal energy more specifically. Simultaneously, the Subsoil Act was amended to allow prioritization of different activities. In many ways the detailed regulation of geothermal energy has approached the regulation of exploitation of conventional oil and gas, but in a less burdensome form.

However, while a specific legal regime in Denmark has been adopted for exploitation of geothermal energy, the rules that govern exploration and production of oil or gas in Germany are also applicable to geothermal resources.[47] The new Dutch Mining Act of 2003 vests the ownership of subsoil minerals in the state and includes geothermal energy under that legislation.[48] The Mining Act, however, only applies to geothermal heat located below 500 m. Also, in Germany geothermal energy has been incorporated into the Mining Code since 1980. Geothermal energy is deemed a free mineral and is thereby excluded from the surface owner's property.[49] However, it should be noted that the Mining Code is only applicable to resources that are located more than 100 m below the surface, whereas the near-surface resources still belong to the owner of the land. Opposed to the Dutch and German legal regimes, the Danish Subsoil Act does not distinguish between the depths where geothermal energy is found in the subsoil. All resources belong to the state regardless of depth.

In Iceland, the issue of ownership is regulated somewhat differently. Ownership of subsoil resources is based on the ownership of land.[50] Thus, it is only public land resources that are the property of the State of Iceland. According to the Act on the Survey and Utilization of Ground Resources the definition of the term 'resource' applies to any element or energy that can be extracted from the earth, whether in solid, liquid, or gaseous form, regardless of the temperature at which they may be found and is thus inclusive of all forms of geothermal resources (Art 1 and 3).[51] The

[46] In order to implement the EC Hydrocarbon Licensing Directive (94/22), it was necessary in 1995 to amend the Subsoil Act substantially.

[47] See chapter 20. [48] See chapter 19.

[49] See chapter 20.

[50] See J. Ketilsson, L. Olafsson, G. Steinsdottir, and G. A. Johannesson, *Legal Framework and National Policy for Geothermal Development in Iceland*, 3, Proceedings World Geothermal Congress 2010, Bali, Indonesia.

[51] Act on Survey and Utilization of Ground Resources, No 57, 10 June 1998 as amended in 2006, available at <http://eng.atvinnuvegaraduneyti.is/laws-and-regulations>. Geothermal energy is defined as 'on the one hand, reserves of energy in the bedrock, and, on the other hand, a constant flow of heat from the bowels of the earth which does not constitute groundwater' (Art 2).

Act explicitly excludes geothermal energy from being considered as a mineral or groundwater. Major amendments have recently been made to ensure that the water and geothermal resources that are in state and municipalities' ownership stay that way, and can no longer be sold. According to the Act, the Minister of Industry is permitted to take the initiative or issue a licence to others on exploration for and subsequent production of resources anywhere in the country. Private landowners are only allowed to initiate activities if a licence has not previously been issued to others. When a licence is issued for private land, the landowner is obliged to allow unobstructed access to the land. Accordingly, although the ownership of resources follows the land, the State of Iceland is still in control of the utilization of the resource.

3. *Legal management regime*

The Danish, German, Dutch, and Icelandic legal management systems are based on a licensing regime.[52] Whereas the Dutch and German licence conditions basically follow the system applicable to oil and gas in their respective countries. Denmark recently adopted a new framework for geothermal energy projects. On the one hand, this has implied new rules in the Subsoil Act and model forms that to some extent resemble those applicable to oil and gas. On the other hand, these new rules are far from being equally restrictive and detailed.

In Denmark exploration for, and production of, geothermal energy requires a licence pursuant to the provisions of the Subsoil Act.[53] This Act merely lays down the framework within which operations under a licence are to be carried out. For geothermal activities up until the Act was amended in 2011, it was the general licence requirement set out in Article 5 that applied, with some limited specific terms included in the issued licence.

A number of licences have been awarded based on this (older) regime, and geothermal energy is produced at a few geothermal plants.[54] In 1983, DONG Energy was awarded an exclusive licence to explore for and extract geothermal energy. This licence expired in 2013 and originally covered the entire Danish onshore area. Parts of the licence were relinquished in 1993 and in 2003. As from 30 September 2010, DONG Energy also relinquished the major part of the unused areas under the licence. The relinquished area has been the subject of a general invitation to submit applications by others.

With the increasing interest in developing geothermal energy and making the application procedures and criteria public, and thus more transparent, as mentioned, in 2010 the Subsoil Act was amended to include a specific Part 4a on 'Special Provisions Regarding Exploration for and Production of Geothermal

[52] See chapters 19 and 20 and the Act on Survey and Utilization of Ground Resources (n 51) Chapter III and IV.

[53] No 541 of 30/05/2011, cf Consolidated Act No 960 of 13/09/2011.

[54] Danish Energy Agency's Annual reports, *Denmark's oil and gas production—and subsoil use*, in which geothermal heat production has been a topic since 2008.

Energy'. Accordingly, licences must be granted subsequent to an open bidding procedure based on published selection criteria (Art 18a and b). The terms are published in advance by the Ministry of Climate, Energy and Buildings in the form of a 'Model Licence for Exploration for and Production of Geothermal Energy'. In addition, a general Invitation Letter to the public has been developed, outlining the main criteria for obtaining a licence to explore for and produce geothermal energy for district heating production. Applications for new licences could be submitted for the first time on 1 December 2010. Subsequent applications for new licences can be submitted twice a year, on 1 February and 1 September.

A licensee is granted one single licence covering both exploration and production of geothermal energy. The licence is not split into two, as in the Netherlands.[55] However, it is still a phased approach, since there is an important division between exploration and production activities. Following the exploration period of up to six years (Art 18c), the licensee is entitled to a prolongation of the licence for a production period of no more than 30 years. The area will, however, be delimited and only cover the part from which production of geothermal energy will take place. As a condition for extending the licence, the Minister may require that an application for approval of a plan for the production activities pursuant to Art 10 must be submitted within a specific time limit. When approving the plan, the date of start of production will be determined (Art 18d). The DEA has published a set of Guidelines concerning the development plan for exploitation.

In principle, the licence grants an exclusive right to explore for and produce geothermal energy within the relevant area. However, this exclusive right is limited in certain respects as other parties may obtain a licence relating to the same area for other activities such as exploration for other natural resources, storage, or pipeline construction (Model Licence Art 3). If the activities cannot take place at the same time, it is up to DEA to prioritize.

In Iceland, exploration and exploitation of geothermal resources is subject to a licence from the Minister of Industry pursuant to the Act on Survey and Utilization of Ground Resources (Resources Act), as well as the Electricity Act.[56] A landowner does not have priority to an utilization licence for resources in the land unless such owner has previously been issued an exploration licence (Resources Act, Art 6). Before a licensee begins extraction on private land it is necessary to reach an agreement with the landowner on compensation for the resource or obtain permission for expropriation. In the event that neither an agreement on compensation nor expropriation take place within 60 days, the licence shall be cancelled (Art 7). The Minister has power to expropriate resources, and necessary land for the extraction necessary for the licence to be of use (Art 29).

[55] See chapter 19.

[56] See Ketilsson et al (n 50), I.G. Haraldsson, *Legal And Regulatory Framework–Barrier Or Motivation For Geothermal Development?*, Short Course on Geothermal Development and Geothermal Well, 2012, available at <http://www.os.is> and the Electricity Act No 65 of 15 March 2003, Chapter II.

4. *Environmental protection*

The Danish Model Licence requires the licensee to perform the operations in such a way that the activities do not cause risk to persons or the possession of others due to pollution or other damaging impact on the environment (Art 8). All installations must be safely constructed and maintained properly to prevent leakage, cable breakage, and the like. Moreover, the licensee must be insured against liability (Art 8), and the DEA has drafted an Operator's Insurance Declaration form to ensure a proper level of insurance. Under the Subsoil Act (Art 35), liability is strict and unlimited and includes personal injury and injury to property. This Act also determines that a licence shall include detailed rules concerning steps to be taken in regard to the licensee's installations when the licence terminates, together with the handling of installations which have fulfilled their purpose.[57]

A licence pursuant to the Subsoil Act does not free the licensee from obtaining licences and permits under other acts (the Model Licence Art 21). Thus the activities connected to geothermal energy production and supply also fall under the regulation of the Heat Supply Act and several environmental protection acts like the Planning Act[58] and the Environmental Protection Act.[59]

The Danish EIA rules for land-based activities in the Planning Act are detailed in an Executive Order on Environmental Assessment of Certain Public and Private Projects[60] and are applicable to mandatory Annex I projects and Annex II projects that, on the basis of an individual screening, require a full EIA. All Annex I and Annex II projects must be reported to the municipal council concerned (Art 2). Geothermal drilling activities are included under Annex II and are thus subject first to a screening procedure. The criteria for the evaluation of whether a full EIA is required are included in Annex 3 and match the EU EIA Directive. The decision on screening must be published (Art 5), but there is no requirement to involve the public in the screening process as such. The publication must, however, include information about where and how relevant informative material about the project may be obtained (Art 6). If an EIA is required, an assessment must be carried out and municipal planning guidelines for the project must be adopted. The responsibility to receive sufficient information rests with the municipality, but the developer is required to submit it.

In Germany, a full EIA must always be implemented if the drilling depth is more than 1,000 m.[61] In Iceland, development of geothermal resources is subject to comprehensive environmental legislation, including the Nature Protection Act No 44/1999. In an appendix to the utilization licence, there is a stipulation for what

[57] The Model Licence provides additional details in Art 19.

[58] Consolidated Act No 937 of 24/09/2009 as amended, available at <http://www.retsinformation.dk/Forms/R0710.aspx?id=127131>.

[59] Consolidated Act No 879 of 26/06/2010 as amended, available at <http://www.retsinformation.dk/Forms/R0710.aspx?id=132218>.

[60] Cf Art 11g and Executive Order No 744 of 28/06/2012, available at <http://www.retsinformation.dk/forms/R0710.aspx?id=134469>.

[61] See chapter 20.

detailed information the licensee should provide to the public authorities in order to monitor the resource and the environmental impact of the activities.[62] An important pillar in this connection is the Act on Environmental Impact Assessment, which also applies to geothermal activities.[63] Accordingly, geothermal power stations with a heat output of 50 MW or more and power installations with an electricity output of 10 MW or more are always subject to an EIA.

IV. Conclusion

Looking at the legal situation in all the countries covered, it is clear from the discussion that legislation is required to manage the exploration and development of geothermal energy. Without such legislation, there are three areas of legal uncertainty: (a) whether ownership of the resource is vested in the state or the surface landowner; (b) what legal management regime applies to the exploitation of the resource; and (c) what environmental controls are applicable.

In the common law countries the ownership issue would be determined by the application of the *cujus est solum* doctrine and the question of whether geothermal energy is classified as a 'mineral', a 'gas', or as 'groundwater'. The *cujus est solum* doctrine was developed in the fourteenth century and was never designed as a rule to determine resource ownership in the modern era.[64] As for the appropriate legal management regime, the legislation on minerals, oil, and gas, and groundwater was also never designed with the issue of geothermal energy in mind. None of these fit comfortably if they are to apply to geothermal energy. In relation to environmental controls, the exploitation of geothermal energy raises special environmental concerns. While many of these could be controlled satisfactorily by general environmental legislation, this will depend on the terms of such legislation, which differ among jurisdictions. It is clear that some of the environmental concerns would not be within the terms of such legislation.

In New Zealand, and in those states and provinces in Australia and Canada where geothermal energy exists in commercial quantities, the legislatures have all, rightly, concluded that common law rules in this area should be replaced by legislation. They have not agreed, however, on the appropriate form of that legislation, which differs widely among the jurisdictions. In relation to the ownership issue, there is general consensus that there should be state ownership of the resource, but no agreement as to the legislative means of achieving this goal. As seen earlier, 'geothermal resource' or 'geothermal substance' is defined by reference to the temperature of the substance when it reaches the surface, but this temperature is variously specified as low as 40°C and as high as 100°C. This difference results in a very significant difference between the jurisdictions as to the scope of application of the legislation. A specified temperature of 100°C excludes the application of the

62 See chapter 20.

63 Act No 106 of 25/5 2000, available at <http://eng.umhverfisraduneyti.is/legislation>. See Annex 1, 2.

64 *Bury v Pope* (1586) Cro Eliz 118; 78 ER 375.

legislation to geothermal steam and all hot groundwater. The exact wording of the definition of the resource would also determine whether the HDR resource would be covered. In relation to the appropriate legal management regime, while some jurisdictions have enacted special legislation designed specifically for the geothermal industry, many jurisdictions leave the matter to be determined by rules designed for minerals, oil and gas, or groundwater exploitation. A similar situation exists in relation to the environmental controls. While some jurisdictions have enacted special controls for all or some of the environmental issues flowing from geothermal energy exploitation, the majority have opted to leave environmental disputes to be resolved under the environmental rules of general application.

A special mention in this regard must be made of New Zealand. As discussed earlier, unlike the Australian states and the Canadian provinces, rather than introducing new legislation governing the resource, the New Zealand parliament repealed nearly all the provisions of the Geothermal Energy Act 1953 and left the legal issues to be resolved by the application of the Resource Management Act 1991, an enactment of general application. The only exception was the resource ownership issue, which is resolved in favour of the state by virtue of section 354 of the 1953 Act, which was not repealed.

Looking at the issue in non-common law countries in Europe, recent legislative amendments or even totally new legislation as in Denmark, Germany, and the Netherlands have been adopted to reflect the increasing public interest in the further developments of geothermal resources in a transparent, resource-efficient and environmentally safe way. The decarbonization of the energy sector has been an important driver in this connection. The European Union, Denmark, Germany, and other major world economies are investing heavily in clean technologies, with major consequences to legal and regulatory frameworks.

The definition of what should be considered geothermal energy differs among the four European countries. The delimitation to various depths as implemented by Germany and the Netherlands seems to lack a proper basis given the constant development of the technology. It seems more appropriate to include all sources, as adopted by Denmark and Iceland, to ensure a proper management regime for the exploitation of geothermal resources.

With respect to ownership of the resources, Iceland is closer to the common law approach where the ownership of the resources follows ownership of the land. In Denmark, Germany, and the Netherlands it has been legislated that the ownership of geothermal resources is vested in the state. The difference, however, may seem bigger in formal terms than when it comes to real terms. Due to the implementation of a comprehensive licensing system and a detailed management system, the exploration and exploitation of geothermal resources in all the surveyed countries are under close control by the state. We do not consider it to be of much importance whether the exploration and production activities are under one common licence as in Denmark or split into two separate ones as in the Netherlands but combined with rights to exploit when a discovery is made. In all cases, the result is the application of a phased approach where moving into the production phase requires public approval and state intervention. It should also be noted that the energy licences are supplemented by the requirement to obtain environmental permits.

Environmental impact assessment procedures have been implemented so that all projects are considered as to their influence and consequences to the environment. It is actually a requirement that flows from EU legislation, although with some national autonomy on whether a full EIA is required for all activities or whether it can be based on an initial screening assessment.

Opinions may differ as to the most appropriate form of new geothermal legislation. Our surveys show that the difference is not connected to whether a country may be characterized as a common law country or not. The goal is surely to promote the sustainable development of the resource, to encourage responsible investment, and to protect the environment.[65] In our opinion, these goals are most satisfactorily achieved by the type of comprehensive geothermal legislation now in effect in Queensland, Victoria, and the Northern Territory (Australia), in British Columbia (Canada), and in Denmark. The very best appears to be that in the Northern Territory and Denmark. These jurisdictions have the most recently enacted legislation and were able to learn from the earlier legislative experiences in the other jurisdictions by ensuring that all possible contentious issues are covered by the new laws. It is submitted that the New Zealand legislation is a retrograde step. While it appears to take account of Maori rights and concerns, these have no relevance to other countries. Moreover, energy policy is of national concern and one in which the regional councils would normally have no role to play.

[65] See section I.B.

17

Siting Nuclear Waste Repositories

Donald N. Zillman

I. Introduction

This chapter examines the use of underground repositories for the permanent disposal of high-level nuclear waste and spent nuclear fuel. While spent nuclear fuel may be reprocessed profitably, for brevity we often use 'waste' to describe both terms. A significant portion of that waste comes from spent fuel currently stored at nuclear electric-generating plants around the world. Sixty years since the start of the age of commercial nuclear electric power, no permanent repository for this waste is yet operating. A primary reason for this has been the difficulty of securing public consent for the siting of such repositories. Siting decisions have become a crucial element in deciding the future or not of the major energy source that is nuclear power.

The harnessing of nuclear fission, primarily for the generation of electricity, is the newest of the major energy sources. Nuclear fission first gained prominence for its role as a weapon of war that ended the Second World War with the bombings of Hiroshima and Nagasaki, and then it shaped 40 years of the Cold War.

In the 1950s, nuclear fission became a source for the production of enormous amounts of peaceful energy for a small investment of refined uranium. Atoms for Peace were promoted, or over-promoted, as the source of bountiful and inexpensive energy for the entire world. While a small portion of non-weapons nuclear energy was dedicated to transportation uses in the nuclear navies of the major military powers, the overwhelming use of the peaceful atom was to provide the fuel to operate electric-generating plants. The nuclear fuel served the same end use as the combustion of coal, natural gas, and petroleum, the use of the power of falling water, and other renewable energies.

Nuclear energy provides 13.5% of total electric generation worldwide. Nuclear energy today produces as much electricity as was produced from all sources of energy in 1960.[1] As of January 2013, 31 countries operated 437 nuclear reactors with a net capacity of 372 GW. Another 68 reactors in 15 countries are under

[1] Available at <http://www.world-nuclear.org/info/Current-and-Future-Generation/Nuclear-Power-in-the-World-Today/#.Uel erhylkb8>. See generally, the World Nuclear Association's Information Library, available at <http://www.world-nuclear.org/Information-Library/>.

construction. In the transportation realm, 180 nuclear reactors power about 150 ships and submarines, primarily in the major navies of the world.[2]

According to the 2012 Key Energy Statistics of the International Energy Agency (IEA), three countries—the United States, France, and Japan—produced about 60% of the world's total nuclear electricity. The United States was the largest producer of nuclear energy, produced from 101 nuclear reactors. France, Japan, the Russian Federation, Germany, South Korea, Ukraine, Canada, the United Kingdom, and Sweden followed in that order. France led the world, with about 75% of its total electricity coming from the nuclear process. It is also the largest exporter of nuclear electricity. Half a dozen other countries produced about half of their electricity through the nuclear process. Japan, Germany, the United States, the Russian Federation, the United Kingdom, and Canada produced between 14 and 30% of their total electric generation from nuclear reactors.

The Executive Summary of the IEA's World Energy Outlook 2012[3] commented on the uncertain future of nuclear power: 'The anticipated role of nuclear power has been scaled back as countries have reviewed policies in the wake of the 2011 accident at the [Japanese] Fukushima Daiichi nuclear power station. Japan and France have recently joined the countries with intentions to reduce their use of nuclear power, while its competitiveness in the United States and Canada is being challenged by relatively cheap natural gas.' However, total nuclear electric output is expected to increase because of production increases in China, India, South Korea, and Russia.

Underground activity plays an important role in nuclear energy.[4] The nuclear fuel cycle begins with the underground mining of uranium. That raw uranium is then processed in a number of steps to produce fissile fuel that can be used as the fuel for a reactor to provide electric generation. Eventually, the nuclear fuel in a reactor reaches a point where it 'is no longer efficient in creating electricity, because its fission process has slowed'.[5]

The various by-products of the nuclear fuel cycle (mining, milling, fuel fabrication, nuclear electric generation) pose health and safety risks to nuclear workers and to the surrounding population.[6] Among the pertinent factors in assessing the risks of nuclear waste are: (1) its immediate radioactive harm to humans; (2) the period for which that risk will continue; (3) the presence of fissile actinides, which are substances that can pose national security risks in the wrong hands; and (4) the continued presence of heat in the waste.

[2] See Nuclear Power in the World Today (n 1).

[3] Available at <http://www.iea.org/publications/freepublications/publication/English.pdf>. See generally, the International Energy Agency's 'World Energy Outlook', available at <http://www.worldenergyoutlook.org>.

[4] The United States Energy Information Administration (EIA) provides good descriptions of the various aspects of the nuclear fuel cycle for the lay reader, available at <http://www.eia.gov/energyexplained/index.cfm?page=nuclear_home>. See generally, the EIA's 'Energy Explained', available at <http://www.eia.gov/energyexplained/>.

[5] See <http://www.nrc.gov/waste/high-level-waste.html>.

[6] See <http://www.eia.gov/energyexplained/index.cfm?page=nuclear_environment>.

Addressing a European audience in 2004, Mohamed ElBaradei, then International Atomic Energy Agency (IAEA) Director General observed: 'The greatest challenge [to nuclear energy's future] lies in the development of clear global and national strategies for the management and disposal of spent fuel and high-level radioactive waste.'[7] A decade later that challenge still stands.

This chapter examines legal aspects of the permanent disposal of dangerous, long-lived nuclear wastes. These wastes include certain military waste, spent fuel from nuclear electric-generating plants, and other high-level wastes. Construction of a permanent nuclear waste repository is a major undertaking. A repository project demands a successful combination of science, technology, financing, political support, and law. The world's initial efforts with permanent, high-risk nuclear waste disposal have shown that the political and legal aspects may be the most challenging parts of the project.

Decisions about nuclear waste storage and disposal are a significant part of one of the overarching energy questions in 2014: what is the future of nuclear electric generation in the world's energy mix? The IEA World Energy Report reflects the uncertain answers to that question. The accident at Fukushima in Japan in 2011 provided support for the anti-nuclear advocates' view that reliance on nuclear energy is too risky to continue. By contrast, nuclear energy's overall safety record over the past 60 years, and its potential to provide ample base-load electric generation on an as-needed basis and to do it without the climate-changing releases of carbon dioxide from burning fossil fuels, persuade pro-nuclear advocates that nuclear power must be a continuing part of the world's energy picture.

II. The nuclear risks

All energy sources pose risks to both human life and the broader environment. Mining accidents, oil fires, natural gas explosions, or hydroelectric dam construction threaten the lives of both energy workers and civilians. Environmental consequences of fossil fuel combustion, petroleum spills, disruption of river systems, and damage to scenic vistas add to the negatives of energy development.

Nuclear power poses a distinctive set of risks to human health and the environment. The two nuclear bomb explosions of 1945 made clear that massive radiation releases pose a threat beyond the initial explosive capability of nuclear weapons. Radiation exposure is a fact of normal life and is often done intentionally for beneficial purposes (e.g., radiation therapy). However, larger doses can be fatal in the short-term or bring about longer-term cancers and other diseases. The World War II and Cold War experiences brought forth the stories of radiation sickness and the premature death of persons who survived the explosion of the Hiroshima and Nagasaki bombs, workers in the mining and processing industries for nuclear materials, and the 'downwinder' citizens exposed to fallout from the above-ground

[7] *Nuclear Power: An Evolving Scenario*, available at <http://www.iaea.org/newscenter/statements/2004/ebsp2004n001.html>.

weapons tests of the 1950s and 1960s conducted in the state of Nevada in the United States.

The development of both nuclear weapons and the peaceful uses of the nuclear process (primarily electric generation) made clear that one aspect of the nuclear cycle would be the safe storage and disposal of various waste products of the nuclear processes. In terms of the civilian uses of the nuclear process, these waste products ranged from mining waste to milling and fuel processing waste to materials exposed to radiation at the nuclear facilities (tools, clothing, rags, etc) to the spent fuel itself.

As noted, the differences in nuclear waste types are considerable. Much low-level waste poses only moderate risks to human health, needs only modest storage protection, and loses much of its capacity for radioactive harm within a century. By contrast, spent nuclear fuel remains dangerously radioactive for times estimated at 10,000, 100,000, or one million years. Estimates vary, based on the ore body used to make a comparison with a naturally occurring substance. Spent fuel typically will decay to near the radioactivity level found in natural ore bodies in 200,000 years. But that does not make spent fuel safe. Natural ore bodies are not automatically safe. The major source of high-level waste in some nations is from the reprocessing of spent fuel from nuclear electric-generating plants.[8]

The United States Nuclear Regulatory Commission (NRC) describes spent fuel as follows: 'Spent nuclear fuel refers to uranium-bearing fuel elements that have been used at commercial nuclear reactors and that are no longer producing enough energy to sustain a nuclear reaction. Once the spent fuel is removed from the reactor the fission process has stopped, but the spent fuel assemblies still generate significant amounts of radiation and heat.'[9]

Since the start of the commercial nuclear age, spent fuel has been temporarily stored at the reactor site in specially designed pools. When pool capacity has been reached, the fuel is transferred to dry cask storage for further storage at the plant site.[10]

Spent nuclear fuel may or may not deserve the description 'waste'. An ongoing public policy debate involves whether spent fuel should be reprocessed. The NRC explains: 'Reprocessing extracts isotopes from spent fuel that can be used again as reactor fuel.'[11] Reprocessing provides vastly more energy potential from the initial nuclear fuel. It also considerably reduces the amount of 'waste' that eventually needs to be disposed of.[12] Russia, Japan, the United Kingdom, and France have been consistent practitioners of reprocessing.

The major argument against reprocessing was invoked by President Jimmy Carter, a veteran of the nuclear Navy programme, when he stopped US reprocessing efforts

8 See generally, the EIA's explanation of nuclear energy, available at <http://www.eia.gov/energyexplained/index.cfm?page=nuclear_home>.

9 Available at <http://www.nrc.gov/waste/spent-fuel-transp.html>.

10 Available at <http://www.nrc.gov/waste/spent-fuel-storage/faqs.html>.

11 See n 5.

12 Greater detail about fuel cycles, including fuel reprocessing, is provided by the US Department of Energy in its Nuclear Research and Development Roadmap, Report to Congress, available at <http://energy.gov/sites/prod/files/NuclearEnergy_Roadmap_Final.pdf>.

in 1977. The danger being avoided is the diversion of material from the reprocessed fuel to weapons purposes or other threats to national security.[13] Economics and public safety also helped end reprocessing ventures in the US. The West Valley, New York commercial reprocessing facility was closed for worker health and environmental concerns. The Department of Energy has engaged in a two-decade cleanup at the cost of billions of dollars. The Barnwell, South Carolina commercial reprocessing facility was cancelled when the discoveries of Canadian and other high-grade uranium deposits made reprocessing uncompetitive with newly manufactured fuel.

A further concern about the 'back end' of the nuclear fuel cycle involves transportation of radioactive material for disposal at a waste repository. Shipments of nuclear waste by truck or train from a nuclear electric plant (where spent fuel is temporarily stored) to a permanent repository may involve travel of hundreds, even thousands, of miles. Citizens along the routes may be uneasy about the potential for an accidental or intentional breach of the storage containers and the release of substantial amounts of radiation in their communities. A National Research Council study makes the case that transport of nuclear materials is extremely safe around the world.[14] But such studies have not answered all concerns.

Numerous facilities have been developed to handle the storage and disposal of low-level waste and some intermediate waste. The greater challenge has involved the more-radiation-potent and long-lived forms of waste. These are either the spent fuel from electric-generating plants, radioactive material remaining after the reprocessing of spent fuel, or certain waste products from the use of the nuclear process for military and research purposes. This chapter concentrates on these permanent disposal issues.

The early decades of the nuclear era explored a number of solutions to nuclear waste.[15] One solution that received some degree of thought and scientific study was sending the waste into outer space. Technological complexity, cost, and the risk of accident (e.g., concerns that if the rocket exploded it would spill radioactive waste over large portions of the earth) terminated this approach. More attention was given to disposal at sea, but the growth of concern over ocean pollution helped to constrain and then terminate this solution. The most acceptable solution became disposal of the waste in secure geological formations far below the land surface of the earth.

[13] The decision to stop reprocessing was not without opposition in the United States. See P. Domenici (former US Senator from New Mexico), *A Brighter Tomorrow: Fulfilling the Promise of Nuclear Energy* (2004).

[14] National Research Council, *Going the Distance? The Safe Transport of Spent Nuclear Fuel and High-Level Radioactive Waste in the United States* (2006).

[15] *The Economist*, 2 June 2012, available at <http://www.economist.com/node/21556100>. The article notes that 270,000 tonnes of high-level waste, mostly spent fuel, are in temporary storage worldwide. For a thorough summary of nuclear waste disposal options, see the World Nuclear Association's overview of nuclear waste management, available at <http://www.world-nuclear.org/info/Nuclear-Fuel-Cycle/Nuclear-Wastes/Waste-Management-Overview/>.

III. Nuclear law

The large majority of nuclear power plants are located in nations that are members of the Organisation for Economic Co-operation and Development (OECD). The OECD's publication, 'Nuclear Legislation in OECD Countries', provides concise summaries of nuclear law in its member states.[16] While no two national legislative programmes are identical, there are considerable similarities in these democratic, economically developed, and free-market nations. Common features of legal regulation of nuclear matters include:

- Nuclear power issues are the subject of nuclear-specific laws at the national level. Lesser units of government (states, provinces, counties, cities, etc) may have some involvement in nuclear issues, but they are clearly subsidiary to the national authority to a far greater degree than is true with other energy sources.
- While the private sector plays a considerable role in nuclear operations (often as the builder and operator of the nuclear electric plants), the privatization directions of the last 30 years have not taken the national government out of the business of regulation in the nuclear field. A familiar legislative approach is to make private commercial operators responsible for many aspects of a nuclear operation (including waste issues). However, further sections of legislation make clear that ultimate authority rests with national government regulators. Even enthusiastic free-market supporters have been hesitant to take government out of nuclear operations.
- Government regulation of nuclear activity (including waste disposal) is often divided among several government agencies. As an example, the United States gives nuclear authority to the Department of Energy, the NRC, and the Environmental Protection Agency.[17] Transportation and worker health and safety matters may involve additional government regulators. Such multiplication has both positive and negative aspects. Specialist agencies may better handle work within their realm than a generalist agency. Multiple agencies also allow for several perspectives on public policy issues. Less favourably, too many agencies may duplicate work or impose conflicting regulations. Lastly, multiple agency responsibility may let important matters be ignored if people are persuaded they are someone else's responsibility.
- More than any other energy source, nuclear regulation has inspired international treaties, agreements, etc. Among nuclear matters that have inspired such international agreements and that have implications for nuclear waste disposal are the risks of nuclear proliferation, ocean dumping of nuclear materials, and waste/spent fuel management. Waste management is now a

[16] Available at <http://www.oecd-nea.org/law/legislation/>. See generally, the Nuclear Energy Agency's webpage on the area of nuclear law, available at <http://www.oecd-nea.org/law/>.

[17] Available at <http://www.nrc.gov/waste/hlw-disposal.html>.

subject for regulation by the European Union,[18] the IAEA, and, most comprehensively, by the IAEA-sponsored 1997 treaty specific to waste disposal, the Joint Convention on the Safety of Spent Fuel Management and on the Safety of Radioactive Waste Management.[19]

- Issues of nuclear waste treatment are typically a significant part of national nuclear legislation and of international nuclear governance. The laws mandate safe storage and disposal practices. Storage typically refers to short- to intermediate-term handling of the waste, and with a potential for its retrieval. Disposal refers to permanent disposition. Laws for both storage and disposal address the various kinds of radioactive products and offer a schedule for planning the permanent disposal of the more dangerous wastes in some form of underground repository. Deep geologic permanent storage is clearly now the disposal mechanism of choice.
- The law often establishes a distinctive financial mechanism for covering the expected costs of permanent nuclear waste disposal. Revenues are gathered in advance or on a 'pay-as-you-go' basis. The goal is to assure that government has the money in hand for disposal, even if the nuclear operators have ceased operation, leaving bills unpaid, or if general government funds are not readily available.

IV. Locating permanent nuclear waste repositories

A. International standards

The IAEA is the leading international body with responsibility for nuclear matters. Its well-publicized work on controlling nuclear weapons proliferation helped earn it a Nobel Prize in 2005. Its work on peaceful uses of the atom may be less visible, but is no less important. The IAEA has led in setting and enforcing standards for the safe handling, transportation, storage, and disposal of spent fuel and other radioactive waste.

The major legal product of the IAEA work is the 1997 Joint Convention, mentioned earlier,[20] which entered into force on 18 June 2001. All of the nations that are major producers of nuclear electricity are signatories.

The Joint Convention reflects practices already in place in most nuclear states, rather than imposing new standards. The 'ultimate responsibility' for nuclear safety 'rests with the State'. Military issues and decisions on reprocessing also rest with the individual states. However, the Convention emphasizes the importance of state standards becoming matters of worldwide acceptance. Safe management of spent

[18] Directive 2011/70/EURATOM Establishing a Community Framework for the Responsible and Safe Management of Spent Fuel and Radioactive Waste [2011] OJ L199/48, 2 August 2011, available at <http://eur-lex.europa.eu/LexUriServ/LexUriServ.do?uri=OJ:L:2011:199:0048:0056:EN:PDF>.

[19] Available at <http://www.iaea.org/Publications/Documents/Infcircs/1997/infcirc546.pdf>.

[20] See n 19.

fuel and radioactive waste are of 'importance to the international community'. A primary objective is 'to promote an effective nuclear safety culture worldwide'. International co-operation in a variety of ways can enhance these objectives.

Articles 6 and 13 address the siting of proposed facilities. In identical language for both spent fuel and for radioactive waste management the articles call for extensive study of site-related factors and the impacts of a 'facility on individuals, society, and the environment'. Information on the safety of a facility is to be made 'available to members of the public'.

Disclosure of information to the public and opportunity for public participation are made more precise in the European Union's 2011 nuclear waste directive.[21] There are 143 reactors in 14 EU Member States.[22] As such, the European Union offers a unique opportunity for multi-national collaboration in a geographically compact area. The Directive mandates that EU Member States with nuclear energy programmes prepare national nuclear waste disposal programmes by 2015 that accord with the language of the Directive. Article 10, Transparency, requires the provision of information to 'workers and the general public'. It further requires 'that the public be given the necessary opportunities to participate effectively in the decision-making process... in accordance with national legislation and international obligations'.

Additional European collaborative efforts on nuclear waste disposal centre on the European Repository Development Organisation (ERDO). ERDO's Model Structure and Plan states that its objective is 'sharing of knowledge, technologies and geological disposal facilities' among the members.[23] It recognizes that the 'most challenging aspect' of waste disposal is the location of appropriate disposal sites. ERDO plans a 'bottom-up process' that starts with identifying communities that may be interested in serving as repository hosts.

The international and multi-national agreements leave wide discretion to individual states as to precisely how public participation will be carried out.[24] But, the mere concept of giving the general public access to information and the ability to participate in nuclear siting decisions is a marked change from the early days of the nuclear age.

B. The United States experience

The majority of the discussion of the siting of geological repositories for the storage of long-lived nuclear waste will examine the United States experience. That reflects

[21] Directive 2011/70/EURATOM (n 18) at 51.

[22] Funding Gap for Nuclear Decommissioning in Bulgaria, Lithuania, and Slovakia, European Parliament News, 22 January 2013, available at <http://www.europarl.europa.eu/news/en/pressroom/content/20130121IPR05429/html/>.

[23] Available at <http://www.erdo-wg.eu/Documents_files/ERDO%20Model.pdf> at 10 and 13.

[24] For a discussion of the evolution of rights to public involvement in major natural resources decisions, see generally, D. Zillman, A. Lucas, and R. Pring (eds), *Human Rights in Natural Resource Development:' Public Participation in the Sustainable Development of Mining and Energy Resources* (2002).

this author's familiarity with US energy and nuclear law. It also reflects the roles of the United States as both the leading nuclear military power and the nation with the largest number of reactors for the generation of electricity.

US nuclear policy has evolved over time. It has been driven as much by political and public policy considerations (often reflected in law) of the moment as it has by scientific and technological ones. A person looking back on 70 years of the nuclear age could fairly ask why the problem of long-term waste disposal was not addressed and solved from the beginning. Military necessity directed otherwise. Similarly, the scientific optimism of the early Cold War period encouraged a mindset that considered that problems like waste disposal for commercial nuclear electric plants could be solved after an 'Atoms for Peace' programme had created a vibrant nuclear electric power industry.

That hopeful world disappeared in the United States starting in the mid-1960s. Both the Vietnam War and the Watergate scandal damaged public trust in the national government. Nuclear power became suspect well before the Three Mile Island accident in 1979. Although that accident resulted in no consequential radioactive release into the atmosphere, it did impose costs in the billions of dollars and left nuclear energy with a negative reputation in the eyes of some citizens that continues to influence policy today. The overall economic promise of nuclear power to provide electricity 'too cheap to meter' also disappeared in the 1970s. Further, President Carter's 1977 decision not to pursue reprocessing of spent fuel because of the proliferation risks also clouded nuclear power's future.

1. The Waste Isolation Pilot Plant

Out of these experiences of the 1970s, two major efforts arose for the permanent disposal of the more dangerous nuclear wastes. The first involved the handling of some long-lived transuranic radioactive wastes created by the defence programmes for the manufacture of nuclear weapons. Transuranic refers to elements heavier than uranium, the heaviest natural element. These elements are created in the process of neutron bombardment of uranium to make weapons or to generate electricity. An important transuranic element is plutonium.[25] Transuranic waste from the military weapons programme was stored temporarily at US government-owned sites around the country.

A scientific consensus arose that this waste would be best disposed of permanently at one or more underground sites in geologically stable locations. In the 1950s, the National Academy of Sciences identified underground salt formations as an attractive permanent disposal facility. The salt formations promised stable geology, an absence of flowing water, and a self-sealing capability that would prevent release

[25] See, the US Department of Energy's description of its Waste Isolation Pilot Plant, available at <http://www.wipp.energy.gov/fctshts/Why_WIPP.pdf>. See also, the US Environmental protection Agency's description of transuranic radioactive waste, available at <http://www.epa.gov/radiation/docs/radwaste/402-k-94-001-tru.html>.

of the radioactive waste to the environment.[26] The deep geologic repository would allow the closure of temporary storage sites and the use of those sites for other purposes. Several of those temporary sites were located close to major population centres. The search to site the Waste Isolation Pilot Plant (WIPP) began.

Journalist Chuck McCutcheon studied 30 years of WIPP location decision-making in his 2002 book, *Nuclear Reactions*.[27] McCutcheon provides a fascinating study of the involvement in WIPP of three levels of government—national, state, and local—and activity in the three branches of the national government—the legislative, the executive, and the judicial. All units were to play a role in the WIPP siting decision.

The WIPP project was advanced by the combination of support from the federal government, eager to see a solution to the military nuclear waste problem, and from the southern New Mexico small city of Carlsbad. In the early 1970s, the federal government had powerful assets for securing a waste site decision. As McCutcheon notes, popular sentiment at the height of the Cold War generally deferred to the military on nuclear defence issues.[28] If Uncle Sam said it needed a military nuclear waste depository, it ought to have one. Second, the plains and mountain states of the western United States provided large geographic areas that were well suited to a WIPP. They combined stable geology, low population, and the advantage of vast federal landownership. A potential project site would not have to struggle with land (and subsurface) acquisition of water and mineral rights from private landowners nor land use regulations imposed by a variety of local and state government units.

The State of New Mexico also offered a history of close affiliation with nuclear activities. The state was home to Los Alamos, one of the crucial sites in the World War II Manhattan Project that produced the first atomic bombs. New Mexico was also home to White Sands, the location of the first test of the atomic weapon before its use over Japan. National laboratories like Los Alamos and Sandia in Albuquerque were highly attractive to professional employers and a source of pride and revenue to a relatively poor state.

Of equal advantage to WIPP development was the City of Carlsbad's economic needs. The town's major industry for half a century, potash mining, had suffered from the closure of several mines that were undercut by foreign producers. One community leader recalls 7 November 1971 as the beginning of the Carlsbad efforts. On that day, he and others learned that a well-advanced plan to locate the military defence nuclear waste repository in a salt deposit in Lyons, Kansas had ended with the discovery of geological flaws in the plan and the resulting political objection. A group of Carlsbad business and political leaders encouraged the

[26] See the US Department of Energy's explanation of why salt was selected as a disposal medium, available at <http://www.wipp.energy.gov/fctshts/salt.pdf>.

[27] C. McCutcheon, *Nuclear Reactions: The Politics of Opening a Nuclear Waste Disposal Site* (2002). Another excellent introduction to WIPP with a greater focus on the science of WIPP is National Academy of Sciences, *The Waste Isolation Pilot Project: A Potential Solution for the Disposal of Transuranic Waste* (2013).

[28] See McCutcheon (n 27) at 32.

opening of discussions with state and federal officials about siting the WIPP near their city.

McCutcheon notes that local leaders made a 'conscious and important early decision not to involve the public' in the early WIPP discussions.[29] This is true in the sense that 'public participation' would be defined today. Formal notifications, public hearings, local veto powers, and the like were not mandated by statute in 1971. Project promoters instead started an informal campaign to sell the community on the economic and community benefits from WIPP. A considerable number of citizens were initially sceptical. A few were outright opposed. But the majority of Carlsbad citizens were willing to be educated on the advantages and disadvantages of nuclear waste disposal before making a final decision.

The WIPP chronology[30] identifies 1974 as the year in which the United States Atomic Energy Commission selected an ancient salt bed 26 miles east of Carlsbad for exploratory work in the search for a repository site. This distanced WIPP from Carlsbad enough to reduce what would later be called NIMBY ('not in my back yard') fears among local residents.

The late 1970s and early 1980s saw WIPP struggle with its identity. McCutcheon notes that 1975 plans for WIPP involved a 'main level [that] would be used for the transuranic waste accumulating at weapons production facilities [and a] second level . . . to be studied for storing high-level spent fuel from commercial power plants'.[31] That was enough to disturb State of New Mexico officials and popular sentiment in New Mexico beyond the environs of Carlsbad. The commercial waste storage site was a particular hot button issue. Unlike the military programmes, New Mexico was not home to a commercial nuclear power plant. 'Why should we take other people's nuclear garbage?', some New Mexicans asked.

The decade that followed saw WIPP under study at most levels and branches of government. Local government in Carlsbad remained supportive of the project. State government officials in New Mexico were not vehemently opposed to WIPP, but they did have concerns over the safety and environmental impacts of the project, the transportation of the waste through New Mexico, the potential that commercial waste eventually might be included in the project, and the lack of the state's regulatory role in the operation of WIPP.

The US Congress supported the project in a 1980 statute,[32] but moved away from a view that WIPP should be managed as a purely military activity. President Jimmy Carter attempted to kill WIPP but was rebuffed by Congress. Presidents Reagan, George H. W. Bush, and Clinton generally supported Congress' steps to move WIPP to completion.

The federal courts were called upon in 1981 and in 1991–92 to respond to State of New Mexico lawsuits demanding more thorough environmental reviews and a

[29] See McCutcheon (n 27) at 26.

[30] Available at <http://www.wipp.energy.gov/fctshts/Chronology.pdf>.

[31] See McCutcheon (n 27) at 37.

[32] Public Law 96–164, available at <http://uscodebeta.house.gov/statutes/1979/1979-096-0164.pdf>.

greater regulatory role for the State. Generally favourable court decisions provided added support for New Mexico's concerns.

In 1992, Congress consolidated much of the work of the prior decades in the WIPP Land Withdrawal Act.[33] The statute's detail reflected political compromises over many of the contentious issues of the previous 15 years. The statute also reflected the growth of worker and public safety and environmental protection laws over that period. One clear purpose of the statute was to shift jurisdiction over the 16-square-mile WIPP site from the US Department of the Interior to the Department of Energy. Oil, gas, and mining activities were forbidden. The statute also gave the federal Environmental Protection Agency authority over determining compliance with radioactive waste disposal regulations.

In considerable detail, the statute specified the kinds of waste that WIPP would handle. Most prominently, the statute forbade the disposal of spent nuclear fuel and other high-level waste at the Carlsbad site.[34] Another section specified the total amount of waste that WIPP could receive. The kinds of military defence transuranic waste that WIPP could handle were defined by reference to precise radiation release from the waste materials. Not every unit of waste produced in the defence weapons programme would be eligible for WIPP disposal.

The WIPP Land Withdrawal Act also promised 'economic assistance' to New Mexico, a portion of which could go to units of local government in the vicinity of WIPP.[35] The federal government committed to 14 years of annual payment of US $20 million and, afterwards, 'such sums' as Congress might choose to authorize. In retrospect, some of the details of the Act appear excessive and may hinder the most efficient operation of the WIPP. In 1992, these were necessary political compromises to allow the legislation to pass.

Construction moved forward, as did plans for shipments of military wastes from various sites to WIPP. On 26 March 1999 the first shipment of waste from Los Alamos National Laboratory arrived at WIPP to an enthusiastic welcome. In the years that followed 1999, WIPP's website chronology highlights further shipments to WIPP from around the nation, rather than litigation or legislation.

By the tenth anniversary of waste shipments, WIPP was being viewed as a success both nationally and internationally. WIPP in 2012 identified among its accomplishments the safe disposal of about 85,000 m^3 of waste, more than 11,000 safe shipments of that waste to WIPP, and the removal of all transuranic wastes from the World War II and Cold War military programmes from 22 sites in 12 states.[36] As of 30 October 2012, WIPP reported it had filled 48% of WIPP's capacity.[37]

Receipt and disposal of qualifying defence transuranic waste at WIPP continues. Events like the 2011 forest fire near the Los Alamos National Laboratory's above-

[33] Waste Isolation Pilot Plant Land Withdrawal Act, Public Law 102–579, available at <http://www.wipp.energy.gov/library/cra/baselinetool/Documents/Regulatory%20Tools/10%20WIPPLWA1996.pdf> (the 'WIPP Land Withdrawal Act').

[34] WIPP Land Withdrawal Act (n 33) at 4.

[35] WIPP Land Withdrawal Act (n 33) at 5.

[36] United States Department of Energy, Carlsbad Field Office, National TRU Waste Management Plan (December 2012) at 3.

[37] National TRU Waste Management Plan (n 36) at 14.

ground storage site for WIPP-eligible waste prompted renewed urgency in the work. WIPP also anticipates serving its role as a site for nuclear storage research. Among the most notable research projects are studies of the impact of heat from nuclear waste on salt formations. This is essential information for making decisions on the location of the repository for heat-releasing waste from some defence projects and from spent fuel from commercial nuclear plants. WIPP officials and local WIPP advocates point out that this research provides valuable information for any potential waste site utilizing salt as a host rock, not just for a future potential expansion of WIPP.

I visited Carlsbad and the WIPP site in February 2013. In addition to a tour of the WIPP site itself, I talked to local officials and community members, some of whom have been involved in the WIPP project since its inception. My major questions were what has worked well, what has not, and what the lessons of the WIPP experience are for government officials, the nuclear industry, and for communities and their citizens about the location of future nuclear waste disposal projects.

Carlsbad is a city of 27,000 people in southeastern New Mexico. It is a four-and-a-half hour drive from either New Mexico's capital, Santa Fe, or its population centre, Albuquerque. Carlsbad is three hours from El Paso, Texas and its cross-border neighbour Ciudad Juarez, Mexico. At an altitude of 3,100 feet, Carlsbad offers warm-weather retirement living with average winter high temperatures near 60°F and 350 days of sunshine yearly. An attractive Chamber of Commerce booklet highlights outdoor recreation, a zoo, a junior college, an arts community, golf courses, a performing arts centre, primary medical care facilities, restaurants, and shopping malls. The average home price is US$85,000. The booklet summarizes: 'Young families, entrepreneurs and retirees all find Carlsbad to be a home that is second-to-none, as they take pleasure in the all-around small-town charm and friendliness discovered here.' Carlsbad is also the nearest city (a 22-mile drive to the west and about 50 miles from WIPP) to spectacular Carlsbad Caverns National Park, one of the United States' 20 World Heritage Sites.

WIPP, with approximately 900 professional and blue-collar employees, and several related businesses, is a major employer and a major presence in Carlsbad. WIPP's headquarters, the Carlsbad Field Office, is located on a main street in Carlsbad in an attractive southwestern-style building. In addition to WIPP offices, the facility houses a small public display describing 'the WIPP Experience'.

The Pilot Plant itself is 26 miles southeast of the City. Views from the roads to the Plant show a growing number of oil and gas wells in the sparsely vegetated landscape. Not only are oil and gas booming, but the potash industry has rebounded strongly since the depression of the early 1970s that first encouraged Carlsbad leaders to explore a nuclear waste repository.

The Plant complex is a series of single- and double-story buildings in the middle of the 16 square miles that were withdrawn in the 1992 Act for the WIPP. The highest structures are connected to the four shafts that provide access and air circulation to the underground repository itself. A small elevator that is partially enclosed travels from the surface to the floor of the repository, 2,150 feet down.

The trip takes three-and-a-half minutes. About 800 feet down, the 2,000-foot deep salt formation begins.

My guide inquired whether I had been in an underground mine before. I responded that my one experience was in a Kentucky coal mine. He replied that after that experience, I'd find the WIPP spacious. Any worries of claustrophobia vanished when I saw the wide corridors and high ceilings. The long corridors encouraged use of a multi-passenger golf cart to move around the dimly lit accessible areas. The side corridors provided the disposal areas. The less harmful waste shipments, 96% of the total, were packed in the open areas of the side corridors from the end of the side corridor to where it joined the main corridor. When the waste packages reach the main corridor, the corridor is closed and a new side corridor is opened to repeat the process.

The 4% of waste that is more hazardous and does not allow direct human handling are stored in cavities drilled into both sides of the side corridors. These cavities were filled with one remote-handled waste package each and then sealed with a large concrete plug. A single side corridor could handle over 100 such cavities.

In addition to the geology, the tour provided a look at the specialized machinery designed for moving the waste from its arrival at the plant surface to its place of final disposal in the WIPP underground. Some direct human activity is necessary to achieve this, but many steps are done automatically and controlled remotely. Constant monitoring for radiation takes place to assure that the waste conforms to what was expected to arrive at the WIPP and to assure that the WIPP facility stays radioactively 'clean'.

Federal employees and contractors, as well as Carlsbad leaders, recognized that WIPP relations with the community have been a continuing educational process. Community groups regularly meet with WIPP officials for discussion of ongoing issues. Few local citizens do not know some WIPP employees. A Rotary Club member reported that a considerable percentage of Club members had taken the underground tour that I had taken. Another citizen described the advantage of having WIPP PhD employees serve as judges and advisers to middle school science fairs. The junior college hosts the Carlsbad Environmental Monitoring Research Center, whose work includes testing for radiation exposure for any citizens who request such a test.

Beyond Carlsbad, one of the most successful community outreach programmes has involved the sensitive issue of transportation of the waste over hundreds of miles. Great care is given to selection and training of the drivers, selection of the highway routes from the waste source to WIPP, packaging of the waste shipments, and monitoring of each step of the travel. Department of Energy officials carry out a programme of training for first responders and others along the transportation corridors. Accident scenarios are game-planned. Lines of authority are explained. In 14 years, no serious accidents have taken place during WIPP transportation activity.

From the perspective of most Carlsbad residents, much has gone well from 1971 (Carlsbad's first interest in the WIPP) to 1992 (the Land Withdrawal Act) to 1999 (the first shipment to WIPP) to the present. WIPP has become a major employer, with well-paying jobs for professionals and labourers alike. Useful commercial spinoffs from WIPP activity have located in the multi-county area. Business has grown overall, and Carlsbad survived the Great Recession of 2007 with few negative impacts.

Was everything perfect? No. As noted, the political manoeuvering to license WIPP may have provided an excess of regulation that is now perceived as unnecessary. Further, the vague federal promise of continuing federal support money after 15 years has not been kept. Even dollars needed for annual WIPP maintenance and replacement of equipment have been hard to acquire in tough national budgetary times.

Local leaders have recognized that they need to be advocates to a variety of audiences. The Carlsbad Mayor's Nuclear Task Force meets regularly for educational and advocacy purposes. An Eddy-Lea Energy Alliance involves leaders of the two counties nearest to the WIPP and that are the homes for its employees. Its major focus has been on the prospect of the location of interim storage for commercial nuclear waste somewhere in the two-county area.

The Mayor's Task Force members and others reach out to the rest of New Mexico at the gubernatorial, legislative, and community leader levels. Considerable time is spent in Washington, DC meeting with federal officials. Ample volunteer work keeps the cost to the city down.

This lobbying work has two broad purposes. The first is to advocate continually for the WIPP budget and for improvements to the existing WIPP. Carlsbad residents support WIPP but are disappointed that Congress and Washington officials have been frugal with dollars needed to fund what they view as a successful and internationally ground-breaking project. Beyond just keeping WIPP operating, the advocates are also mindful of expanded opportunities in nuclear waste storage for WIPP and for the two county 'nuclear corridor' area. These ventures range from research projects (like the study of the impact of heat upon salt formations) to additional disposal of defence waste to interim storage sites for commercial spent fuel, and, possibly, even to a permanent high-level commercial waste repository. A common response to inquiries about the future emphasizes the need for full scientific study and further thorough education of the community. But that is usually followed by the observation that if that went well, Eddy and Lea Counties would be hard to match for geologic and hydrologic attraction, professional expertise, community familiarity with nuclear issues, and well-organized political support. The Carlsbad Chamber's booklet contains a half-page feature for WIPP headlined 'Solving a national problem . . .'. Carlsbad is entitled to take pride in doing that.

2. *The commercial high-level waste repository*

By the mid-1970s, nuclear power had become an important contributor to America's production of electricity. As a consequence, the growing volume of spent nuclear fuel forced the issue of waste disposal on the federal government, the private businesses engaged in nuclear power production, and the public at large. Storage of the spent radioactive fuel in pools at the nuclear electric plant site had its physical limits and safety risks.

Several other factors also demanded a decision on a permanent and secure disposal site for spent nuclear fuel. The first was President Carter's decision to reject the reprocessing of the spent fuel. As noted, new fuel fabricated from the old spent fuel considerably reduced the amount of 'waste' needing permanent disposal. A second factor pressing federal action was the action of the State of California. California public policy-makers had become sceptical of nuclear power. While they recognized that California could not override federal safety decisions in the licensing and operation of nuclear plants, California could and did condition future nuclear licences in California upon the existence of a federally approved plan for the permanent disposition of spent nuclear fuel. The federal authorities had to admit that no such plan existed. Finally, the 1979 Three Mile Island accident in Pennsylvania awakened fears of a massive radiation release in populated areas. Rightly or wrongly, millions of Americans became uneasy about nuclear plants in their neighbourhoods or states.

The result was the enactment by Congress of the Nuclear Waste Policy Act (NWPA) of 1982,[38] in which the Congress placed responsibility in the federal government for the eventual disposal of commercial nuclear waste. Site review of possible repository locations had been ongoing since at least 1976, when the federal Energy Research and Development Administration announced that 36 states were under review. It frankly noted that prior federal efforts to find a 'permanent solution to the problem of civilian radioactive waste disposal have not been adequate'.[39]

The NWPA directed the Secretary of Energy to advance a process that would study multiple sites around the country that might eventually be selected as the 'permanent solution'. That solution would be a 'repository' used for 'permanent deep geologic disposal of high-level radioactive waste and spent nuclear fuel'.[40] Review of sites would consider such factors as geologic media, hydrology, seismic activity, and proximity to populations.[41]

Times had changed since the early days of the WIPP venture. Quiet dealings with local leaders were likely to be an unsuccessful approach to siting the repository for the more long-lived and dangerous commercial wastes. The NWPA provided ample provision for notification and consultation with state and Indian tribal officials.[42] Public hearings were a part of the review process.

The statute directed the Secretary of Energy to recommend three repository sites to the President. Both practical and political reasons drove the multiple sites requirement. Practically, the prospective expansion of nuclear power could mean that a single site would be insufficient for all the waste that eventually would be

[38] NWPA, Public Law 97–425, available at <http://www.gpo.gov/fdsys/pkg/STATUTE-96/pdf/STATUTE-96-Pg2201.pdf>.

[39] NWPA (n 38) at 2207.

[40] NWPA (n 38) at 2204.

[41] NWPA (n 38) at 2208.

[42] NWPA (n 38), see ss 117 and 118.

produced. Further, worries about accidents during transportation of the waste from power plant to repository prompted efforts to reduce total travel miles. Politically, an early commitment to a single site lessened the perception that all states had an obligation to be considered for a controversial federal facility.

Study moved forward and the Secretary put forth three sites in rural Deaf Smith County, Texas, near Hanford in Washington State, and at Yucca Mountain adjacent to the Nevada Test Site (now the Nevada National Security Site), about 100 miles from Las Vegas, Nevada. Despite varying degrees of local community support, no home state embraced the offer to remain on the selection list. Delay became the order of the day and political clout probably trumped geological evaluation.

A frustrated Congress amended the NWPA in 1987.[43] The legislators boldly reduced the contenders to one—the Yucca Mountain site in Nevada. The statute also made clear that no other repository was to be planned without Congressional approval.[44] The new statute spelled out the financial rewards to Nevada and its local governments.[45] A further section spelled out a lengthy list of 'impacts' from the repository location that might be supported by federal dollars.[46] Among the impacts were education, public health, law enforcement, medical care, cultural and recreational needs, social services, transportation, tourism and economic development, and 'other needs . . . that would not have arisen but for the [repository location]'. Officials and members of the public in 49 states breathed collective sighs of relief. Nevada Senator Harry Reid removed any facade of his state having 'won' the nuclear waste lottery with his characterization of the new statute as the 'Screw Nevada Act'. Few, if any, contenders for statewide office in Nevada for the next three decades disagreed with Reid's characterization. Local officials and popular sentiment in host Nye County, however, remained supportive of the project for its economic benefits to the lightly populated region.

During those three decades most parts of the federal government moved ahead with the study, construction, and licensing of the Yucca Mountain site. Over the objection of the State of Nevada, Congress and President George W. Bush approved the process in 2002.[47]

Nevada continued its opposition on several fronts. Lawsuits raised numerous issues that encouraged either cancellation or delay for further study. Scientific and technical studies countered positive studies from the proponents of the project. Media cultivation by opponents of Yucca Mountain sought to make the points that the science was bad and the politics unfair. The continuing upscale growth of Las Vegas and the gaming industry suggested a repository accident would combine 'nuclear catastrophe' and 'Las Vegas' in worldwide media coverage.

[43] Public Law 100–202, available at <http://history.nih.gov/research/downloads/PL100-202.pdf>, and Public Law 100-203, available at <http://www.nwtrb.gov/mission/1987aa.pdf>.

[44] 42 U.S.C. § 10172a. [45] 42 U.S.C. § 10173. [46] 42 U.S.C. § 10174a(b).

[47] Public Law 107–200, available at <http://www.gpo.gov/fdsys/pkg/PLAW-107publ200/pdf/PLAW-107 publ200.pdf>.

Most significantly, politics changed. Senator Reid advanced in the Democratic Party leadership. In 2004, the Senator helped secure Democratic Presidential candidate John Kerry's opposition to Yucca Mountain. The Bush re-election ended that hope. But two years later Democrats took control of the US Senate. Their new Majority Leader was Harry Reid.

Politics had clearly turned against Yucca Mountain.[48] In 2008, Democratic Presidential candidate Barack Obama followed John Kerry in public opposition to Yucca Mountain. Upon his election, Obama appointed Nobel laureate Steven Chu as Secretary of Energy. Chu and President Obama took a number of steps to decouple the Department of Energy from Yucca Mountain. Majority Leader Reid led an effort to defund Yucca Mountain in Congress.[49]

Secretary Chu also chartered a Blue Ribbon Commission (BRC) on America's Nuclear Future. The Commission's report appeared early in 2012 and offered a 'new strategy to manage used nuclear fuel and high-level radioactive waste'.[50] Crucial to the process was a 'consent-based approach' for the selection of the repository site. WIPP and programmes in France, Finland, Spain, and Sweden were offered as promising examples of the consensual approach. The BRC report was largely adopted by Secretary Chu in January 2013, two months after President Obama won a solid re-election victory (including swing state Nevada) and Majority Leader Reid retained control of the Senate.[51]

The BRC report and Secretary Chu's Strategy paper were clear that the 'new strategy' required securing popular support for the repository in its state of location. Both documents endorsed 'a siting process that is consent-based, transparent, phased, adaptive, standards-and science-based, and governed by legally-binding agreements between the federal government and host jurisdictions'.[52] As the WIPP experience points out, local support does not automatically guarantee statewide support. While the NWPA and its amendments remain on the statute books, a new approach to commercial waste disposal will demand a major rewrite of present legislation.

In Spring 2013, Secretary Chu resigned. His replacement, Ernest Moniz, is an MIT scientist with Department of Energy experience, including work on nuclear issues. It is uncertain how high on the national agenda a solution to nuclear waste problems may be. Utilities are suing the Department for taking their money to fund a permanent repository but not delivering. The considerable cost to the taxpayers of this fiasco may prod a budget-conscious Congress to act. A bipartisan Nuclear Waste Administration Act of 2013 (Senate Bill 1240) is working its way through the

[48] A concise summary of Yucca Mountain developments is available at <http://en.wikipedia.org/wiki/Yucca_Mountain_nuclear_waste_repository>.

[49] For further efforts to terminate the Yucca Mountain project, see <http://www.nrc.gov/waste/hlw-disposal.html>.

[50] Strategy for the Management and Disposal of Used Nuclear Fuel and High-Level Radioactive Waste, United States Department of Energy, January 2013, available at <http://energy.gov/sites/prod/files/Strategy%20for%20the%20Management%20and%20Disposal%20of%20Used%20Nuclear%20Fuel%20and%20High%20Level%20Radioactive%20Waste.pdf> at 3.

[51] See Strategy (n 50).

[52] See Strategy (n 50) at 9.

Chamber. The Bill essentially adopts many of the suggestions of the prior Department of Energy reports.

Even if nuclear waste becomes a legislative priority, however, it is doubtful whether Congress is inclined to do more than approve a process that will correct the alleged failings of the Yucca Mountain programme. And many scientific and political leaders are reluctant to abandon an investment in Yucca Mountain that may have reached US$20 billion dollars over the past three decades. In summary, while the United States has spent the most technical, scientific, legal, and political effort of any nuclear nation on commercial high-level repository issues, its returns to date are modest.

C. Other nations' repository experiences

Other nuclear nations provide different experiences in attempts to site repositories. I emphasize here nations with market economies and representative democracies. Each of these nations needs to recognize varying degrees of popular opposition to nuclear power in general, and to the location of high-level nuclear waste repositories, in particular. The sections that follow briefly examine, as of mid-2013, the experiences of France, Japan, the United Kingdom, Sweden, and Finland. The repository siting experiences of each country merit detailed study well beyond the page limitations of this chapter. I also recognize that we omit creative, and sometimes controversial, repository location activity in other nuclear nations. The five nations studied, however, provide a variety of experiences that is useful for any nations addressing repository siting.[53] All five are signatories to the 1997 Joint Convention.

1. France

France can make a solid claim for being the world's most committed nuclear electric nation.[54] The United States Public Broadcast System programme, Frontline, examined the French popular attitudes to nuclear power and to waste disposal.[55] Two factors helped to explain the solid popular support for nuclear power. The first was the lack of domestic fossil fuels and the unease over dependence on Middle Eastern imports. The second was a national admiration for large-scale, high-technology projects and the scientists and engineers who make them work.

[53] Unless otherwise cited, all information is drawn from nuclear laws in OECD countries, available at <http://www.oecd-nea.org/law/>, as well as the IEA's Key World Energy Statistics, available at <http://www.iea.org/publications/freepublications/publication/kwes.pdf>.

[54] See Nuclear Power in the World Today (n 1). See also, Katherine Ling, 'Is the Solution to the U.S. Nuclear Waste Problem in France?', *The New York Times*, 18 May 2009, available at <http://www.nytimes.com/cwire/2009/05/18/18climatewire-is-the-solution-to-the-us-nuclear-waste-prob-12208.html?pagewanted=all>.

[55] See <http://www.pbs.org/wgbh/pages/frontline/shows/reaction/readings/french.html>.

The disposal of nuclear waste, however, challenged the pro-nuclear consensus. Communities that were pleased to have a nuclear power plant in the neighbourhood felt very differently about a nuclear graveyard. The French parliament appointed Christian Bataille, who had experience as both a Member of Parliament and a mayor, to study the problem and recommend a solution. Monsieur Bataille's interviews with concerned citizens found that talk of 'permanent' disposal suggested to them that government would be abandoning all responsibility for the waste. Objections lessened if government spoke of 'stocking' waste in a way that could be reversed if encouraged by new technologies or economics.

These findings helped shape the fundamental French legislative framework for nuclear waste. The 1991 Bataille Act sets out a research programme to assess the handling of several kinds of nuclear wastes, including high-level wastes. The Planning Act No 2006–739 concerning the Sustainable Management of Radioactive Materials and Waste expands on the framework of the 1991 Act.[56] The Act and amendments mandate a public review and consultation process for the selection of a repository site for high-level waste. The National Radioactive Waste Management Agency (ANDRA) published technical safety studies that are written in plain language to help citizens understand the siting decision.

Government studies, backed by international peer review, have now centred on a repository site in the Meuse and Haute-Marne districts of eastern France.[57] ANDRA has already undertaken considerable research in the area at the Bure Underground Laboratory. ANDRA anticipates that after further public consultation, Parliament will approve plans for a deep geological waste repository in 2015, for which operation will begin in 2025. ANDRA also expects to open a repository for low-level, but long-lived, radioactive waste in 2020. ANDRA is already operating repositories for less harmful low-level wastes.

ANDRA's earlier experience with siting a disposal facility for long-lived, low-level nuclear waste may suggest that all political and public problems have not been solved. In June 2008, ANDRA invited 3,115 communities with favourable geology to express an interest in the low-level waste facility. Only 40 communities expressed an interest. The two most geologically attractive sites drew strong anti-nuclear opposition and the communities withdrew their desire to move further.

2. *Japan*

In 2010, Japan ranked third in the world, behind the United States and France, in the number of nuclear plants and in total nuclear generation. Prior to the 2011 Fukushima accident Japan relied on nuclear power for about one-quarter of its electricity. Like France, Japan reprocesses its spent fuel.

[56] Available at <http://www.andra.fr/download/andra-international-en/document/editions/305va.pdf>.

[57] See <http://www.world-nuclear-news.org/WR-Next_phase_for_French_geological_disposal-0501127.html>.

The Law on Final Disposal of High Level Radioactive Waste of 2000 committed Japan to deep burial of its high-level waste.[58] The Nuclear Waste Management Organization of Japan (NUMO) was designated as the government agency to plan and construct a repository. In 2002, NUMO actively solicited municipalities to volunteer for the waste site location.[59] By 2007, however, only one such candidate had emerged and, worse still, that municipality later retracted its offer due to a change in opinion by the mayor.[60] In an effort to have a site selected in 2030, NUMO recently began an open solicitation process through which those sites that are proffered and potentially suitable will be subject to detailed investigation.[61]

More than two years after the March 2011 earthquake, tsunami, and consequent damage to the Fukushima-Daiichi nuclear complex, the future of nuclear power in Japan remains uncertain. The World Nuclear Association's publication, *Nuclear Power in Japan*, summarizes:

> However, following the tsunami which killed 19,000 people and which triggered the Fukushima nuclear accident (which killed no one), public sentiment shifted markedly so that there were public protests calling for nuclear power to be abandoned. The balance between this populist sentiment and the continuation of reliable and affordable electricity supplies is being worked out politically.[62]

In October 2011, a Japanese Government White Paper supported reducing 'Japan's dependency on nuclear energy... as much as possible in the medium-range and long-range future'.[63] The new cabinet office, the Energy and Environment Council, recommended a phase out of nuclear power by 2040, in a strategy paper released in September 2012.[64] The Cabinet initially backed the recommendation. But, strong business opposition and political opposition from the head of the Liberal Democratic Party changed minds. The decisive victory of the Liberal Democratic Party in the November 2012 elections appeared to endorse a policy of continued nuclear use with increased attention to safety issues and greater consultation with local governments. The new Abe government continues to advocate a policy that nuclear power must remain a part of Japan's energy programme.

Japan's response to the Fukushima accident continues to evolve and to impact waste disposal policy. The accident has assuredly prompted a greater concern about earthquakes. The Science Council of Japan has expressed concern about permanent subsurface disposal of nuclear waste in earthquake-prone Japan. A Council member has expressed the view that 'the best possible option is temporary storage [that would] secure time to find ways to more appropriately handle the matter'.[65]

58 Available at <http://www.japanfs.org/en/mailmagazine/newsletter/pages/032508.html>.

59 See <http://rt.com/news/japan-nuclear-waste-disposal-934/>.

60 See n 59.

61 See the 'High-Level Wastes' heading in the World Nuclear Association's profile of Japan, available at <http://www.world-nuclear.org/info/Country-Profiles/Countries-G-N/Japan/>.

62 See <http://www.world-nuclear.org/info/Country-Profiles/Countries-G-N/Japan/#.Ue8Crhylkb8>.

63 World Nuclear Association's profile of Japan (n 61), under 'Energy for a growing economy'.

64 World Nuclear Association's profile of Japan (n 61), under 'Post-Fukushima energy policy change, 2011 on'.

65 Available at <http://www.upi.com/Business_News/Energy-Resources/2012/09/13/Japan-ponders-how-to-dispose-of-nuclear-waste/UPI-21661347560441/>.

3. *The United Kingdom*

The United Kingdom currently produces between 15 and 20% of its electricity from nuclear generation. It ranks tenth for overall generation of nuclear electricity. The government's posture towards further nuclear development has shifted from generally negative to generally positive over the past 15 years. A de facto ban between 1989 and 2006 changed to become support for new nuclear construction. The need to address climate change has been a major pro-nuclear factor. In 2006, the United Kingdom also committed to a new generation of nuclear reactors. The United Kingdom's attitude to permanent disposal of high-level waste has mirrored that of other major nuclear nations: 'It is a very important problem that we need to solve. Someday.'

Modern attention to high-level waste management can be traced to the Government's decision in 2003 to create the Committee on Radioactive Waste Management.[66] In July 2006, the Committee reported recommending geological disposal, secure interim storage in the meantime, and continuing research and development. The Government accepted the recommendations and on 12 June 2008 published its *Managing Radioactive Waste Safely* White Paper to direct English, Welsh, and Northern Irish policy.[67] The Scottish government opposes geological storage. The major goal of the White Paper was finding the single permanent repository site that would serve UK disposal needs.

Government public relations to find the willing community portrayed the venture in highly positive terms. 'Construction and operation of a geological disposal facility will be a multi-billion pound project that will provide skilled employment for hundreds of people for over a century. It will contribute greatly to the local economy and wider socio-economic framework. There are also likely to be spin-off industry benefits, infrastructure benefits, benefits to local education or academic resources, and positive impacts on local service industries that support the facility and its workforce. It is also likely to involve major investments in local transport facilities and infrastructure, which would remain after the facility had been closed . . . '[68]

However, the proposal also described the community hosting the repository as providing 'an essential service to the nation' and noted the care that needed to go into dealing with intergenerational decisions.[69]

The White Paper directed an approach 'based on voluntarism and partnership' between Government and interested local communities. The Government promised 'an open and transparent approach', which allowed public involvement throughout the process. The community's 'Right of Withdrawal' was a 'key part

[66] Available at <http://webarchive.nationalarchives.gov.uk/20130503173700/http://corwm.decc.gov.uk/en/crwm/cms/about_us/our_history/our_history.aspx>.

[67] See the Department for Environment, Food, and Rural Affairs and the Department for Business Enterprise and Regulatory Reform, and the devolved administrations for Wales and Northern Ireland, 'Managing Radioactive Waste Safely: A Framework for Implementing Geological Disposal', June 2008, available at <http://www.official-documents.gov.uk/document/cm73/7386/7386.pdf>.

[68] 'Managing Radioactive Waste Safely' (n 67) at 6.

[69] 'Managing Radioactive Waste Safely' (n 67) at 6.

of the voluntarism approach'. At any point up to the beginning of construction, the community could withdraw.[70]

Government recognized that the various studies involved in a siting decision could impose costs on the candidate community. Government promised to enter into Engagement Packages with the community to meet some or all of those costs. Details were for negotiation between the parties.

Despite the promises of major economic development, only Cumbria in northwest England expressed an interest in being a possible host for the repository. Cumbria brought nuclear experience to its inquiries. It is the site of the Sellafield nuclear plant. In the 1990s, the Nirex Plan explored the prospects of an underground nuclear waste laboratory. The project died when a planning inspector found the geology to be unsafe,[71] a finding that stopped the project, but which was not widely supported as scientifically well-based. Following the Nirex decision, the United Kingdom reorganized its nuclear waste programme, placing the national government directly in charge and creating a Nuclear Decommissioning Authority. That prompted a second look at a Cumbria location for a repository.

Experts divided sharply over whether it was sensible to seek community support before resolving geological and other feasibility issues.[72] Feasibility aside, local residents and others worried that even the geologically safest repository might not be a compatible neighbour in the tourist-popular English Lake District.

In late January 2013, Cumbria County Council vetoed going further with the waste repository. The seven-to-three Council vote effectively ended the four-year exploration process.[73] Council leader Eddie Martin expressed concern over the geology and feared that 'if the area becomes known in the national conscience as the place where nuclear waste is stored underground, the Lake District's reputation may not be so resilient'. He further noted that the Council was worried that moving forward with planning might have jeopardized Cumbria's legal right of withdrawal.

The Secretary of State for Energy and Climate Change expressed disappointment but reiterated Government's support for nuclear power and for the selection of an underground permanent repository. For the moment, however, the United Kingdom finds itself in the same position as the United States and Japan. Despite considerable national government solicitation and promises of financial assistance, local government objections have killed the hope of finding a willing host community.

4. *Sweden*

Sweden poses a particularly interesting study of high-level waste disposal. It has been an active participant in nuclear electric generation for decades, ranking tenth worldwide in installed capacity in 2010. However, from 1980–2010 Sweden pursued a government policy initiated by popular referendum to phase out nuclear power as an

[70] 'Managing Radioactive Waste Safely' (n 67) at 5.
[71] Available at <http://www.bbc.co.uk/news/uk-england-cumbria-19816861>.
[72] See n 71.
[73] Available at <http://www.bbc.co.uk/news/uk-england-cumbria-21253673>.

energy source. Political and popular sentiment, however, shifted as nuclear power emerged as a climate-friendly energy option. In 2010, the Swedish Parliament narrowly approved a backing away from the phase out of nuclear power.[74]

The Swedish Constitution places control over peaceful nuclear uses in the national government. The Nuclear Energy Act of 2003 sets out familiar divisions of responsibilities between the private commercial sector and the government. Waste management is an important subject of that regulation.

In the 1970s, the nuclear power companies created the Swedish Nuclear Fuel and Waste Management Company (SKB) to safely manage and dispose of all radioactive wastes.[75] SKB has conducted active research on this topic for over 30 years. Repositories for low-level waste and interim storage for higher-level waste have already been established. For over 20 years research has also planned for a repository for the permanent storage of high-level spent nuclear fuel. After ample study, in March 2011 an application was submitted to the Radiation Safety Authority and to the Environmental Court to build the repository at the nuclear plant at Forsmark.

The submission of the application triggered an extensive study process that is expected to be completed by 2015. The process includes international advice and review within Sweden from government officials, environmental groups, local governments, and universities and colleges. As reviews are completed, they will be open for further review and public hearings. Eventually, the Radiation Safety Authority and the Environmental Court will offer their recommendations to the Government. The involved municipalities will have the opportunity to veto the recommendations. Despite the comprehensive timetable, a decision to begin construction of the repository is expected by 2019.

SKB's website promises that the repository will provide 'safety for 100,000 years' and notes that its research has considered the potential impacts of earthquakes, future ice ages, and climate change. The website observes: 'For most people, 100,000 years is an enormously long time. However, the Spent Fuel Repository is to be placed in an environment that has been stable for billions of years: the Swedish crystalline basement rock. With such an environment, it is possible to make predictions on development in the very long term.'[76] Reflecting on the possible end of the commercial nuclear age in Sweden, SKB notes: 'Our generation has benefited from nuclear power and therefore we also have a responsibility to solve the issue of final disposal.'[77]

5. *Finland*

Finland has four nuclear reactors at two geographic sites, an additional reactor approved and moving towards completion, and two others in the planning stage. The Finnish government has committed to continuing a nuclear programme for

[74] See <http://www.world-nuclear.org/info/Country-Profiles/Countries-O-S/Sweden/#.Ue8sOxylkb8>.
[75] Available at <http://www.skb.se/default____24417.aspx>.
[76] Available at <http://www.skb.se/Templates/Standard____24058.aspx>.
[77] Available at <http://www.skb.se/Templates/Standard____33922.aspx>.

the foreseeable future. Popular opinion has been consistently pro-nuclear, with a 2012 (post-Fukushima) poll showing 65% support for nuclear power. The Finnish plans for a permanent repository for spent nuclear fuel may be the most advanced of any nation. Finland hopes to open the first such repository as early as 2022.[78]

Finland's Nuclear Energy Act requires that all nuclear waste generated in Finland must be stored and disposed of in Finland. The Act details the familiar division of responsibility between the commercial operators and the government that ends with final ownership of spent fuel in government hands. However, the Finish legal structure gives greater authority over the repository process to the commercial nuclear plant operators than is present in other nations. An ongoing dispute involves where the spent fuel from the newest nuclear plant will be stored. The commercial operators of the existing nuclear plants have refused to agree to take the spent fuel from a new commercial operator. Government officials have encouraged a solution. But, the prospect remains of a new repository to handle the spent fuel from the new nuclear plant.[79]

Final disposal facilities for low-level and intermediate-level waste are already in operation. They are located in bedrock.

Preparations for the permanent disposal of spent nuclear fuel began in the early 1980s. Initial hopes were to select a site by 2000. That date proved too optimistic but a steady programme of research and review endorsed a plan to encapsulate the waste and place it in bedrock 500 m below the earth's surface[80]

Six sites were investigated. The Finish Radioactive Waste Management and Decommissioning plan provides that 'Consent of the proposed host municipality is required for the construction [of the repository]'.[81] A site near the Olkiluoto nuclear plant site was identified. The host municipality approved the application by a 20 to 7 vote of its Council in 2000. The Government approved the proposal in December 2000 and the decision was ratified by Parliament in May 2001.[82] Construction has advanced for an underground 'rock characterization facility' and a construction licence application for the disposal facility is expected shortly. Current plans are to begin receiving spent fuel in 2022 and continue for almost a century, with final sealing of the repository in 2120.[83]

V. Future directions

Despite much research and public discussion, as of 2014 few nuclear nations can claim to have 'solved' the problem of permanent disposition of spent fuel and other

78 See <http://www.world-nuclear.org/info/Country-Profiles/Countries-A-F/Finland/#.Ue8vjBylkb8>.
79 See n 78.
80 Available at <http://www.stuk.fi/ydinturvallisuus/ydinjatteet/loppusijoitus_suomessa/kapselointi_ja_ls_laitos/en_GB/laitos/>.
81 Available at <http://www.oecd-nea.org/rwm/profiles/Finland_report.pdf>.
82 See n 81.
83 Available at <http://www.posiva.fi/en/final_disposal/general_time_schedule_for_final_disposal>.

high-level nuclear waste. One thing is certain: whatever the future direction of commercial nuclear power, a waste disposal issue will remain. Even if every nation abandons nuclear power tomorrow (a highly unlikely prospect), a significant amount of spent fuel and high-level waste exists in temporary storage, hardly a satisfactory long-term solution. As nuclear plants are shut down, the prospect of decades of waste lingering on site above ground becomes increasingly troubling. Abandoned business enterprises are hardly attractive caretakers of previously generated waste. Furthermore, if nuclear expertise dies out with its present generation of workers, who can be counted on for the eventual safe disposal of the waste? Swedish experts stated the matter well: our generation created the waste and our generation should permanently dispose of it as safely as possible.

On the other hand, if nuclear energy remains an important part of future electric generation, even greater amounts of waste will need to be disposed of. And if nuclear power is in serious competition with other generation sources (renewables, increased amounts of natural gas, coal bolstered by carbon capture and storage projects), resolution of the permanent waste disposal issue may decide the economic and political attractiveness of nuclear power. A refusal to solve the waste disposal issue may effectively decide nuclear power's future.

Several decades and billions of dollars have been spent in the United States to indicate that repository siting by government fiat does not work. The importance of public participatory decision-making will probably shape most nations' repository laws and policies. Public disclosure, educational programmes, public hearings, solicitation of volunteer communities, and veto powers are all sensible. But, they do not guarantee that a good permanent waste site will be selected and constructed.

Both sides have a case to be made in the question of whether science should precede political and popular support or vice versa. An initial search for the ideal geologic, hydrologic, and seismic repository is useful, but it may fail if the popular support is not there initially or cannot be developed. But, equally relevant, compiling a lengthy list of prospective volunteer communities may be pointless if many of them will fail basic scientific tests or would not be ready for a long selection process in which political administrations will change and a vigorous anti-repository campaign will likely be launched. Government site selectors may want to create an early screening process to eliminate clearly scientifically unqualified locations promptly and at limited expense. Selectors should also be cautious of proposals from government officials in economically depressed, but geologically doubtful, areas in which the repository may look like a last hope to save the town.

One positive factor for a selection decision is a community's and a state's familiarity with nuclear matters. The Swedish, Finnish, United Kingdom, and New Mexico experiences suggest that living with aspects of nuclear science and enterprise can help build and sustain community popular and political support. The repository becomes part of a nuclear economy rather than the single and new nuclear presence in the area. Nuclear power plants, fuel fabrication facilities, and other nuclear business enterprises look like solid engines of economic development. They may smooth the way for a repository.

That model also helps to define national government financial support for a repository project. Most national governments understand the need for initial financial aid to cover the costs of a reasonable investigation of a community's bid for a repository. Few lightly populated communities (an attractive factor for repository location) can afford the significant expense of research and consultation that may come to naught. That should be the national government's responsibility.

Once a site has been selected, the community should also be entitled to help with the costs of infrastructure and services for new employees made necessary by the coming of the repository project. Needs for schools, social services, law enforcement, and health care may rapidly expand. It is unfair to ask the community to bear those costs up front and by itself.

What about even larger expenditures that may have no direct relation to the siting of the repository? Suppose the community insists that the national government shall also locate a military base or a major medical research facility as a part of the repository agreement? An initial national government response is likely to be negative. So is the political reaction from other jurisdictions bidding for the military base or the research facility. But suppose the national government has only one willing community bidder for the repository?

These matters cover only some of the challenges facing the drafters and implementers of new laws that reflect participatory democracy in the selection of repository sites. One hopes that the next three decades will evidence more progress than the previous three.

18

Electricity Undergrounding in Russia: The Case for Underground Substations

Sergey Seliverstov

I. Introduction

Although electrical substations have been located underground in Japan and the United Kingdom since the late 1960s, the practice is still rare. The first underground substation in the United States was opened in California as recently as 2006.[1] Such rare and complex technology requires engineering and land planning specific to each new project.

While underground substations will probably remain the exception rather than the rule, several factors encourage their expanded use. Land in growing megalopolises is becoming increasingly expensive. An underground electrical substation allows the use of the surface for other valuable urban uses. Harsh weather and dangers of possible terrorism may also make attractive an underground location for important electricity infrastructure.

This chapter discusses the first and recent cases of underground electrical substation construction in Russia and the prospects for replication of those cases in the future. Two underground substations are being built in the Skolkovo Innovations Centre near Moscow. The Innovations Centre is often advertised as the 'Russian Silicon Valley'. Construction of the Innovations Centre relied on substantial exemptions in terms of land management and urban planning law and regulations. Those exemptions greatly favoured the construction of underground substations. We examine how the construction of these and future underground substations fit into Russian electricity sector regulation and land law.

Russia is not actively pursuing some of the new or innovative underground energy activities discussed in other chapters of this book. Russia's ample conventional oil and natural gas reserves supply both domestic and export purposes and provide little incentive to develop the unconventional reserves of those hydrocarbons that have attracted support in other nations. Also, neither carbon capture and storage nor geothermal energy is a Russian priority.

[1] H. Cohen, *The Neighborly Substation* (2008) 23, available at <http://www.manhattan-institute.org/html/crd_neighborly_substation.htm>.

II. Economic and technical background

In addition to its vast oil and natural gas reserves, Russia has the fourth largest and most extended electricity system in the world, which is spread over eight time zones. The major part of the Russian electricity system is connected into the United Power System of the Russian Federation (UPS). The UPS is defined in the Federal Law 'On electricity sector'[2] (the Law 'On electricity sector') as the 'complex of production and other material assets of the electricity sector connected by means of the single process of production and transmission of electricity within the framework of centralized operational dispatch management'.[3]

The total installed capacity of the UPS in 2012 amounted to 223,070.8 MW.[4] Of that total, 68.1% is provided by fossil fuel generation, 20.6% by hydropower stations, and 11.3% by nuclear power stations. The UPS includes more than 600 power stations, 124,000 km of transmission lines, and countless substations between Vladivostok in the Far East of Russia and Kaliningrad Region on the border with Poland. The UPS operates in synchronous mode with the power systems of nine neighbouring states—Azerbaijan, Belarus, Estonia, Georgia, Kazakhstan, Latvia, Lithuania, Mongolia, and Ukraine. The single synchronous zone extends further to Kirgizstan, Moldova, and Uzbekistan.[5]

The electrical substations are an important technological element of the UPS, more specifically of its transmission and distribution elements. The substations serve for switching from the high voltages needed for efficient long-distance transmission to the lower voltages appropriate for shorter-distance transmission and for distribution to residential and commercial end users. The voltage level (there are more than a dozen voltage levels in Russia) determines the capacity of the substation.

The need to minimize the loss of electricity encourages the siting of the substations close to the final customers. This is the key challenge for the majority of large urban residential and commercial areas, since according to the urban planning rules, substations usually fall in the category of industrial facilities. There is always a need to find the proper balance between economic and energy efficiency on the one hand and administrative and environmental regulations on the other.

III. Electricity sector development and investment programmes

The development of the electricity sector in general and especially of its network segments is done in accordance with the countrywide 'general scheme of the

[2] Federal Law dated 26 March 2003, No 35-FZ 'On electricity Sector'.

[3] Article 3 of the Law 'On electricity sector'.

[4] 'Official Report on the Functioning of the UPS of Russia in 2012', prepared by the System Operator of the UPS, 3, available at <http://so-ups.ru/fileadmin/files/company/reports/disclosure/2013/ues_rep2012.pdf>.

[5] Official Report (n 4) at 2.

electricity sector objects' (the 'General Scheme') and the 'UPS development scheme and programme' (the 'UPS Programme'). The construction of the high-capacity substations also falls within their scope because the overwhelming majority of the substations are being constructed by the open joint-stock company 'Federal Grid Company of the Unified Energy System' (the 'Federal Grid Company'). We outline here the legal framework for the General Scheme and the UPS Programme and their influence on the activities of the Federal Grid Company.

The use of schemes and programmes has both technological and historical bases. In the Soviet times, the entire economy had been developed in accordance with centralized plans. This was especially the case for the electricity network segment, which unlike some other sectors of Russian industry, greatly benefited from such an approach. The centralized development of the transmission and distribution networks, as well as the coordination of such development with the growth of generation and demand areas, allowed operators to avoid interregional mismatches, bottlenecks, or excessive reserve capacities in the majority of situations.

Since perestroika and the breakup of the Soviet Union, the electricity sector in Russia has undergone substantial changes. Privatization in the sector was followed by liberalization, resulting in full ownership unbundling and the creation of a vast variety of market mechanisms on the basis of wholesale and retail electricity markets.[6] Nevertheless, the major elements of centralized network development have been preserved in the liberalized open market.

The approval process for both the General Scheme and the UPS Programme is currently governed by the Government Regulation 'On Schemes and Programmes of the Prospective Development of the Electricity Sector',[7] adopted in 2009. The main principles, which are currently applied to the formation of the schemes and programmes are, with certain exceptions, not unusual for a planned economy. They are:

(1) economic efficiency of the proposed solutions based on the optimization of the modes of the UPS;
(2) application of new technological solutions;
(3) coordination between the schemes and programmes of the prospective development and the investment programmes of the electricity and network companies;
(4) coordination between the development of transmission and distribution networks;

[6] For details, see S. S. Seliverstov, 'The Electricity Sector Reforms in Russia: European Legal Concepts and Russian Reality' in *EU Energy Law and Policy Issues* (B. Delvaux, M. Hunt, and K. Talue, eds, 2nd edn, 2010) Vol 2, 37–50; S. S. Seliverstov and I. V. Gudkov, 'The Development of Electricity and Gas Networks in Russia' in M. M. Roggenkamp, L. Barrera-Hernandez, D. N. Zillman, and I. del Guayo, *Energy Networks and the Law* (2012) 394–417.

[7] Government Regulation dated 17 October 2009, No 823, 'On Schemes and Programmes of the Prospective Development of the Electricity Sector'.

(5) coordination between the development of the transmission infrastructure and the power generation sector; and

(6) openness to the public of the state investment strategies and solutions.

The General Scheme is a strategic document. With a duration of 15 years, it is periodically amended at least once every three years on the basis of the long-term prognosis of electricity demand. The General Scheme is elaborated by the Ministry of Energy with the participation of the Federal Tariff Service, the state corporation 'Rosatom', which operates all nuclear power stations in Russia, the fully state-owned open joint-stock company, 'System Operator of the United Power System' (the 'System Operator'), and the Federal Grid Company. The General Scheme shall then be approved by the government of the Russian Federation.

The UPS Programme represents the second level of planning. It defines the seven-year plan for the coordinated and balanced development of the network infrastructure and the generation capacities. It is elaborated by the System Operator and the Federal Grid Company annually on the basis of the General Scheme and is approved by the Ministry of Energy. The UPS development scheme (the 'UPS Scheme') becomes part of the UPS Programme and includes, inter alia, existing and planned substations of the voltage class 220 kV and higher. The two Skolkovo substations— 'Skolkovo' and 'Smirnovo' (also called 'Soyuz')—have been included in the UPS Schemes and UPS Programmes, as adopted by the Ministry of Energy in 2011[8] and in 2012, respectively.[9]

In addition to containing a general explanation of UPS development, the relevant Orders of the Ministry of Energy also outline the timeframes and investments for commissioning the two substations and serve as a basis for the Investment Programme of the Federal Grid Company.

The Investment Programme is composed of all investment projects executed or being executed by the company. It is a key strategic document for electricity companies with state capital (though not necessarily state-controlled) and network companies.[10] The approval of the Investment Programmes, including the Investment Programme of the Federal Grid Company, is based on the relevant Government Regulation[11] and outlines an 'administrative' phase of the decision-making process.

The Investment Programmes should reflect the basic parameters of the UPS Scheme and the UPS Programme. They should also contain the overall description of the Investment Programme of the given company, the construction and

[8] Order of the Ministry of Energy of Russian Federation dated 29 August 2011, No 380, 'On the Approval of the Scheme and the Programme of the Development of the United Power System of Russia for the Period of 2011–2017'.

[9] Order of the Ministry of Energy of Russian Federation dated 13 August 2012, No 387, 'On the Approval of the Scheme and the Programme of the Development of the United Power System of Russia for the Period of 2012–2018'.

[10] Item 24(a) of the Government Regulation dated 17 October 2009, No 823, 'On Schemes and Programmes of the Prospective Development of the Electricity Sector'.

[11] Government Regulation dated 1 December 2009, No 977, 'On Investments Programmes of the subjects of the Electricity Sector'.

financing schedules of each investment project, and a report on the fulfilment by the company of previous investment projects. These sections of the Investment Programmes are usually not disclosed to the public. What is disclosed is the overall list of investment projects with indicative costs and time estimates.

The Investment Programme of the Federal Grid Company is approved by the Ministry of Energy upon agreement of the Ministry of Economic Development, the State Corporation 'Rosatom', and the Ministry of Regional Development. The two Skolkovo substations have been included as separate investment projects in the Investment Programmes of the Federal Grid Company since 2010. It is interesting to note that the Skolkovo substations were first mentioned in the Investment Programme and only afterwards in the UPS Scheme.[12] This is not the usual administrative procedure. At the same time, the UPS Scheme preceding the Investment Programme outlined the abstract necessity of the transformation capacities in general terms. One way or another, the inclusion in the Investment Programme of the Skolkovo substations gave the green light to financing and construction of those unusual facilities.

IV. The law on Skolkovo: exemptions from land and urban planning regulations

The first initiatives to build underground electrical substations in Moscow and Saint Petersburg date back to 2006 and 2008, respectively. The substation in Moscow was planned for the Belorussky railway station area. This area underwent and still is undergoing major reconstruction and is among the most expensive business and residential districts in Europe. The substation in Saint Petersburg was planned to be part of an underground parking area underneath one of the squares in the historic part of the city. Neither of these pioneering projects was put into effect, in part due to the 2008 financial crisis, technical and regulatory complexities, and lack of administrative support.

Two Skolkovo underground substations have similar technical characteristics. Their voltage is 220/20 kV, and each has two gas-insulated 63 MW transformers. One of the reasons for using gas-insulated transformers is to minimize fire risks in the underground premises, where it is more difficult to put out fires than on the surface. Waterproofing was also one of the major necessities and major difficulties in the Skolkovo construction.

The fact that all the equipment is located inside a building and that operation and control are handled remotely increases the level of safety. However, due to the rarity of such projects, there is no statistical record on how underground location influences the overall level of security of such installations.

[12] Order of the Ministry of Energy of Russian Federation dated 15 July 2010, No 333, 'On the Approval of the Scheme and the Programme of the Development of the United Power System of Russia for the Period of 2010–2016'.

Substation Skolkovo is only partially underground. The burial depth is 10 m. The substation complex occupies six stories with a total area of more than 6000 m^2. Above ground, the facility is covered by green planting and landscaping. The substation was scheduled to begin operation in 2013.

Substation Smirnovo is of even more exceptional construction. It is buried 24 m deep. This makes it a 'unique capital construction' within the meaning of the Russian Urban Planning Code.[13]

Eventually there will be a five-story office building called 'Forrest Office' above the substation. After the completion of the Forrest Office, its first floor will host the control centre of both Skolkovo substations and the museum of the Federal Grid Company.

There will be a number of new energy efficiency applications in the building, including solar panels and a special lighting system. The heat created by the transformers will be used for heating the premises during the winter. The geothermal system will provide cooling in the summer. The building is expected to correspond to the Platinum standards of the Leadership in Energy and Environmental Design.

The Skolkovo projects are included in the Investment Programme of the Federal Grid Company approved by the Ministry of Energy, which provides the necessary administrative support and the necessary financing for the projects. Their construction is seen as a crucial part of the overall infrastructure development of the Skolkovo Innovations Centre and adjacent area.

The Skolkovo Innovations Centre is currently the Russian Government's most promoted centre for research and innovations. It is advertised as the 'Russian Silicon Valley'. There are other dedicated research and innovation locations in the Moscow region. However, Skolkovo seems far ahead in attracting financing and administrative support. A specific Federal Law (the 'Law on Skolkovo') details the environment for the functioning of the Innovations Centre.[14] A number of those legal provisions have been applied to the construction of the Skolkovo underground substations.

The Law on Skolkovo grants substantial autonomy to the Management Company of the Innovations Centre. The Management Company has exclusive title to the land and facilities within the territory of the Innovations Centre. The Management Company is entitled to unilaterally transfer the land plots of different land categories to the category of community lands. The Management Company cannot dispose of land plots other than by leasing them to the resident companies. The sublease of land plots or accommodation facilities is prohibited.

The territory of the Innovations Centre is exempt from general urban planning, land use, and construction requirements. The Management Company prepares and uses its own General Plan and Construction and Land Use Regulations. No public hearings are necessary for the approval of those plans and regulations.

[13] Article 48.1 of the Urban Planning Code of the Russian Federation dated 29 December 2004, No 190-FZ.

[14] Federal Law dated 28 September 2010, No 244-FZ, 'On Skolkovo Innovations Centre'.

The Management Company also approves territorial planning documents and issues construction permits and permits to put the capital constructions into effect. The Management Company is also responsible for the creation of infrastructure, including electricity infrastructure, and for supplying electricity to the population. Therefore, the Management Company in Skolkovo represents a kind of universal authority, which has significantly simplified the overall administrative process connected with the construction of the substations.

In practice, however, given the unique character of the Smirnovo substation, its technical parameters were specifically approved by the Agency of the Ministry of Regional Development, which was responsible for the construction supervision. The Federal Grid Company received the following approvals from the Skolkovo Management Company: expert approval of the project documents, the construction permit, and the permit to put the capital construction into operation in the form adopted by the Management Company.

V. The line between land law and subsoil regulations

There is a clear distinction between land law and subsoil regulation in Russia. As envisaged in the Land Code 2011, '[t]he land legislation governs the relationship regarding the use and protection of lands in the Russian Federation considering them as the basis for life and activities of the nations living on the respective territory (land relationship) . . . Property-related relationships regarding ownership, use and disposal of land plots as well as regarding transactions therewith are governed by the civil legislation, unless otherwise provided by the land, forestry, water legislation, legislation on subsoil, on environmental protection, by specific federal laws.'[15]

The subsoil is governed by a separate set of legislative and regulatory acts, the most important of which is the Law 'On subsoil'.[16] Unlike land plots, subsoil in Russia is in the exclusive ownership of the state. Private companies and individuals can only be granted the right to use identified parcels of the subsoil, such a right being formalized in subsoil use licences. The subsoil use presupposes the entire set of specific administrative and technical regulations. In short, land and subsoil represent two different spaces in both physical and regulatory terms.

The physical, and hence the legal, borderline between the two spaces, however, is not clearly marked. Neither the Land Code nor the Law 'On subsoil' contain any provisions making that distinction. In practice, however, underground oil and gas storage facilities, tunnels, underground motorways, and the metro require a subsoil use licence to be constructed.

The question of whether the construction of underground electrical substations requires a subsoil licence and whether the whole set of subsoil regulations applies to

[15] Article 3 of the Land Code of the Russian Federation dated 25 October 2001, No 136-FZ.
[16] Federal Law of 21 February 1992, No 2395-1, 'On subsoil'.

them is still open. On the one hand, the so-called Methodical Guidelines and Recommendations issued by different bodies responsible for the subsoil management,[17] and strictu sensu not being legally binding, establish a number of distinguishing criteria.

The Recommendations of the Committee on Geology and the Use of Subsoil dated 1992, for example, envisage that the underground engineering constructions with a burial depth up to 5 m and not connected with the extraction of mineral resources do not require a subsoil licence.[18] This, in turn, presupposes that constructions to a greater depth are indeed subject to licensing requirements. It should also be reiterated here that, according to the Urban Planning code, the capital constructions with a burial depth greater than 15 m are considered 'unique', which also triggers a specific regime of project expertise and construction approvals for them.

The Methodical Guidelines adopted by the Ministry of Natural Resources in 1998 introduced the notion of the 'mine opening'. The Guidelines further stated that they apply to constructions located in such mine openings. The electric power stations and substations are expressly cited as examples of such constructions requiring a subsoil licence. The definition of 'mine opening', however, is absent from the legal and administrative acts. Therefore, the formalistic question still remains, whether the licensing requirement applies to substations located in such openings or to all types of underground substations.

The Skolkovo substations do not provide a clear-cut answer to that question. In practice, the construction of Skolkovo, and even of the unique Smirnovo substation, did not require the subsoil licence. This can be explained, in part, by the specific land management and urban planning regime envisaged by the Law 'On Skolkovo'. We say 'in part' because strictu sensu the Law 'On Skolkovo' granting specific rights to the Management Company of the Innovations Centre does not grant any rights to subsoil use or management. Therefore, it may be argued that under normal conditions, i.e. if constructed outside the scope of the Law 'On Skolkovo', the underground substations with burial depths of more than 5 m, and especially of more than 15 m, should serve as a test case for line drawing between 'land' and 'subsoil' under Russian law.

[17] See, e.g., Methodical Guidelines on Licensing of the Subsoil Use for the Purposes not Connected with the Extraction of the Mineral Resources, adopted by the Ministry of Natural Resources on 22 June 1998 (not officially published); Recommendations on the Order of Licensing of the Use of Subsoil Executed by the Working Undertakings with Regards to Underground Waters, Dumping of Harmful Substances, Waste, Sewage Disposal in the Subsoil and the Use of Subsoil not Connected with the Extraction of the Mineral Resources, annexed to the Letter of the Committee on the Geology and the Use of Subsoil of 5 November 1992, No BIII-61/2714.

[18] Para 1(d) of the Recommendations on the Order of Licensing of the Use of Subsoil Executed by the Working Undertakings with Regards to Underground Waters, Dumping of Harmful Substances, Waste, Sewage Disposal in the Subsoil and the Use of Subsoil not Connected with the Extraction of the Mineral Resources, Annexed to the Letter of the Committee on the Geology and the Use of Subsoil of 5 November 1992, No BIII-61/2714.

VI. Financing of the development projects

Financial attractiveness is a key driver for development of the underground electrical substation technology. So far, the figures do not look inspiring. According to the latest Investment Programme of the Federal Grid Company for 2013–17,[19] the overall investments for the construction of the Skolkovo substation is 3,648 million rubles (US$117.7 million), and of the Smirnovo substation, it is 3,445.7 million rubles (US$111.2 million). The costs would be substantially lower for regular above-the-ground substations. It is also worth noting that the initial estimates provided in the UPS Programme for 2011–17 were 1,018,7 million rubles (US $33.39 million) for each substation.[20]

It is also interesting to compare these figures with the directly interconnected project of reconstruction of electricity transmission lines between Moscow and the Skolkovo in Odintsovo area. The overhead high-voltage 500 kV and 220 kV lines, with the total length of about 11 km (total length of the cable is about 44.5 km), as well as a number of 110kV lines, are being replaced by the underground cable lines. The overall amount of investment is estimated at 14,000 million rubles (US$451.6 million). The useful effect of the later project would, according to the estimates of the Federal Grid Company, consist of the release of about 180 hectares of land in Moscow and in the region right on the Moscow border.[21]

Not all of the 180 hectares will be used for industrial or residential construction. There will be a protective zone for the cable line and other related limitations for the use of the land. Nevertheless, the savings effects of substituting overhead lines for cable lines is more obvious than for building an underground substation. On the other hand, in dense urban areas the underground electrical cables already exist and underground substations would represent a 'point-like' solution for the land saving. The use of low-capacity substations and technological advances may make underground electrical substations economically viable in the future.

VII. Conclusion

The successful construction of two relatively high-capacity 220 kV underground substations in the Russian Silicon Valley represent a 'shop-window' rather than the start of a wide-ranging application of that technology. Skolkovo is not so densely populated as to make the underground substation technology vital or even economically justifiable.

[19] The Investment Programme of the Federal Grid Company for 2013–2017 approved by the Order of the Ministry of Energy dated 31 October 2012, No 531, <http://www.fsk-ees.ru>.

[20] Order of the Ministry of Energy of Russian Federation, dated 29 August 2011, No 380. 'On the Approval of the Scheme and the Programme of the Development of the United Power System of Russia for the Period of 2011–2017'.

[21] Available at <http://www.fsk-ees.ru/investments/electricity_innovation_centre_skolkovo/>.

The specific regime of land management and urban planning established by the Law 'On Skolkovo' eliminated many administrative obstacles for the construction of these distinctive projects. At the same time, such experience does not allow for an accurate estimate of the difficulties to be confronted by similar projects needing to operate under the standard regulatory regime. Neither does it allow a clear-cut answer to whether the construction of underground substations generally can be qualified as a subsoil use within the meaning of the relevant legislation and would therefore need to meet an additional set of regulations.

The development of the underground electrical substation technology in Russian cities will depend on its commercial attractiveness and a political willingness to implement the technology. In the near future, application of such technology is likely to occur in the form of low-capacity substations in the most luxurious or historical urban areas of Moscow and Saint Petersburg, or in the form of 'shop-windows' accompanying large urban development projects.

PART V

RESOLVING UNDERGROUND RESOURCE CONFLICTS AROUND THE WORLD

19

New Uses of the Underground in the Netherlands: How to Manage a Crowded Subsoil?

Martha Roggenkamp and Danielle Hanema[1]

I. Introduction

The subsoil of the Netherlands has been used for many centuries—and is still being used—for the purpose of energy production. After a period of open cast mining, underground mining activities, particularly coal mining, started in the fourteenth century in the southern part of the Dutch province of Limburg.[2] Coal mining was terminated in the 1970s[3] following the discovery of onshore petroleum resources,[4] and the discovery of large quantities of natural gas in the Groningen area in 1959.[5] This was followed by the discovery of numerous other gas fields onshore as well as offshore. Whereas the Groningen gas field is considered a major gas field and currently accounts for some 60% of total Dutch gas production,[6] all other Dutch

1 This chapter was written as part of the Energy Delta Gas Research project.

2 J. Voncken, 'Ontstaansgeschiedenis van de steenkolenwinning in Nederland' (History of Coal Mining in the Netherlands), 31 December 2009, available at <http://www.kennislink.nl/publicaties/ontstaansgeschiedenis-van-de-steenkolenwinning-in-nederland> (Dutch).

3 The last coal mine was closed in 1974. TK 1969–1970, 10 312, number 2 at 13:TK 1973–1974, 58, at 3001, 3014. 'Laatste kolenmijn in Limburg gesloten' (Last Coal Mine in Limburg Closed), *De Waarheid*, 2 January 1975, at 3 (Dutch).

4 The first oil in the Netherlands was shown to be present in the Winterswijk area (eastern Netherlands) in February 1924. See 'Aardolie bij Winterswijk. Een belangrijke vondst'. (Oil at Winterswijk. An Important Discovery), *Het Centrum*, 28 February 1924 at 5 (Dutch). This was followed by the discovery of several other oilfields and minor gas fields in the following decades.

5 'Rijke aardgasader in Slochteren ontdekt. Bij de Knijpsbrug' (Abundant Natural Gas Discovered in Slochteren at the Knijpsbrug), *Nieuwsblad van het Noorden*, 25 September 1959, at 1 (Dutch). Besides the discovery of several natural gas and oil fields, there was another reason for closing the coal mining industry: the Dutch coal mines were not able to compete on the very competitive coal market. Therefore the Dutch government decided in 1965 to terminate the coal mining industry in the Netherlands: 'Nota inzake de mijnindustrie en de industriële herstructurering van Zuid Limburg' (Memorandum regarding the mining industry and the industrial restructuring of Southern Limburg), TK 1965–1966, 8424, numbers 1–9 (Dutch).

6 In 2011, the Groningen field produced 49,400 million m^3. The total gas production in the Netherlands (both onshore and offshore) accounted for 78,600 million m^3, available at <http://www.nlog.nl/en/production/production.html>.

fields are considered to be small fields. As at 1 January 2013, a total of 49.3% of the Dutch territory—41,785 km^2—was utilized for the exploration for and production of hydrocarbons.[7] In addition, 54.03% of the area of the Dutch continental shelf—56,814 km^2—was under exploration and production.[8]

Given that most of the Dutch oil and gas fields are relatively small, an increasing number of these fields are reaching the stage at which production ceases and the fields are abandoned and installations removed. Depleted oil and gas fields, however, create possibilities for new uses of the subsoil, most particularly reuse for storage purposes. Subsoil gas storage has taken place onshore since the 1990s in Grijpskerk and Norg for reasons of security of supply, i.e., additional availability in cold winter periods.[9] More recently, new storage facilities have been developed in Alkmaar (Bergermeer)[10] and Zuidwendige[11] for meeting demands for flexibility in the gas market. In Zuidwendige, gas storage is in a salt cavern rather than a (depleted) gas field.

New market developments, as well as the growing number of depleted oil and gas fields, pose questions regarding other uses of the subsoil for energy or energy-related purposes. This entails the possibility of storage of nuclear waste or CO_2 as part of the final part of the Carbon Capture and Storage (CCS) chain, and which may be relevant for electricity generators, refineries, etc. Apart from this, the need to secure long-term energy supplies has triggered new techniques and policies regarding subsoil energy developments. First and foremost, this involves the exploration and production of geothermal heat and shale gas. In addition, the subsoil can also be used for storage of heat and cold.

This chapter examines the Dutch legal framework applying to these new subsoil energy developments. We first discuss the legal framework applying to the use of the so-called deep underground, and thereafter consider whether the existing legal regime is adequate to govern these developments. We then discuss the need to introduce a regime of subsoil planning and end with a conclusion.

II. The law regulating the use of the subsoil: Mining Acts

When discussing the law governing the subsoil, we need to distinguish between the period before and the period after the passage of the Mining Act in 2003. Before the Act was passed in 2003, the use of the subsoil in the Netherlands was governed by a French Act drafted by Napoleon Bonaparte, i.e., the *Loi concernant les Mines, les*

[7] 'Koolwaterstof VERGUNNINGEN, Nederlands Territoir per 1 januari 2013' (Hydrocarbon Licences, Dutch Territory as at 1 January 013), available (in Dutch) at <http://www.nlog.nl/resources/Jaarverslag2012/VergunningenE&Pkwst_Mutaties2012NL_20130101.pdf>.

[8] 'Koolwaterstof VERGUNNINGEN, Nederlands Continentaal Plat per 1 januari 2013' (Hydrocarbon Licences, Dutch Continental Shelf as at 1 January 2013), available (in Dutch) at <http://www.nlog.nl/resources/Jaarverslag2012/VergunningenE&Pkwst_Mutaties2012NL_20130101.pdf>.

[9] See further <http://www.nam.nl/nl/our-activities/norg.html> (Dutch).

[10] See further <http://www.alkmaargasstorage.nl/Alkmaar%20PGI.htm>.

[11] See further <http://www.agbzw.nl> (Dutch).

Minières et les Carrières du 21 Avril 1810 (or Mining Act 1810). The Mining Act 1810 was introduced in the Netherlands during the French reign. When the Netherlands regained its independence in 1813 it was decided that this Act would remain 'provisionally, until further measures are taken'.[12] In the meantime, however, additional legislation had entered into force. Onshore, the Mining Act 1810 was, inter alia, supplemented with the Mining Act 1903 and the Minerals Exploration Act of 1967. Offshore, the Continental Shelf Mining Act applied as of 1965.[13] The latter Act is a framework Act and has been supplemented with several Royal Decrees organizing in greater detail the exploration and production of oil and gas.[14]

In 2003, these Acts were replaced by one new law: the Mining Act of 2003.[15] This Act is basically an implementation of the Hydrocarbons Licensing Directive (EC Directive 94/22).[16] Consequently, exploration and production activities depend on prior authorizations issued on a competitive basis by a competent authority, while taking into account the protection of the environment, health, and safety. Notably, the Hydrocarbons Licensing Directive does not include provisions regarding the construction and use of upstream pipelines, the abandonment of installations, and closure of reservoirs, nor the possibility of using depleted fields for storage purposes.

The 2003 Mining Act and the accompanying Decree and Regulation govern the exploration for and the production of oil and gas and other subsoil resources, both onshore and offshore.[17] Onshore, the Act applies to the subsurface below 100 m, as otherwise the ownership rights of landowners would be hampered.[18] Exploration and production of subsoil resources are based on a licensing regime where licences are awarded by the Ministry of Economic Affairs. An interested party will usually first apply for an exploration licence, which is awarded on the basis of an 'open door' regime where the Ministry will invite others to submit competitive applications after an application has been made. The licence will be awarded to the applicant with the best technical and financial capabilities and the best work plan. The holder of an exploration licence can apply for a production licence if

[12] Staatsblad 1813, 3.

[13] Continental Shelf Mining Act of 23 September 1965, Staatsblad 428.

[14] The most important Royal Decrees dated from 1967 (Staatsblad 24), 1976 (Staatsblad 102), and 1996 (Staatsblad 212, 213, 214).

[15] Wet van 31 oktober 2002, houdende regels met betrekking tot het onderzoek naar en het winnen van delfstoffen en met betrekking tot met de mijnbouw verwante activiteiten (Act of 31 October 2002, regarding regulations concerning the exploration for and the production of minerals and concerning mining related activities (Mining Act)), *Staatsblad* 14 November 2002, number 542 (Dutch). For a (non-authoritative) translation of this Act in English, see <http://www.nlog.nl/en/legal/legislation.html>

[16] Directive 94/22/EC of the European Parliament and of the Council of 30 May 1994 on the conditions for granting and using authorizations for the prospection, exploration and production of hydrocarbons. This Directive was published in OJ L 164/3 on 30 June 1994.

[17] M. M. Roggenkamp, 'Energy Law in the Netherlands' in *Energy Law in Europe. National, EU and International Regulation* (M. M. Roggenkamp, C. Redgwell, I. del Guayo, and A. Rønne, eds, 2007, vol 2) 783 at 794.

[18] Mining Act, NL 2003, s 2 states that the state owns the mineral resources located below 100 m of the surface.

an economically exploitable quantity of (energy) resources has been discovered.[19] A production licence is awarded for a specific period,[20] a specific resource, and a specific area that is delimitated at the surface only. After production has ceased, the licensee is obliged to remove the installation according to specific standards set by the government. The entire process of exploration, production, and abandonment is supervised by the health and safety authority called the State Supervision of Mines.[21] Work plans, soil movement measurement plans, abandonment plans, etc. need to be submitted to and approved by this authority.[22]

When drafting the 2003 Mining Act the legislators intended not only to regulate existing activities like oil and gas exploration and production but also to provide for new and/or future developments such as subsoil storage and the production of geothermal heat.[23] The Act therefore provides for a licensing regime for these two activities as well. This licensing regime was based on the experiences gained in the past with hydrocarbons exploration and production. However, it has become clear that changes may be needed to the regulatory framework. Section III reviews the regime set up by the Mining Act and why specific changes were made and/or are still in the process of being made.

III. Subsoil storage

A. Introduction

Although subsoil gas storage started in the 1990s, the Mining Act of 2003 provided the first proper legal basis for such activity.[24] While drafting the provisions on subsoil storage, the legislator recognized the need for using depleted fields for storage purposes. The legislator also recognized that storage in the long term probably would not be limited to natural gas and could be extended to other substances as well.[25] The Act therefore refers to storage of 'substances', i.e., the act of 'conveying or keeping substances at a depth of more than 100 meters below the earth's surface, or recovering these substances [...]'.[26] Consequently, the Act applies to underground storage in all types of geological structures, such as depleted oil/gas fields, salt caverns, and aquifers. Moreover, it regulates not only the subsoil storage of natural gas but also that of CO_2, waste, and possibly even nuclear waste. Whatever the substance, subsoil storage is made dependent on a licence. The

[19] Mining Act, NL 2003, s 8. It is the Minister of Economic Affairs who decides whether the reservoir is economically exploitable.

[20] The duration of the licence depends on the size of the reservoir. A licensee can apply for an extension of the duration of the licence, but only if necessary for production purposes.

[21] See further, <http://www.sodm.nl/english/organisation>.

[22] Other advisory bodies such as the Mining Council and the Technical Committee on Soil Movement must also be consulted.

[23] TK 1998–1999, 26 219, number 3, at 7, 8.

[24] TK 1998–1999, 26 219, number 3, at 11, 12.

[25] TK 1998–1999, 26 219, number 7, at 19.

[26] Mining Act, NL 2003, s 1(i). An exception is included for the conveyance into or keeping therein or retrieval therefrom of substances aimed at the production of terrestrial heat from the subsurface.

following sections first discuss the licensing regime and thereafter how this regime applies to the subsoil storage of gas and the possible subsoil storage of CO_2.

B. Storage licence

Underground storage is made dependent on a storage licence specifying the substances, area, and time period for which it applies.[27] A storage licence is exclusive, since it will not be granted if a storage licence already exists or if an exploration or production licence has been granted for the same reservoir to another person.[28] In other words, as long as a production licence has not yet expired, a storage licence can only be awarded to the person holding the production licence. The legislator wished to avoid a situation where different persons would hold licences for exactly the same subsoil strata. However, as the reservoirs most suited for underground storage are situated onshore and most onshore production licences have been awarded in perpetuity, few storage licences will be awarded to others than the holder of a production licence. Unless the licensee opts for a voluntary splitting and transfer of part of the licence, this situation may reduce the establishment of underground storage facilities considerably.

In 2009, the Mining Act was amended in order to stimulate active use of licences.[29] As a result, the Minister of Economic Affairs has power to limit the scope of a licence (relinquish part of the area) or to withdraw a licence if it has not (properly) been used for the activities governed by the licence.[30] Such a limitation or a withdrawal has multiple consequences. First, others would be given the opportunity to apply for a licence for the relinquished part of the area. Such an application would probably entail a request for a storage licence. If the Minister uses its powers onshore, another consequence would be that the holders of production licences, who legally own the minerals,[31] would face a (partial) or a full expropriation of these as a result of the limitation or withdrawal. The legislator has decided that such licensees should be compensated for damages regarding these expropriations.[32]

27 In order to be able to start operating the storage facility, the holder of a storage licence also needs to submit to the Minister a storage plan for approval. In addition, all provisions in the Mining Act regarding earth movements and decommissioning apply to storage as well.

28 Mining Act, NL 2003, s 26(1)(2). In addition, the Minister may refuse a storage licence if the applicant is considered not to be financially and technically capable of carrying out the intended activities. Mining Act, NL 2003, s 27.

29 Wet van november 26, 2009 tot wijziging van de Mijnbouwwet in verband met het stimuleren van een actief gebruik van vergunningen voor opsporing, winning en opslag (Act of 26 November 2009 amending the Mining Act regarding stimulation of active use of exploration, production and storage licences), *Staatsblad* 8 December 2009, number 508 (Dutch). See also TK 2007–2008, 31 479, number 3, at 1.

30 Mining Act, NL 2003, ss 32a, 32b, 32c on limitation and Mining Act, NL 2003, ss 31a, 21 on withdrawal.

31 This only concerns licensees who have been granted a licence under the old regime (prior to the entry into force of the Mining Act of 2003). These licensees have ownership of all subsoil resources as of the moment the concession was awarded. This status has been continued under the current Mining Act. Mining Act, NL 2003, s 143(2,4).

32 The legislator has stated that the licensee will be compensated for possible damages, because Mining Act, NL 2003, ss 143(4), 150(1) would apply. TK 2007–2008, 31 479, number 3, at 8.

Finally, the Mining Act distinguishes between temporary and permanent storage.[33] Permanent storage will, for example, be required for storing waste products. Temporary storage, however, applies to underground gas storage for peak shaving or other short-term supply purposes. In this situation, the licence must specify a period in time within which the substances should be recovered. It is noteworthy that the ownership of substances retrieved under a storage licence is transferred to the person who owned these substances immediately prior to underground storage.[34] This clause was included in order to avoid any discussion about ownership upon retrieval.[35] It does not make clear, however, the ownership of the substances during the storage period.

C. Gas storage

In the Netherlands, gas is usually stored in depleted gas reservoirs or salt caverns, which are located at a depth between approximately 3,500 and 4,000 m and 1,500 and 4,000 m, respectively.[36] Subsoil gas storage is considered as temporary storage in the sense that gas is injected into the reservoir with the aim of recovering it after a specific period of time. The storage licence will therefore include provisions on the amounts and pace of gas to be injected and recovered each year. Creating a gas storage is also dependent on the amount of cushion gas available. Making use of a nearly depleted reservoir has an advantage that cushion gas is likely to be available. If not, the operators of the storage facility need to buy the required amounts of cushion gas on the open market. The need for subsoil gas storage has increased following the process of gas market liberalization and the subsequent demand for flexibility services. Several supply companies have therefore established subsoil gas storage reservoirs not only in the Netherlands but also abroad, for example in Epe, Germany. Due to its role in gas market liberalization, the regulation of the subsoil reservoirs is not limited to the Mining Act, which governs the establishment of storage facilities. The Gas Act[37] regulates the way in which underground gas storages (UGS) are used, i.e., the issue of third-party access to subsoil storages.

The current Gas Act applies a regime of negotiated third-party access (TPA) to all UGS.[38] Operators of UGS are entitled to refuse TPA but only on limited grounds,

[33] Mining Act, NL 2003, s 28. [34] Mining Act, NL 2003, s 3(3).

[35] TK 1998–1999, 26 219, number 3, at 51.

[36] According to the geological division of the Nederlandse Organisatie voor Toegepast Natuurwetenschappelijk Onderzoek (Netherlands Organisation for Applied Scientific Research) (TNO) depleted gas reservoirs are categorized under Layer 1: 'the Rotliegend Group' and salt caverns are part of Layer 2: 'the Zechstein Group'. See further <http://www.nlog.nl/resources/VRODO/provinciaal/Algemeen.pdf> (Dutch).

[37] Wet van 22 juni 2000, houdende regels omtrent het transport en de levering van gas (Act of 22 June 2000, regarding regulations concerning the transport and the supply of gas (Gas Act)), *Staatsblad* 20 July 2000, number 305 (Dutch).

[38] Gas Act, NL 2000, s 18g. The regime on third party access was changed in 2012 by an amending Act: *Staatsblad* 19 July 2012, number 334 (Dutch). Before 2012, a regime of more regulated access was applied for UGS having a dominant position, i.e. UGS established before the entry into force of the Gas Act in 2000. A regime of purely negotiated access applied to all other gas storage facilities. The legislator amended the Gas Act in 2012 as the market for gas storage had changed and

such as where there is no capacity available or when the requested access would hinder the operators in carrying out their tasks, including the flexibility services.[39]

Although UGS is considered to be of growing importance for the Netherlands, some legal obstructions potentially still apply. Most particularly, this involves the issue of to whom a storage licence can be awarded.[40] Until 1988, all onshore concessions (now production licences) were awarded in perpetuity, and because most suitable UGS are located onshore, storage licences could only be awarded to the holders of a production licence. Moreover, the holders of these onshore concessions also had ownership of all subsoil resources as of the moment the concession was awarded. In the situation where a storage licence was awarded to another party, arrangements had to be made concerning compensation for the minerals (i.e. gas) in situ and not yet produced and used as cushion gas and/or working gas. Although the Mining Act was amended in 2009 to allow for others to be awarded a storage licence and to ensure that the holder of the previous production licence will be paid damages if such a situation occurs,[41] it remains to be seen whether such a situation will take place, because it will be extremely difficult to assess the financial basis for such compensation.

D. Carbon dioxide storage

1. The need for a legal framework

A new type of subsoil storage was introduced more recently. This involves the geological storage of CO_2, which is in fact part of a new technology consisting of carbon capture and storage (also known as CCS) and which is aimed at combating climate change while continuing to use fossil fuels. CCS is part of EU climate policy, which aims to reduce CO_2 emissions by 2020 by at least 20%, based on 1990 levels.[42] In this process, CCS is considered as a transitional instrument as it limits the emission of CO_2, but not the use of fossil fuels. CCS may be used until other reliable means of clean energy can be applied on a larger scale.

On the EU level, the geological storage of CO_2 is governed by Directive 2009/31/EC.[43] This Directive amends a number of existing Directives and Regulations affecting CCS,[44] but its main focus is—as the title indicates—the geological storage of CO_2. Subsoil storage under the Directive is limited to storage in geological

sufficient storage alternatives are available. A system of negotiated third-party access for all UGS reflects this change in the gas market. See TK 2010–2011, 32 814, number 3, at 46.

[39] Gas Act, NL 2000, s 18ga. [40] Mining Act, NL 2003, s 26.

[41] TK 2007–2008, 31 479, number 3, at 8.

[42] The EU Council agreed to these targets in a Council Meeting of March 8–9, 2007, Presidency Conclusions presented on 2 May 2007, 7224/1/07 REV 1, available at <http://register.consilium.europa.eu/pdf/en/07/st07/st07224-re01.en07.pdf>.

[43] (CCS) Directive 2009/31/EC of the European Parliament and of the Council of 23 April 2009 on the geological storage of carbon dioxide and amending Council Directives 2000/60/EC, 2001/80/EC, 2004/35/EC, 2006/12/EC, 2008/1/EC, and Regulation (EC) No 1013/2006. This Directive was published in OJ L 140/114 on 5 June 2009.

[44] These Directives and Regulations affect parts of the CCS chain and include the IPPC Directive and the Environmental Liability Directive.

formations, i.e., lithostratigraphical subdivisions within which distinct rock layers can be found and mapped.[45] Underground storage of CO_2 thus depends on the availability of suitable storage formations.

Member States intending to allow for CO_2 storage will need to make an assessment of the possible storage capacity, but are free to decide whether such storage will be developed and which areas will be selected for storage.[46] In order to assess the suitability of a potential site, it may be necessary to carry out geological surveys and/or drilling activities. The Directive therefore introduces the concept of an exploration permit prior to the award of a storage permit.[47] In addition, the Directive imposes strict requirements with regard to the monitoring of the injection and storage of CO_2, given the risks involved.[48] Since this type of storage aims at permanent storage, and considering that a licensee cannot be held responsible for the reservoir in perpetuity, the Directive also addresses the duration of the storage licence, i.e., the moment when a licensee will be able to transfer the licence and the accompanying obligations to the state.[49] Last but not least, the Directive provides for some rules for third-party access to the storage facility and any connected pipeline systems.[50]

The Directive was implemented in Dutch law on 6 June 2011.[51] The Dutch legislature wished to avoid any major delays in the implementation process and therefore decided to implement the CCS Directive (almost to the letter) in the Mining Act, as this Act already provided for a regime on the storage of substances (including the storage of CO_2).[52] Although it does not present a definition of the term 'substances', the preparatory works to the Act clearly indicate that the Act was also intended to apply to the storage of CO_2.[53] The Mining Act, nevertheless,

[45] CCS Directive, EU 2009, s 3(1)(4).

[46] The selection procedure needs to take into account the criteria listed in annex I of the CCS Directive. These criteria, and thus the selection process, are based on the idea that the use of selected storage sites will not lead to a significant risk of leakage and/or any significant negative environmental or health impacts. CCS Directive, EU 2009, s 4.

[47] CCS Directive, EU 2009, s 5. Storage permits are regulated by CCS Directive, EU 2009, ss 6–11.

[48] CCS Directive, EU 2009, ss 13–16.

[49] CCS Directive, EU 2009, ss 17–18.

[50] CCS Directive, EU 2009, s 21 provides that potential users should be able to negotiate access and that such access can be denied, for example, in case of a lack of capacity, incompatibility of technical specifications and duly substantiated reasonable needs of the owners/operator of the site. A similar provision can be found in Mining Act, NL 2003, s 32.

[51] Wet van 6 juni 2011 tot wijziging van de Mijnbouwwet in verband met implementatie van richtlijn nr. 2009/31/EG van het Europees Parlement en de Raad van april 23, 2009 betreffende de geologische opslag van koolstofdioxide en tot wijziging van richtlijn 85/337/EEG van de Raad, de richtlijnen 2000/60/EG, 2001/80/EG, 2004/35/EG, 2006/12/EG, 2008/1/EG en verordening (EG) nr. 1013/2006 van het Europees Parlement en de Raad en van OSPAR Decision 2007/2 on the storage of carbon dioxide streams in geological formations (Act of 6 June 2011 to the amendment of the Mining Act regarding the implementation of Directive 2009/31/EC of the European Parliament and the Council of 23 April 2009 on the geological storage of carbon dioxide and amending Council Directive 85/337 EEC, European Parliament and Council Directives 2000/60/EC, 2001/80/EC, 2004/35/EC, 2006/12/EC, 2008/1/EC, and Regulation (EC) No 1013/2006 and of the OSPAR Decision 2007/2 on the storage of carbon dioxide streams in geological formations), *Staatsblad* 19 August 2011, number 381 (Dutch).

[52] TK 1998–1999, 26 219, number 7, at 20 and TK 2009–2010, 32 343, number 3, at 4.

[53] TK 1998–1999, 26 219, number 7, at 20.

needed some particular amendments because the Directive included some additional requirements. The regime for subsoil storage of CO_2 regulated by the Mining Act is discussed briefly in the next section.

2. *The licensing regime*

In order to implement the Directive, a separate chapter governing CO_2 storage was introduced in the Mining Act.[54] As provided by the Directive, and following the existing regime of the Dutch Mining Act, two separate licences may apply, i.e., one licence for exploring suitable sites and another licence for subsoil storage. These licences are, in principle, available to all entities possessing the necessary technical and financial capacities and are issued on the basis of objective, published criteria.

Whereas the Directive presents quite detailed provisions regarding exploration permits, the chapter on CO_2 storage in Mining Act is less detailed.[55] The reason for the absence of such specific detailed provisions is that the Netherlands anticipated making use of depleted oil and gas fields and, consequently, sufficient knowledge of the subsoil should be available for granting storage licences.[56]

A storage licence is required if, with or without an exploration permit, a site has been found to be suitable for the storage of CO_2. Again, the general principles in the Directive correspond to those in the Mining Act, which means that the application procedure needs to be based on transparent and objective criteria and that the storage licence needs to be awarded on a non-discriminatory basis.[57] By contrast to other storage licences, a CO_2 storage permit can only be awarded if the competent authority has considered the Commission's opinion on the draft licence.[58] When awarded, a storage licence must contain the details of the operator, the precise location of the site, the total quantity of CO_2 to be stored and the maximum injection rates,[59] the approved monitoring plan, the conditions for closure, the approved provisional post-closure plan, and a requirement to maintain financial security or any other equivalent to ensure that all obligations arising under

[54] Mining Act, NL 2003, ss 25–32.

[55] In case of exploration, the general licensing principles of the Mining Act will apply, which means that a CO_2 exploration licence can be granted exclusively and for a limited volume area and not extend the period necessary for exploration. The duration of an exploration permit may be extended, however, if the permit period is insufficient to complete the exploration activities and the exploration has been performed in accordance with the provisions of the permit.

[56] TK 2009–2010, 32 343, number 3, at 5.

[57] CCS Directive, EU 2009, ss 6 to 9 and Mining Act, NL 2003, ss 25–31d.

[58] Member States are required to make available to the Commission all applications for storage permits, including all material that will be taken into account when awarding a permit, and all draft permits. The Commission may then issue within a specific period of time a non-binding opinion on these draft permits. Subsequently, the competent authority shall notify the final decision to the Commission and where it deviates from the Commission's opinion it will state the reasons for doing so. CCS Directive, EU 2009, s 10.

[59] According to CCS Directive, EU 2009, s 12, a CO_2 stream must consist overwhelmingly of carbon dioxide.

the permit, including closure procedures and post-closure provisions, can be met.[60] As is the case with other licences, a storage licence can be updated or withdrawn.[61]

Although the implementation process was facilitated by the fact that a storage regime was already in place and the fact that the general principles included in the Directive corresponded with those in the Mining Act, one important change needed to be made to the Mining Act. That involved the competitive bidding procedure and how that affects the holders of production licences who might be interested in re-using the reservoir for storage purposes. Following the requirements in the Directive, licences must be awarded in competition. If a storage licence is awarded directly, without an exploration licence, competitive bidding must take place when awarding a storage licence. This does not work well for storage purposes, and especially not if the reservoirs are part of an area for which a concession (now production licence) has been awarded in perpetuity. Preferably, the holder of a production licence should compete with all other applicants and does not have a priority right. This situation will not promote the interest of existing licensees in re-using their reservoirs for CO_2 storage. However, if licensees for that reason opt to apply merely for gas storage licences, the Minister may reject such a storage licence in the general interest,[62] if the storage reservoir would be relevant for CO_2 storage and meets the climate mitigation obligations.

3. *Storage operations, closure, and post-closure*

The aim of CO_2 storage is to avoid emissions of this greenhouse gas by storing it permanently and safely, i.e., without leakages during the storage process and thereafter. The Directive and the Mining Act present an elaborate system of monitoring and reporting, which means that on the basis of a monitoring plan, an operator has to monitor the injection and storage facilities in order to detect migration and/or leakage of CO_2 and any harmful effects on the environment.[63] In case of significant irregularities or leakages, the operator must notify the competent authority immediately and take the necessary corrective measures.[64] The authorities are required regularly to inspect the storage sites.[65]

[60] Mining Act, NL 2003, s 31b.

[61] Mining Act, NL 2003, s 31h. A renewal may be necessary in case of substantial changes to the operations of the site. The first review will take place five years after the award of the permit and thereafter every 10 years. If a permit has been withdrawn, the competent authority must either issue a new storage permit or close the storage site.

[62] Mining Act, NL 2003, s 27.

[63] CCS Directive, EU 2009, s 13, Mining Act, NL 2003, ss 31b–31h and Mining Decree, NL 2003, s 4. These provide that the monitoring will be based on a monitoring plan which is approved by the competent authority and updated every five years in order to take account of technical developments. On the basis of this monitoring plan the competent authorities may assess the effectiveness of any corrective measures of leakage and whether the stored CO_2 will be completely contained for the indefinite future.

[64] CCS Directive, EU 2009, s 16 and Mining Act, NL 2003, s 31d.

[65] CCS Directive, EU 2009, ss 14 and 15. In the Netherlands, the State Supervision is charged with this responsibility: Mining Act, NL 2003, ss 126–130. Inspections may include visits to the storage complex and the injection facilities, as well as a check of all relevant records of the storage site kept by

A crucial phase in the process of creating permanent geological storage of CO_2 is the closure of the storage site after completion of the injection.[66] This needs to be based on a post-closure plan designed by the operator and approved by the authorities on the basis of best practice.[67] The operator is responsible for sealing the storage site and removing the injection facilities, as well as for any leakages and damages occurring thereafter. Does closure of the site entail that the injected CO_2 is permanently stored? In other words, how long should the operator and/or licensee be responsible for the reservoir? This responsibility could, for example, cease after the sealing of the reservoir on the basis of the closure plan, or it could be indefinite. The Directive has opted for a compromise, and rules that the responsibility for the storage site may be transferred to the authorities after a period of at least 20 years on its own initiative or upon request from the operator, but only if and when all available evidence indicates that the stored CO_2 will be completely and permanently contained[68] and the operator has made a financial contribution covering at least the anticipated costs of monitoring for a period of 30 years.[69] After the transfer of responsibility to the authorities (i.e., the Dutch State), in principle, the (former) operator will be immunized from liability from any costs incurred after the transfer of responsibility, unless there has been fault on the part of the operator.[70]

4. *Carbon dioxide storage in practice*

When the Dutch government started to develop its energy transition policy, it included the ambitious idea that the Netherlands could be turned into an EU CO_2 hub because of the expected availability of an ample number of depleted oil and gas fields.[71] Initially, the government focused on developing CO_2 storage locations onshore as suitable reservoirs are available and this is the least-cost option. Despite

the operator. Whereas routine inspections must be carried out at least every year, non-routine inspections will be carried out if the competent authority has been notified of leakages or significant irregularities and/or the reports show insufficient compliance with the permit conditions or if necessary to investigate serious environmental complaints and any other situations where the competent authority considers this appropriate.

66 CCS Directive, EU 2009, s 17 and Mining Act, NL 2003, s 31j provide that a storage site or part of it will be closed (a) if the relevant conditions stated in the permit have been met; (b) at the request of the operator, after authorization of the competent authority; or (c) if the competent authority decides so after the withdrawal of a storage permit.

67 CCS Directive, EU 2009, s 17(3), In addition, the Directive envisages post-closure monitoring of the site in accordance with the requirements laid down in Annex II 2.

68 CCS Directive, EU 2009, s 18(2,3,4). As in the case of the award of a storage licence, the Commission will be informed about a draft decision of approval of the transfer of responsibility and may issue a non-binding decision.

69 CCS Directive, EU 2009, s 18(1). CCS Directive, EU 2009, s 20 provides for financial compensation to be paid by the operator for post-closure costs after the transfer of responsibility. Mining Act, NL 2003, s 31j.

70 CCS Directive, EU 2009, s 18(7) and Mining Act, NL 2003, s 31k(5). This means that the financial security is only valid and effective until the moment of transfer of responsibility (CCS Directive, EU 2009, s 19).

71 See Advice of Working Group CO_2 storage of Platform New Gas (Nieuw Gas) to the Task Force on Energy Transition, March 2006, at 11, 25.

several attempts, however, no licences have yet been awarded. The main reason is the lack of public acceptance. Consequently, projects offshore are now being considered, but due to a lack of government funding, no progress has yet been made.[72]

E. Underground heat and cold storage

Increasingly, use is also being made of the subsoil to store heat and cold. Heat and cold can, *inter alia*, be stored in aquifers, hard rock surrounding boreholes, and flooded mines or caverns. Such storage is based on the ability of the earth to even out variations in temperature naturally, taking into account that at depths between 6 and 50 m, the temperature is generally constant all year round. By making use of this natural ability, heat can be collected and injected in the subsoil in the summer and then used in the winter season. Similarly, cold from winter air can be stored for air conditioning in the summer. Generally, it is possible to store heat or cold in the subsoil for periods for up to several months.

In the Netherlands, heat and cold storage has been carried out since the 1990s and is usually conducted at a depth between 20 and 200 m. It requires two boreholes: one to inject the heat or cold and one to extract it. Given the drilling techniques used, and the fact that the storage activities often take place below 100 m from the surface, one would expect the Mining Act to apply. However, the legislature has exempted this type of storage from the scope of the Mining Act.[73] According to the legislature, it is not necessary to apply a licensing regime for heat and cold storage because the industry does not need it, and it would lead to unnecessary administrative costs.[74] Apart from the fact that the needs of the industry as such are not a convincing argument, we note that the exemption corresponds with the regime applied to the production of geothermal heat. The absence of a licence to store heat and cold may nevertheless lead to uncertainties when considering and/or making decisions about different uses of the subsoil.

IV. Geothermal heat

A. The role of the Mining Act

Geothermal heat differs from heat storage as it involves 'heat that is present in the subsoil and *also originates from it*' [emphasis added].[75] The Mining Act applies to

[72] Green Hydrogen is a project by Air Liquide which aims to inject and store the captured CO_2 on the Danish continental shelf. The so-called ROAD project is an undertaking by EON Benelux, Electrabel and GdF Suez and entails capture of CO_2 at the Maasvlakte in Rotterdam and subsequent injection at a depleted field on the Dutch continental shelf. Both projects have been awarded EU subsidies, but either these subsidies or the matching finance by the Dutch authorities are too low to get the projects started. See further <http://www.globalccsinstitute.com/projects/12706> (Green Hydrogen) and <http://www.road2020.nl/en/> (ROAD).

[73] Mining Act, NL 2003, s 25(2) and Mining Decree, NL 2003, s 28(e).

[74] Mijnbouwbesluit (Mining Decree), *Staatsblad* 24 December 2002, number 604 (Dutch). For a (non-authoritative) translation of this Decree into English, see <http://www.nlog.nl/en/legal/legislation.html>.

[75] Mining Act, NL 2003, s 1(b).

the exploration for and extraction of geothermal heat[76] due to the similarities with the other uses of the subsoil, i.e., the same kind of techniques are used, and involve something valuable that exists in the subsoil and belongs to society as a whole.[77] There is one major difference, however, and that is that the Mining Act only applies to geothermal heat located below 500 m.[78] In the Netherlands, geothermal heat can be economically extracted at depths between approximately 1,500 and 3,500 m.[79] Consequently, the production of geothermal heat from old mine shafts located between 100 and 500 m below the surface is excluded from the application of the Mining Act.[80]

Since large-scale development of geothermal heat is subject to the Mining Act, the same licensing regime applies. This means in short the need to apply for two separate licences (an exploration and subsequent production licence), which are awarded according to a competitive bidding system.[81] When awarded, the licences are exclusive[82] and need to specify the type and duration of activities, as well as the area to which they apply.[83] So far, two geothermal production licences and 68 exploration licences have been awarded.[84] Several of these licences have been applied for by and awarded to municipalities. Although the state—via the state participant Energiebeheer Nederland (EBN)—could, in principle, participate in the production of geothermal heat, this is not yet the case. The reason might be the interest by local governments and thus the regional approach to the production of geothermal heat.[85]

Compared to the exploration and production of oil and gas, and despite the increased need for using renewable energy sources,[86] few licences have been issued for exploring and producing geothermal heat. The lack of progress in developing geothermal heat was therefore one of the issues addressed in the evaluation of the

76 Mining Act, NL 2003, s 6. 77 TK 1998–1999, 26 219, number 3, at 11.

78 Mining Act, NL 2003, s 2(3). The legislator was of the opinion that smaller projects in the upper underground do not need to be regulated by this act. TK 1998–1999, 26 219, number 3, at 50 and number 7, at 78. As economically viable amounts of geothermal heat probably are present at locations much deeper than 500 m, the demarcation for applying the Mining Act was set at 500 m below surface.

79 According to the TNO geothermal heat can be found in the following geological strata: layer 1: 'the Rotliegend Group'; layer 3: 'the Trias Groups'; layer 4: 'the Jura Groups'; or layer 5: 'the Rijnland Group'. See further <http://www.nlog.nl/resources/VRODO/provinciaal/Algemeen.pdf> (Dutch).

80 Policy Research Corporation (PRC) (commissioned by the Dutch Ministry of Economic Affairs, Agriculture and Innovation), *Evaluatie van de Mijnbouwwet. Eindrapport* (2007) 55. PRC suggests that this situation should be covered by the Mining Act.

81 See Mining Act, NL 2003, s 15. However, it is possible to exempt certain geothermal activities from the existing licensing system. See Mining Act, NL 2003, s 6(2).

82 Mining Act, NL 2003, s 7; see Roggenkamp (n 17) at 796. 83 Mining Act, NL 2003, s 11.

84 See Annual Report of 2012 of the Ministry of Economic Affairs, Agriculture and Innovation, available at <http://www.nlog.nl>. The number of exploration licences were presented by Ronald Jansen, Ministry of Economic Affairs, on 14 December 2012 at a seminar organized by the Dutch Energy Law Association. At 1 April 2013 (in 2012), some 34 applications were pending, see (Dutch) <http://www.nlog.nl/resources/Geothermie/VergunningenAardwarmte_Mutaties2013NL_20130401.pdf>

85 See also M. M. Roggenkamp and I. M. Brinkman, 'Evaluatie van de Mijnbouwwet: is het veld halfvol of halfleeg?' (2008) 29 Nederlands Tijdschrift voor Energierecht 254 at 263.

86 On the basis of Directive 2009/28/EC on the promotion of the use of energy from renewable sources ([2009] OJ L140), the Netherlands has a target of 14% renewables in 2020.

Mining Act in 2007.[87] The main reason for the lack of success was found to be the fact that the licensing regime of the Mining Act was too complex and did not fit well with the specific requirements relating to the production of geothermal heat.[88] In other words, the licensing regime did not correspond with industrial needs and practice. We will now discuss these shortcomings further.

B. Shortcomings in the licensing regime

The basic principle that the exploration for and production of subsoil minerals and geothermal heat should be based on two separate licences has proven to be an important obstacle, since in the case of geothermal heat, it is not efficient to make such a clear distinction between exploration and production.[89] As the same well can be used for exploring and producing geothermal heat, it would be more efficient to start the production process immediately after a successful exploratory drilling, using the same well.

Another concern involves the size of the licence area. By contrast to oil and gas which are trapped in a reservoir, geothermal heat can flow freely within the subsoil geological strata. When awarding a licence, it is therefore very likely that the licensed area is more limited in scope than the subsoil geological structure from where geothermal heat is extracted. Consequently, the holder of a production licence will often extract heat which originally was not part of the licensed area.[90]

Finally, there is an imbalance between the high costs of producing geothermal heat and the low revenues from its sale. This is currently being taken into account, as no levies are imposed for extracting geothermal heat. However, since the Mining Act in principle does allow for such levy,[91] there is some financial uncertainty for (possible) investors in this specific market.[92] It should be noted that as of 2012, investors have been given an additional incentive as the production of geothermal heat is now included in the government support scheme for promoting renewable energy sources, the Stimulering Duurzame Energie (SDE).[93] Although such subsidies will probably stimulate the production of geothermal heat, they do create a problem when considering the basic principle for awarding a production licence, i.e., that production should be economically viable. The award of a subsidy seems to disregard this basic assumption and could be an obstacle to awarding a production licence.

[87] Mining Act, NL 2003, s 191 requires an assessment after five years after the Act entered into force. This assessment has been done by the Policy Research Corporation (n 80).

[88] Policy Research Corporation (n 80) at 52, 53.

[89] Roggenkamp and Brinkman (n 85) at 264.

[90] Policy Research Corporation (n 80) at 54.

[91] Mining Act, NL 2003, s 98.

[92] Policy Research Corporation (n 80) at 54, 55. PRC suggests that instead of a legal provision, terms and conditions about possible levies should be included in the exploration licence.

[93] The subsidy regime distinguishes between geothermal heat extracted from below and above 2,700 meters below surface. The subsidy regime is incorporated into the Besluit stimulering duurzame energieproductie (Decree regarding stimulation of the production of renewable energy), *Staatsblad* 30 October 2007, number 410 (Dutch) and the Algemene uitvoeringsregeling stimulering duurzame energieproductie (General regulation regarding stimulation of the production of renewable energy), *Staatscourant* 3 March 2008, number 44 (Dutch).

C. Suggestions for amendment of the Mining Act

Following the review of the Mining Act in 2007 and the presentation of the shortcomings as discussed earlier, the legislature presented a draft Bill in 2010 to amend the Mining Act.[94] This draft has not been sent to Parliament and will be replaced by a new draft Bill.[95] It can assumed that the new Bill will address some of the issues discussed here.

One of the issues involves a simplification of the licensing regime. The draft Bill proposed the introduction of a new licensing regime consisting of a geothermal start licence and a geothermal sequel licence.[96] In contrast to the current regime, a geothermal start licence will entitle the licensee to start producing geothermal heat immediately after the geothermal heat has been discovered.[97] By introducing these two new geothermal licences, the legislature can simplify the licensing regime[98] without infringing the basic principles of the existing licensing regime.[99]

The draft Bill also raised the issue of the size of the licence area. In the proposal, the legislator suggested linking the licence area to the location of the drill holes. Usually a licensee makes use of multiple geothermal wells, i.e., a combination of a production well and an injection well pumping the heat-depleted brine into the source reservoirs. If such multiple wells are situated at the borders of a licence area, the neighbouring licensee could be negatively impacted as the injection brine reduces the temperature of the geothermal heat in the subsoil. When taking this situation into account, when redrafting the provision for awarding a geothermal production licence, it could be ensured that a licensee of an adjacent area would not be hampered in the extraction of geothermal heat. As a consequence, the area of the geothermal production licence could also be much smaller than the area for which an exploration licence or geothermal start licence was awarded.[100]

Last but not least, the draft Bill refers to the issue of 'by catch'. The current Mining Act rules that subsoil minerals are property of the state and that ownership is transferred to the holder of the production licence upon production.[101] However, in case of geothermal heat, several examples are known of situations where the licensee producing geothermal heat has also accidentally extracted oil and/or gas which was licensed to another party.[102] This is referred to as 'by catch'. The Mining

[94] The draft and the Explanatory Memorandum are published on this website (Dutch): <http://www.internetconsultatie.nl/geothermievergunningen>.

[95] It is not clear when this new draft will be presented.

[96] Explanatory Memorandum, section I.2.2.1, at 2.

[97] Mining Act, NL proposed, s 24a and Explanatory Memorandum, section I.2.2.1, at 2.

[98] Explanatory Memorandum, section I.1, at 1.

[99] PRC suggested in its review (n 80 at 53) that a solution could be to grant a production licence automatically if certain terms and conditions laid down in the exploration licence are met. Roggenkamp and Brinkman disagree because this would be an infringement of the systematics of the Mining Act (n 85 at 264).

[100] Explanatory Memorandum, section I.2.2.2, at 3.

[101] Mining Act, NL 2003, s 3. Please note that a different regime applies to onshore concessions awarded before 2003. The 'old' Mining Act ruled that the ownership was transferred upon award of the concession.

[102] In 2012, such 'by catch' occurred five times in eight projects. See presentation by Ronald Jansen, Ministry of Economic Affairs, on 14 December 2012 at a meeting of the Dutch Energy Law Association.

Act contains a specific condition with respect to 'by catch' as it rules that a licence may apply to other resources than specified in the licence so long as their production is unavoidable and coincides with the licensed resources.[103] Depending on the actual situation, 'by catch' may thus be lawful. However, the law does not state who should be considered as the owner of this 'by catch'. Is this the holder of the gas/oil production licence or the holder of the geothermal production licence? This issue becomes more prominent if the 'by catch' is significant.

So far the issue of 'by catch' has been settled amicably, but a more permanent solution is required. One possibility would be the withdrawal of the geothermal production licence as the licensee has not met the conditions set in the licence. But then a situation could arise where the oil and gas may remain in situ, especially if the holder of the oil and/or gas licence has no economic incentive for production. Another option could be to use some sort of a 'unitization' approach, i.e., an agreement between the two licensees involved, similar to the agreements already used in the case of a straddling oil and/or gas field. At the time of writing, it is unclear which approach the legislature will choose. It is clear, however, that 'by catch' is, in practice, often the result of a lack of information and knowledge of the subsoil. Moreover, despite the fact that conventional geothermal wells are often drilled under different standards than those used for oil and gas wells, serious safety concerns exist.[104] The new Bill will therefore also include additional requirements regarding the quality of information and the technical capabilities of the licensees.[105] By doing so, 'by catch' will be reduced and safety in general will be enhanced, and, ultimately, two of the hurdles for geothermal heat development will be overcome.

V. Shale gas

A. Introduction

A new energy development involving the deep underground is shale gas. Shale gas is natural gas that is trapped within shale formations, which can either be source rock or the cap rock of an oil or gas reservoir. Shale is a sedimentary rock that consists of consolidated clay and silt-sized particles. The fact that natural gas is tightly confined within the shale makes it hard to produce.[106] The production of shale gas depends on two well-known techniques that have been used since the 1980s, i.e., horizontal

[103] Mining Act, NL 2003, s 11(1).

[104] The State Supervision of Mines has therefore introduced new/specific safety standards. See <http://www.sodm.nl/onderwerpen/aardwarmte> (Dutch).

[105] M. L. Stoffers and S. J. W. H. Reintjes, 'Jubileumcongres "Energie en energierecht de komende 10 jaar—de rol van techniek en recht"', (2013) 34 Nederlands Tijdschrift voor Energierecht 31 at 35.

[106] G. Thonhauser, 'Shale and Tight Gas Development for Europe' in *Unconventional Gas: Potential Energy Market Impacts in the European Union. A Report by the Energy Security Unit of the European Commission's Joint Research Centre* (I.L.G. Pearson, P. Zeniewski, F. Gracceva, P. Zastera, C. McGlade, S. Sorrell, J. Speirs, G. Thonhauser, C. Alecu, A. Eriksson, M. Schuetz, and P. Toft, 2012) 56 at 56, 57.

drilling and hydraulic fracturing (or fracking).[107] Horizontal drilling implies drilling a vertical well to the desired depth and then drilling horizontally through the shale. Hydraulic fracturing involves the use of explosives, which induce fracs within the shale, while the injection of a mixture of water, sand, and chemicals[108] keeps the fracs open, allowing the gas to 'escape' and to be extracted.

Although hydraulic fracturing and horizontal drilling are already used on a regular basis in the Netherlands for the development of conventional natural gas, they have not yet been used for shale gas production. The government estimates, however, that some 500,000 billion m^3 of (shale) gas could be developed in the Netherlands,[109] although precise figures are unknown because there is currently a moratorium on the exploration and production of shale gas.[110] This moratorium has been linked with the outcome of a research project on shale gas addressing the potential risks and consequences of the exploration for, and production of, shale gas in terms of environmental and personal safety.[111]

Section B discusses the position of shale gas in the current Mining Act, before briefly examining some of the environmental consequences of the production of shale gas.

B. The Dutch Mining Act

Because shale gas is just a type of natural gas, it differs from conventionally produced natural gas only in regards to the production process.[112] As explained

[107] Thonhauser (n 106).

[108] This mixture consists of approximately 90% water, 9.5% sand, and 0.5% chemicals: Philippe and Partners, *Final Report on Unconventional Gas in Europe. In the Framework of the Multiple Framework Service Contract for Legal Assistance* (2011) 8.

[109] See 'Slochteren is mini-gasbel vergeleken met bij de nog onontdekte voorraden; Gas EBN noemt immense getallen' (Slochteren has Minor Gas Reserves Compared to Yet Undiscovered Reserves. Gas EBN Mentions Enormous Numbers), *De Pers*, 23 June 2009. By contrast, the size of the Groningen gas field was estimated in 1959 to be 2.9 trillion normal m^3. See <http://www.nlog.nl/en/reserves/Groningen.html>.

[110] The Minister of Economic Affairs, Agriculture and Innovation has stated this in a letter to the House of Representatives on 20 June 2011, available at <http://www.rijksoverheid.nl/onderwerpen/gas/documenten-en-publicaties/kamerstukken/2011/06/21/kamerbrief-winning-schaliegas.html> (Dutch).

[111] On 26 August 2013, the Minister of Economic Affairs published the results of the research project on shale gas. According to the Minister, the results show that the possible consequences and risks of the production of shale gas for nature, human health, and the environment are manageable and can be sufficiently addressed within the current legal framework. See <http://www.rijksoverheid.nl/documenten-en-publicaties/kamerstukken/2013/08/26/brief-aan-de-tweede-kamer-schaliegas-resultaten-onderzoek-en-verdere-voortgang.html> (Dutch). On 18 September 2013, the Minister of Economic Affairs announced that further research is needed in order to identify suitable locations for the exploration and production of shale gas, thus allowing the government to offer these locations to interested companies. This would be a new development, as up to now interested parties (companies) were able to identify themselves the areas for which an exploration licence could be applied for. The Minister estimates that the intended additional research can take up to 18 months. No licences will be awarded during this period. See <http://www.rijksoverheid.nl/documenten-en-publicaties/kamerstukken/2013/09/18/brief-aan-de-tweede-kamer-vervolgstap-schaliegas.html> (Dutch).

[112] Stoffers and Reintjes (n 105). See also S. Lechtenböhmer, M. Altmann, S. Capito, Z. Matra, W. Weindorf, and W. Zittel (commissioned by the European Parliament's Committee on Environment, Public Health and Food Safety), *Impacts of Shale Gas and Shale Oil Extraction on the Environment and on Human Health* (2011) 13.

earlier, a more complicated production process applies due to the low permeability of the shale gas reservoirs.[113]

Dutch shale gas is located approximately between 1,000 and 4,500 m below the surface[114] and is therefore subject to the regime of the Mining Act.[115] So far, no specific rules have been included in the Mining Act regarding the exploration and production of shale gas, so the general rules governing the exploration for and the production of gas apply.

A party wishing to develop shale gas will need an exploration licence[116] and subsequently a production licence, but only if an economically viable quantity of gas has been discovered.[117] These licences will determine the type of minerals (in this case, natural gas),[118] the period, and the area they relate to.[119] The licence area is indicated in square meters and identified by referring to a set of boundaries at the surface.[120] The area consists of both the surface area indicated and its subsoil.[121] So far, no vertical divisions have been included in the licences awarded.[122] Consequently, the current regime does not provide for a distinction to be made between the exploration for and production of natural gas and shale gas, although the search and production may require different techniques. Although the production of conventional natural gas may possibly involve fracking, unconventional gas depends on the use of this technique. Some of the consequences of the increased use of the technique of fracking are considered in section C.

C. Fracking

In order to explore for and produce shale gas, it is necessary to induce fracs into the tight soil layers in order for the shale gas to 'escape'. Fracking requires the use of enormous quantities of water and chemicals[123] and may thus lead to water and land contamination, as well as greenhouse gas emissions and noise issues. In addition,

[113] Conventional gas can be found in reservoirs with a permeability greater than 1 millidarcy and unconventional gas is found in reservoirs with relatively low permeabilities (less than 1 millidarcy). The low permeability does not allow producing via conventional methods: Thonhauser (n 106) at 56.

[114] In the Netherlands, shale gas is expected to be located between approximately 1,000 and 4,500 m below the surface, depending on the geological strata. See <http://www.tno.nl/downloads/Zijp_TNO_Gea2012_juni_Schaliegas.pdf>.

[115] Mining Act, NL 2003, ss 1(a), 2(2).

[116] The exploration licence will be awarded in competition.

[117] Mining Act, NL 2003, s 8.

[118] The licences will therefore not distinguish between conventional gas and unconventional gas or shale gas.

[119] Mining Act, NL 2003, s 11.

[120] Whereas onshore use is made of the official map of the land registry, offshore use is made of geographical coordinates, calculated in accordance with the system of European equalization (block system). See Mining Regulation, NL 2003, s 1.2.2.

[121] Mining Act, NL 2003, s 11(3).

[122] It should be noted that the Ministry of Economic Affairs upon advice of the Mining Council recently has included such a vertical division when awarding an exploration licence for geothermal heat (*Staatscourant*, 10 April 2013, number 9330 (Dutch)). It may well be that such vertical division will be used more often in order to distinguish between subsoil strata and licence area.

[123] Fracking fluid consists of 99.5% water/sand and 0.5% chemicals. See R. Herber (Professor in geo-energy in the University of Groningen), presentation on shale gas in the Netherlands at a seminar organized by the Dutch Energy Law Association on 14 December 2012. See also n 108.

fracking requires more operating sites and an increased use of roads in order to transport the necessary amounts of water and waste products.[124]

A point of concern is the impact of the chemicals used underground for fracking.[125] If the chemicals remain underground, they could harm the subsoil (for instance, by leakage) and thus jeopardize the production of other energy resources. In addition, these chemicals may contaminate drinking water.[126] Although the Mining Act itself does not oblige the licensees to publish a list of chemicals and the quantities used,[127] the Mining Regulation[128] addresses some of these issues. The Mining Regulation contains, for example, provisions on the construction of bore holes and the use of chemicals for the production of shale gas. In addition, each work plan needs to include details of the drilling fluids used and why they are used.[129]

As mentioned earlier, the production of shale gas also involves the use of considerable quantities of water to help the fracs to remain open. This may jeopardize public water supply, and may also result in water contamination. The required quantities of water for producing shale gas are still being investigated.[130] Although, as a general rule, all licensees are obliged to produce according to a previously approved production plan,[131] the use of water is not part of the production plan but governed by the Water Act, which governs all use of water in the Netherlands.[132] For the purpose of using, injecting, and re-injecting waste-water, a licence is required on the basis of the Water Act. Another concern is the

124 See Lechtenböhmer et al (n 112) at 56.

125 Stichting SchalieGASvrij Haaren, *De risico's van onconventioneel aardgas* (2011) 9, available at: <http://www.schaliegasvrij-haaren.nl/wp-content/uploads/2011/09/Factsheet-Milieudefensie-over-Schaliegas-September-2011-De-risicos-van-onconventioneel-gas.pdf> (Dutch).

126 The research on shale gas has included this point of concern. Witteveen and Bos have identified some risks, but they consider those risks to be manageable: Witteveen and Bos (commissioned by the Dutch Ministry of Economic Affairs), *Aanvullend onderzoek naar mogelijke risico's en gevolgen van de opsporing en winning van schalie- en steenkoolgas in Nederland. Eindrapport onderzoeksvragen A en B, 2013* at 6, 60–2, available at <http://www.rijksoverheid.nl/documenten-en-publicaties/rapporten/2013/08/26/aanvullend-onderzoek-naar-mogelijke-risico-s-en-gevolgen-van-de-opsporing-en-winning-van-schalie-en-steenkoolgas-in-nederland-eindrapport-onderzoeksvragen-a-en-b.html> (Dutch, with an English summary at 5–7).

127 Stichting SchalieGASvrij Haaren (n 125) at 9. The research mentioned earlier on shale gas will address this issue. See Witteveen and Bos (n 126) at 99–104.

128 Mijnbouwregeling (Mining Regulation), *Staatscourant* 19 December 2002, number 245 (Dutch). For a (non-authoritative) translation of this Regulation in English, see <http://www.nlog.nl/en/legal/legislation.html>.

129 Mining Regulation, NL 2003, s 8.2.1.1(2j). According to s 8.2.1.1(2k) a list of chemicals should also be included in the work plan in case a bore dust cleaning system is to be used.

130 Witteveen and Bos (n 126) at 51–8. It is estimated, however, that some 15,000–20,000 cubic metres of fracking fluid (water and chemicals) is needed per frac-job. See presentation by Rien Herber (Professor in geo-energy in the University of Groningen) on 14 December 2012 at a seminar of the Dutch Energy Law Association.

131 Mining Act, NL 2003, s 34(1). Mining Act, NL 2003, s 35 and Mining Decree, NL 2003, s 24 determine the scope of the production plan and do not refer to the use of water for drilling purposes.

132 Wet van 29 januari 2009, houdende regels met betrekking tot het beheer en gebruik van watersystemen (Waterwet) (Act of 29 January 2009, regarding regulations concerning the management and use of water systems. Waterwet)), *Staatsblad* 12 March 2009, number 107 (Dutch).

possibility of contamination[133] of, for example, groundwater, which is an important source of drinking water in the Netherlands. The fear of a lack of suitable drinking water is one of the sources of objection to shale gas.[134] For environmental and health purposes, it is therefore important to closely monitor the impact of shale gas production on groundwater.[135] In the Netherlands, the protection of groundwater (and the subsoil in general) is governed by the Soil Protection Act.[136]

Another concern is that if the fracs get too large or are situated at non-favourable sites, they could cause earthquakes. This is of particular concern in the Netherlands, where the number and size of earthquakes and the subsidence of land are increasing. When drafting the new Mining Act, Parliament discussed in detail how these negative impacts could be avoided and possible damages could best be addressed. Although the issue of liability is still governed by the Civil Code, the Mining Act presents a special regime on earth movements that aims to assist private persons in their claims. The technical committee on earth movements plays a crucial role in this process.[137] Whereas the Ministry of Economic Affairs is currently assessing the existing regime, given the recent earthquakes in the North of the Netherlands, it is too early to say whether changes will be made to the regime. It would not be surprising if even stricter rules are introduced if shale gas is developed.

D. Emissions

As shale gas is natural gas, it includes greenhouse gases like methane and CO_2.[138] It is possible that leakage may occur during or after the production process. Because emissions of methane and CO_2 may cause damage to the environment, health, and safety, the Environmental Protection Act[139] provides a regime of careful monitoring within the framework of a system of emissions trading in the EU (EU ETS).[140] Currently, it is not clear whether shale gas production is governed by the EU ETS.[141]

[133] AEA Technology Plc estimates the chances of ground water contamination to be either moderate or high, depending upon the distance between the fracturing zone and the ground water. AEA (commissioned by the European Commission DG Environment), *Support to the Identification of Potential Risks for the Environment and Human Health Arising from Hydrocarbons Operations Involving Hydraulic Fracturing in Europe* (AEA/ED57281/Issue Number 17c 2012) 43–7 [Nogepa].

[134] 'Winning schaliegas vervuilt drinkwater' (Production of Shale Gas Leads to Water Contamination), *NRC Handelsblad*, 25 June 2013, available at <http://www.nrc.nl/nieuws/2013/06/25/winning-schaliegas-vervuilt-drinkwater-klankbordgroep-schaliegas-valt-uit-elkaar/> (Dutch).

[135] AEA (n 133) at 158–60.

[136] Wet van 3 juli 1986, houdende regelen inzake bescherming van de bodem (Act of 3 July 1986, regarding rules concerning the protection of the soil), *Staatsblad* 1986, number 374 (Dutch).

[137] Mining Act, NL 2003, ss 113–122.

[138] Typically shale gas consists of methane, CO_2, and heavier hydrocarbons. The accurate chemical composition of shale gas depends on the geology of the shales. AEA (commissioned by the European Commission DG Environment), *Climate Impact of Potential Shale Gas Production in the EU* (AEA/R/ED57412/Issue Number 2, 2012) 10.

[139] Wet van 13 juni 1979, houdende regelen met betrekking tot een aantal algemene onderwerpen op het gebied van de milieuhygiëne (Act of 13 June 1979, regarding regulations concerning some general issues regarding environmental hygienics), *Staatsblad* 1979, number 442 (Dutch). Chapter 16 of the Environmental Protection Act governs emission trading.

[140] Stichting SchalieGASvrij Haaren (n 125) at 9.

[141] AEA (n 138) at 70.

VI. Subsoil planning

A. Introduction

The discussion in this chapter has shown that the Dutch subsoil can and will be used for various activities in the energy sector. In practice, it may be difficult to conduct all these activities simultaneously in or around the same subsoil strata. This could result in a situation where interested parties will need to compete for subsoil space.

Within the current licensing system there is no obligation for the government to take into consideration any subsoil or mining activities other than the ones applied for, even if any other such activity would be more beneficial to society. This means that there is a risk of not producing minerals as efficiently as possible or, even worse, losing some potential uses of the underground altogether. One possible way to prevent this is to introduce some sort of subsoil planning. A regime of subsoil planning does not yet exist in the Netherlands, although attempts are being made by some provinces and the national government to commence subsoil planning.[142] Section VI discusses the extent to which the Spatial Planning Act could be applied to subsoil planning in the Netherlands and the obstacles that could arise.

B. Spatial planning

1. Spatial Planning Act

Spatial planning in the Netherlands is governed by the Spatial Planning Act 2006.[143] This Act is based on the principle that planning should take place as far as possible on the local level unless provincial or national interests are involved.[144] All governments (national, provincial, and local) may issue spatial policy plans, which are referred to as 'structural visions' (*structuurvisie*).[145] These plans are a first step in the spatial planning process.[146] They are non-binding and present a purely indicative outlook of proposed spatial developments regarding a specific area or

[142] The province of Drenthe has already published a draft on subsoil planning regarding its territory: *Structuurvisie Ondergrond 2.0* (2013). This publication can be downloaded from <http://www.provincie.drenthe.nl/actueel/bekendmakingen/@91110/concept> (Dutch). The province of Groningen has published an agenda in order to start a project on subsoil planning, The *Strategische Agenda voor de Structuurvisie Ondergrond* (2012) can be downloaded from <http://www.provinciegroningen.nl/fileadmin/user_upload/Documenten/Brief/2011-56964.pdf> (Dutch).The Dutch government has set up a project called STRONG (*Structuurvisie Ondergrond*), with the aim of drafting a governmental plan on subsoil planning. For more information on this project, see <http://www.rijksoverheid.nl/onderwerpen/bodem-en-ondergrond/structuurvisie-ondergrond> (Dutch).

[143] Wet van 20 oktober 2006, houdende nieuwe regels omtrent de ruimtelijke ordening (Wet ruimtelijke ordening), Act of 20 October 20, 2006, regarding new rules concerning spatial planning (Spatial Planning Act), *Staatsblad* 28 November 2006, number 566 (Dutch).

[144] TK 2002–2003, 28 916, number 3 at 11.

[145] Spatial Planning Act, NL 2006, ss 2.1 (municipalities), 2.2 (provinces) and 2.3 (government).

[146] Spatial Planning Act, NL 2006, ss 2.1, 2.2, 2.3.

public entity involved.[147] Once drafted, a '*structuurvisie*' can be used by the competent authority for decision-making, i.e., issuing specific spatial plans such as zoning plans.[148] Unlike a '*structuurvisie*', these planning decisions are binding.

Attempts have been made recently to draft structural visions for the deep subsoil. The Sections that follow discuss the extent to which the Spatial Planning Act applies to the deep subsoil and thereafter consider how governments at the national and provincial levels intend to plan energy activities in the deep subsoil.[149]

2. Subsoil planning at national and provincial level in the Netherlands

The Dutch government clearly recognizes the importance of the subsoil for current and future energy activities, as well as that other interests are at stake such as archaeology, soil containment, and groundwater quality. All these functions influence each other, and without some sort of subsoil planning, the use of the subsoil and, in particular, mining activities and the subsequent use of minerals would become inefficient.[150] Can such subsoil planning be based on the Spatial Planning Act? Although the Act explicitly states that the term 'land' includes both the surface and the subsurface at different levels, it does not state explicitly that 'land' also includes the use of the deep subsoil.[151]

Such doubt apparently does not exist at the governmental level. The national government has expressed the need for subsoil planning and such policy plans could be included in a '*structuurvisie*'.[152] Subsequently, the Dutch government announced that it intends to present a draft governmental '*structuurvisie*' on the underground by the end of 2013.[153] Some provinces have also started to draft a regional structural vision. In 2012, the province of Groningen announced its intention to present in 2013 a '*structuurvisie*' aimed at developing a sustainable use of the underground,[154] and the province of Drenthe published a draft regional '*structuurvisie*' on subsoil planning in early 2013.[155] In this structural vision, Drenthe presented a tool called 'the stairs of Drenthe',[156] which should assist decision-makers in prioritizing the different uses of the subsoil.[157] The idea is

[147] TK 2002–2003, 28 916, number 3 at 91. The *structuurvisie* is only binding the public entity that has constituted it.

[148] TK 2002–2003, 28 916, number 3 at 12, 14.

[149] In this section, subsoil planning on municipality level is not discussed because of its limited relevance and the fact that there are more than 400 municipalities in the Netherlands.

[150] TK 2010–2011 32 660, number 17 at 29.

[151] Spatial Planning Act, NL 2006, s 1.1(2a). In the Explanatory Memorandum of this Act, the legislator has indicated that the reference to subsoil layers is included in order to make sure that a certain piece of land can be used at different levels and for different purposes (see TK 2002–2003, 28 916, number 3 at 91). The examples used of activities in the subsurface are limited to activities such as the laying of cables and pipelines and the construction of parking garages.

[152] TK 2010–2011, 32 660, number 17 at 29.

[153] The Minister of Infrastructure and Environment and the Minister of Economic Affairs informed the Dutch parliament on 21 March 2013 of this intention. See TK 2012–2013, 33 136, number 5.

[154] See n 142 (regarding Groningen) and <http://www.provinciegroningen.nl/beleid/water-milieu-en-veiligheid/bodem/diepe-ondergrond/> (Dutch).

[155] See n 142 (regarding Drenthe).

[156] In Dutch: *de ladder van Drenthe.*

[157] See n 142 (regarding Drenthe) at 51.

that the exact position of an activity on those 'stairs' represents the importance of that activity. As a result, important activities prevail over those activities with a lower ranking and will thus not be influenced by them. However, as all mining activities are positioned on the same step of the stairs,[158] the usefulness and effectiveness of this tool for subsoil planning seems very limited.

3. *Issues concerning subsoil planning in the Netherlands*

Although in 2013 some attempts have been made to submit '*structuurvisies*' for underground planning within the scope of the Spatial Planning Act, the automatic application of the Act to the deep underground can be questioned. In this process, little attention has been paid to the Mining Act, which actually governs all activities in the deep underground.

First, it should be noted that the preparatory works to the Spatial Planning Act when discussing the activities in the subsurface only refer to constructions and installations located in the shallow underground, such as pipelines, cables, and tunnels.[159] What is more, the legislature has not yet given a decisive answer on the issue of the relationship between the Mining Act and the Spatial Planning Act, which was raised in Parliament some years ago.[160]

Even if the Spatial Planning Act applies to the deep underground, one could question the extent to which the existing planning instruments suffice, and whether some specific instruments should be incorporated in the Act. For example, is a '*structuurvisie*' drafted by a lower government actually the right instrument to govern deep underground planning? As mentioned earlier, a '*structuurvisie*' only binds the public entity that has constituted it. A provincial structural vision therefore only binds the provincial government. However, the provincial government has no competence with regard to the deep subsoil. On the basis of the Mining Act, the Minister of Economic Affairs has the sole responsibility to issue licences for the use of the subsoil below 100 m. Therefore a provincial structural vision seems to be an empty tool without any legal significance for the deep underground (although it may have an impact on the associated installations aboveground). Contrary to the basic assumption of the Spatial Planning Act that spatial planning should be done on the lowest level possible,[161] we would argue that a different approach should apply to the deep underground so that a structural vision (if any) is at least presented by the national government. This would be in line with another important recent amendment to the Spatial Planning Act, i.e., the introduction in 2010 of new provisions on National Coordination of Planning Procedures.[162] According to this regulation, the Minister of Economic Affairs may

158 The storage of CO_2 is located one step below other mining activities: see n 142 at 52.

159 TK 2002–2003, 28 916, number 3 at 91.

160 This issue was raised at the time the Mining Act of 2003 was drafted. The legislator did not see reason to deal with this at that time: TK 1998–1999, 26 219, number 3 at 6, 7.

161 TK 2002–2003, 28 916, number 3 at 11.

162 In Dutch: *rijkscoördinatieregeling*. The legal basis of this regulation is Spatial Planning Act, NL 2006, ss 3.35, 3.36. All infrastructural projects that are currently covered by this regulation can be consulted at: <http://www.agentschapnl.nl/programmas-regelingen/rijksco%C3%B6rdinatieregeling> (Dutch).

decide to take over the process of permitting from lower governments if it involves infrastructural projects of national interest. These projects are designated by law and include energy projects such as mining installations and installations necessary for subsoil storage of substances.[163]

We would therefore advocate that the national government be the designated authority for spatial planning in the deep subsoil. After all, it is the national government that awards all licences under the Mining Act and has the right to coordinate and award the necessary planning permits if they concern related projects of national interest, i.e., projects involving the exploration and production of oil and gas and subsoil storage. Consequently, all decision-making on how and for what purpose the deep underground will be used and the associated infrastructure would then be governed by the same authority.

VII. Conclusion

The use of the deep underground is increasing. Energy development is directly or indirectly (as in the case of CO_2 storage) the reason for using the deep underground in a more 'unconventional' way. In this chapter we have discussed some of these new developments, namely the storage of gas, CO_2, and heat and cold, as well as the production of 'new energy sources' like geothermal energy and shale gas.

In the Netherlands, the Mining Act, which entered into force in 2003, is governing the use of the subsoil. The Act provides for a licensing regime based on general EU principles of competition, non-discrimination, and transparency. The intention of the legislature to introduce one licensing regime which applies equally to existing and new resources and developments has proven to be unrealistic. The regimes applying to both storage and production of geothermal heat need to be amended. The production of geothermal heat can play an important role in reaching the Dutch renewables targets, but is currently hampered by the existing licensing regime. Amendments to the Mining Act have been announced and will also include provisions regarding 'by catch' and higher standards for the safety and technical capacity of the licensee.

Given the increasing number of subsoil activities, it is clear that the Act does not provide for instruments to streamline and coordinate the different uses and the way in which these uses interact. When awarding a licence, the government cannot take into consideration subsoil or mining activities other than those applied for, even if other such activities would be more beneficial to society. A production licence applies to a specific resource and the licence area is only demarcated at the surface. Within that surface area, several licences may apply, each having an impact on a specific geological subsoil strata. So far this has not resulted in a vertical geological demarcation of the subsoil, but it seems that a first step may have been taken in this

163 The legal basis for this specific project is the Mining Act, NL 2003, s 141a(1b).

direction after a subsoil demarcation was included in a geothermal exploration permit in April 2013.

The need for such subsoil demarcation and balancing of subsoil interests also shows the necessity for subsoil planning. Again, some initial steps have been taken, but mostly at the provincial level. Some provincial governments have published some draft policy plans and the national government aims to present a first policy plan ('*structuurvisie*') at the end of 2013. So far, these plans seem to be based on the principles included in the Spatial Planning Act. The extent to which this Act should be strictly applied to the deep underground has not yet been raised. We argue that the Spatial Planning Act at least should be considered in conjunction with the Mining Act and that the national government should draft a structural policy plan ('*structuurvisie*') rather than the provincial or local governments, as the use of the deep underground primarily involves energy projects of national interest. Only if the national government has the authority to coordinate and regulate all planning and licensing activities involving the deep underground can an efficient use of the minerals and reservoirs located in the deep underground be ensured.

20

German Legal Responses to New Subsurface Technologies

Gunther Kühne

I. The German 'Energiewende' (energy switch) and underground technologies

It was in autumn 2010 that the Federal German Government formally adopted the plan to reorientate its energy strategy: gradual expansion of the share of electricity generation from renewable energies (wind, solar energy) at the expense of electricity production from fossil fuels (coal) and nuclear energy. This strategic shift was even further accentuated after the Fukushima catastrophe: phasing out of nuclear energy as early as 2022 and gradual expansion of renewable energies up to 2050 (35% 2020; 50% 2030; 65% 2040; 80% 2050).[1] The expansion of renewables is to concentrate mainly on wind and solar energy. It is obvious that such a reorientation of energy strategy is bound to have repercussions on the use of energy-related underground technologies. Thus, for example, all technologies that aim at the recovery of additional fossil fuels (hydraulic fracturing or 'fracking') or at reducing emissions from fossil fuels (carbon capture storage or 'CCS') will lose much of their appeal in the new energy scenario, with its rapid expansion of renewables.

II. Subsurface technologies from energy and environmental perspectives

Notwithstanding this relatively recent turn of events, Germany has experienced an extensive discussion over the past decades about whether and how to use the potential of underground resources. This chapter, in a short historic retrospect, reviews the relevance and interconnection of the two dominating policy objectives underlying the use of underground resources other than water. (Water, both legally

[1] For an overview of the 2010/2011 German 'energy switch', see G. Kühne, 'Regulating the Extension of Electricity Networks: A German Perspective' in *Energy Networks and the Law* (M.M. Roggenkamp, L. Barrera-Hernández, D.N. Zillman, and I. del Guayo, eds, 2012) 371, 373–7.

and economically, would require a separate and extensive discussion.) The two dominating objectives are energy policy and environmental policy. This order of the two policies is already indicative of their chronological relevance.

A. Underground technologies from an energy perspective

Historically, underground technologies in Germany almost exclusively have been driven and supported by *energy* considerations and strategies. Since the nineteenth and for most of the twentieth centuries, Germany developed underground hard coal mining to an extent that it became the backbone for both private and industrial energy consumption. The most important areas of coal mining were the Ruhr area and—until the end of World War II—Upper Silesia. After World War II and during the reconstruction period, the overwhelming economic importance of underground mining of hard coal continued, along with the mining of lignite, which is also an underground energy resource but which is extracted by way of open-cast mining.

It was around the middle of the twentieth century that the underground became increasingly used for obtaining additional energy resources: the exploitation of oil and gas reservoirs concentrated in the Lower Saxonian basin around Hanover.

The legal basis for these energy-related extractive uses of the underground was mining law. Since the Middle Ages, it had evolved out of traditional non-energy-related mining (iron ore, silver) into a highly developed set of principles and rules. The development of mining law reached its climax in 1865 when the Prussian General Mining Code (Preussisches Allgemeines Berggesetz, ABG)[2] was enacted. This piece of legislation was to become by far the leading source of German mining law.[3] It remained in force until 1 January 1982, when the new Federal Mining Law (Bundesberggesetz, BBergG)[4] came into force.

During the 1960s, a new perspective started to emerge: the use of the underground for non-extractive purposes. The underground space as such, both man-made and natural, began to gain significance as part of the energy supply system: the installation of underground oil and gas storage facilities became an increasingly vital element in order to secure the uninterrupted availability and reliability of energy supply.[5] The legal framework governing this was, and stayed, rather inchoate and was formulated as an appendix to mining law.[6]

[2] Of 24 June 1865, Prussian Gazette 705.

[3] For a review of German mining law history see, e.g., F. Trelease and G. Kühne, 'The New West German Mining Law' (1984)19 Land & Water L Rev 371 at 377. For a brief overview of German mining law, see also J.-C. Pielow, H.-M. Koopmann, and E. Ehlers, 'Energy Law in Germany' (M. Roggenkamp, C. Redgwell, I. del Guayo, and A. Rønne, eds, 2007), *Energy Law in Europe* 646.

[4] Of 13 August 1980, Bundesgesetzblatt (BGBl) (Federal Gazette) I, 1310.

[5] This is particularly true in the case of oil after the oil crisis of the 1970s. The statutory basis for keeping a strategic reserve is the 'Gesetz über die Bevorratung mit Erdöl und Erdölerzeugnissen' of 25 July 1978, BGBl I 1073. The most recent version dates from 16 January 2012, BGBl I 74. The oil reserve is stored in specifically created salt caverns at a depth of between 1,000 and 1,500 m.

[6] BBergG, s 126, paras 1, 2.

B. Underground technologies from an environmental perspective

The idea that underground space may be used for environmental purposes is a relatively recent discovery, dating back to the advent of the environment age around 1970. Underground waste disposal is the prototype of environment-related underground uses, in particular for highly toxic waste. For example, in 1972 the underground waste disposal site at Herfa Neurode was opened. It was to become the world's largest repository for highly toxic waste. During the early 1970s subsurface waste disposal was widely regarded as progress compared to above-ground disposal. Over the years, this 'out of sight, out of mind' attitude has changed. One essential reason is the endless controversy over the exploration and installation of underground nuclear waste repositories in sites such as decommissioned iron ore mines or in salt domes.[7] Scepticism has grown in connection with the former salt mine of Asse, where in the 1960s an experimental repository was operated and 125,000 barrels with low- and medium-level radioactive waste were stored. For decades, water has penetrated into the caverns and plans are being made for a retrieval of the barrels.[8] Whether this is possible is still an open question. In any case, these incidents and failures have greatly contributed to undermine public confidence in using the underground for the disposal of toxic substances. There is, however, one aspect of subsurface use that is viewed positively: the construction of electricity grid lines below surface in order to avoid the destruction of landscape and the electromagnetic waves associated with above-surface electricity grid lines.[9]

The new uses presently also under discussion in Germany (unconventional gas exploration and production through fracking, geothermal energy generation, CCS) are fields where energy-related and environment-related aspects are intertwined and controversial.

C. Political and public responses to new subsurface technologies (fracking, geothermal energy, CCS)

The attitude towards these new subsurface technologies, as shown by German political circles and by the German public in general, is ambivalent at best. This is particularly true in light of the so-called 'Energiewende' or 'energy switch', which the Federal Government had already embarked on in 2010 and which was significantly boosted under the impact of the Fukushima disaster in March

[7] For a review of the German political and legal situation with regard to nuclear waste repositories, see G. Kühne, 'Judicial Progress in Germany's Nuclear Waste Disposal Policy, The Konrad Repository Decisions of March 26, 2007' (2007/2) 80 Nuclear Law Bulletin 9.

[8] Recently a 'Statute on the Acceleration of the Retrieval of Radioactive Waste and of the Decommissioning of the Asse II Mine' was enacted: BGBl 2013 I 921.

[9] This is now covered by the Electricity Grid Expansion Act (*Energieleitungsausbaugesetz*, or ENLAG): BGBl 2009 I, 2870, s 2. Certain high-voltage grid lines are selected as potential pilot projects to test the use of subsurface cables.

2011.[10] The 'energy switch' is overwhelmingly focused on the abandonment of nuclear energy and on the substitution of electricity generation from fossil fuels by the use of renewable energy sources, especially wind and solar energy.

The discussion of the new technologies is dominated by their environmental implications. One reason is that, currently, the procurement of energy on world markets does not pose grave problems—neither the procurement as such nor the price factor. This is partly due to the shale gas boom in the United States. The German perspective, accordingly, is much more concentrated on the presumed or real risks this technology involves than on the energy opportunities it has to offer. The same is true of geothermal energy. There have been incidents in connection with geothermal projects, namely earth tremors presumed to have been caused by the use of fracking technology.[11] In addition, the German potential for deep thermal energy generation for electricity is rather limited.

In contrast to fracking and geothermal energy, CCS derives its relevance exclusively from the environmental aspect. Despite its strong general pro-environment stance, the German public here, too, is very reserved, to say the least. CCS, in addition to its unclear economic feasibility, raises the same suspicions regarding technical risks as fracking or geothermal projects do. Moreover, CCS is a technology designed to make the use of fossil fuels cleaner—a form of energy Germany wants to phase out altogether in favour of renewable energies.

D. Conclusion

All in all, German public opinion, for a variety of reasons, is not very favourable towards an offensive implementation of new subsurface technologies. There is one additional constitutional-political reason for German hesitation and inaction in this field, as in many others: the division of power between the federal and the state levels. Often both levels are dominated by opposing majorities of the more opportunity-oriented conservative-liberal 'camp' vs the environmental risk-oriented red-green 'camp'. The result on the federal legislative level, where federal and state majorities confront each other through the existing two-chamber-system—Bundestag: federal; Bundesrat: state—is often either a stalemate or a lame compromise.

III. Conceptual basis for implementing new subsurface technologies under German private and public law

One of the central problems to be dealt with when it comes to underground uses is the demarcation between the legal spheres of the real property (surface) owner and

[10] For a brief review of the German post-Fukushima energy policy scenario, see G. Kühne, 'Regulating the Extension of Electricity Networks: A German Perspective' in *Energy Networks and the Law* (M. M. Roggenkamp, L. K. Barrera-Hernández, D. N. Zillman, and I. del Guayo, eds, 2012) 371 at 375–7.

[11] See section IV.A.

the subsurface user. In this respect, the German legal system provides for a staged set of rules consisting of both private and public law components.[12]

A. The property law basis (Section 905 Civil Code, BGB)

Under s 903 sentence 1, Civil Code (Bürgerliches Gesetzbuch, BGB), the owner of property may deal with it at his or her discretion and exclude others from every influence—the classical nineteeth-century definition of property. According to s 905, sentence 1, BGB, the rights of the owner of a plot of land extend to the subsoil under the surface. However, under s 905 sentence 2, BGB, the owner may not prohibit influences that are exercised at such a depth that he or she has no interest in excluding them.

It is no surprise that there is a case law discussion about the meaning and character of 'exclusionary interest' (only freedom from physical interference or also economic interests?).

Courts have generally shown a tendency to favour a wide interpretation of 'exclusionary interest'.[13] It may be material or immaterial, for example, aesthetic. In a judgment of 23 October 1980, the Federal Supreme Court (Bundesgerichtshof, BGH)[14] had to decide a case involving underground storage: the surface owner had sued a mining company which held mineral rights for salt mining. After depletion of the deposit, the company had used the caverns for the storage of oil. The Court held that the underground storage activity was unlawful because the mining title did not encompass the storage right and that the surface owner had a general, maybe even remote, exclusionary interest with regard to a third party's business activity underneath his or her own property. This demonstrates the weakness of the legal position of a third party which is using the underground of a real property owner. That is why, normally, such underground uses as, for example, laying of underground pipelines in the gas industry, are based on contractual arrangements, i.e. easements.

There is, however, a line of jurisprudential authority that bars injunctions against such third-party property users if their activity is supported by a vital public interest.[15] Courts have applied this reasoning to commercial underground gas storage facilities serving an important supply function.[16] In such cases, the user (storage operator) has to compensate the surface owner through payment of a market-based fee.[17]

12 For a review of the system, see G. Kühne, 'Unterirdische Grundstücksnutzungen als Gegenstand des Zivil-, Berg-, Energie- und Umweltrechts—Zugleich zur rechtssystematischen Einbindung der CO_2-Speicherung' (2009) 17 Recht der Energiewirtschaft 14.

13 See Bassenge in Palandt, *Bürgerliches Gesetzbuch* (72nd edn, 2013) s 905, marginal note 2.

14 Reported in Wertpapier-Mitteilungen 1981 129. The decision is analysed in depth by J. Baur, 'Der Konflikt zwischen Eigentümer und Dritten bei der Tiefennutzung von Grundstücken—Eine Untersuchung zur Reichweite des § 905 BGB am Beispiel der Untertagespeicherung' (1986) 150 Zeitschrift für das gesamte Handelsrecht und Wirtschaftsrecht 507 ss.

15 See Bassenge in Palandt (n 13) s 906, marginal note 36 with court references.

16 See Decision of the Oberlandesgericht (Regional Appellate Court) Celle, 17 October 1980, (1981) 122 Zeitschrift für Bergrecht 449.

17 Decision of the Bundesgerichtshof of 21 December 1989, Amtliche Sammlung der Entscheidungen des BGH (Official Collection of the Decisions of the BGH), BGHZ 110, 17, 21.

B. Legalization through licensing

The third-party underground user has a stronger position vis-à-vis the surface owner where the activity in question has been approved and legalized within a comprehensive licensing procedure. In Germany, the licensing procedure is the planning approval procedure (Planfeststellungsverfahren). Under s 75, para 2, sentence 1 of the Administrative Procedure Code (Verwaltungsverfahrensgesetz, VwVfG),[18] the approval decision has the effect of barring all prohibitory actions by the real property owner against the approved facility. This, for example, applies to waste disposal facilities, including underground sites (Section 35 para 2 of the Closed Substance Cycle and Waste Management Act, Kreislaufwirtschaftsgesetz, KWG).

In other instances, the legislature has conferred on operators of energy facilities, whether on surface or underground, the right to expropriation. This, for example, applies to underground gas storage facilities, which are highly important for the energy supply system. Section 45 of the Energy Act[19] confers such a right, which may be implemented by an expropriation decree imposing the grant of an easement on the property owner.

C. Separate quasi-proprietary mining law regimes

The most radical form of curtailing the legal sphere of a surface owner is to create a separate and comprehensive legal framework for parts of the underground. This has been the case for centuries in Germany with regard to mining law. As part of a long tradition, the economically important minerals such as salt, coal, and, in more recent times, oil and gas, have been legally separated from surface ownership.[20] Under such a system, any claim of the surface owner to these minerals is even conceptually unthinkable. These minerals are subjected to a framework that is totally disconnected from surface ownership. The state, through mechanisms of administrative procedures, confers licences and titles governing the exploration and exploitation of the mineral deposits. These licences and titles are quasi-proprietary in character. All this is dealt with in the Federal Mining Law.[21] In certain ways, it also determines the legal regime for new subsurface uses such as oil and gas exploration and production through fracking, geothermal energy, and CCS.

IV. Unconventional gas and hydraulic fracturing ('fracking')

Among the modern subsurface uses in connection with energy presently under discussion, the complex of unconventional gas (shale gas) and its exploration/

[18] Of 25 May 1976, Bundesgesetzblatt (BGBl) (Federal Gazette) I, 1253.

[19] Gesetz über die Elektrizitäts- und Gasversorgung (Energiewirtschaftsgesetz—EnWG) of 7 July 2005, BGBl 2005 I 1970.

[20] See s 3, para 2, sentence 2 of the Federal Mining Act. It reads: 'The surface property does not extend to the free minerals.'

[21] See n 4.

exploitation through hydraulic fracturing (fracking) takes centre stage. The discussion underway worldwide has also reached Germany during the past two years. The confrontation between energy aspects and environmental considerations is particularly controversial, both within the political arena and in the general public.

A. The energy relevance

The potential for shale gas production in Germany is considerable. According to a study released by the Bundesanstalt für Geowissenschaften und Rohstoffe (BGR, Federal Agency for Geo-Sciences and Raw Materials) in May 2012[22] the ascertained shale gas reserves in clay formations total between 6.8 and 22.6 billion m^3. Supposing a recoverability factor of 10%, 0.7 to 2.3 billion m^3 of shale gas is technically exploitable. These quantities significantly exceed Germany's gas resources (0.15 billion m^3) and gas reserves (0.146 billion m^3). According to these figures, production from domestic reserves has the potential to significantly contribute to Germany's natural gas supply and to make up for the declining production from conventional gas deposits. Domestic security of gas supply could be considerably enhanced. However, from a global point of view Germany is lagging far behind the United States as to its shale gas reserves. It takes only the twentieth position.[23]

B. The legal framework

The shale gas discussion in Germany, to the extent that it is a legal discussion, is centred around mining law and water law.

1. Mining law

The exploration and production of natural gas in Germany fall within the ambit of mining law. This applies to conventional and unconventional gas indiscriminately. The statutory basis is the mining code (Federal Mining Law, Bundesberggesetz (BBergG)).[24] Unlike in many other jurisdictions, there is no separate set of rules for mining solid minerals and hydrocarbons.

Since natural gas—like other minerals of economic importance—is legally separated from surface ownership,[25] any title in this respect has to be acquired from the state. The way to achieve this is the award of a mineral title. For exploration, this is an exploration licence (Erlaubnis)[26] and, for production, a production licence (Bewilligung)[27] which, under certain conditions, may be transformed into mining property (Bergwerkseigentum).[28] These licences or rights are

[22] Bundesanstalt für Geowissenschaften und Rohstoffe (BGR), Abschätzung des Erdgaspotentials aus dichten Tongesteinen (Schiefergas) in Deutschland (Assessment of the Natural Gas Potential from Dense Shale Formations (Shale Gas) in Germany), Hanover, May 2012, 29, 30, 48.

[23] BGR (n 22) at 31.

[24] See n 4.

[25] Section II.C.

[26] BBergG, s 7.

[27] BBergG, s 8.

[28] BBergG, s 9.

awarded upon applications within established administrative proceedings. The prerequisites to be met for an award are exhaustively listed in the Mining Code (BBergG, ss 11, 12). Among these prerequisites are the availability of the necessary financial resources and the presentation of a realistic work programme (BBergG, s 11 nos 3, 7; s 12). The issuance of a licence may be denied if exploration or production is excluded for the entire field because of overriding public interests (BBergG, s 11, para 10). During recent years, a number of licences for shale gas exploration have been issued.[29] These awards have been criticized because they were made without participation of the surface owner, without an environmental impact assessment, and without notifying the respective municipalities of the awards.[30] But this procedure is not specific to shale gas projects. Rather, it reflects the normal licensing procedure under German mining law: the licence itself is not an authorization to actually perform mining activities. For that purpose the licence holder has to undergo a second level of administrative proceedings, the operations plan procedure (Betriebsplanverfahren). As an essential part of this procedure, the Mining Authority has to control whether the intended project will be executed in accordance with good mining practice and whether it is not harmful to third persons or to public welfare.[31] It does not, however, encompass a comprehensive Environmental Impact Assessment (EIA). On the basis of the EIA Directive of 27 June 1985,[32] German mining law has enacted the EIA requirement for certain projects listed in s 1 of the 'Ordinance on EIA for Mining Projects' (Verordnung über die Umweltverträglichkeitsprüfung bergbaulicher Vorhaben, UVP-V Bergbau).[33] Under this Ordinance, the only project requiring an EIA in the field of hydrocarbons is 'production of oil and gas for commercial purposes with a production volume of more than 500 tons of oil per day or 500,000 m^3 of natural gas per day'.[34] Shale gas exploration does not fall within this category. As a result, shale gas exploration projects do not require an EIA under present German law.[35]

2. *Water law*

Exploration and production activities very often have an impact on water resources. This is also relevant for boring in unconventional gas reservoirs. Boring may result in toxic substances leaking out into the groundwater system, in particular through

[29] By 1 July 2011 in Northrhine-Westphalia, the largest state, 20 exploration licences for unconventional gas existed and nine such licences had been applied for: see W. Grigo et al, 'Aufsuchung und Gewinnung von Kohlenwasserstoffen aus unkonventionellen Lagerstätten in Northrhine-Westphalia', in *Chancen und Risiken von unkonventionellem Erdgas* (W. Frenz and A. Preusse, eds, 2011) 21 at 26, 27.

[30] See, e.g., M. Terwiesche, 'Berg-, wasser- und bauverwaltungsrechtliche Hürden des Frackings' in *Unkonventionelle Gasgewinnung in NRW* (W. Frenz, P. Kukla, and A. Preusse, eds, 2012) 61 at 62, 65.

[31] BBergG, s 48, para 2, 55.

[32] Council Directive 85/337/EEC of 27 June 1985 on the assessment of the effects of certain public and private projects on the environment, OJ L 175/40.

[33] Of 13 July 1990, BGBl I 1420.

[34] UVP-V Bergbau, s 2(a).

[35] There is a legal discussion in Germany on whether this state of law constitutes a correct implementation of the EEC Directive. W. Frenz, 'Fracking und UVP' (2012) Umwelt- und Planungsrecht (UPR) 125 at 126 argues that the present EIA Directive requires an EIA whenever there are environmental dangers in question, regardless of any production thresholds.

casing and cementing. Any activity through which such substances might be released into the groundwater system is subject to a licence under water law (Water Resources Act—Wasserhaushaltsgesetz, WHG, s 9, para 1, no 4). Such a licence will be denied wherever there is concern that the water balance might be adversely affected (WHG, s 48, para 1, sentence 1). To what extent shale gas activities using methods of hydraulic fracturing pose such dangers for groundwater quality is a matter for expert debate, and there is a trend towards diverging judgments between geologists and environmentalists.

C. Recent political and legal reform moves

The political and legal controversies that have characterized the debate for more than two years mainly focused on two points: the absence of an EIA at the licence award level and, during the control phase, over boring projects involving hydraulic fracturing methods. Reports about possible dangers and film presentations such as 'Gasland' have sparked off demonstrations in potential exploration areas and radicalized the discussion in a way that total rejection of hydraulic fracturing gained ground in some political circles. This is all the more so in some areas where licences for shale gas exploration had already been issued without public participation, such as in Northrhine-Westphalia.[36] This practice was discontinued once the Red-Green coalition in that state came to power in 2010. Regardless of the positive experience over decades with fracking in conventional gas, exploration and production studies were commissioned on the potential and on the environmental risks of hydraulic fracturing. In the meantime, the issuance of exploration licences and boring permissions was suspended until publication of the study results.

In summer 2012, two studies by the most important Federal Agencies (Federal Agency for Geo-Sciences and Raw Materials, BGR,[37] and Federal Environmental Agency, Umweltbundesamt, UBA[38]) were published. The conclusions diverged. The BGR study evaluated the unconventional gas technology as positive and the environmental risks as manageable.[39] In contrast, the UBA study raised serious concerns and proposed an outright prohibition in drinking water and spa protection zones.[40] Both evaluations were reflected accordingly on the political level (Federal Economics Ministry vs Federal Ministry for Environmental Affairs).

In order to reach a common position, the Federal Government engaged in lengthy consultations from autumn 2012. On 25 February 2013, both Ministries presented a joint proposal: projects for exploration and production of oil and gas for commercial purposes and involving hydraulic fracturing have to undergo a mandatory EIA within the framework of mining law. Within drinking water and spa protection zones, such activities would be prohibited under water law. During the

[36] Grigo et al (n 29). [37] BGR (n 22).

[38] See Umweltbundesamt, Gutachten (Expert Opinion): Umweltauswirkungen von Fracking bei der Aufsuchung und Gewinnung von Erdgas aus unkonventionellen Lagerstätten, 2012, available at <http://www.umweltbundesamt.de>.

[39] BGR (n 22) at 48. [40] See Umweltbundesamt (n 37) sub D.

ensuing parliamentary deliberations, a working group of the majority parties (Christian Democrats and Liberals) reached an agreement not to ban shale gas exploration involving fracking in principle, but to forbid fracking in catchment areas of drinking water lakes, to require the consent of water authorities for drilling operations, and to restrict the terms of operation to certain chemical liquids. Finally, in May 2013, the Sachverständigenrat für Umweltfragen (SRU) (Expert Council for Environmental Questions) published a very critical opinion on the potential of shale gas production for the German energy portfolio and on the environmental acceptability of fracking. The increasingly negative attitude of experts and public opinion towards fracking in Germany are probably responsible for the final failure to find a legislative solution. As a result of the September 2013 general elections, Germany is heading towards a grand coalition of Christian and Social Democrats. According to the coalition agreement, still to be approved by the members of the Social Democratic Party, fracking is to be put on hold until further research has proved that this technology has no detrimental effect on the environment, especially the water balance. The new Government intends to open a transparent dialogue with all parties concerned and to initiate legislation subjecting all projects involving fracking technology to a mandatory EIA and to public participation.

V. Geothermal energy

In recent times in Germany, interest in promoting the use of geothermal energy has noticeably increased. To a certain extent this is due to the fact that geothermal energy shares the charisma of a renewable energy.

A. General observations and potential

Unlike New Zealand, Germany is not an obvious country for using geothermal energy. This form of energy was more or less ‘discovered’ around the turn of the century when climate policies and, with them, renewable energies, became the order of the day. When considering the benefits of geothermal energy, one has to differentiate between two kinds of uses:

- near-surface geothermal energy that can be used for heating of buildings and for water heating;[41] and
- deep geothermal energy, which can be used for electricity generation.

Presently, the share of geothermal energy in covering German demand of heating and electricity is rather modest: in 2010, geothermal heating only amounted to 0.42% of final energy consumption for heating purposes. Its share in total

[41] For a discussion on near-surface geothermal energy and its legal implications, see S. Benz, *Rechtliche Rahmenbedingungen für die Nutzung der oberflächennahen Geothermie*, 2007.

electricity consumption of 0,005% was even smaller.[42] Over recent years, however, investment incentives have significantly improved.[43] The promotion package, in essence, consisted of the following elements:

- the inclusion of geothermal energy in the subsidization scheme under the Renewable Energies Act (Erneuerbare-Energien-Gesetz, EEG) and increased feed-in tariffs, especially within the recent amendment in 2012;
- a market incentive programme for the promotion of deep geothermal energy;
- the promotion of research and development;
- the introduction of an obligation to use renewable warmth in new housing construction—an obligation that can be implemented through installation of geothermal facilities.

It is the risk-prone deep geothermal energy where, since 2009, investment conditions have improved considerably. In July 2012, 19 heating plants and heating and power plants were already in operation, 20 were under construction, and 74 were in the planning stage.

The potential is considerable: supposedly, by 2020, 280 megawatts of power will be installed and the generation of electricity from deep geothermal energy will have risen to 1.8 billion kilowatt hours. By the same year, the capacity to generate warmth from deep geothermal energy facilities will stand at 8.2 billion kilowatt hours. It is assumed that after 2020 the increase will accelerate and reach a level of 850 megawatts by 2030.[44]

Despite this generally positive outlook, even geothermal energy and its utilization are perceived negatively by segments of the population. This is the result of several accidents that drew attention in the media. In one case, bore holes were drilled for the installation of bore hole heat exchangers for the purpose of providing heat for the city hall in the town of Staufen (Baden-Württemberg) in 2007.[45] The city hall itself and adjacent buildings were affected by cracks, causing double-digit million Euro damage. Moreover, in the city of Landau on 15 August 12009, earth tremors occurred at a distance of 2 km from the bore holes of the local geothermal power plant. There is a high probability that these tremors were caused by the increase in pore water pressure following the injection of water into deep rock layers.[46] Hydraulic fracturing technology is used for both unconventional gas

[42] See Bundesministerium für Umwelt, Naturschutz und Reaktorsicherheit (Federal Ministry of the Environment, Nature Conservation and Reactor Safety), Erneuerbare Energien in Zahlen (Renewable Energies in Figures), as of December 2011, 7.

[43] See the Report of the Federal Government to Parliament on a Concept to Promote, Develop and Introduce Electricity Generation by Geothermal Energy and the Use of Geothermal Heat, in Bundestag Document 16/13128 of 14 May 2009, 3.

[44] See Bundestag Document 16/13128 of 14 May 2009, 3.

[45] See U. Ehricke, 'Verkehrssicherungspflichten im Hinblick auf Geothermiebohrungen' (2009) Umwelt- und Planungsrecht (UPR) 281.

[46] See Das seismische Ereignis bei Landau vom 15.8.2009 (The seismic event near Landau of 15 August 2009)—Abschlussbericht der Expertengruppe 'Seismisches Risiko bei hydrothermaler Geothermie', Hanover, 29 October 2010, available at <http://www.mwkel.rlp.de/File/Landau-Abschlussbericht-Expertengruppe-pdf/>.

activities and geothermal energy projects. From there it is understandable that reservations and opposition against unconventional gas ventures are carried over to the utilization of geothermal energy.

B. The legal regime

The principal legal framework for exploring and producing geothermal energy in Germany is mining law. When enacting the Federal Mining Code in 1980[47] the legislature took the decision to incorporate geothermal energy into mining law. Geothermal energy was treated as a deemed free mineral (BBerg, s 3, para 3), thereby excluding it from the surface owner's property.

Consequently, the exploration and 'production' of geothermal energy are basically subject to the same rules that govern exploration and production of oil or gas: the operator needs a mining licence and the performance of exploratory or production activities is subject to approval of operation plans by the Mining Authority. However, while these procedures may be adequate for coal, oil, or gas projects, they can be disproportionately burdensome for geothermal activities, especially near-surface operations. Therefore, the legislature departed from the regular framework for this category.

Under BBergG, s 4, para 2, no 1, the production of minerals, including geothermal energy in connection with building use of the surface, does not fall within the realm of the Mining Code.[48] This means that such activities (producing geothermal energy for heating purposes on the same plot of land) are exempt from mining law rules. But once boring reaches a depth of more than 100 m, such activities are again required to be notified to the Mining Authority (BBergG, s 127). Such near-surface projects do not require a mining licence.

Depending on the individual case, other provisions regarding administrative control may come into play. This applies, in particular, to water law whenever exploration and production of geothermal energy may affect the groundwater system.

C. Evaluation of the legal regime

There is no basic opposition to subjecting geothermal energy to the principles and rules of mining law. But there are problems with regard to details. As indicated earlier, near-surface and deep geothermal energy both differ as to their technology and to their respective range of application. For near-surface geothermal energy the mining law regime is widely regarded as overly complicated and intensive.[49] On the

[47] See n 4.

[48] This effect is achieved through definition: the extraction of minerals (here the deemed mineral of 'geothermal energy') in a plot of land in connection with its use for building purposes is held not to constitute a 'production'.

[49] See, e.g., F. von Hammerstein, 'Wann ist das Bundesberggesetz auf die Nutzung von Erdwärme anwendbar?' in *Festschrift (Liber Amicorum) for Peter Salje*, (A. Klees and K. Gent, eds, 2013) 201 at 208; also sceptical: E. Gurlit, 'Geothermie—Suche nach einem Ordnungsmodell für die Gewinnung

other hand, the exception to this regime in favour of the surface owner, as far as the utilization for heating of surface structures is concerned, is also unsatisfactory because then it is confined to the boundaries of the individual plot of land.[50] This means that the exception in favour of the surface owner does not work in case of facilities with cross-boundary energy generation. Accordingly, other criteria for differentiating between near-surface and deep geothermal energy have been put forward, such as heat output.[51]

Within the mining law regime geothermal energy has a problem because mining law does not provide for mining licences to be issued for certain (strata) layers ('floors').[52] By definition, the theoretical spatial validity of a mining licence, under the definition of 'field' in BBergG, s 4, para 7, extends from the surface to the centre of the earth.[53] In this respect, mining law will have to be amended.

Hydraulic fracturing is also a controversial topic within the complex of geothermal energy exploration and production. The recent incidents reported here generally are associated with the use of fracking technology. Not surprisingly then, the joint proposal presented by the Minister of Economics and the Minister for Environmental Affairs on 25 February 2013[54] also addressed geothermal energy, stating:

> A mandatory Environmental Impact Assessment (EIA) shall be introduced for all deep level drilling activities from a depth of 1000 m and more
>
> —within designated nature reserves or special nature reserves designated in accordance with Directives 2009/147/EC or 92/43/EEC,
>
> —involving hydraulic fracturing technology.

VI. Carbon capture and storage (CCS)

Germany's attitude towards CCS technology—as in the case of unconventional gas exploration and production—has been and still is tortuous and ambivalent. It took Germany years to enact a statute that follows a minimalistic approach.

A. Legislative history

Germany's legislative efforts were prompted by the enactment of Directive 2009/31/EC of the European Parliament and of the Council of 23 April 2009 on the

von Erdwärme' in *Festschrift (Liber Amicorum) for F.J. Säcker* (D. Joost, H. Oetker, and M. Paschke, eds, 2011) 712 at 713.

[50] See von Hammerstein (n 49) at 201, 208. [51] See von Hammerstein (n 49) at 201, 214.

[52] See Bundestag Document 16/13128 of 14 May 2009, 16.

[53] BBergG, s 4, para 7 reads: 'Field of an exploration licence, a production licence or of a mineral property is a segment of the earth demarcated by straight lines at the surface and vertical layers to the depth unless the borders of the applicability of this law require another demarcation.'

[54] See section III.C.

geological storage of carbon dioxide.[55] Under the Directive, Member States retain the right to determine the areas within their territory from which a storage site may be selected. This includes the right of Member States not to allow any storage in parts of or on the whole of their territory.[56] But if Member States allow such storage, the Directive provides a framework for the installation and operation of such facilities in order to give operators the necessary planning and investment security.

CCS technology has not yet sufficiently matured to allow a routine industrial use. Since 2007, Germany has three test/pilot plants in operation. On 28 June 2012, the German Parliament passed the Law on Demonstration and Application of Technologies for Capture, Transport and of Permanent Storage of Carbon Dioxide.[57] The legislative history was turbulent. The factual background is that there is widespread opposition within the population and political circles to the introduction of this technology. The result was that the text that was voted into law falls significantly short of earlier drafts. In contrast to the final text, which only concerns demonstration facilities, these earlier proposals included the eventual installation of storage facilities for commercial use. The parliamentary passage of this piece of legislation has been made possible through a compromise with the states. They have conceded the right to ban the installation and operation of such devices in parts or all of their territory.[58] The states most affected by this clause are Schleswig-Holstein and Lower Saxony, where a number of potential sites are located. The effect of this exemption clause may be that, in the end, there will not be a sufficient number of candidate sites to test this technology.[59]

B. The legal framework

The German CCS statute encompasses both capture and storage, the latter being the only subject of interest in this context.[60]

The statute specifically addresses the four phases of the life cycle of storage facilities: nationwide evaluation and registering, exploration of the underground, installation and operation of such facilities and, finally, their decommissioning. The exploration phase raises the question of the relationship between the exploration operator and the surface owner.

In this respect, mining law was the model (BBergG, ss 39, 40). Under s 10, para 1 of the Statute, the surface owner's consent is required whenever an operator of exploratory activities has to use the surface. In case of denial, the consent may be

[55] OJ L 140/114 of 5 June 2009. For a discussion see, e.g., D. Greinacher, 'CCS—Europarechtlicher Rahmen für eine neue Technik', in *Festschrift for Gunther Kühne* (J. F. Baur, O. Sandrock, B. Scholtka, and A. Shapira, eds, 2009), 557.

[56] Recital 19 of the Directive (n 55).

[57] Gesetz zur Demonstration und Anwendung von Technologien zur Abscheidung und zum Transport und zur dauerhaften Speicherung von Kohlendioxid, BGBl 2012 I 1726.

[58] Section 2, para 5 of the Statute.

[59] N. Dieckmann, 'Das neue CCS-Gesetz—Überblick und Ausblick' (2012) Neue Zeitschrift für Verwaltungsrecht 989 at 995.

[60] For a review see Dieckmann (n 59).

granted by the competent authority if the exploration is supported by overriding public interests. This means that opposing surface owners are not in a position to prohibit such activities, but can only delay them. This is what had already happened.

The main focus of the storage section of the statute is on the installation and operation of CO_2 storage facilities. During the entire legislative process, the conflict between storage operator and surface owner played an important role. It was suggested at some point that storage rights be treated as 'deemed mineral rights' with the effect of totally incorporating storage into the body of mining law (see section III.C). That was the legal regime applicable to the storage of oil and gas in East Germany during the early 1990s after reunification. In the case of the CCS statute, the legislature did not follow this path. Instead, for the installation and operation of storage facilities, the new law requires licensing through a comprehensive planning approval procedure (see section III.B). This procedure absorbs all other statutory requirements and procedures under environmental law such as water law or nature conservation law. An EIA is also an integral part of the procedure.

The legislature went as far as to include provisions on the decommissioning of storage facilities. Decommissioning requires a separate licence and a specific EIA.

C. Perspectives

Today in Germany, CCS technology is viewed as highly problematic. This relates both to its high costs and to its uncertain environmental effects. The most relevant factor, however, is the rapid reorientation of German energy policy over the past three years towards renewable energies. CCS technology derives its rationale from the idea of making energy (electricity) generation from fossil fuels environmentally compatible. Present German policy, however, aims to abandon fossil fuels altogether or, at least, to marginalize them within the energy portfolio for a transitional period. For such a low priority, the high financial investment for making this technology commercially viable is widely held to be disproportionate.

VII. Conflicts between subsurface uses

The increasing variety of subsurface technological uses raises a new problem: what are the legal tools to resolve conflicts between different kinds of uses? This is a problem that is well known for above-surface uses of land.

A. Increase of conflicts between uses

Over the last decades, most notably in recent years, underground uses have significantly increased in various forms. Apart from the most modern examples discussed earlier (unconventional gas, geothermal energy, CCS), there are more traditional uses such as underground storage of oil and gas, underground waste disposal, and the classic underground mining. The space underneath the surface gets crowded and conflicts are bound to arise. This calls for legal solutions.

B. Conflict solutions on an individual case-by-case basis

In the eventual case of conflicting uses, present German law offers mechanisms under public law to solve such conflicts and to determine priorities. Normally, the prerequisites for obtaining a licence for a commercial activity contain a provision that such an activity may be restricted or denied if it runs counter to an overriding public interest. Such interests, in our time, are very often of an environmental nature. But colliding uses of a public interest may also work as an overriding public interest. In a case decided in 2008, the Administrative Appellate Court (Oberverwaltungsgericht) for Lower Saxony[61] had to deal with the legality of an operations plan approval (Betriebsplanzulassung) for salt mining. The reservoir in question was part of the Gorleben salt dome, which for decades has been under exploration as a candidate site for the installation of a high-level radioactive waste repository. The execution of the salt production plan would have put at risk the repository exploration activities and the potential later installation of the repository itself—this was, indeed, the ultimate goal of the salt production project. The Court held that the salt mining project was illegal because it ran counter to the overriding public interest in an unhampered continuation of the exploration activities for the repository (BBergG, s 48, para 2).

This example shows that existing public (administrative) law is in a position to deal with conflicting uses on an individual case and conflict basis. Theoretically, there is also the possibility of using private law mechanisms for resolving underground conflicts. Property law contains an elaborate set of rules and principles for accommodating conflicting uses of surface property (ss 906, 1004 Civil Code): the law of private nuisance. This body of law may apply to underground conflicts by way of analogy. This would, however, presuppose the at least quasi-proprietary character of underground rights, which presently applies only to mineral rights. To design a general system of underground rights (including, for example, CCS) as being of a quasi-proprietary nature would have had the ingenious effect of making available the law of private nuisance in all its refinements.

All these devices—under public or private law—can only deal with concrete and individual conflicts. What is needed, however, is a body of law that can serve as an instrument to prospectively avoid conflicts, i.e. a law of underground planning or zoning.

C. Underground planning (zoning) law

The statutory basis for regional land use planning in Germany is the Federal Regional Planning Act (Raumordnungsgesetz, ROG).[62] It sets forth principles

[61] Oberverwaltungsgericht Lüneburg, Judgment of 17 July 2008, (2008) 149 Zeitschrift für Bergrecht 257; L. Dietrich, 'Nutzungskonflikte unter Tage' in *Bergrecht zwischen Tradition und Moderne* (G. Kühne and U. Ehricke, eds, 2010) 139 at 152, 153.

[62] BGBl 2008 I 2986.

for regional planning and for regional planning procedures that are implemented by state organs with regard to individual areas and projects.

The principles of regional planning are based on surface planning. They also concern the underground, but only to the extent that surface use has an impact on the underground. It is planning—so to speak—from top to bottom effects. Underground planning would require the opposite order: from bottom to top effects. Meanwhile, there are early manifestations of a change in perspective: in 2009, one of the ROG principles was reworded so as to take into account the spatial requirements of climate change and climate protection. The ROG now obligates planning authorities to take into account the spatial requirements of climate protection: 'In doing so the geographic conditions for an expansion of renewable energies, for an economic use of energy as well as for the conservation and the development of natural sinks for climate-damaging substances and for *storage of those substances* shall be secured.'[63] The last words were deliberately directed at CCS.

One important instrument of prospective planning and coordination of different land uses is the designation of priority areas (Vorranggebiete): s 8, para 7, no 1 ROG, and of reserve areas (Vorbehaltsgebiete): s 8, para 7, no 2 ROG. It is still a matter of debate whether these instruments are presently applicable to underground uses.[64] In any event, a meaningful planning procedure requires that there is a reliable basis for a demand estimate both in quantity and in time. A procedural mechanism for establishing such a reliable demand estimate still remains to be put in place.[65] Finally, it has to be borne in mind that underground planning is much more difficult than surface planning, since it is much more money- and time-consuming to ascertain the suitability of the underground for a certain use than with regard to surface uses. From a realistic standpoint, planning, in its initial phases, will have to concentrate on exploration planning rather than on installation and operation planning. The new German coalition government (see section IV.C) has committed itself to adapt planning law so as to more effectively cope with conflicting land uses, including production of raw materials.

VIII. Conclusions

Subsurface uses of (modern) technologies, to the extent that they are factually and economically relevant, pose the basic problem of accommodating the legal spheres

63 ROG, s 2, no 6, sentence 8.

64 See the discussion in W. Erbguth, 'Unterirdische Raumordnung—zur raumordnungsrechtlichen Steuerung untertägiger Vorhaben' (2011) Zeitschrift für Umweltrecht (ZUR) 121 at 122. In a most recent publication—J. Schilling, *Planerische Steuerung von unterirdischen Raum- und Grundstücksnutzungen* (2013) 243—the author concludes that the instruments of present planning law are already a valid legal basis for comprehensive underground planning strategies and procedures.

65 Dietrich (n 61) at 139, 161; M. Hellriegel, 'Rechtsrahmen für eine Raumordnung zur Steuerung unterirdischer Nutzungen—Konkurrenzkampf unter der Erde' in Neue Zeitschrift für Verwaltungsrecht (NVwZ) (2013) 111 at 115; P. Franke, 'Die Einlagerung von CO_2 in unterirdischen geologischen Formationen unter besonderer Berücksichtigung des Bergrechts' in Kühne and Ehricke (eds) (n 61) at 99, 137.

and interests of the surface owner and the (potential) subsurface or underground user.

- As in many other jurisdictions, in Germany there is an interest in and (controversial) discussion about the potential and the feasibility of using new underground technologies. These discussions have significantly increased in recent years. Among the technologies, one can distinguish between those serving energy objectives and those serving environmental objectives.
- The use of the underground for energy purposes has a long tradition in Germany, represented, in particular, by hard coal underground mining since the nineteenth century. During the last decades, other non-extractive forms of uses have appeared and established themselves. This is the case with the underground storage of oil and gas, especially in the wake of the energy crisis of the 1970s.
- The use of underground technologies for environmental objectives is a relatively recent innovation in connection with the advent of the environment age. One example is underground toxic waste disposal facilities.
- Technologies motivated by energy and by environmental objectives (unconventional gas exploration and production, geothermal energy, CCS) encounter mixed positive/negative reactions from political circles, experts, and the general public.
- The principal legal tool to enable the use of underground technologies under German law is a staged system of negating the surface owner's access to the underground sphere: the denial of prohibitory action because of lack of exclusionary interest, the legalizing effect of licensing under public (administrative) law, and the establishment of a separate quasi-proprietary underground regime.

This range of legal approaches is well reflected by the various rules that are being discussed relating to the new technologies:

- The determining role in dealing with unconventional gas (hydraulic fracturing) and geothermal energy is taken by mining law. One reason may be that, because of its long historic tradition, this area of law had produced a framework of well-established and functional rules, especially for separating the legal spheres of the surface owner and of the mining industry. But it should be realized that mining law mainly addresses mining proper, through a system of legal tools that are burdensome and may not be adequate for all the new technologies.
- Thus, in some aspects, present mining law appears not to be perfectly adjusted to the unconventional gas technological procedures (injection of chemical substances into the underground) because certain risks were not dealt with adequately. Provisions should have been and certainly will be made to ensure that hydraulic fracturing operations require an EIA.

- In the case of geothermal energy, mining law is not suited for the specificities of near-surface geothermal energy. And deep geothermal energy, which is totally governed by mining law, would need a licensing system which allows the issuance of different licences for different depths, prohibited under present mining law. Insofar as near-surface geothermal energy is part of the surface owner's legal sphere, the vertical limitation to the individual plot of land does not take into account the horizontal trans-boundary extension of this energy production.
- In the case of CCS, the pertaining statute is not modelled on mining law, but legalizes the CCS operator through licensing procedures.
- Given the increasing number of modern underground technologies, conflicts between different uses are bound to arise. In the case of individual conflicts, the criterion of 'overriding public interests', normally contained in the various licensing regimes, may be an appropriate administrative tool to resolve such conflicts. What is lacking is a comprehensive regime for a prospective underground planning system. Present planning law provides for an elaborate regional planning system which deals with surface planning and which takes into account the underground only to the extent that it is affected by surface planning. What is required is the reverse planning order: a cohesive underground planning system, including its effects on the surface.

This discussion has shown that in Germany, the use of new energy-related technologies (fracking, geothermal energy, CCS) will encounter both legal and serious political obstacles. Legally, most of the perceived or real obstacles can be attributed to the unpopular and old-fashioned image of mining law (lack of EIA in the exploration phase, low level of public participation, lack of stratigraphic subdivision of mineral titles). But these obstacles could be removed by legislative reform. The main obstacle, however, is of a socio-political nature. In most jurisdictions, the attitude towards these technologies is determined by the relationship between general energy and environment policies. As a general characteristic, a shift from energy supply enhancement to environmental awareness has taken place. This general trend is subject to modifications according to the energy portfolio in a given national context. Thus, for example, a strong policy in favour of energy independence and attraction of domestic, as well as foreign, industrial investments through lower energy prices will work towards encouraging exploitation of unconventional hydrocarbon resources—a process that presently is in full swing in the United States. Where there is a substantial reliance on fossil fuels, as in China and Australia, there will certainly be a stronger interest in and support of CCS technologies.

In Germany, we observe almost exactly the opposite. The 'Energiewende' (energy switch) has geared general energy policy towards switching from fossil fuels to renewables (meaning wind and solar energy). From this perspective, there is limited interest in shouldering the high investment costs and environmental risks of developing CCS technologies only for a relatively limited transitional period of time. And in a social and political environment that is characterized by a considerable level of risk aversion, sun and wind represent an appeal of superior environmental acceptability as compared to the unknown dangers of the underground.

21

Australian Responses to Subsurface Conflicts: Greenhouse Gas Storage v Petroleum

Michael Crommelin

I. Introduction

This chapter examines Australian responses to the recent environmental challenge of storage of greenhouse gases[1] in natural underground reservoirs. Technological development[2] significantly increases the prospect of long-term storage of greenhouse gases, with substantial environmental benefits.[3] The best storage reservoirs, however, contain petroleum. This inconvenient fact places greenhouse gas storage in competition with petroleum exploration, production, and storage. The chapter describes the Australian legal framework for management of underground natural resources, based upon government proprietorship of most of these resources, and the use of statutory regimes (rather than the common law) to provide the necessary authority for private exploitation of each of them. The proliferation of these statutory regimes, each relating to a specific resource, inevitably gives rise to conflicts among them. The difficulties encountered in resolving these conflicts are severe enough to suggest that a major reappraisal of the existing approach to management of underground resources in Australia is required, perhaps leading to consolidation rather than fragmentation of the established statutory regimes.

II. The historical context

Australian law retains vestiges of Australia's colonial history. For almost 150 years after 1788, Australia comprised a number of British colonies. Early in this period, English law was introduced into all of these colonies.[4]

1 Terminology has evolved during this period, from 'geological sequestration' (sometimes 'geo-sequestration') to 'carbon capture and storage' (CCS) to 'greenhouse gas storage' (GGS).

2 J. Bradshaw, 'Some Technical Practicalities and Legal Implications of Geological Storage of CO_2: A Geologist's Perspective' in [2009] *AMPLA Yearbook* 280.

3 I. Havercroft and R. Macrory, 'Pulling the Threads Together' in *Carbon Capture and Storage: Emerging Legal and Regulatory Issues* (I. Havercroft, R. Macrory, and R. Stewart, eds, 2011) 297.

4 For example, Australian Courts Act 1828 (UK), s 24: 'All laws and statutes in force within the realm of England at the time of the passing of this Act . . . shall be applied in the administration of

Although colonial Australia had little, if anything, in common with medieval England, the feudal model of English land law was initially applied to the Australian colonies.[5] The Crown (initially on behalf of the UK government) acquired radical title to all land in Australia, as an incident to the sovereignty derived from occupation.[6] This title was residual in nature, conferring no present beneficial interest in the land. In 1992, the High Court of Australia held that the Crown's acquisition of radical title did not, of itself, extinguish native title, the interests in land held by the indigenous inhabitants of Australia at the time of occupation. However, radical title allowed the Crown to obtain or convey beneficial title to land, and to extinguish native title, by legislative or executive act.[7] Substantial extinguishment occurred throughout the colonial period and thereafter; even so, native title remains in force over large areas of Australian territory.[8]

The law of England that was applied in the Australian colonies at that time had no concept of absolute ownership of land. Instead, it recognized a limited number of estates or interests (titles) in land, such as freehold (the estate in fee simple, now almost indistinguishable in fact from absolute ownership), leasehold (conferring entitlement to exclusive possession of land for a term of years), profit à prendre (conferring a right of entry upon land together with a right to extract natural resources from the land), easement (conferring a right of way across land for the benefit of adjoining land), and licence (conferring a mere right of access to land; its status as an interest in land still remains uncertain).[9] Nevertheless, English land law included an important presumption that freehold title to land included rights to most land-based resources on and beneath the surface of the land,[10] unless such rights were reserved to the Crown upon the initial grant of the freehold title, or subsequently assigned by the holder of that title.

At first, the UK government exercised control over land in Australia, by virtue of its inherent executive power.[11] Colonial Governors, acting in accordance with instructions issued from London, were authorized to grant freehold titles to private landholders. Most of the early grants included no express reservation of any underground resources, although from 1828 there was a practice in some colonies of specifically reserving gold, silver and (occasionally) coal. Later, the UK

justice in the courts of New South Wales and Van Diemen's Land respectively, so far as the same can be applied within the said colonies.'

5 S. Hepburn, 'Feudal Tenure and Native Title: Revising an Enduring Fiction' (2005) 27 Sydney LR 1.

6 T. P. Fry, 'Land Tenures in Australian Law' (1946–47) 3 Res Judicatae 158.

7 *Mabo v Queensland (No 2)* (1992) 175 CLR 1, 50; *Western Australia v The Commonwealth (Native Title Act Case)* (1995) 183 CLR 373, 422.

8 *Wik Peoples v Queensland* (1996) 187 CLR 1. In 1993, 14.25% of Australian land was subject to native title: see <http://www.ga.gov.au/education/geoscience-basics/land-tenure.html>. Since then, claims established under the Native Title Act 1993 (Cth) have increased that figure.

9 Hepburn (n 5).

10 *Cujus est solum, ejus est usque ad coelum et usque ad inferos.* The royal metals (gold and silver) were exceptions to this presumption. The presumption is examined in detail in chapters 2–4.

11 E. Campbell, 'Crown Land Grants: Form and Validity' (1966) 40 Australian LJ 35. This inherent executive authority is often described as 'prerogative' power; its source lies in the executive (rather than the legislative) branch of government.

Parliament assumed control over land management in Australia with the enactment of the Sale of Waste Lands Act 1842 (UK). Following this enactment, the uneven practice of specifically reserving some minerals from grants of freehold title was largely discontinued.[12]

The control over land management in Australia then passed from the United Kingdom Parliament to the legislatures of the various Australian colonies, as those colonies obtained self-government. Typically, the constitutions of the newly self-governing colonies proclaimed that the 'entire Management and Control of the Waste Lands belonging to the Crown in the [Colony] . . . shall be vested in the legislature of the said Colony'.[13]

These provisions went well beyond the mere transfer of control over land management from the UK Parliament to the colonial legislatures. Following self-government, the Crown's title to lands in each of the Australian colonies was held on behalf of the government of that colony rather than the government of the United Kingdom. In addition, inherent executive power over Crown land and underground resources was entirely abrogated by the conferral of exclusive authority upon the colonial legislatures to manage and control Crown lands and underground resources within their territorial boundaries.[14] This remains so today in the Australian States, although apparently not in the Australian Capital Territory,[15] while the situation in the Northern Territory seems uncertain.

The colonial legislatures soon used this constitutional authority to break away from English land law and practice by designing and granting entirely new land titles.[16] Although these titles were frequently called 'leases' or 'licences', they differed substantially in legal character from their English namesakes.[17] Their origins were statutory; accordingly, their legal attributes (rights and obligations) were determined by the provisions of their relevant statutes, rather than the principles of English land law.[18] The result was 'a bewildering multiplicity of tenures'[19] with few shared characteristics beyond their statutory nature and the fact that they established an enduring legal relationship between the colonial government and the holder of a statutory title. Unlike the freehold title derived from English land law which conferred exclusive possession of the land and rights

[12] A. C. Veatch, *Mining Laws of Australia and New Zealand* (1911); see A. G. Lang and M. Crommelin, *Australian Mining and Petroleum Laws* (1979) 11–17.

[13] New South Wales Constitution Act 1855 (UK), s 2; the term 'waste lands' referred to lands in which no private interests had been granted by the Crown.

[14] *Cudgen Rutile (No 2) Ltd v Chalk* [1975] AC 520; *Wik Peoples v Queensland* (1996) 187 CLR 1.

[15] *Johnson v Kent* (1975) 132 CLR 164.

[16] Fry (n 6) at 160–9; *Wik Peoples v Queensland* (1996) 187 CLR 1.

[17] Fry (n 6) at 169–70. In *Stewart v Williams* (1914) 18 CLR 381, 390, Griffith CJ described these titles as 'new forms of tenure'.

[18] *R v Toohey; Ex parte Meneling Station Pty Ltd* (1982) 158 CLR 327; in that case, Mason J observed (at 344) that a statutory grazing licence 'has to be characterized in the light of the relevant statutory provisions without attaching too much significance to similarities which it may have with the creation of particular interests by the common law owner of land'; see also *Wik Peoples v Queensland* (1996) 187 CLR 1.

[19] *Millard on Real Property (N.S.W.)* (4th ed) 474; quoted in Fry (n 6) at 163.

Table 21.1 Australian Land Title Categories by State and Territory

	QLD	NSW	VIC	SA	WA	TAS	NT	ACT	**Total**	%
	(area in thousand km^2)									
Title										
Statutory	959	310	0	419	1,026	0	686	1	3,401	44.3
Freehold	648	406	155	347	205	27	523	0	2,311	30.1
Reserves	120	86	73	218	1,295	41	137	1	1,971	25.6
Total	**1,727**	**802**	**228**	**984**	**2,526**	**68**	**1,346**	**2**	**7,682**	**100**

Source: <http://www.ga.gov.au/education/geoscience-basics/land-tenure.html>. Figures for Reserves are approximate.

to exploit a wide range of land-based resources, these statutory titles (such as 'pastoral leases') were usually granted for limited, specified purposes.

Today, the pattern of land titles varies substantially from State to State (and Territory) in Australia. Statutory titles are particularly significant in Western Australia, Queensland, the Northern Territory, and South Australia, which together represent more than 85% of the Australian continent. Freehold titles remain predominant in the smaller States of New South Wales and Victoria. Reserves are retained by State and Territory governments (and acquired by the Commonwealth government) for various public purposes including nature conservation, forestry, and defence; they represent a significant proportion of land in Tasmania, Western Australia, the Australian Capital Territory, and Victoria (see Table 21.1).

Later in the nineteenth century, there was a further significant break from English land law and practice when the Australian colonies decided to retain control over underground resources at the expense of private landholders. First, the prerogative right of the Crown to the royal metals (gold and silver) established in England in 1567[20] was confirmed in the Australian colonies,[21] with the result that each colonial government had title to gold and silver within private (as well as public) lands unless those metals were explicitly included in Crown land grants. Next, colonial legislatures required the reservation of all minerals from future land grants, thereby maintaining government proprietorship of these resources too within private (as well as public) lands.[22] A further mechanism, adopted only in Victoria, was the limitation of Crown grants of freehold title to land to a distance of

[20] *Case of Mines* (1567) 1 Plowd 310, 75 ER 472; see chapter 2.

[21] *Woolley v Attorney-General of Victoria* (1877) 2 App Cas 163; *Cadia Holdings Pty Ltd v New South Wales* (2010) 242 CLR 195.

[22] For example, Crown Lands Act 1884 (NSW), Lands Act 1891 (Vic); M. Crommelin, 'Resources Law and Public Policy' (1983) University of Western Australia LR 1; chapter 2. This policy was also a departure from the established practice relating to public lands in the United States of America: see Veatch (n 12); chapter 3.

50 feet[23] from the surface of the land, with title to the land below that stratum remaining in the Crown.[24]

The trend towards government proprietorship of underground resources has continued unabated. In some States and the Northern Territory, government mineral proprietorship has been bolstered by expropriation of minerals that had previously been privately owned as a result of early colonial land grants.[25] As well, legislation in all States and the Northern Territory now declares that petroleum in its natural state on or below the surface of the land is the property of the Crown (in right of the relevant government), without exception, regardless of proprietorship of the land.[26] In addition, legislation recently enacted in three States—South Australia,[27] Victoria,[28] and Queensland[29]—declares that the Crown owns all underground geological storage formations.

As a consequence, most underground resources in Australia are now the property of (or are otherwise controlled by)[30] State and Territory governments, despite any freehold title to the land in which they are located. Exploitation of these resources requires statutory authorization by the relevant State or Territory legislature.[31] Remarkably, in New South Wales[32] and Queensland[33] statutory authority is even required for the exploitation of minerals which remain privately owned as a consequence of colonial land grants made prior to the adoption of the policy of reservation of mineral resources.

As Barton demonstrates,[34] the extensive rights conferred upon the holders of freehold title to land are likely to include property in pore space. However, in Australia freehold title is the exception rather than the rule. The limited scope of rights conferred by statutory titles to land and underground resources in Australia generally ensures that State and Territory governments are entitled to the pore space in underground geological formations onshore and within the seabed beneath their coastal waters,[35] whether or not their legislatures have asserted property in those formations. Pursuant to the *Seas and Submerged Lands Act 1973* (Cth), the Commonwealth government has 'sovereign rights' over the pore space in offshore underground reservoirs outside coastal waters.[36]

[23] 15.24 metres. [24] Lands Act 1891 (Vic), s 11.

[25] Northern Territory (all minerals): Mineral (Acquisition) Ordinance 1953 (Cth); South Australia (all minerals): Mining Act 1971 (SA); Victoria (all minerals): Mines (Amendment) Act 1983 (Vic); New South Wales (coal): Coal Acquisition Act 1981 (NSW); see *Durham Holdings Pty Ltd v New South Wales* (2001) 205 CLR 399.

[26] For example, Petroleum Act 1998 (Vic), s 9.

[27] Petroleum and Geothermal Energy Act 2000 (SA), s 5.

[28] Greenhouse Gas Geological Sequestration Act 2008 (Vic), s 14.

[29] Greenhouse Gas Storage Act 2009 (Qld), ss 27–28.

[30] For example, in relation to waterways and groundwater: Water Act 1989 (Vic), s 7.

[31] See n 14.

[32] Mining Act 1992 (NSW); see *Wade v New South Wales Rutile Mining Co Pty Ltd* (1969) 121 CLR 177; *Cadia Holdings Pty Ltd v New South Wales* (2010) 242 CLR 195.

[33] Mineral Resources Act 1989 (Qld). [34] See chapter 2.

[35] The status of coastal waters is considered at n 53.

[36] This matter is considered at n 38.

III. The constitutional context

In 1901 the Australian colonies entered into a federal union under the Australian Constitution, which established the Commonwealth of Australia.[37] The colonies became States in the new federation. The Constitution distributes legislative, executive, and judicial powers among the Commonwealth and the States.[38] Commonwealth legislative powers are conferred in relation to a number of specified matters; most of these powers are concurrent[39] rather than exclusive.[40] In the event of inconsistency between a law of the Commonwealth and a law of a State, the law of the Commonwealth prevails.[41] State legislative powers are not specified in the Australian Constitution; instead, States retain the legislative powers vested in them at the time of federation, to the extent that the Constitution does not prescribe otherwise.[42]

The Australian Constitution also provides that State constitutions continue in force at the establishment of the Commonwealth, subject to any changes made by the Constitution.[43] It makes no reference to proprietorship of land or underground resources. Accordingly, the Crown's title to land (radical and beneficial) within the Australian States is still held on behalf of the various State governments; the Northern Territory achieved a similar position upon self-government in 1978.[44]

The legislative authority of the Commonwealth Parliament now extends to particular aspects of the management of Crown land and underground resources in the States and the Northern Territory, including exports,[45] taxation,[46] uranium,[47] employment and industrial relations,[48] indigenous land title,[49] and environmental protection.[50] Nevertheless, these powers do not entirely supplant the overall authority of State legislatures to manage and control Crown lands and underground resources within their territorial boundaries, derived from colonial

[37] Commonwealth of Australia Constitution Act 1900 (UK).

[38] For a more detailed account of the allocation of powers under the Commonwealth Constitution, see M. Crommelin, 'Australia' in *Oil and Gas in Federal Systems* (G. Anderson, ed, 2012) 35 at 39–48.

[39] Constitution, s 51.

[40] The exclusive powers of the Commonwealth are listed in s 52 of the Constitution; they include 'all places acquired by the Commonwealth for public purposes' and certain types of taxation (duties of customs and of excise).

[41] Constitution, s 109. [42] Constitution, s 107. [43] Constitution, s 106.

[44] Northern Territory (Self-Government) Act 1978 (Cth).

[45] Constitution, s 51(i): 'Trade and commerce with other countries, and among the States'; *Murphyores Inc Pty Ltd v The Commonwealth (Fraser Island Case)* (1976) 136 CLR 1.

[46] Constitution, s 51(ii): 'Taxation; but so as not to discriminate between States or parts of States'; note also Constitution, s 114: '. . . the Commonwealth [shall not] impose any tax on property of any kind belonging to a State'; *Fortescue Metals Group Limited v The Commonwealth* [2013] HCA 34.

[47] Constitution, s 51(vi): 'The naval and military defence of the Commonwealth and of the several States'; Atomic Energy Act 1953 (Cth.).

[48] Constitution, s 51(xx): 'Foreign corporations, and trading and financial corporations formed within the limits of the Commonwealth'; *New South Wales v The Commonwealth (Work Choices Case)* (2006) 229 CLR 1.

[49] Constitution, s 51(xxvi): The people of any race, for whom it is deemed necessary to make special laws; *Western Australia v The Commonwealth (Native Title Act Case)* (1995)183 CLR 373.

[50] Constitution, s 51(xxix): External affairs; *The Commonwealth v Tasmania (Tasmanian Dam Case)* (1983) 158 CLR 1.

history and their proprietorship of those lands and resources.[51] In particular, State and Northern Territory legislatures continue to provide the statutory regimes governing exploration for and development of underground resources within their territorial boundaries and coastal waters.

Offshore, the Commonwealth has the constitutional authority to control exploration for and exploitation of the underground resources within Australia's territorial sea, exclusive economic zone, and continental shelf.[52] However, pursuant to a complex political arrangement concluded in 1979 between the Commonwealth and the States (and Northern Territory), the Commonwealth Parliament has conferred jurisdiction over coastal waters upon the States and the Northern Territory, together with property in the seabed and subsurface beneath those waters.[53] Coastal waters extend three nautical miles offshore from the territorial boundaries of the States and the Northern Territory.[54]

The Commonwealth Parliament has exercised Australia's exclusive sovereign rights, derived from international law,[55] to control exploration for and exploitation of the underground resources of the seabed beyond coastal waters to the limits of Australia's offshore jurisdiction.[56] In doing so, however, Parliament chose not to assert proprietorship of those resources,[57] preferring instead merely to prohibit exploration and exploitation activities other than those authorized by the statutory regimes established for these purposes.[58]

The Australian Constitution also confers power on the Commonwealth Parliament to make laws with respect to 'the acquisition of property on just terms from any State or person for any purpose in respect of which the Parliament has power to make laws'.[59] The High Court has long construed this provision as requiring the Parliament to provide 'just terms' in relation to any acquisition of property by virtue of Commonwealth legislation, such as a Commonwealth statute which prohibited the exercise of statutory mining rights within the extended boundaries of a national park in the Northern Territory.[60] Nevertheless, in 1998 the Court held that a Commonwealth statute which cancelled (in part) an offshore petroleum exploration permit did not amount to an 'acquisition of property' by the Commonwealth (or anyone else), even though the permit conferred a statutory right on

[51] The constitutional allocation of authority over onshore mineral resources was recently considered by the High Court of Australia in *Fortescue Metals Group Limited v Commonwealth* [2013] HCA 34.

[52] Seas and Submerged Lands Act 1973 (Cth); the constitutional validity of this Act was confirmed in *New South Wales v The Commonwealth (Seas and Submerged Lands Act Case)* (1975) 135 CLR 337.

[53] Offshore Constitutional Settlement 1979; see M. Crommelin, 'Offshore Mining and Petroleum Constitutional Issues' (1981) Australian Mining and Petroleum LJ 191.

[54] These boundaries are constituted by the ordinary low water mark, except where straight baselines are drawn across coastal indentations in accordance with international law.

[55] See chapter 6.

[56] Offshore Minerals Act 1994 (Cth); Offshore Petroleum and Greenhouse Gas Storage Act 2006 (Cth).

[57] Ownership of underground seabed resources is discussed in chapter 6.

[58] Offshore Minerals Act 1994 (Cth), s 38; Offshore Petroleum and Greenhouse Gas Storage Act 2006 (Cth), ss 97, 160, 193, 210, 289, 356.

[59] Constitution, s 51(xxxi).

[60] *Newcrest Mining (WA) Ltd v The Commonwealth* (1997) 190 CLR 513.

the holder to the grant of a production licence in the event of identification of a petroleum pool in the permit area and recovery of petroleum from that pool.[61] Surprisingly, perhaps, the decision did not turn on legal characterization of the statutory petroleum title. Regardless of whether or not the permit was 'property' for the purpose of section 51(xxxi) of the Constitution, the Court decided that partial cancellation of that title did not amount to an 'acquisition of property', since the Crown in right of the Commonwealth had no radical title to the continental shelf beyond Australia's territorial boundaries. The Court noted that, unlike the onshore situation, where the States and the Northern Territory had radical title to land and property in underground resources within their territorial boundaries, the Commonwealth had not obtained radical title to the continental shelf or asserted proprietorship of underground resources therein. Instead, the Court said, Australia had mere sovereign rights derived from international law to explore and exploit the seabed resources of the continental shelf, with the consequence that the Commonwealth acquired no property from the cancellation of the petroleum exploration permit.[62]

State legislatures are not required by their constitutions to provide compensation in respect of legislative expropriation of property. However, as a matter of statutory interpretation, Australian courts demand a clear demonstration of legislative intention in the language of the State statute to effect an expropriation of property without compensation.[63] Nevertheless, as previously noted,[64] there are several examples of State expropriation of private property in mineral resources with limited or no provision of compensation that have avoided or withstood legal challenge.[65]

IV. Multiple resource regimes

If 'a bewildering multiplicity of tenures'[66] was the result of the rejection of English land law in favour of statutory titles confined to limited land uses, the subsequent development of statutory title regimes for specific underground resources further complicated the management of government resources in Australia. In the middle of the nineteenth century, statutory regimes were established for gold, and then extended to all minerals.[67] Statutory regimes for water soon followed.[68] Petroleum

[61] *The Commonwealth v WMC Resources Ltd* (1998) 194 CLR 1.

[62] M. Crommelin, 'The Legal Character of Resource Titles' (1998) 17 Australian Mining and Petroleum LJ 1.

[63] *Durham Holdings Pty Limited v New South Wales* (2001) 205 CLR 399.

[64] See n 25.

[65] Mining Act 1971 (SA); Coal Acquisition Act 1981 (NSW); Mines (Amendment) Act 1983 (Vic). In addition, both the Mineral Resources Act 1989 (Qld) and the Mining Act 1992 (NSW) severely curtail the proprietary rights of private mineral owners within their jurisdictions, with limited compensation.

[66] See n 19. [67] See Lang and Crommelin (n 12) at 2–7.

[68] For example, Water Act 1885 (Vic).

regimes were next, early in the twentieth century;[69] and more recently came geothermal energy regimes[70] and greenhouse gas storage regimes.[71]

This proliferation of land and resource management regimes demanded legal mechanisms determining relationships between them; a similar requirement had long been recognized in English land law and met by common law rules governing land-use conflicts.[72] Initially, the State legislatures largely ignored this requirement in establishing the statutory resource regimes,[73] leaving the courts with the invidious task of resolving such conflicts on a case-by-case basis as an exercise of statutory interpretation with little, if any, statutory guidance.[74] The recent introduction of greenhouse gas storage regimes in some Australian jurisdictions is noteworthy insofar as these regimes attempt to redress this neglect by including some explicit provisions defining their relationship with the existing petroleum regimes.

V. Petroleum regimes[75]

Despite their proprietorship of (or exclusive sovereign rights over) petroleum resources, all Australian governments engage private enterprise to locate and develop these resources.[76] The terms of engagement are prescribed by legislation. There are no fewer than 15 statutory regimes in Australia governing petroleum exploration and production. Each State (and the Northern Territory)[77] has two regimes, one applicable onshore,[78] the other to its coastal waters.[79] A Commonwealth regime applies to all offshore areas beyond coastal waters.[80]

Although they differ considerably in detail, these statutory regimes have significant common characteristics.[81] They usually provide three principal titles authorizing specified petroleum operations: exploration, retention (appraisal), and production. All of these titles confer exclusive rights and substantial obligations to

[69] See Lang and Crommelin (n 12) at 6–7.

[70] For example, Geothermal Energy Resources Act 2005 (Vic).

[71] For example, Greenhouse Gas Geological Sequestration Act 2008 (Vic).

[72] See chapter 2.

[73] An exception was made in the case of the inherent conflict between miners and landowners. Statutory mineral (and petroleum) regimes conferred a right to compensation upon landowners (and, often, occupiers) for interference with enjoyment of their rights to the land, unlike the common law: see chapter 2. See Lang and Crommelin (n 12) ch 10.

[74] For example, see *Associated Minerals Consolidated Ltd v Wyong Shire Council* (1974) 48 ALJR 464.

[75] For a more detailed description of these regimes, see Crommelin (n 38).

[76] Crommelin (n 22).

[77] The Northern Territory acquired self-government in 1978: Northern Territory (Self-Government) Act 1978 (Cth).

[78] For example, Petroleum Act 1998 (Vic).

[79] For example, Offshore Petroleum and Greenhouse Gas Storage Act 2010 (Vic). Pursuant to the Offshore Constitutional Settlement 1979, these statutory regimes must conform closely to the Commonwealth regime established by the Offshore Petroleum and Greenhouse Gas Storage Act 2006.

[80] Offshore Petroleum and Greenhouse Gas Storage Act 2006 (Cth).

[81] M. Crommelin, 'Mining and Petroleum Titles' (1988) 62 Australian LJ 863.

conduct the relevant operations within defined areas.[82] In general, overlapping petroleum titles are precluded.

The allocation process for an exploration title is discretionary, allowing the relevant government to take account of a wide range of factors in deciding when to grant a title, to which applicant, on what conditions. An exploration title may initially be granted over a relatively large area, although that area is usually reduced at prescribed intervals by obligatory relinquishment of parts thereof. The holder of an exploration title is required to perform specified works (such as the drilling of wells) or to spend specified sums on approved exploration operations, or both. Failure to fulfil these obligations will render the title liable to cancellation.[83] The holder of an exploration title who makes a commercial petroleum discovery usually has a statutory right upon application to the grant of a production title in respect of that discovery.

A production title applies to a relatively small area, but if necessary to allow exploitation of the entire petroleum deposit, an applicant can obtain several production titles in relation to a discovery. The holder of a production title is required to develop the deposit and produce petroleum in accordance with a plan approved by the government.[84] Petroleum becomes the property of the holder of a statutory petroleum title when the petroleum is recovered in the title area, rather than upon grant of the petroleum title.[85]

If the recovery of petroleum is not commercially viable at the time of discovery but is likely to become so within 15 years, the holder of the exploration title is usually entitled upon application to obtain a retention title authorizing further exploration and appraisal of the discovery on terms much less onerous than those applicable to the holder of a production title.[86]

Overall, these statutory title regimes confer a large measure of discretionary power on ministers and government officials at all stages of exploration, retention, and production operations, from the initial application for an exploration title to the abandonment of a reservoir upon exhaustion of commercial petroleum deposits.[87] Although all governments engage private enterprise to exploit their petroleum resources, they retain the capacity to subject private petroleum operations to close scrutiny and supervision, and to influence the timing and scale of exploration, development, and production.[88] Government approval is also required for most commercial dealings with interests in statutory petroleum titles.[89]

[82] Subordinate titles (such as special prospecting authorities and access authorities) allow others to explore upon or gain access to principal title areas, but the rights conferred by these subordinate titles are very strictly limited: for example, Offshore Petroleum and Greenhouse Gas Storage Act 2006 (Cth), Parts 2.7, 2.8.

[83] For example, Offshore Petroleum and Greenhouse Gas Storage Act 2006 (Cth), Part 2.2.

[84] Offshore Petroleum and Greenhouse Gas Storage Act 2006, Part 2.4.

[85] For example, Offshore Petroleum and Greenhouse Gas Storage Act 2006 (Cth), s 285; cf chapter 19).

[86] Offshore Petroleum and Greenhouse Gas Storage Act 2006 (Cth), Part 2.3.

[87] T. Daintith, *Discretion in the Administration of Offshore Oil and Gas* (2006).

[88] Offshore Petroleum and Greenhouse Gas Storage Act 2006 (Cth), chapters 2, 6.

[89] Offshore Petroleum and Greenhouse Gas Storage Act 2006, chapter 4.

VI. Greenhouse gas storage regimes

Like the United Kingdom,[90] Australia has incorporated greenhouse gas storage within its energy and climate change policies.[91] Australia relies heavily upon its extensive fossil fuel resources for electricity production.[92] Greenhouse gas storage has the potential to allow Australia to continue to do so while still achieving reductions in greenhouse gas emissions. The economic incentive for Australia to overcome technical and economic impediments to greenhouse gas storage is therefore considerable.

In 2005, the Ministerial Council on Mineral and Petroleum Resources[93] advocated regulatory consistency for greenhouse gas storage regimes among the Australian States and Territories in its Carbon Dioxide Capture and Storage Australian Regulatory Guiding Principles.[94] So far, consistency has proved elusive. There are now several statutory regimes governing greenhouse gas storage in Australia, offshore and onshore.[95] Structurally, these regimes fall into four distinct categories.[96]

The first category comprises legislation enacted solely for an identified project. Many major resource projects in Australia have unique legal foundations derived from agreements between private developers and State and Territory governments in their capacity as resource proprietors. Each of these agreements has, as it must,[97] statutory ratification.[98] One of these statutes, the Barrow Island Act 2003 (WA), authorizes the developers of the Gorgon liquefied natural gas (LNG) project in Western Australia to store substantial quantities of greenhouse gas underground on Barrow Island.

The second category consists of legislation establishing a specific regime for greenhouse gas storage distinct from the petroleum regime applicable in that jurisdiction. Victoria established such an onshore storage regime in 2008[99] and Queensland did so in 2009.[100] Each of these statutes applies generally throughout the State rather than simply to an identified project.

The third category also establishes a comprehensive regime of general application for greenhouse gas storage within a jurisdiction but does so by way of extensive

[90] See chapter 13.

[91] J. McLaren and J. Fahey, 'Key Legal and Regulatory Considerations for the Geosequestration of Carbon Dioxide in Australia' (2005) 24 Australian Resources and Energy LJ 45.

[92] M. Gibbs, 'The Regulation of Geological Storage of Greenhouse Gases in Australia' in *Carbon Capture and Storage: Emerging Legal and Regulatory Issues* (I. Havercroft, R. Macrory, and R. Stewart, eds, 2011) 159.

[93] Now the Standing Council on Energy and Resources (SCER) comprising Commonwealth, State, Territory and New Zealand Ministers with responsibility for energy and resource matters.

[94] S. Singleton and R. Gawrych, 'Overlapping Land Interest Issues for Greenhouse Gas Grants and Activities' [2009] *AMPLA Yearbook* 283.

[95] See Gibbs (n 92) at 160–6.

[96] Chapter 15 provides an innovative approach to the regulation of greenhouse gas storage.

[97] See n 14.

[98] M. Crommelin, 'State Agreements: Australian Trends and Experience' [1996] *AMPLA Yearbook* 328.

[99] Greenhouse Gas Geological Sequestration Act 2008 (Vic).

[100] Greenhouse Gas Storage Act 2009 (Qld).

amendment to its established statutory regime for management of petroleum resources. The Commonwealth adopted this approach for greenhouse gas storage in offshore areas outside coastal waters in 2008 by extensive amendment of its Offshore Petroleum Act 2006.[101] Victoria enacted virtually identical legislation in 2010[102] with regard to its coastal waters, in accordance with the requirements of the Offshore Constitutional Settlement 1979.[103]

The last category is represented by the South Australian Petroleum and Geothermal Energy Act 2000, which establishes a management regime for underground resources applicable not only to petroleum and other 'regulated substances' such as hydrogen sulphide, nitrogen, helium, and carbon dioxide, but also to 'regulated resources' such as sources of geothermal energy and natural storage reservoirs. This approach differs from the second and third categories in its adoption of a more integrated approach to multiple resource management.

All categories (save perhaps the first) have a significant feature in common. The statutory regimes established for greenhouse gas storage are modelled closely upon the petroleum regimes established in the relevant jurisdictions, with three principal titles conferring exclusive rights and substantial obligations to conduct assessment, appraisal, and injection operations within defined areas, granted by the relevant minister or authority according to statutory requirements incorporating a significant measure of administrative discretion.[104]

VII. Competition, choice, and coordination

It is widely acknowledged that the best prospects for greenhouse gas storage in Australia lie in depleted petroleum reservoirs.[105] Accordingly, competition between greenhouse gas storage and exploitation of petroleum resources seems inevitable. Statutory regimes for greenhouse gas storage deal with this competition in various ways.[106]

A threshold issue is whether existing statutory petroleum titles are entitled to any constitutional protection against interference with rights conferred by those titles, consequent upon the grant of greenhouse gas storage titles. Given the very considerable extent to which Australian sedimentary basins, offshore and onshore, are already subject to petroleum exploration titles, this issue has great practical significance.

As previously discussed, the constitutional limitations upon statutory authority to curtail or interfere with existing resource exploration and production titles are meagre.[107] State legislatures are merely obliged to demonstrate their intention,

[101] Offshore Petroleum and Greenhouse Gas Storage Act 2006 (Cth).
[102] Offshore Petroleum and Greenhouse Gas Storage Act 2010 (Vic).
[103] See n 53. [104] See Gibbs (n 92).
[105] M. Gibbs, 'Greenhouse Gas Storage in Offshore Waters: Balancing Competing Interests' (2009) 28 Australian Resources and Energy LJ 52 at 53.
[106] J. Minchinton, 'Overlapping Tenure Issues-Legislative Regimes' [2012] *AMPLA Yearbook* 493.
[107] See n 59 and following.

without equivocation, to impinge upon such titles. The Commonwealth Parliament appears to be similarly unconstrained with respect to offshore petroleum titles, although it may not have the same latitude regarding onshore titles.[108]

It is therefore surprising to observe the sensitivity demonstrated towards existing petroleum titles by some Australian legislatures in their design of greenhouse gas storage regimes. The most striking example is found in the Offshore Petroleum and Greenhouse Gas Storage Act 2006 (Cth),[109] which confers an effective veto over competing greenhouse gas storage operations upon the holders of offshore petroleum titles in force at the date of commencement of the storage regime,[110] thereby relinquishing a large measure of government control over the exploitation of depleted petroleum reservoirs to the holders of those petroleum titles.

The Petroleum and Geothermal Energy Act 2000 (SA)[111] also affords considerable protection to the holders of existing petroleum production titles, insofar as their titles relate to gas storage.[112]

Otherwise, Australian legislatures have not established clear priority rules for determining competition between petroleum titles and greenhouse gas storage titles; neither have they imposed compensation requirements upon greenhouse gas title holders who, in exercising their statutory rights, infringe upon the rights of the holders of existing petroleum titles, or vice versa; nor have they introduced strata title schemes designed to diminish competition and conflict between holders of statutory titles for the different resources.[113] Instead, they have encouraged the negotiation of arrangements between title holders, and have relied heavily upon the exercise of administrative discretion as the ultimate means of making difficult choices.

The Greenhouse Gas Storage Act 2009 (Qld) allows the grant of greenhouse gas storage titles over areas subject to petroleum titles[114] and provides for the holders of competing petroleum and greenhouse gas storage titles to enter into 'coordination arrangements' to resolve differences between them.[115] These arrangements must be approved by the Minister.[116] In a similar vein, the Offshore Petroleum and Greenhouse Gas Storage Act 2006 (Cth) provides for a wide range of 'designated agreements' between the holders of (and applicants for) petroleum and greenhouse gas storage titles which alleviate potential conflicts between them.[117]

Administrative discretion is clearly the mainstay of Australian statutory resource management regimes for resolution of conflicts between competing title holders. The critical issue is always the scope of the discretionary power conferred by the

108 See n 60.

109 The Offshore Petroleum and Greenhouse Gas Storage Act 2010 (Vic) is essentially identical.

110 See Gibbs (n 105).

111 Sections 34, 67–70.

112 See Singleton and Gawrych (n 94) at 285–6.

113 See chapter 22.

114 See Singleton and Gawrych (n 94) at 287.

115 Greenhouse Gas Storage Act 2009 (Qld), Ch 4; see M. Klapper, 'Negotiating the Overlapping Tenure Agreement' [2012] *AMPLA Yearbook* 514.

116 Greenhouse Gas Storage Act 2009 (Qld), s 187.

117 Offshore Petroleum and Greenhouse Gas Storage Act 2006 (Cth), s 32.

statute. Tests such as 'significant risk of a significant adverse impact'[118] or 'public interest'[119] are prescribed in the Offshore Petroleum and Greenhouse Gas Storage Act 2006 (Cth). However, explicit bounds are not always imposed upon the exercise of discretionary power. Whatever statutory approach is adopted, discretionary power is never unlimited in scope.[120] The issue of limits is determined ultimately by the courts, as an exercise of statutory interpretation, drawing upon the text, context, and purpose of the statute.[121]

VIII. Conclusion

The unbroken history of proliferation of statutory regimes for the management of underground resources is now under close scrutiny in Australia, no doubt as a consequence of the failure to resolve inevitable tensions between them. There is renewed interest in the development of integrated statutory regimes governing the exploitation of a number of resources within sedimentary basins.[122] This approach, while probably no panacea, has the distinct advantage of confronting the difficult challenge of multiple resource management at the design stage of statutory regimes by incorporating specific mechanisms for resolving resource conflicts. It also offers prospects for achieving greater accountability for the public policy choices that must be made in the management of government resources, and providing increased security for the holders of resource titles.

[118] Offshore Petroleum and Greenhouse Gas Storage Act 2006 (Cth), ss 25–29; see also Gibbs (n 92) at 173; Singleton and Gawrych (n 94) at 287; Gibbs (n 105) at 60.

[119] Offshore Petroleum and Greenhouse Gas Storage Act 2006 (Cth), s 362; see also Singleton and Gawrych (n 94) at 289; Gibbs (n 105) at 66.

[120] *BHP Petroleum Pty Ltd v Balfour* (1987) 180 CLR 474.

[121] *Project Blue Sky Inc v Australian Broadcasting Authority* (1998) 194 CLR 355 at 384.

[122] 'Modernising Queensland's resource tenure legislation', Industry discussion paper, Queensland Department of Natural Resources and Mines (2012).

22

Disputes Between the Owners of Different Subsurface Resources

Nigel Bankes

I. Introduction

This chapter deals with disputes between the owners of different subsurface resources. It draws on examples from Canada and especially from the Province of Alberta, which has a long history of oil and gas development. The chapter principally deals with ownership conflicts within the same geographical space or tract of land. Thus the chapter does not deal with the problems that arise between adjoining owners with respect to the ownership of fugacious mineral resources that migrate from one tract of land to another within the same reservoir. These problems concern the rule of capture (and its modification) and are already well treated in the literature.[1]

Section II describes how subsurface resource disputes arise as a result of the severance of the ownership of different mines and minerals. Section III offers a typology of the different types of disputes that may arise with examples from the decided cases, and section IV describes some of the solutions that have been developed to resolve disputes between subsurface ownership interests.

Disputes between the owners of different subsurface resources have their origins in the decision of the owner of the entire subsurface estate (i.e., the owner of all the 'mines and minerals') to create entitlements to different resources within that bundle of rights. The owner of the entire mines and minerals estate may be the state (or the Crown) or the owner may be a private party. The new entitlement created by the holder of the mines and minerals estate may be in the nature of a severed estate, i.e., the ownership of (some of) the minerals in place. Alternatively, it may be in the nature of the right to remove (some of) the minerals, with ownership

[1] See T. Daintith, *Finders Keepers? How the Law of Capture Shaped the World Oil Industry* (2010); and also B. Kramer and O. Anderson, 'The Rule of Capture; an Oil and Gas Perspective' (2005) 35 Environmental Law 899 and C. Low, 'The Rule of Capture: Its Current Status and Some Issues to Consider' (2009) 46 Alta L Rev 799.

of those minerals only passing (as personal property) as and when reduced to possession.[2] Some examples follow.

The first example is provided by the conveyancing practices of the Canadian company Canadian Pacific Railway (CPR). The CPR as a private owner routinely created severed mineral estates out of its land holdings in western Canada conferred on it as part of a large land grant from the federal government to support the construction of a transcontinental railway. As discussed in several decided cases, but in particular *Anderson v Amoco Canada Oil and Gas*,[3] CPR's resource management practices evolved over the years. Initially, it simply reserved coal from its grants to individual settlers, later reserving 'coal, petroleum, and valuable stone', before finally reserving out 'all mines and minerals'. The reservation in the form of 'coal, petroleum, and valuable stone' has been at the root of many disputes.

The oil and gas leasing practices of the Province of Alberta provide a second example. The government of Alberta has used a variety of leasing strategies over the past 70 years. For example, beginning in 1951, the Crown allowed the creation of separate tenures for natural gas rights.[4] While the Crown subsequently reversed that decision on a prospective basis (1976), the implications of that policy are still being worked through insofar as separate petroleum and natural gas rights remain extant. Similarly, the province also created a separate tenure regime for oil sands rights, recognizing that the exploration for and development of the oil sands resource may have more in common with the development of mineral properties than it does with the development of oil and gas properties. While the logic was sound, its implementation required the province to distinguish between conventional petroleum resources and the oil sands resource and resulted in different lessees holding rights to related substances in the same lands.[5] This ultimately led to the so-called 'gas over bitumen' dispute discussed in more detail later.

The province has also created separate tenures on the basis of the depth of producing formations within a location. The province introduced the 'deep rights reversion' rules in 1976.[6] Under these rules, a Crown petroleum and natural gas agreement is only continued after an initial term with respect to those areas of the agreement that are considered to be capable of production, and then only down to the deepest producing formation. The balance of the lands covered by the agreement revert to the Crown.[7] More recently, the province has followed this up with shallow rights reversions with the aim of ensuring that the agreement holder is only

[2] In common law jurisdictions such an interest is referred to as an incorporeal estate or hereditament; within the international oil and gas industry the interest may be referred to more generally as a working interest.

[3] 2004 SCC 49.

[4] Alberta Energy, *Alberta's Oil and Gas Tenure*. See also M. Crommelin, 'Government Management of Oil and Gas in Alberta' (1975) 13 Alta L Rev 146.

[5] For some discussion, see *Canadian Natural Resources Limited v Jensen Resources* 2012 ABQB 786 (a case holding that a royalty created by the lessee of petroleum rights continued to bind the subsequent replacement oil sands lease).

[6] SA 1976, c 33.

[7] See Petroleum and Natural Gas Tenure Regulations, Alta Reg 263/97, s 15.

allowed to hold rights to the zones that are capable of production.[8] This allows the Crown to re-lease the inactive rights to other parties who may be interested in exploring these 'fallow' lands. This may create the potential for conflict in several ways. First, it may make it easier to trespass on another party's rights even if only to acquire potentially valuable geological knowledge rather than actually producing from another party's formations.[9] Second, limited geological knowledge may make it difficult to be precise about the zone designations on which horizontal severances of petroleum and natural gas rights are premised. A number of disputes have arisen as to whether a particular producing formation in a particular location is included in the shallow rights or the deep rights.[10]

There are other ways in which resource use conflicts between the owners of different resources may arise. For example, working interest owners with rights to the entire mineral estate may create the potential for resource use conflict by entering into separate unitization arrangements for petroleum and for natural gas.[11] Other private arrangements, such as 'farmout' agreements, may also divide rights in relation to natural resources. This may happen in a farmout agreement where the owner of the petroleum and natural gas rights farms out only part of that bundle allowing, for example, the farmee to earn an interest in the natural gas rights but not the petroleum rights. This seems to be relatively rare but farmors invariably practice another form of severance insofar as the farmee typically only earns an interest in a particular formation or only down to a particular target formation.[12]

II. Types of disputes that may arise

The case law and practice suggest that the creation of multiple rights in the mines and minerals estate may give rise to a number of different types of dispute.[13] For expositive purposes they might be categorized as follows. First, there may be disputes as to the *content* of individual rights within the bundle. Such disputes

[8] A. Ingelson and W. Randall, 'Shallow Rights Reversion: Uncertainty and Disputes' (2010) 48 Alta L Rev 397.

[9] *Xerex Exploration v Petro-Canada*, 2005 ABCA 224.

[10] See ERCB Decision 2009-050, leave to appeal denied 2010 ABCA 258 and *Nexxtep Resources Ltd v Talisman Energy Inc*, 2012 ABQB 62, aff'd 2013 ABCA 40, and for further related proceedings, see 2013 ABCA 186.

[11] See, e.g., *Prism Petroleum Ltd v Omega Hydrocarbons Ltd*, 1994 ABCA 97.

[12] This practice is widespread in the industry. For an example from a decided case, see *Canadian Natural Resources Limited v Encana Oil & Gas Partnership* 2007 ABQB 460 (rev'd on appeal 2008 ABCA 267), where the agreement provided that 'the Farmee will earn.... to the base of the deepest formation evaluated by drilling to Contract Depth, but no lower than the Bluesky formation'.

[13] There may also be a preliminary question as to whether particular resources are included within the surface title or the mineral title. This type of issue is most likely to arise with respect to quarrying and other aggregate materials that are commonly used for building and construction purposes. See, e.g., *Western Minerals Ltd v Gaumont* [1953] SCR 345 discussing, *inter alia*, retroactive legislation in which the province declared that a reservation of mines, minerals, and valuable stone did not include sand and gravel. The current version of this legislation (Law of Property Act, RSA 2000, c L-7 ss 55–58) clarifies what is included in a mineral title and what is included in a surface title (sand, gravel, clay, and marl).

principally present interpretive problems, but they may also raise questions as to the working rights associated with a particular right in the bundle. Second, the dispute may take the form of a priority dispute. That is to say, it may not be possible to produce both resources or accommodate two different uses at the same time. Which resource or which use should take priority and which resource (or use) will be 'sterilized'? And third, there may be compensation issues to the extent that the owner of one right in the mineral resource bundle is unable to exploit its resource as a result of a decision to accord priority to the owner of another resource.

A. Disputes as to the content of individual rights within the bundle and the scope of any associated working rights

Disputes as to the content of individual rights within the bundle may take several different forms. For example, in *Borys v Canadian Pacific Railway Co*,[14] one of the questions for the Canadian courts and ultimately for the Privy Council was the question of whether the term 'petroleum' in a reservation of 'coal, petroleum, and valuable stone' included natural gas or whether the natural gas rights passed to the transferee on the basis that that which had not been reserved passed with the transfer. The Court held that petroleum and natural gas were two separate substances and that the CPR did not own the natural gas contained in the gas cap in the oil and gas reservoir. This led to an additional difficulty since it was acknowledged that in the ordinary course of reasonable operations 'some of the gas in the gas cap emerges with the petroleum'.[15] In such a circumstance, should the owner of the gas cap be entitled to enjoin the petroleum lessee from further production? The Privy Council concluded that CPR's reservation of the petroleum when it granted the balance of the estate to the Borys' interests 'necessarily implies the existence of power to recover it [the petroleum] and of the right of working'[16] and went on to say:[17]

> [We] are not prepared to hold that [CPR and its lessee] are under an obligation to preserve [Borys'] gas with the consequent denial of their right to recover the petroleum in the usual way. Even if it be conceded that the respective rights of the two parties are to work for and recover each his own property . . . it does not follow that neither can act without the consent of the other and that only by mutual agreement can they work at all.

Thus, provided that the CPR and its lessees were acting reasonably, they could not be restrained by the gas owner. The Privy Council was at pains to point out that it was not determining whether or not the gas owner might also be able to produce its gas using 'any usual or customary method', since that issue was not before it.[18] In addition, the decision has nothing to say about whether or not the petroleum lessee has any duty to compensate the natural gas owner.[19] *Borys* is thus an important

[14] [1953] AC 217 (PC) (*Borys*).

[15] *Borys* (n 14) at 227 (this was in addition to solution gas in the reservoir that is produced at the well-head in gaseous form).

[16] *Borys* (n 14) at 228. [17] *Borys* (n 14) at 230. [18] *Borys* (n 14) at 230.

[19] We might infer that there is no duty to compensate in the event that the natural gas is just being vented or flared. It might be different if the gas were being recovered and marketed.

decision with respect to both the content of the rights in the bundle and the associated working rights.

There are other common examples of disputes as the content of the rights included within particular sticks of the ownership bundle. The ownership of coal bed methane has proven problematic in many jurisdictions where there exist separate titles to coal and to natural gas.[20] Similarly, the ownership of pore space for the purposes of natural gas storage and for disposal purposes[21] (especially in the context of the geological sequestration of carbon dioxide or indeed for other purposes)[22] may be a source of dispute as between surface owners and mineral owners.[23]

B. Priority and sterilization issues

Priority and sterilization disputes between different resource owners arise because it may not be possible to exploit both resources (either at the same time or at all). Consider, for example, the *Borys* decision discussed earlier.[24] The case confirmed that the gas owner owns the gas cap gas and that the petroleum owner can produce its petroleum. The case did not decide that the gas owner could produce its gas because that issue was not before the court, though it would seem to follow as a matter of property law that the natural gas owner should be able to produce its natural gas. But in practice, and for good technical reasons relating to maximizing the recovery of the oil in place, this is not the case. Indeed, conservation authorities the world over seek to prevent the concurrent production of natural gas with oil so as to maintain reservoir pressure and to use the drive from the natural gas to assist in producing the oil.[25] In most cases, conservation authorities insist that producers recover natural gas that is produced in association with the oil and re-inject it into the reservoir in order to help maintain reservoir pressure—at least where it is economic to do so.[26] It is apparent that this result is obtained not by the application of property norms but by the application of legislation in the general public interest, justified by a clear scientific understanding of the serious negative implications (reduced recovery of petroleum in place) of failing to restrict the production of natural gas.

20 See, e.g., *Amoco Production Co v Southern Ute Indian Tribe*, 526 US 865. In that case, the Court concluded that a statutory reservation of coal from grants of land to settlers in the western United States did not include coal bed methane, i.e. the methane that is adsorbed onto the surface area of the coal pores and may be produced when the pressure on the coal bed is decreased and the gas is released from its 'connection' to the coal.

21 Relevant pore space includes the pore space in depleted oil and gas reservoirs and pore space within saline aquifers.

22 Other purposes include the use of pore space for the disposal of other gases (e.g. hydrogen sulphide derived from the processing of sour natural gas) and oilfield wastes or other chemical wastes.

23 See chapter 2. 24 *Borys* (n 14).

25 Various provisions in Alberta's Oil and Gas Conservation Act, RSA 2000, c O-5 (OGCA) authorize such an approach, including s 33 (designation of pools and zones), s 38 (power to require re-injection), and s 39 (prior approval required for concurrent production of oil and associated gas cap).

26 D. H. Breen, *Alberta's Petroleum Industry and the Conservation Board* (1993).

At some point the operator of the reservoir and the regulator[27] may well conclude that further recovery of petroleum is uneconomic and the decision will be made to blow-down or produce the natural gas cap. At this point in time (which may be several decades after production began), the natural gas owner may be able (through its lessee) to produce its natural gas.[28] It does not appear that the natural gas owner has any claim to compensation or other cause of action for having been denied the opportunity to produce for a number of years. There can be no cause of action against the petroleum owner or lessee, since the decision to prevent production of the natural gas was made by the regulator and not by the petroleum owner. And the regulator will typically have immunity from a civil cause of action provided that it has acted in good faith.[29]

For the most part, these rules which afford priority to petroleum owners and effectively sterilize gas production and deny or seriously delay the opportunity of the gas owner to earn a return are no longer contentious, perhaps because the science is so clearly established and the public policy objective of maximizing recovery of the reserves in place is unassailable.[30] Such was definitely not the case, however, when Alberta's conservation authority, the Energy Resources Conservation Board (ERCB), attempted to extend the same policy and the same line of reasoning to shut-in natural gas production where natural gas reserves were found in association with oil sands resources. In the end, the Board decided to defer natural gas production in favour of oil sands production,[31] but there was extensive regulatory and court litigation on the matter, as well as claims for compensation from the natural gas owners (discussed later).[32]

There are a number of reasons why the ERCB's preference for bitumen over gas production proved to be so much more contentious than the general rule that precludes concurrent production of natural gas and petroleum. One reason is that the science seemed far less definitive in demonstrating that the prior production of

[27] The singular term 'operator' assumes that at some point the operation has been successfully unitized. If not there will be multiple operators who may have conflicting views about whether and when to commence production of the natural gas.

[28] Note that there may still be complex ownership issues to be resolved. For example, at this point the petroleum rights owners have no right to produce the natural gas and thus must acquire those rights from the gas owners. Alternatively should the gas owners seek to take over the operation, the petroleum owners will undoubtedly seek to recover some of the costs associated with drilling the wells which the gas owners seek to use to produce their resource. For discussion, see N. Bankes, 'Compulsory Pooling under the Oil and Gas Conservation Act of Alberta' (1997) 35 Alta L Rev 945.

[29] See *Hunt Oil v Galleon Resources*, 2010 ABQB 212 (an unsuccessful action for damages by one owner in a pool, who contended that the other owner in the pool had unreasonably delayed the successful consideration of its application by the ERCB and was therefore responsible for the resulting damages.)

[30] The introduction of these measures, however, was very contentious. See Breen (n 26).

[31] EUB Decision 2000–22, Gulf Canada Resources Limited, Request for the Shut-in of Associated Gas, Surmont Area. This chapter refers throughout to the ERCB for ease of reference. The Board also has been known historically as the Alberta Energy Utilities Board (EUB) and is currently known as the Alberta Energy Regulator (AER). However, the jurisdiction of this regulatory body has not changed in relation to the matters under discussion here. For further discussion of the AER see chapter 7.

[32] *Giant Grosmont Petroleums Ltd v Gulf Canada Resources Ltd*, 2001 ABCA 174 (the Court concluded that the ERCB had the authority to issue regulations requiring natural gas owners to obtain Board approval before producing natural gas found in association with oil sands).

natural gas would prejudice the ultimate recovery of the bitumen. A second reason was that in this instance the natural gas owners had got out in front of the bitumen owners and had drilled and completed hundreds of producing wells in formations associated with the bitumen resource. Thus, the decision to shut-in gas production had dramatic consequences in terms of the sunk investments of gas lessees in drilling wells and developing the necessary infrastructure to get their product to market.[33] This was not a case of persons who knew when they acquired the drilling rights to natural gas that they would not be able to produce until the oil sands resource had been recovered. The then practice justified an entirely different set of expectations on the part of gas owners, who therefore felt ambushed by the application of this rule in the context of oil sands production. Third, the scale of the problem was significant both geographically and temporally. Geographically the conflict involved a large number of wells facing shut-in orders and the in situ oil sands resource covers a large area of the province. The temporal scale issues were perhaps equally problematic since the bitumen resource, while well known in its broad parameters, will be produced sequentially over a period of decades, if not centuries, given the capital costs associated with the development.[34] Thus the delay until gas owners might be able to produce meant in practice that they would have to write off these reserves. By the same token, delays in bringing the bitumen to production means that a cost–benefit analysis is unlikely to definitively favour producing bitumen, perhaps decades into the future as opposed to monetizing the value of natural gas now.[35]

A form of priority dispute may also arise where different owners disagree as to whether a proposed new activity will cause risk to the activities of an incumbent. An example of this may be a dispute between the operator of an existing natural gas storage project (A) and another party (B) which owns oil and gas exploration rights to adjacent properties. B wishes to drill for, explore, and potentially produce from those lands. Both A and B likely agree that it would be unlawful for B to produce A's gas,[36] but B may well take the view that it should be able to drill and explore on adjacent lands because on its view of the geology there is little or no risk for A's storage operation from its proposed activities. On the other hand, A may take the view that the risk is significant and that therefore B should not be allowed to drill. Such was the case in *Kallisto Energy Corporation, Application for a Well Licence, Crossfield East Field*.[37] In that case, Kallisto was 'B' and 'A' was CrossAlta, the

[33] In addition, operators would have sunk costs associated with acquiring the natural gas rights at Crown sales on a bonus bid basis.

[34] And, of course, some of the resource may never be produced either because it is not economic or (and this may be related) because of the greenhouse gas emission costs associated with production.

[35] For development of this point, see M. W. Wenig, 'Valuing Energy Resources: Reflections on the EUB Decision in the Surmont "Gas over Bitumen" Controversy' (2002) 80 Resources 1.

[36] There is no Canadian authority precisely on point but there seems to be broad acceptance that the rule of capture does not extend to allowing an adjacent owner to produce somebody else's injected gas. See, e.g., *Kallisto Energy Corporation, Application for a Well Licence, Crossfield East Field*, 2012 ERCB 005 at para 58, where Kallisto 'acknowledged that it does not have the right to remove or convert storage gas and has no intention of doing so'.

[37] *Kallisto* (n 36); see also the sequel to this decision, 2013 ABAER 013.

operator of the natural gas storage facility approved by the ERCB in 1994. CrossAlta argued that the ERCB should deny Kallisto's application for a well licence to drill for and produce an oil well some 1.2 km from the closest part of the reservoir. The Board ultimately granted Kallisto's application but subject to certain terms and conditions that were designed to protect CrossAlta.[38]

C. Compensation issues

In some cases, the decision to favour one set of resource entitlements over another emerges from the background rules of property law. Thus it seems well understood, at least in common law jurisdictions, that the owner of the subsurface estate has an implied right to use as much of the surface estate as reasonably necessary in order to get at the mineral estate, and furthermore may do so without owing a duty to compensate the surface owner, at least unless its operations cause subsidence.[39] The basis for this remarkable rule appears to be that the subsurface owner ultimately acquires its rights from a common owner of the surface and subsurface, and thus it would be a derogation from the grant for the surface owner to purport to withhold consent.[40] To use the conceptual terms of Calabresi and Melamed,[41] it is as if the surface owner is left with neither a property entitlement nor a liability entitlement—just a Hohfeldian liability.[42]

It is hardly surprising that this result has proven to be politically unacceptable in many oil- and gas-producing jurisdictions, including Alberta, and that legislatures have taken steps to change the nature of the entitlement, if not reverse it. For example, Alberta's Surface Rights Act[43] affords the surface owner a Calabresian liability entitlement against an oil and gas lessee seeking surface access rights for the purpose of drilling a well. The surface owner has no veto (no property entitlement), but does have a right to compensation.

Compensation also emerged as an important issue in the gas over bitumen dispute. The Executive (the Lieutenant Governor in Council) responded to the Board's decision to shut in natural gas producers by relying upon a little used provision in the Oil and Gas Conservation Act[44] (OGCA) to instruct the Board to

38 Discussed in section III.D.

39 See *Borys* (n 14). See also chapter 3, especially section III.B, 'The dominance of the mineral estate'.

40 See *Borys* (n 14).

41 G. Calabresi and D. Melamed, 'Property Rules, Liability Rules and Inalienability: One View of the Cathedral' (1972) 85 Harv L Rev 1089. A property entitlement affords the holder of the entitlement a veto (the right to withhold consent); the holder of a liability entitlement cannot veto the development but is entitled to be compensated.

42 W. Hohfeld, 'Some Fundamental Conceptions as Applied in Judicial Reasoning' (1913) 23 Yale LJ 16. In Hohfeld's conception of jural relations the term liability connotes the idea that the person (here the surface owner) is vulnerable to the exercise of a power by another person (here the owner of the mineral rights).

43 RSA 2000, c S-24. See in particular s 12 (which reverses the common law rule that affords the mineral owner and its licensees a right of entry without paying compensation), s 19 (which provides for an entry fee) and s 25 (which details how compensation is to be determined if the parties cannot agree).

44 OGCA (n 25) s 91.

prepare a scheme to compensate persons who are injured or who suffer a loss as a result of the shut-in order. The Order went on to instruct the Board to determine 'those persons, *not including the Crown*' who 'should pay such compensation'.[45] The oil sands lessees sought judicial review of the Order in Council, arguing that the section did not give the Executive the authority to limit the scope of the Board's review by excluding the Crown from any potential liability under any scheme that the Board might develop. 'The role of the [Executive] is to trigger the process via a direction to the [Board] and to make the ultimate decision with respect to whether the scheme should be established. All matters relating to the substance of the scheme are . . . within the purview of the Board.'[46] The Court agreed.

The brief reasons of the Court are properly framed in administrative law terms and thus focus on the division of responsibility between the Board and the Executive. However, the Court's recitation of the facts suggests that it was fully aware of the undercurrents behind the litigation and the apparent unfairness of shielding the Crown from any potential contribution to the compensation scheme, especially given that it was the beneficiary of revenues from both oil sands developments and natural gas developments, and that it was the Crown's decision to create split titles, which was the source of the problem. As the Court reflected in its opening paragraphs:[47]

> Her Majesty the Queen in Right of Alberta is the owner of all of the hydrocarbon resources . . . including bitumen and natural gas. The mineral title for this area is split into two distinct titles for each of natural gas and bitumen which create separate, independent interests in those resources. The Province of Alberta is entitled to receive royalties from both natural gas and bitumen production.

Defeat in Court (and the case was not appealed) led the province to reconsider its position and it ultimately entered into a compensation agreement with its natural gas lessees.

III. Some strategies to lessen or resolve disputes between different owners

This section examines different arrangements that may be adopted, either by affected parties or by governments and regulators, to resolve the types of disputes identified earlier. The strategies and solutions include statutory and other declarations as to the scope of different resource rights, the enactment of clear ex ante priority rules, indemnity arrangements, terms and conditions associated with regulatory approvals, setback rules, strategies for recombining property rights, and strategies to forestall claims to compensation.

[45] *Gulf Canada Resources Limited v Alberta*, 2001 ABQB 286 [emphasis added].
[46] *Gulf Canada Resources Limited v Alberta* (n 45) at para 28.
[47] *Gulf Canada Resources Limited v Alberta* (n 45) at para 3.

A. Statutory and other declarations as to the scope of rights

One way to resolve or anticipate interpretive disputes as to the content of particular rights is by way of a legally binding declaration as to the scope of competing rights. One or both parties to a particular dispute may seek a binding judicial declaration as to their entitlements. Such a declaration will bind the parties to the particular outcome and, depending on the authority of the Court, the declaration might also serve as a binding authority for subsequent decisions on similar facts. An application to an energy regulatory tribunal may provide a less definitive outcome, partly because of the relative authority of the decision of a tribunal, but perhaps more importantly because the issue will typically arise indirectly rather than directly. Parties adopted both avenues in Alberta in attempting to resolve the ownership of coal bed methane.

Encana, one of the most important owners of coal in the province, sought relief from both the ERCB and the Courts.[48] Before the ERCB it took the view that gas owners were not entitled to a well licence to drill for and produce natural gas because they were not the relevant owners. In issuing its decision (ultimately rejecting Encana's contentions), the Board emphasized that it was not making a definitive decision on ownership; it was merely deciding the particular issue entrusted to it under the Oil and Gas Conservation Act, namely whether the gas owners were entitled to a well licence.[49] Encana also initiated a number of test cases in the ordinary courts seeking declarations as to its ownership interest in coal bed methane.[50]

Another alternative is the adoption of a statutory declaration if the legislature can be convinced that the problem is a problem of general application that can best be resolved that way. The law and practice in Alberta offers several examples, including an early decision to define authoritatively the scope of the surface estate in terms of the aggregate and other minerals that might be considered to form part of the surface owner's set of entitlements rather than the mineral owner's.[51] Other more recent examples include declaratory enactments designed to clarify ownership of natural gas storage rights,[52] the ownership of coal bed methane,[53] and the

[48] Encana is the successor in interest to CPR and thus the beneficiary of the reservation of 'coal, petroleum and valuable stone'.

[49] OGCA (n 25) s 16; and see *ERCB Bearspaw Decision*, ERCB Decision 2007-024, ss 5–7.

[50] See *Encana Corporation v Devon Canada Corporation*, 2012 ABCA 271, and for further litigation see 2013 ABQB 96 and 2013 ABQB 352; these cases, which were commenced before the enactment of declaratory legislation, have largely been summarily dismissed on the basis that the declaratory legislation discussed later in this chapter has resolved the issue definitively in favour of the natural gas owners.

[51] See discussion at n 13 (*Western Minerals*).

[52] Mines and Minerals Act, RSA 2000, c M-15 (MMA) s 57. For commentary, see Glen Acorn and Michael W. Ekelund, 'An Overview of Alberta's Recent Legislation on Natural Gas Royalty Simplification and Gas Storage' (1995) 33 Alta L Rev 342, and Nigel Bankes, Jenette Poschwatta, and E. Mitchell Shier, 'The Legal Framework for Carbon Capture and Storage in Alberta' (2008) 44 Alta L Rev 585.

[53] MMA, s 10.1, as amended by SA 2010, c 20. This provision declared that coal bed methane is, and always has been, natural gas.

ownership of pore space for geological sequestration purposes.[54] Such provisions typically speak retroactively, as well as prospectively, and go to some pains to extinguish any cause of action for compensation that might otherwise arise as a result of an interference with vested rights.[55] For example, Alberta's legislation on the ownership of pore space for geological sequestration purposes provides as follows:

> 15.1 (1) It is hereby declared that
> (a) no grant from the Crown of any land in Alberta, or mines or minerals in any land in Alberta, has operated or will operate as a conveyance of the title to the pore space contained in, occupied by or formerly occupied by minerals or water below the surface of that land,
> (b) the pore space below the surface of all land in Alberta is vested in and is the property of the Crown in right of Alberta and remains the property of the Crown in right of Alberta. . . .
> (5) No person has a right of action and no person shall commence or maintain proceedings
> (a) to claim damages or compensation of any kind, including, without limitation, damages or compensation for injurious affection, from the Crown, or
> (b) to obtain a declaration that the damages or compensation referred to in clause (a) is payable by the Crown, as a result of the enactment of this section.

Such a declaratory statement will not resolve all difficulties and there may still be room for interpretive arguments as to the scope of the declaration. The *Star Weald*[56] decision is a case in point.[57] In that case, one of the issues before the court related to the proper interpretation of a provision in the UK petroleum legislation of 1934, which vested all petroleum in the Crown. Similarly, amendments to the Mines and Minerals Act in Alberta offering an authoritative statement to the effect that coal bed methane is and always has been natural gas have not completely resolved the situation since the declaratory provisions are made subject to any relevant express agreement to the contrary.[58]

B. The enactment of clear ex ante priority rules

One way to reduce the opportunity for conflict between different uses of the subsurface is to enact clear priority rules from the outset. While it is easy to support such an approach in principle, it may not always be possible to anticipate the need to enact such a priority rule, perhaps because the conflict that emerges has not been

[54] MMA, s 15.1.

[55] It is perhaps relevant to note that there is no constitutional protection of property rights in Alberta.

[56] *Star Energy Weald Basin Limited v Bocardo SA* [2010] UKSC 35.

[57] This decision is discussed in detail in chapter 2, especially Part IV, 'Subsurface activity as trespass: *Bocardo v Star Energy*'.

[58] See cases referred to in n 50 (largely resolving issues in favour of the natural gas owners).

anticipated. The conflict between the production of natural gas and the future recoverability of bitumen is a case in point. There the priority rule was developed ex post in response to technological developments which permitted the recovery of in situ bitumen resources that were not formerly recoverable.

In other cases, the legislature has been more proactive, as in the case of amendments to the Oil and Gas Conservation Act adopted in 2010 to deal with the review and approval of carbon capture and sequestration (CCS) projects.[59] Under these amendments the CCS proponent must be able to satisfy 'the Board that the injection of the captured carbon dioxide will not interfere with (a) the recovery or conservation of oil or gas, or (b) an existing use of the underground formation for the storage of oil or gas'[60] before the Board can recommend a scheme approval.[61] Several observations may be made about this particular language. First, it casts a heavy onus (proof of a negative) on the CCS proponent. Second, the choice of which values to protect is significant. Here the legislature has chosen to protect current and *prospective* hydrocarbon recovery operations and *current* natural gas storage operations. The legislation does not offer the same statutory assurance with respect to other values, such as the protection of potable groundwater. The official government position seems to be that this is so obvious that it does not need to be specifically referenced in the statute.[62]

C. Indemnity arrangements

One way to resolve potential conflicts or to allow potentially competing activities to take place concurrently might be through indemnity arrangements structured to protect the incumbent from the possible adverse consequences of a newcomer's activity. The willingness of the newcomer to provide such an indemnity is likely to be directly related to the default rules of the relevant legislation. An example may make this clearer. Under the relevant rules governing the approval of natural gas storage projects in Alberta, the applicant must file information with the Board showing that it has served its application upon all those persons 'who may be impacted either negatively or positively [by the proposed project] and that they have no objection or concerns'.[63] In the event that a party with standing objects to the proposal, the matter cannot be dealt with as a desk matter but must proceed to a

[59] See OGCA (n 25) s 39(1.1). [60] OGCA (n 25) s 39(1.1).

[61] See 2012 AERCB 008, Shell Canada Limited, Application for the Quest Carbon Capture and Storage Project, 26.

[62] Other legislators are less sanguine. For example, the licensing of underground injection wells in the United States occurs within the framework of the federal Safe Drinking Water Act, which is designed to ensure that underground injection wells do not contaminate underground sources of drinking water. For the details of the Underground Injection Control Program, see <http://water.epa.gov/type/groundwater/uic/index.cfm>.

[63] ERCB Directive 65, Resources Applications for Oil and Gas Reservoirs, Unit 4.3, Application for Underground Gas Storage. The Directive contemplates that the applicant must notify at least all lessees and lessors within the area of the storage pool and adjoining offsetting sections, and all well licensees. Notifications must cover all zones, including those zones that underlie or overlie the storage pool.

hearing unless the difference between the parties can be resolved beforehand. One way in which an applicant may address a party's objections could be by agreeing to indemnify that party from any loss that it may suffer as a result of the proposed activity.

Similar notification rules apply to acid gas injection wells and to CCS projects.[64] One concern relates to the potential liabilities associated with abandoned wells that penetrate the storage formation and which are within the disposal plume or pressure plume for the injection project. Under the Oil and Gas Conservation Act, the licensee of those legacy wells retains liability for any necessary remedial operations, even post-abandonment.[65] It seems reasonable to think that the licensee of such a well might have good grounds to object to the licensing of an injection well that increases the risks associated with its legacy well unless and until the applicant for the CCS scheme approval agrees to take a transfer of the legacy well licence or agrees to indemnify it for all harms or additional expenses it may incur as a result of the CCS operation.[66]

D. Terms and conditions

If the parties cannot resolve their differences privately,[67] the matter will proceed to a Board hearing, at which point the Board will have to decide whether to grant or reject the application. If the Board grants the application, it will have to decide whether to include terms and conditions that offer the incumbent a measure of protection. Such was the case in the Kallisto/CrossAlta Storage decision of the Board discussed earlier. The Board recognized that it was engaged in a balancing act and that the terms and conditions that it was including were one way in which it was able to authorize continuing oil and gas exploration while protecting both CrossAlta's private interest and the more general public interest in ensuring the safety and availability of gas storage sites:[68]

> The panel recognizes the benefits that gas storage brings to the province, the public, and industry... The panel notes that these benefits must be weighed against potential resource sterilization and interference of other legitimate property rights including the mineral rights of Freehold owners in this case. The panel is of the view that the risk to the integrity of the storage reservoir must be balanced against the right to explore for and develop hydrocarbon resources in proximity to the storage reservoir and, where the risk can be appropriately and responsibly managed, such development is in the public interest and should occur.

The terms and conditions included a prohibition on fracture stimulation above a certain pressure without Board approval, as well as testing conditions that were designed to provide all parties with an information base on which it might be

[64] ERCB Directive 65 (n 63) Unit 4.2. [65] OGCA (n 25) s 29.

[66] The former is a more definitive and therefore attractive solution.

[67] The party proposing the activity may simply view the request for an indemnity as too demanding and unreasonable.

[68] 2012 ERCB 005 (n 36) at para 74.

possible to assess whether there was communication between Kallisto's well and CrossAlta's storage unit.[69]

E. Setback rules

Another way to avoid conflict is for the relevant regulator to stipulate setback rules, for example, a minimum distance between, say, the boundaries of a natural gas storage site and the bottom hole location of an exploratory or producing well. Setback distances are commonly adopted by North American oil and gas conservation authorities as a means of protecting adjacent properties from drainage under the rule of capture,[70] as well as to protect other values,[71] but there is definite difference of opinion with respect to using prescribed setback distances to protect natural gas storage projects.

The principal objection to setback rules or buffer zones is that they unnecessarily sterilize adjacent lands which may be productive of oil and gas (or other resources). This may have a significant impact on the owner of the resource rights within the buffer zones, whether that person is the Crown or a private owner. Furthermore, the regulatory creation of a buffer zone effectively confers a benefit on the holder of the storage rights for which it has not paid. One response therefore is that the owner of the storage project should acquire its own buffer zone, but this may be more easily said than done. It may be possible where the storage rights are privately owned, but a storage operator (at least in Alberta) has no compulsory rights of acquisition. And if the storage rights are owned by the Crown, the province takes the view that it will only include lands in a storage agreement to the extent that the lands are being used for these purposes.[72] Neither can the lands be held on conventional petroleum or natural gas leases (Crown or freehold), since at some point such leases will demand production if they are to continue in force.[73]

[69] The Board decision required Kallisto to report on the various tests, after which the Board concluded (see updated action plan on the Board's website) that there was no communication between the well and the unit.

[70] A setback rule may not prevent drainage but it might put all parties in a similar position. Such rules are rarely absolute. In some cases, a party may drill an off-target well but subject to a production penalty (typically waived for the first well in the pool). See Oil and Gas Conservation Regulations, Alta Reg 151/71, Part 4.

[71] For example, regulations (or the regulator) may establish setback rules in relation to water bodies, public facilities, occupied dwellings, etc. In some cases, there will be a dispute as to whether setback requirements have been triggered or should have been triggered. See, e.g., *Big Loop Cattle v Alberta (Energy Resources Conservation Board)*, 2012 ABCA 64. The issue in that case (which arose in relation to a pipeline rather than a well), was whether an Indian reserve qualified as an 'urban centre' for the purposes of triggering a setback requirement.

[72] This is the position in both British Columbia and Alberta. For more detailed discussion, see N. Bankes and J. Gaunce, *Natural Gas Storage Regimes in Canada*, ISEEE Research Paper, December 2009, available at <http://www.iseee.ca/media/uploads/documents/pdfs/researchreports/Nat_gas_storage_cdn_survey.pdf> and discussing the position in British Columbia, at 27–30 but noting (at 31) that the Crown did agree to create a protective corridor in one case, the large Aitken Creek project.

[73] Some of these challenges are referred to in *Kallisto* (n 36) at para 61.

One Canadian regulatory authority, the Ontario Energy Board, does, however, take into account the importance of establishing a buffer zone for designated natural gas storage areas in order to protect against the inadvertent penetration of the storage area. Under the Ontario scheme, the Board has the authority to designate an area as a gas storage area (DSA). In doing so, the Board[74] has indicated that it takes account of three matters: (1) whether the underlying geological formation is appropriate for storage; (2) whether the tract of land is appropriately sized to provide for safe operation; and (3) possible effects of designation on directly affected landowners and whether the storage developer has the necessary leases and agreements in place. As to the question of sizing, the Board observed in one decision that:[75]

A DSA is established to protect a storage reservoir from future third party drilling and other subsurface activities. A DSA represents a reasonable balance between the protection of the reservoir storage from other subsurface activities and the retention of as much land as possible for future oil and gas exploration and drilling.

Board decisions establish the boundary based on pool boundaries with an allowance for a buffer zone, an area between the boundary of the pool and the edge of the designated area.[76] The Board typically relies heavily on reports filed by the provincial Department of Natural Resources, as well as by the applicant, but in one decision the Board declined to extend the Designation Boundary to meet the Department's request to have the boundary coincide with spacing boundaries on the grounds that the designation should remain 'a purely technical determination'.[77]

Setback rules or rules that provide for a broader prohibition on drilling may be developed to protect other resources. For example, the province of Saskatchewan hosts important potash resources, as well as oil and gas resources, and has thus taken special measures to ensure that oil and gas operations do not interfere with the recovery of potash reserves. The regulations contain two types of provisions.[78] First, there is a provision which authorizes the Minister, by order, to create potash restricted drilling areas. In these areas, no person may drill a well without the written approval of the Minister and the written consent of 'every potash disposition holder' within the restricted drilling area, and such consent 'not to be unreasonably withheld'.[79] Second, and in addition to the provision on restricted

[74] EB-2008-0002, In the Matter of an application by Market Hub Partners Management Inc. and AltaGas Ltd for an Order designating the area known as the Sarnia Airport Gas Storage Pool, in the Geographic City of Sarnia in the County of Lambton, as a gas storage, 28 July 2008.

[75] EB-2008-0002 (n 74) at 7.

[76] RP-2003-0253, Tribute Resources Inc and Tipperary Gas Corp, Partial Decision with Reasons, 25 October 2004 at 11.

[77] RP-2003-0253 (n 76) at 12; and boundaries should protect against 'inadvertent penetration into the storage area'. See also Century Pools II, Designation Order Decision, RP-1999-0047, 30 March 2000, para 3.2.5, where the Board rejected an argument from an owner that the boundary should include an entire unitized area. The Board agreed with the applicant and the Department that it was not necessary to include the lands to ensure the integrity of the storage reservoir.

[78] Oil and Gas Conservation Regulation, 2012, RRR, c O-2, Reg 6, ss 26–27.

[79] A potash disposition holder includes a fee simple potash owner as well as any person holding right to recover potash, whether derived from a private owner or the Crown.

drilling areas, there is a provision which authorizes the Minister to establish protective measures within designated commercial potash areas aimed at operations for drilling for oil and gas *below* the top of the Prairie Evaporite. The goal of the protective measures is to effectively isolate the Prairie Evaporite zone from any contamination associated with oil and gas drilling activities through the zone.

F. Strategies for recombining property rights

The anticommons literature suggests that once Humpty Dumpty (i.e., ownership of the entire bundle of rights representing full ownership) has been disaggregated, it may prove difficult to put Humpty back together again, principally because of the transaction costs associated with dealing with multiple owners.[80] This is likely to become more rather than less difficult over time, especially if ownership interests are held by natural persons rather than corporate entities.[81] That said, private lawyers and policy advisers to governments have created several ways to facilitate recombining ownership to permit the rational exploitation of mineral resources.[82] The best-known examples are the arrangements that have been developed to deal with the fragmentation of ownership rights with respect to the same resource as between adjacent owners. These arrangements include pooling agreements and unitization agreements. These agreements put Humpty back together again by re-aggregating rights (typically only with respect to specific mineral formations) by giving each working interest owner a share (a tract participation factor) in either a particular drilling spacing unit (a pooling agreement) or within an entire reservoir or pool (a unitization agreement).[83] In some cases, governments may take these arrangements a step further and provide for compulsory pooling and unitization.

These arrangements may be adapted to deal with other situations that fall more directly within the scope of this chapter. For example, parties have been able to find

[80] The seminal article is M. A. Heller, 'The Tragedy of the Anticommons: Property in Transition from Marx to Markets' (1998) 111 Harv L Rev 621. This and other contributions are discussed in J. Watson Hamilton and N. Bankes, 'Different Views of the Cathedral: The Literature on Property Law Theory' in *Property and the Law in Energy and Natural Resources* (A. McHarg, B. Barton, A. Bradbrook, and L. Godden, eds, 2010) 1.

[81] The paradigmatic example here is the division of tribal ownership that was created in Indian reservations in the United States through the adoption and application of the so-called allotment policy of the Dawes Act. This policy transferred the ownership of individual tracts of collectively owned tribal lands to individual tribal members. Titles were further fragmented when tribal members died intestate, leaving property to family members as tenants in common: Heller (n 80).

[82] The most important example in the common law (not specific to mines and minerals and very rare in the mineral context) is the institution of the joint tenancy which simplifies the ownership structure of land automatically over time by virtue of the right of survivorship. Under the right of survivorship, the surviving joint tenant(s) take the balance of the entitlement until there is but a single owner. The right of survivorship operates immediately upon death and before the operation of the deceased's will or intestacy: see K. Gray and S. F. Gray, *Elements of Land Law* (5th edn, 2009) 915.

[83] For Canada, see N. D. Bankes, 'Pooling Agreements in Canadian Oil and Gas Law' (1995) 33 Alta L Rev 493 and 'Compulsory Pooling' (n 28); for the international practice, see D. Asmus and J. Weaver, 'Unitizing Oil and Gas Fields Around the World: A Comparative Analysis of National Laws and Private Contracts' (2006) 28 Houston J Int L 3.

commercial solutions to the ownership issues associated with coal bed methane by negotiating pooling agreements in which coal owners and gas owners pool their rights (whatever they may be) to gas with a view to achieving the legal certainty necessary to support an application for a well licence.[84] Pooling agreements and pooling orders have also been discussed in the context of disputes between the owners of deep and shallow rights.[85] More prosaically, the government of Alberta allows the working interest owners of oil sands rights to acquire any outstanding natural gas rights with respect to the same tract(s) of lands and on the basis of average bidding prices in the area and without having to go through a Crown posting and competitive auction (which might result in a third party picking up the natural gas rights).[86]

G. Forestalling claims to compensation

One of the ways to forestall claims to compensation under both domestic law and international investment law is to warn parties that they acquire their interests subject to the possibility that they may not be able to exercise their rights. This is the position that the Province of Alberta has adopted in relation to the disposition of petroleum and natural gas rights in the oil sands region of the Province following the ERCB decision (discussed earlier) to shut in natural gas production. The terms and conditions of Crown sales now routinely contain a warning to potential bidders to the effect that:[87]

> . . . all land(s) is/are within an oil sands area as designated by the [ERCB]. Solution gas is expressly excluded from the petroleum and natural gas rights granted under crown agreements issued in respect of oil sands areas. Moreover, production of gas from the land(s) in this agreement may be disallowed or precluded by order of the ERCB or otherwise, on the grounds that such production may detrimentally affect the recoverability of oil sands from those lands. By accepting this agreement for the petroleum and natural gas rights in these lands, the lessee/licensee hereby acknowledges all of the above, and that production of gas from the lands in this agreement may by order of the ERCB or otherwise be precluded or disallowed, and hereby waives any recourse, action, cause of action or claim that the lessee/licensee may have against the Crown in right of Alberta as a result of or in relation to its inability for any of the above reasons or for any other reason whatsoever to produce gas from the lands in this agreement.

84 See *ERCB Bearspaw Decision*, ERCB Decision 2007-024, s 9.2.1. There is also discussion in the Decision (s 10.3.2) of 'coal certainty agreements' pursuant to which coal owners might quit claim any interest that they might have in coal bed methane in return for a share of production.

85 See discussion in Bankes, 'Compulsory Pooling' (n 28). Vertical pooling is also briefly discussed in the *Bearspaw* decision (n 84) s 10.2.

86 For the details, see Alberta Energy, Information Letter, IL 2006–12, Electronic Bidding and Posting of Rights for the Public Offering of Oil Sands and Petroleum and Natural Gas Rights, 3 May 2006, available at <http://inform.energy.gov.ab.ca/Documents/Published/IL-2006-12.pdf>.

87 Details of Crown offerings are posted on the website of the Department of Energy, available at <http://www.energy.alberta.ca/Tenure/1314.asp>.

IV. Conclusions

This chapter has examined a range of disputes that may arise between owners of different subsurface rights. In some cases, the rights of those owners may pertain to the same tract of land (as in the gas over bitumen examples), while in other cases an owner of one resource entitlement may be proposing to engage in an activity that affects a neighbouring resource entitlement (as in the case of an owner of oil and gas rights who wishes to drill close to a gas storage operation or the more common case of an owner of mineral rights who needs to use surface lands to carry out its operations). These disputes often have their origins in the decision of a current or a former owner to create severed or split estates in different resources. These disputes often present themselves as priority issues and as right-to-work issues.

The chapter has demonstrated that some of the priority and right-to-work rules are deeply embedded in the default rules of property law, most notably in the case of the relationship between surface owner and mineral owners. But the chapter also showed that such rules are contingent and may be subject to alteration by competent legislatures. Finally, the chapter described a number of different ways in which governments and private parties may be able to manage right-to-work and priority issues as between the owners of the rights to different resources.

23

Spain's Approach to New Technologies: From Underground Structures to Carbon Dioxide Storage

Iñigo del Guayo and José Alenza

I. Introduction

A. The Spanish Act on CO_2 geological storage within an EU law context

This chapter analyses the evolution of the legal framework for underground activities in Spain. This analysis is offered in the light of the latest step in that evolution, which is Act No 40 of 29 December 2010, on the geological storage of carbon dioxide (GSCA). The Act was passed to implement Directive No 2009/31/EC of the European Parliament and of the Council of 23 April 2009, on the geological storage of carbon dioxide (CCD), and to amend a number of previous Directives.[1] In addition to the adoption of the CCD, two funding instruments were set up: (i) the European Energy Programme for Recovery (EEPR); and (ii) the NER 300 programme funded by the Emissions Trading System (ETS) allowances to channel substantial EU funding to large-scale demonstration projects.[2] One of the six carbon capture and storage (CCS) projects that will receive funding (€1 billion, in total) under the EEPR is in Spain (the so-called *Compostilla* project, discussed later).

The starting point of the analysis is Act No 22 of 21 July 1973, on mines (MA), followed by Act No 34 of 7 October 1998, on hydrocarbons (HA). This chapter tries to identify the main characteristics of the changes which have taken place in the past 40 years within the Spanish legal order in relation to underground structures.

[1] OJ L 140/114 of 5 June 2009.

[2] The AAG has paid attention to this issue: see N. Bankes and M. Roggenkamp, 'Legal Aspects of Carbon Capture and Storage', in *Beyond the Carbon Economy* (D. Zillman, C. Redgwell, Y. Omorogbe, and L. K. Barrera-Hernández, eds, 2008) 339. There is little literature about the legal structure for this activity in Spain, even in Spanish: J. F. Alenza, 'El nuevo regimen legal del almacenamiento geológico del dióxido de carbono' (2011) 185 Revista de Administración Pública 289; and M. Gámez Mejías, 'El marco jurídico del almacenamiento geológico profundo de dióxido de carbono en el contexto de la lucha contra el cambio climático. Perspectivas y reflexiones tras la transposición al derecho interno' (2011) 20 Revista Aranzadi de Derecho Ambiental 49.

'In the transition to a fully low-carbon economy, the Carbon Capture and Storage (CCS) technology is one of the key ways to reconcile the rising demand for fossil fuels, with the need to reduce greenhouse gas emissions. Globally CCS is likely to be a necessity in order to keep the average global temperature rise below 2 degrees.' These words are a quotation from the recent report of the European Commission on the Future of Carbon Capture and Storage in Europe.[3]

Despite efforts at the EU level, CCS has not yet taken off in Europe for a variety of reasons, the main one being that with 'current ETS prices well below €40/tCO_2, and without any other legal constraint or incentive, there is no rationale for economic operators to invest in CCS'.[4] The Commission recognizes that CCS is at a dangerous crossroads and invites Member States to make proposals.

Both the CCD and the GSCA are instruments to fight climate change, since the underground storage of CO_2 reduces the emission of greenhouse gases into the atmosphere.

B. Developments of CO_2 underground storage in Spain

In Spain, so far there are four research projects for underground structures to be used for the geological storage of CO_2, that have obtained, or that will require, a permit for research from the competent authorities.

The most ambitious project is the *Compostilla*, which is promoted by a consortium formed by the Spanish Ministry of Industry's Energy City Foundation (CIUDEN), the Spanish company Endesa, and the Finnish company Foster Wheeler Energia Oy. This is a comprehensive project in the province of Burgos for the commercial demonstration, including capture, transport, and storage of CO_2. The location of the experimental plant is Hontomín and the research permit for the underground structure is called Huérmeces. In its first phase (2009–2012), it included the construction of three plants at pilot scale; it includes the geological characterization of a structure for the proper and safe storage of CO_2. Phase II (2013–2015) envisages the construction of a demonstration plant (with a scale 300 MW). This project is one of the six CCS demonstration projects funded by the EEPR. The *Compostilla* project, however, currently lacks the necessary financing for the demonstration phase. The phase subsequent to the demonstration phase would also require that Spain adopt legislation for planning and building the CO_2 transport corridor.[5]

[3] *Communication from the Commission to the European Parliament, the Council, the European Economic and Social Committee and the Committee of the Regions, on the future of carbon capture and storage in Europe*, Brussels, 27.3.2013, COM (2013) 180 final, 3.

[4] *Communication on the future of carbon storage* (n 3), at 3.

[5] *Communication on the future of carbon storage* (n 3), at 28. See <http://www.compostillaproject.es>. The research permit was published in the Official Bulletin of the Autonomous Community of Castilla and León, no 19 of 28 January 2002, and the licence for preliminary work within the underground storage was published in the Official Bulletin of the Autonomous Community of Castilla and León, No 157 of 16 August 2010. Consequently, both the permit and the licence were awarded according to the MA and not the GSCA. The Environmental Research Assessment, prior to the awarding of the concession, was published in the Spanish Official Bulletin No 242, of 8 October 2012.

In the province of Palencia, Royal Decree No 1733/2010 of 17 December declared a provisional reserve area in favour of the state for the investigation and possible exploitation of underground structures likely to be effective for CO_2 storage.[6]

In Asturias, the publicly owned company Hunosa (the biggest company in the area of coal production) has four projects for geological storage of CO_2. Two of them, located in coal mine sites, have already obtained permits from the Autonomous Community of Asturias.[7] Since the other two involved both inland and off-shore locations, it will be for the central government to award the necessary permit.[8]

In Aragon, a survey has been conducted for the geological storage of CO_2 by Endesa. As a result, three research permits were awarded to the company by the Autonomous Community of Aragon.[9] The company has come to the conclusion that they are not suitable locations for underground storage of CO_2.

Finally, the company Cepsa has also requested a research permit for a CO_2 storage project called La Rabida. The project is located partly on land, in the province of Huelva, and partly in the sea off the coast of the province. The permit request is currently pending in the Ministry of Industry.[10]

II. Public Domain and *dominio público*

An important remark must be made from the outset. In some countries (like the Anglo-Saxon ones), the expression 'public domain' belongs to the realm of intellectual property law. It refers to works which are no longer protected by copyright law or which have never enjoyed said protection. In other countries (like the Latin ones, including Spain), the expression 'Public Domain' (*dominio público*, in Spanish) has the same meaning, but also has another primary meaning, when it refers to state property. Rooted in the Roman law concepts of *res communis omnium*, *res nullius*, or *res extra commercium*, certain interests belong to the state (or, in English legal terminology, 'are vested in the state'), such as beaches, rivers, and mines. Spanish law regulates those goods not only from a negative perspective (no private individual may become the owner of them), but also from a positive

6 The area is called *Almacén 3* (Spanish Official Bulletin No 310 of 22 December 2010).

7 C02-2 in 11 municipalities and CO2-4 in six municipalities, all of them in the Autonomous Community of the Principado de Asturias.

8 See RD No 1999, of 11 December 2009, by which the central government reserves for itself an area to research for geological formation suitable for storage of CO_2 in Asturias and its continental shelf.

9 The surveys took place in the Municipalities of Bujaraloz, Monegrillo, and Pina de Ebro. The names of the three permits are Monegrillo 1, Monegrillo 2, and Intermedia 3. See the Official Bulletin of the Autonomous Community of Aragon No 48, of 8 March 2011, and No 217, of 7 November 2012, respectively.

10 See Resolution of the Directorate General for Energy Policy and Mines publishing the research permit application for CO_2 storage called La Rabida (Spanish Official Bulletin No 181, of 29 July 2011), for the purpose of allowing the submission of competing offers.

perspective (the actual owner of said goods is the state or any of the infra-state political organizations, such as the Autonomous Communities or Municipalities).

III. Constitutional provisions relating to the Public Domain and its application to underground structures for the storage of CO_2

In accordance with the Spanish Constitution, every kind of resource, whatever its form may be, is subject to the general national interest, whether it is privately owned or belongs to a public power.[11] This is a general statement, which applies to goods belonging to either private individuals or companies and to public entities.

Public entities can own properties of two kinds: (i) goods which enjoy the same nature and which are subject to the same rules as goods owned by private individuals or companies; and (ii) goods which are subject to a special legal framework, since they belong to the Public Domain. With regard to the latter kind of goods, the Spanish Constitution states that a Parliamentary Act may declare that a particular kind of natural resource belongs to the Public Domain (for example, rivers, minerals, and hydrocarbons such as oil and natural gas). Article 132 of the Constitution refers to those resources that are to be considered as part of the Public Domain. Among them are the tideland, beaches, territorial waters, and the natural resources of the Exclusive Economic Zone and of the continental shelf. It is for future Acts to include within the Public Domain any other resources, with the legal framework based on the following principles: (i) the state cannot dispose of them in any way; (ii) they cannot be seized; and (iii) they cannot be acquired by individuals.

An example of the application of that constitutional provision is the HA. Its Article 2 declares oil and gas deposits and underground storages, located within the Spanish territory or the Continental Shelf, to be part of the Public Domain of the state. Another example is the GSCA Article 3, under the heading *Dominio Público*, which declares that 'the geological formations which are part of the storage sites' in Spanish territory, as well as in the subsoil of the territorial sea and in the seabed which is under the sovereignty of Spain (the 'underground structure' to be considered, in turn, part of a 'geological formation'), are part of the Public Domain.

The declaration of a good or of a group of goods to be part of the Public Domain does not mean that private individuals or companies are excluded from the use of it. On the contrary, they can apply for a permit or concession to use a portion of the Public Domain. However, the Spanish Constitution states that 'from time to time, a Parliamentary Act may reserve to the public sector, essential resources or services especially those of a monopolistic nature'.[12] The meaning and consequences of 'reserve' (or 'reservation') have been subject to several discussions. It is clear to us

[11] Art 128(1) of the Spanish Constitution.
[12] Art 128(2) (first part of the second sentence) of the Spanish Constitution.

that the 'reserve of an essential service' has a different meaning than the 'reserve of an essential resource'.[13] The latter means that private companies or individuals cannot apply for a permit or concession to use the 'reserved' resource. Once the resource (the whole or portions of it) has been reserved, no applications from private individuals or companies will be allowed to proceed, and it will be only for the central government, either itself or by means of a public institution, to use the reserved property.

An example of this reservation can be found in Royal Decree No 1999 of 11 December 2009, by which central government reserved for itself the exploration of underground structures capable of hosting an underground storage facility for CO_2. It was under the competence of the central government, since it involved the continental shelf. Though this Royal Decree was passed before the entrance into force of the GSCA, it used provisions already in force in the MA. An application for judicial review was submitted by some environmental organizations, but the Supreme Court dismissed the plaintiff, since the reservation, by itself, could not have any harmful effect on the environment.[14]

Public domain can be central (state), regional (Autonomous Communities), or local (Municipalities and Provinces).[15] Main natural resources (rivers and coasts) are declared to be part of the Public Domain of the state. However, this does not mean that neither the Autonomous Communities nor the Local Authorities have competences over those resources. On the contrary, Parliamentary Acts regulating natural resources included within the Public Domain of the state award competences to both the Autonomous Communities and the national Government. An example of this can be found in the GSCA. The GSCA is based on the distinction between research permits and exploitation concessions. The research permits are awarded by the Autonomous Communities (unless the research will take place in the territory of two Autonomous Communities or when it applies to the marine subsoil: in either case the permit has to be awarded by the national government), whereas concessions are awarded by the national government. Since research permit holders enjoy a preference to be awarded a concession if they show the place is suitable for a CO_2 storage site, in actual terms, the decision of the Autonomous Community strongly influences that of the national government.

[13] I. del Guayo, 'Energy Law in Spain' in *Energy Law in Europe. National, EU and International Regulation* (M. M. Roggenkamp, C. Redgwell, I. del Guayo, and A. Rønne, eds, 2nd edn, 2007) 1077.

[14] Decision of the Supreme Court of 17 May 2011.

[15] As a result of the constitutional provisions about the territorial organization of the state, the entire Spanish territory is now divided into 17 Autonomous Communities (such as Catalonia, the Basque Country, and Galicia), together with two Autonomous Towns located in Africa (Ceuta and Melilla). The Constitution guarantees a level of autonomy to Municipalities, Provinces, and Islands. There are more than 8,000 Municipalities, 50 Provinces, and 11 main islands. See Arts 140 and 141 of the Spanish Constitution.

IV. Spanish mining law

The MA lays down the legal framework for the search for and the use of mineral deposits and any other geological resource, whatever its origin and physical state may be.

A. Mines and geological resources as part of the Public Domain

All mines and other geological resources located in the Spanish national territory, in the territorial waters, or in the continental shelf are declared by the MA to be vested in the state (i.e., they are part of its Public Domain).[16] As a consequence, the state has the exclusive right to search for, drill for, work, and dispose of for profit minerals in the whole Spanish territory (including the continental shelf, the territorial waters, and the Exclusive Economic Zone).

Spanish mining law relies also upon the principle of promoting private initiative and investment in this sector,[17] giving private individuals or companies the right to apply for an authorization to search for minerals or for a concession to work a mine, save in those areas where the state has reserved this right for itself (either to search for and/or exploit a specific mineral in an area, or to search for and/or exploit any/every mineral which is found in an area). In fact, the exploitation of mines is usually carried out by private concessionaires, except for valuable minerals of a strategic nature, such as uranium[18] and, to a certain extent, coal.

After Spain's entry into the European Communities, the MA was modified in order to allow individuals and companies from other states belonging to the European Union to enjoy the rights of the Act,[19] save for strategic minerals, which are subject to the general rules of foreign investments in Spain. According to both the Constitution and the Statutes of the Autonomous Communities, while the state lays down the basic mineral law, it will be for the Communities to develop such law and to exercise most of the competencies for the area, including the awarding of authorizations and concessions.

The search for and exploitation of oil and gas is not covered by the Mines Act, but rather by the Hydrocarbons Act, though the former acts as a supplementary law to the latter, whenever it is found to lack detailed rules on certain issues. For example, the MA acts as a supplementary law to the HA in relation to rules governing underground gas storage; there are also general provisions within the HA, and

[16] Art 2.1 of Act No 22 of 21 July 1973. It was developed by RD No 2857 of 25 August 1978. See also arts 334, 349, and 350 of the Spanish Civil Code (1889).

[17] Act No 6 of 4 January 1977, an Act to encourage the operation of mining activities, as amended by Act No 43 of 27 December 1995, which was developed by RDs nos 1167 of 2 May 1978 and 2485 of 23 December 1994. This legislation settles, among some other provisions, a number of fiscal benefits for mining companies.

[18] The National Undertaking for Uranium (*Enusa*) is charged with the task of exploiting this mineral, and treats it and supplies it to the Spanish nuclear power plants. It belongs to the central government, through SEPI (60%) and CIEMAT (40%).

[19] RLD no 1303 of 28 June 1986.

further details are to be found in the MA, where it addresses rules applying to the use of underground structures.

B. Classification of mineral resources

The MA classifies mines and geological resources into three sections.

Section A refers to those mineral resources which have a low economic value and hence are used only in their immediate geographical area, and to those mineral resources which are suitable for use in the construction of infrastructure and no further treatment—or a simple treatment—is needed for that purpose. Section A includes most of the minerals which are called 'rocks'.

Section B refers to mineral waters, thermal springs, underground structures, and those resources formed as a consequence of the exercise of any mining activity regulated by the Act. Article 23(3) of the MA defines underground structures as any natural geological deposit, or artificially produced as a result of the development of activities regulated by the same MA, of such a kind which retain naturally and thoroughly any product or waste which has been injected within said deposit.

Section C refers to all minerals and geological resources not included in the two previous sections.

A new section, D, was created in 1980,[20] under which the following minerals ceased to be included within section C and are now subject to the special rules of section D: (i) coal; (ii) radioactive minerals; (iii) geothermal resources; (iv) bituminous stones; and (v) any other minerals or geological resources which the government may decide in the future to include within the section.

V. The storage of CO_2 and Public Domain

In order to properly understand the scope of the GSCA, with regard to what is considered to be part of the Public Domain, it is useful to compare the MA, the HA, and the GSCA.

A. Underground structures as part of the Public Domain in the 1973 Mining Act

In accordance with the MA, all mines and other geological resources are part of the Public Domain and, consequently, so are underground structures.[21] The scope of the MA is therefore very wide.

When it was passed 40 years ago, the Act was intended to have the widest possible scope, in order to include everything that was considered a mineral or a geological resource. Subsequent technical developments made it possible to use

[20] Act No 54 of 5 November 1980, an Act to modify the Mining Act 1973, with special regard to mineral resources suitable for energy uses.

[21] Articles 2(1) and 23(3), of Act No 22 of 21 July 1973.

underground structures for purposes which could not have been foreseen at the time the Act was passed, such as natural gas storage and, in particular, CO_2 storage. As a result of these developments, new uses of underground storages became regulated in new special norms, outside the MA.

B. Underground storage of natural gas

In accordance with Article 2(1) of the HA, underground storage in the territory of the state and in the subsoil of the territorial sea and seabed under the sovereignty of Spain belong to the Public Domain. Though it is not clear from the wording of the HA, the natural gas itself is not part of the Public Domain, but only the subsoil structure containing it.[22] A slightly different situation is that of the water underground aquifers, where both the cavity and the water belong to the Public Domain, in accordance with Article 2 of the Royal Legislative Decree No 1 of 20 July 2001, approving the Water Act. However, the Act states that the aquifer belongs to the Public Domain only in relation to disposal and affection of water resources.

C. Storage sites, geological formations, and underground structures as part of the Public Domain in the GSCA

Article 4 of the GSCA contains a number of definitions. For the purpose of understanding the scope of the GSCA in relation to Public Domain, five definitions are relevant here: (1) the 'geological storage of CO_2' is the injection and confinement of CO_2 within underground geological formations; (2) a 'storage site' is the volumetric structure within a geological formation used for the geological storage of CO_2, as well as the associated superficial and injection installations; (3) a 'geological formation' is a lithostratigraphic subdivision where distinct rock layers can be found and mapped; (4) a 'storage complex' is the storage site and the surrounding geological formations that may affect the integrity and overall safety of storage (secondary containment formations); and (5) an 'underground structure' is a cavity or permeable rock (rock with hydraulically connected pores) in which the transmission of the pressure can be measured by technical means and is delimited by flow barriers (saline formations, lithologic facies changes) or by the wedging or the formation outcrop.

What the GSCA declares to be part of the Public Domain in Article 3 are 'the geological formations which are part of the storage sites' in Spanish territory, as well as in the subsoil of the territorial sea and in the seabed which is under the sovereignty of Spain, in accordance with legislation in force and international

[22] Some commentators have been misled by the poor grammar of the legislature. In the Spanish language there is a distinction between the stored materials (*almacenamiento*) and the place where those materials are stored (*almacén*). However, the HA incorrectly uses the word *almacenamiento* instead of *almacén*. In fact, the word *almacén* is not used in any single Article of the Act. No one has denounced that situation. On the contrary, the whole of the energy law community uses the word *almacenamiento* to refer to both to the place where the gas is stored, as well as to the gas stored.

treaties and conventions. It is the 'geological formation', and not the 'storage site', which is considered to be part of the Public Domain. This would imply that the scope of the Public Domain has been narrowed in comparison with the MA, and that the 'underground structures' are no longer part of the Public Domain. That conclusion, however, is not correct, for various reasons.

First, the distinction laid down by the GSCA between a storage site, a geological formation, and an underground structure is artificial.[23] They are, in reality, elements of the same concept or various aspects of the same concept. Second, the definition of 'underground structure' of the MA is wider than the definition of 'underground structure' in the GSCA, and the former includes the latter. Third, the terms 'storage site' and 'geological formation' of the GSCA can also be considered to be covered by the term 'underground structure' as defined in the MA. An exception would be 'the associated superficial and injection installations' of a storage site, which would not be covered by the definition of 'underground structure' of the MA. As a result, in reality, the GSCA neither narrows nor widens the scope of the Public Domain, except for 'the associated superficial and injection installations'. The definition of Public Domain in the GSCA, in relation to geological storage of CO_2, is no more than a portion of the General Mining Public Domain, as defined in the MA.

We can see in the GSCA changes in the traditional legal framework of the Public Domain. It could be argued that the legal order has evolved from a static view of the Public Domain to a dynamic understanding of the institution, the GSCA being an example of the latter. Under a static view, groups of goods are declared by a particular Act to be part of the Public Domain. Under this static view, there is no need to actually declare that each of the goods of the same nature is a part of the Public Domain. In other words, there is no need to individually declare that this or that other good is part of the Public Domain, since the declaration has been made in general terms by the Act, affecting an homogeneous number of goods (for example, roads, rivers, buildings hosting governmental offices, etc). With regard to underground structures, the MA is static in that all underground structures in the country are part of the Public Domain, irrespective of whether they are actually used or not. The GSCA is dynamic in that only those underground structures which are actually used for storage of CO_2 are considered to be part of the Public Domain.

D. Who owns the CO_2?

In any case, the GSCA does not consider the CO_2 itself to be part of the Public Domain. Rather, CO_2 is something that is in the Public Domain, but which is not part of it. In this sense, the GSCA follows the path of the HA, according to which the underground structure is part of the Public Domain while the stored natural gas is not. As the objective sought is permanent containment of CO_2 in the

[23] See further Mejías (n 2).

underground structure, however, it is likely that the CO_2 will dissolve into the reservoir rock or that it will become a mineral. In either of these cases, CO_2 will have transformed itself and incorporated by accession to the Public Domain.

As it is not incorporated by accession to the underground structure, CO_2 is not part of the Public Domain. But who owns it? Does it still belong to the concessionaire who injected it? Obviously, the concessionaire is still responsible for the CO_2, but does the concessionaire still own it? In our opinion, it can be understood that, as happens with waste, the CO_2 has been abandoned into the underground structure. It is injected in order to abandon it, and abandonment is a way of losing property. The gas would become res nullius. Anyway, the issue of ownership does not seem so relevant. The law introduced a system of responsibility, which is what really matters.

VI. Authorizations and concessions

In Spanish law, the gradual intensity of public intervention within the economic sector is translated into three different legal techniques: communications, authorizations, and concessions. In some cases, the law imposes upon individuals or legal persons the obligation to communicate to the competent Public Administration the founding of a business; communicants are free to develop it unless they are instructed otherwise by the relevant authority because of a violation of the existing rules for the development of such business.

In other cases, the law imposes upon individuals or legal persons the obligation to obtain an authorization prior to the founding of a business (authorizations can also be designated, among other names, as licences or permits). It is assumed that the competent Public Administration does not enjoy any kind of discretion in granting or denying the authorization; rather, it must grant it whenever the applicant fulfils the exigencies laid down in the legal norms.

Concessions operate in the realm of the Public Domain and public services, as well as in the area of public works, and public procurement. Any individual or legal person who intends to operate in any of those areas must obtain a prior concession. Whereas an application to get a concession for the exclusive use of a portion of the Public Domain can be submitted at any time by the interested individual or company, applications to operate a public service can only be submitted when and if the relevant Public Administration opens a tender procedure. Public Administration enjoys a level of discretion (depending on the sector in which the concession is to operate) to grant or deny the concession, based on the personal, financial, and technical circumstances of the applicant.

Due to the disparate areas of public intervention in economic sectors, and due to the remarkable number of existing legal norms, the abovementioned characteristics of communications, authorizations, and concessions may be subject to a number of specific rules. Notwithstanding those remarks, there are three ideas which define the respective scope for authorizations and for concessions. Authorization is a legal technique more compatible with the idea of a free market economy, and thus with freedom of business and of investment. The right to carry on a particular business is not awarded by the authorization, but rather the applicant enjoys this right prior to obtaining the authorization. The authorization simply removes a number of obstacles to the exercise of the right. Conversely, no individual or legal person has a pre-existent right to use the Public Domain in an exclusive way or to run a public service. Such a right is awarded by the Public Administration, by means of the concession. Whereas authorizations declare the right to exist, concessions bring the right into existence. The different nature of these two legal techniques shows that while authorizations are awarded in an indefinite manner, concessions are of a temporary nature.

VII. Authorizations for the use of underground storage in accordance with the Mining Act 1973

For the exploitation of mineral resources included within sections A and B of the Act, authorization is required. In regard to the minerals in section C, a division needs to be made between exploration and production. The exploration for these minerals is subject to an authorization, which is given for short periods of time (one to three years) and does not create any contractual relation between the individual or company and the Public Administration. The exploitation of minerals in section C, however, is subject to a concession. A concession is awarded for 30 years, its duration may be extended, and it has the nature of an administrative contract. With regard to the mineral resources of section D, the scope for private initiative is narrowed and, in general terms, both the exploration for and the exploitation of those resources will be carried out by the state. The MA also deals with the expiration of mining rights, which may be caused by the improper fulfilment of the duties of the concessionaire. Mining rights can be transferred, subject to a previous authorization of the Public Administration.

In accordance with the MA, the use of resources of section B (such as underground storage) is subject to prior authorization. When the MA was passed in 1973, there was no available technology allowing the storage of valuable goods (such as natural gas) in an underground structure, which explains why only an authorization was needed, instead of a concession. The Act establishes priorities among the three types of resources that are included in section B. The Act creates safeguard zones for the use of underground structures, which are important to protecting the environment, similar to those established for mineral waters.

VIII. Concession for the storage of natural gas in an underground storage

The natural gas industry is a relatively new industry in Spain. Between 1850 and 1960, a number of Spanish towns enjoyed town gas, manufactured from coal or oil at local factories. This industry declined in the 1960s and was replaced by alternative fuels, such as oil and bottled gas. The development of the natural gas industry goes back to the end of the 1960s when liquid natural gas started being transported from Libya and Algeria by methane tankers, and distributed and supplied in some towns of Catalonia. For several reasons, the development of the natural gas industry stopped and was not revived until 1985. From 1985 to 2005, the promotion of natural gas was the core of the Spanish Energy Policy, which was accompanied by a liberalization process stemming from the approval of the HA.

As for other infrastructure needs, the Government has promoted the construction of natural gas underground storages, initially in former gas fields, once depleted, and later in new underground sites. It should be noted that gas production in Spain has been almost insignificant, and when we refer to 'former gas fields', we mean two small gas fields, already depleted, and acting now as underground gas storages (one in the Bay of Biscay, another one in the Valley of the Guadalquivir River).

Neither within the 1987 Gas Act, nor within the original version of the HA (which derogated and substituted the former), were there specific provisions about natural gas underground storage. It should be understood that the MA was to operate as a supplementary law with regard to underground storage. However, whereas the MA subjects the use of underground structures to a prior authorization, the 1987 Gas Act stated that strategic storage of natural gas (i.e., underground storage) was subject to a prior concession.[24] Therefore, there was limited scope for the MA to be applied.

The 1987 Gas Act stated that underground gas storage was subject to a prior concession; therefore, although the MA states that the use of underground structures is subject to a prior authorization, in the case of underground structures used as gas storage, a concession was needed instead of an authorization. The HA repealed the 1987 Gas Act and stated that all existing concessions in the natural gas sector were transformed into authorizations, upon the entry into force of the Act (which took place on 9 October 1998). That decision tried to underline the liberalizing character of the new HA, since indefinite authorizations are more compatible with the free market than temporal concessions. The transformation of concessions into authorizations applied to underground gas storage. As a result, the HA was in line with the MA, since in both Acts the use of underground structures was subject to a prior authorization.

The original wording of the HA was obscure with regard to underground storage of natural gas, so that it was not clear whether it was subject to a prior concession or to a prior authorization. Notwithstanding this obscurity, there are several reasons to state that in accordance with the original wording of the HA, the underground storage of natural gas was subject to a prior authorization. That being so, there were more robust arguments to accept the supplementary application of the MA.

[24] Article 2 of the 1987 Gas Act.

By means of a 2007 reform contained within Parliamentary Act, Article 24 (*bis*) of the HA has since stated that the underground storage of natural gas is subject to a prior concession.

IX. Research permits and concessions for the underground storage of CO_2

Chapter II of the GSCA contains the key provisions of the Act, related to both research permits (Articles 8 and 9) and storage concessions (Article 10).

A prior research permit is required whenever there is the need to do research to find out the storage capacity or the suitability of a location for storage. Such a research permit holder can check injections in the location. The Government may ask that the fulfillment of the permit holder's legal obligations be guaranteed. The permit lasts for no more than four years, but exceptionally can be extended for two more years. Research permits will be awarded on the basis of objective, public, and anti-discriminatory criteria, among which attention must be paid to the amount of investment, as well as the speed in the execution of the programme and its technical characteristics. In case there is more than one application covering the same area, it must be guaranteed in the procedure that all entities enjoying the necessary capacities can participate. Once an application for a research permit has been submitted, the relevant authority (Autonomous Community or National Government) must publish an announcement in the Official Bulletin, so that other applications in the same area can be submitted. The GSCA foresees the possibility that either the Central Government or the Autonomous Community, whenever they think it is needed, can call for a public tender to award a research permit in areas where no application has been submitted.

According to both Articles 5(2) and 6(2) of the CCD, Member States must ensure that the procedures for the granting of exploration permits and storage permits, respectively, are open to all entities possessing the necessary capacities, and that the permits are granted on the basis of objective, published, and transparent criteria. This provision applies in Spain to both exploration permits and storage concessions. The CCD does not impose on Spanish authorities, when implementing the CCD, the obligation to design a permit or licence for storage purposes and, consequently, the CCD does not prohibit the use of a concession for storage purposes. Spain is free to decide which legal technique it uses to allow an applicant to store CO_2 in an underground storage. What the CCD imposes upon Spain is that, whatever technique is used, the procedure is open to all interested and capable parties.

Underground storage of CO_2 is subject to a prior concession, which is to be awarded in accordance with Chapter II of the GSCA. Underground storage concessions award to the holder an exclusive right to storage of CO_2 in an underground location. No underground location can be used to store CO_2 before an underground storage has been awarded in accordance with the GSCA.

The suitability of the geological formation of a storage site must be determined through a characterization and assessment of the potential storage complex and surrounding geological formations, in accordance with the criteria specified in Annex I of the Act. A geological formation may only be selected as a storage site if, in the proposed conditions of use, there is no significant risk of leakage or any significant risk to the environment or human health.

Holders of a concession may be all those individual or legal persons who show sufficient technical and economic solvency needed to execute the storage project for which they have submitted an application.

There can be only one holder of the concession in each storage location. In this regard, the Ministry for Industry, Tourism and Commerce must check that the holder is financially and technically solvent to develop the activity of CO_2 storage. If there is more than one storage site within the underground structure, it must be checked to see that pressure interaction among those various sites does not interfere in the proper functioning of storages.

No other uses can be authorized in the storage location that are incompatible with the storage of CO_2. While the procedure to award the concession is being developed, no other use incompatible with the storage can be authorized. In this sense, once an application has been submitted, the Ministry for Industry, Tourism and Commerce will inform the Ministries and Public Administrations in order to avoid the authorization of incompatible uses.

The storage concession cannot last more than 30 years. However, it can be extended for two periods of 10 years each. Article 10(6) foresees an exceptional extension of 10 years more, whenever the holder shows within the last year of the second extension that at the end of the second extension the total capacity of the storage is not going to be filled.

The holder of the concession must give financial guarantees of the fulfilment of its obligations in the underground storage of CO_2 (art 12 of the GSCA).

X. Concluding remarks

The legal framework for underground storage of CO_2 in Spain allows for the following four conclusions.

A. The conversion of the general mining law into supplementary law

The evolution and development of new technologies making underground structures available for purposes which could not have been foreseen by the legislator in 1973 implied a departure from the assumption that the country could have a common framework for underground structures, whatever the purpose of the structure was. As a result, the availability of the new technologies meant the elaboration of a specific legal framework for each of them and, therefore, the transformation of the Mines Act from a common framework into a supplementary act, to be applied if and only if the new framework lacks an answer to an unforeseen problem. Moreover, the MA becomes supplementary, but only at second instance, since the supplementary law of the GSCA, at first instance, is the Hydrocarbon Act, which regulates concessions for the underground storage of natural gas.

B. The European law on CCS has led to the construction of a new kind of concession

The 2009 European Directive on CO_2 storage was passed within a wider context, consisting in longstanding efforts of EU institutions to liberalize the internal market, including the energy market. Therefore, one of the underlying principles of the 2010 GSCA is the need to guarantee competition and transparency within the procedures aimed at awarding the exploration and storage permits (it is not the exclusive, nor the main one). Insofar as the GSCA is directed to implement the Directive, it includes provisions to guarantee competition and transparency. However, after the approval of the GSCA, former authorizations for the use of underground storage are substituted by concessions for the use of the underground storage of CO_2. The substitution means both a higher degree of state control and the use of a technique (concession) which traditionally involves a higher level of governmental discretion. In the light of the discussion in this chapter, in relation to the distinction between authorizations and concessions, one might come to the wrong conclusion that the GSCA meant a step back in the path of liberalization; on the contrary, the result of this legal evolution is that EU law has forced the Spanish legal order to create a new legal technique: a concession is no longer to be awarded on a discretionary basis (as opposed to the traditional concessions), but rather according to objective, published, and transparent criteria. In that context, 'discretionary basis' means that the government enjoys discretion to judge whether an applicant for a concession has a sufficient economic, technical, and financial background to be awarded the concession.

By means of a concession, public authorities keep stronger and tighter control of the activities of the concessionaire, in comparison with an authorization. In addition, the concession is, by definition, temporary, as opposed to the general indefinite character of authorizations. Due to the remarkable security and environmental issues surrounding CO_2 storage (including the long period of the storage cycle), it seems sensible that the GSCA opted for a concession, instead of an authorization, but one must remember that some aspects of the traditional legal framework for concessions must be considered to be ruled out by the European Directive, such as the discretion in awarding them.

C. The GSCA is an example of the combination of public and private regulatory components to encourage new technology

The GSCA is an example of the combination of disparate regulatory techniques. In the light of traditional regulation theory, public property is clearly a way to regulate. Actually, it was the main way of regulation in Europe between the end of the Second World War and the wave of privatization of the 1990s. With ideological dogmas aside, the best regulatory options rely upon three pillars: (i) a balance between public and private interests, such as in the Private Public Partnership or other projects involving both the private and the public sector; (ii) a combination of the most useful regulatory techniques in light of energy policy objectives; and (iii) a regulatory structure which is designed in accordance with the technical specificities of each regulated activity.

The creation of a public enterprise devoted to the storage of CO_2 would have been an option for the Spanish government. That option could have relied upon a double assumption: on the one hand, that public finance was needed, the private sector not being interested in investing in a new (not mature) and expensive technology; on the other hand, that environmental aspects surrounding the storage of CO_2 in underground structures were of too much importance to be left in the hands of private initiative. Actually, that was the option the government took in 2005, when Enresa was transformed from a commercial company into a public institution,[25] and the management of radioactive residues was declared to be an essential service reserved for the state. However, the CCD ruled out the creation of a public monopoly charged with the task of storing CO_2 in underground structures.

When implementing the CCD, the Spanish government created a framework which allows the private sector to get involved in the business, but that also reinforces governmental control over the activity. Though it may sound contradictory, the GSCA tries to attract private investment by means of the creation of a concessional structure. A concession structure subjects the concessionaire to a stricter governmental control, but, at the same time, it expressly awards to the concessionaire an exclusive right. One of the most remarkable provisions to make investment attractive is the transfer of responsibility over the storage from the concessionaire to the government. Under certain conditions, the transfer can take place 20 years after the award of the concession, though it can take place earlier. Given that the concession lasts 30 years (and can be extended to two periods of 10 years each), and that the confinement of CO_2 in the storage facility is designed to last much, much longer, the responsibility which the concessionaire incurs is (too) generous, and has been subject to criticism. Such kind of generosity was understood to be the only way to attract private investment within this no-profit activity. When the responsibility of a concessionaire comes to an end, it is passed on to the state.

D. An inheritance of privatization and liberalization?

Privatization, deregulation, and liberalization, which were the main characteristics of energy regulation between 1980 and 2007, are under scrutiny, particularly after the start of the financial crisis in 2007. Under the Keynesian paradigm (1945–1980), the monopolistic character of some parts of the energy industry (transport and distribution) meant that many countries decided to set up legal

[25] Act No 24 of 18 November 2005.

monopolies, run by public enterprises, applying not only to transport and distribution but also to the whole of the energy chain, including supply. This wave of privatization starting in 1980 was applied in some countries not only to those parts of the energy chain that are suitable to competition (production and supply), but also to natural monopolies. A more realistic situation is reached when policymakers and lawmakers understand the disparate nature of the components of the energy industry. When that happens, there is scope to reinforce the public nature of essential facilities and, simultaneously, to foster competition in areas of the energy business where it can actually take place. The Spanish GSCA is an example of that, since it widens the scope of Public Domain, a trend which seems to belong to the old paradigm and, at the same time, tries to create a favourable atmosphere for private investment, which is a more modern development.

E. A law encouraging CCS technology

Several provisions of the Spanish GSCA actually encourage CCS technology. However, the whole institutional and legal system for this technology in Spain relies too much on the CO_2 tonne price. There should be a more aggressive approach to the promotion of this technology, since the CO_2 tonne price will never be attractive enough make it possible to rely completely upon market forces to drive the technology forward. Consequently, Spanish law could be better shaped to actually encourage this technology, cutting much red tape. There should be a stronger allocation of public funds. The involvement of many different levels of government must be better coordinated. We need to recognize that the role of law is limited, but we should let the law do what it can.

24

Energy Underground and Water Sustainability: African Strategies for a Changing Environment

Yinka Omorogbe

I. Introduction

It is always a difficult task to write about 'Africa', thus conveying the perception that it is one big amorphous continent with similar problems, needs, and solutions. This could not be further from the truth. In fact, Africa is a very complex continent, with sometimes convoluted responses to seemingly simple issues. Even the question of how many countries there are in Africa doesn't throw up a simple answer. It has 55 sovereign states, 54 of which are members of the African Union,[1] and a territory—Somaliland—which remains unrecognized by African states but which has both government and control over its land area. Africa also still retains vestiges of its recent colonial partitioned past, with Spain, France, Portugal, and the United Kingdom still retaining islands off its coast as territories.[2] As to weather and terrain, it has great diversity, ranging from snow in the north and south, such as in Lesotho, Morocco, Tunisia, and South Africa; to dryness and great heat in the countries of the Sahara Desert (which is the largest hot desert in the world); and temperate to hot weather in grasslands of the Savannah, right next to the large and humid tropical forests of west and central Africa. Whilst most Africans are black, all are not. Indigenous populations are of both Negro and Arab extraction, whilst there are generations of Indian and Caucasian Africans. In terms of resources and wealth, it is again a land of great contrasts. It is the wealthiest continent in terms of natural resources, and the poorest in terms of economic and development indicators. It is also a continent of great apparent contrasts, with opulence often co-existing with

[1] All the sovereign states are members, with the exception of Morocco, which withdrew from membership in protest in 1984, after the Organisation of African Unity (predecessor to the African Union) admitted the Saharan Arab Democratic Republic as a member, which Morocco refused to recognize.

[2] Ceutta, Melilla, and the Canary Islands—Spain; Mayotte, and Reunion—France; the islands of Saint Helena, Ascension, and Tristan da Cunha (one territory)—United Kingdom. See Countries in Africa>List of African Countries, at <http://www.answers.org>.

abject poverty. It is not uncommon to see shantytowns right in the middle of affluent neighbourhoods.

Writing collectively about Africa is therefore not such a straightforward matter because the countries comprising the continent are so different. One would venture to say, however, that this chapter deals with a topic that it is relatively easier to generalize about. This is because practically all African countries suffer, in varying degrees, from problems related to access to modern energy, and to water and sanitation. Here, the focus is on new uses of underground energy resources that can potentially provide much-needed services, but which negatively impact the world's most precious natural resource: water.

This chapter strives not to be criticized for giving an 'African' perspective that is in fact slanted or concentrated on one aspect of this multi-faceted and multi-layered continent.[3] It takes what the present author hopes is an Afrocentric perspective to the issues dealt with, striving not to be myopic, and particularly striving not to over-generalize, over-mystify, or over-simplify. Therefore, as much as possible, generalizations are avoided by giving regional or country-specific examples where they are seen as necessary or relevant, even as it discusses the need for conventional energy and the effect that underground technologies are likely to have on the various economies of Africa. Against this background, this chapter considers the new ways of unlocking geothermal energy, and energy from shale formations, and considers whether they hold any promise for Africa in general and for developing states in particular. It considers possible strategies for the various African countries, based on present needs, realities, availability of knowledge, and current legislative and regulatory frameworks.

II. Energy in Africa

Africa is the continent that uses the least energy, and thus may collectively be described as energy poor, in terms of utilization, with great problems related to the achievement of universal access to energy services.[4] Even the African countries that have achieved the most access still lag significantly behind their average western counterparts. The statistics for Africa and Asia are dismal. More than half of the population in developing Asia and 80% of the population in sub-Saharan Africa rely on traditional biomass fuels such as wood, crop waste, dung, and (mainly for the urban poor) kerosene, all of which are used to cook on inefficient local stoves that emit a lot of smoke and particulate matter. These are unhealthy and inefficient fuels, quite unlike cleaner and more efficient options such as liquefied petroleum gas, natural gas, and biofuels. The 10 largest populations without access to clean

[3] The western press regularly does that, by focusing on one particularly (often negative) aspect and proclaiming that this is 'Africa'. This author is a vociferous critic of this practice, which she perceives as being a subconsciously prejudicial practice.

[4] 'Energy in Africa: Overview', available at <http://www.web.worldbank.org>. The World Bank rightly states that there is an energy crisis in Africa, with about half its countries suffering from an energy famine.

cooking facilities are found in Asia and Africa, and include Nigeria, the Democratic Republic of the Congo, and Ethiopia.[5] In respect of electricity, 29% of the population of sub-Saharan Africa has access to electricity, compared with 40% in other low-income countries in other parts of the world. Excluding South Africa, the World Bank identifies low entire installed generation capacities for selected African countries, stating by way of comparison that the entire installed capacity of sub-Saharan Africa is 28 gigawatts, which is equivalent to that of Argentina.[6] South Africa is the best in terms of generating capacity, with an average generation of 40,000 GwH, and 4,803 kWh per capita for 2008–2012.[7] In comparison, cumulative figures for 2008–2012 show that Ethiopia has one of the lowest figures for Africa, at 52 kilowatt hours per person (kWh). Nigeria is not much better, with a low generating capacity of 135 kWh, behind Kenya (155 kWh), Cameroon (258 kWh), Ghana (299 kWh), and Gabon (972 kWh).[8]

Paradoxically, Africa is awash with energy. Huge fossil energy resources are located all over the continent. Nigeria, Libya, Angola, Gabon, Equatorial Guinea, Egypt, and South Sudan are the better-known and major producers, but half the countries have some exploration currently ongoing, and promising discoveries have been made in, for example, Ghana and Kenya. Mozambique, Kenya, Madagascar, and Sierra Leone are up-and-coming producers, whilst countries such as Ethiopia and Namibia are believed to hold sizeable reserves. East Africa holds tremendous promise, with Lake Albert in Uganda stated as having 3.5 billion barrels of oil reserves.[9] It is still a relatively unexplored continent and therefore it is not unreasonable to expect upward revisions of reserve estimates, as well as new discoveries and more African producers/exporters in the near future. Even now, Africa can conveniently meet all its energy needs solely from conventional fossil fuels.[10]

Africa also has renewable energy resources, which are widely distributed and enormous in quantity. It has abundant hydropower. Whilst hydroelectricity is the biggest source of electricity, its potential remains largely underutilized. Africa has

[5] Countries with the largest populations without access to electricity in 2010: Congo, Pakistan, Tanzania, Kenya, and Uganda. Countries with the largest population relying on traditional biomass in 2010: India, China, Bangladesh, Indonesia, Nigeria, Pakistan, Ethiopia, Democratic Republic of the Congo, Vietnam, and the Philippines. Source: World Energy Outlook 2012, 'Measuring Progress towards Energy for All: Power to the People?' Chapter 18, 533–4, available at <http://www.worldenergyoutlook.org>.

[6] World Energy Outlook 2012 (n 5).

[7] On South Africa, see 'Electricity Generated and Available for Distribution (Preliminary)' (2012), available at <http://www.statssa.gov.za/publications/P4141/P4141February2012.pdf>.

[8] 'Electric Power Consumption (kWh per Capita)', available at <http://data.worldbank.org/indicator/EG.USE.ELEC.KH.PC>. The website of the Nigerian Presidential Task Force on Power describes Nigeria as amongst the most electricity-deprived people in the world, and gives similar statistics—see 'Nigeria's Power Reform', available at <http://www.nigeriapowerreform.org>.

[9] Michael Hall and John Diggens, 'The African Rift System—A View from Space', (2001) 4(8) ExPRO, available at <http://www.geoexpro.com>.

[10] *Oil and Gas in Africa*, Joint Study by the African Development Bank/African Union (2009), which estimates that Nigeria alone can meet all of Africa's energy needs.

some of the largest watercourses in the world such as the Nile, Niger, Zambezi, Limpopo, and Volta Rivers, which are more than sufficient for the electricity needs of the various countries. It can also harness energy from wind and ocean currents, as it is surrounded by the Indian Ocean on the east and the Atlantic Ocean on the west. Ocean-current turbines along the 2,000-km northwest coastline from Morocco to Senegal could potentially generate all of Africa's energy needs. Its most abundant renewable energy source, however, is the sun, which shines all year round in most of the African countries. Solar energy could easily be used to provide off-grid energy to inaccessible remote communities.

Africa has extensive geothermal resources. The East African Rift Valley is one of the major tectonic structures[11] of the earth, where the heat energy of the earth escapes to the surface. It is very extensive and runs through several countries in East and Central Africa. As most of these countries are net importers of energy, geothermal resources thereby hold a lot of promise for them.[12] Activities in this sector should increase in these countries, all of which are presently net importers of petroleum. Geothermal resources in the Red Sea Valley, between Nigeria's Atlantic southeast coast and Cameroon's Atlantic southwest coast, remain unutilized. South Africa, though relatively less well endowed, is said to be seriously considering the option of geothermal energy.

All evidence indicates that large amounts of shale resources abound all over Africa. However, since conventional energy in most of the countries is still underexplored, there has apparently been little or no impetus to critically consider its use in most of these countries. Thus a 2011 US study shows substantial deposits of shale gas in various regions of the world, including the African countries of Morocco, Algeria, Tunisia, Libya, Egypt, Mauritania, Western Sahara, and South Africa.[13] Both this study and its 2013 update[14] note that Russia, Central Asia, the Middle East, South East Asia, and Central Africa were not included, primarily because there were either significant quantities of conventional natural gas reserves noted to be in place (i.e., Russia and the Middle East), or because of a general lack of information to carry out even an initial assessment. Most of the sub-Saharan countries contain at least modest reserves, and so it is reasonable to expect more discoveries of shale deposits.

These statistics show that African energy is largely underexplored and underutilized, and that one of the most pressing problems of the continent must be how to tap its extensive energy resources. Since energy directly impacts development, some of the greatest problems of underdevelopment are also to be found in these

[11] Tectonics is the branch of geology that studies the folding and faulting of the earth's surface. The term 'tectonic structure' is applied to various parts of the earth's crust that are formed by the combination of a number of different smaller structural forms. See 'Tectonics': <http://www.definitions.net/definitions/tectonics>.

[12] See section III.A.

[13] *World Shale Gas Resources: An Initial Assessment of 14 Regions Outside the United States,* April 2011, available at <http://www.eia.gov>.

[14] *Technically Recoverable Shale Oil and Gas Shale Resources: An Assessment of 137 Shale Formations in 41 Countries Outside the United States*, June 2013, available at <http://www.eia.gov/>.

energy-deficient countries. It is therefore obvious that there is a critical need to increase energy use in accordance with principles of sustainable development, taking long-term environmental matters into consideration.

III. Underground energy

Advances in technology coupled with sustained high energy prices have led to increased interest in, and use of, geothermal and shale resources in countries all over the world. This section briefly discusses the processes involved in the extraction of these underground energy resources, and their possible impacts on the environments and the communities within which they are exploited.

A. Geothermal energy

Geothermal energy involves the use of energy from inside the earth.[15] Hot rocks under the earth's surface heat water underground, thereby producing steam which is brought up to the earth's surface through holes, purified, and then used as a fuel. It is an important source of energy in the volcanically active countries of New Zealand and Iceland, and it is currently in use in countries such as the United States, Japan, the Philippines, and Italy (where the first geothermal station was built). In East Africa, the East African Rift System contains large amounts of geothermal resources. It extends for 6,500 km, passing through Eritrea, Djibouti, Ethiopia, Kenya, Tanzania, Uganda, Rwanda, the Democratic Republic of the Congo, Zambia, Malawi, Mozambique, and Madagascar, It is estimated to have a geothermal resource potential of more than 15,000 MWe.[16] Kenya and Ethiopia presently have installed geothermal capacity, whilst some other countries, including Djibouti, Uganda, and Rwanda, are at various exploratory stages.[17] It is expected that more countries in that area will utilize this resource, particularly as none of them are yet established petroleum producers (with the exception of the Congo). South Africa, which is not regarded as having much geothermal potential,

[15] Geo = earth, thermal = heat. The centre of the earth is 6,000°C. For basic primers see, e.g., <http://www.darvill.clara.net/altenerg/geothermal.htm>; <http://www.renewableenergyworld.com/rea/>; 'Geothermal Energy: Tapping the Earth's Heat' <http://environment.nationalgeographic.com/environment/global-warming/geothermal-profile>.

[16] MWe = Megawatts of electricity. See Meseret Teklemariam Zemedkun, 'Overview of Geothermal Resource Exploration and Development in the East African Rift System', presented at Short Course VII on Exploration for Geothermal Resources, organized by the United Nations University Geothermal Programme (UNU-GTP), Geothermal Development Company (GDC), and KenGen, at Lake Bogoria and Lake Naivasha, Kenya, 27 October–18 November 2012; 'Full Steam Ahead to Sustainable Energy: Tapping Geothermal Power in Kenya's Rift Valley', available at <http://www.un.org/africarenewal/magazine/april-2012/full-steam-ahead-sustainable-energy.>.

[17] See Zemedkun (n 16). See also Jean d'Amour Mbonyinshuti, 'Rwanda: Hope for Geothermal Power as Drills Charge', 19 July 2012, <http://www.allafrica.com>.

is also seriously examining its geothermal prospects.[18] It currently has very little installed capacity.[19]

Geothermal energy uses naturally occurring steam and hot water trapped in various reservoirs under the surface of the earth and, therefore, it is no surprise that such energy impacts water resources. The process of extraction of geothermal fluids (which include gas, steam, and water) depletes heat from natural reservoirs at 10 times their rate of replenishment.[20] Natural features such as hot springs and geysers may be irreparably damaged. In New Zealand, the first geothermal plant in Wairekei has had negative impacts on the water resources in the Geysa Valley, the nearby Waiora Valley, and the Karapiti blowhole.[21] The ground has gradually sagged to as much as 3 m in some places, and the hot springs have declined and died. The land at the centre of the subsistence bowl is sinking by 0.5 m per year, and in 2005 was 14 m lower than it was before the power station was built.[22] Arsenic pollution as a result of geothermal waste is another concern. In addition to these negative impacts on water systems and quality, there is evidence that the processes for the retrieval of geothermal energy can lead to greater earthquake frequency.[23] Clearly, the exploitation of geothermal resources negatively impacts water resources, but not to the extent of those processes employed for the recovery of shale resources.

B. Shale resources

Shale is a sedimentary rock that is predominantly comprised of consolidated clay particles.[24] Shales are typically deposited as mud in environments such as tidal flats and deep-water basins where these fine-grained clay particles fall out of suspension in these quiet waters. During the deposition of these fine-grained sediments, there can also be deposition of organic matter in the form of organic debris derived from algae, plants, and animals. The naturally tabular clay grains tend to lie flat as the sediments accumulate and subsequently become compacted as a result of additional sediment deposition. This results in mud with thin laminar bedding that solidifies into thinly layered shale rock. The very fine sheet-like clay mineral grains and laminated layers of sediment result in a rock that has limited horizontal permeability and extremely limited vertical permeability, which means that oil and gas

[18] 'Despite geological limitations, South Africa begins to weigh its geothermal options', <http://www.engineeringnews.co.za> (posted on 15 December 2010). Also, 'Full Steam Ahead? Geothermal Energy can be Africa's Game-Changer', <http://www.bdlive.co.za> (posted on 4 March 2013).

[19] Interestingly, it has a little hotel that uses geothermal energy for heating and cooling: the My Pond Hotel, Port Alfred, <http://www.africanecosystems.co.za>.

[20] This may be partially improved by injecting waste fluids back into the geothermal system.

[21] 'Story: Geothermal Energy', available at <http://www.teara.gov.nz>.

[22] 'Story: Geothermal Energy' (n 21).

[23] See this article on the website of the Union of Concerned Scientists: 'Environmental Impacts of Geothermal Energy', available at <http://www.ucsusa.org>.

[24] For further understanding of shale gas and its processes, see 'Modern Shale Gas Development in the United States: An Update', available at <http://www.netl.doe.gov/File%20Library/Research/Oil-Gas/shale-gas-primer-update-2013.pdf>; 'Hydraulic Fracturing 101', available at <http://www.earthworksaction.org>.

trapped in shale cannot move easily within the rock, except over the course of millions of years. These formations are found all over the world. The United States, which has major gas shale basins located all over the country, is presently the world's largest producer of this gas, commonly known as shale gas.

Improvements in technologies, the use of horizontal drilling, and high oil prices over the past few years make it economically feasible to produce large volumes of shale gas, mainly through a process known as hydraulic fracturing, commonly known as 'fracking'. This term describes the processes whereby a high-pressure cocktail of water, sand, and chemicals is injected into geological formations, such as those described earlier, fracturing the formations and thereby releasing natural gas. One estimate is that the drilling and hydraulic fracturing of a horizontal shale gas well may typically require between 2 and 4 million gallons of water.[25] As a result of fracking, the United States is now an even larger producer of petroleum and natural gas, 70% of which is said to be produced through fracking. This has led to a new 'oil boom' in the United States.

Fracking is, however, a highly controversial practice, and has met with a very mixed reception in various states because of the negative environmental and health effects that it is reputed to have. It is being vigorously debated in New York, which overlays sizeable shale deposits, and has been banned by the state of Vermont, which is said not to have any deposits.[26] California is making moves to impose a moratorium on fracking,[27] and Mora County in New Mexico, and several cities in the United States have banned the practice.[28] However, at federal level, it has been embraced and even incentivized for almost a decade. Notwithstanding the obvious dangers that the release of chemicals into the environment poses, fracking companies are exempted from the provisions of the Safe Drinking Water Act, the Clean Water Act, and the Clean Air Act, which would have made it mandatory to declare what chemicals are used as part of the process because of the various negative effects on the environment.[29] These exemptions certainly aided the growth of this practice, leading to allegations by environmentally concerned people and groups that political and pecuniary reasons have prevailed over and above the wellbeing of the ordinary person. The author wonders why exemptions in favour of fracking were made as far back as 2005, and at the time when a former CEO of Halliburton (the company which was granted an exclusive licence in 1949 by the patent holder,

25 *Modern Shale Gas Development in the United States: A Primer*, April 2009, ES-4, prepared for the US Department of Energy and the National Energy Technology Laboratory, available at <http://www.netl.doe.gov>.

26 'Vermont First State to Ban Fracking', 17 May 2012, available at <http://edition.cnn.com/2012/05/17/us/Vermont-fracking/>: 'Vermont Becomes First State to Ban Fracking', 17 May 2012, available at <http://www.foxnews.com>.

27 'California Fracking Ban; Golden State Moratorium on Controversial Practice Moves Forward' 17 May 2013, available at <http://www.huffingtonpost.com>.

28 'First County in the US Bans Fracking to Save its Water', available at <http://www.thinkprogress.org>; 'New Mexico County First to Ban Fracking in US', available at <http://www.huffingtonpost.com>; 'Bans on Horizontal Fracking', available at <http://www.greeleyandstone.com>; 'Local Actions Against Fracking', available at <http://www.foodandwaterwatch.com>.

29 The US oil and gas industry is exempted from the Safe Drinking Water Act and is therefore allowed by the Environmental Protection Agency to inject known hazardous substances. This exemption, known as the Halliburton Loophole, operated as an incentive, and clearly facilitated the widespread practice of fracking, and the increase in production of shale gas.

Stanolind Oil Company, and which is one of the three largest manufacturers of fracturing fluids)[30] was Vice-President of the USA.[31]

The most significant developments and exploitation of shale gas and other unconventional types of natural gas have taken place in Canada and in the United States. It has just commenced in the United Kingdom and in South Africa, notwithstanding great outcries from environmentalists.[32] Conversely, shale gas use has been banned in Bulgaria, and there is a moratorium on its use in France.

In both the United Kingdom and South Africa, arguments as to economic benefits, coupled with suggested strategies to mitigate possible environmental hazards, have led to substantial government support for shale gas production that involves hydraulic fracking, despite outcries from environmentalists. The environmental and health problems associated with fracking surround three issues:

(1) The introduction of large amounts of methane into the atmosphere—in areas where fracking is conducted, there are allegations that water from water pipes has burst into flames when taps were opened.

(2) Assertions that areas where fracking occurs are more prone to earthquakes than they would otherwise be.

(3) The danger posed to water quality through the introduction of chemicals used in the course of the fracking process, which has led to allegations of ill health, death, and a contaminated environment. Many of these chemicals are stated to be carcinogens.[33]

[30] There are currently numerous patents over different aspects of the fracking process. The original patent, US Patent no 59,536 was given to Col Edward A. L. Roberts for a fracking process that became known as the Roberts Torpedo. It was used for oil production. On 17 March 1949, a team of petroleum production experts converged on an oil well about 12 miles east of Duncan, Oklahoma—to perform the first commercial application of hydraulic fracturing. Later that same day, Halliburton Oil Well Cementing Co (HOWCO) and Stanolind company personnel successfully fractured another well near Holliday. Stanolind patented the technology and Halliburton was granted a 20-year exclusive licence, thereby enabling the consistent edge that it has maintained in the hydraulic fracking process. See 'Shooters: A "Fracking" History', available at <http://aoghs.org/technology/shooters-well-fracking-history>; the website of the American Oil and Gas Historical Society: 'Hyrdaulic Fracturing: History of an Enduring Technology', available at <http://www.spe.org>.

[31] Then Vice-President Dick Cheney. See 'What is the Halliburton Loophole?', available at <http://www.independentwatertesting.com/education-center/148-what-is-the-halliburton-loophole.html>; 'The Halliburton Loophole', available at <http://www.earthworksaction.org>; 'The Fracked-up Shale Gas Bubble', 13 March 2013, available at <http://www.globalresearch.ca/the-fracked-up-usa-shale-gas-bubble/5326504>.

[32] On South Africa, for a description of the fracking process and companies involved, see David Fig, 'Fracking and the Democratic Deficit in South Africa', available at <http://www.tni.org>. See also 'Debate Heats Up over Karoo Fracking', available at <http://www.havemanninc.com/wp-content/uploads/2011/04/Bulletin.pdf>. But see 'The Other Side of the Karoo Fracking Debate', available at <http://www.25degrees.net>; 'Fracking It in South Africa: An Argument for Shale Gas Production in the Karoo', John Schellhase, 15 November 2012, available at <http://www.africanarguments.org>.

[33] 'Chemicals Used in Hydraulic Fracking', available at <http://www.fracfocus.org> (the website of the Chemical Disclosure Registry). 'List of 78 Chemicals Used in Hydraulic Fracturing Fluid in Pennsylvania', available at <http://marcellusdrilling.com> (quote: 'There are many nasty chemicals on this list, BUT . . .'); Michael Kelley, 'The 10 Scariest Chemicals Used in Hydraulic Fracking', 16 March 2012, available at <http://www.businessinsider.com>.

The complaints are numerous, as are the lawsuits that have been instituted all over the country. So far, none has been decided in favour of the complainant, but complaints are on the increase, as are the litigations.[34] At least one study has shown that there is in fact a link between hydraulic fracturing and earthquakes,[35] and there is little controversy that chemicals from the fracking process are contaminants. It is thus a process that is yet to be adjudged safe.

C. Environmental impacts of the extraction processes

The processes for the extraction of geothermal and shale resources affect both water habitats and resources, and fracking almost certainly negatively affects water quantity and quality. These are issues that can be mitigated, and do not have to be a reason for discontinuing or not commencing exploitation. Where mitigation can be identified and implemented in an effort to ensure that health and safety are not compromised, then there is no cause for alarm. However, in most African countries the capacity to mitigate issues pertaining to water use and health is questionable, as almost all the countries suffer from major problems related to basic water quality and safe sanitation. As the next section attempts to make clear, water issues in the developing world are fundamentally different from those in the developed world.

IV. Water resources in the developing world

With the exception of North Africa,[36] the average poor rural dweller in a typical African (or South Asian country) lives a life that is totally devoid of modern energy, sanitation systems, and clean water. Basic energy needs are sourced from firewood or, at best, kerosene. In many instances, the water source is a good distance away, and is fetched by hand, bucket-by-bucket, from an often-contaminated river, stream, or brackish well. Toilet facilities are non-existent or, at most, rudimentary. Where there is a toilet, it is invariably a pit latrine. More often than not, the bush or pieces of paper out in the open comprise the rural dweller's toilet. Under these unsanitary and unhygienic conditions, poor health and early death are common, and contribute to the low life expectancies and high mortality rates in these countries.

There are few municipal water and sewage systems for the poor rural dweller in sub-Saharan Africa and South Asia. Where they do exist, they remain at a

[34] Barclay R. Nicholson and Stephen C. Dillard, 'Analysis of Litigation Involving Shale and Hydraulic Fracturing: Part 1', [2013] IELR 50. For environmentalist activists' perspectives, see <http://www.nofrackalmanac.com>.

[35] 'Fracking Causes Earthquakes—UK Government: It's Worth the Risk', available at <http://www.globalresearch.ca/fracking-causes-earthquakes/30522>. See also Paul Ishaya Amaza. 'Exploring Barriers to Financing Shale Gas Production on a Limited Recourse Basis' [2013] IELR 67.

[36] See Figure 24.1. The North African countries have some of the highest coverage rates in the world for water and sanitation.

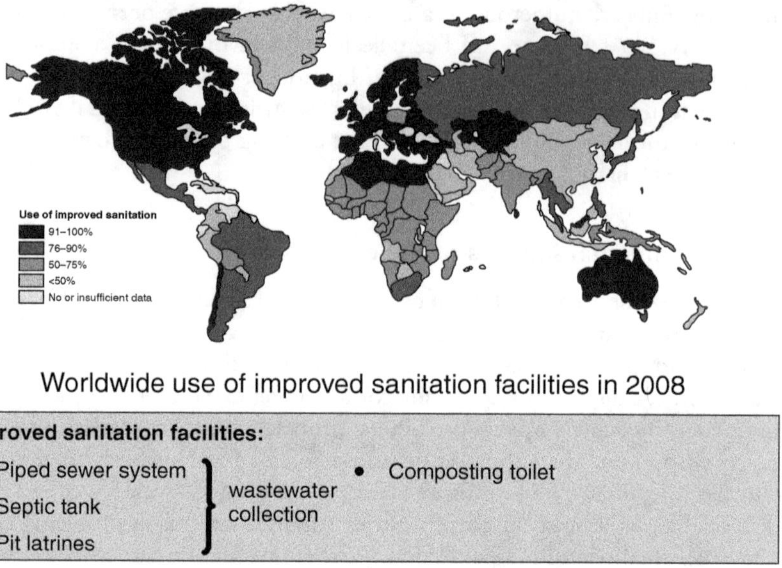

Fig. 24.1 Sanitation around the world

Source: Sarantuyaa Zandaryaa PhD, UNESCO Division of Water Sciences, 'Global Challenge of Water: Examples from Different Continents', available at <http://www.worldwaterweek.org>.

rudimentary stage. The more affluent rural dwellers build their own sewage systems and dig their own boreholes, to which they attach treatment systems, if necessary, so as to guarantee water quality. This aids the lucky poor villagers who will usually be allowed to fetch water from that compound and thus be freed from the drudgery and contamination still suffered by the less fortunate ones. Where are the modern public water and sanitation systems? They are unevenly distributed in the urban areas in the more affluent neighbourhoods, where even there they often function imperfectly, with toilets frequently not flushing and taps not providing water.

Problems of water and sanitation management therefore loom large in the developing world, and are likely to worsen in consequence of increasing population and the effects of climate change, if no meaningful actions are taken to tackle these issues. Such issues lie at the heart of the rights to life and dignity, and explain why there are constant and concerted efforts by the United Nations and its specialized agencies to promote the existence of the international human right to water. It has been proclaimed as such, via a 2010 United Nations General Assembly Resolution that recognizes 'the right to safe drinking water and sanitation as a human right that is essential for the full enjoyment of life and all human rights'.[37] It is 'deeply

[37] Res. A/RES/64/292 of 3 August 2010. See also General Comment No 15, 'The right to water (arts 11 and 12 of the International Covenant on Economic, Social and Cultural Rights)'. In recognition of the importance of these issues, the United Nations, through the General Assembly and its specialized agencies, has established various programmes and activities to stimulate awareness and encourage measures to positively impact on water and development issues. We are currently nearing the end of the 'International Decade for Action: Water for Life 2005–2015', proclaimed by the

concerned' that approximately 884 million people lack access to safe drinking water, that more than 2.6 billion do not have access to basic sanitation, that 1.5 million children die annually and 443 million school days are lost each year, all because of this problem.[38] However, outside the United Nations, the concern may be less so, because the existence and status of this right remains controversial, particularly for developed countries, which appear wary of the obligations that invariably flow from the existence of a right, which are also articulated by the United Nations.[39] Without delving into this issue (since it is outside the scope of this chapter) the position taken here is that, irrespective of whether or not the right to water exists as an international human right, water issues in fact lie at the heart of the rights to life and to human dignity, and are therefore of critical importance.[40] The 2.6 billion people without access to safe sanitation cannot be said to be enjoying the right to adequate housing in the absence of this basic requirement. The lack of sanitation accounts for one-quarter of all deaths of children under five years.[41] They have all died as a result of the attendant violations of their rights to life and to health. Female children are more affected. They suffer violations of their right to education because of the absence of clean water and safe sanitation, as parents will often not allow their daughters to attend schools without toilets, particularly once they have started menstruating.[42] Problems of water are closely linked to poverty, with women carrying a disproportionate share of the burden. In addition to the violation of the right to education, women are traditionally assigned the task of fetching water, which translates into working five to seven hours more each week.[43] Issues such as these, directly traceable to inadequate access to and management of water and sanitation, effectively limit choices and freedoms of females, and ultimately affect development.[44]

United Nations General Assembly (UNGA); 2012 was the year of 'Sustainable Energy for All', 2013 was the International Year of Water Cooperation, and 2014 to 2024 has been proclaimed as the 'Decade of Sustainable Energy for All'.

38 In the Preamble to the UNGA Resolution.

39 In *The Right to Water*, Fact Sheet No 35, a joint publication of the Office of the High Commissioner for Human Rights, UN HABITAT, and the World Health Organization, available at <http://www.ohchr.org>.

40 See John Scanlon, Angela Cassar, Noemi Nemes, *Water as a Human Right?* IUCN Policy and Law Paper No 51 for a clear overview of the content and scope of a possible right to water. See also *The Right to Water* (n 39). South Africa and Armenia contain constitutional provisions that acknowledge the right to water. Chile, in recognition of this right but without explicitly declaring it as such gives water stamps to people below a certain threshold. See Salman M. A. Salman and, Daniel D. Bradlow, *Regulatory Frameworks for Water Resources Management: A Comparative Study* (2006) 161, available at <http://www.worldbank.org>.

41 1.8 million children die every year from diarrhoea and other diseases caused by unclean water and poor sanitation. See *The Right to Water* (n 39) 13.

42 UN-Water, 'Sanitation Contributes to Dignity and Social Development', Fact Sheet No 3 (2009) quoted in *The Right to Water* (n 39).

43 In rural areas of the Republic of Benin, girls aged 6 to 14 spend an average of an hour a day fetching water, compared with 25 minutes spent by their brothers. In Malawi, women spent five times more time fetching water than the boys. See Box 2.2, 'Water, gender, and time-poverty' in *Human Development Report 2006: Power, Poverty, and the Global Water Crisis* 35, available at <http://www.hdr.undp.org>.

44 Often a woman will be faced with 'no-win choice dilemmas'. Should she care for a sick child or spend two hours fetching water? Should her daughter be kept at home so that she can fetch water,

There is a gulf in water and sanitation usage between developed and developing countries. The United States, Australia, Italy, Japan, Mexico, and the North African countries of Algeria, Tunisia, Morocco, Egypt, and Libya are some of the countries at the upper end of the scale, with the United States topping the list with an average of 575 litres used per person per day.[45] Bangladesh, Kenya, Burkina Faso, Nigeria, Angola, Cambodia, Ethiopia, Haiti, Rwanda, Uganda, and Mozambique are at the other extreme, below the water poverty threshold of 50 litres per person per day,[46] with Mozambique averaging 10 litres per person per day.[47] Eight of the countries with the worst indices are in Africa.

The result is that in much of the developing world, apart from in the more affluent urban areas, the management of and access to safe water and sanitation is about a century behind what currently exists in the developed nations of the world. The following quote from the Human Development Report 2006 states as much.

> Few people in the industrial world reflect on the importance of clean water and sanitation in shaping the history of their countries or their life chances. Not too many generations ago the inhabitants of London, New York and Paris were facing the same security threats as those of Lagos, Mumbai and Rio de Janeiro today. Water polluted with raw sewage killed children, created health crises, undermined growth and kept people in poverty. New technologies and finance made universal access to clean water possible. But the crucial change was political. Social reformers, physicians, municipal leaders and industrialists formed powerful coalitions that elevated water and sanitation to the top of the political agenda. They forced governments to acknowledge the curing of diseases caused by unsafe water was inefficient and wasteful: prevention through clean water and sanitation was the better cure.

The train of events described in this quote did not occur in the developing world. Instead, the trend of colonialism to subjugate everything to the interests of the colonizing country worked against the spread of modern water and sanitation infrastructure through the territories. Whilst in Europe and America, the critical importance of universal access to safe water and sanitation was realized and adopted as a goal, and therefore networks were designed to have total coverage of the populations; in colonial territories this was not so. For example, in colonial Lagos, at the beginning of the twentieth century, great investments were made in urban and sanitation infrastructure in wealthy white-inhabited areas. Poorer areas and those that were not inhabited by expatriate communities were left out. Sewage disposal was done manually, and waste disposed of via open trucks which would wind down the roads, fouling the atmosphere as they passed.[48] This differential treatment of sewage in colonial and indigenous areas was no doubt partially due to discrimination, although the obvious and often stated cause was lack of funding.

thereby freeing her (the mother) for income-generating activities? Or, should her daughter go to school to acquire skills necessary to escape poverty? See *Human Development Report 2006* (n 43) 35, Box 2.2.

[45] Celine Kaufmann, 'Access to Drinking Water and Sanitation in Africa', Policy Insights No 41, April 2007, available at <http://www.oecd.org/dev/insights>.

[46] See *Human Development Report 2006* (n 43) 34 for how the threshold figure was arrived at.

[47] *Human Development Report 2006* (n 43) 34.

[48] Night soil men (popularly known as *agbepo*) were a regular feature in Lagos until the 1970s and were only phased out when the law made it mandatory for there to be a change in toilet systems.

The result was that needed expansion into poorer neighbourhoods never occurred. This was the typical pattern,[49] and it had the effect of creating segregation and dividing the haves from the have-nots. Briefly, modern water infrastructure in much of the developing world was not created to serve the poor.

Several decades later, the status quo remains in sub-Saharan Africa, with the presence or absence of modern water and sewage systems effectively defining class, status, and neighbourhoods in the various cities and villages. In the absence of adequate water systems, houses for the poor continue to be built without toilets, or with outhouses containing pit latrines. Schools in both urban and rural areas often have broken or no toilets. In Nigeria, even the camps for graduates serving their mandatory National Youth Service are in this category, leading the less rugged participants to manufacture all types of excuses not to stay in residence.

Breaking out of this situation has proved difficult for several reasons, with problems of under-financing, under-maintenance, and the inability of poorer communities to pay for water services often being cited. However, this author's opinion is that the primary reasons for the present situation are as highlighted in the earlier quote, and have to do with internal dynamics in many of the developing states. Positive change in water and sanitation in developed countries occurred because of activities by those who helped to prioritize and bring the problems of water and sanitation to the attention of the governments. Conversely, such pressure groups—which should normally be found among the more affluent and educated members of society—do not exist, or are so few as to only exert a negligible influence. Instead, those managing the inefficient water and sanitation systems in their houses and offices have failed to appreciate the severity of the problem. It is the belief of this author that water and sanitation issues have become rooted in stratified class and income systems, under which the poor are not expected to have modern water systems because of the expense. Water and sanitation infrastructure serve to distinguish between the haves and the have-nots, with their absence being seen primarily as a by-product of poverty and underdevelopment, and not as a critical lapse with huge implications for the sustainable development and health of the citizenry. Therefore, the water problems of the poor are seen as resolved once a well (or borehole) and a pit latrine are provided for the community, and the creation of modern water and sanitation systems are not treated as priority items.

Again, there has to be a determination by the various impacted governments to prioritize and elevate issues of sanitation and clean water to the top of the development agenda. This is still a slow work in progress. Rwanda has made appreciable progress and is touted as the 'poster child' for improved hygiene and sanitation, with more than half the population now having decent sanitation, nearly four times that in 1990.[50] Ghana also has made clear improvements. Other

[49] *Human Development Report 2006* (n 43) 86, particularly Box 2.1, 'The burden of history: many networks were not designed to reach the poor'.

[50] *3 Years of the Economic Development and Poverty Reduction Strategy (EDPRS): A Summary Implementation Report 2008–2010*. See also John Vidal, 'Water and Sanitation Still not Top Priorities for African Governments', *The Guardian*, Thursday 30 August 2012, available at <http://www.theguardian.com>, where a UN official is quoted as saying, 'In Rwanda, political prioritization for

countries, such as Nigeria, seem to have plans that are long on talk and short on action.[51] As a result, several decades later, services and expansion have not improved, or have improved only marginally, in many of the countries. Previously existing infrastructure has decayed, the result being that in many previously well-served areas, irregular or no water supplies are the norm. Expansions of networks rarely occur. Even brand new purpose-built cities, such as Abuja, have not provided for the poorer areas around their environs. Thus, water and sanitation infrastructure may be provided for middle-class estates but not for the local communities that reside minutes away. Decaying infrastructure in established affluent areas, no infrastructure for newer neighbourhoods, and the total absence of networks in poorer and rural areas mean that the people often have to resort to their own resources. For the very poor, water is provided by human water carriers who charge per bucket, the result being that they pay considerably more—up to five to ten times more—than their more affluent residents.[52] For those who can afford it, boreholes are sunk. In the absence of regulations, rules, or planning permission, they are sunk indiscriminately, with sole determinants being need and affordability. As for sanitation, the surrounding environment is the toilet of the poor in the developing world, leading to unhealthy, unsanitary environments in poorer urban and rural areas.

A third problem arises from the state of the laws to regulate issues of water and sanitation. Generally speaking, not only do many of the countries lack physical infrastructure, they also have inadequate legal and regulatory environments that should provide the frameworks for the management of domestic water resources.

The question arises: if the problems associated with geothermal production and hydraulic fracturing are thrown into this already problematic mix, what will the effect on water resources be for of some of the world's most vulnerable people? Major disadvantages surround the fact that fracking processes utilize great amounts of water, contaminating it in the process. A knowledgeable source states that the water needed may be obtained from surface water, groundwater, municipal wastewater suppliers, treated wastewater from treatment facilities, power plant cooling water, and recycled produced water.[53] In the average developing country, where would this water be sourced? Most likely, it would come from the already contaminated rivers, lakes, and underground aquifers, thereby placing even greater strains on these water resources, further impairing quality and access.

sanitation and hygiene has come from the very top. This unprecedented level of support has been critical.'

[51] I. J. Goldface-Irokaibe, 'Water Management in Federal and Federal-Type Countries: Nigerian Perspectives' available at <http://www.forumfed.org/en/global/thematic/water_papers/Joe%20Goldface_en.pdf>; O. B. Akpor and M. Muchie, 'Challenges in Meeting the MDGs: The Nigerian Drinking Water Supply and Distribution Sector', (2011) 4(5) Journal of Environmental Science and Technology 480–9, available at <http://www.core.kmi.open.ac.uk/download/pdf/1048403>: H. O. Nwankwoala, 'Improving Water Resources Management in Nigeria: Policy Imperatives and Emerging Realities' (2011) 10(1) Scientia Africana 46–7.

[52] For example, people living in the slums of Jakarta, Manila, or Nairobi. See *The Right to Water* (n 39).

[53] 'Energy from Shale', available at <http://www.energyfromshale.org>.

V. Water vs energy: reconciling tensions

Issues relating to development, water, and energy are intertwined. Sustainable development is an impossibility in the absence of safe and available water supplies, and without people having access to modern energy services. Whilst energy impacts standards of living and quality of life, human and animal life on earth are not possible in the absence of water, and disease-free existence and productive longevity are unattainable if that water is contaminated. However, improved access to modern energy services enhances health and wellbeing through, for example, refrigeration, which ensures the preservation of vaccines and drugs, even as good health is necessary for one to harness the productivity and increased quality of life that improved access to energy brings. Where conflicts arise regarding the use of water resources for energy, or for other areas which impact on health or wellbeing, or where the use of energy impacts water quantity and quality, it is only logical for issues surrounding the preservation of water access and standards to prevail.

Both access to clean water and to improved energy services have been recognized as among the rights to development.[54] They are now best expressed in the Millennium Development Goals (MDGs), which were agreed upon by the world's sovereign states at the 2000 World Summit on Sustainable Development.[55] All these goals are dependent on access to clean water and sanitation, and to improved access to energy services. Even more than energy services, none of these goals are realizable in the absence of access to clean and uncontaminated water. So when tensions arise between these two important issues, what should the approach be? Faced with the development challenges of many African countries, which include lack of access to clean potable water, and the lack of access to modern energy services for the majority of the African population, can fracking be introduced into what is already a delicate and fragile mix? For example, should fracking be recommended in an environment where people are already suffering health challenges, including infant and maternal mortality, as the result of factors that include the use of water that is contaminated, but that is the only available source; or that is utilized in the absence of a regulatory framework that imposes standards for its use?

[54] First articulated by a Senegalese jurist, Keba M'baye and several years later, in 1986, proclaimed by the international community, in the United Nations Declaration on the Right to Development. See Keba M'baye, 'Le Droit du Developpement comme un Droit de l'Homme', (1972) 5 Revue des Droits de l'Homme 503–34. See also General Assembly Resolution A/RES/41/128 of 9 December 1986, available at <http://www.un.org>. This Declaration relied on the Universal Declaration of Human Rights, and the International Convention on Economic Social and Cultural Rights. See General Assembly Resolution 217A/III of 10 December 1986, available at <http://www.ohchr.org>; and United Nations Treaty Series, Vol 993, 3, <http://www.unhcr.org> and <http://www.un.org>.

[55] This momentous conference was held in Johannesburg, South Africa, 26 August–4 September 2002. See <http://www.un.org> and <http://www.millenniumproject.org>. These goals, which were to be attained by 2015, strike at the heart of extreme poverty and are as follows: Goal 1: Eradicate extreme poverty and hunger; Goal 2: Achieve universal primary education; Goal 3: Promote gender equality and empower women; Goal 4: Reduce child mortality; Goal 5: Improve maternal health; Goal 6: Combat HIV/AIDS, malaria, and other major diseases; Goal 7: Ensure environmental sustainability; Goal 8: Develop a global partnership for development.

Under such scenarios, will fracking improve or reduce the standard of living of the people in the poorer communities within most of the countries in Africa, if they decide to explore their shale reserves?[56]

Tensions exist between practices that adversely affect human life and the environment. So far, fracking is practised mainly in developed economies, which have regulatory and administrative procedures in place. In places lacking these frameworks, the effects are likely to be more devastating, with negative effects being disproportionately experienced by the poor. Going by the weight of evidence, the negative environmental and health effects of fracking are not in doubt. Its growth appears to be fed by needs of energy security on the part of the countries within which it is practised, the promise of great revenues to be earned by the companies, the prospects of jobs, and the presence of strong and wealthy lobbyist groups. There are clearly linkages between fracking and falling standards of health and safety in areas of operation. It is also clear that the practice involves the use of large amounts of water, a reduction in underground water supplies, and an increased risk of arsenic contamination. These are not issues that can be adequately dealt with in countries that presently lack an effective legal and administrative infrastructure. Introducing this will simply create a poisonous anti-environmental cocktail of terrifying proportions that will impact upon the already worrisome situation.

It appears that debates on whether or not to utilize technologies such as fracking subconsciously presuppose the existence of developed and viable legal and regulatory frameworks and infrastructure (similar to what pertains in the developing world) for the management and use of water. In fact, however, in many instances the existing frameworks and infrastructure fall far below these standards, and are therefore incapable of managing these new technologies.

VI. Legal frameworks for the regulation of water resources

The authority and ability of a state to regulate any sector, including its water resources, depends on the existence and content of its legal framework. This is a comparatively recently recognized fact that is growing in importance. Article 2 paragraph 1 of the Covenant on Economic, Social and Cultural Rights requires states to utilize 'all appropriate means, including particularly the adoption of legislative measures' in the implementation of their obligations under it. The position of the United Nations Economic and Social Council (ECOSOC) in General Comment No 15 goes further, stating that the right to water not only

[56] 'World Shale Gas Resources: An Initial Assessment of 14 Regions Outside the United States', April 2011, available at <http://www.eia.gov>; Technically Recoverable Shale Oil and Shale Gas Resources: An Assessment of 13 Formations in 41 Countries Outside the United States, 10 June 2013, available at <http://www.eia.gov>. It is noteworthy that every country that has been investigated has been found to have shale deposits. The reports did not assess sub-Saharan Africa at all, but the assumption here is that, based on the existence of shale in practically every area with hydrocarbon deposits, it is logical to reason that, even as practically all African countries have conventional petroleum deposits, so do they also have shale deposits.

exists, but is fundamental for securing an adequate standard of living. After showing the link between water and various articulated and non-controversial rights, it notes the imposition of the duties of Article 2 paragraph 1 and then proceeds to outline legislation, policies, and strategies in the same section.[57] However, it effectively de-emphasizes the role of legislation. Of the seven paragraphs in that section,[58] only one is on legal frameworks, and that section only mildly suggests the use of legislation as a means of ensuring national implementation, providing that 'states parties *may find it advantageous*[59] to adopt framework legislation to operationalize their right to water'. This non-assertive language is easy to ignore. However, the 1977 Action Plan of the Mar del Plata Water Conference, containing detailed recommendations for the enactment of water laws that are simple yet comprehensive, and that can be easily implemented by present administrative capacity, is phrased in stronger language and has been followed by several other pronouncements and declarations on the centrality of the law as an essential prerequisite for sustainable water management.[60]

Notwithstanding these, developing countries are often characterized by an absence of, or the existence of weak, legal frameworks.[61] A perusal of water and sanitation policies of some heavily impacted countries shows serious deficiencies. Whilst most countries have policies, road maps, and GoAL WaSH[62] documents, a 2012 status report on integrated water resources management, based on country self-assessments of progress made (which will predictably be more positive than independent assessments), still shows that many countries lack water laws, are not administering the laws they have, or have no plans for international water resource management.[63] Clearly, many have 'not found it advantageous' to enact effective legislation or to make the necessary reforms of their existing laws on water and sanitation. As a result, legal, regulatory, management, and administrative frameworks in countries that are severely impacted by problems of safe water and sanitation are totally incapable of producing meaningful change.

Various reasons are given for the poor state of the law. There is the widespread belief that:

> 'The water crisis is essentially a crisis of governance.' Lack of adequate water institutions, fragmented institutional structures, excessive diversion of public resources for private gain have impeded the effective management of water supplies.[64]

[57] Part V. 'Implementation at the National Level'.

[58] Section V of ECOSOC General Comment No 15.

[59] Emphasis added.

[60] For a succinct summary of the various calls for the adoption on functional water laws and policies at international conferences, see Salman and Bradlow (n 40). See also Report on the United Nations Water Conference, Mar del Plata, 14–25 March 1977, available at <http://www.internationalwaterlaw.org>.

[61] Salman and Bradlow (n 40).

[62] Governance, Advocacy and Leadership for Water, Sanitation and Hygiene, the water governance programme of the United Nations Development Programme (UNDP).

[63] *AMCOW 2012: 2012 Status Report on the Application of Integrated Approaches to Water Resources Management in Africa.*

[64] See Scanlon, Cassar, and Nemes (n 40) 17. The World Bank suggests that 20% to 40% of water sector finances are lost to dishonest and corrupt practices, which also lead to a 30% increase in

However, whilst problems of poor institutions and corruption represent real challenges, the biggest obstacles appear to be a lack of awareness by the general public of the critical importance of water and sanitation to sustainable development, coupled with the lack of political will at the highest levels to address the problem. This writer therefore agrees with an analysis of the self-assessments by various African governments in the 2012 report of the African Ministers' Council on Water as follows:[65]

> The reasons African governments cite for not implementing integrated water management policies or meeting commitments they have made to provide sanitation are many and varied . . . A survey of officials by UNEP in 40 African countries suggests they are not mainly constrained by a lack of money.
>
> Congo-Brazzaville, Nigeria and Sierra Leone don't even have a formal water policy . . . São Tomé and Principe said it did not have the necessary laws in place; Cameroon said it had no one to champion the cause of water provision, and 25 countries, including Namibia, Swaziland, Rwanda and Mozambique, said they did not have enough human capacity.
>
> Some governments were brutally honest about their failings. Congo-Brazzaville said it could not get the private sector or civil society interested, Burundi that it had experienced too many changes of ministries, and Ghana that it had problems collecting revenue from local sources. Liberia said it had difficulty accessing donor funds, and Libya and Zimbabwe said they did not have the infrastructure.

Legal and regulatory frameworks, which provide standards and guidelines aimed at ensuring universal access for all, and are in line with established criteria and guidelines, are essential and exist in all the developed countries. These clearly defined legal frameworks are utilized to achieve desired aims and objectives, and to regulate and ensure conformity with established parameters. The United States has a very developed legal framework, and the average industry is subject to stringent regulations. In addition to enunciated policy statements, laws are enacted in line with the directives of federal policy. Under US environmental law, there are stringent rules of disclosure. In an effort to circumvent this, the only lawful mechanism was to amend existing laws, and to make an exception for the practice (fracking) in the industry (shale gas production) that the government wanted to encourage. The solution? The Halliburton Loophole, which exempted industry from the current rules of disclosure. In a country with an undeveloped legal framework, various companies would simply have conducted their practices without adequate guidelines and standards, with attendant negative consequences upon people and the environment. If fracking is introduced into jurisdictions with weak legal controls, one shudders to think of what could happen.

household connection costs: 'WIN, UNESCO Partner to Fight Corruption in Water Sector', eWash, Nigeria's News on Water, Sanitation and Hygiene, available at <http://assemblyonline.info/eWASH>.

[65] 'Water and Sanitation Still not Top Priorities for African Governments', Water Sports Blog, 31 August 2012, <http://www.water-sports.blogsport.com>, commenting on *Status Report on the Application of Integrated Approaches to Water Resources Management in Africa 2012,* available at <http://www.unwater.org> and <http://www.amcow-online.org>.

Compromise positions aimed at continuing the exploitation of shale gas and providing optimal protection for the environment must revolve around legal mechanisms, such as the following:[66]

- promoting maximum contaminant levels allowed in water for all chemicals used in fracking;
- closing the Halliburton Loophole through an Act of Congress;
- mandating public disclosure of all chemicals used in fracking in the United States;
- mandating the inspection of concrete casing inside well bores;
- mandating storage of toxic fluid from fracking into tanks;
- mandating the injection of tracers in the fracking fluid so that inspectors can easily see whether any of the fluids end up in the water used in residential homes;
- mandating tests of aquifers and drinking water wells for chemicals before drilling begins, and then during the process of gas extraction, so that the changes in groundwater are evident.

These can only be achieved through legal mechanisms that involve the use of primary and subsidiary legislation. They also presuppose the existence of an already fairly developed water and sanitation system, which is still lacking in many African countries. Until there is some improvement, affected developing countries simply cannot cope with the extra stress that the underground technologies will bring, and they risk exacerbating already adverse environmental conditions that militate against sustainable development.

VII. Needed: a strategic approach

African countries need to take a strategic approach to whether or not to utilize the underground technologies that have been the focus of this chapter. The decision to allow the use of these processes must be based on a realistic assessment of needs, capabilities, and existing legal and administrative structures. First, from preceding sections, it is apparent that both the exploitation of geothermal resources and the processes of fracking can have negative effects on the environment and health of people. Second, it has been made clear that access to water and safe sanitation are major issues plaguing the developing world, including most African countries. Third, existing water and sanitation infrastructure and legal frameworks in the majority of these countries cannot cope with present problems, and thus cannot cope with additional problems, particularly those that incorporate comparatively high technology. The average sub-Saharan country is unlikely to be able to provide

[66] 'Safety First, Fracking Second: Drilling for Natural Gas has Gotten Ahead of the Science Needed to Prove it Safe', available at <http://www.scientificamerican.com/article.cfm?id=safety-first-fracking-second>.

mitigation against the additional pressures that will arise from the use of fracking and geothermal processes. Whilst many of these countries are in need of modern energy, whether it has to come from geothermal or shale gas is another matter. Increased energy access should be in line with principles of sustainable development, and with the need to uphold fundamental human rights, and to protect the people and their environments. Africa is a continent with many energy options; one need not be at the expense of the other.

Each country's approach must, of necessity, be driven by its particular needs, backed by adequate and effective legal and regulatory frameworks that allow for the successful implementation of the country's chosen strategy. Considering the basic needs for sustainable development, improved energy access, and access to clean water, three broad groups of countries are identifiable. The first group consists of fuel-deficient countries that remain dependent on exports for their modern fuel needs, which are presently primarily derived from petroleum and natural gas. As discussed in the preceding sections, this is an increasingly dwindling group, as promising discoveries continue to be made all over the continent. The second group consists of petroleum-producing countries that have not yet attained self-sufficiency, or have not become exporters. The third group is made up of petroleum-exporting countries. Each of these groups contains two sub-groups, consisting of those that are found to have commercial shale deposits and those that do not. Exactly which countries are in which group cannot presently be ascertained with great accuracy, as the borders are constantly shifting, and will continue to do so as exploration for the various energy sources continues.

All countries have to recognize the need to improve their policy, legal, and administrative frameworks if they are to achieve success in issues of water access and sanitation. In addition, they need to realize that undeveloped policy and legal frameworks mean that they have fewer responsible options as to energy sources. Having a functional legal and administrative framework in place means that a country can then decide on what its best options are, based more on its needs and less on its capability.

Established exporters, such as Nigeria, Gabon, Angola, and Equatorial Guinea, remain energy poor and plagued by problems of energy and water access. All still contain territory that has not been explored for petroleum resources and—like all of sub-Saharan Africa—shale resources. For these countries, impacts of fracking may lie in the effects that the resulting increased self-sufficiency of major trading partners have on their economies. After all, President Barack Obama of the United States told African countries with oil deposits that the United States did not need their oil because of the recent increases in oil and gas production, largely driven by advances in technology for hydraulic fracturing.[67] For these countries, what do the

[67] 'Can Obama's Africa Power Plan Hold a Candle to China?' available at <http://www.reuters.com/article/2013/07/02/africa-investment-idUSL5N0F821520130702>. Obama's remarks were widely reported in the Nigerian press. See, for example, Sam Nda Isaiah, 'Obama's Stark Message to Nigeria', available at <http://www.thescoopng.com/sam-nda-isaiah-obamas-stark-message-to-nigeria/.>

new underground technologies portend for their economic progress and development? The opinion of this author is that many of them are yet to adequately utilize existing conventional reserves, and so have no immediate need for the comparatively expensive unconventional technologies that are unlikely to translate into energy for the use of those that presently have no access to conventional sources. However, the economies of these countries will definitely be impacted by reduced sales to major trading partners. For these countries, fracking also impacts their economies and sustainable development, albeit in a different way. Their challenge, from the moment of realization (which hopefully will occur sooner rather than later), is to develop strategies that encourage energy self-sufficiency, develop new trading relationships, and diversify their economies so as to reduce present dependencies on petroleum.

All African countries have one positive feature in common: the existence of sizeable untapped renewable energy resources. Irrespective of circumstances, a major focus should therefore be on measures that encourage their utilization, such as the creation of investor-friendly environments incorporating legal and administrative frameworks that promote stability, protect investor funds, and guarantee a safe return on investments. African states are better off utilizing other options apart from fracking. It should also be remembered that present economics make it an economically viable alternative. In a lower priced era—and fluctuating prices are an inevitable feature of the petroleum industry—fracking will be less viable. It is probably in the interests of less affluent countries to consider energy sources that will be relatively sustainable when economic conditions change. Maybe then the voices of environmentalists will finally be heard, and fracking will be seen as an environmentally hazardous practice that is a violation of the rights to life, and to a healthy environment.

25

Conclusion

Donald N. Zillman, Aileen McHarg,
Lila K. Barrera-Hernández, and Adrian Bradbrook

I. Introduction

Scientific, technological, economic, and political developments in the past decade have changed important assumptions about what the world energy picture will look like in the near future. As we discuss in *The Law of Energy Underground*, many of these developments involve subsurface activities like unconventional oil and gas extraction, carbon capture and storage, geothermal energy, disposal of nuclear waste and spent fuel, carbon fuel storage, and undergrounding of electricity and other energy infrastructure.

Some of these underground developments offer the potential to increase the supply of energy worldwide and to change long-standing balances of power. Most notably, this is true for the growth in the production of unconventional oil and gas resources—shale oil and gas, tight gas, coal bed methane, and methane hydrate among others. Geothermal energy, which is a renewable, climate-friendly source, also offers an increase in total energy production. Other underground developments promise to mitigate some of the objections to the continuing use of existing energy sources. Carbon capture and storage (CCS) and deep underground repositories for nuclear waste disposal are examples. These developments share legal issues such as insurance, long-term liability, and damage resulting from leakage.

Law has played an important role in the development of all uses of energy. Part I of this book reviewed the growth of national laws governing property rights in and ownership of energy found underground. Part II discussed the increasing significance of international law in energy underground issues. Part III examined the potentially game-changing boom in the production of unconventional oil and gas. Part IV examined manners in which the underground has been employed to advance sustainable solutions to environmental problems. Part V provided case studies of where the law can offer guidance and possibly resolution to national and regional conflicts, which often involve multiple uses of the underground.

In this concluding chapter, we summarize in Sections II to V the work of the authors who have contributed to writing this book. In Section VI, we examine important implications of new developments in the law of energy underground. In particular, we emphasize the connectedness of energy decisions. A change in the supply of one energy resource may have implications for other energy resources, for instance. Likewise, objections to the environmental impacts of one energy resource may have implications for the prospects of an alternative energy resource.

Our conclusion, in Section VII, centres on the law and looks to the future. What are the challenges that the law and legal institutions must meet if the continued economic growth of energy development is to be balanced with environmental quality and social equity? Achieving sound policies for striking this balance will require an alignment of science and technology, economics and finance, and legal and political frameworks. We hope that attention to these values can guide the energy world of the next decade and beyond.

II. Property rights in underground resources

As explored in Part I, 'Property Rights in Underground Resources', the law has played an important role in the development of all energy uses. Property law is one of the major legal pillars of the law relating to energy. AAG authors considered the development of property law in its application to energy and natural resources in previous studies, most notably in *Property and the Law in Energy and Natural Resources* (2009).[1] As stated by the editors of that volume:

> The law of energy and natural resources has always had a strong focus on property as one of its components. Property law has had a strong influence on the development of core legal principles in the governance of energy and natural resources, from the definition of rights of control and access, to the institutional structures for resource exploitation and conservation.[2]

The 2009 volume made two important general findings: (1) As time has gone on, the state has played a greater role in the management of natural resources in most legal systems, co-existing with, but generally not displacing, systems of private property rights; and (2) whilst property law may have ancient origins, it has proven to be highly resilient and capable of adapting to the technological developments of various energy sectors.[3]

To what extent, however, do these findings hold good for the new technologies that are the subject matter of *The Law of Energy Underground?* Do the same property law principles that apply to traditional ('conventional') fossil fuel development extend to 'unconventional' oil and gas production, as well as to gas storage, geothermal energy, CCS, and nuclear waste disposal? Have governments been more interventionist in legislating specifically to establish new legal management regimes for new underground energy developments?

[1] A. McHarg, B. Barton, A. Bradbrook, and L. Godden (eds), *Real Property and the Law in Energy and Natural Resources* (2009).

[2] McHarg et al (n 1) at 1.

[3] McHarg et al (n 1) at 1–2.

The application of property law to underground energy resources is assessed by Barry Barton. He makes the point that property law provides default rules to regulate resources in situations where the legislature has failed to establish legal management regimes and where no other legal framework (such as contracts or trusts) exists.

The primary common law rule really is ancient! The *cujus est solum* doctrine (whoever owns the soil also owns, without limitation, the airspace above it and the subsurface below) has its origin in Roman law or Jewish law. It was first applied by the common law in 1586.[4] It continues to serve as the default rule in the common law, and indeed in other legal 'families' studied in Part I, placing all subsurface rights in the hands of the surface owner. In contemporary practice, however, the rules of ownership are set by either a grant between (or among) the parties or by legislation putting those rights in state hands.

A major contribution made by Barton's chapter is the resolution of the issue as to whether the downwards application of *cujus es solem* extends indefinitely in application, or whether there are limitations in its application to areas near the surface. This issue has been in doubt for a long time. These doubts have been strengthened in modern times by cases deciding that in respect of the maxim's upward application, there is a limitation to the airspace that the landowner can effectively use.[5] Barton's case analysis shows that the underground application of the *cujus es solum* doctrine has no such limitation and the maxim is unfettered. In effect, absent intervening legislation, the surface owner's rights to minerals and other substances underground are increased vis-à-vis those of other claimants. Barton also explains that the vacant spaces left by extraction of minerals do not belong to the owner of the minerals but rather to the surface owner. This principle also extends to pore spaces. These conclusions have far-reaching implications for the development of gas storage and CCS.

In practice, legislation in the vast majority of jurisdictions, during the late nineteenth and twentieth centuries, has vested all minerals in the state. That vesting leaves the *cujus est solum* principle untouched, as is shown by Barton's discussion of the *Bocardo* case.[6] But, if the subsoil, as opposed to the minerals in it, is so vested, then *cujus est solum* is displaced. The major exception is the United States. As discussed by Terence Daintith, except on those public lands retained by state or federal government, private mineral ownership still predominates and is still regulated by common law principles. Unlike in other common law jurisdictions, the rule of capture is still of prime importance in resolving ownership rights to fluid resources in the United States. Daintith goes on to explain how the common law has or is likely to resolve ownership and other legal issues (such as liability for leakage) involving new initiatives like horizontal drilling and hydraulic fracturing for shale oil and gas, tight gas, and coal bed methane. Whilst common law principles

[4] *Bury v Pope* (1586) Cro Eliz 118; 78 ER 375.

[5] See, e.g., *Bendal Pty Ltd v Mirvac Project Pty Ltd* (1991) 23 NSWLR 464; *LIP Investments Pty Ltd v Howard Chia Investment Pty Ltd* (1989) 24 NSWLR 490.

[6] See chapter 2.

exist to resolve these issues, it appears that in disputes between the surface owner and the mineral owner, the states' (e.g., Texas, New York) courts are currently divided, complicating the condition of the law and introducing uncertainty into investors' decisions.

Chapters in Part V add to the discussion of property rights. Nigel Bankes addresses the issue of conflicts between and among different potential users of the same underground space. These are important matters given the expanded underground uses that are the subject of the book. Quite plausibly, the same parcel of underground land could simultaneously be of interest to explorers of unconventional oil and gas, to existing producers of conventional oil and gas, to companies wishing to store petroleum and natural gas temporarily, and to developers of CCS projects. What rules of priority and deference should apply? Bankes offers a number of legal techniques that may be used to reduce the risk of conflicting uses of underground spaces including declaratory legislation, regulatory terms and conditions, and indemnity arrangements.

These Canadian common law issues find their counterpart in Dutch civil law, as Martha Roggenkamp and Danielle Hanema discuss. The large percentage of the Dutch underground that already hosts commercial activity emphasizes the importance of the topic. Many jurisdictions may provide solutions to existing conflicts in individual situations. But, as argued by Gunther Kühne, as well as by Roggenkamp and Hanema, there is a need to develop underground planning law principles in order to cope with potential conflicts prospectively.

The relevant property issues involving new energy technologies in civil countries, as well as mixed civil and common law countries, are considered in separate chapters in Part I by José Juan González and by Hanri Mostert and Meyer van den Berg. A fundamental point made by González is that in many civil law countries, most natural resources are ruled by the national property doctrine. As a result, new underground activity has to be the subject of new regulatory schemes. In many jurisdictions, particularly in Spain and its former colonies, all mines and minerals were declared to be the property of the state. In some countries, such as Indonesia, state mineral ownership is mandated by the country's constitution; in others, such as France, the state has reserved or retaken mineral ownership by legislation. Mostert and Van den Berg's study of the Republic of South Africa, Namibia, and the Roman-Dutch and German legal legacies provides a fascinating blend of common law and civil law approaches. It emphasizes the broad state interest expressed in the emerging custodianship doctrine and it recognizes that property law concepts begun in colonial and Apartheid eras have needed to change to provide the benefits of national energy resources to the entire population.

All the chapters lead to the unlikely conclusion that as to the ownership of minerals, there is now more similarity between civil law jurisdictions and English and Commonwealth law than between English and United States' common law. Except in the United States, state ownership or, at the least, control has become the norm. Perhaps, as noted by Daintith in other contexts, state ownership is thought to be un-American!

From a conceptual framework, it appears that there is a difference in understanding between common law and civil law countries as to the meaning of 'public domain'. Iñigo del Guayo and José Alenza explore this difference in Part V. The concept is broader in civil law jurisdictions. In Spain, for example, 'Public Domain' refers not only to intellectual property but also to property in common areas such as beaches, rivers, and mines. Based on Roman law concepts of *res communis omnium*, *res nullius*, or *res extra commercium*, 'Public Domain' ensures that there is no private ownership in these areas and that, instead, ownership is vested in the state. The Spanish Constitution declares that every type of resource, whatever its form may be, is subject to the general national interest. This type of reasoning seems foreign to common law, which focuses on the protection of individual property rights.

Another concept that may be less familiar to the common law is that of the social function of property. In Latin America and other jurisdictions, as explained by González, an owner's unfettered right to use, enjoy, and dispose of land is generally subject to the public interest. The distinction is of significance, particularly in relation to the public interest in environmental protection vis-à-vis new uses of the underground.

There are several lessons to be drawn from Part V. First, except in the United States, the trend to move away from private ownership of resources continues. In common law jurisdictions, this means there are fewer applications of common law principles and, instead, more legislative intervention. Second, whilst conceptual differences remain, in practical terms, there is a convergence between common law and civil law jurisdictions in relation to the property rights in resources. Third, as González argues convincingly, strategic public interest considerations are more important in civil law than in common law jurisdictions in the development of resources law. Fourth, the idea of rating resources as *res publicae* (public property) is fundamental to the thinking of civil lawyers. Finally, we are moving closer to establishing a clearer understanding of the property law rules for determining underground energy resources, as well as to determining how these rules might respond to technological change.

III. The international law treatment of subsurface resources

Catherine Redgwell and Lavanya Rajamani introduce the overall structure of international law in 2014 and its particular implications for energy underground law and policy. The authors remind us of the connectedness of energy matters around the world. The chapters discussing property and unconventional oil and gas emphasize the change in oil and gas law as it has gone from having once been a matter of interest and right only for land owners, mineral owners, and extraction companies to now being a realm in which government—as regulator, facilitator, and property owner—plays a more significant role. In similar fashion, international law has become a very relevant part of energy law in a growing number of facets beyond oil and gas.

The major factor driving the growth of international law in energy has been the increasing number of matters that are undeniably more than just the concern of a single nation. Concerns over climate change provide the most powerful example. What China and the United States do and do not do with regard to greenhouse gas emissions from their respective vehicles, industries, and militaries seriously impacts on the entire world. But even the most environment-friendly nation cannot solve the problem of climate change by itself. Other environmental issues of international concern include threats or damage to oceans, rivers, rain forests, and biodiversity.

Beyond environmental matters, international trade in energy resources continues to grow, and it demands a legal structure that can effectively cross national boundaries. Whether issues are addressed via private law agreements among residents of many nations, or by government-to-government agreements, or by universal statements of principle backed by legally binding enforcement, energy law has an international flavour.

Redgwell and Rajamani recognize the evolution of international law moving from traditional customary law (often created by diplomatic negotiations between and among nations) to an increasing number of written treaties between and among nations. They also examine the growth of 'understandings' crafted and implemented by governments, private businesses, established non-governmental organizations (NGOs), and ad hoc coalitions of citizens. The product of this work can be legally binding 'hard law' or non-binding—but often highly important—'soft law'.

These frameworks set out by Redgwell and Rajamani are reflected in other chapters. As Kazuhiro Nakatani shows, Japan's expansion of mineral extraction capabilities has been aided by international rules on ocean jurisdiction. Lila K. Barrera-Hernández explains that Argentina's efforts to develop shale gas need to deal with international standards of the acquisition of property by governments. Wang Mingyuan and Jin Feng stress the potential for domestic advancements in CCS technologies to become export industries. Kühne, McHarg and Poustie, del Guayo and Alenza, and Roggenkamp and Hamena all explore aspects of the European Union's supranational direction or guidance over what would once have been merely national energy decisions. Yinka Omorogbe examines the potential for international development standards to build healthier and wealthier societies for some of the least-favoured citizens of the world. Finally, almost every country that we have studied keeps a close eye on present and potential development of climate change mitigation standards.

IV. Unconventional oil and gas extraction

No aspect of underground energy development in the past decade has received greater public attention than the remarkable growth in the production of oil and gas from unconventional underground sources. Production of these two resources has been made possible by the improvement of techniques such as horizontal drilling and hydraulic fracturing. This boom in unconventionals is also attributed to attractive investment in the industry, as well as satisfactory political and legal arrangements.

The chapter by Alistair Lucas, Theresa Watson, and Eric Kimmel, and that by LeRoy Paddock and Jessica Wentz, examine aspects of the United States and Canada experience with unconventionals. The two North American countries lead the world in the actual implementation of unconventional oil and gas production. Unconventional activity in the Province of Alberta has added to the already rich energy reserves of that Province. Production from other Canadian Provinces may add to the nation's wealth. The site of production of unconventionals in the United States ranges from the traditional oil and gas state of Texas, to shale oil production in the state of North Dakota, and to the Marcellus shale gas belt, which itself is spread across the states of Pennsylvania, New York, Ohio, and West Virginia. Paddock and Wentz provide a fascinating compare-and-contrast study of unconventional development on federal land (i.e., land owned by the United States government), which has occurred primarily in the western states, and unconventional development in the eastern states of New York and Pennsylvania, where there is far less federal land. Whilst Pennsylvania has embraced the shale gas boom, New York has resisted it. Other state and municipal governments are currently facing similar decisions.

Unconventional oil and gas development is less prevalent in other nations. Studies of potential for such development indicate that numerous nations around the world have the ability to increase (or initiate) oil and gas production from unconventional sources. Parts III and V provide case studies that range from South America to Africa to Australia to East Asia and to Europe. Those studies in Part III—Milton Montoya on Colombia, Barrera-Hernández on Argentina, Mohammed Bekhechi on Algeria, and Nakatani on Japan—involve countries that have expressed a strong interest in moving forward with unconventional oil and gas development.

Sceptics or outright opponents of unconventional development include such diverse nations as France, Russia, Germany, and some of those comprising sub-Saharan Africa. A mix of economic, environmental, and political reasons is cited for this scepticism or opposition. Sergey Seliverstov reports that Russia has deemed unconventionals to be simply unnecessary, given that its conventional resources of oil and gas are vast. Kühne explains that Germany regards unconventional oil and gas development as contrary to its *energiewend*, which calls for the nation to decrease its reliance on all fossil fuels and nuclear power and, in turn, to replace them with carbon-free renewables. Omorogbe's assessment of sub-Saharan Africa concludes that unconventional oil and gas development would harm water needs and democratic growth.

Colombia and Algeria are exemplary of those nations that desire to expand oil and gas production from unconventionals. As Montoya and Bekhechi emphasize, a boom in unconventional production could have enormous positive implications for the respective national economies. These authors also explain, however, that both countries are wrestling with how to protect the environment without discouraging investment in unconventionals.

The studies of Canada and the United States recognize the value of well-established property law in advancing the new unconventional enterprises. That property law has identified the issues involved in determining property rights of surface owners and owners of subsurface resources. These understandings have provided the bases for either private contractual agreements that adopt or modify long-standing property understandings or legislative amendments of prior legal standards. All of the studies emphasize that governmental interest will play a large role in the development (or not) of unconventional oil and gas resources. The chapters examine the different roles that government can play.

In the United States, where oil and gas regulation is a matter primarily of state—not federal—competence, early legislation and case law focused on the prevention of wasteful and dangerous practices in the interests of neighbouring oil producers and royalty owners. Whilst some legislatures recognized a general public interest in the conservation of these resources, it was not until the 1930s that courts fully accepted that such an interest could provide a constitutionally acceptable basis for government regulation of oil and gas production.

Different governmental objectives inspired worker health and safety legislation. The hazards to workers in underground coal mines and nuclear facilities provide strong justifications for government involvement. Land use and zoning laws address the impacts of oil and gas developments on surrounding human habitation. These laws were an early recognition of the importance of the NIMBY ('not in my back yard') principle. The impacts of unconventional oil and gas extraction should not be allowed to take place where they would have too negative an impact on human habitation. Extraction remains subject to government regulatory mandates and prohibitions.

A highly important question is who benefits from production of unconventional oil and gas. Traditional oil and gas law has shaped the rewards structure between the owner of the subsurface minerals or the right to extract them (often the farmer, rancher, other private landowner, or a unit of government) and the enterprise doing the actual exploration for and extraction of the oil and gas. The normal rewards to the resource owner are a combination of an initial bonus for allowing the extraction company to explore and produce, a regular series of rental payments to keep the lease operative, and royalties from or a percentage of the financial benefits of any production that actually occurs. The approach places most of the economic risk on the oil and gas company. If it takes no exploratory action (for example, because the prices for oil and gas are too low), it still must pay the signing bonus and rentals. The mineral rights owner pays nothing and takes those financial benefits. Normally, however, both the oil and gas company and the owner want to see production. That is the primary source of substantial revenue for both parties potentially for decades into the future.

These forms of revenue sharing will characterize most unconventional oil and gas activities. However, what has become increasingly important is what benefits governments and their citizens will receive. Nakatani's chapter on Japan and Barrera-Hernández's chapter on Argentina consider different aspects of the broad rights of the national government. The revision of the venerable 1950 Mining Act in Japan makes clear that the wide variety of mineral resources (including oil and gas) is to be developed for the benefit of Japan. Argentina moves forward with unconventional development in the interesting posture of recently having taken over private interests in existing oil and gas ventures. Judicial actions will decide the legitimacy of Argentina's actions and what, if any, compensation it will owe to the former private owners.

Another inquiry is which unit(s) of government will benefit from development revenues? As discussed by Lucas, Watson, and Kimmel, and by Paddock and Wentz, for countries like Canada and the United States, both the federal (i.e., national) government and the state (New York or Pennsylvania) or provincial (Alberta) government desire a share of the revenues—and, of course, one as large as possible. Michael Crommelin offers Australian perspectives on control and benefit at the national and sub-national realms. In some situations, long-standing constitutional provisions or assumptions of sovereignty may decide who gets what money. Even if rules have been promulgated, legislation can shift revenues to another unit of government.

The chapters make clear the importance of environmental issues in unconventional development. Even advocates for aggressive unconventional oil and gas development recognize that techniques such as hydraulic fracturing place burdens on environmental values beyond those arising from conventional oil and gas extraction practices. A list of prominent 'fracking' harms includes the contamination and the (excessive) consumption of water resources, the release of air pollutants (e.g., greenhouse gases), the stimulation of seismic activity, and heavy surface disruption (e.g., air, light, and noise pollution) from the development of the wells. Different authors are concerned with different factors—both in terms of how likely the risk of harm may be and of how serious that harm may be. They also recognize that, on the one hand, new technologies improve with experience, but on the other, limited experience has not revealed all of the risks for and harms to the environment.

Fracking debates have also put the right to know, access to information, and other public participation issues on the front burner. Around the world, the availability of full and reliable information on the potential impacts of fracking is at the centre of public and governmental attitudes towards the acceptability of unconventional development. Thus, some governments, such as those in Germany and the state of New York, have put the development of unconventionals on hold until its environmental impact is assessed more thoroughly. Not surprisingly, in some jurisdictions where developers are required to submit more information, such as in Alberta where fracking fluid disclosure is required, the developers seem to face less public resistance. In Argentina, conversely, closed-door negotiations concerning the shale gas development of Vaca Muerta have been conducted among federal authorities, provincial authorities, and Chevron and YPF. This lack of transparency has been a source of increasing opposition to the development of unconventionals in Argentina.

V. Renewable and sustainable underground uses

The chapters that comprise Part IV suggest that with the right technology and legal framework, the potential of earth's subsoil to contribute to energy sustainability is considerable. As explained by Donald N. Zillman, deep underground nuclear waste repositories provide the best solution to the issue of how to dispose of nuclear waste and spent nuclear fuel. Expanding the potential of nuclear energy is directly tied to political and legal decisions on how to use the underground. Likewise, other critical infrastructure siting decisions, such as underground electricity substations, or 'cleaning up' the fossil fuel sector through reliance on CCS, also require a set of rules dealing with the subsoil. In addition, according to Adrian Bradbrook and Anita Rønne, the earth's subsoil may harbour enormous renewable energy. However, this 'may' in the authors' statement points to another significant and pervasive theme throughout the book: uncertainty.

As explained by Seliverstov, by creating a special ad hoc regime and leaving the existing regulations untouched, Russia's approach to siting its first underground electricity substations in Skolkovo, near Moscow, avoided the opportunity to provide regulatory answers on how to achieve the difficult balance between efficient energy development and environmental protection in underground siting decisions. Nor does it provide a clear-cut answer to whether the construction of underground substations falls under Russia's legislation on the use of the subsoil. In the end, though interesting, the case study 'does not allow for an accurate estimate of the difficulties to be confronted by similar projects' in the future.

Moreover, Zillman's account of the inability of democratic governments around the world to find a replicable approach to nuclear waste disposal is striking. Not even the US, the world's largest nuclear power, with a successful nuclear waste siting experience under its belt (WIPP), has been able to design a political and legal framework to provide a definitive answer to dealing with the permanent disposal of commercial nuclear waste.

'Uncertainty' is also the word of the day when it comes to the future of CCS. Effective development and commercial deployment of CCS is essential if the continued use of fossil fuels for electricity generation is to be compatible with serious climate change mitigation efforts. It is therefore particularly relevant for developing economies (such as China) as a means of reconciling their legitimate desire for increased energy use, whilst constraining their carbon emissions. However, whilst China's intentions to develop cleaner fossil energies of high-efficiency and near zero emission of CO_2 are laudable, it is clear from the chapter written by Wang and Jin that the country is 'hitting a wall' in its CCS efforts. Indeed, the uncertainty derived from the international community's inability to move ahead in setting new climate change targets is reflected in legal inaction at home. The authors point to the lack of national abatement targets and a regulatory framework for CCS as significant barriers to CCS development in China.

In contrast, McHarg and Poustie describe the United Kingdom's considerable and leading efforts to advance CCS. They observe that government must serve as both a promoter/facilitator of the technology and a regulator of its environmental and social consequences. Nevertheless, the technological, economic, and environmental uncertainties involved in the development of CCS pose particularly challenging political and regulatory problems. Despite extensive efforts, it is not clear that the United Kingdom has yet done enough to make CCS a commercial reality.

In a chapter that steps back from the specifics of any particular jurisdiction, Lital Helman, Endre Stavang, and Gideon Parchomovsky offer a staged approach to developing CCS policies that are more environmentally friendly—in the sense of ensuring net environmental gains. They make optimistic assumptions that CCS will eventually gain traction as a meaningful tool to bridge the gap between fossil fuel use and environmental sustainability. However, echoing McHarg and Poustie's findings, the authors admit that '[b]ecause of the considerable uncertainty concerning the scope of risks associated with CCS at this stage, and the low (or non-existent) cost of carbon relative to it, even the most effective regulatory systems cannot provide sufficient incentive for private parties to engage in CCS'. Further, they stress the often understated fact that at the current stage of CCS technological development, its true environmental effect is as yet unknown.

Notwithstanding the above, dealing with uncertainty is often the motor behind developments in the legal landscape. That is the case of Australia and other common law jurisdictions tackled by Bradbrook and Rønne and by Crommelin, where the development of the legal framework for geothermal energy responds to the need to move away from the uncertainty derived from applying common law principles to regulating the use of new natural resources. Likewise, the decision-making framework for CCS implementation proposed by Helman, Stavang, and Parchomovsky aims to close the uncertainty gap faced by potential investors in any given jurisdiction by proposing policy and regulatory solutions to problems of technology, siting, and liability.

The sure-and-steady support of geothermal energy development in Denmark and other EU Member States, as reflected in their legal frameworks, stands in stark contrast to the uncertainty that prevails in connection to other uses of the underground. That is due to the Community's early commitment to climate change action under the Kyoto Protocol. Following prompts from EU law, the Netherlands, Denmark, and Germany offered advanced legal frameworks for geothermal energy development. However, as Kühne demonstrates in the case of Germany, those jurisdictions that rely on principles of mining law have to face two problems: (1) the traditional and undynamic character of mining law in general; and (2) the inadequacies of that law with regard to the specifics of geothermal energy—as opposed to solid or fluid minerals.

In the face of uncertainty, governments are willing to trust technology and science to deliver sustainable solutions to complex environmental problems. Indeed, governments around the world seem to approach the uncertainty that pervades the energy and sustainability connection with a willingness to accept increasingly higher levels of risk concerning their use of the underground. Persistent reliance on nuclear energy, development of pilot CCS projects, and even the development of geothermal resources (sometimes involving fracking-like technologies) seems to reflect an unwavering and naïve or stubborn trust in humanity's ingenuity in the face of uncertainty. As reported in this Part, no tightening of the environmental law framework has been introduced to accompany the development of underground energy activities. Unlike in the responses to hydraulic fracturing for oil and gas, there are yet no moratoria on potentially earthquake-producing activities, like CCS and geothermal energy production. Rather, governments seem to operate from the premise that the sustainability of current policy choices can be achieved, eventually, through funding R&D. Existing environmental laws and regulations, equipped with standard tools such as requirements of emissions caps and environmental impact assessments, suffice. However, the question needs to be asked: at what point do the principles of sustainable development, such as the precautionary principle and intergenerational equity, come into play? Like Sweden's SKB, discussed in chapter 17 on nuclear waste, is it enough to declare that the generation that benefited from the nuclear power has an obligation to solve the problems left in its wake? Where and when should a country draw the line and stop prioritizing the present over the future? These and similar questions are being asked by a global civil society increasingly reluctant to play the part of the silent bystander.

Accordingly, most jurisdictions reviewed in *The Law of Energy Underground* seem to pick up on the need to promote inclusiveness. Authors refer to public participation as an essential component of the legal and regulatory framework for underground development. Although there may be a tension between the desire to provide certainty for investors in developing major underground infrastructure and the provision of opportunities for public participation which could potentially derail those plans, a transparent and inclusive process that takes into account legitimate public interests and concerns ultimately poses fewer political risks. Remarkably, despite the negative connotation usually attached to the idea of nuclear waste disposal, Zillman's account of the US experience with the City of Carlsbad demonstrates that good faith consultations combined with full disclosure and adequate environmental review can ultimately deliver solutions to address even the hardest energy-related problems. Experience in the United States also reinforces the idea that when dealing with fracking, opposition to it is stronger when the projects are for-profit and do not offer tangible, long-term benefits to host communities.

Finally, international cooperation in the form of agreements, pilot projects, and technology transfer plays a significant role in many of the underground uses reviewed in this Part. According to Zillman, for instance, '[m]ore than any other energy source, nuclear regulation has inspired international treaties, agreements, etc'. Additionally, EU law is a significant driver behind the development of geothermal capacity and the regulation of carbon capture across that continent. Climate change negotiations, and the development of carbon pricing mechanisms, have a significant impact on all current uses, and on the future of CCS in particular.

VI. What happens next?

The projections of both the US Energy Information Administration and the International Energy Agency regarding energy supplies and energy uses a quarter-century into the future recognize the wide range of factors that can influence the energy big picture in 2040. The ground-breaking changes considered in *The Law of Energy Underground* make such predictions even more difficult. With those caveats, where are the developments in unconventional oil and gas, geothermal, and underground waste disposal likely to lead?

Canada and the United States have proven that large reserves of gas and oil shale, coal bed methane, tight gas, and other unconventionals can be extracted for profit. Worldwide geological studies indicate that at least several dozen other nations spread widely across the world have similar reserves that can be developed.

The experiences of the United States and Canada also indicate the potentially transformational nature of unconventional oil and gas development. North America could become self-sufficient in both oil and natural gas. Both Canada and the United States could also become major exporters. These are changes with major impacts on the world economy and on geo-politics.

The studies from Argentina, Colombia, Algeria, and Japan reflect similar enthusiasm for unconventional development on the part of national leaders, businesses, and portions of the citizenry of the countries. Other nations, like Poland, China, and the United Kingdom, join that list.

The potential for development in many countries is dependent on adequate responses to the numerous environmental concerns. Proposals like the OECD's *Golden Rules* and Pennsylvania's Center for Sustainable Shale Development attempt to mitigate the concerns. Certainly, these and other proposals will not satisfy all fracking opponents. They may, however, persuade governments, businesses, and a solid majority of people that unconventional development is necessary and preferable to other alternatives.

As the discussion around the impact of unconventionals continues, significant attention will need to be placed on the interface of unconventional extraction and water resources. Currently, the debate seems to be taking the shape of energy versus water. As Omorogbe indicates, whether this is a true or false dilemma will have important consequences for the planet's energy future.

Done properly, unconventional oil and gas expansion can advance some very important energy goals. First, an overall increase in supplies of oil and natural gas could allow the world's most important energy fuels to reach those nations that presently lack in production—whether in the developing or developed world—in greater amounts and at manageable prices. This could reduce costs to manufacturers and consumers alike. Second, the ability of natural gas to replace coal as a primary fuel for electricity generation could have large environmental benefits because coal is the dirtiest of all energy sources and, of course, is a major contributor to greenhouse gas emissions. Third, the marked increase of nations that are self-sufficient (if not exporters) of oil and natural gas eases reliance on Middle Eastern petroleum at a time when the Middle East appears be more politically volatile than ever. Assuredly, from the perspective of major exporters of conventional oil and gas (Russia and Saudi Arabia, for instance), the growth of competitors worldwide is a challenging new development.

The change in the United States' reliance on imported oil also has significant energy security impacts. Since the end of the Second World War, the United States has been the sole nation able to project substantial military force worldwide. In so doing, it has allowed sea lanes to remain open for oil shipments around the globe. It has also provided some protection against threats of regime change that might have had a major impact on international energy markets. The US-led military response to Iraq's conquest of Kuwait in 1990 is a vivid example.

This picture is changing in crucial ways. The US military continues to downsize. The entire military force (Army, Air Force, Navy, and Marines) today is smaller than the Army alone was during much of the Cold War. Some of this is due to geopolitical decisions and to popular fatigue after a highly unsatisfactory decade-long military effort in Afghanistan and Iraq. But a good deal comes from overall US budgetary woes. The long-time congressional attitude that 'whatever defence is needed, must be funded' no longer prevails in considerable portions of either Democratic or Republican parties.

US oil and gas self-sufficiency or export capability further changes the military dynamic. Why should the US armed forces remain ready to protect shipment lanes or overturn governments hostile to a free-market flow of energy resources when the beneficiaries will not be US business enterprises or US citizens? At the extreme, the use of US military force may aid nations that are direct competitors of American exporters and give flexibility to foreign consumers who would otherwise buy from American exporters.

On balance, unconventional oil and gas development appears likely to continue. Major producers and exporters of conventional oil and gas will continue to rely on lower production costs to keep a degree of market control. However, the presence of new exporters in the market may limit that control.

If unconventional oil and gas development appears very likely to move ahead in a considerable number of nations, CCS development appears to be a much trickier proposition. The primary purpose of CCS is to mitigate fossil fuels' contribution to greenhouse gas release and consequent climate change. The most significant beneficiary of CCS is coal, the dirtiest of the fossil fuels, although, in the long-term, gas-fired generation will also need to be fitted with CCS in order to meet emissions reduction goals. If CCS can provide an answer to greenhouse gas release (and the release of other pollutants), coal's advantages of abundance and low cost can keep it competitive for good portions of, at least, the electricity generation market. If CCS cannot fulfil those promises or if regulation of greenhouse gas releases remains politically and legally more aspirational than mandated, then CCS makes little sense. Where CCS will be used is likely to be in nations in which governments, rather than the workings of the market, demand it.

Efforts to mitigate climate change by reducing greenhouse gas emissions will be hindered less by unconventional oil and gas development than they will be by the continued use of coal, but it seems that if such efforts are to be taken seriously, then it is nuclear power and renewable energy, and perhaps CCS, as well, which must lead. As the experience of the United Kingdom demonstrates, promotion of unconventionals may be in significant tension with promotion of low carbon alternatives, and is a major source of policy uncertainty. Nuclear power remains the primary steady-state alternative to the fossil fuels. Despite nuclear power's considerable environmental negatives, if reduction of greenhouse gas release were the imperative, nuclear expansion would continue. As with renewables and CCS, however, the unconventional oil and gas boom may adversely affect the economics of low carbon energy sources, thus requiring greater public subsidy than might otherwise be the case, perhaps producing greater public opposition. As already noted, however, unconventionals have their own public image problem. It remains to be seen, therefore, which version of the energy future will come to fruition, and which concerns—whether climate change, affordability, or energy security—prove to be stronger.

VII. The role of law

The individual chapters highlight the extent to which the law governs underground energy. Constitutional statements of grand principles become implemented in more specific legislation that sets guidelines for fields of law and often are quite detailed in the rules and enforcement measures. More commonly, the legislation leaves room for enormous explication of detail by administrative bodies at sub-national, national, or international levels. These bureaucracies do essential work when broad objectives are to be actually carried into practice.

We will not detail all these sources of existing law and law in the making. The individual chapters do that. Rather, in what follows, we note five challenges and opportunities for the legal profession. No single sector of the legal profession has sole responsibility for solving them. We would hope that the sometimes collaborative and sometimes independent work of all legal community members would assist progress. Legal community players include private and corporate lawyers arranging transactions for their clients, legally trained government officials in energy and environmental ministries, and, in the sub-national and national legislatures, members of the judiciary and members of the legal academy.

This is work that is neither the exclusive province of lawyers nor work that should always be run by lawyers. However, legal skills are of great value in bringing together business and government leaders, representatives of citizen groups and established NGOs, scientists and technicians, and other stakeholders, all of whom can shape policy. Lawyers have a wonderful opportunity to exercise their talents to gather and digest knowledge from many professions and shape that knowledge in ways that serve problem solving. Lawyers can also call on their abilities to assess conflicting views and, in turn, to help adversaries seek workable solutions to challenging energy problems.

With those factors in mind, let us consider the five broad areas in which legal wisdom will be highly useful in addressing problems raised in the previous pages of *The Law of Energy Underground.*

First, we have discussed the need for thoughtful work in the international aspects of energy and environmental law. At present, there is relatively little hard or soft international law that specifically addresses energy issues as they relate to the environment. Sole reliance on general international environmental law is helpful, but not ideal.

Many of the matters raised throughout the book have international impacts. That is not to say that only international law can solve them. More often, a balance is needed among strong national, regional, and local problem solving in areas where those governments can make a contribution and areas in which even the strongest of national policies alone cannot solve a matter that crosses national boundaries.

Along with other authors, Redgwell and Rajamani in particular have highlighted some of the areas where this collaboration is needed, as well as where it is already working. *The Law of Energy Underground* has also captured the various forms in which international law can be created and implemented. We call special attention to the growing role of non-governmental actors in the process. Corporations, established NGOs, and citizens groups can play a valued role in both hard and soft law work.

The second crucial legal contribution to addressing energy underground problems is in balancing the inevitable conflicts between the development and uses of energy sources with the adverse environmental impacts such development creates. Objections to unconventional oil and gas development (captured in public perception by the single term 'fracking') have dominated both media and governmental realms in the past decade. But, as Bradbrook and Rønne emphasize, even seemingly benign renewable geothermal energy brings negative environmental consequences in its wake.

We have also seen that energy underground uses aimed at mitigating the environmental harms of energy uses have their own set of environmental negatives. CCS raises a mixture of fears. Likewise, permanent disposal of nuclear waste and spent nuclear fuel pose a variety of concerns.

Our colleague in an earlier AAG work, Rock Pring, borrowed Robert Heinlein's TANSTAAFL principle—'there ain't no such thing as a free lunch'—as a useful starting point for examining the interaction of energy production and use, on one hand, and preservation or improvement of the environment, on the other.[7] All gains from energy use and development have their negative impacts. Useful discussion starts from an understanding of both the benefits and the costs. Sadly, much of the citizenry and policy makers of the world (including representatives of government, industry, and law) have only a limited sense of 'how energy works'. Intelligent policy-making for unconventional oil and gas development, CCS, geothermal resource exploitation, undergrounding electricity substations, nuclear waste disposal, or other underground energy ventures is difficult if the citizen's

[7] D. N. Zillman, C. Redgwell, Y. O. Omorogbe, and L. K. Barrera-Hernández (eds), *Beyond the Carbon Economy: Energy Law in Transition* (2008) at 14–15.

knowledge stops at 'motor fuel comes out of the gas pump' or 'electricity works when I flip the light switch'. We need a more energy-literate public.

Modern environmental law is only a half-century old. Some of its early statutes reflected a world in which environmental harms were not taken seriously by large portions of industry, government, and the public. The early days may have pitted 'good environmentalists' against 'bad polluters' and proffered a model of tightly written statutes and regulations to protect the environment regardless of the costs of doing so. The task of making these 'command and control' laws work often fell to government administrators who were strong supporters of the environmental values and to judges ready to enforce the letter of the law.

Over the past half-century, approaches that have intentionally moved away from command-and-control have been implemented with considerable success. Lucas, Watson, and Kimmel explore Canada's recognition of the need to allow the emerging unconventional industry to have input into its regulation. Scientific and technical expertise about unconventional oil and gas resides, in considerable part, within the unconventional industries. Helman, Stavang, and Parchomovsky cite similar market thinking in the development of CCS ventures. They urge a regulatory model that anticipates continuing improvement of scientific and technological expertise about CCS. Generally, an important role for the law in this area is to provide sufficient certainty—both for investors in new technologies that they will see a return on their investments and for governments and publics that policy goals will be achieved—whilst maintaining sufficient flexibility to adapt to new developments, to allow for experimentation, and to cope with inevitable uncertainty. This balance may be better achieved by seeking legal commitment to broad policy goals and frameworks, and through the establishment of robust regulatory processes, rather than through the elaboration of detailed regulatory rules.

That said, the third broad area that needs legal input is the decision on whether new statutory law is needed to address new underground technologies. Crommelin, Montoya, Bekhechi, Kühne, Roggenkamp, McHarg, and Poustie answer that question in the affirmative. Seliverstov makes the case for new project-specific law being crucial to the success of the Skolkovo underground substation project. Wang and Jin, as well as Roggenkamp and Hanema, address particular planning law needs.

This issue also raises the question of who implements the new law. Bekhechi's description of Algerian law and Montoya's description of Colombian law identify a number of national government agencies with some responsibility over unconventional oil and natural gas. If each agency can slow or derail an unconventional oil and gas project, investors may be wary. On the other hand, it may be difficult to ask a single agency to properly represent economic development, environmental protection, and other social interests. Lawyers can be helpful in assessing and resolving such questions. At the same time, moreover, not every government has an adequate understanding of what unconventional development involves. In Colombia, for instance, 'one of the main concerns in relation to developing projects in unconventional reservoirs is that of strengthening the [government's] technical knowledge in order to issue environmental licences without unjustified delays or excessive conditions'.

The fourth broad area that needs legal input is the contest between national and sub-national authority over underground energy decisions. The topic has appeared frequently in the chapters. Struggles within Nevada and New Mexico over nuclear waste disposal sites featured national laws and perspectives differing from or conflicting with state laws, and both or one of which also differed from or conflicted with local laws or expressions of public will. Argentina's reassertion of control over national oil and gas resources is controversial, both for its claimed expropriation of private property and for its removal of provincial authority over important energy decisions.

Easily demarcated 'rights and wrongs' in disputes among local, regional, and national governments are few and far between. Each side can make a plausible case for its claims of legal powers and sensible public policy results. Different cases should be able to lead to different results. The job of the good lawyer in such matters will be to carefully present the facts of the particular dispute and the consequences of different awards of authority. The good lawyer may also need to channel diplomatic skills in order to keep the opposing parties working together.

The fifth theme is the role of public participation in many of the energy decisions that we face. The AAG's first collaboration with Oxford University Press in 2002 examined public participation in its many forms at the beginning of the new millennium.[8] Common themes in public participation were the need for early disclosure of major energy projects to stakeholders and the opportunity for those stakeholders to participate at an early stage in the governmental vetting of the projects. Major international agreements like the Aarhus Convention began to give public participation shared legal content.

The Law of Energy Underground has examined public participation issues in many chapters. Most authors recognize that 10 years on from the *Public Participation* book, public participation as a concept has grown remarkably. Sensible energy project developers today recognize that early disclosure and opportunity to participate are wise strategic moves for the eventual success of their project. Often the concerns raised by opponents can be addressed and then either corrected or, at least, mitigated. In some cases, the public participation will unearth issues that should doom the project before enormous wealth is invested in it or environmental damage is caused. Developers also should recognize that 'opponents' come in a range of shapes and sizes. Some may be core opponents of big business or all aspects of an energy technology. Others may be candid and firm in their NIMBY stance—happy to have the project occur somewhere else. Still others may fear that the success of the project or the technology may undercut local industries.

Public participation has been richly advanced in the past decade by the growth of the interconnection of the world citizenry. Today's advocates can simply employ the Internet—via blogs, Twitter, Facebook, and other social media—to promote

[8] D. N. Zillman, A. Lucas, and G. Pring (eds), *Human Rights in Natural Resource Development: Public Participation in the Sustainable Development of Mining and Energy Resources* (2002).

any cause of their choosing and muster opposition in a way that allows them to bypass the more cumbersome avenues of having to contact or lobby a government official or agency, or having to make use of traditional organized media outlets. No longer is it safe to assume that 'if it isn't on BBC or CNN, it didn't happen'. Now, in today's world, the way of personalized networking may drive what *does* appear on BBC or CNN.

The growth of public participation is not wholly positive. Whilst channels of communication have increased to provide greater opportunities to ventilate issues, they may miss the moderating advantages of experienced government officers or sophisticated news reporters. They may also enhance the perception that there are always two sides (or more) to every issue. The disregard of established scientific research is one negative consequence. Government and industry are often as—if not more—guilty of this. The lawyer needs to insist on hard evidence in order to advocate for the client. The lawyer also needs to help define the limits on public input and involvement in the decision-making process. Prompt release of comprehensive information is necessary. Serious opportunity to influence governmental decision-makers is also necessary. Additionally, unbiased appellate review by courts is necessary. But there need to be limits. Endless review of decided matters or insistence on resolving every possible objection to or approval of development is not productive and encourages delay, often undercutting the financing or public support of worthwhile projects.

In conclusion, we hope that *The Law of Energy Underground* will stimulate lawyers, public policy makers, citizens, and other stakeholders, and encourage them to become more engaged with the fascinating and ever-changing worlds of energy and the environment. The consequences of intelligent policy-making in these changing worlds are massive. We hope this work will contribute to that.

Index

Page numbers in italic refer to figures.

The manufacturer's authorised representative in the EU for product safety is Oxford University Press España S.A. of el Parque Empresarial San Fernando de Henares, Avenida de Castilla, 2 – 28830 Madrid (www.oup.es/en or product.safety@oup.com). OUP España S.A. also acts as importer into Spain of products made by the manufacturer.

www.ingramcontent.com/pod-product-compliance
Lightning Source LLC
LaVergne TN
LVHW011857200926
848484LV00002B/469
* 9 7 8 0 1 9 8 7 0 3 1 8 1 *